IV International Scientific Conference "The Convergence of Digital and Physical Worlds: Technological, Economic and Social Challenges (CC-TESC2018)

SHS Web of Conferences Volume 44 (2018)

St. Petersburg, Russia
16 – 18 May 2018

Editors:

A. Sarygulov
V. Sergeev
L. Ungvari
W. Semmler

ISBN: 978-1-5108-6414-6

Printed from e-media with permission by:

Curran Associates, Inc.
57 Morehouse Lane
Red Hook, NY 12571

Some format issues inherent in the e-media version may also appear in this print version.

Printed by Curran Associates, Inc. (2018)

For additional information, please contact EDP Sciences – Web of Conferences at the address below.

EDP Sciences – Web of Conferences
17, Avenue du Hoggar
Parc d'Activité de Courtabœuf
BP 112
F-91944 Les Ulis Cedex A
France

Phone: +33 (0) 1 69 18 75 75
Fax: +33 (0) 1 69 28 84 91

contact-edps@webofconferences.org

Additional copies of this publication are available from:

Curran Associates, Inc.
57 Morehouse Lane
Red Hook, NY 12571 USA
Phone: 845-758-0400
Fax: 845-758-2633
Email: curran@proceedings.com
Web: www.proceedings.com

TABLE OF CONTENTS

Preface

Fourth International Conference «Convergence of digital and physical worlds: technological, economic and social challenges» (CC-TESC2018) was held at the St. Petersburg Polytechnic University named after Peter the Great, with the participation of the two strategic partners - the University of Applied Science Wildau (THW, Germany) and St. Petersburg State Economic University (SPSEU) with the support of the Russian Science Foundation (RSF).

The conference aimed to exchange views, organize scientific discussion and dialogue between representatives of universities, academic institutions and industry representatives in such areas as: industrial Internet and industry 4.0; diffusion of technologies and the formation of a new technological platform; ensuring information security when processing large data; the economic potential of the new industrial base and the structure of the future economy; social consequences of the convergence of the digital and physical worlds; business management model and entrepreneurship in the new industrial base. The subject of a broad discussion was the question about significance of the breakthrough technologies, especially information and communication technologies, which become the basis for a new technological and digital infrastructure of society. The latter circumstance should play a key role in the creation of a new industrial base, which received such names as "Internet of Things" or "Industry 4.0". Scientific discussions at the conference were aimed at mobilizing intellectual forces to clarify the concept (platform) of the new industrial base (taking into account already accumulated international experience), as well as to systemic consideration of the issues of creating and developing a new industrial base, which we understand more widely than mentioned above the concept of "Internet of Things" and "Industry 4.0". Also during the conference it was suggested to consider technological, economic and social components as a single and integral platform for shaping the structure of the future economy. This conference has become a regular platform for the international exchange of views of scientists and is the continuation of the 3-rd conference, held in 2016.

All submitted to the conference bt21states were double-blind peer review of qualified experts. The program committee of the conference, after careful study, selected 77 articles from the 139 submissions. 160 people from 7 countries representing 21 universities, academic institutes, industrial companies and research organizations took part in the work of the scientific forum.

We would like to express special gratitude to EDP Sciences - SHS Web of Conferences for their cooperation and the presented opportunity for wide and open access of the conference proceedings to the international scientific community.

We would also like to thank all members of the program and organizing committees, reviewers, rapporteurs, authors of articles and participants for their contribution to the work of the conference. We hope that the results obtained during the work of our conference will be in demand by the scientific community and industry practice to solve the pressing problems of technological and economic development.

Professor Andrei Rudskoy

Chairman IV International Scientific Conference «Convergence of digital and physical worlds: technological, economic and social challenges» St. Petersburg, Russia, May 2018

Conference Chairman

Prof. A.I. Rudskoy

Scientific Committee

Chairman

Prof. A.A. Akaev

Scientific Committee members

- Prof. T. Devezas, University of Beira Interior, Covilhã (Portugal)
- Prof. J. Leitão, , University of Beira Interior, Covilhã (Portugal)
- Prof. W. R. Thompson, Indiana University and Concordia Colle (USA)
- Prof. André van Stel, Trinity Business School, Trinity College Dublin (Ireland)
- Prof. U. Gartner, Jena University (Germany)
- Prof. A. Coad, Institute for Prospective Technological Studies (IPTS), Joint Research Centre European Commission (Spain)
- Prof. M. Pianti, University of Urbino (Italy)
- Prof. C.L. Magee, Massachusetts Institute of Technology (USA)
- Prof. L. Ungvari, University of Applied Sciences Wildau, Germany
- Prof. Sergeev, Peter the Great St.Petersburg Polytechnic University, Russia
- Prof. A. Bukhanovsky, National Research University of Information Technologies, Mechanics and Optics (ITMO University), Russia
- Prof. N. Shabrov, Peter the Great St.Petersburg Polytechnic University, Russia
- Prof. A. Budrin, National Research University National Research University of Information Technologies, Mechanics and Optics(ITMO University), Russia
- Prof. V. Sokolov, St. Petersburg State Economic University, Russia
- Prof. A. Popovich, Peter the Great St.Petersburg Polytechnic University, Russia
- Prof. W. Semmler, New School for Social Research, New York (USA)
- Prof. H. Dyja, Czestochowa University of Technology (Poland)
- Prof. Ch. Apostolopoulos, University of Patras (Greece)
- Prof. B.Behrens, Gottfried Wilhelm Leibniz University of Hannover (Germany)
- Prof. Liu Wei, Tsinghua University (China)

Organizing Committee

Chairman

Prof. A.I. Rudskoy

Organizing Committee members

- Prof. D. I. Kuznetsov
- Prof. V.V. Korablev
- Prof. V.N. Sokolov
- Prof. A.I. Sarygulov
- Prof. A.N. Kobyshev
- Head of Dept A.L. Smirnova
- Deputy Head of Dept. L.M. Papina

Technical Committee

- V.B. Rapgof
- D.I. Gigauri

Statement of Peer review

In submitting conference proceedings to *Web of Conferences*, the editors of the proceedings certify to the Publisher that

1. They adhere to its **Policy on Publishing Integrity** in order to safeguard good scientific practice in publishing.
2. All articles have been subjected to peer review administered by the proceedings editors.
3. Reviews have been conducted by expert referees, who have been requested to provide unbiased and constructive comments aimed, whenever possible, at improving the work.
4. Proceedings editors have taken all reasonable steps to ensure the quality of the materials they publish and their decision to accept or reject a paper for publication has been based only on the merits of the work and the relevance to the journal.

Title, date and place of the conference

IV International Scientific Conference "The Convergence of Digital and Physical Worlds: technological, economic and social challenges". May 16-18, 2018. St. Petersburg, Russia

Proceedings editor(s):

1). Dr. Askar Sarygulov, Saint Petersburg State University of Economics, St. Petersburg, Russia. cfr@engec.ru

2) Prof. Vitaliy Sergeev, Peter the Great Saint Petersburg Polytechnic University, Russia. vitaly.sergeev@spbstu.ru

3) Prof. Dr. László Ungvári, Professor, Technical University of Applied Sciences, Wildau, Germany. laszlo.ungvari@th-wildau.de

4) Willi Semmler, Henry Arnhold, Professor, New School for Social Research, NY, USA. Semmler@newschool.edu

Date and editor's signature

16th of May, 2018

Neurobiological studies within the framework of highly technological teaching

Marianna Ababkova[1*], and *Veronica* Leontyeva[1]

[1] Peter the Great St. Petersburg Polytechnic University, 195251 Polytechnicheskaya st. 29, Russian Federation

Abstract. Modern highly technological teaching widely uses neurotechnologies related to creating new educational products, expanding the content of education and establishing objective feedback with students. One of the most promising neurotechnologies in the sphere of education is the method of biological feedback (BFB) based on studying the current psychophysiological state of students and using this information for further correction of the educational process, improving its quality and efficiency. This article presents the results of the studies based on the method of biological feedback to investigate the influence of the form of presentation of the educational material on the current psychophysiological state of students. During the BFB-studies, we used the PEN method developed by Hans and Sybil Eysenck to form focus groups of students and the CMS method to process the results of the studies. The research resulted in quantitative values of parameters of the current psychophysiological state of students reflecting the degree of intensity of such properties as the general adaptive resource, the degree of mobility (instability) of psychological processes, neuroticity, psychic productivity etc. (a total of 19 parameters).The study's results based on the biological feedback method showed that studying educational materials that are different in form influences the parameters of the current psychophysiological state of students. The indicators of reserve of control of psychological activity, regulating and adapting the psychological sphere, as well as the indicators of reserve of syndromologicaladaptiveness of the current state if students study the textual material on their own, will improve as compared to studying graphical material only. Different types of educational material can cause anxiety and increased apprehension, with textual material contributing the least to these effects.

1 Introduction

Development of highly technological teaching is related to such key cognitive technologies of the future as neuro-interfaces, Neuronet and biological feedback (BFB). Using devices based on neuro-technology will make it possible to create new educational products, expand the content of education by transiting from the textual, graphical or audio content of the educational process to include tactile, motoric, emotional and other content. Developing

*Corresponding author: ababkova_myu@spbstu.ru

and copying physiologic interfaces that can be used to improve the activities in the spheres of corporative marketing, medicine, sports, gaming etc., the potential of the entire body (body position and facial expression scanners – Kinect, LeapMotion, MYO etc.), sight direction (Eye Tribe), controllers of the current health state (heartbeat frequency, blood pressure), monitors of the level of physical activeness (Fitbit, Jawbone), electric encephalographs for sending messages (Emotiv) will inevitably lead this set of tools to become widely used in the sphere of education in the near future [1].

Neurotechnologies using biological feedback are more and more widely used in the modern educational process [2]. The market of evaluation and training cognitive abilities based on BFB methods, which was USD 1.7 billion in 2013, is expected to grow to USD 5.7 billion by 2018, according to predictions of experts [3].

The essence of the BFB method is visualization for the tested person using a screen, or in the audio form, of the current values of his/her physiological parameters determined by the clinical protocol, that are divided into two large groups:

- "neuronic feedback" (neurofeedback, neurotherapy) based on modifying different parameters of the electroencephalogram (EEG) of the brain (amplitude, power, coherence etc. of the basic rhythms of EEG;

-biological feedback (biofeedback) measuring the values of the vegetative (sympathic-parasympathetic) activation (skin conductivity, cardiogram, pulse frequency, electromyogram, temperature, photopletizmogram etc.).

2 Overview of literature

Currently, BFB methods are used in education in the following cases:

- achieving high functional ability of participants of the educational process (studying adaptability of students to the educational process [4], measuring the actual psychologicalstate of high school pupils in the conditions of interactive studying [5], relieving apprehension of students during the exams, relaxation and positive attitude, speech correction) [6];

- optimizing physical or mental activity (general improving of health and harmonizing the performance of the nervous and vascular systems);

- therapy of addictive behavior, treatment of hyper-active schoolchildren [7].

In the foreign literature there are articles describing the use of BFB methods in education [8, 9, 10].

In some foreign educational organizations, teachers and students are offered courses of BFB for health improving and harmonizing the nervous and vascular systems. For example, in Japanese universities, BFB methods are used during exam periods to relieve students' apprehension. In schools of the state of South Dakota (USA), these methods are used within the framework of the program "Self-Awareness through Training with BFB Methods" [7]. The Charity fund Melinda & Bill Gates Foundation (specializing in improving the educational system) issued a grant in 2011 for Clemson University (South Carolina, USA) to carry out pilot studies of students' involvement into the educational process by changing the galvanic resistance of skin [11].

Russian specialists, like their foreign colleagues, actively investigate projects based on BFB methods. For example, a monitoring research on students' adaptedness for studying at Saint-Petersburg polytechnic university Named after Peter the Great showed that the process of students' adaptation for studying at a technical higher school can be deteriorated not only due to their particular features in the emotional and communicative spheres but also due to various deficiencies in the development of their intellectual capabilities, the most important of which is the logical, abstract and 3D engineering thinking [4].

Within the framework of another project, the actual psychological state of senior high school students was studied in the conditions of interactive teaching. Differences were detected in well-being, activeness and mood in class with interactive methods of introducing new educational material [5].

With the use of BFB-based diagnostics of physiological changes for students in the conditions of educational stress, methods of stress states correction are being developed in relation to teaching [12].

Focused instrumental measurement of the psychophysiological state of students will help find out which time of day and which conditions are the most favorable for studying and tune individual regimes of the educational process, as well as efficiently control the well-being of students and teachers [1].

Therefore, BFB methods can be used as a means to promote an individual method of improving the well-being, as a tool that can help to bring up healthy generations, as a set of methods and forms of education without negative impact on the state of health, as an efficient method to evaluate pedagogical technologies [13].

3 Method of studies

Within the framework of the research carried out by the "Advertising and PR" department of the Institute of Humanities of Saint-Petersburg polytechnic university named after Peter the Great in the spring of 2017, a study was conducted to evaluate the emotional state of the 2 grade students of the course "Advertising and PR" in the practical seminars on the "Basics of Advertising". The purpose of the study was investigating the inter-relation between the forms of presenting the educational material and the current psychological state of the students using the measured results with the method of biological feedback. The tasks of the study were as follows:

- preliminary evaluation of the psychophysiological state of students on the basis of BFB method before the educational presentation.
- final evaluation of the psychophysiological state of students on the basis of BFB method after the educational presentation.
- comparing the obtained data for the experimental and the reference groups and forming the conclusions.

A hypothesis for the study was the assumption that presenting the educational material in the graphical form improves comprehension and memorizing, has a positive effect on the psychological state of students as compared with the textual form of presentation.

For the experiment, two focus groups of students were formed, equal in the number (12 people each), similar in the age and sex. Besides, the participants had similar distribution in psychological parameters estimated with the help of a PEN questionnaire to measure such psychological features as neuropsychological instability, extraversion and psychoticism.

Collecting the data on the emotional state of students was based on psychophysiological methods of CMS (Current Mental State – of the current psychological state) implemented in the form of a hardware-software complex (HSC) for CMS. This method makes it possible to carry out an objective evaluation of the psychological state by the data from cardiorhythmography, as well as monitor the changes in the state during various time periods and evaluate the effect of various influences onto the psychological state. The hardware-software complex includes a microcardioanalyzer and CMS software. The results of the investigation were quantitative (in per cent) values for parameters of the current psychological state of the examined persons (in 19 scales) reflecting the degree of the feature of the current psychological state. In these scales (in per cent) the similarity or difference is determined between the state of the examined person and the reference samples.

4 Processing the studies' results

Before class, both focus groups passed a preliminary evaluation of the psychophysiological state with the biological feedback method on the basis of the HSC for CMS. Then each group was given a lesson with studying theoretical material presented in various forms. The experimental group was given a lesson in self-studying of the material on the "Basics in advertising" in the direction "Brand mapping. Compiling Brand Comprehension Maps" in the form of a presentation containing graphical illustrative material (animated schemes, tables), video and sound. The reference focus group was given the same theoretical material but presented in the textual form only. The students studied the theoretical material on their own during 45 minutes, without interference from the tutor. After independently studying the theoretical material, the experimental and the reference groups were given a theoretical test to check their comprehension of the educational material on the topic "Brand mapping. Compiling Brand Comprehension Maps".

It was expected that the experimental group would have better results of the theoretical test after self-study of the presentation. However, the average mark of the theoretical testing of the experimental group was 2.91, with 4 "poor" marks, 5 "satisfactory" marks and 3 "good" marks, with no "excellent" marks. The reference group had the average mark 3.25, with 4 "poor" marks, 3 "satisfactory" marks, 3 "good" marks and 2 "excellent" marks. In our opinion, such results can be related to student poor ability to work with diagrams and tables, as well as lack of comments and explanations from the tutor. It appears that, for efficient studying of theoretical materials containing diagrams, tables and video, a somewhat different approach is required than for studying textual materials.

After studying theoretical materials, each focus group was investigated again with the psychophysiological method of CMS by the data from cardiorhythmography. Then the data was entered into a computer and processed with the specialized software (Fig. 1).

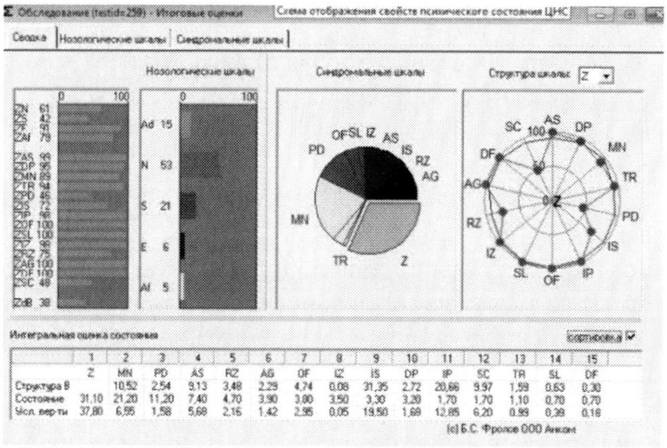

Fig. 1.A screenshot of the results of testing with the CMS software.

Table 1 shows the main average marks for the experimental and reference groups by the results of data processing comparable to reference values.

Table 1. Summary of the experiment results.

Experiment number	Nosological scales					Syndromological scales				
	Af	E	S	Ad	N	IS	MN	PD	OF	Z
1.1	14.83	13.55	16.11	15.22	7.16	5.38	12.44	7.86	5.7	15.10
1.2	16.94	7.72	10.66	23.33	7.94	2.58	5.52	5.41	3.74	28.63
2.1	20.69	21.53	28.38	21	8.30	6.62	22.67	10.41	4.41	20.81
2.2	23.61	19.15	9.46	35.77	11.69	3.34	14.45	5.93	4.84	35.84
Reference value	4.8	7.6	6.3	73.3	8.1	1	1.1	1.3	1.1	88.4

The overall compensation of the state of students groups. This value reflects the reserve of control of the psychological activity, the optimal adaptive regulation (and adaptation) of the mind. Before the experiment, the experimental group showed a larger limitation of the reserve of nosological adaptability in the current state (scale $Ad_{1\text{-}1}$=15.2) than the reference group (scale $Ad_{2\text{-}1}$=21), with the reference norm Ad=73.3 (Fig. 2).

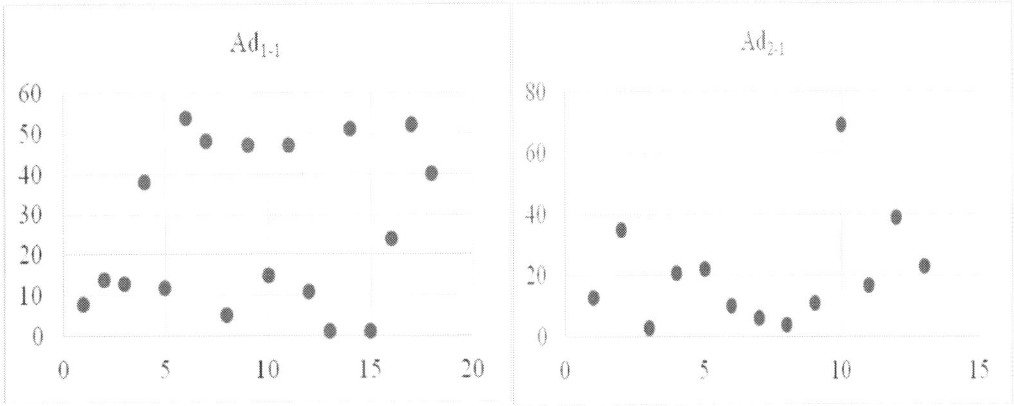

Fig. 2. Comparison of the values for the reserve of adaptability Ad for the experimental and reference groups before studying the educational materials.

We can also note the current limitation of the reserve of syndromological adaptability in the current state for the experimental group $Z_{1\text{-}1}$=15.10 (this value for the reference group was even higher, $Z_{2\text{-}1}$=20.81) as compared to the reference norm (Z=88.4), Fig. 3.

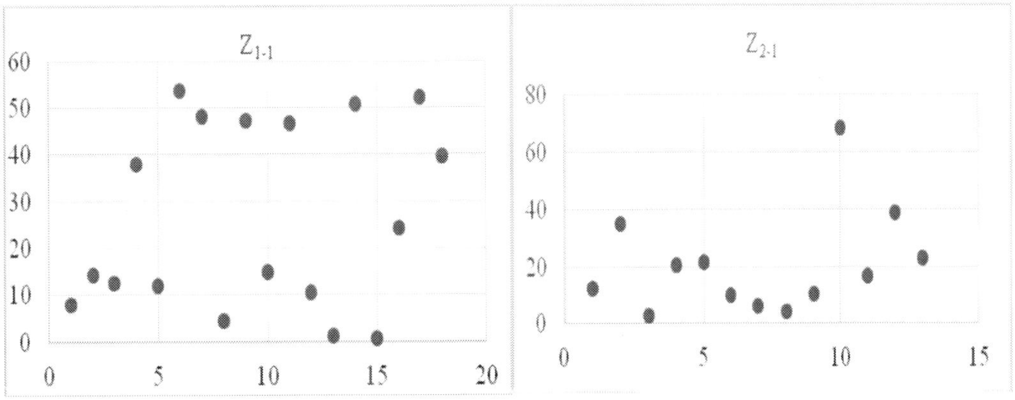

Fig. 3. Comparison of the values for the reserve of syndromological adaptability in the current state Z for the experimental and reference groups before studying the educational materials.

After studying the educational materials, the values for the reserve of nosological adaptability in the current state for the experimental group slightly increased (scale Ad_{1-2}=23.3); for the reference group, the value increased more abruptly (scale Ad_{2-2}=35.77) (Fig. 4).

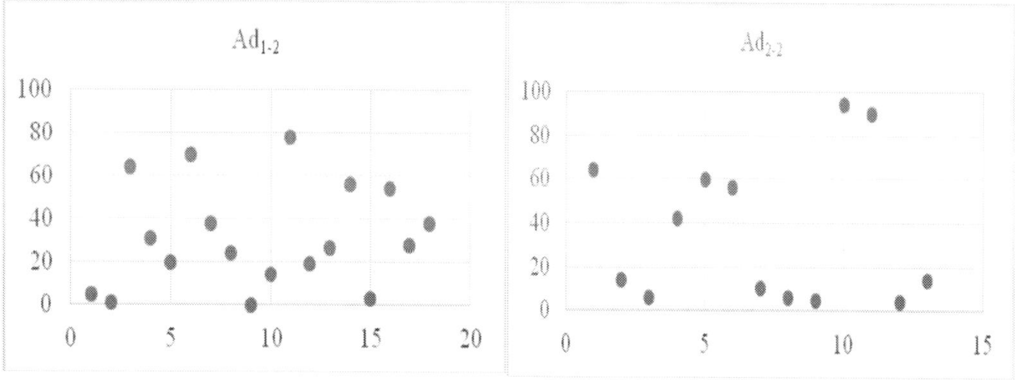

Fig. 4. Comparison of the values for the reserve of adaptability Ad for the experimental and reference groups after studying the educational materials.

The current limitation of the reserve of syndromological adaptability for the experimental group increased Z_{1-2}=28.63 (for the reference group, this value increased even more, Z_{2-2}=35.84), Fig. 5.

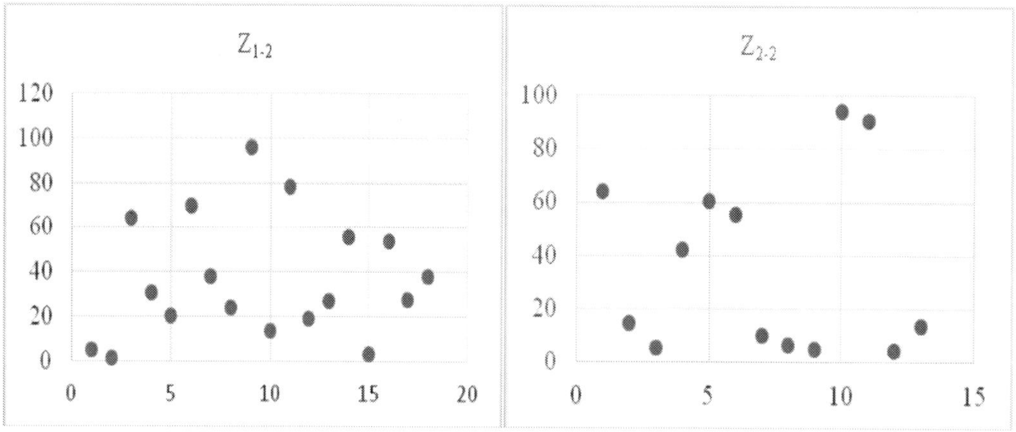

Fig. 5. Comparison of the values for the reserve of syndromological adaptability in the current state Z for the experimental and reference groups after studying the educational materials.

State of health (psychological and physical). Before the experiment, the experimental group had the average value in the scale of hypochondria equal to 2.01, and the reference group had the value of 6.5.Before the experiment, both groups had not a very good state of health and state of physical and psychological comfort (the reference value is 1), which can be explained by the end of the academic year and general tiredness. However, upon completion of the experiment, this value for the reference group slightly increased (scale IP, the reference group had 5.1, the experimental group had 3.4). Studying new material presented in the schematic form decreased the well-being of the experimental group.

Emotional sphere. This value reflects the character of the emotional reaction or emotional component (mental balance, emotions intensity). Before the class study, for both groups, the value of the emotional (and, therefore, the indirectly-volitional, mental etc.) psychological deviation or stress (scale Af, the reference value of 4.8) was increased

(Af_{1-1}=14.8, Af_{2-1}=20.69). After the class study, both groups show an increased affectivity value (scale Af, values 16.9 and 23.6, respectively).

In regard of the value DP (depression of the psychological state, opposite to vigor, the feature of depression, the reference value is 1.4), it can be noted that, before the experiment, the experimental group had 2.57, and the reference group had 2.13. After studying the educational material, both groups had slightly decreased values for vigor in the form of inclination for seriousness and apprehension with the generally high level of the positive attitude (scale DP, values DP_{1-2}=2.68 and DP_{2-2}=3.13, respectively).

Before the class, both groups showed a clearly expressed degree of the current excitement, vivacity and intensive emotions, increased movement activity, faster speech and increased self-esteem (scale MN_{1-1} = 12.4, MN_{2-1} = 22.67) as compared to the reference sample (MN= 1.1). As a result of different forms of the study material, both groups had this value improved and decreased almost twofold (MN_{1-2} = 5.52 and MN_{2-2} = 14.45).

Before the experiment, both groups showed the current limitation of the assuredness, exaggerated trend to be cautious, manifestations of anxiety and apprehension (TR_{1-1}=1.51 and TR_{2-1}=3.45, the reference norm being 1.3). Upon completion of the experiment, the experimental group had this value increased, whereas the reference group had it comparable with the reference value (TR_{1-2}=2.21 and TR_{2-2}=1.3, respectively).

Before the experiment, the experimental and reference groups showed the current emotional intemperance, disturbed balance "Myself-Others" (IS_{1-1}=5.38 and IS_{2-1}=6.62, the reference norm being 1). After the experiment, both groups had this value improved almost twofold (IS_{1-2}=2.58 and IS_{2-2}=3.34).

Before the beginning of the class studies, the value of the degree of limitation of the current spontaneity and productivity of the mind when reflecting the reality for the experimental and reference groups differed by several times (SL_{1-1}=1.63 and SL_{2-1}=4.31, the reference norm being 1). After the experiment, this value decreased for both groups; for the reference group is came close to the norm (SL_{1-2}=0.37 and SL_{2-2}=1.31).

Perceptive-thinking sphere. This value reflects the particular features of comprehension and thinking. During the preliminary series of testing, both groups had this value close to the reference value (N_{1-1}= 7.16, N_{2-1}= 8.3, the reference norm being 8.1). After the experiment, this value, which characterizes the presence of risk of actual psycho-traumatizing emotions, as well as a slight limitation of vulnerability and increased sensitivity remained almost unchanged for the experimental group, whereas for the reference group it was increased as compared to the reference sample (N_{1-2}= 7.94, N_{2-2}= 11.69).

A well-expressed degree of a decrease in specificity (pragmatism, reality) of thinking before the experiment for the experimental group was lower than that of the reference group; this value for both groups was higher than normal (S_{1-1}= 16.11, S_{2-1}= 28.38, the reference norm being 6.3). After classes, this value was improved for both groups; for the reference group it was decreased more and came closer to the normal (S_{1-2}= 10.66, S_{2-2}=9.46).

Before the experiment, a higher degree of a decrease in self-criticism for own opinion and actions was manifested in both groups (PD_{1-1}=7.86, PD_{2-1}=10.41, the reference norm being 1.3). After classes, the value of assuredness of correctness (reality, accuracy, faultlessness) of own opinion was decreased in both groups, with a more noticeable change in the reference group (PD_{1-2}=5.41, PD_{2-2}=5.93).

Before the experiment, the degree of manifestation of repeated (obsessive, arising unwillingly) emotions, decrease in the ability to willingly change over to other emotions was higher in both groups (OF_{1-1}=5.7, OF_{2-1}=4.41, the reference norm being 1.1); after the experiment, it was decreased for the experimental group, and it slightly increased for the reference group (OF_{1-2}= 3.74, OF_{2-2}= 4.84).

Before the experiment, both groups showed some degree of limitation of the current spontaneity, differentiation and productivity of mind when reflecting the reality ($SL_{1\text{-}1}$=1.63, $SL_{2\text{-}1}$=4.31, the reference norm being 1); after the experiment, this value was closer to normal for the reference group ($SL_{1\text{-}2}$=0.37, $SL_{2\text{-}2}$=1.35).

*The sphere of will.*This value mainly reflects an intention, direction, strength and intensity of psychological reaction. Before the experiment, both groups showed a small degree of slowing down in the psychological reactions; however, the experimental group slowed down more ($E_{1\text{-}1}$=13.55, $E_{2\text{-}1}$=21.53, the reference norm being 7.6). After the experiment, the experimental group had this value close to normal, and the reference group had it somewhat lower ($E_{1\text{-}2}$=7.72, $E_{2\text{-}1}$=19.15).

The value of rigidity of mind before the experiment and after it changed insignificantly in both groups; for the experimental group, it came close to the reference norm ($IZ_{1\text{-}1}$=0.89, $IZ_{2\text{-}1}$=2.8, the reference norm being 1.2; $IZ_{1\text{-}2}$=1.45, $IZ_{2\text{-}2}$=2.72).

Before the experiment, both groups showed a somewhat limited psychological tonus; there could be a feeling of general weakness and fatigue ($AS_{1\text{-}1}$=2.86, $AS_{2\text{-}1}$=3.66, the reference norm being 1.2); after classes, this value was significantly increased in the reference group $AS_{1\text{-}2}$=3.19, $AS_{2\text{-}2}$=5.31). After the experiment, the indicator of restraint of emotions and the mental balance "Myself-Others" for both groups was improved almost twofold; for the experimental group, it was closer to the reference norm ($IS_{1\text{-}1}$=5.38, $IS_{2\text{-}1}$=6.62, $IS_{1\text{-}1}$=2.58, $IS_{2\text{-}1}$=3.34, the reference norm being 1).

5 Conclusions and recommendations

As a result of the previous pilot study, it was estimated that using active methods of teaching, unlike the traditional ones, is more efficient in respect of influence on the state of health, adaptability and productivity of mind for students [14].

A series of further experiments with the use of preliminary measurements showed that studying various forms of educational materials causes improvement or deterioration in different groups of values of the current psychological state of students. For example, the value of reserve of control of psychological activity, regulation and adaptation of mind, as well as the value of reserve of syndromological adaptability in the current state of students when self-studying textual material is improved more than that when studying only graphical materials.

The indicators of psychological and physical state of health of students also depend on the form of presentation of the material. For example, the indicators of the emotional sphere of students change during studying various forms of educational materials; there can be an increase in the intensity of emotion, as well as a decrease in vigor in the form of some tendency towards seriousness and apprehension with generally high level of the positive attitude; however, the indicators of mania are decreased and the balance "Myself-Others" is improved. Various forms of educational materials can cause anxiety and increased apprehension, with the textual material contributing the least to this effect.

It is noteworthy that the indicators of a degree of limitation in the current spontaneity and productivity of mind of students when reflecting the reality are improved when studying textual material, whereas the indicators characterizing the risk of presence of actual psycho-traumatizing emotions, as well as a slight limitation of vulnerability and higher sensitivity are deteriorated.

As the experiment result showed, studying textual presentations deteriorates the values of specificity (pragmatism and reality) of thinking, as well as the reality, accuracy and faultless of the opinion.

When studying the illustrated presentations, the indicators of the degree in expressiveness of repeated (obsessive, arising unwillingly) emotions and the decrease in the ability to willingly change over to other emotions are improved, whereas the indicators of productivity of mind when reflecting the reality are improved when reading texts.

Basing on our experiment, we can draw the conclusion that working with new educational materials always increases the stress, disregarding of the presentation form of that material. Obviously, in order to achieve the optimal results of the educational process, it is necessary to alternate the presentation forms of the educational material between the textual and the graphical forms; interactive presentations cannot be considered an alternative to studying educational texts.

Despite the fact that educational neurobiology has quite a long history, there is still a lot to be done to implement the results of neuro-studies into the educational process. In order to improve the functioning of the educational system on the basis of the data of neuro-science and better understand their importance for teaching, an open dialogue is required between professionals in these two spheres.One of the directions for cooperation in the inter-disciplinary context "biology– neuro-science – cognitive neuro-science – psychology–educational studies –organization of educational process" [15].

As BFB technologiesare developed, the focused instrumental monitoring of the state of body and mind and subsequent adaptation to them makes it possible to find out, for example, which time of day and which conditions are the most efficient for teaching a particular person, and tune in the individual regimes of studies, teach the person to self-controlling own states (relaxing, concentration etc.) [1].

Further investigations using the methods of biological feedback can help answer the important questions about comprehension of the educational material; about students' motivation, their emotional state and involvement of capabilities to memorize the material; about the optimal time-schedule of classes, alternating between "active" and "passive" hours (for example, between physical training and lectures); about the time required for restoration (relaxation) after difficult classes and exams. Plans for further experiments presume investigations of the role of the teacher in influencing the psychophysiological state of students.

In general, the results of the experiments make it possible to draw the conclusion that using the biological feedback method is efficient from the viewpoint of obtaining the actual data on the current psychological state of students to better tune the parameters of the educational process; on the other side, due to the fact that, during classes, the students run the risk of developing psychological deviations, therefore, to maintain the psychological health and improving the stress-resistance, the method of biological feedback can be used, as well as methods of relieving psycho-emotional stress and BFB training sessions.

The authors of this article would like to acknowledge the assistance from the department "Physical training and adaptation" of the Institute of physical culture, sports and tourism of Peter the Great St. Petersburg Polytechnic University and, personally, Oleg Yevgeniyevich Piskun for the equipment and assistance in carrying out the studies.

References

1. P. Luksha, D. Peskov, Global Education Futures: Agenda, **206** (2014)
2. M. Yu. Ababkova, V. L. Leontieva, Conflictology: quarterly scientific and practical journal, **1** (2016)
3. Analysis of the state and dynamics of the world market of neurotechnologies [online], Available at: http://sibfrontier.ru/wp-content/uploads/2015/04/RVK_Analiz-sostoyaniya-i-dinamiki-mirovogo-ryinka-neyrotehnologiy_2015.pdf (2015)
4. O.E. Piskun, The scientific-theoretical journal "Uchenyezapiski", **11 (81)** (2011)
5. E.V. Kovalevskaya, Psychological Science and Education, **7** (2015)

6. T.I. Velichko, Living psychology, **4** (2017)
7. T.S. Vartanova, *Application of the biofeedback method in the practice of foreign health care, social assistance and education* (SPbJSC "Bio-Svyaz", Saint Petersburg, 2008)
8. P. Ratanasiripong, N. Ratanasiripong, D. Kathalae, ISRN Nursing, **2012** (2012)
9. P. Chaló, A. Pereira, P. Batista, L. Sancho, ApplPsychophysiol Biofeedback, **42 (3)** (2017)
10. D. Oman, S. L. Shapiro, C. E. Thoresen, T. G. Plante, T. Flinders, Journal of American college. Health, **56** (2008)
11. V. Strauss, $1.1 million-plus Gates grants: "Galvanic" bracelets that measure student engagement. The Washington Post [online], Available at: http://www.washingtonpost.com/blogs/answer-sheet/post/11-million-plus-gates-grants-galvanic-bracelets-that-measure-student-engagement/2012/06/10/gJQAgAUbTV_blog.html (2017)
12. Yu.V. Yumatova, Science and education: a new time, **5 (10)** (2015)
13. O.V. Silantieva, *Biological feedback technology (BFR) in the work of an educational psychologist. Actual problems of science and education: Theory and practice* (Petite, Moscow, 2015)
14. M.Yu. Ababkova, V. L. Leontyeva, Education and science, **7**(2017)
15. D.L. Schwartz, K.P. Blair, J.M. Tsang, British Journal of Educational Psychology, **II (8)** (2012)

SHS Web of Conferences **44**, 00003 (2018) https://doi.org/10.1051/shsconf/20184400003
CC-TESC2018

On competitive potential of organization under conditions of new industrial base formation

Timur Ablyazov[1],and *Veronika* Asaul[1*]

[1] Saint Petersburg State University of Architecture and Civil Engineering, Faculty of economics and management, 190005 2-ya Krasnoarmeiskaya st. 4,Russian Federation

Abstract. The world data volume will increase 10 times by 2025 to equal 163 ZettaByte. More than 95% of data will be transmitted in real time by the devices incorporated into network, which is the key feature of new industrial base formation [1]. Even today the information technology gap between economies of the developed and developing countries spells not only a reduction of competitiveness of organizations and individual branches of economy, but the loss of national technological sovereignties. This article considers a system of providing competitiveness of an organization, which is connected with the innovative business model of development and is supported by such a component of entrepreneurial business, as the information technology interaction of entities of social and economic relations.

A transition to the sixths technological mode, which takes place under conditions of intensification of globalization processes and risks, is connected with formation of "digital economics" with the new scientific knowledge and competencies, information and communications technologies and innovative production as the most important factor of its development.

In spite of the widely used term "digital economics", no universally accepted scientific definition has been elaborated. The article authors have worded the following definition: digital economics is a controlled system of social and economic relations, where the involvement of resources, interaction of subjects and objects as well as acquisition of valuable result are provided in the way of exchanging digital data on the parameters and properties of every system element by means of information and communications technologies.

Mastercard and Fletcher School of Law and Diplomatic Activity [2] have provided Digital Evolution Index 2017 rating. The study reflects a progress in formation of digital economics in different countries as well as a level of global network penetration into social and economic links of billions of people. Nowadays more than a half of the world population uses Internet. The study results show competitiveness and potential of development of digital economics in 60 countries. Digital Evolution Index 2017 rating appraises every state by 170 unique parameters.

They describe 4 basic factors, which determine the rate of digital economics elements incorporation:

---

*Corresponding author: asaul@inbox.ru

https://doi.org/10.1051/shsconf/20184400003

- offer level (availability of access to Internet and degree of infrastructure development);
- demand of customers for digital technologies;
- institutional environment (state policy, legislation, resources);
- innovative climate (investments into R&D and digital-startups).

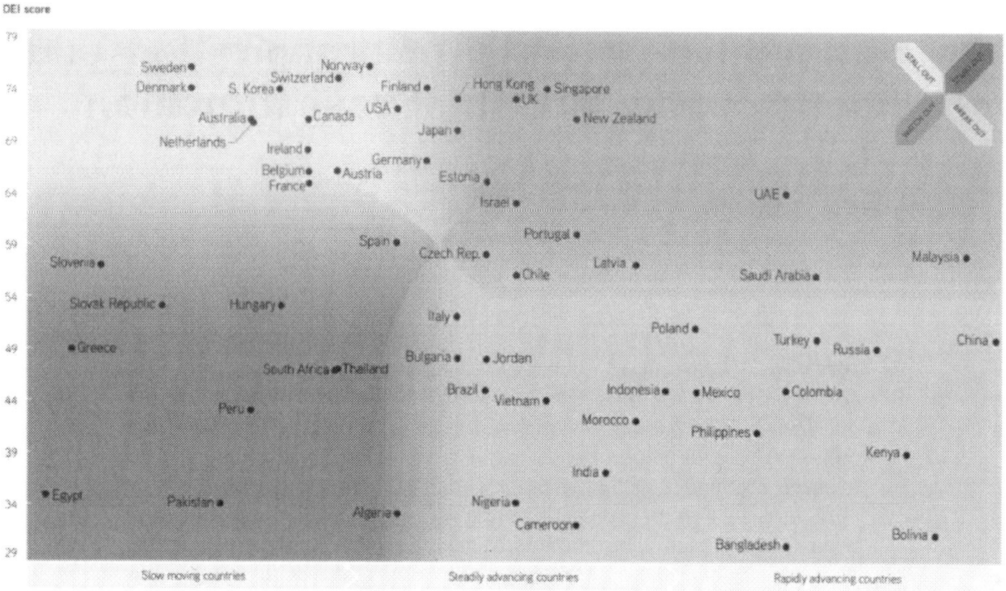

Fig. 1. Assessment of development of digital economics by combination of four factors [2].

Proceeding from the results of this study Singapore, Great Britain, New Zealand, the United Arab Emirates, Estonia, Hong Kong, Japan and Israel have become "digital nobles": these countries get characterized by high level and high rate of development of digital development. Owing to such speed of incorporating innovations at all levels of peoples' lives, business and interaction with state, these progressive markets can serve an example of successful technological progress and milestones for future growth.

Russia belongs to a group of promising countries with rather low level of penetration of elements of digital economics due to undeveloped infrastructure and low quality of institutional environment. In this case significant dynamics and great potential of economic development are observed. In order to use the existing social and economic potential a program "Digital economics of the Russian Federation" has been developed to be approved by the Resolution of the Government No.1632-r dated July 28, 2017. The adoption of this document determines a necessity of developing new methods of entrepreneurial business development, since the classical principles of interaction of entrepreneurial business entities can not provide for necessary speed of information transmission and taking managerial decisions as well as required level of production cost and transaction expenses.

According to this program the digital economics is represented by three following levels, which influence in the close rapport the life of people and community as a whole:

- markets and branches of economy (sphere of activity), where interaction of particular entities (suppliers and consumers of goods, works and services) takes place;
- platforms and technologies, where the competencies for development of markets and branches of economy (sphere of activity) get formed;
- environment creating conditions for the development of platforms and technologies and efficient interaction of entities of markets and branches of economy (sphere of activity) encompassing regulatory control, informational infrastructure, human resources and informational safety [3].

The formation of new conditions for social and economic interaction entailed a change of forms and methods of organization of business entities as well as labor market. Fig. 2 shows the intensity of everyday use of information and communication technologies (ICT) in work.

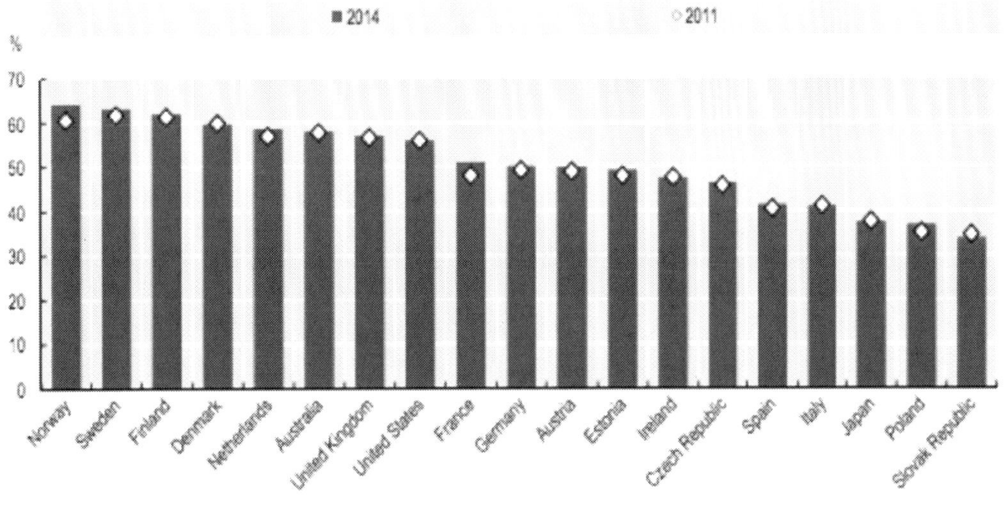

Fig. 2. Share of persons using ICT in everyday activity [4].

Figure 2 shows that the work intensity on a scale of the entire economy differs greatly in different countries. In 2014 the intensity of using ICT ranged from 64% of all occupations in Norway and 33% in SlovakRepublic. The employment share under conditions of ICT intensive use was stable in the period since 2011 till 2014 or in the majority of countries except Denmark, Ireland, Italy, Japan and Slovakia, where a minor reduction was noticed. The most significant growth has been noticed in Norway (3.7%), next France (2.9%) and Poland (1.7%) are to follow.

The development of digital economics makes it possible to organize remote working places and compensate for shortage of manpower due to people from the other countries that has brought about the increase of international and multinational enterprises (MNE), who boast simpler ways of entering global markets. The information and communication technologies represent one of the most important triggers of international productiongrowth, since it simultaneously brings about intensification and development of cohabitation between ICT and international production[5]. Fig. 3 shows the architecture of digital economics formed by MNE.

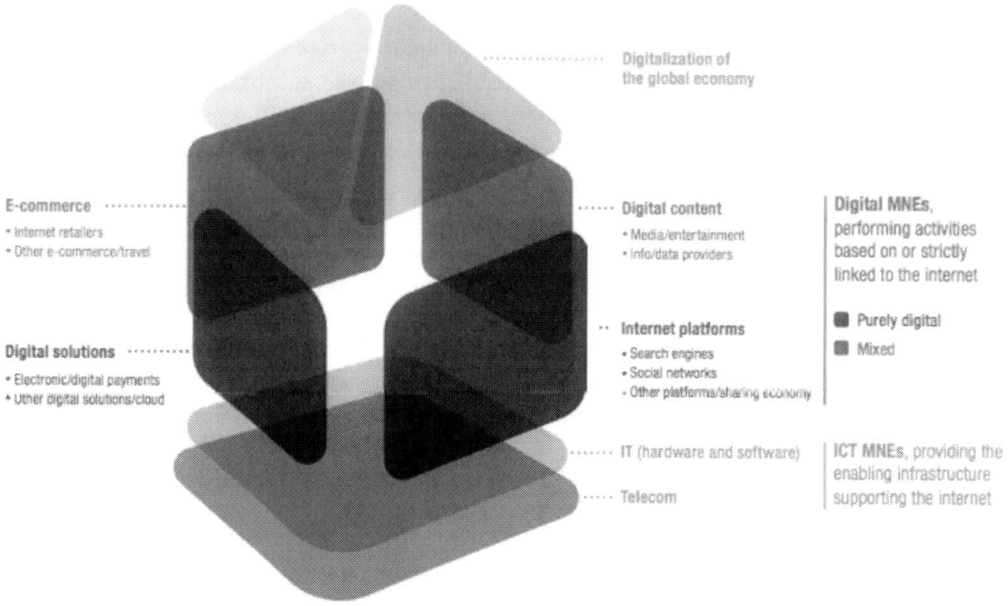

Fig. 3. Architecture of digital economics [5].

Analyzing this architecture one can come to a conclusion that the development of digital economics and MNE provides wider opportunities for restructuring processes and sales channels, reforming management mechanisms in global production networks, forming absolutely new models of international business and transition from traditional transnational corporations to virtual MNE, which international consequences of activity are absolutely different.

Under conditions of forming new industrial base the success of any organization in the market is provided in a great measure by the capacity of its competitive opportunities featuring rather dynamic than static character, since despite association of component elements of competitive opportunities to particular conditions and reasons of process of their formation and development, [6].

Presently, several scientific schools have been formed, the subject of which are the substance, composition of elements and structure of organization competitive opportunities. The article of B. Vernerfelt "Resource interpretation of company", which pointed out for the first time "profitability of analysis of a company rather from the point of view of its resources than products" has laid a basis of the "school of resources, capabilities and competencies". The articles of K. Prakhalad [7] and G. Khamel "Key competence of corporation", [8] R. Grant "Resource theory of competitive advantages. Practical findings for formulating strategy" [9] and D. Ties "Dynamic company's capabilities and strategic management" have made strong contribution into development of the resource-based theory[10].

The use of such notion as "production potential", which was used for the first time by A.I. Anchishkin in the 70s of XX century, was characteristic for the Soviet and Russian economic science for many years. The scholar considered it as a "set of resources, which take a shape of production factors in the process of production" [11].

The representatives of this school proceeded from the fact that the competitive opportunities get formed due to organization's individual characteristics, first of all, its capabilities, resources and competences (potentials). At the same time the competitive opportunities correspond to a combination of internal and external competitive opportunities of a company, which make it possible to run an effective competitive activity in the market due to manifestation of competitive opportunities based on using material and non-material resources [12, 13].

At present, an unalterable opinion has been formed in the economical science stating that competitiveness of organization depends to ever greater extent on the efficiency of using internal resources, than from an external environment[14].

The competitive opportunities feature two basic sources:

- exploitation of natural resource potential of the territory as well as production factors;
- innovation-based development.

This group of researchers divides competitive opportunities into two basic types: resource-factor and innovative-technological assuming a reasonable combination thereof.

Taking into account the definition of "digital economics", the authors offer in Fig. 2 a structure of competitive opportunities of organization under conditions of forming digital economics, which correspond to a system of interrelation of economical, social, financial, technical, technological and innovative aspects.

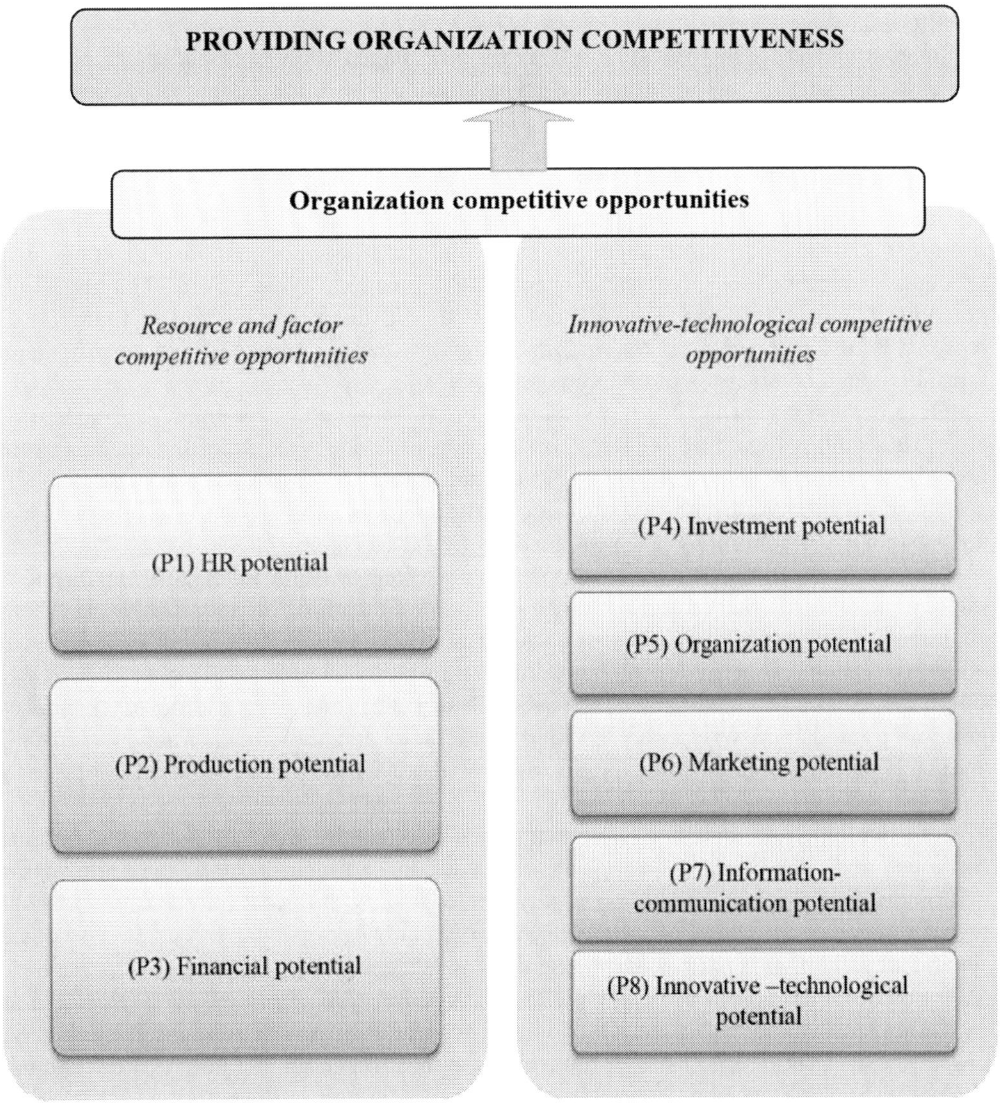

Fig. 4. Structure of competitive opportunities of organization under conditions of forming digital economics.

Resource-factor competitive opportunities are different sources of formation and elements of the production and economic system of the organization.

The HR potential (P1) is a combination of competences and characteristics of organization employees as the main resource, which is closely connected with an effective execution of assigned tasks and attaining strategic goals of organization development. It should be noted that the main difficulty during incorporation of elements of digital economics and forming digital ecosystems will be not the selection of new promising technologies, but a high demand for new specialists (carriers of digital culture, which can emerge in digital community only) in the course of developing a system of knowledge management in this environment.

Production potential (P2) stands for the available and potential production capabilities, availability of very production factors, its provision with determinative types of resources, which depending on the branch of economy consist of the fixed assets, current assets and other resources, which are used or will be used directly in the production process.

Financial potential(P3) is characterized by availability and accessibility of sources of financing organization activity [15]. The following can be attributed to the elements of financial potential: sales volume; net profit; profitability of sales; capitalization; financial stability index, etc.

Innovative and technological co-advantage advantages allow not only to use new forms of marketing, production or after-sale services, but also to increase the period of retention of competitive advantages.

Investment potential(P4) is a maximum possible volume of investments, both internal and external, which are necessary and sufficient for providing financial-economic activity of organization in case of an effective use ofproduction capacities, human and other resources, streamlined investment activity and attractiveness of organization under particular conditions of investment climate and business cycle phase. The investment potentialof organization corresponds not only to organization's capability to invite and reasonably use internal and external investments, but an important function of scaled reproduction of enterprise's production capacity [16].

Organization potential (P5) is a system of organization and economical relations of the enterprise entities regarding efficient combination of production factors in space and time with the aim of establishing and distributing added value [17]. Digital platforms providing access and processing big volumes of information and its security shall become a basis of this system under conditions of forming a new production base.

Marketing potential (P6) is a combination of facilities and enterprise capabilities in implementation of marketing activity, i.e., a combination of indicators and factors characterizing its strength, sources, opportunities, means, capabilities and other abilities and other production resources, which can be used in economical activity [18].

Under conditions of digital economics the organizations gain additional channels of promoting goods and services to the market, methods and tools of interaction with target audience (Internet portals, social media, etc.), without which it is impossible to provide its competitiveness.

Information-communication potential (P7) denotes a level of used technologies, methods and conditions making it possible to efficiently use the information-communication reserves, including a level of providing information security, providing regulation and coordination of actions of all participants of organization business processes, set and attain common goals, system extension and, if necessary, scaling.

Innovative–technological potential (P8) is a combination of organization resources and capabilities providing incorporation of innovations both in production and in the business processes and making a basis for a model of organization economic potential development considering its influence on the growth of efficiency of organization activity.

In spite of the fact that the competitive capabilities are the basic component of organization competitiveness and boasts the features of a complex dynamic social-economic system, it is possible to influence the advantageous competitive positions of organization in the market only under condition of an efficient interaction of all resources, potentials and taking into account factors of external and internal environment, where a new industrial base gets formed. The formation of such an environment, as practice of great Britain [19], Denmark [20], Singapore [21] and other developed countries shows, is possible only under condition of state-level incorporation of utilization of innovative and information-communicationtechnologies in all key branches of economy: industry, transport, financial sector, trade, housing and utilities infrastructure, education, public health service and state management, which help organizations get timely adapted to the changing conditions of social-economic relations and entrepreneurial activity.

References

1. D. Reinsel, J. Gantz, J. Rydning, Data Age 2025: The Evolution of Data to Life-Critical[online], Available at: https://www.seagate.com/files/www-content/our-story/trends/files/Seagate-WP-DataAge2025-March-2017.pdf (2017)
2. B. Chakravorti, R. Shankar, Digital Planet 2017: How Competitiveness and Trust in Digital Economies Vary Across the World[online], Available at: https://sites.tufts.edu/digitalplanet/files/2017/05/Digital_Planet_2017_FINAL.pdf (2017)
3. Program "Digital Economics of the Russian Federation"approved by the Resolution of the Government No.1632-r (2017)
4. New skills for the digital economy measuring the demand and supply of its skills at work. Ministerial meeting on the digital economy [online], Available at: http://www.oecd-ilibrary.org/docserver/download/5jlwnkm2fc9x-en.pdf?expires=1516737638&id=id&accname=guest&checksum=125AF889D7A773AFB386F570FF717AF4 (2016)
5. UNCTAD,Investment and the Digital Economy World Investment Report [online], Available at: http://unctad.org/en/pages/PublicationWebflyer.aspx?publicationid=1782 (2017)
6. I.V. Savenkova, M.I. Kulsh, MolodoyUchenyi, **20** (2014)
7. B.A. Wernerfelt, Strategic ManagementJournal, **5 (2)** (1984)
8. K.K. Pakhalad, G. Khamel, Bulletin of St. Petersburg State University (Management), **3** (2003)
9. R.M. Grant, Bulletin of St. Petersburg State University (Management), **3** (2003)
10. D.J. Ties, G. Pizano, E. Shuen, Bulletin of St. Petersburg State University (Management),**3**(2003)
11. A.I. Anchishkin, *Forecasting Rates and Factors of Economic Development of Socialist Economics* (Ekonomika, Moscow, 1973)
12. I.A. Arenkov, Ya.Yu. Salikhova, M.A. Gavrilova, Problemy Sovremennoi Ekonomiki, **4** (2011)
13. A.A. Suska, Molodoy Uchenyi, **12** (2012)
14. I.V. Savenkova, *Competitive Advantages in a System of Market Relations* (Konstanta, Belgorod, 2011)
15. M.V. Kudina, *Theory of Company's Cos t*(Infra-M, Moscow,2013)
16. A.V. Kozik, *Investment Potential of Enterprises (Ways and Factors of its Strengthening and Effective Use)* (Orel, 2000)

17. V.N. Belkin, O.A. Antonova, V.D. Gorbunov, *Organizational Capital of an Enterprise*(Institute of economics, the Ural branch of Russian Academy of Sciences, Ekaterinburg, 2011)
18. D.V. Tolstykh, *Marketing Potential as a Factor of Territory Social and Economic Development* (Moscow, 2013)
19. UK Digital Strategy [online], Available at: https://www.gov.uk/government/publications/uk-digital-strategy (2018)
20. About the Digitalization Strategy 2016-2020 [online], Available at: https://digst.dk/strategier/digitaliseringsstrategien/om-digitaliseringsstrategien-2016-2020/ (2018)
21. Official site of Data.gov.sg [online], Available at: https://data.gov.sg/about(2018)

Digital technologies: new forms and tools of business activity[a]

Timur Ablyazov [1*], *Julia* Asaturova[2], and *Vadim* Koscheyev [1]

[1] Saint Petersburg State University of Architecture and Civil Engineering, Faculty of economics and management, 190005 2nd Krasnoarmeiskaya st. 4, Russian Federation

[2] Peter the Great Saint Petersburg Polytechnic University, University, Institute of Industrial Management, Economics and Trade, 195251, Politechnicheskaya st., 29, Russian Federation

Abstract. The digital transformation of business activity is characterized by diffusion of innovative technologies, integration of physical and digital systems. The unprecedented digital revolution has substantially transformed forms of business activity and has given auxiliary options for implementation of new business ideas laying the groundwork for investment climate. The new forms of business activity have different propagation dynamics and they generate in most cases quite different patterns of growth and evolution. The innovative tools and operating models of business activity have got a significant effect on geography and size of prospective market, competitive environment and speed of goods substitution. Changes in global economics in the last ten years have shown that technology companies are the leaders by rates of growth and market capitalization. At the same time, their digital products and developments are key factors in the dynamic development of traditional industries of their economics. The processes of forming and development of business (entrepreneurial) initiative under conditions of introduction of digital economics' elements in different spheres of socioeconomic interaction have been covered in the article.

The perception of the concept of "entrepreneur" was largely influenced by the level of development of society and the technological setup. If in the 18-19 centuries, first of all, in the definition of entrepreneurship, the resources used (land, labor and capital) were reflected, then with the development of science and society the role of innovations and the entrepreneur's personality becomes more important. Systematization of theoretical approaches for business activity research achieved on the bases of chronological approach has a descriptive character and therefore doesn't give expected results in case of its application. The systematization based on peculiar properties of methodological approach of different economic schools is more fruitful. The given criterion enables selecting two groups of business activity concepts:

[a] The article was prepared as part of the work on the grant of the President of the Russian Federation NSh-4028.2018.6

*Corresponding author: 3234969@mail.ru

- Concepts using a functional approach;
- Concepts using an interdisciplinary approach.

It should be noted that in all of the above approaches to the study of entrepreneurship there are three components that characterize this phenomenon: personal, economic and organizational and managerial. They are organically interconnected, which is seen in a special type of reproduction, which is called the reproduction of the entrepreneurial type. At the same time, these theoretical approaches to the analysis of entrepreneurship differ in the degree of concentration of attention on one of the components. In particular, in the methodology of the study of entrepreneurship, the German historical school emphasizes the personal component [1]; the innovative concept –economic and personal components [2]; the classic and neoclassic concepts – economic component [3]; the Neo-Austrian school – personal as well as on institutional and managerial components [4]; the institution concept – institutional and managerial component [5].

The methodology of this study differs from existing concepts in that of analyzing the development of entrepreneurship, in addition to the components listed above, much attention is paid to the component of information and technological interaction between subjects of socio-economic relations. The given component has not been accounted for in previous theories due to significant difference of scientific-and-technological progress between the periods of scientific views formation. The role of the given component at present is significant due to formation of the 6th technological setup and a new industrial base. Based on the foregoing, the authors have formulated the following definition of the term "entrepreneur": it is a subject of socio-economic relations that realizes individual opportunities to achieve the desired result by manifesting an initiative of interaction with resources and other economic entities using available and innovative tools of the current technological setup.

Digital revolution results in transformation of not only separate companies, but entire sectors of the world economy. Just as the creation of radio telegraph, steam engine and transistors led to a structural change in the global industry, the Internet, BIG-data, artificial intelligence (AI), robotics and other innovative technologies are forming the 6th technological setup before our very eyes. The peculiarity of current changes is unprecedented rates of technology changes. Critics of the early project of mapping of the human genome were confident that it would take 10,000 years to study DNA base pairs. In fact the project was completed in 10-year period with the level of costs below targeted budget. For the period from 2001 to 2007 the cost of mapping was reduced 10 times, and from 2007 to 2014 the cost fell down 10,000 times [6].

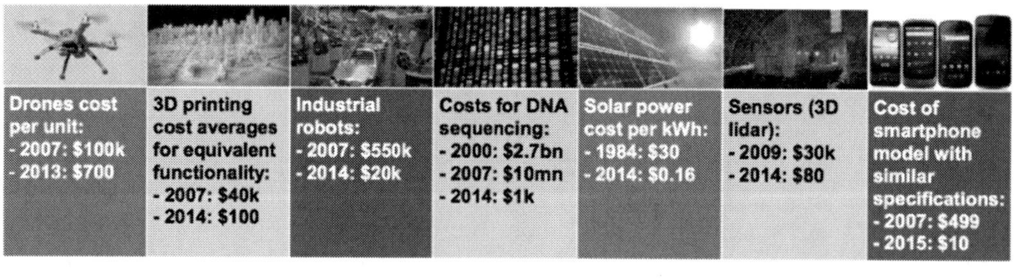

Fig. 1. Change in cost of key technologies [7].

Scientific and technological progress and the development of local and global digital platforms have contributed to the emergence of new forms of entrepreneurship, strengthening their economic and business activities at national and international levels. Moreover, in this context, the forms of entrepreneurship are understood not as a legal status, but as a level of penetration of entrepreneurship into the social and economic interaction of the person who carries out business and the external environment, and also the principles on which this interaction is built.

According to the report of the European Fund, five new forms of entrepreneurship are actively formed and are developing: one-person enterprises, part-time entrepreneurs, parallel entrepreneurs, serial entrepreneurs and business transfers [8].

One person enterprises and individual entrepreneurs (enterprises in which there are no employees).This form of entrepreneurship includes persons engaged in entrepreneurial activities, which, regardless of their legal status, makes an important contribution to a person's income and, therefore, goes beyond the hobby. Self-employment is not a new phenomenon, although the industries where such business activity is widely spread have changed over time. In several sectors such as information and communication technologies and services connected with them, handicraft industry, and services in construction sphere and transport the level of enterprises with one person and self-employment is especially high. For example, organizations consisting of one person make up more than 50 percent of all Austrian companies and motivations for starting an entrepreneurial activity, along with self-fulfillment and work without superiors, are economic reasons: displacement from the labor market due to automation and job cuts (self-employment becomes an alternative to unemployment) [9]. An important characteristic of this form of entrepreneurship is that the entrepreneur conducts his business activities without permanent employees. However, such entrepreneurs frequently cooperate with other entrepreneurs and organizations.

Part-time entrepreneurs. There is no generally accepted definition of part-time entrepreneurs. The definitions in the EU Labor Force Survey [10] distinguish between full and part-time employment or entrepreneurship based on the spontaneous response of respondents. Thus, in some countries the part-time entrepreneur is defined as a person working less than 35 hours per week. Other sources, such as "Entrepreneurship in Missouri", identify part-time entrepreneurs in terms of how much of their income is generated by individual entrepreneurial activities. The average income of full-time entrepreneurs is $ 29,998, while the average income of part-time entrepreneurs is $ 4,294 [11]. However, part-time entrepreneurs are also often considered primary entrepreneurs with a transition economy testing the market to make sure that their business is economically sustainable before becoming a full-fledged entrepreneur. Other authors, such as Frederick Welter [12], believe that the key factor in the emergence of part-time entrepreneurs is the need to generate additional income to meet household everyday needs. Such enterprises, as a rule, have low growth rates and low survival rate. Part-time entrepreneurs can work, retire, participate in educational, training programs or do household activities along with doing business. The examples are a government employee, engaged in a part-time working day who runs a farming enterprise for commercial purposes as well as business consultants and IT consultants that are engaged in a part-time working day and also execute individual contracts. Students engaged in a part-time working day can be engaged in business activity in parallel with training.

Parallel entrepreneurs (Two or more enterprises work at the same time). In addition to part-time entrepreneurs, there are examples of entrepreneurs who run several different companies in parallel [13]. Digital technologies have allowed faster interaction with consumers and partners and, therefore, provided additional business opportunities. This factor allows particularly active entrepreneurs to create and manage several business projects simultaneously. These organizations can be based on general synergy effects. For example, using the same customer base which offers different goods and services. These companies can be at different stages of the life cycle; an entrepreneur can, for example, start a new business when it becomes obvious that the existing one at some point will not be competitive in the future. When this happens, the definition of a parallel entrepreneur may coincide with the category of the serial entrepreneur.

Series entrepreneurs (starting a new business after selling, closure or introduction of new leadership in the previous one).Entrepreneurs can realize that they will not need to devote 10, 20 or 30 years to their business. In the conditions of digital economy formation, there is a rapid replacement of products in the market, a dynamic and profound change in the competitive environment, which makes business cycles in the economy much faster. A modern entrepreneur understands that his experience is to launch entrepreneurial processes, rather than consolidate them [14]. You can build a successful business in a short period, perhaps in five to eight years, and then sell it. The market of purchases and investments to these types of companies has dramatically changed over the last years. In other words, an entrepreneur who prefers the process of creating a company can sell his young company or transfer its property or management to another entrepreneur, and then start again.

Business transfers and legal successions (transfer of management or ownership to a new entrepreneur, while the business continues to operate). Transfer of business means transferring the right of its ownership (to the whole or a large part) or transferring management from one entrepreneur to another, while the business itself continues to function, including labor relations with its employees and any other agreements concluded by it. Business transfers can exist in different situations. They include:

- Transfer from parents to children , traditional change of generations [15];
- After passing the entrepreneurial stage of business development, the company, as a rule, faces new strategic options and management problems that are likely to require new managerial competencies and skills;
- Transfer of ownership or part of it through redemption of top management or partial sale of business or shares.

According to the study of "Global Entrepreneurship Monitor (GEM)" [17], exactly the existing opportunities for entrepreneurial activity served as the main motives for launching business projects. The highest rates are in North America – 82.6% of respondents answered that the opportunity factor was the basis for starting their entrepreneurial activities.

Digital technologies have provided additional opportunities not only for starting an entrepreneurial activity, but also tools for the dynamic growth of companies, product replication, scaling and access to international markets. According to the White Book of the World Economic Forum "Digital transformation of industries" [7], which was prepared together with Accenture company, digital networks and channels of interaction with customers can create significant additional business value and generate new sources of income, among which one can distinguish:

1. Sale – transaction. Sale, i.e. payment and transfer of ownership of traditional industrial goods is carried out via digital platforms.

2. Leasing of power. It is monetized as remote use of human time, computing machines or other assets.

3. Licensing. Technology, brand or intangible assets are licensed for periods of time. Sale is carried out independently through digital channels without involving authors of the invention to direct sales of goods or services.

4. Subscription. The buyer prepares an automatic re-purchase of goods or services for a short or long period.

5. Commission fee. Agents collect commissions for services to organize interaction between buyers and sellers of goods and services via digital platforms.

6. Advertising. It is often used in mass media and entertainment services as a method of distribution and exchange of information about relevant goods and services, sold via digital environment.

Companies that at the beginning of their business had an analog business model in their core and during the period of their work accumulated significant information about their customers, digital transformation allowed to monetize data through their systematization and processing using BIG-data technologies. Citigroup, for example, has created a separate company, the business model of which is based on promotion of marketing programs of insurance companies via their channels of operation with clients.

Young companies that have introduced digital technologies in their business, increasing their sources of income, outperform their peers and successfully compete with large, more mature companies. Previously, the company required an average of 20 years to reach an estimate of a billion dollars. At present startup companies achieve this plank much earlier: Google – in 8 years, and such companies as Uber, Snapchat and Xiaomi in 4 years or less (see Fig. 2). They achieved such rates to the great extent due to successful use of digital technologies. According to research of Digital IQ in Price Waterhouse Coopers, 57% of surveyed IT executives believe that an improvement in the company's digital opportunities is a top priority for the organization grows revenue [18].

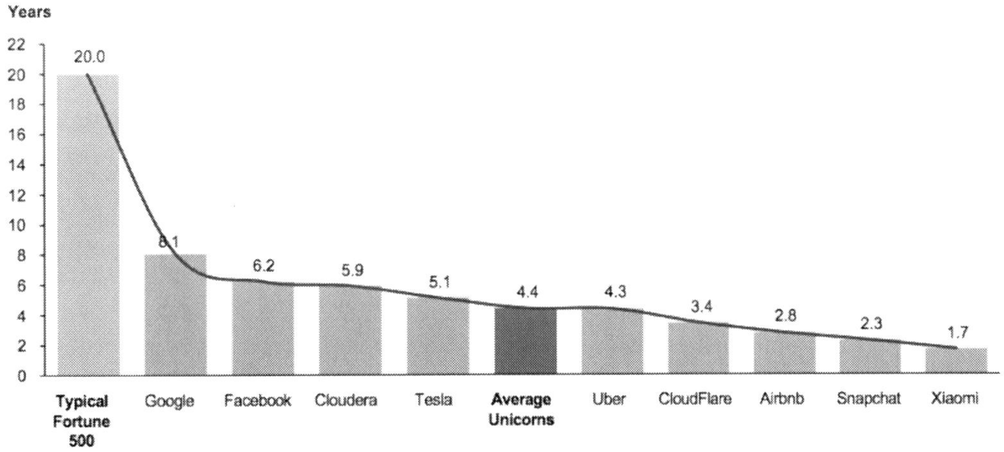

Fig. 2. Time to reach a market valuation of $ 1 billion or more [7].

Innovative tools and methods of entrepreneurship affect not only the speed of increase in the market capitalization of companies, but also its size. In 2008, the most expensive company according to the Global Top 100 survey conducted by Bloomberg and PwC analysis was Exxon Mobil Corp [19] from the oil and gas sector with a capitalization of $ 337 billion. After eight years, its capitalization grew by only $ 3 billion, and the company went down to the 7th place in the ranking. Technology companies, such as Apple Inc and Alphabet Inc-Cl A, showed capitalization growth of $ 660 billion and $ 469 billion, respectively, and ranked first in the rating. All-in-all technological companies take 25% in rating of 20 most expensive companies in 2017, though this rate was equal to 5% 8 years ago.

Company name	Nationality	Industry	Rank +/-	31 March 2017		31 March 2009	
				Rank	Market Cap ($bn)	Rank	Market Cap ($bn)
Apple Inc	United States	Technology	32	1	754	33	94
Alphabet Inc-Cl A	United States	Technology	20	2	579	22	110
Microsoft Corp	United States	Technology	3	3	509	6	163
Amazon.Com Inc	United States	Consumer Services	-	4	423	NA	31
Berkshire Hathaway Inc-Cl A	United States	Financials	7	5	411	12	134
Facebook Inc-A	United States	Technology	-	6	411	-	-
Exxon Mobil Corp	United States	Oil & Gas	-6	7	340	1	337
Johnson & Johnson	United States	Health Care	0	8	338	8	145
Jpmorgan Chase & Co	United States	Financials	19	9	314	28	100
Wells Fargo & Co	United States	Financials	45	10	279	55	60
Tencent Holdings Ltd	China	Technology	-	11	272	-	13
Alibaba Group Holding-Sp Adr	China	Consumer Services	-	12	269	-	-
General Electric Co	United States	Industrials	11	13	260	24	107
Samsung Electronics Co Ltd	South Korea	Consumer Goods	39	14	259	53	61
At&T Inc	United States	Telecommunications	-8	15	256	7	149
Ind & Comm Bk Of China-A	China	Financials	-12	16	246	4	188
Nestle	Switzerland	Consumer Goods	-2	17	239	15	129
Bank Of America Corp	United States	Financials	69	18	236	87	44
Procter & Gamble	United States	Consumer Goods	-9	19	230	10	138
China Mobile Ltd	Hong Kong	Telecommunications	-15	20	224	5	175

Fig. 3. The rating of companies by the size of market capitalization in Q1 2017 [19].

According to the Accenture study [20], companies that use the right combination of new technologies can increase their market capitalization by an average of more than $ 6 billion. Accenture conducted economic modeling after its initial studies showed that only 13% of leaders from more than 900 large companies said that investing in digital technologies not only increased business efficiency but also provided new tools for its growth. Accenture believes that this low value of this indicator is mainly due to the separate deployment and implementation of investments in digital technologies. Objects of economic modeling of Accenture are companies with sales income of $ 1 billion or more in the automotive, chemical industries, manufacturers of electronic and high-tech, energy, biological, household and communal goods and services. To develop technology combinations that could best help companies reduce their costs per employee and increase their market capitalization, Accenture surveyed 931 managers from large companies in 12 industries from 21 industrialized countries to understand how companies are implementing digital technologies and what benefits they receive from them. Then a set of 10 critical technologies has been specified: 3D-printing, AI (artificial intellect), AR/VR (mixed and virtual reality), autonomous robots, autonomous vehicles, BIG-data, block chain, digital replica (twins) of physical assets, machine learning and mobile computing. Survey data and financial data of companies were used to model economic value and identify combinations of technologies with the greatest impact on costs per employee, the maximum and minimum cost of output and its impact on market capitalization. The results of researches have been obtained by using of tools of machine computing, analysis of technological components, financial and business processes. For example, a company in sector of industrial equipment can implement additional cost saving by more than $ 43,000 per one employee, if they combine robot engineering, technologies of 3D-printing, AI, BIG-data and block chain. Energy companies can increase market capitalization by more than $ 16 billion if they combine technologies such as virtual reality, BIG-data and AI.

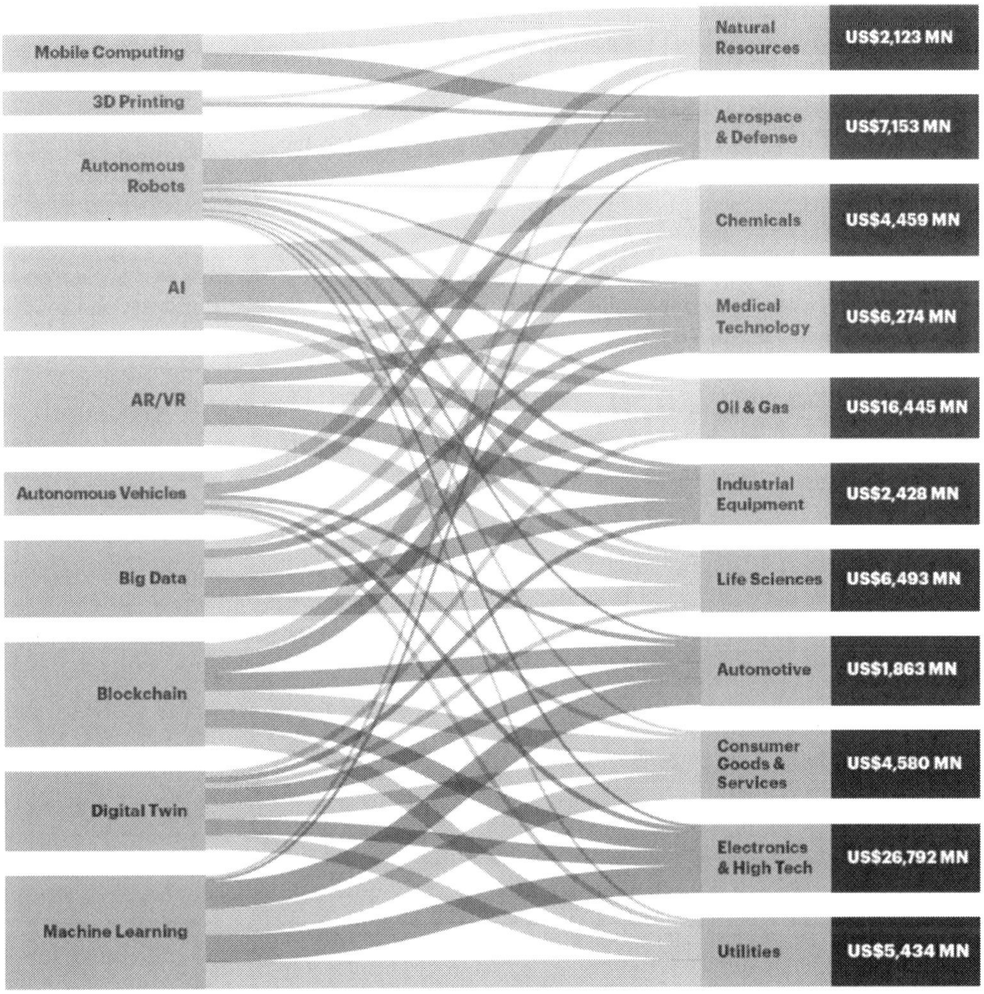

Fig. 4. Influence of the optimal combination of digital technologies on increasing the market capitalization of companies [20].

It should be noted that the initiative of digital transformations must come from the company's management and be implemented at all levels of operational activities. It is impossible to realize a successful transformation by introducing a staff unit and hiring an employee to implement this program. Successful digital transformation requires an appropriate corporate culture in which management supports innovation, encourages the introduction of new technologies, changes its own daily approach to the work process and shares risks with the company's employees. More than 80% of top managers, participating in Gartner opinion poll expect that their companies will become digital organizations by 2019 [21]. This includes both introduction of digital operations research model and acceptance of new technologies for definition of operating efficiency. According to methodology, developed by Capgemini Group [22] architecture of digital operating system consists of 6 components:

1. Channels of interaction with clients, making it possible to customize communication with due account for history of client request.
2. Business processes. They enable shaping of maximal added value of a good and services support continuous development of company.

3. Structure of organization. It opens up capabilities and reserves of improvement of company's efficiency by hierarchy of interaction and accountability with application of information and communication technologies.

4. Physical infrastructure, including property, entities, equipment and other assets.

5. IT-architecture. It coordinates interaction of infrastructure elements (for example, web-spaces, and storage clouds) for functioning of business processes.

6. Data and information. There are raw materials for analysis and understanding that can give the business a competitive advantage. Modern customer data analytics or operation can also contribute to efforts regarding introduction of other innovations in operations.

One of the main goals of building of digital operating system is provision of company's "transparency" due to the fact that under conditions of formation of digital economy this is one of the major factors of successful development. Accessibility of information about company provides its competitive ability, helps both in promotion of goods and services in the market and in search of employees and investors. Transparency and open communication at the workplace contributes to development of creative and innovative approach to execution of tasks. Clear Company research has shown that in companies with high levels of interaction and communication with employees the performance rate is 22% higher than in similar companies. They also have lower level of employees' turnover [23] in 50% of cases.

Innovations have made corrections to generally accepted concepts, principles and essence of entrepreneurship. The evolution of digital technologies makes both start-up entrepreneurs and leading companies rethink the possible ways of their development. Along with the key economic indicators of the performance of companies, a significant role is played by digital indicators, which characterize the opportunity to provide unprecedented speed of scaling and growth. Digital technologies have changed the way how entities and objects of socio-economic relations interact between themselves. The growing expectations of consumers of goods and services, the formation of new business and operational models pushes organizations to perceive digital technology as a new focus of their development strategy.

References

1. M. Weber, (ed.) The theory of social and economic organization (1964)
2. E. N. Fetisov, I. G. Yakovlev, About social aspects of business activity (conceptual introduction in a problem), **1** (1993)
3. V. Avtonomov, O. Anan'in, N. Makasheva, *History of economic doctries*, **784** (2003)
4. I. M. Kirtsner, translated from English, edited by professor A. N. Romanov, *Business competition and business activity* **239** (2001)
5. L. V. Grishaeva, Bulletin of Omsk University. Series "ECONOMICA", **1** (2012)
6. DNA Sequencing Costs: Data from the NHGRI Genome Sequencing Program (GSP) [online], Available at: www.genome.gov/sequencingcostsdata (2018)
7. World Economic Forum White Paper Digital Transformation of Industries: In collaboration with Accenture [online], Available at: http://reports.weforum.org/digital-transformation/wp-content/blogs.dir/94/mp/files/pages/files/digital-enterprise-narrative-final-january-2016.pdf (2018)
8. European Monitoring Centre on Change, *Emerging forms of entrepreneurship* [online], Available at: https://www.eurofound.europa.eu/sites/default/files/ef_files/docs/erm/tn1009034s/tn1009034s.pdf (2018)

9. D. Bogenhold, Andrea Klinglmair, Micro-Entrepreneurship: Tendency towards Precarious Work? Empirical Findings for Austria, *Athens Journal of Business and Economics*, **1(2)**, 107-121 (2015) [online], Available at: https://www.researchgate.net/publication/274717669_Micro-Entrepreneurship_Tendency_towards_Precarious_Work_Empirical_Findings_for_Austria (2018)
10. Eurostat, *The European Union Labour Force Survey* [online], Available at: http://ec.europa.eu/eurostat/web/microdata/european-union-labour-force-survey (2018)
11. Associate of Applied Science in Entrepreneurship [online], Available at: https://wp.missouristate.edu/ctp/entrepreneurship.htm (2018)
12. F. Welter, *Policy delivery: Challenges and opportunities for entrepreneurship and* (SME 2009)
13. OECD/The European Commission, *The Missing Entrepreneurs: Policies for Inclusive Entrepreneurship in Europe* [online], Available at: http://dx.doi.org/10.1787/9789264188167-en (2018)
14. M. Peris-Ortiz, J.-M. Sahut, *New Challenges in Entrepreneurship and Finance: Examining the Prospects for Sustainable Business Development, Performance, Innovation, and Economic Growth* (2015)
15. C. Aronoff, S. McClure, J. Ward, *Family Business Succession. The Final Test of Greatness* (2011)
16. C. Holland, *The Art of Business Succession: Who will fill your shoes?* (2012)
17. Babson College and the London Business School, *Global Entrepreneurship Monitor. Global Report 2017/18* [online], Available at: http://www.gemconsortium.org/report (2018)
18. PriceWaterhouseCoopers, *Global Digital IQ 3® Survey* [online], Available at: https://www.pwchk.com/en/consulting/digital-consulting/digital-iq-2017/pwc-digital-iq-report.pdf (2018)
19. PriceWaterhouseCoopers, *Global Top 100 Companies by market capitalisation)* [online], Available at: https://www.pwc.com/gx/en/audit-services/assets/pdf/global-top-100-companies-2017-final.pdf (2017)
20. D. Abood, A. Quilligan, R. Narsalay, *Industry X.0. Combine and conquer. Unlocking the power of digital* [online], Available at: https://www.accenture.com/t20180112T093917Z__w__/us-en/_acnmedia/Accenture/Conversion-Assets/DotCom/Documents/Global/PDF/Dualpub_26/Accenture-Industry-XO-whitepaper.pdf (2018)
21. J. Lopez, J. Tully, P. Meehan, M. Burkett, D. Scheibenreif, *Agenda Overview for Digital Business* [online], Available at: https://www.gartner.com/doc/2955218/agenda-overview-digital-business- (2018)
22. R. Cade, M. Buggie, *Operating Model in a Digital World. An introduction to Digital Operating Model* [online], Available at: https://www.capgemini.com/consulting-nl/wp-content/uploads/sites/33/2017/08/dcx_operatingmodelinadigitalworld_0.pdf (2018)
23. S. Pollock, *Final Destination: Organizational Transparency* [online], Available at: http://blog.clearcompany.com/final-destination-organizational-transparency (2018)

Digital economy and the models of income distribution in the society[a]

Askar Akaev[1*], *Andrew* Rudskoi[2], and *Tessaleno* Devezas[3]

[1] Moscow State University, 119991 Leninskie Gory 1, Russian Federation
[2] Peter the Great St. Petersburg Polytechnic University, 195251 Polytechnicheskaya st. 29, Russian Federation
[3] Atlantica School of Management Sciences, Health, IT & Engineering C-MAST (Center for Aerospace Science and Technologies), 2730-036 Atlantica, Fabrica da Polvora de Barcarena, Portugal

Abstract. Digital technologies, robotic automation and artificial intelligence are becoming the main drivers of technological and economic development. In this regard, it is quite natural that the demand for justification of such threats for the employment market appears, and also the question arises whether it is possible to foresee and analyze the level of inequality and distribution of income in the society where the proportion of artificial intellectual systems in creating new costs will be exceptionally large.

NBIC – technological revolution has led to creating highly-efficient digital technologies, intellectual computers and robots which are able to generate major changes in industrial forces many times superior to the achievements of the third industrial revolution based on microelectronics and informational technologies. Thatiswhythe world is talking about the fourth industrial revolution [1] and creating the Industry 4.0 [2]. The basic infrastructure of Industry 4.0 is industrial internet [3] – a digital platform which provides for effective cooperation of all objects of industrial production on the basis of the Internet. Simultaneously a multifunctional digital information technology has appeared which is designated for reliable account of assets and operations with them – Blockchain-technology, able to become a reliable economic software in the Internet maintaining online payments, decentralized digital exchange of assets, release and execution of "clever contracts" [4]. Internet-technologies enable total automatization of the process of manufacturing goods starting from production of utilities and assembly works up to making electronic orders and delivering finished products to end-consumers, completely forcing human labor out of the production field. As digital technologies and platforms play the key role in the Industry 4.0 and in general in the new digitalized economy it is no wonder that transition to "Digital Economy" is being mentioned lately with increasing frequency.

One of the main innovations created by NBIC – technological revolution – is, without any doubt, nanochips, biochips and quantum computers [5]. They have significantly raised the computing capacity of computers which has led to breakthrough achievements in the

[a] The article is prepared with financial support from the Russian Science Foundation (Grant No. 18-18-00099)
[*] Corresponding author: askarakaev@mail.ru

field of machine education and artificial intelligence (AI) [6]. It has become possible to create intellectual computers and robots which are able to cooperate with the human being, study and improve in the process of production activity.

Three main production technologies lie in the basis of producing goods within the framework of the Industry 4.0 or digital economy: automatized system of three dimensional digital design of complicated systems; additive technologies of layered growth (3D-printing) of complicated objects on the basis of their three dimensional digital models; intellectual industrial robots. All these technologies give unprecedented flexibility to the Industry 4.0 thanks to the easiness with which parameters of product design can be changed using digital program methods both at the design stage and at the production stage. Thus, the Industry 4.0 or digital economy solves the problem of transition from the mass production of standard goods to creating qualitative goods and services meeting individual requirements and preferences. In its turn it conforms with the tendency of moving to variety of goods and services, to expanding their assortment, that is, it takes into account the consumers' behavior [7].

It goes without saying that the digital economy doesn't exist apart from the real economy. Digital economy is the developed real economy in which the key role is played by digital technologies and platforms that are aimed at increasing the productivity of factors, optimizing equipment operation, minimizing consumption of materials and resources, improving the quality of goods as well as increasing the accuracy of forecast of consumers' demand.

At the same time digital technologies also have disadvantages, intensive labor saving is most important of them. Digital economy will create very few new working places and destroy many jobs including entire professions [1]. Erik Brynjolfsson and Andrew McAfee, the Massachusetts Institute of Technology scientists claim: "The XXI century economy will qualitatively change. Mass replacement of qualified labor with capital will begin and, as a consequence, there will be a sharp decrease of labor activity" [8]. As you can see, new technologies come laden with the evidences of the new quality of growth but also they hold the serious danger of releasing a great number of employed people from the production field and forming a new structure of the entire employment market. The actuality of such a threat is demonstrated by the increased volume of publications about potential social consequences of the new technical revolution [9-12]. In this regard, it is quite natural that the demand for justification of such threats for the employment market appears, and also the question arises whether it is possible to foresee and analyze the level of inequality and distribution of income in the society where the proportion of artificial intellectual systems in creating new costs will be exceptionally large.

As a first step we suggest using the following model of labor employment and income taking into account technological replacement of working places.

$$L(t) = \lambda \cdot \left(\frac{k}{\gamma}\right)^{\frac{1}{(1-\theta)(1-\tilde{\alpha}+\delta)}} \cdot K(t)^{\frac{1-\tilde{\alpha}-\theta(1-\tilde{\alpha}+\delta)}{(1-\theta)(1-\tilde{\alpha}+\delta)}}, \tag{1}$$

where $L(t)$ – is the number of workers and office staff employed; $K(t)$ – physical capital; $\lambda = \alpha^{\frac{1}{1-\theta}}$ – normalizing coefficient; θ – the parameter which characterizes the efficiency of education $(0 < \theta \le 1)$; α – normalizing coefficient; δ – capital input-output coefficient. If we set the constant present value in model (1) $\tilde{\alpha} = \alpha_0 = 0.38$ then, using this model, we can calculate the predictive dynamics of the potential number of working places in the USA economy – $L_p(t)$. Its diagram is presented in Fig. 1.

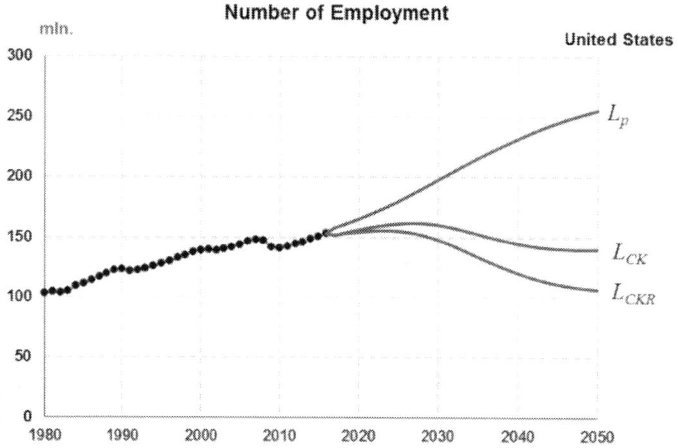

Fig. 1. The expected number of the people employed in the USA economy taking into account technological replacement of working places (L_{CK}) and robotization of production (L_{CKR}).

D. Acemoglu and P. Restrepo analyzed the USA labor market and determined that there is an empirical regularity: the appearance of one new robot for 1000 workers reduces employment – even if it increases in related branches – by 0.18% and the average salary reduces by 0.25% [13]. Later the same authors specified the indicated numbers to the higher side: employment is reduced to 0.34%, and wages are reduced to 0.5%. These empirical regularities are formalized in the following way:

$$\begin{aligned} &\text{a) } L_{CKR}(t) = L_{CK}(t)\cdot\left[1-\varepsilon_L\cdot\left(R(t)-R_0\right)\right],\ T_0 = 2018 \\ &\text{b) } \bar{\omega}(t) = \bar{\omega}_0\cdot\left[1-\varepsilon_\omega\cdot\left(R(t)-R_0\right)\right]\cdot\exp\left[\bar{q}_p\cdot\left(t-T_0\right)\right] \end{aligned} \tag{2}$$

Here $\bar{\omega}_0$ is the average annual salary of an employee in the USA in the moment T_0 (in the USA in 2016 $\bar{\omega}_0$ = 60 thousand dollars); $\bar{q}_p$ – the average expected inflation rates which can be taken as equal to 2% per year (that is $\bar{q}_p$ = 0.02); R_0 = 1.88 mln robots used in the USA economy by the beginning of 2018; $\varepsilon_L = (0.18 \div 0.34)\cdot 10^7$ and $\varepsilon_\omega = (0.25 \div 0.5)\cdot 10^{-7}$ – empirical coefficients.

As $\bar{\omega}(t)$ (2b) isthe nominal average annual expected salary of one worker per year, the expected dynamics of the total annual income of all workers employed in the economy can be calculated using both the empirical regularities (2):

$$\bar{Y}_{ph}(t) = \bar{\omega}(t)\cdot L_{CKR}(t) \tag{3}$$

Additional reduction of working places caused by robotic automation of production and calculated with the help of the formula (2a) isreflectedbythecurve $L_{CKR}(t)$ inFig. 1. As you can see in this figure, digital technologies reduce four times more working places than robots (if we take $\varepsilon_L = 0.34\cdot 10^{-7}$, then – two times more) though we can witness for ourselves the work of robots when the action of digital technologies takes place in the real world.

Now we address the work [14] in which, on the basis of the general statistic data, it was shown that distribution of the annual income of families with one and two working parents is well enough described by the exponential and Rayleign distribution laws:

$$\begin{aligned} &a)\ Y_{ph1} = \frac{1}{r_{m1}} \cdot \exp\left(-\frac{r}{r_{m1}}\right) \\ &b)\ Y_{ph2} = \frac{1}{r^2_{m2}} \cdot \exp\left(-\frac{r}{r_{m2}}\right) \end{aligned} \tag{4}$$

where r is the annual family income in thousands of US dollars; r_{m1} and r_{m2} – mathematic expectations (average values) of family income. At that, it turned out that these distributions are fair for the income up to 120 thousand US dollars.

The distribution of income of rich families with the income more than 120 thousand dollars, as expected, turned out to be a power parameter – like the Pareto principle with the power coefficient $h = 2.7$:

$$Y_{sp}(t,r) = \frac{h(t)-1}{Y_{sp_0}} \cdot \left(\frac{Y_{sp_0}}{r}\right)^{h(t)}, \tag{5}$$

where Y_{sp_0} is the lower limit of income of rich families. According to our calculations the numerical values of parameters turned out to be equal to: $h = 2.5$ for 2017; $Y_{sp_0} = 570$ thousand dollars. As we can see they have significantly changed during the last 20 years.

Besides, we have empirically determined that $h(t)$ is inversely proportional to $\tilde{\alpha}(t)$:

$$h(t) = \frac{h_1}{\tilde{\alpha}(t)},\ h_1 = const. \tag{6}$$

Using the known data of the Pareto factor $h(t)$ we have determined the value $h_1 = 0.95$. At that, $h(t)$ decreasing, asymptotically tends to the value of 2.

The total income of private households $\bar{Y}_{ph}(t)$ defined by us earlier (3) is distributed between households with one and two workers:

$$Y_{ph}(t,r) = \bar{Y}_{ph}(t) \cdot \left[\upsilon_1(t) \cdot Y_{ph_1}(r) + \upsilon_2(t) \cdot Y_{ph_2}(r)\right], \tag{7}$$

Where υ_1 and υ_2 are shares of families with one and two workers and $\upsilon_1 = 1 - \upsilon_2$. It is known that in 1996 theincomeof American households could be well described by approximation $0.45 \cdot Y_{ph_1} + 0.55 \cdot Y_{ph_2}$ [14]. In the 2010s there already was the correlation $0.5 \cdot Y_{ph_1} + 0.5 \cdot Y_{ph_2}$.

The peak of women's economic activity in the USA came to 2000 when 60% of them worked equally with men [15]. Since then this indicator continues decreasing. As a result of intensive technological replacement of working places the number of families with two workers υ_2 will decrease from now forward. It is quite logical to admit that this will happen according to the logistic law:

$$\upsilon_1 = \frac{\upsilon_{10}}{\upsilon_{10} + (1-\upsilon_{10}) \cdot \exp\left[-\vartheta_\upsilon \cdot (t - T_{0\upsilon})\right]}, \tag{8}$$

where υ_{10}, ϑ_υ are constant parameters. Let us suppose that by 2050 the absolute majority of families will have one worker, then, knowing that in the 2010's $\upsilon_{10} \cong 0.5$, out of (8) we determine: $\vartheta_\upsilon \cong 0.067$.

Thus, we have defined the distribution of family income of the middle class including poor (7) and also rich families (5). Their mathematical expectations are important for comparative study; it is not hard to obtain them from the above mentioned distributions:

$$\begin{aligned} &\text{a) } r_{mph}(t) = v_1(t) \cdot r_{m1} + 2v_2(t) \cdot r_{m2} = \left[v_1(t) + 2z \cdot v_2(t)\right] \cdot r_{m1} \\ &\text{b) } r_{msp}(t) = \frac{h(t)-1}{h(t)-2} \cdot Y_{sp0};\ r_{m2} = z \cdot r_{m1} \end{aligned}, \tag{9}$$

Here is the coefficientz taking into account difference in salaries of men and women in families. If their salaries are equal then $z = 1$.

As r_{m1} we can take the average annual expected salary of a worker which we have already determined (2b):

$$r_{m1} = \bar{\omega}_0 \cdot \left[1 - \varepsilon_\omega \cdot (R(t) - R_0)\right] \cdot \exp\left[\bar{q}_p \cdot (t - T_0)\right], \tag{10}$$

This average income can nominally increase slightly, although in real terms it will only decline. As for rich families their average income (9b) will only grow because the Pareto factor $h(t)$ will decrease, asymptotically tending to 2, and Y_{sp_0} will slowly grow but we don't know the regularity of its growth.

Let us introduce a crude measure of inequality as the relation of the average income of rich families (9b) to the average income of families from the middle class including poor ones (9a):

$$\xi(t) = \frac{r_{msp}(t)}{r_{mph}(t)} = \frac{h(t)-1}{h(t)-2} \cdot \frac{Y_{sp_0}}{\left[\upsilon_1 + 2z \cdot (1-\upsilon_1)\right] \cdot r_{m1}}, \tag{11}$$

Here, $h(t)$ is calculated using the formula (6), υ_1 – the formula (8) and r_{m1} – the formula (10). Thegrowthcurveof income inequality $\xi(t)$ calculated using the formula (11) with the conservative value $Y_{sp_0} = 570$ thousand dollars and also the minimum value $\varepsilon_\omega = 0.25 \cdot 10^{-7}$ is represented in Fig.2a. As you can see from the diagram, if drastic measures on redistributing income will not be taken, then inequality of income which represents more than a tenfold break already will grow and exceed a twenty-fold break in the 2030's, and by 2050 this value will exceed a fifty-fold break. And this is without taking into account the tendency to increase the lower limit of income of rich families Y_{sp_0}.

a) b)

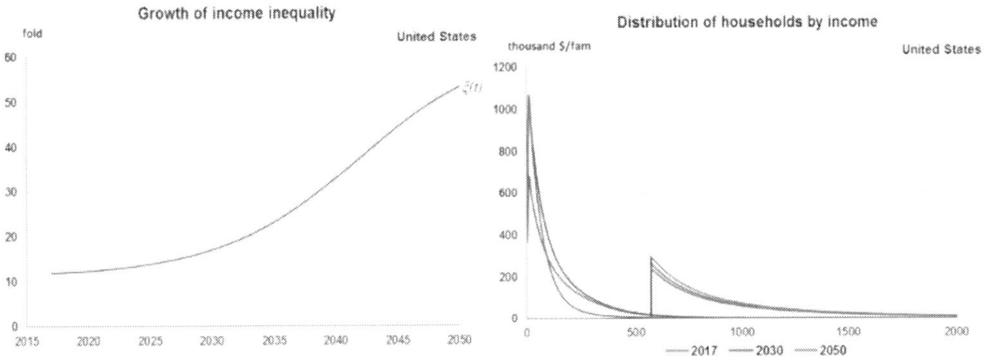

Fig. 2. Growth of inequality and polarization of income of the USA population.

The polarization of income is especially well seen in Fig. 2b where the curves of distributing the annual income of middle class representatives are demonstrated, including poor ones (in Fig.2b – to the left) and also rich ones (in Fig. 2b – to the right); the curves are built relatively using the formulas (7) and (5) for 2017, 2030 and 2050. As you can see, families with the average income within the limits of 300 thousand dollars to 600 thousand dollars will practically disappear by 2050. This speaks of the devastation of the middle class from the society of the future, which at all times has been the backbone of democracy and stability in society.

In his fundamental book "The Great Divide", Joseph Stiglitz, the Nobel prizewinner, has disclosed to the fullest extent the true picture of income inequality in the USA and polarization of the American society and its harmful effect on the American nation and the whole world [16]. He appeals to adopt real decisions for preserving the middle class: increase of taxation for corporations and rich people; more investments in education and healthcare and also in science; assistance for households and not for banks; repairing economy to the full employment. That's just the possibility of making such decisions in the era of the digital economy remains a big question.

References

1. K. Schwab, *The Fourth Industrial Revolution* (World Economic Forum, Cologne, 2016)
2. H. Kagermann, W. Wahlster, J. Helbig, Recommendations for implementing the strategic initiative INDUSTRIE 4.0. [online], Available at: http://www.acatech.de/fileadmin/user_upload/Baumstruktur_nach_Website/Acatech/root/de/Material_fuer_Sonderseiten/Industrie_4.0/Final_report__Industrie_4.0_accessible.pdf (2013)
3. S. Greengard, *The Internet of Things* (The MIT Press, Cambridge, 2015)
4. M. Swan, *Blockchain: Blue-print for a New Economy* (O'Reilly Media, Sebastopol, 2015)
5. T. Devezas, J. Leitão, A. Sarygulov A., *Industry 4.0 – Entrepreneurship and Structural Change in the New Digital Landscape* (Springer International Publishing, Cham, 2017)
6. R. Kurzweil, *How to Create a Mind: The Secret of Human Thought Revealed*, (Brilliance Audio, New York, 2012)

7. P. Saviotti, Journal of Evolutionary Economics, **11** (2001)
8. E. Brynjolfsson, A. McAfee, *The Second Machine Age: Work, Progress and Prosperity in a Time of Brilliant Technologies* (W.W. Norton & Company New York, 2014)
9. E. Jacobs, What Do Trends in Economic Inequality Imply for Innovation and Entrepreneurship? [online], Available at: http://cdn.equitablegrowth.org/wp-content/uploads/2016/02/16094329/021616-innovation-jacobs.pdf (2016)
10. C. M. Mody, Responsible Innovation: The 1970s, Today, and the Implications for Equitable Growth [online], Available at: http://cdn.equitablegrowth.org/wp-content/uploads/2016/02/04175810/020816-resp-innov.pdf (2016)
11. G. Valenduc, P. Vendramin, ETUI Working paper (2016)
12. C. Degryse, ETUI Working paper (2016)
13. D. Acemoglu, P. Restrepo, NBER Working Paper No. 23285 (2017)
14. A. Dragulesku, V. M. Yakovenko, Physica A., **299** (2001)
15. M. Ford, Basic books, **2** (2015)
16. J. E. Stiglitz, *The Great Divide: Unequal Societies and What We can Do About Them* (W.W. Norton & Company, New York, 2015)

Digital economy: backgrounds, main drivers and new challenges[a]

Askar Akaev[1], *Askar* Sarygulov[2*], and *Valentin* Sokolov[2]

[1] Moscow State University, 119991 Leninskie Gory 1, Russian Federation
[2] Saint Petersburg State University of Economics, 191023 Sadovaya st. 21, Russian Federation

Abstract. The industry development over the last hundred years has had a huge impact on the development of technological infrastructure and life change. Three main components of this development are related to personalization: a car as a personal vehicle and greater personal freedom; a personal computer as a means of intellectual autonomy; a personal phone as a means of freedom of communication and access to information. These three development factors significantly changed the employee psychology and created the conditions for diffusion of qualitatively new, synthesized (cyber-physical) technologies that became the basis of the Industry 4.0 and the Internet of Things – two main working concepts of industrial and infrastructural development for the next 20 years. The conventional or classical industrial systems that are dominant to the present day have mainly been based on the principles of human muscle energy replacement, but the technological changes of our days raise the question of the substantial scale of displacement of the living manpower both in production and in management and services. The process of technological and industrial transformation that has already begun will inevitably lead to the transformation of social and economic systems, and here the key problem will not only be the provision of a new quality of economic growth, but also the solution of the employment problem interfacing a new technological platform, the information and social infrastructure of society.

Significant efforts made by financial regulators to overcome the consequences of the 2008-2009 crisis did not lead to a noticeable revival of the economy of the industrialized countries. As applied to the US economy, this phenomenon was characterized as "secular stagnation" [1]. Researchers who analyzed more than 10-year stagnation in the Japanese economy, as a reason, indicated the low efficiency of capital use [2-3]. The same process was called "stagnation traps" [4], when under pessimistic expectations, a gap between large volumes of production and low growth rates can coexist.Japanese and Korean economists in their joint study see the reason for the Japanese economy stagnation at an extremely low rate of capital expenditure connected with its development [5].

---

[a]This article was prepared under financial support of the Russian Science Foundation (Grant No. 18-18-00099)

[*]Corresponding author:cfr@engec.ru

The most recent crisis (2007-2009) was predetermined not only by the presence of "bubbles" in the sphere of finance, but also by the allometric character of the sectoral development, when disproportionately high shares in national economies fell on one sector (finance, services), while the share of other industries first of all processing) catastrophically reduced. This structural imbalance accumulated over the years was the result of non-conjugation of a new technological platform, control forms and methods, and practices of social development.

All this predetermined two options for solving the accumulated problems: widespread use of economic policy methods to overcome the stagnation is aggregate demand stimulation, the policy of low interest rate and new investments support in the economy, and a number of other regulatory measures. In addition, another way has been outlined to solve the problem of economic stagnation: search for new technological solutions that could qualitatively change the entire economic landscape and give a new impulse to development. Here, it is necessary to note the recommendations for the development strategy "The Industry 4.0" for German manufacturers [6], two American concepts: "The Industrial Internet" [7] and "The Internet of Things" [8]. The paper on artificial intelligence [9] published in 2003 laid the foundations for the industrial development of the systems with artificial intelligence. At the World Economic Forum 2016, K. Schwab initiated a broad discussion on the Fourth Industrial Revolution [10]. The well-known book [11] assesses the positive consequences of the use of digital technologies primarily in the form of increase in performance and provision of more creative character of employees' compensation. Other researchers warn of the potentially high risk of new industrial systems, firstly, in the area of economic inequality [12]. In general, the world industry and services sector are accumulating the necessary "critical mass" of new knowledge and technologies, which can create new conditions for development like an explosion. And consumption personalization and social demands individualization can be considered as a point of transition to a new machine era which includes: a) the Industry 4.0; b) the Internet of Things; c) AI elements based systems.

These qualitative changes have matured over the past 25-30 years – a period that can be characterized as a zigzag of history and economic divergence. A key feature of world development in this period was the slowdown in economic growth in industrialized countries at simultaneous social and economic polarization. The actual locomotives of the world economy were rapidly growing China and India. Another important feature was the qualitatively new role of information and communication technologies which became the basis of a new digital infrastructure of society. The analysis of the structural dynamics of the world's developed countries shows that a set of conditions (information-technological, managerial-organizational, financial, consumer) is maturing in them, the combined effect of which provides a qualitatively new trend of economic development. In our view, a long stagnation period, especially in the industrial development of the world's leading economies (G-7 countries), which covers the last 20 years, is largely due to the structural unpreparedness of their economic and industrial systems to a qualitatively new stage of development. Our previous analysis of the manufacturing industry structure in terms of technologies and employment structure of the G-7 countries showed that there is a decrease in the employment rate in the industry and the manpower flow to the service sector for 1980-2010 and practical invariance of industry sectors rate in terms of the technologies level for the same period. [13] With regard to changes in the labor nature, they are characterized by three main trends: a) direct substitution of human functions based on robotic and computer application; b) rapid depletion of certain types of professions due to the availability of global information and social networks; c) rapid growth of the parallel labor market. Therefore, the key question is how to ensure the development of those types of technologies which will continue to provide human participation in the production process, without making it an "appendage" of new intellectual systems. This problem solution will reduce the risk of increasing inequality and financial instability.

The technological breakthrough taking place presently has not arisen without reason. It was preceded by the stage of a rather long period of decrease in growth rates and significant reduction in the share of industry in the GDP of all industrialized countries. However in the depths of these processes, new scientific ideas matured and applied research was carried out which were later materialized in several key lines.

The first line was directly related to the development of the technologies themselves – in the field of new materials and methods for their obtaining. Here it is necessary to identify nanotechnologies that significantly extended the potential for obtaining new materials with predefined properties and technology of layered synthesis (3D printing).

The second line is based on the development of data processing technologies (BigData, cloud computing, augmented reality, neural systems) and exploratory studies on the creation of quantum computers, new generation supercomputers.

The third line is to find a synergistic effect from the convergent nature of the use of advanced technologies and new knowledge which led to the creation of not only new (NBIC) technologies, but also gave wide opportunities for the development of the life science, human genome research, creation of a new generation of medicines and prolongation of human life.

The fourth line focuses on the studies for creation and operation of industrial systems with the artificial intelligence elements and global digital infrastructure that allows practical tasks such as the creation of "smart factories", "smart cities", "digital currencies" or robotic cars. In the most concentrated form, this was reflected in the following concepts: "Digital Economy" (2001), "Crypto-Currency" and "Blockchain" (2008), "Industrial Internet" (2012), "Internet of Things" (2012), "Industry 4.0" (2013), "Second Machine Age" (2014) and "The Fourth Industrial Revolution" (2016).

The next line is related to the commercialization of those technological solutions that fundamental and applied science transferred to the industry. A special feature of this process was the qualitatively new role of outsourcing when new diagrams of production cooperation led to a wide diffusion of technologies and a sharp decrease in costs. The consequence of all this was the emergence of broad capabilities and relatively inexpensive technical gadgets. Their accessibility and availability of global information networks have opened new opportunities for both the consumer and business.

A separate line was studies on the impact of new technologies on the level of employment and the processes of economic inequality. The dominant characteristic of studies in this line is the formulation of the problem itself and recognition of the need for deep institutional and legal reforms.

The next line of research is connected with the formation of a parallel labor market under new opportunities provided by electronic platforms. New opportunities for self-organization of labor activity have a significant impact on the character of mutual relations between the manufacturer of goods and services and the consumer, since they often change roles and erase previously existing tight bounds in the conventional diagrams: "manufacturer-seller-consumer".

Modern trends in industrial development are largely based on the digital technologies. In this regard, it is not unexpected that there is a question on the stability of this trend. Especially in the context of the relatively recent (2000-2001) crisis in IT companies, when the market capitalization of the Internet and telecommunications companies fell by 1.775 trillion dollars and led to a massive bankruptcy of about 300 large companies [14]. It should be noted that among these companies there were not only Internet providers, but also engaged in e-commerce (Cyberian Outpost, eToys.com, Pets.com, Webvan), social networking (theGlobe.com), digital currency trading (Floos .com), online video and audio hosting (Pixelon, Ritmoteca.com). Such high-tech companies as Cisco, Qualcomm, eBay, Amazon.com, Google emerged the crisis with significant losses. The crisis cause laid not only in the context of broad market speculation in the shares of IT companies, but also in the unreasonably high expectations of investors and consumers from the sphere of IT services, the absence of developed digital infrastructure, powerful and capable of on-line data retrieval systems oriented tomass consumer. As well as there were no high-tech and affordable gadgets that significantly reduced the field of new technologies application. Now, almost 15 years later, this technological gap has been overcome. The practice of industrial development and management in recent 5-10 years demonstrates the specific examples of technological breakthroughs: creation of robotic cars (Google, Tesla), voice recognition technologies (Siri, Alexa), a new generation of storage robots (Amazon Kiva), exponential growth of microchip density, data load and process rate, capacity of data warehouses and their energy efficiency. Rapid development of the Internet and the associated growth in e-commerce led to the creation of new technologies for bank transactions – blockchain. This allowed reducing the terms for the funds transfer from 5-6 banking days to 20 seconds [15]. The growth of digital technologies, social networks and smart phones has contributed to faster and more targeted customer satisfaction, creation of new companies (Uber, Amazon, Alibaba, Facebook, Netflix, iTunes) and bankruptcy of others (for example, Borders, Blockbuster, Kodak, as a result of which 250 thousand people in total lost their jobs). Rapid growth rates of a number of different robots and systems with artificial intelligence (AI) shall be specially mentioned. On the one hand, global investments in start-ups related to AI development have reached their five-year peak in 2016 and amounted to 5.02 billion dollars [16]. On the other hand, the US practice for development of high-tech industries has showed that only 8.8% of manpower in the 1980s, 4.4% in the 1990s and only 0.5% in the 2000s have transferred to these sectors [17]. The banking sector susceptible to innovation has already announced future large-scale staff reductions: the American CitiBank will reduce 30% of employees until 2025; three largest Japanese banks (Mizuho Financial Group Inc, Sumitomo Mitsui Financial Group Inc and Mitsubishi UFJ Financial Group Inc) for the same period will reduce 33 thousand employees. The American researchers consider that it quite possible that almost 47% of workplaces are under direct threat of automation and substitution by robots, software products or artificial intelligence [18], for Germany, this figure is even higher – up to 59% [19], and, for countries of Southern Europe, it varies from 45 to 60 percent [20]. The specialists from MIT assess that in the near future one robot will substitute 3.2 to 5.4 workers [21]. It should be noted that robots are increasingly used not only in industry, but also in services and households. So, according to the International Federation of Robotics, 2.6 mln. industrial robots and 42 mln. services and households robots will be used in the world in 2019. Thus, technological transformation will inevitably lead to the transformation of social and economic systems.

The conventional or classical industrial systems that are dominant to the present day have mainly been based on the principles of human muscle energy replacement (steam force, internal combustion engine, electricity). Intellectual abilities were fully used and their replacement with machines in the course of production, management or design was minimal. However, the technological changes of our days raise the question of the substantial scale of displacement of the living manpower both in production and in management and services. And this cardinally changes the entire economic and social landscape.

Another important component lies in the plane of the forms of organization and conduct of business. The system existence for years a priori proceeded from the fact that people shall be organized into certain structures with internal rules and their hierarchy, and the results of their activities shall be mediated by a multitude of agents before they reach the end user. This inevitably caused complex systems of production, supply, storage, sale, trade and imposed certain mutual obligations on both parties in case of hiring and firing. Actual technologies offer ample opportunities for self-employment that already leads to the creation of a parallel labor market, blurring the line between the concepts "work" and "home". The latter circumstance raises the question of reviewing many regulatory standards in the field of employment, taxation, medical insurance and pension coverage. For example, in the EU countries, almost 55% of self-employed people (13% of the overall number of labor force) are at risk of losing unemployment benefits and 37.5% are at risk of losing sick benefits [22]. Modern giants of the digital industry (Google, Amazon, Twitter) actively use information generated by network users for commercial purposes. This process is called "Digital Taylorism" or "Crowd sourcing". Many researchers consider these processes as extremely negative, but their comprehensive and systematic study has not yet been made.

New technologies also provide ample opportunities for rapid and direct economic exchange of goods and services between the manufacturer and the end user, often separated by thousands of kilometers. And this forms a new type of relationship, without intermediaries, with a high level of individualization of the request and the targeting and accuracy of its satisfaction by the manufacturer. In classical economic systems there was a close-out separation of labor into living and materialized, the latter has a purely production, but not a creative nature. Modern complex software products (it is not yet artificial intelligence) are able to replace a person, for example, in the analysis of standard banking transactions or stock trading on the stock exchange or, as Uber's experience shows – to replace entire companies. While carrying out such functions, embodied labor already changes its character and is capable of variability and generation of new added value. More complex systems, for example oriented to pattern recognition are able to control technical means (for example, cars) and in this case, the scale of replacement of living labor already look frighten. All of these raise the question of the nature of capital accumulation, since new intellectual systems with a high capitalized value can potentially create conditions for the dominance of machines over man, not only in the sphere of production, but also in the sphere of services and social communication.

Many processes in the economy acquire a qualitatively new character due to the trunk nature of digital technologies, which:

– Constantly expand the range of economic activities, creating conditions for the growth of return on capital at practically zero marginal costs;

– Promote the emergence of new business models based on the market competition of digital goods and services;

– Offer ample opportunities for the network principle of production organization, actually blurring the lines between manufacturers, sellers and consumers;

– Create an unprecedented amount of data and at the same time provide various tools for processing and using this resource that transforms data numerically into a strategic resource and makes it one of the main organizational principles of both the economy and society as a whole.

In June 2015 MIT Technology Review published the Open Letter on Digital Economy, initiated by an international group of scientists and representatives of private companies. During the wide discussion of this letter, a future program of action and research emerged, which can be divided into three major areas:

- Changes in government policies in education, infrastructure, entrepreneurship, trade, immigration, research and other key areas that will help create jobs and improve the economy.
- Business and organizational models that will help to achieve not only higher productivity and profit for companies, but also greater prosperity for their managers, investors, workers and society as a whole.

• Study of the economic and social consequences of the digital revolution, so that innovative and long-term solutions can be adopted.

Several centers have been created by now, that study various aspects related to the formation of the economy based on a new technological platform.

The Massachusetts Institute of Technology (MIT) performs extensive studies in the field of assessing the impact of workplace automation and robots application [20]; the same questions are in the purview of scientists at the Boston Columbia University [22].

The University of Oxford [18] conducted extensive studies and assessed the probabilities of full computerization of many professions with respect to the American economy. The University of Oxford together with Citibank (Citi Global Perspectives & Solutions) in 2016 published the results of extensive studies on the state of the economy of key countries and the problems of transition to a digital economy (Technology at Work v2.0).

The problems of technological development, jobs future, inequality and productivity are constantly monitored by the McKinsey Global Institute (MGI) and are reflected in a number of scientific reports [24-27].

The European Trade Union Institute focuses on studies of employment issues, new forms of business organization, performance of institutional reforms and protection of workers' interests. This was reflected in two working documents of the Institute for 2016 [28-29].

The problems of economic inequality are studied under the auspices of the Washington Center for Equitable Growth. Here, first of all, it is necessary to mention the following papers: E. Jacobs [30] and C. M. Mody [31].

The platform of the World Economic Forum initiated two important reports on the possibilities and consequences of the new industrial revolution [32-33].

The issues of economic and technological challenges are conventionally in the purview of major international organizations: Organization for Economic Co-operation and Development (OECD) that with an interruption of 16 years published two reports having the direct relation to the problems of the digital economy [34-35]. The same issues are monitored by the United Nations Industrial Development Organization (UNIDO) which were reflected in the document for 2016 [36-37].

Among the European countries it is necessary to allocate Germany that not only proposed in 2013 the concept of "The Industry 4.0" prepared by the representatives of the Federal Government, academic and business groups, but also the Action Program to provide a smooth transition to a new type of economy that was reflected in the document of the Federal Ministry of Labor and Social Affairs [38].

As for the Russian research segment, it should be noted the following:

– The program "Digital Economy of the Russian Federation" [39] adopted in 2017;

– Survey report "Digital Economy: Global Trends and Practice of Russian Business" prepared by the HSE Institute of Innovation Management (HSE IIM) [40];

– The results of joint comprehensive studies on the problems of "Industry 4.0" performed by Russian and foreign scientists and published in a separate monograph in the Publishing House "Springer Verlag" in 2017 [41].

The non-profit, private found Ewing Marion Kauffman Foundation (USA) opened an on-line platform for an open discussion on the problems of development and support of entrepreneurship and innovation under new technological challenges, and invited the representatives of academic and business circles to participate.

The analysis of the most recent publications and literary sources, as well as trends in production shows that new conditions have practically been created that can provide the structural transformation of industrial and economic systems since:

– a digital infrastructure has been formed that includes the public Internet and a set of technically simple gadgets, social networks, systems for on-line "big" data process and exchange;

– a new technological platform was created based on the technologies of the "microcosm" and biological systems with elements of artificial intelligence;

– the mass consumer has real possibilities for "personalization" of its requests, and the technological platform is able to satisfy them.

Such structural transformation can be probably achieved by creating a new industrial base that will connect the Internet of Things, smart factories and digital infrastructure. At the level of separate firms and companies, technological and industrial trends are forming, which determine the future nature of system development as a whole.

It is obvious that the development of a new industrial base will require significant amounts of capital and costs to maintain human resources. In this regard, a number of issues arises, the solution of which is not only relevant, but is also complex scientific problems. First of all, it is necessary to include the following:

– Study of the fundamentally new nature of the capital accumulation process in the context of individual components (human, intellectual and physical), in conditions when new revolutionary technologies and innovations become the dominant and driving force affecting economic development in the first half of the 21st century;

– Assessment of changes in the employment market caused by the widespread use of new intelligent computers and global computer networks that create the conditions for both free job search and partial replacement of human knowledge with machine intelligence;

– Justification of the mechanisms of protection against the intensification of social polarization and growth of economic inequality under conditions of potentially high replacement of human labor with machines and intellectual systems, which leads to the development of regulatory measures to ensure a conflict-free transition to a new industrial base;

– The role of a new industrial base in changing the structure of the world economy. The emergence and development of the Industry 4.0, new products and sales markets will result in changing the structure of employment in the leading countries that means a change in the system of the already established international division of labor.

The process of technological and industrial transformation that has already begun will inevitably lead to the transformation of social and economic systems, and here the key problem will not only be the provision of a new quality of economic growth, but also the solution of the employment problem interfacing a new technological platform, the information and social infrastructure of society.

References

1. L. H. Summers, U.S. Economic Prospects: Secular Stagnation, Hysteresis, and the Zero Lower Bound, *Business Economics*, **49(2)**, 65-73 (2014)
2. A. Ando, D. Christelis, T. Miyagawa, Inefficiency of Corporate Investment and Distortion of Savings Behavior in Japan, *NBER Working Paper,* **9444** (2003)
3. F. Hayashi, The Over-Investment Hypothesis, in Lawrence R. Klein, ed., Long-Run Growth and Short-Run Stabilization: Essays in Memory of Albert Ando, Edward Elgar (2006)
4. G. Benigno, L. Fornaro, Stagnation Traps, *IMF Conference on Secular Stagnation, Growth, and Real Interest Rate held at Florence* (2015)
5. H. Chun, T. Miyagawa, H. K. Pyo, M. Takizawa, K. Tonogi, *Declining Rate of Return on Capital and the Role of Intangibles in Japan and Korea, The Fourth World KLEMS Conference Asia KLEMS session* (2016)

6. H. Kagermann, W. Wahlster, J. Helbig, Recommendations for implementing the strategic initiative INDUSTRIE 4.0., *Industrie 4.0. WorkingGroup* (2013)
7. P. C. Evans, M. Annunziata, Industrial Internet: Pushing the Boundaries of Minds and Machines (2012)
8. M. Swan, Sensor Mania! The Internet of Things, Wearable Computing, Objective Metrics, and the Quantified Self 2.0., *J. Sens. Actuator Netw.*, **1**, 217-253 (2012)
9. S. J. Russel, P. Norvig, Artificial Intelligence: A Modern Approach (2nd ed.), Prentice Hall (2003)
10. K. Schwab *The Fourth Industrial Revolution: what it means, how to respond, World Economic Forum* (2016)
11. E. Brynjolfsson, A. McAfee. The Second Machine Age: Work, Progress and Prosperity in a Time of Brilliant Technologies, W.W. Norton & Company (2014)
12. D. Spencer, Work in and beyond the Second Machine Age: the politics of production and digital technologies. *Work, EmploymentandSociety*, **31(1)**, 142-152 (2017)
13. A. Akaev, S. Rumyantseva, A. Sarygulov, V. Sokolov, Structural-cyclic processes of economic dynamics, 462 (2016)
14. D. Kleinbard, The $1.7 trillion dot.com lesson, CNN Money (2000)
15. K. Shiba Central Banks' New Approach to AI: New Settlement System Applying Blockchain Technology and Issuance of Digital Currency. Institute for InternationalMonetaryAffairs (IIMA). *Newsletter*,**3**,(2017)
16. J. Ogawa, Global AI startup financing hit $5bn in 2016, Nikkei Asia Review (2017)
17. J. Lin, Technological Adaptation, Cities, and New Work, *Review of Economics and Statistics*, **93(2)**, 554–574 (2011)
18. C. B. Frey, M. A. Osborne, the Future of Employment: How Susceptible are Jobs to Computerization? (2013)
19. C. Brzeski, I. Burk, Die Roboterkommen. Folgen der Automatisierungfür den deutschenArbeitsmarkt, *Economic Research* (2015)
20. J. Bowles, The computerisation of European jobs, Bruegel (2014)
21. D. Acemoglu, P. Restrepo,Robots and Jobs: Evidence from US Labor Markets (2017)
22. M. Matsaganis, E. Özdemir, T. Ward, A. Zavakou, Non-standard employment and access to social security benefits (2016)
23. S. G. Benzell, L. J Kotlikoff,G. LaGarda, J. D. Sachs, Robots Are Us: Some Economics of Human Replacement, Boston University, Columbia University (2015)
24. ManufacturingtheFuture: The next era of Global Growth and Innovations, McKinsey Global Institute (2012)
25. Disruptive technologies: Advances that will transform life, business, and the global economy McKinsey Global Institute (2013)
26. Poorer Than Their Parents? Flat of Falling Incomes in Advanced Economies, McKinsey Global Institute (2016)
27. A Future That Works: Automation, Employment, and Productivity, McKinsey Global Institute (2012)
28. G. Valenduc, P. Vendramin. Work in the digital economy: sorting the old from the new, *ETUI Working paper* (2016)
29. C. Degryse. Digitalisation of the Economy and its impact on Labor Markets, *ETUI Working paper* (2016)
30. E. Jacobs. What Do Trends in Economic Inequality Imply for Innovation and Entrepreneurship?, Washington Center for Equitable Growth (2016)
31. C. M. Mody, Responsible Innovation, Washington Center for Equitable Growth (2016)
32. *The Fourth Industrial Revolution: what it means, how to respond, World Economic Forum* (2016)

33. *Realizing Human Potential in the Fourth Industrial Revolution An Agenda for Leaders to Shape the Future of Education, Gender and Work, World Economic Forum* (2017)
34. The New Economy Beyond the Hype, *OECD Report* (2001)
35. Future of Work and Skills, *OECD Report* (2017)
36. IndustrialDevelopment, *Report UNIDO* (2016)
37. The Role of Technology and Innovation in Inclusive and Sustainable Industrial Development, *Report UNIDO* (2016)
38. Re-imagining Work. White Paper Work 4.0, German Federal Ministry of Labor and Social Affairs (2016)
39. The Digital Economy of the Russian Federation, Government Report (2017)
40. Digital Economy: Global Trends and Practice of Russian Business, Moscow, HSE (2017)
41. T. Devezas, J. Leitão, A. Sarygulov A., *Industry 4.0 – Entrepreneurship and Structural Change in the New Digital Landscape* (Springer International Publishing, Cham, 2017)

Application of hierarchic authentication to isogenies of elliptic curves for providing safety of data routing in the systems of analysis of digital production traffic[a]

Elena Alexandrova[1], *Maria* Poltavtseva[1*], and *Anastasia* Yarmak[1]

[1]Peter the Great St. Petersburg Polytechnic University, Institute of Computer Sciences and Technologies, 195251 Polytechnicheskaya st. 29, Russian Federation

Abstract. The article discusses the peculiarities of the process of information routing in the course of acquisition and processing big data of digital production, including systems of traffic analysis. Such a specific features variability of physical nodes-processors with the retention of functional stringency of order of information processing is distinguished. Inordertoprovidesafetyofthedescribedprocessofinformationprocessingand possibility of restoration of a chain of processing every fragment of data, the authors offer a protocol of hierarchic authentication developed thereby on isogenies of elliptic curves. The work includes algorithms of shaping parameters, generation of keys, generation and checking signature. The evaluation of signature stability again basic types of attacks has been performed. A solution offered by the authors can be used both in traditional and, in future, in quantum systems. A simulation of corresponding signature dimensions has been performed in the work.

1 Introduction

A current development of industrial manufacture, "the 4th industrial revolution" [1] and computerization of production processes have brought about a necessity of occurrence of unique information systems encompassing activity of enterprises and organizations from management of physical objects to business processes [2]. They are based on a set of new solutions, both in the field of element base (quick controllers, data processing centers, in future – quantum computation equipment), and in the field of software (virtualization, cloud technologies, analytical systems, big data processing systems).

According to current analytical and industrial investigations the big data technologies are one of the main technologies making a basis of digital production. They appear as one

[a] With financial support from the Ministry of Education and Science of the Russian Federation in the framework of the Federal targeted program "Investigations and developments in the priority field of development of Russian science and technology complex for 2014-2020", Agreement No. 14.578.21.0231, agreement unique identifier RFMEFI57817X0231)

[*]Corresponding author: poltavtseva@ibks.spbstu.ru

of fundamentals of digital economics both in private [3], and in state [4] sources. From the point of view of informational safety the big data systems of digital production take on two roles:

1) as an instrument of protection strategy implementation;
2) as an object of ensuring safety.

In the first case the big data technology is used for providing security of digital economics system as a whole. The assessment of security of big heterogeneous system of digital production requires analysis of a great number of poorly structured parameters correlated with different management levels (physical level, SCADA level, corporate network level, etc.). The analysis of traffic of highway network with the aim of revealing intrusions can be used as an example of such application. This, generally speaking, private task of security analysis already requires processing of terabytes and petabytes of information.

In the second case it is referred to security of the transferred data proper, ensuring confidentiality of processing thereof. The digital production contemplates enormous volumes of transferred data from the parameters and indicators of sensors to confidential documentation. Not only the places of origin, processing and final use of such sort of information are mutually spaced from one another logically and geographically, but some individual steps too, such as processing and storage of information encompass a plurality of heterogeneous computation nodes [5].

At that it is important that the data of systems of ensuring security shall be protected in the same way, if not more than the other data. The influence of ill-minded person on the system of providing informational security and detecting intrusions throw into question a possibility of its application as a whole. Therefore, a relevant task consists in the development of means of enhancing security of systems of big data processing taking into account the prospects of technologies development.

2. Specific features of data routing in the course of acquisition and processing thereof in digital production systems

The traditional components of architectures of analytical systems mixing takes place in the up-to-date big data systems, including systems of processing network traffic. The classical analysis includes sequentially: data sources; components of extraction and conversion; components of storage; sampling, restructuring and delivery; presentations of data and information receivers in the form of analysts or business proposals. The modern architectures make it possible to distinguish three architectural layers:

1. Data sources.
2. Heterogeneous environment of data transfer and processing.
3. Data consumers.

The components of processing, such as conversion, storage, restructuring, etc. appear to be distributed between these layers (Fig. 1), at that, a distribution can differ depending on architecture of a particular system.

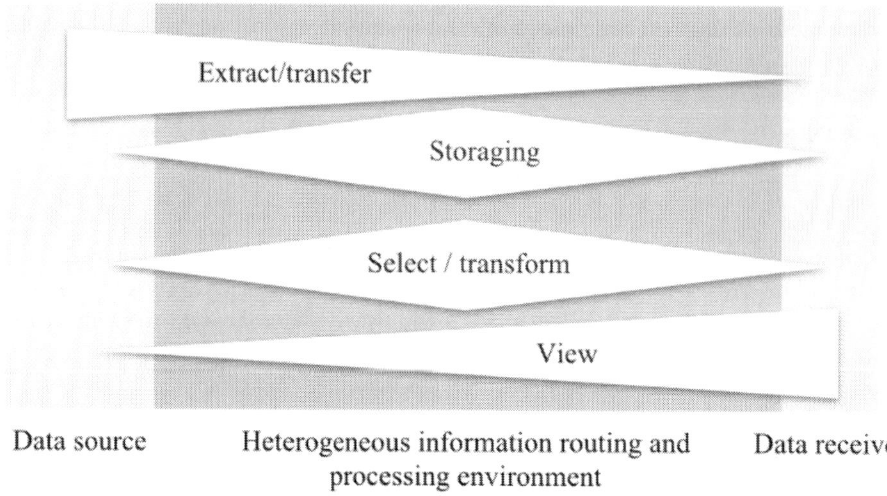

Fig. 1. Distribution of data processing components.

Such a distribution contemplates information processing at different stages with the use of distributed nodes and systems, when the movement of a particular information fragment with respect to computation system can differ depending on a great number of parameters, such as:

- data source;
- data type;
- temporary data characteristics;
- work load of different fragments of information transmission network;
- work load of computation nodes

and others. Since the source and type of data are not the only determining factors for forming a route, it is impossible to forecast in advance, where particularly, at what particular nodes they are going to be processed. A variability of routes of processing information is shown in Fig. 2.

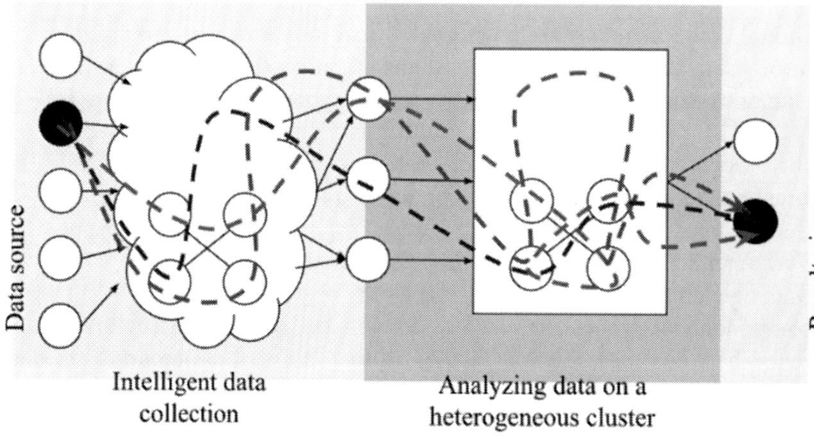

Fig. 2. Variability of routes of processing information of one source.

The highway routers can come forward as a source of data in the systems of traffic analysis, while a client part of SIEM system of security analysis will come forward as a receiver [6]. The source and receiver of data in Fig. 2 are highlighted in black color, different paths of information routing between them in the course of processing are shown. In this case the system of traffic analysis features the following peculiarities:

1. Data processing takes place according to a predetermined diagram, set of functionally type-safe nodes on the basis of data-driven approach.
2. Number of functional types of processor nodes is countable and small.
3. Particular physical processor node can differ for every data fragment.

In other words, the typical set of processor nodes does not depend on the system characteristics, but on the initial data only (e.g., whether the information was fragmented or not), and features low variability. Thus, in order to provide for security of such sort of system from influence in the chain of processing data of external nodes, it is necessary to have a possibility to establish the entire chain of processors (both ideological and physical). In order to do so, the authors suggest using a mechanism of hierarchical digital signature. The following can be referred to as the requirements to a signature:

1. Possibility of tracing an entire chain of data processing.
2. Applicability of the offered algorithm of hierarchical signature with the advanced solutions of element base (in particular, with quantum calculations).

In order to attain these requirements, the authors suggest using a hierarchical authentication on isogenies of elliptic curves.

3. Hierarchical authentication on isogenies of elliptic curves

3.1. Authentication in classical and quantum systems

As of today there exist several classes of cryptographic systems presumably resistant to attacks on quantum computer:

1. Patterns of signature based on hash functions (pattern of signature of Merkle [7], Lemport [8], et al.).
2. Encryption schemes based on coding theory (cryptosystems of Mac-Elis [9], Niederwriter [10], et al.).
3. Cryptosystems based on noncommutative groups [11], e.g., braid groups, polycyclic groups, etc.
4. Cryptosystems based on grids (e.g., NTRU [12]).

The significant drawbacks obstructing the use of such systems in practice is a big size of the signature and cryptotext as well as low rate of data conversion as compared with the well-known classical cryptographic systems. The rapidly advancing technologies in the field of quantum calculations on the one hand, make it possible to increase the calculations rate, while on the other hand, they can endanger the available cryptosystems with an open key, which security is based, as a rule, on factorization task and calculation task of discrete logarithm in the cyclic group of elementary order. After invention of quantum computer these tasks can be solved during multinomial time by means of P. Shore algorithm. Therefore, it is necessary to use the other mathematical structures and build new protocols, which could remain relevant in case of inventing quantum computer of sufficiently big digit capacity.

The use of isogenies as the main mathematical structure gives a chance to design different diagrams: key derivation protocols, evidences with zero footprints, encryption with an open key, electronic digital signature (impossible-to-deny signal, blind signature) have been proposed as of today. However, as of the present moment there are no known examples of using isogenies for building diagrams of hierarchical authentication.

The application of rank-order digital signature makes it possible to solve a problem of creating signature on behalf of several entities and monitor the order of procedure of forming a message signature, providing by the same hierarchical authentication taking into account the structure of the group itself.

It is necessary to take into account a number of requirements, when developing a diagram of rank-order signature, in particular, the length of signature shall be invariable with respect to dimensionality of the group of signatories, while a check of the signature shall be simplified as much as possible demanding no verification of a chain of all signatures of the group participants.

3.2. Hierarchical Authentication on Isogeny of Elliptic Curves

Let us assume that $E(\mathbb{F}_{p^2})$ is a supersingular elliptic curve, where, $p = l_A^{eA} l_B^{eB} f \pm 1$,$< P_A, Q_A > \; = E[l_A^{eA}]$, $< P_B, Q_B > \; = E[l_B^{eB}]$. A unique isogeny φ: $E \rightarrow E'$ with nucleus Rexists for curve $E$and finite subgroup $R \subset E$. Let us designate $E^{'} = \varphi(E) = E/< R >$. The following computationally complex assumptions are used when building protocols on isogenies of supersingular curves [13].

Decisional Supersingular Isogeny (DSSI) problem: Let us assume that $E_A(\mathbb{F}_{p^2})$ is the other supersingular curve. Make definite, whether curves E_A and E are connected by isogeny of degree l_A^A.

*Computational Supersingular Isogeny (CSSI) problem:*Let us assume that $\varphi_A: E \rightarrow E_A$ is isogeny with nucleus$< R_A >$, where $R_A \in_R E, \# < R_A > = l_A^{eA}$. Use data E_A, $\varphi_A(P_B)$, $\varphi_A(Q_B)$ to find generatrix $< R_A >$of isogeny nucleusφ_A.

Supersingular Computational Diffie–Hellman (SSCDH) problem: Let us assume that $\varphi_A: E \rightarrow E_A$ is isogeny with nucleus$< m_A P_A + n_A Q_A >$,$\varphi_B: E \rightarrow E_B$ is isogeny with nucleus$< m_B P_B + n_B Q_B >$, where m_A, n_A (m_B, n_B) are random normal numbers of $\mathbb{Z}/\, l_A^{eA}\mathbb{Z}$ (accordingly $\mathbb{Z}/\, l_B^{eB}\mathbb{Z}$), not divisible by l_A^{eA}(accordingly l_B^{eB}). Use these curves E_A, E_B as well as points $\varphi_A(P_B)$, $\varphi_A(Q_B)$,$\varphi_B(P_A)$, $\varphi_B(Q_A)$ to find *j*-invariant of a curve $E/ < m_A P_A + n_A Q_A, m_B P_B + n_B Q_B >$.

Supersingular Decision Diffie–Hellman (SSDDH) problem: Having data taken with a probability of 1/2 from one of two finite sequences:

$(E_A$, $E_B, \varphi_A(P_B)$, $\varphi_A(Q_B)$,$\varphi_B(P_A)$,$\varphi_B(Q_A), E_{AB})$, where $E_{AB} \cong E_0/ < m_A P_A + n_A Q_A, m_B P_B + n_B Q_B >$;

$(E_A$, $E_B, \varphi_A(P_B)$, $\varphi_A(Q_B)$,$\varphi_B(P_A)$,$\varphi_B(Q_A), E_C)$, where $E_C \cong E_0/ < m^{'}_A P_A + n'_A Q_A, m'_B P_B + n'_B Q_B >$;

define, what finite sequence they have been taken from.

Suggested authentication network includes four procedures:

1. *Algorithm of parameters generation*, which results in initialization of generally-known network parameters
2. *Algorithm of keys generation*, which effects generation of open key–closed key pair for a user by means of protocol parameters
3. *Algorithm of shaping signature*, receiving a closed key of the user, message m, as well as a list of open keys of the users, who have signed the message earlier, and a current signature value σ_i. to the input. As a result of work the algorithm returns a new value σ_{i+1} or an error, if the input data appeared to be incorrect;
4. *Algorithm of checking signature*, receiving a list of open keys of the users, message m and a current signature value σ. to the input. As a result of successful verification

the algorithm returns value 1, and otherwise – it returns 0.

Let us assume that $E(\mathbb{F}_{p^2})$ is a supersingular elliptic curve set over characteristic field $p = l_A^{e_A} l_B^{e_B} l_S^{e_S} f \pm 1$with a number of points equal $(l_A^{e_A} l_B^{e_B} l_S^{e_S} f)^2$.

Let us also register points being the generatrices of torsion subgroups: $< P_A, Q_A > = E[l_A^{e_A}]$, $< P_B, Q_B > = E[l_B^{e_B}]$,$< P_S, Q_S > = E[l_S^{e_S}]$. According to a suggested protocol points P_A, Q_A and $P_B, Q_B$are used for generation of nuclear of users' isogenies, while points P_S, Q_S are used for shaping a secret isogeny φ_S.

Generation of network parameters takes place according to the following algorithm:

1. Select security parameter λ and generate field characteristic with a specified number of points $(l_A^{e_A} l_B^{e_B} l_S^{e_S} f)^2$.
2. Generate elliptic curve $E(\mathbb{F}_{p^2})$.
3. Find points $\{P_S, Q_S\}$ forming the torsion subgroups$E[l_S^{e_S}]$.
4. Generate a random point $P_M \in E[l_S^{e_S}]$.
5. Determine hash function $H: \{0,1\}^* \to \mathbb{Z}$.

Subsequently, the open network parameters equal: $p, E, \{P_S, Q_S\}, P_M, H$.

In order to shape an open key of a group with number n of participants, where every one represents a node – data processor as well as personal keys of the group users, it is necessary to perform the following actions.

1. Generate a secret isogeny $\varphi_S: E \to E_S$ by means of a nucleus $< m_S P_S + n_S Q_S >$, where $m_S n_S \in \mathbb{Z}/l_S^{e_S}\mathbb{Z}$ are random numbers not divisible by l_S, $< P_S, Q_S > = E[l_S^{e_S}]$.
2. Plot a chain of isogenies $\varphi_1 \to \varphi_2 \to \ldots \to \varphi_n$, where $\varphi_i: E_{i-1} \to E_i$, $E_0 = E, i = 1, \ldots, n$, by means of random selection of generatrices $P_i, Q_i \in E_i[l_i^{e_i}], i = \{A, B\}$, and nucleus coefficients $m_i, n_i \in \mathbb{Z}/l_i^{e_i}\mathbb{Z}$, not divisible by$l_i$.
3. Calculate: $\psi(P_M) = \varphi_n \circ \varphi_{n-1} \circ \ldots \circ \varphi_2 \circ \varphi_1(P_M)$, where $\varphi_i: E_{i-1} \to E_i, E_0 = E$, " $\circ$ " is an operation of composition of isogenies. Set an open key of a group $gpk = (E_s, \psi(P_M), deg\psi)$.
4. For every node processor or user $u_i, i = 1, .., n$, set open key–closed key pair (pk_i, sk_i) in the following way: $pk_i = (E_i, P_i, Q_i), sk_i = (m_i, n_i, m_S, n_S)$.

In order to sign message M the first user u_1 of the chain will carry out the following actions (Fig. 3):

1. Calculates hash value from a message: $h = H(M)$.
2. Generates a random point $Q \neq P_M$, $Q \in E[l_S^{e_S}]$ and assumes$Q_M = hQ$.
3. Generates isogeny $\varphi_1: E \to E_1$ on the basis of a personal closed key by means of nucleus $< m_1 P_1 + n_1 Q_1 >$and calculates the values$\varphi_1(Q_M), \varphi_1(P_s), \varphi_1(Q_s)$.
4. Generates isogeny $\varphi_{1s}: E_1 \to E_{1s}$ on the basis of a closed key of the group by means of nucleus$< m_s \varphi_1(P_s) + n_s \varphi_1(Q_s) >$.
5. Assumes: $Q_{M,1} \leftarrow \varphi_1(Q_M), P_{s,1} \leftarrow \varphi_1(P_s)$, $Q_{s,1} \leftarrow \varphi_1(Q_s)$.
6. Shapes a signature $\sigma_1 = (E_{1s}, Q, Q_{M,1}, P_{s,1}, Q_{s,1})$ and hands it over to the next user.

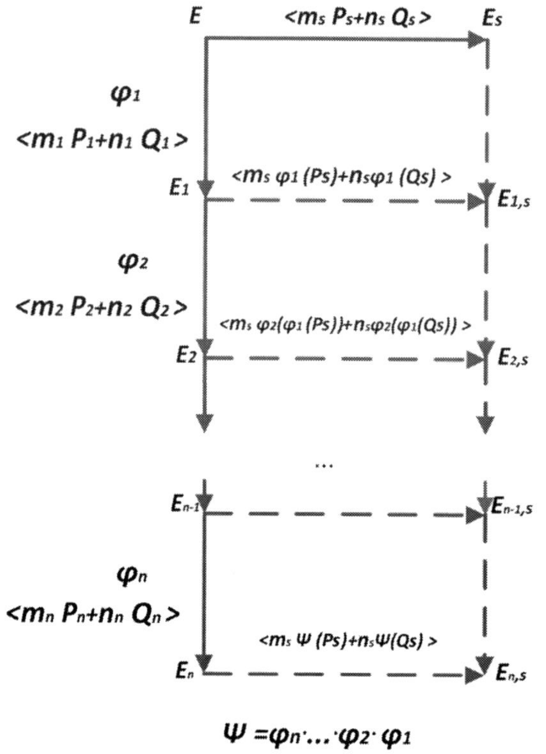

Fig. 3. Rank-Order Collective Signature Generation Network.

A user (node – processor) u_i performs the following actions on the basis of a signature $\sigma_{i-1} = (E_{i-1,s}, Q, Q_{M,i-1}, P_{s,i-1}, Q_{s,i-1})$ received from the previous user:

1. Generates user's isogeny $\varphi_i: E_{i-1} \to E_i$ by means of nucleus $< m_i P_i + n_i Q_i >$and calculates values$\varphi_i(Q_{M,i-1}), \varphi_i(P_{s,i-1}), \varphi_i(Q_{s,i-1})$.
2. Using an open key of the previous user E_{i-1} and value $E_{i-1,s}$ obtained from signature σ_{i-1}, it checks knowledge of secret isogeny φ_s by the user u_{i-1}, as in the evidence circuit [13]. In order to do so, it calculates isogeny $\varphi_{i-1,s}: E_{i-1} \to E'_{i-1,s}$ by means of nucleus $< m_s P_{s,i-1} + n_s Q_{s,i-1} >$ and checks equation $E'_{i-1,s}$and $E_{i-1,s}$.
3. Finds curve $E_{i,s}$ in the way of plotting isogeny $\varphi_{is}: E_i \to E_{is}$ by means of nucleus$< m_s \varphi_i(P_{s,i-1}) + n_s \varphi_i(Q_{s,i-1}) >$.
4. Assumes: $Q_{M,i} \leftarrow \varphi_i(Q_{M,i-1}), P_{s,i} \leftarrow \varphi_i(P_{s,i-1}), Q_{s,i} \leftarrow \varphi_i(Q_{s,i-1})$.
5. Shapes signature $\sigma_i = (E_{is}, Q, Q_{M,i}, P_{s,i}, Q_{s,i})$ and submits it to the next user.

Based on the calculated signature $\sigma_n = (E_{ns}, Q, Q_{M,n}, P_{s,n}, Q_{s,n})$ the last user of the chain of processing datau_n shapes a collective signature of a message:

$\sigma = (Q, Q_{M,n})$.

The following actions are to be performed when checking a signature:

Having message M, signature $\sigma = (Q, Q_{M,n})$ and open key of the group $\psi(P_M)$ an inspector calculates the following values of Weil coupling:

$$e_{l_S^{es}}(\psi(P_M), Q_{M,n}) \stackrel{?}{=} e_{l_S^{es}}(P_M, hQ)^{deg\psi},$$

where, ψ is an isogeny corresponding to composition of the user's isogenies, i.e. $\psi = \varphi_n \circ \varphi_{n-1} \circ \dots \circ \varphi_2 \varphi_1$, $deg\psi = deg\varphi_n \cdot \dots \cdot deg\varphi_1$.

If the equality has been fulfilled, the result will be: signature is correct, otherwise the result will be: signature is incorrect.

This check is correct, since with respect to bilinear mappings the following interrelations are met:

$$e_{l_S^{es}}(\psi(P_M), Q_{M,n}) = e_{l_S^{es}}(\psi(P_M), \psi(Q_M)) = e_{l_S^{es}}(\psi(P_M), \psi(hQ)) = e_{l_S^{es}}(P_M, hQ)^{deg\psi}.$$

3.3. Analysis of suggested solution security

The isomorphism of groups of classes of isogenies and groups of classes of ideals exists for supersingular and non-supersingular curves. A ring of endomorphisms of elliptic curve is cumulative for supersingular curves, while a group of classes of ideals is Abelian. This property has been used in attack [14] for solving an analog of the CSSI task for non-supersingular curves over subexponential time on quantum computer. In case of supersingular curves a ring of endomorphisms is noncommutative, while the group properties are not met for the classes of ideals, therefore, an attack from work [14] can not be applied, and the task of finding isogenies of supersingular curves features an exponential stability in this case.

Opening the user's personal closed key. Let us assume that there are open parameters of the system p, $E, \{P_S, Q_S\}, P_M, H$as well as open keys $gpk = (E_s, \psi(P_M), deg\psi)$ and $pk_i = (E_i, P_i, Q_i)$. Then cracking the user's personal closed key is confined to a task of finding a generatrix of isogeny nucleus $\varphi_i$with respect to available images $\varphi_i(Q_{M,i-1}), \varphi_i(P_{s,i-1}), \varphi_i(Q_{s,i-1})$,, which is complex for calculation.

Since the points (P_S, Q_S) are generatrices of the subgroup $E_{i-1}[l_S^{es}]$, the values $\varphi_i(P_S), \varphi_i(Q_S)$ help an intruder calculate the action φ_i for the entire subgroup $E_{i-1}[l_S^{es}]$, since any element $E_{i-1}[l_S^{es}]$ is a linear combination of generatrices P_S, Q_S. However, there is no algorithm making it possible to use this information for determiningisogeny φ_i. If the intruder has a possibility of calculating action φ_i in the points of subgroup $E_{i-1}[l_i^{e_i}]$, where the generatrices $< P_i, Q_i >= E_{i-1}[l_i^{e_i}]$are used during generation of nucleus φ_i, then it is possible to open isogeny $\varphi_i$by means of quantum computer. Besides, in such case it is possible to launch an attack using a classic computer too by calculating generatrix of dual isogeny nucleus. Thus, it is not realistic to transfer action φ_i to $E_{i-1}[l_S^{es}]$ to values at $E_{i-1}[l_i^{e_i}]$ and, by the same, come to know a secret isogeny of the user φ_i.

Incorporation of intruder's signature into a chain. Let us assume that the illegal intruder possesses signature $\sigma_{i-1} = (E_{i-1,s}, Q, Q_{M,i-1}, P_{s,i-1}, Q_{s,i-1})$, which has been received from a previous user u_{i-1}, and wants to build in its own signature before sending it to the next user u_i. In order to do so, it needs to have its own elliptic curve E_{adv} in the list of open keys of the group users. Then it is obliged to provide the next user with an evidence of awareness of secret isogeny $\varphi_s$in the way of plotting isogeny $\varphi_{adv,s}: E_{adv} \rightarrow E_{adv,s}$ including value $E_{adv,s}$into a signature. However, the attacker should know for this purpose the closed key values m_s, n_s, which are known to the legitimate group users only. If the legitimate system user possessing an open key and a closed key corresponding to it, is the intruder, it succeeds to prove to the next user that it is a legitimate group member. But the final isogeny ψ'will look as follows in case of embedding signature into a chain:

$$\psi' = \varphi_n \diamond \varphi_{n-1} \diamond \varphi_{adv} \diamond \dots \diamond \varphi_2 \varphi_1,$$

while its degree will increase $deg\varphi_{adv}$ times. In this case in the course of checking signature the equation

$$e_{l_M}(\psi[P_M], \psi'[hQ]) = e_{l_M}(P_M, hQ)^{deg\psi}$$

will not be fulfilled, since the open group key $\psi(P_M)$ comprises an image of a legitimate chain, and the value $deg\psi \neq deg\psi'$.

Changing order of message signing. In case of a confederacy involving a group of users, who want to violate a hierarchy of signature formation, value $deg\psi'$ will be equal $deg\psi$, however, the resulting isogeny ψ'will differ by an order of succeeding of the user's isogenies, therefore, the check interrelation will not be used too. Any additional signature incorporated by an intruder will bring about the increase of degree of the resulting isogeny, which legitimate value is provided in the open key of a group. Therefore, a complete signature falsification is possible only under condition of incorrect generated system parameters.

*Message false representation.*Let us assume that there is a signature $\sigma = (Q, Q_{M,n})$ of message$M$and the intruder has an intention to find a document M'corresponding to this signature σ. For this purpose it will calculate its hash $h' = H(M')$ trying to find such a value $h'Q$in order to fulfill the check interrelation. Since Q is a part of signature, it can not be substituted, therefore, the message false representation is confined to solving task of finding hash function collision.

The authors have performed simulation of the offered pattern with the use of computerized algebra system Sage for a group consisting of five users. As a result, an evaluation signature length has been obtained that will vary depending on the security level for classical (Table 1) and quantum computer (Table 2).

Table 1. Size of signature taking into account security requirements for classic computer.

Parameterλ	Character length, bit	Signature size, bit
80	480	1,920
112	672	2,690
128	768	3,074
192	1,152	4,610

Table 2. Size of signature taking into account security requirements for quantum computer.

Parameterλ	Character length, bit	Signature size, bit
80	720	2,882
112	1,008	4,034
128	1,152	4,610
192	1,728	6,914

Standard GOST R 34.10-2012 [15] is based on the discrete logarithm problem in group of points of elliptic curve and specifies the algorithm of forming message signature. The length of signature depends on the order of subgroup of points of elliptic $q$and equals. The value $q$also depends on security level and can assume values: $2^{254} < q < 2^{256}$for$\lambda = 128$ or$2^{508} < q < 2^{512}$for$\lambda = 192$. Thus, the size of a signature formed according to GOST R 34.10-2012 equals 512 bit or 1,024 bits.

An offered pattern of the signature is inferior to standard GOST R 34.10-2012 with respect to criterion of signature size, however, it helps provide group authentication and form a collective signature from several participants. At that, the size of collective digital signature is equivalent to signature size, formed by one user. The offered pattern also additionally helps check the order of signature formation, which makes it possible to trace a chain of data processing.

4. Conclusion

As a result of performed work the authors offer a diagram of hierarchical authentication on the basis of isogenies of elliptic curves for ensuring security of data routing in the systems of analysis of digital production, in particular, in the systems of traffic analysis. Thepeculiaritiesofinformationrouting in the course of processing big data in such systems demanding application of participants' hierarchical authentication have been revealed.

In order to solve the assigned tasks, a decision has been taken to use a collective signature with introduction of an additional property of checking order of forming it. The authors have developed a corresponding pattern of authentication and a set of algorithms providing its functioning. A pattern offered in the work comprises a description of algorithms making it possible to effect generation of parameters according to an assigned security level, forming keys of the users and a group, forming a signature and its check.

The security analysis has been carried out, in which context consideration has been given to the scenarios of attacks aimed at violating the order of signature, message false representation, opening user's keys and incorporating intruder's signature into a chain. It has been established that the offered pattern is stable with respect to these attacks taking into account assumptions complex for calculation.

As a result of simulation of a developed pattern in the computerized algebra system Sage, the digital values signature size for characteristics of different length have been received, both for quantum and for traditional systems. A comparison made with the existing impossible-to-deny signal on isogenies of elliptic curves shows that the proposed pattern helps create a signature of lesser length. In case of adhering with the requirements to selecting field characteristic the developed pattern although gives up the standard of digital signature GOST R 34.10-2012 with respect to signature size, but it helps provide verification of the order of forming a signature; in this case the signature length does not depend on the group dimensionality, and the used task of finding isogenies grants a possibility of providing stability with respect to quantum computer.

References

1. K. Shwab, *The fourth industrial revolution* (Crown Business, New York, 2016)
2. Yu. S. Vasiliev, D. P. Zegzhda, M. A. Poltavtseva, Computer systems, **4** (2017)
3. Industry 4.0 How to navigate digitization of the manufacturing sector. McKinsey Digital [online], Available at: http://www.cloud-finder.ch/fileadmin/Dateien/PDF/Themenkategorien/industrie40/McKinsey_Report_Industry_4.0_s.pdf (2015)
4. Program "Digital economics of the Russian Federation" has been approved by the Resolution of the Government of the Russian Federation No. 1632-p dated July 28, 2017 [online], Available at: http://static.government.ru/media/files/9gFM4FHj4PsB79I5v7yLVuPgu4bvR7M0.pdf (2017)
5. D. Pudov, Open systems. DBMS, **4** (2017)
6. D. S Lavrova, Automatic Control and Computer Sciences,**50(8)** (2016)
7. R. C. Merkle et al., *Secrecy, authentication, and public key systems* (UMI Research Press, Ann Arbor, 1979)
8. L. Lamport, SRI International, **238** (1979)
9. R. J. McEliece, Coding Thv, **4244** (1978)
10. H. Niederreiter, Problems of control and information theory,**15 (2)** (1986)

11. I. Anshel, M. Anshel, D Goldfeld, Mathematical Research Letters,**6** (1999)
12. J. Hoffstein, J. Pipher, J. H. Silverman, International Algorithmic Number Theory Symposium (1998)
13. L. De Feo, D. Jao, J. Plut, Cryptology ePrint Archive, report, **2011/506** (2011)
14. A. Childs, D. Jao, V. Soukharev, Math. Cryptol.,**8 (1)** (2010)
15. GOST R. R 34.10-2012– Federal Technical Regulation and Metrology Agency.Information technologies.Cryptographic protection of information.Processes of forming and checking electronic digital signature. Instead of GOST – P. 34.10-2001 (2001)

Industry 4.0 and basic principles of a new architecture for control of power plants processes

Nikolay Amosov[1], *Alexander* Andryushin[2], *Edik* Arakelyan[2*], and *Anatoliy* Kosoy[2]

[1] Peter the Great St. Petersburg Polytechnic University, 195251, Politechnicheskaya st., 29, Russian Federation
[2] National Research University "MPEI", Thermal and Atomic Power Engineering Institute, 111250, Krasnokazarmennaya st., 14, Russian Federation

Abstract. The results of the level analysis of intellectuality and efficiency of up-to-date automated process control systems (APCS) based on software and hardware systems (SHS) are presented. It was demonstrated that, despite the widespread implementation of modern software and hardware systems during the construction of new APCS and upgrading the existing ones for thermal power plants (TPP), improvement of the process control quality, optimization of their modes and parameters take place generally at the equipment and power unit level and to a far lesser extent – at the power plant level and as a result – insufficient level of automation and low technical and economic efficiency. Another conclusion from the performed analysis – when implementing control algorithms in the APCS based on the up-to-date SHS, their wide data and software capabilities are not fully used. The main ways of further APCS improvement for the purpose of further increasing of their efficiency and the level of intelligence of SHS based APCS of power plants are presented. The possibility of their implementation is considered with application of the basic principles laid in the concept Industry 4.0. The possible economic effect from the implementation of the proposed solutions for increasing the intelligence and efficiency of the SHS based APCS was assessed. A brief description of the configuration of the proposed SHS based control system is given.

The technological process of up-to-date TPP differs by the complexity of the interrelationships between a large number of equipment, high parameters of the working environment, stringent requirements for the accuracy of their regulation, and this has led to the constant search and implementation of new methods for improving the control systems based on the new automatic control hardware. The analysis shows that the current stage of power plants APCS development is moving in two main directions [1, 2]:

– Improvement of the automation equipment itself, first of all, software and hardware system (SHS), on the basis of which new (conventional) APCS are created and the existing ones are upgraded;

*Corresponding author: edik_arakelyan@inbox.ru

– Increase in the processes automation level, providing a significant improvement in the quality and efficiency for maintenance of technological modes of equipment both in the range of workloads, and in the processes of equipment start and stop.

Both lines are closely interconnected: the higher the hardware development level is, the higher the intellectuality level can be achieved, and the automation level shall correspond to the technical level of promising high-efficiency power plants. Trends in the development of modern control systems based on the widespread implementation of software and hardware system (SHS) have provided for creation of the unified power unit control system in all modes of operation, that, in addition to direct control of the power unit, is capable of blocking operator mistakes, controlling intelligent regulation strategies, fully integrated power control and generation using digital process control, etc.

The analysis of the functional capabilities of modern APCS built on the basis of domestic and foreign SHS performed by the scientists of the National Research University "MPEI" shows that improving the process performance quality, optimizing their modes and parameters take place mainly at the equipment and power unit level and significantly to a lesser extent – at the power plant level [3-6]. The scientists of the Institute of Control Sciences of RAS have reached the same conclusion, and they state in [7] the following: "Unfortunately, the practice for APCS creation has developed "by prototype", the essence of which lies in the transfer of functions "prototype" to new hardware and software. In this case, it is clear that the APCS functional capabilities remain at the same level and, as a rule, are limited to the control of separate parameters and local control of separate production mechanisms.The author notes in the paper "Research and development of methods for automated control of processes and their configurations in flow-line production" [8]: "However, the analysis of many operating APCS (for example, APCS of site facilities) shows that today the APCS functionality is used at the same level – mostly SCADA (Supervisory Control and Data Acquisition) is actually the simple display of the process status. Currently, as a rule, only the parameters monitoring and local control of separate production facilities are automatically performed. At the same time, the coordination of processes and operations, interaction with related systems and services, process control as a whole and decision-making in extreme situations are still laid upon a person".

As a result, an insufficient level of automation and low technical and economic efficiency, as the costs required for actual hardware and software are difficult, and in some cases it is impossible to compensate for gains from the processes automation. Another conclusion from the performed analysis – when implementing control algorithms in the APCS based on the up-to-date SHS, their wide data and software capabilities are not fully used. Under these conditions, the problem is highly actual for development of methodological provisions, technical and process solutions, the implementation of which will ensure further increase in a degree of intelligence of energy production control systems at power plants up to a certain (optimum) level by developing and implementing new innovative technologies, algorithms and systems for optimum control of operation modes for power plants equipment and the power plants in general.

In order to search for possible ways to improve the intelligence of the SHS based control systems and to improve their efficiency, we carried out calculations to assess the technical-and-economic practicability of full-scale upgrade of 200 and 300 MW condensing type power units APCS based on the domestic SHS "Kvint" provided that optimization tasks of all control levels are implemented based on SHS data support [9, 10]. The calculations have shown that if the entire economic effect from the introduction of the full-scale APCS with solving the block and plant level tasks are taken as 100 percent, then it is distributed among its components approximately as follows:

– Improvement of equipment process control quality and partial optimization of their parameters – 17.5%;

– Optimum control of equipment operating modes (including automated starts from different thermal states) – 17.5%;

– By solving the problems for ensuring the optimum strategy of power unit application in the electricity and capacity market – 35.0%.

– By increasing the reliability of the equipment functioning and reducing operating costs by optimizing the terms and scope of repairs and maintenance – 30.0%.

The specified data show that the trends for development of intelligent automated process control systems (IAPCS) shall be aimed at creating the unified system for optimum control of technical and production processes in all modes of operation of equipment, power units and the plant as a whole.

The question arises – how to be out of the current APCS condition to a higher level in terms of intellectual and efficiency, i.e. how to implement the transition to the creation of a "smarter and more efficient" APCS. Is it possible to apply the basic principles of the Industry 4 to achieve this goal?

The term "Industry 4.0", as the next, the 4th stage of the industrial revolution, was meant as informatization of the assembly process and components move under supervision and machines interaction, but now this concept has more widely meaning and proposes rational use of natural and technical resources, the most effective energy saving based on maximum automation and intellectualization of production processes, control decisions, etc. [11, 12].

Although there is currently no clear algorithm for applying the concept of Industry 4.0 in various industries, its main principles are stated and can also be interpreted with regard to automated power generation at power plants [13].One of the Industry 4.0 principles is the possibility of transition from the conventional vertical integration of production processes characterized by the centralization of production processes to the horizontal integration of various parts of the production process interacting with each other, while a significant part of production will be carried out automatically without human participation, i.e. the human role is reduced to the minimum. In the process of production control, an important place is given to the Internet of Things, i.e. the possibilities of using Internet information technologies for coordination and maintaining production processes.

The process of electric power generation at power plants in principle corresponds to the principle of processes interconnection between each other, but from the point of view of these processes control, if the APCS is built on the basis of SHS, a centralized control system is often applied, when all control decisions are made in the central server, where the whole information flows from measuring gages and instruments. For real, this does not apply to automatic control systems (ACS), which for the most part function in the autonomous mode. In this system, the process of production process optimization becomes more complicated due to the heavy workload of mid-level controllers that receive and process a huge amount of information.

The application of the horizontal principle of TPP processes control means the transition to geographically and functionally distributed control systems when a part of controllers is installed near the control facility and partly takes over the functions of data processing and processes controlling of this particular facility. The territorial distribution of the main generating units, auxiliary power facilities and technological assemblies is a compulsory necessity to ensure the vital activity of any large energy complex.The use of APCS local software systems supplied by manufacturers of completed main and auxiliary equipment has become a real necessity, but in this case, a certain complexity takes place in the installation of any complex geographically distributed system.

Nevertheless, the process of decentralization in the control process in the APCS built on the SHS is currently implemented during the design of new APCS and modernization of existing ones by setting the so-called peripheral, low-power controllers, but mainly for distant facilities. When applying the ideas of the Industry 4.0 such a control principle shall be extended to all the main units of the power unit, but in this case, it is necessary to ensure their interconnection in accordance with the process and with the operational control level. This will relieve the controllers at the level of operational control, especially in terms of data processing to solve common optimization tasks. In addition to purely technical and technological advantages – the improvement of operational and other conditions, it becomes possible to develop modern APCS in the line of their intellectualization by using high-precision mathematical models in the control circuit based on the typical diagnostic algorithms and optimum control.

The APCS design in accordance with this principle creates favorable conditions for the application of the basic concept Industry 4.0 – widespread implementation of IP technologies and the fullest automation of processes to increase the efficiency and intelligence of the production control system. The concept implementation with regard to the power plants SHS based APCS at current level of APCS, even if they are built on the SHS basis, is a complex problem due to the above mentioned, the application software ASW functions primarily to solve block control tasks, and the main economic effect of a full-scale APCS can be obtained when solving the plant level optimization tasks.

Taking into account this fact, the principle for building the control system to implement the concept Industry 4.0 can be suggested:

– Transition to control of technological and production processes of energy production at TPP by the criteria of energy and technical efficiency. Contrary to the proposals of separate solution of optimization tasks of unit, block and plant level existing in the technical literature leading in most cases to contradictory results, the problems solution in total will allow using the results obtained in the hierarchical approach "unit-block plant" at the lower hierarchies when solving the tasks at the upper levels; in this case, a clear separation of the solved optimization tasks shall take place at each hierarchical level approximately in the following form [4, 9]:

at the unit level – optimization of the parameters and indicators adjusted at the given unit (boiler efficiency, condenser pressure, steam pressure at sliding control of primary steam pressure, etc.); determination of the current technical condition (state coefficient) on the basis of parametric analysis (diagnostics);

at the block level – calculation and analysis of current and rated energy indicators (PI) of each unit and block as a whole, determination of the reasons for their deterioration and development of recommendations for their elimination; optimal distribution between parallel units operating included in the unit (double blocks, two, three-shaft CCP); operative and long-term diagnostics of unit equipment with optimization of terms of units repair and maintenance; optimum distribution of heat load between network heaters of the heating unit, etc.;

at the plant level – calculation and analysis of current and rated SHS of power units and the plant as a whole, taking into account the plant's own needs; selection of the composition of generating equipment, taking into account the possibilities of units back-up and optimal distribution of thermal and electrical load for SHS, and optimal distribution of electrical load for the condensing plant between generating units, taking into account the peculiarities of power plant output to the electricity and capacity market; choice of the optimal strategy for the scope and terms of repairs and maintenance, taking into account the current state of equipment with the development and implementation of automated systems for technical diagnosis, etc.

– Development and implementation of the concept of operational control of the power plant operating modes as part of the SHS application software in the automatic (or semi-automatic) mode, with the creation of tasks for the block and local APCS. In this case, the problem of the expediency for solving any optimization task at the given time, based on the current needs of the power plant.

– In the framework of the above principle of interaction between the hierarchical levels of the distributed APCS, an algorithm shall be developed for optimal distribution of the APCS information support between peripheral, block and plant level controllers by the criterion of maximum speed.

An important aspect in the implementation of the principles of the Industry 4.0 in modern APCS is the current state of APCS hardware and a degree of their readiness for solving the above tasks.

Since the beginning of distributed microprocessor systems development, a certain possibility of their spatial distribution has been seen. With the development of microprocessor means and the accumulation of experience development, these opportunities have significantly expanded. Quite a large number of manufacturers of SHS with various own technical solutions has been appeared.

To implement the above tasks, the SHS shall meet certain requirements for hardware and software [4, 14]. However, not all SHS meet these requirements. Thus, the network interface of remote modules can not be reserved, and the high-speed response of network interfaces in some SHS is not enough to implement protection and security locks, and controllers require forced ventilation that is not permissible when placed in contaminated industrial premises. Remote modules can often be installed only in the controller cells reduced in size that does not allow creating a truly distributed system.

Nevertheless, in Russia there are several domestic and imported SHS that fully meet the requirements for high-speed distributed systems of responsible control. The positive experience of field controllers operation is accumulated; typical solutions are developed for creation of local control systems on their basis. Several manufacturers serially produce drives smart control cabinets, intelligent sensor stands have been developed and begin to be used in projects. In this case, it can be stated that advanced domestic developments are as good as the characteristics and quality of products of the world's leading manufacturers.

The use of microprocessor technology along with SHS also affected field technical means of APCS: primary measuring instruments, shut-off and regulating actuators, local control devices and secondary indicating gages. There was such a thing as the intelligence of field control and monitoring hardware that allowed not only to increase the own hardware functionalities, but also to expand the APCS network architecture having included it to field equipment. A degree of intellectual security of the field level means that it performs the functions of preliminary processing of technological parameters, self-diagnostics, reconfiguration of measuring ranges and control in the on-line mode, parameter simulation. The use of switches – field bus protocol converters provides logical consolidation in not only a group of technological parameters into a single network node, but also technological functions of APCS.

Thus, when analyzing the effectiveness of development and implementation of the proposed APCS architecture and the structure of software and hardware of the TPP APCS, the following aspects shall be taken into account:

1. Installation of peripheral (field) controllers in the immediate vicinity of control objects and transferring the functions of primary data processing, partial control of local control systems (LCS), and a number of other functions to them. To reduce the data volume transferred to the upper level of data control and freeing CPU from solving particular problems, is accompanied under other equal conditions by reducing the reliability of the measurement systems as a whole.
2. The transition (partial or full) to the digital interface of data exchange between sensors and controllers using modern digital gages including intelligent sensors, actuators, etc. leads, on the one hand, to instruments cost increase, but, on the other hand, to disposal (partially or completely) of electromechanical communication devices and assemblies (when installing field semiconductor switches).

3. Widespread introduction of field controllers, intelligent instruments and digital data transfer interface will lead to the need for a more clear-cut solution of the problems of redundancy and information security;

4. Extension of LCS application and functions increasing volume performed can lead to the possibility of a significant increase in the automation level and a volume of optimization tasks of the block and system nature to be solved at the upper level of control that will lead to increase in the APCS efficiency.

A special place in the process of SHS based APCS intellectualization is the problem of the level of technological and production processes automation. The current monitoring and control hardware allows automating rather complex processes. The most difficult processes are transient regimes: start, stop, load relief and extreme regulation modes. In addition, modern power plants operation in conditions of variable load schedules leads to the need for the operation of TPP power equipment in the modes of minimum safe, shutdown and subsequent start-up. Of course, these modes can be automated, but it requires a lot of material and intellectual costs.

In accordance with the above objectives and problems setting, a degree of automation of geographically distributed APCS is significantly increased, primarily, due to the solution of complex tasks. Nevertheless, at the block level this issue is solved in different ways. Most often, depending on the availability of material assets and misunderstanding of the long-term prospects for the energy complex development [14].

Conceptual provisions by a degree of energy facility automation shall be built under the conditions of "reasonable sufficiency" based on the theory and technological experience of maintaining the equipment operating modes.

According to the preliminary assessment, this approach can provide for the following: increase in power plants operation economy by optimizing the equipment operating modes within 2%, decrease in fuel costs for declaration conditions by 20-30%; – increase in power plants maneuverability by reducing the turbines start-up time by 40-50%; increase by at least 40% of the reliability of equipment technical condition assessment; decrease in a number of emergency stops by 15%; increase in the power equipment resource by at least 10%.

APCS intellectualization by controlling the plant technical and production processes with applying the Industry 4.0 principles will require:

– Development and implementation of new approaches in the theory of automatic control of complex technical systems as applied to energy facilities when integrating the control circuits of processes of operational (at the equipment level) and station (pre-forecast) levels;

– Expansion of the SHS functional capabilities in terms of optimal control of technical and production processes at the block and station levels by integration of calculation algorithms of above tasks into the SHS software applications;

– Large computing power and powerful methodological and algorithmic base, necessary for calculations in the mode as close as possible to real time.

Below there is a brief description of the possible configuration of the proposed SHS based control system [15]. The system consists of mandatory and additional modules. The mandatory system modules are: calculation database, calculation server, data collection server. All these modules can be local, i.e. implemented on one computer. Such implementation will increase the system reliability and operation rate, but will reduce its scalability and significantly increase the computational load to a separate physical module. The system modularity will avoid large costs for its maintenance, allow for flexible configuration, provide interfaces to create the own modules for advanced users and third-party developers. Such implementation will increase the system reliability and operation rate, but will reduce its scalability and significantly increase the computational load to a separate physical module. The main requirement for the command control system of equipment operation modes is the presence of multiple I/O interfaces for data exchange that requires special attention to information protection. For this purpose, it is necessary to provide the possibility for creation of a user with access rights to the built-in functions only. This will provide for testing the request before submitting the information. High network loading due to the applying the unified database requires the input of requests optimization algorithms. The calculation server is used for periodic or signal tasks start, which implies task program start. The data collection server performs the functions for data collection from the APCS and other systems and downloads the received information to the calculation database. For this module, it is necessary to provide multiple network communication protocols for access to other systems. Manual input, if necessary, can be performed using the clients' data collection server. The data transfer server is not a mandatory SHS module. In this case, its installation will significantly increase the system reliability. It serves to transfer operational information between the plant shift supervisor, power unit operators and other operational personnel in the automatic mode or on request. Data decoupling between different modules allows talking about the extensibility and interchangeability of system parts. In this case, data concentration in the unified database will prevent their duplication. Thus, all modules, both logical and physical, can be replaced, added or removed from the system.

The "archive" and "user interface" modules serve as additional ones. The main purpose of the archive is to back up the data. It is not a mandatory module, but in case of link broken it can serve as a backup storage and data provider for other modules. Such communication involves laying of redundant communication lines. In case of database server failure, all modules will change over the archive. When restoring the communication, the archive will start synchronizing the data with the calculation database.

User interface modules allow monitoring and controlling the software system behavior, making adjustments to the initial data, manual setting some parameters, adjusting the calculation results, sending tasks to the turbine engine operators' workstations, visualizing data in the form of graphs and tables.

Conclusion

Thus, the problem of increasing the energy efficiency of energy production at power plants can be solved by the intellectualization of the control system throughout the entire production chain of energy generation by applying the basic concepts of the "Industry 4.0" by implementing innovative, energy- and resource-saving technologies and algorithms for optimum control of technical and economic indicators, equipment operation modes when entering the station to the market of electricity and power, algorithms of implicit and long-term diagnostic of unit equipment with optimizing the terms and amounts of maintenance and repair.

The proposed principle for building the control system to implement the concept Industry 4.0 will increase the intellectual level of systems control and accelerate the creation of intelligent equipment and intelligent power plants

The developed methods will be effective in the design and optimization of processes and equipment, as well as building of high-quality power plants control systems. Using the methods and algorithms developed in the project will increase the intellectual level of the control systems and accelerate building of intelligent equipment and intelligent power plants.

References

1. Yu. S. Tverskoy, S. A. Talamanov, *Teploenergetika.* **10**, (2010)
2. V.A. Bilenko, *El. st.*, **1**, 13-18 (2004)

3. T. M. Arutyunyan, E. K. Arakelyan, V. A. Makarchian, *Vestnik of MPEI,* **6**, 114-117 (2007)
4. E. K. Arakelyan, E. D. Vasiliev, S. R. Khurshudyan, *Vestnik of MPEI,* **1**, 15-20 (2014)
5. E. K. Arakelyan, E .D. Vasiliev, *Energosberezhenie I vodopodgotovka,* **5 (97)**, 21-30 (2015)
6. G. Krokhin, A Pestunov, E Arakelyan, V Mukhin, *IOP Conf. Series: Journal of Physics: Conf. Series* **891**, (2017)
7. I. V. Prangishvili, A. A. Ambartsumyan, A. G. Poletykin, G. G. Grebenyuk, I. B. Yadykin, State of energy facilities automation level and technical system solutions aimed at its improvement, Problems of Control (2003)
8. S. A. Branishtov Research and development of methods for automated control of processes and their configurations in flow-line production, diss. Ph.D. In science Moscow, **20** (2008)
9. E. K. Arakelyan , A. V. Andryushin , V. R. Sabanin , S.V. Mezin, F. F. Pashchenko, *IOP Conf. Series: Journal of Physics: Conf. Series,* **891**, (2017)
10. E. K. Arakelyan, M. A. Panko, A. Sh. Aslanyan, *Teploenergetika,*(2010)
11. Katerina Bondar *What is reality Industry 4.0 InnovaCima,* 9 November, 2017 [online] Available at: http://www.en.unir.net (2018)
12. Bernar Marr *What Everyone Must know about the Industry 4.0 Forbes* June 20, 2016 [online], Available at: http://www.gitex.com (2018)
13. R. Rakhmanulov, *Results of the conference "Industry 4", Control Engineering, Russia, August* (2017)
14. V. S. Nevzgodin, V. A. Bilenko, A. G. Svidersky, P. A. Gorozhankin, *Energy Reliability and Safety*, **3**, 19-27 (2011)
15. A. Chernyaev, Papers of International Scientific Seminar Networked embedded and control system technologies: European and Russian R&D cooperation, Italy, Milan, (2009)

Digital transformation and optimization models in the sphere of logistics[a]

Vladimir Anisimov[1], *Evgenii* Anisimov[2], *Tatiana* Saurenko[2*], *Artem* Smolenskiy[2] and *Oleg* Yastrebov[2]

[1] Peter the Great St. Petersburg Polytechnic University, 195251 Polytechnicheskaya st. 29, Russian Federation
[2] Peoples Friendship University of Russia (RUDN University), 117198 Miklukho-Maklaya st. 6, Russian Federation

Abstract. The efficiency, optimization, speed and time limits have always been of crucial importance for the logistics system, while saving of speed and time in the real-time mode are the key factors with transition to digital technologies and establishment of Industry 4.0 since they become the competitive advantages. The innovative use of technologies in such fields as data analysis, Internet of things and cloud calculations significantly change the logistical and transportation systems as a result of mating digital and existing supply chains becoming the catalyst of transition to "Logistika 4.0". This work offers a model and method of shaping an optimal plan of fulfilling a complex of interrelated logistical operations for such changing conditions.The model is based on the presentation of optimization procedure as a non-linear task of discrete programming consisting in minimization of time of fulfilling the above complex of operations by a limited number of contractors partially interchangeable under conditions of limited budgeting. A model obtained thereat for establishing an optimal plan will belong to the class of nonpolynimially challenging tasks. In order to solve these tasks, a method has been suggested supported by a procedure of branches and boundaries. Thealgorithmisbasedon dichotomous branchingdiagram. Itsapplicationprovidesforreceivingboth quasi-optimalandoptimallogisticsplansfor the finite number of steps. Atthat, theassessmentofaccuracy is provided for quasi-optimal plans. The proposed model and method help solve a wide spectrum of practical tasks of logistical planning under conditions of digital transformation.

[a]The publication was prepared with the support of the "RUDN University Program 5-100"
* Corresponding author: tanya@saurenko.ru

1 Introduction

The problems of minimizing time of fulfilling a complex of interrelated logistical operations having restrictions for the number of contractors, interchangeability and cost there of make a class of problems widespread in the practice of organization logistical management. Inparticular, theproblemsof industrial production logisticalplanning, development and implementation of innovative projects, planning scientific work in the research establishments and many othersbelong to this class [1-3]. The complexity of such like problems and considerable material and time expenses determined by planning miscalculations bring about the fact that the solution thereof shall be supported not only by the experience and intuition, but by impersonal scientific substantiations too. The applicable mathematical models can be used as tools for such substantiations. The development of structure of such a model and optimization method of the logistical plan is the purpose of this article.

2 Structure of model of logistical plans optimization

It is reasonable to reflect composition and interrelation of logistical operations in the form of a network when building models of logistical plan optimization:

$$H = \{(i, j)\}, \quad i, j = 0, 1, \cdots, m, \quad i < j, \tag{1}$$

where, i, j – numbers of network nodes.

Every logistical operation in the network (1) is assigned with an arch (i, j) connecting i -n and j -n nodes. Node $i = 0$ corresponds to an event of commencing fulfillment of complex of logistical operations presented by this network. Nodes $i = 1, 2, \cdots, m$ correspond to the events corresponding to completion of all logistical operations described by the arches included into each of these nodes. The total number of logistical operations (arches) equals$N$.

Thesequenceof logistical operations obeystherule: operation corresponding to an arch outgoing from any node can not be launched before finishing all operations corresponding to the arches included into this node.

Every logistical operation (i, j) is characterized by a required number $n(i, j)$ of operators and duration $\tau(i, j)$.

Let us present a set K^* of operators engaged for fulfillment of a complex of logistical operations in the following form:

$$K^* = \{1, 2, \cdots, k, \cdots, K\},$$

where, k - conventional order number (identifier) of operator,
K – number of operators.

Let us present an interchangeability of operators in the formalized form as the matrix:

$$\Delta = \left\|\delta_k(i,j)\right\|,\ k = 1,2,\cdots,K,\quad (i,j) \in H\ , \tag{2}$$

where,

$$\delta_k(i,j) = \begin{cases} 1, & \textit{if } k-n \textit{ operator can be engaged in fulfilling} \\ & (i,j) \textit{ logistical operation}, \\ 0, & k-n \textit{ operator cannot be engaged in fulfilling} \\ & (i,j) \textit{ logistical operation}. \end{cases} \tag{3}$$

Let us present the financial expenditures related to engaging operators in fulfilling logistical operations in the form of vector components:

$$C = \left\|c_k(i,j)\right\|,\quad k = 1,2,\ldots,K,\quad (i,j) \in H\ , \tag{4}$$

where, $c_k(i,j)$ - cost of time unit of engaging k - noperator to fulfilling (i,j) -n logistical operation.

Thelogisticalplanof fulfilling complex of logistical operations formallycan be presented by a set:

$$Y = \left\{A_Y(i,j), r_Y(i,j) \middle| (i,j) \in H\ , r_Y(i,j) \subset K^*\right\}, \tag{5}$$

where, $A_Y(i,j)$ - Y plan – determined moment of time corresponding to beginning of (i,j) - n logistical operation;

$r_Y(i,j)$ – set of operators engaged in fulfilling (i,j) - n logistical operation according to plan Y .

Capacity (number of operators) of set $r_Y(i,j)$ equals $n(i,j)$.

Let us suppose that interruption of every launched logistical operation $(i,j) \in H$ is impermissible and the composition $r_Y(i,j)$ of a allotted operators will not change until it is completed.

Taking into account the adopted designations, the financial expenses $W_Y(i,j)$ for fulfilling logistical operation (i,j) will be calculated according to formula in the course of implementing plan Y :

$$W_Y(i,j) = \sum_{k \in r_Y(i,j)} c_k(i,j)\tau(i,j) \tag{6}$$

Let us designate by means of H_L a set of all network (1) routes connecting its initial and final vertexes.

Timeoffulfillingtheentirecomplexof logistical operations when implementing plan (5) will be equal to maximum duration T_L of route $L \in H_L$ from an initial vertex $i = 0$ of network (1) to a final one $j = m$.

Taking into account the adopted designations, the model of forming an optimal plan of fulfilling the complex of logistical operations will take the following form:

Determine logistical plan

$$Y^* = \left\{ A^*_Y(i,j), r^*_Y(i,j) \;\middle|\; (i,j) \in H,\ r_Y(i,j) \subseteq K^* \right\} \tag{7}$$

of fulfilling the complex of operations $H = \{(i,j)\}$, $i,j = 0,1,\cdots,m$, $i < j$,

providing fulfillment of condition

$$T^* = T(Y^*) = \min_{Y} \max_{L \in H_L} T_L(Y) \tag{8}$$

with restrictions

$$A_Y(i,j) \geq \max_{l,i} \{ A_Y(l,i) + \tau(l,i),\ (i,j) \in H \}; \tag{9}$$

$$\sum_{k \in r_Y(i,j)} \delta_k(i,j) = n(i,j); \tag{10}$$

$$\sum_{(i,j) \in G_Y(t)} r_Y(i,j) \leq K; \tag{11}$$

$$\sum_{k=1}^{K} \delta_k(i,j) \geq n(i,j); \tag{12}$$

$$\sum_{(i,j) \in H} W_Y(i,j) \leq W^*, \tag{13}$$

where, $G_Y(t)$- set of operations being fulfilled at every moment of time$t$ in case of implementing the logistical plan Y;

W^* – maximum permissible financial expenditures for fulfilling a complex of logistical operations (1).

Inproblem (7) – (13) condition (8) formalizes a commitment of minimizing time of fulfilling a complex of logistical operations.

Limitation (9) reflectsaruleofintegrating logistical operations identifying that operations outgoing from any network node (1) can begin only aftercompleting all operations included into this node.

Limitation (10) formalizesarequirementof allocation of an established number of operators for every logistical operation.

Limitation (11) reflects a natural planning condition consisting in that the number of operatorsinvited for fulfilling logistical operations simultaneously can not exceed a total number thereof.

Limitation (12) formalizes a requirement consisting in that the number and interchangeability of operatorsshall provide for a possibility of fulfilling every logistical operation of complex (1).

Limitation (13) denotes that total financial expenditures in the course of fulfilling a complex of logistical operations (1) can not exceed an established limiting level.

3 Optimization method

Problem (7) – (13) belongs to the non-linear problems of distributing discrete on-uniform resources in the random network. It is NP – a complex problem of discrete programming [4-6]. Precise methods of solving problems of such class have been offered for the first time in [7-8]. However, renewableresourcesonlyhave been taken into account in the models given consideration in these works. At the same time it is necessary to take into account the necessary non-renewable resources too in the course of planning actual logistical processes in economicalones. In model (7) – (13) the financial resources belong to this type. Relation (13) formallyreflectsthelimitationoftheseresources.

Model (7) – (13) obtained as a result of introducing this relation is a further generalization considered in model [8]. The precise optimization algorithms for model of (7) – (13) type are absent presently. At the same time the demands of practices of planning logistical processes determine a necessity of developing thereof.

For the existence of solution of problem (7) – (13), it is necessary and sufficient that the composition and interchangeability of operators and the established limiting level of Ω^* of financial expenses provide for a possibility of fulfilling all logistical operations of complex (1).

In the formalized form the fulfillment of the first of these requirements consists in fulfilling limitation (12).

In order to check fulfillment of the second requirement, one can use the following set:

$R^* = \{r^q(i,j) | (i,j) \in H, q = 1,2,\cdots\}$ of all possible variants of allotting resources for the applicable logistical operations. The following set is connected with this set:

$$\hat{W} = \{W^q(i,j), \quad q = 1,2,\ldots, \quad (i,j) \in H\} \tag{14}$$

Of financial expenses $\Omega^q\ (i, j)$ for fulfilling logistical operations with the corresponding variants of engaging operators. The elements of set (14) will be determined by the relation:

$$W^q(i,j) = \tau(i,j) \sum_{k \in r^q(i,j)} c_k(i,j). \tag{15}$$

Taking into account (15) these condrequirement providing for existence of a solution of problem under consideration (7) – (13) is presented in the formalized form by the relation:

$$\sum_{(i,j) \in H} \min_q W^q(i,j) \le W^*, \quad q = 1,2,\ldots\ . \tag{16}$$

It is reasonable to check practicability of conditions (12) and (16) evenbeforecommencementofformationprocedurewith the use of model (7) – (13) of optimal plan of fulfilling a complex of interrelated logistical operations. If these conditions are met,an algorithm including the following actions can be used for optimizing a plan of fulfilling a complex of logistical operations (1):

a) presentation of set $V = \{S\}$ of fragments S of logistical plan Y permissible with respect to limitationsin the form of a tree of subsets (branching);

b) calculating tree branches (dedicated subsets) lower boundary of target function (8);

c) search for permissible variants of logistical plan;

d) checking established permissible variants for optimality.

Thebranchingofatreeofvariantsis effected on the basis of dichotomous diagram. In case of implementing it every vertex of v_s S – n branch of a tree of variants corresponds to an element of logistical plan. Inthiscase, ifthe logistical operation (i, j) corresponding to this element begins at the moment of time $A_S(i,j)$ a $tr_S(i, j)$-n variant of assigning operators, we suppose:

$$v_S=\{A_S(i,j), r_S(i,j)\}. \tag{17}$$

Ifthe logistical operation (i,j) does not begin at the moment of time $A_S(i, j)$ a $tr_S(i, j)$-m variant of assigning operators, we suppose:

$$v_S=\emptyset. \tag{18}$$

For every branch $S \in V$ values $A_S(i, j)$, $(i, j) \in H$, (moments of beginning logistical operations) shall be selected from an increasing sequence corresponding to this branch:

$$t_S = \{t_S^n\}, \quad n = 1, 2, \cdots .$$

In this case, $t_S^1 = 0$, while the subsequent moments t_S^n, $n = 2, 3, \cdots$, will be determined on the basis ofinterrelation:

$$t_S^n = \min_{(i,j) \in G(t_S^{n-1})} \{A_S(i, j) + \tau(i, j)\}, \tag{19}$$

where, $G_S(t_S^{n-1})$ – set of logistical operations (i, j), include dearlier into S -n branch and incomplete by the moment of time t_S^{n-1}, i.e.:

$$G_S(t_S^{n-1}) = \{(i, j) \mid (i, j) \in H, A_S(i, j) \le t_S^{n-1} \le A_S(i, j) + \tau(i, j)\}. \tag{20}$$

Thus, t_S corresponds to a sequence of time moments, in to which logistical operations included into the next tree branchare completed and the corresponding operators get released.

Condition $t_S^1 = 0$ reflects a fact that all the variants of a logistical plan begin at the moment of time $t = 0$.

In the interests of implementing the adopteddichotomousdiagramofbranchinglet us introduce a set for consideration:

$$D = \{d_q | q = 1, 2, \cdots\}, \tag{21}$$

where, $d_q = 1$, if for fulfilling (i, j) -n logistical operation a variant $r^q(i, j)$ of assigning operators is used, otherwise $d_q = 0$.

In this case the order number q of element $d_q = 1$ of set D characterizes both fulfilled logistical operation and a variant of appointing operators, and financial expenses.

Taking into account (21) the process of branching in the interests of compiling an optimal logistical plan (7) consists in selecting permissible variables $d_q \in D$ for every following moment of time t_S^n and setting values thereof, i.e., an interrelation takes place $v_S = \{t_S^n, d_q = 1\}$, if the logistical operation $(i, j) \in G$ corresponding to a variable d_q begins at the moment of time $A_S(i, j) = t_S^n$ at $r^q(i, j)$ -n variant of allotting resources or $v_S = \{t_S^n, d_q = 0\}$, if the specified logistical operation does not begin during a variant of allotting resources under consideration at moment t_S^n.

Set P_S^n of variables $d_q \in D$, which can be included into S -n fragment of the logistical plan (7) at the moment of time t_S^n, comprises values $d_q \in D$ corresponding to logistical operations meeting conditions $(i, j) \in G$, not included earlier into branch S under consideration:

$$A(l, i) + \tau(l, i) \le t_S^n, \quad (l, i) \in H; \tag{22}$$

$$r^q(i, j) \subseteq R_S^n, \tag{23}$$

$$W^* - \sum_{d_m \in D_S(t_S^{n-1})} d_m W^m + W^q \ge 0, \quad q = 1, 2, \ldots, \tag{24}$$

where, R_S^n – set of free operators for S-nplan fragment at the moment of time t_S^n;

$D_S(t^{n-1}_S)$ – set of variables d_q included into branch S of the tree of variants by the moment of time t^{n-1}_S.

Condition (22) distinguishes logistical operations, for which all the preceding conditions have been met by the moment t_S^n. Condition (23) distinguishes logistical operations, for which there exist permissible job orders of operators, while (24) – permissible job orders of free operators permissible with respect to financial expenses.

A maximum route duration from the initial vertex of graph H to a final one being determined without taking into account life restrictions (11), (13) for logistical operations not included into S can be taken for evaluating Q_S of the lower boundary of target function (8) for every fragment S of calendar plan. At that, if at the next branching step corresponding to moment t_S^n, $d_q = 1$, is established, in order to determine $W_S(d_q = 1)$ the following proceeds:

a) logistical operations $(l,i) \in H$, include dearlier into S -n plan fragment (i.e., operations, for which $A_S(l,i) < t_S n$) begin at the corresponding moments $A_S(l,i)$ and come to an end at moments $A_S(l,i) + \tau(l,i)$;

b) for logistical operation $(i, j) \in H$, corresponding to variable $d_q = P_S^n$ and, hence, included at the step under consideration into S -n branch of variants tree – $A_S(i, j) = t_S^n$;

c) for logistical operations $(e,h) \in H$, corresponding to variables $d_u \in P_S^n$, $u \ne q$, which with respect to life restriction (24) can not be included into plan at the moment t_S^n simultaneously with (i, j), commencement time equals t_S^{n+1}, while duration is determined by the relation $t_S^{n+1} + \tau(e,h)$.

If $d_q = 0$, is established at the considered branching step, in order to determine $Q_S(d_q = 0)$ the following is due additionally:

a) logistical operations $(l,i) \in G$, include dearlier into S -n fragment of the logistical plan (i.e., operations, for which $A_S(l,i) < t_S^n$), begin during corresponding moments $A_S(l,i)$ and come to an end at moments $A_S(l,i) + \tau\ (l,i)$;

b) logistical operation (i, j), corresponding to a variable $d_q \in P_S^n$, begins at the moment of time t_S^{n+1} and comes to an end at moment $t_S^{n+1} + \tau(l, i)$;

c) the rest logistical operations $(e, h) \in G$ corresponding to variables $d_u \in P_S^n$, $u \neq q$, begin at moment t_S^n and come to an end at moments $t_S^n + \tau(e, h)$.

Animportantelementof optimization algorithm under consideration for model(7) – (13) significantly influencingits reproducibility is the method of selecting the nextlogistical operation and variant of allotting resources for it. Formally, it consists in selection of variables $d_q \in P_s^n$ to be included into S -n branch at the moment of time t_s^n. Selection of d_q will be effected in the offered algorithm at the next branching step in two stages: logistical operationis selected at the first one, and a variant of allotting resources is selected at the second one.Thenext logistical operation will be selected in accordance with the following sequence of preferences:

$$\min T_j^{(n)} \to \max \tau(i, j) \to \min i \to \min j,$$

i. e. logistical operation is the first to be included into plan with the less late completion time $T_j^{(n)}$ corresponding to it. In case there are several such logistical operations an operation of maximum volume will be chosen from this number. In case there are also several such logistical operations an operationwith the least numbers i, j will be chosen. At that, later completion periods are to be determined taking into account fragment S of the logistical plan under consideration.

Variant $r(i, j)$ of assigning operators for the selected logistical operation (i, j) will be determined proceeding from the condition of value minimum:

$$\sum_{k \in r(i,j)} \sum_{(l,h) \notin S} \delta_k(l, h),$$

i.e., the least universal operators get assigned for the remaining logistical operations $(l, h) \notin S$.

The logistical operation (i, j) selected in this way and variant $r(i, j)$ of assigning operators unanimously determine the next variable $d_q \in P_S^n$, included into S -n branch of plan variants tree at the moment t_s^n.

Thetreegoing around is organized in accordance with "go right" rule. Ithelpskeepthe current fragment of the logistical plan, the least value of target function received earlier and a permissible plan corresponding to it in PC memory when solving a problem.

The indicated rule in combination with the considered method of selecting logistical operations and operators constitutes an approximate algorithm of logistical plan optimization, which helps acquire the first permissible solution over the finite number of steps equal to number N of logistical operations in network (1).

Every S -n branch comes to an end, if it has included all N logistical operations, i.e., a permissible logistical plan Y, was received or if

$$Q_s \geq T^0(1 - \mu), \quad 0 \leq \mu \leq 1, \tag{26}$$

where, T^0 – the least value of target unction for permissible logistical plans received earlier;

μ – specified permissible target function deviation from an optimal one (optimization accuracy).

Fulfilling condition (26) means that it is impossible to improve a record received earlier by more than $100\mu\%$ in the branch being considered and its continuation in the framework of a specified accuracy of optimization has no sense.

A procedure of searching solution comes to an end, if condition (26) is met for all the remaining branches. In case of an established method of going around a tree of variants the second return to the root vertex corresponds to such a situation. In this case the last record is the sought value of target function (8), while a permissible logistical plan corresponding to it–an optimal plan Y^*.

In general the offered model and method of planning logistical processes provide for an automatic viewing and assessing all possible plan variants and receiving on this basis both accurate and approximate solutions of the planning problem. In this case repetitions are excluded in the course of viewing permissible variants. It significantly reduces the time of solving problems.

4 Conclusion

The offered model and method can be used in the systems of supporting decisions-making used in the practice of logistical management of organizations. They help formalize complexes of logistical operations different by the nature thereof. In this case the system approach to forming a plan of logistical process, reviewing it as a unified non-separable complex of interrelated logistical operations and the life support thereof aimed at attaining general final goals, make it possible to reduce material and time expenses of the participants of logistical process, reduce time limits of resources delivery and increase the quality of servicing.

References

1. G.Y. Silkina, Proc. of the 29th IBIMA Conf. – Sustainable Economic Growth, Education Excellence, and Innovation Management through Vision 2020, (2017)
2. A.S. Ksenofontov, I.V. Savon, V.Y. Serba, D.V. Shkurkin, International Journal of Economics and Financial Issues, **6(S1)** (2016)
3. V.G. Anisimov, E.G. Anisimov, T.N. Saurenko, M.A. Sonkin, Journal of Physics: Conference Series, **803** (2017)
4. A. O. Alekseyev, O. G. Alekseyev, V. G. Anisimov, Ye. G. Anisimov, N. I. Yachkula, Soviet Journal of Computer and Systems Sciences, **5**(1988)
5. M. D. Maslakov, A. K. Chernykh, Risk Management Problems in Technosphere, **1 (29)** (2014)
6. V. G. Khalin, G. V. Chernova, A. V. Yurkov, Economical Analysis: Theory and Practice, **7 (406)** (2015)
7. V.G. Anisimov, Ye. G. Anisimov, The Magazine of Computational Mathematics and Mathematical Physics., **32 (2)** (1992)
8. V.G. Anisimov, E.G. Anisimov, The Magazine of Computational Mathematics and Mathematical Physics., **37(1)** (1997)

Industrial Internet in the concept "Industry 4.0": world experience and perspectives of development in the conditions of Russian economy[a]

Julia Asaturova [1*], and *Anna* Mikhailova[2]

[1] Peter the Great St. Petersburg Polytechnic University, Institute of Industrial Management, Economy and Trade, Higher Engineering-Economical School, 195251 Polytechnicheskaya st. 29, Russian Federation

[2] Saint Petersburg State University of Architecture and Civil Engineering, Faculty of economics and management, 190005 2-ya Krasnoarmeiskaya st. 4, Russian Federation

Abstract. At present, the world economy is at the stage of formation of the fourth industrial revolution, which is called to raise the industry to a new qualitative level. In this article we contemplated the history and prerequisites of the industrial revolution, defined its basic features and the most progressive technologies. We analyzed the particular features of development of the industrial revolution in Russia and abroad. We inspected the experience of foreign countries in implementing state programs in the sphere "Industry 4.0". We investigated the concept of the Industrial Internet as a basis for developing of a new wave of the industrial revolution. We studied its main advantages, its influence on the world economy and the anticipated consequences. We investigated the factors hindering the implementation of the project related to the Industrial Internet in Russia. We formulated the primary tasks and evaluated the perspectives for development of the industrial Internet in the Russian economy.

1 Introduction

During the last decades, the mankind entered the path of the fourth industrial revolution [1]. Studies of many modern scientists are deal with implementation of new progressive technologies in industry and other spheres to increase productivity and economic efficiency. The Industrial Internet, which is a component and a very important direction in development of the industrial revolution, is being actively implemented at industrial enterprises bringing radically new cyber-physical approaches in organization of works, services and management. And, as a result, future changes will affect not only the industrial sphere but many other aspects of social life, such as the labor market, the system of

[a] The article was prepared as part of the work on the grant of the President of the Russian Federation NSh-4028.2018.6

[*] Corresponding author: asaturova_yum@spbstu.ru

education, the environment, political systems and many others. We will need to reconsider many notions and, in a certain way, the role of a man in the modern world will be changed.

The general problems of the new industrial revolution are discussed in works [2, 3, 4]. The work [5] investigates the influence of the Internet of Things onto the transformation of industry. Issues related to implementing the Internet of Things in industry are discussed in the work [6]. The influence of the Internet of Things onto the competitive advantage of some industries was discussed in [7]. Some issues related to processing large arrays of data using internet technologies were investigated in the work [8]. Studies of social, psychological and economic consequences of intellectual technologies were discussed in works [9, 10].

2 Characteristic of the fourth industrial revolution

Historically, four main stages are highlighted in the industrial revolution development. *The first* industrial revolution was related to inventing the steam engine that conditioned the transition from manual to machine works and greatly increased the labor efficiency in early XIX century. *The second* industrial revolution was related to the introduction of electricity in industry and introduction of conveyors for mass production by Henry Ford. *The third,* "digital" industrial revolution started during the 70-ies of the XX century and developed from introduction of computers to further evolution of information technologies. Its particular features are: industrial automation, introduction of industrial robots, transition to renewable energy sources and digital industry. Even though not all the components of the "digital" revolution have spread widely in the world, we can now see a radically new breakthrough in the evolution of digital technologies that has conditioned the transition to *the fourth*, "informational" industrial revolution. Its particular feature is wide introduction of cyber-physical systems into manufacturing, everyday life and entertainment. The technologies of data processing are being substituted by information technologies to form a completely digital industry based on information technologies.

For the first time, the concept of the fourth industrial revolution under the name "Industry 4.0" was formulated at an exhibition held in Hannover in 2011, defining it as implementation of "cyber-physical systems" into manufacturing processes. Industrial systems will be integrated into one network, interact in real time, self-adjust and learn new models of behavior. Such networks can support manufacturing with less errors, interact with the manufactured products and, if necessary, adapt to new requirements of the customers. This will promote development of global industrial networks. The most important technologies being the basis of cyber-physical systems are the following:

1. *Big data.* It is a method of collecting and analyzing data from a large number of various sources to become the standard for making solutions in real time.
2. *Cloud calculations.* Using cloud technologies will make it possible to create platforms for cooperation and data exchange between partners located at great distances from one another.
3. *Internet of Things.* Creating a sophisticated system of communication between things, which implies the ability of things to identify one another, exchange the required information, use it and make solutions. After implementing into industry, the Industrial Internet of Things will make it possible to greatly increase the manufacturing efficiency.
4. *Autonomous robots.* Robots are becoming more and more flexible and autonomous. A system of computer vision will make it possible for robots to interact with one another, automatically adjust their activity and work together with people.

5. *Virtual and supplemented reality*. Supplemented reality means the ability to add virtual properties to physical objects, for example by correlating them with some information that can be individualized for particular subjects of perception.
6. *3D modeling and 3D printing*. 3D modeling will make it possible to virtually model a physical process with consideration of the available raw materials and workforce, with decreasing the equipment adjustment time and improving the quality as the result. Inherent advantages of 3D industry will make it possible to cut the costs of transportation and stored reserves.
7. *Distributed lists. Block-chain*. Introducing technologies distributed lists creates the possibility to make management less centralized by delegating some functions to a certain network community, which will promote the trust of system's participants into its activity.

On the basis of a questionnaire answered by top managers of technological companies within the framework of the World Economy Forum in Davos, the key trends are cloud calculations, methods of collecting and processing of big data, the Internet of Things, robot technologies, quantum calculations, biotechnologies and medicine based on 3D printing. As it was noted at the forum, developing the basic directions can bring the profit amounting over USD 30 trillion for the world economy during the next 10 years [11].

3 World experience in implementing state programs in the sphere "Industry 4.0"

The state of the program "Industry 4.0" can be described as an actually started and irreversible process. According to the forecast of McKinsey Global institute, by 2025 the input of the Industrial Internet of Things into the world economy can be up to 11 % of the world GDP. An average yearly growth of GDP in the optimistic and optimistic scenarios of development of the Internet of Things by 2025 can be 3.9 to 11.1 USD trillion [3].

Germany was the first country to employ "Industry 4.0" [12] that, within the framework of their own "High-Tech Strategy" based on intensive implementation of the Industrial Internet of Things, started investing 40 billion Euros per year into the new Internet infrastructure. In order to promote new ideas, a consortium of the largest industrial companies was formed in Germany, such as BMW, Siemens and Bosch. By 2030, Germany plans to completely transit to a new stage of industrial development, where the Internet is used for maximizing the industrial efficiency.

In 2011, the USA started developing the program "Cloud Strategy" [13] aimed at implementing modern technologies to create "smart" industrial plants, shops, cities and transport systems, as well as solutions to the tasks of social communication, e-commerce and monitoring global logistic flows. The world leaders in the cloud technologies market are American companies IBM, Microsoft, Google, HP, AT&T. In 2014 a non-commercial consortium "Industrial Internet" was formed founded by General Electric, AT&T, IBM, Intel and others.

In the European community in 2010, the program "Digital Agenda for Europe" was started [14], with the purpose of developing the internet-economy; it is the first of seven initiatives within the framework of the strategy "Europe 2020". Complete implementation of this program is expected to increase the GDP of the European countries by 5%, or € 1500 per person. In 2016, the European economic committee presented a program to develop digital industry "Digital Market – Digitizing the Industry: Questions and Answers" [15].

In China in 2015 a concept "Internet-Plus" was adopted, which included the best initiatives from world-leading countries to implement internet-management functions into materials processing industry, finance, medicine and agriculture [16]. Using mobile Internet technologies, the traditional manufacturers can install hardware and software on road vehicles, household devices and other industrial products to enable remote control, automatic data collection and analysis.

Analyzing the world experience in implementing the program "Industry 4.0", we can draw the conclusion that implementing new technologies in industry is currently in the active stage. In order to increase the competitive advantage of Russian economy, it is necessary to ensure the transition of the national industry to a new digital technological platform.

4 Industrial internet as a key factor for developing the program "Industry 4.0"

The concept of the Industrial Internet based on wide implementation of digital and internet technologies in industry can be considered the main driving force of the program "Industry 4.0". The Industrial Internet of Things (IIoT) presumes creating the informational communication infrastructure based on the Internet connection of equipment, sensors, devices and automated systems for controlling technological processes to ensure active interaction between them. Such organization of the industry will cause forming new business models for providing products and services and delivering them to customers. The most promising spheres for introducing IIoT solutions and platform are housing services business, transport, medicine, machine-building industry, as well as power generating that, due to the active attitude of the Ministry of Power-Generating Industry, has already developed a "road-map" for using the Industrial Internet technologies.

The main result of implementing the concept of Industrial Internet is increasing the efficiency of the existing industrial and technological processes and decreasing the required capital and operational costs. After implementation into industry, the Internet of Things will bring a few advantages, such as:

- *flexibility* of production that is achieved through refusing to use rigid configurations of conveyor lines, which makes it possible to take and fulfill individual orders and implement new solutions;
- *adjustability* of production that is achieved through using a united technological platform and monitoring on all levels;
- *efficiency* of production that is achieved through minimizing the costs related to the human factor: the high cost of human labor, errors and idle time.

The Industrial Internet is used more and more widely in the world practice. Analysts from the company Ericsson predict that, out of approximately 28 billion connected devices worldwide by the year 2021, about 16 billion will be related to the IoT. According to the assessment from "DirectINFO", the total volume of the Russian market of IoT in 2016 was 17.9 million devices, which is 42 % more than in 2015. It is expected that the total number of IoT devices will be 79.5 million by 2021 and 164.7 million by 2026. [17].

According to the forecasts from specialists of General Electric, the Industrial Internet can already be used in such sectors of economy as transport, power generating and medicine, ensuring the world GDP by USD 32.3 trillion. Becoming the basis for new economy, the Industrial Internet will bring the world economy the effect in the amount 11% of GDP, will enable an increase in the labor efficiency by 25% and decrease the energy consumption by 20% by the year 2030 [18]. The key factor for the growth will be continuous decrease in the cost of sensors and equipment, as well as the cost of communication, data processing and system integration.

Therefore, implementation of the Industrial Internet is the main factor to increase the production efficiency, the level and quality of life. However, development of this process will bring certain difficulties and will require reconsidering many notions and renovating many spheres of life. First of all, we can mention the transformation of the labor market and a possible growth of unemployment. In this respect, it is necessary that the state starts reforming the system of education and creating new jobs as soon as possible.

5 Tasks and perspectives of implementing the industrial internet in Russia

The Russian market for implementing the Industrial Internet technologies is in the beginning of development. However, the statistical data in the RF show that the specific weight of the industrial segment in the Russian market of the Internet of Things is prevailing. In 2015, its share was 64%, which means good perspectives for development of the Industrial Internet technologies in Russia [19]. According to the results of polling the top managers in different spheres of economy, in the RF in general, about 30% of companies are planning to implement the technologies of the Internet of Things or are already implementing them in their companies, and 11% of companies have already implemented projects that use the Internet of Things [19].

We can also mention that, currently, its use is more characteristic for the systems of automated data collection from devices installed at industrial objects. For example, it deals with the machine-building industry, power generating and mining. The interaction between machines develops more in transport companies that intensively use navigation systems. A positive trend is the growth of the share of the organizations that use information systems in manufacturing. From 2010 to 2015, their percentage grew from 25 to 30 %. Most of all, they are implemented in the spheres of communication, chemistry, electric equipment manufacturing and smelting industry [20].

The main factors hindering integration of the Internet of Things into manufacturing are: low level of knowledge and availability of technologies, limited investment and shortage of skilled workforce capable of working with new technologies, deficiencies in the legislation in the sphere of IT technologies, insufficient elaboration of safety issues and data protection, issues related to psychology and the red tape. Ensuring the availability and safety of using progressive technologies for big data processing, cloud and quantum calculations systems, the ability to use "smart" devices, robots and computer control systems are the priority tasks for businessmen and the state to attract more enterprises to the system of the Industrial Internet in Russia.

The Russian companies that are planning to implement the technologies related to the Industrial Internet of Things should start with creating a digital model of the industrial business process to eliminate digital gaps in the manufacturing cycle. One of the leaders in this sphere in Russia is the company Rostelecom acting as an engineering center for digital support during the life cycle of products. Rostelecom is developing a platform for the Industrial Internet on the basis of the analysis of foreign experience with consideration of the specific features of the Russian market [17]. With participation of the company Rostelecom, the "National Association of Market Participants" has been formed. The strategy of development of the Industrial Internet in the RF is being carried out by the Ministry of Trade of the RF (development of the road map for the Internet of Things, with participation of the "Fund for Developing Internet Initiatives"). However, the issues of organizational and legal support for industries related to the development of information technologies require still more elaboration. Therefore, the primary tasks for developing the Industrial Internet in the RF are as follows:

1. Creating an information-telecommunication infrastructure ensuring a technological possibility to use innovative internet technologies.

2. State or state-private financing to implement projects related to the Internet of Things. Support to pilot projects.
3. Support to domestic developers of high-tech products and research in the sphere of artificial intellect, information systems of management and cooperation through networks.
4. Ensuring the availability of IoT platforms for data collecting and processing.
5. Reforms of the system of education and training the IT specialists.
6. Developing the legal base promoting development of new technologies and ensuring their legal status and data protection.
7. Developing universal standards and requirements for new products. Ensuring compatibility with other IT systems, developing the export.

6 Conclusion

Transition of the national industry to the digital technological platform is becoming a topical issue for the competitive advantage of the Russian economy. Currently, the most perspective technologies are related to the Internet of Things, methods of dealing with large volumes of data, cloud and quantum calculations, robots, biotechnologies, digital 3D modeling and 3D printing. The Industrial Internet based on using the technologies of the Internet of Things is becoming the primary driving force of the industrial revolution. Implementing the projects in the sphere of the Industrial Internet is the main factor for increasing the efficiency of production, as well as the level and quality of life.

The first-priority task for efficient implementation of the Industrial Internet into the Russian economy is ensuring the availability of modern technologies for industrial plants. Solving this task is related to providing the state support of domestic developers and manufacturers of modern high-tech products, financing the implementation of projects in the sphere of the Industrial Internet of Things. Another prerequisite for development is creating the normative and legal base and standardization, as well as ensuring data safety. At the level of development of the society as a whole, it is important to maintain balance between development of various industries and spheres of life. Renovating the system of education, timely training of IT specialists, transforming the labor market is a necessity.

References

1. K. Schwab. The Fourth Industrial Revolution [online], Available at: https://cdn.eksmo.ru/v2/ITD000000000819325/PDF/ITD000000000819325.pdf (2016)
2. E. Brynjolfsson, A. McAfee, *The Second Machine Age: Work, Progress, and Prosperity in a Time of Brilliant Technologies* (Norton, New York, 2014)
3. McKinsey Global Institute. Manufacturing the Future: The next era of global growth and innovation [online], Available at: https://www.mckinsey.com/~/media/McKinsey/Business%20Functions/Operations/Our%20Insights/The%20future%20of%20manufacturing/MGI_%20Manufacturing_Full%20report_Nov%202012.ashx (2012)
4. V. V. Korablev, A. I. Sarygulov, V. N. Sokolov, Economic sciences, **6 (256)** (2016)
5. K. A. Gulin, V. S. Uskov, Problems of territory development, **4 (90)** (2017)
6. V. P. Kupriyanovsky et al., International Journal of Open Information Technologies, **4 (12)** (2016)
7. A. V. Babkin, O.V. Chistyakova, Russian Entrepreneurship, **18 (24)** (2017)

8. J. Lichy, M. Kachur, T. Khvatova, Journal of Marketing Management, **33 (9-10)** (2017)
9. McKinsey Global Institute. Disruptive technologies: Advances that will transform life, business, and the global economy. Mc.Kinsey & company [online], Available at: https://www.mckinsey.com/~/media/McKinsey/Business%20Functions/McKinsey%20Digital/Our%20Insights/Disruptive%20technologies/MGI_Disruptive_technologies_Full_report_May2013.ashx (2013)
10. J. Lichy, K. Pon & T. Khvatova, Journal of Management Development, **33 (7)** (2014)
11. World Economic Forum. The Fourth Industrial Revolution. Davos [online], Available at: https://www.weforum.org/agenda/2016/01/the-fourth-industrial-revolution-what-it-means-and-how-to-respond (2016)
12. Industrie 4.0: Mit dem Internet der Dinge auf dem Weg zur 4. industriellen Revolution [online], Available at: https://www.vdi-nachrichten.com/Technik-Gesellschaft/Industrie-40-Mit-Internet-Dinge-Weg-4-industriellen-Revolution (2011)
13. V. Kundra, Federal cloud computing strategy. U.S. Chief Information Officer [online], Available at: http://itlaw.wikia.com/wiki/Federal_Cloud_Computing_Strategy (2011)
14. Digital Agenda for Europe: 2010-2010. Annual Progress Report 2011 [online], Available at: http://eur-lex.europa.eu/legal-content/EN/ALL/?uri=CELEX:52010DC0245R(01) (2011)
15. Analysis of the world experience in the development of industry and approaches to the digital transformation of the industry of the member states of the EEC [online], Available at: http://www.eurasiancommission.org/ru/act/prom_i_agroprom/dep_prom/SiteAssets/Forms/AllItems.aspx (2016)
16. China unveils targets for 2015: Li Keqiang's speech as it happened South China Morning Post [online], Available at: http://www.scmp.com/news/china/article/1729846/live-li-keqiang-unveils-chinas-annual-work-report (2015)
17. The Internet market of things in Russia and the World [online], Available at: http://www.directinfo.net (2017)
18. The Internet of things is the basis of a new economy [online], Available at: https:// www.pcweek.ru/iot/article/detail.php?ID=182807 (2016)
19. V. N. Knyaginina, Expert-analytical report, **136** (2017)
20. Forecast of long-term socio-economic development of the Russian Federation for the period until 2030 (developed by the Ministry of Economic Development of the Russian Federation) [online], Available at: http://base.garant.ru/70309010/#ixzz54TCSsftr (2018)

Digital model of sharing economy: blockchain technology management[a]

Alexander Babkin[1*], *Tatiana* Golovina[3], *Andrey* Polyanin[3], and *Yuliya* Vertakova[2],

[1] Peter the Great St. Petersburg Polytechnic University, 195251, Politekhnicheskaya st., 29, Russian Federation
[2] Southwest State University, Kursk, 50 let Oktyabrya, 94, Russian Federation
[3] Mid-Russian Management Institute – branch of RANEPA, 302028, Orel, Pobedy Boulevard, 5a, Russian Federation

Abstract. The modernization of traditional process and service industries, organization of trading and procurement procedures, related financial and logistical operations, change in the structure of consumption associated with the through penetration of information technologies and digitization of economic processes creates the basis for formation of new markets and conditions for their functioning. As employees, consumers, businesses, and manufacturing processes become increasingly related as a single digital space, digitalization offers wide possibilities for new decision-making models being the basis for ongoing global economic and social transformations which change business and consumer models, one of which is the sharing economy. The digital model of sharing economy will be developed and transformed in the next few years to achieve the main purpose – the use of unengaged or underused assets in the economy. In this regard, the search for new tools and technologies for business models development is vital. The authors present the content, advantages, current state and prospects for development of the distributed registry technology (blockchain). It is presented that it will increase transparency, security and efficiency of transactions of economic entities in various financial and non-financial fields. A transactional model of the economic system based on the blockchain technology is presented. The sharing economy features and characteristics are given.

1 Introduction

The modern economy is post-industrial, and it is often called a new, innovative economy of knowledge, competences, networking. It should be noted that this list of definitions on the one hand brings a different meaning, and on the other hand it characterizes the same period of economic activity. Recently, the digital economy concept has appeared both in the economic theory and in the practical activities of a number of countries. This is due to the

* Corresponding author: al-vas@mail.ru
[a] This paper was prepared in the studies for RFBR project No. 18-010-01119 "Management of digital transformation of innovation-industrial cluster as a strategic element of the industrial digital platform: methodology, tools, practice".

fact that the beginning of the XXI century provided the development of digital technologies based on the information revolution and the processes of economy globalization. The society and economy management processes information has become the main resource. In the person's hands, it is transformed into knowledge, and socioeconomic relations are increasingly transferred to the network space. The key factor of digital transformation in the activity of market entity is the digital culture development.

Currently, the digital economy is included in the list of the main aspects of the strategic development in Russia and many foreign countries. The task for creating the conditions for deep system digitalization of the life style and economic structure in Russia [1, 2], China [3], the EAEU countries [4], Japan [5] and other foreign countries is specified at the government levels. The digital economy development can affect the internal and external business environment, the patterns of its behavior including using the technology to maintain the distributed registry or blockchain technology. The blockchain is a technology that is at the top of the entire digital economy. In the blockchain there are several very important innovations – assets decentralization and tokenization. However, today it is still difficult to implement such models in practice. In any case, the technology itself, which allows us to build up blockchains, has not yet reached the required level of maturity and continues its development.

Up-to-date scientists and practitioners have not formed a common opinion on the content of the digital model of sharing economy: some consider it as an effective platform for transactions within a network that combines equal participants, while others see it as a source of corruption and shadow money flows, and other negative events which put the brakes on the economic growth. However, none of the economists will deny that the sharing economy has great prospects and already has a significant impact on the global economic processes.

With the development of the digitalization processes, the interest in studying the sharing economy only increases. The fact is that many economists, as one of the digital economy characteristics, call its distribution in the world. The following scientists made the particular contribution to the study of the sharing economy theory and its role in the modern ecosystem: Don Tapscott [6], A. Stephany [7], M. Vidas-Bubanja [8]. The scientific papers of scientists and professional associations are devoted to the study of the information society, formation of new technological modes, models of electronic business, implementation of digital technologies and development of digital sharing economy: S. Asharaf [9], T. Issa [10], U. B. Vertakova [11], Boston Consulting Group [12], and also I. Belk [13,14], R. Botsman [15], A. Sundararajan [16], T. Weber [17], C. Lamberton [18], V. Mohlvann [19].

In this case, the matters of sharing economy development and digitalization are mainly considered in whole without studying their mutual interaction and mutual influence.

Study purpose is to substantiate the nature, features and characteristics of the digital sharing economy, which is based on the "blockchain" technology, and also determination of the aspects of its development in Russia. The study was performed based on materials featuring the development of this concept both in the whole world and its spread in the Russian economy.

2 Main results of the study

The studies of the authors [11, 20, 21, etc.] show that in the current context the set of conditions and factors of information globalization has led to the formation of new economic terms which are commonly called as the "digital economy", the formation intensity of which is different for separate countries. Big data, artificial intelligence technologies, and other digital technologies lead to high decision-making speed, forming communications with buyers or suppliers and control of both supply and demand. The economy has gradually diverged the conventional model of centralized organizations, where large operators, which often hold a dominant position, are responsible for rendering services to a group of passive consumers. For the first time, Lawrence Lessig, a Professor of Law at the Stanford University implemented the sharing economy concept in 2008 when he described how many Internet users significantly save while organizing a group in the network and buying the sharing things at very large discount. And by 2010, the Internet services for exchanging the services and things between individuals has been rapidly risen so that they started speaking of the sharing phenomenon everywhere [12].

Currently, the civilization is going towards a new model of increasingly decentralized organizations, where large operators are responsible for aggregating the resources of many people to provide services to a much more active group of consumers. This shift signifies the appearance of a new generation of "dematerialized" organizations which do not require physical offices, assets and even employees. The sharing economy characteristics in the age where the digitalization processes development are shown in Fig. 1.

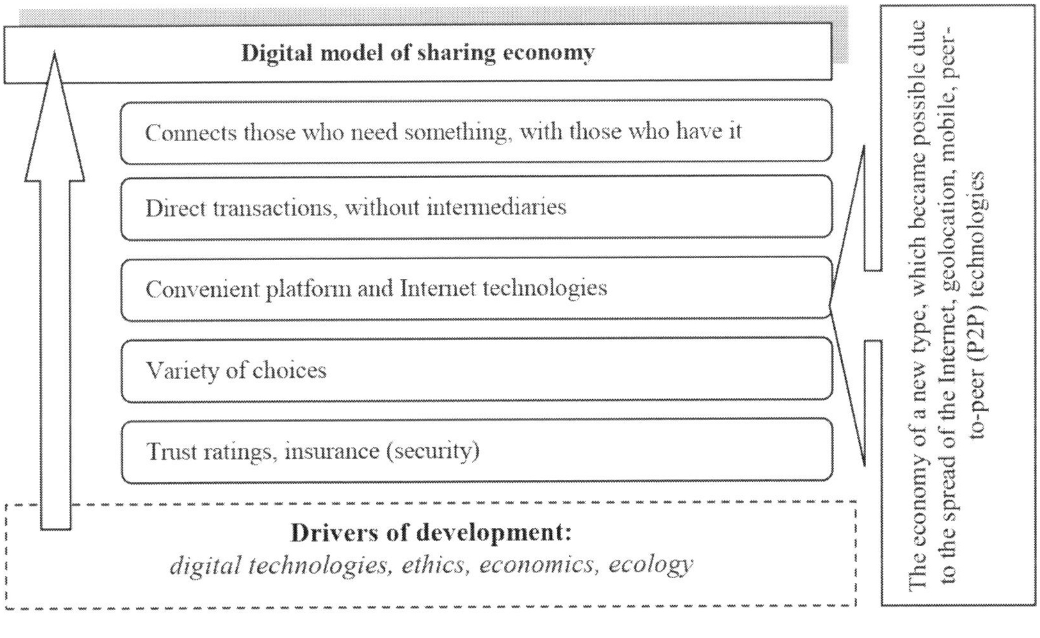

Fig. 1. Characteristics of the sharing economy (compiled by the authors).

The problem with the functioning of this model is that the value produced by the group generally is not distributed in equal shares among all those who contributed to its production; the large intermediaries managing the platforms form the profit.

To remove this imbalance, the new digital economy technology is used. The distributed registry system (Blockchain) is a special technology that is based on the platforms for operations between equal participants operating without intermediaries and in which decentralized information storage is used to reflect all transaction data. The new digital business models are aimed at reducing costs, obtaining additional revenue from digital solutions, optimizing customer interaction and improving customer service by means of studying their experience [20, 21].

For the first time, the "blockchain" technology was used in the financial sector, where it served as the basis for the initial creation of the digital currency "bitkoyn", and later other types of digital currencies [20].

Recently, there are more and more applications that expand the key function of this technology – the decentralized storage of transaction data – by means of integration of the mechanisms allowing real transactions in the decentralized manner. These mechanisms, which are called as "smart contracts", operate based on the individual rules (for example, specific requirements for quantity, quality, price), and which allow automatic selection of potential customers for suppliers and vice versa based on the distributed registries (Fig. 2).

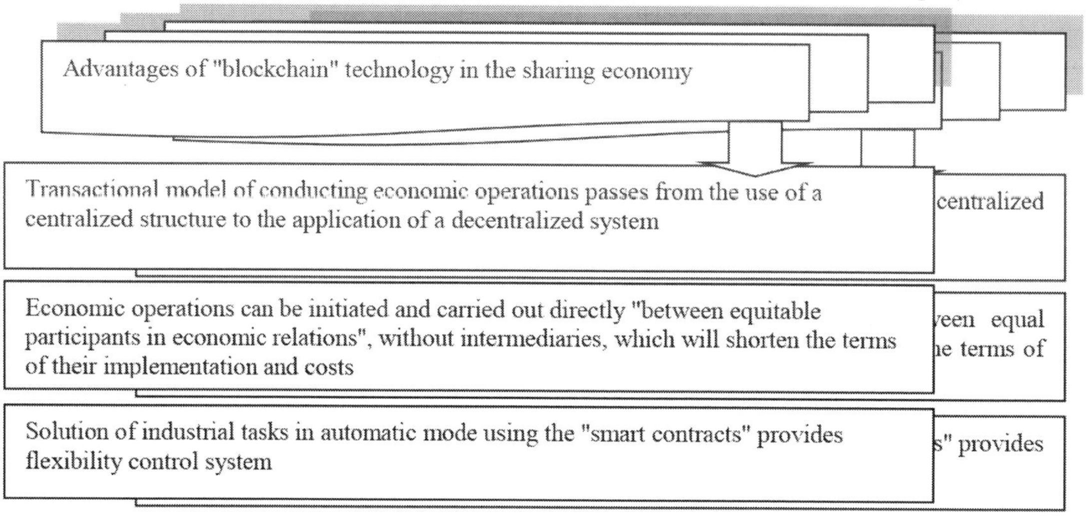

Fig. 2. Advantages of "blockchain" technology in the sharing economy (compiled by the authors).

At the same time, the following factors shall be classified as the factors that currently prevent the implementation of blockchain based applications [20]:

– lack of methodological support for regulatory and legal requirements that shall be met when implementing the blockchain-projects;

– complexity of applying the collective voice of all the parties involved in the blockchain system, in connection with the lack of the best practices;

– low operation speed;

– complexity in setting up and managing the infrastructure;

– lack of reliable and effective process solutions.

Thus, the technology itself, which ensures the sharing economy functioning, has not yet reached the necessary maturity level and continues developing. Overview of the current state of the distributed registry system and its development prospects are given in Fig. 3.

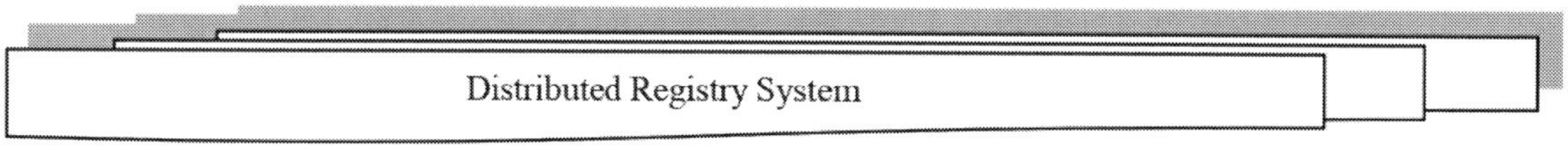

PLAYERS OF THE WORLD MARKET	PILOT PROJECTS WITH BLOCKCHAIN IN THE RUSSIAN FEDERATION	THE VOLUME OF THE WORLD MARKET OF BLOCKCHAIN-TECHNOLOGIES, CRYPTOCURRENCIES AND DIGITAL ASSETS (billion $)
Microsoft Deloitte IBM Linux Foundation Chain Inc. Circle Internet Financial Ripple Ethereum	CB VEB Sberbank VTB S7 Alfa Bank FAS	2016 – 49 ***Prediction*** 2018 – 143 2020 – 230
RUSSIAN MARKET PLAYERS	**INTEREST TO BLOCKCHAIN IN THE RUSSIAN FEDERATION**	
Qiwi Financial Cryptography Waves Platform FinTech Association	FTS ROSREESTR Government of Moscow Government of the Republic of Tatarstan	

Source: prepared by the authors according to the data of IDS Worldwide Semiannual Blockchain Spending Guide, 2017 [22, 23]

Fig. 3. The current state of the distributed registry system.

The blockchain technology can principally change the economic system to which we are accustomed, first by transforming individual sectors, and ultimately through the transforming the entire digital market.

This technology is truly effective in those systems where full data synchronization and confirmation of authorship of the performed actions are required. The "blockchain" technology innovation is the transactions information is no longer stored in the centralized database, but transferred to the computers of all network members who store data locally. The "Bitcoin" application was the first application based on the blockchain technology for so-called crypto currency (bitcoin). In recent years the bitkoyne has served as the basis for creation of other blockchain applications, most of which are currently being developed in the financial sector. More recently a number of companies have been created and some projects have been launched, the purpose of which is to apply the blockchain principles in other industries.

The blockchain was created as a niche product in secondary markets, but recently this technology has attracted the attention of experts from different industries, and also caused the increased interest from the media side. However, many specialists and managers of state and private organizations are not sure what measures they shall take based on this trend [20].

The transactional model based on the blockchain technology reflecting the procedures of the transactions in the economic system is shown in Fig. 4.

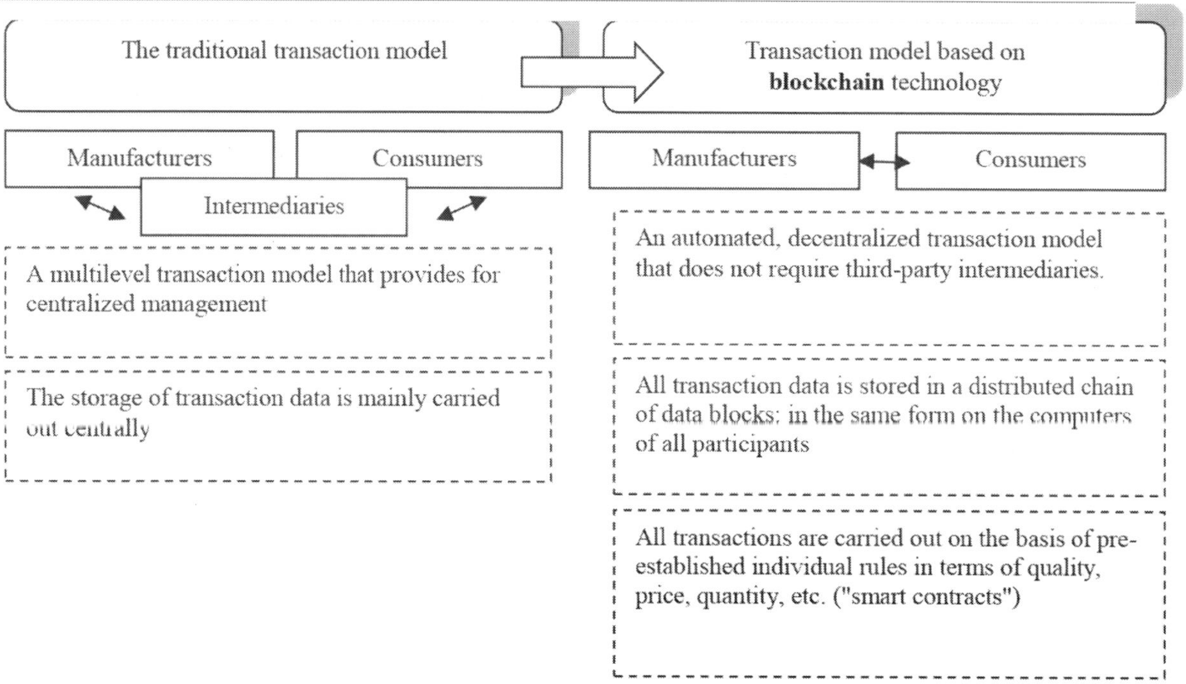

Fig. 4. Transactional model based on blockchain technology.

Now the digitalization has become an irreversible process, the most important factor for development of almost any industry. In modern terms, the innovation driver is not only the state or large social and industrial groups. The transition is formed through the consumer sector, which concentrates the innovative approaches and practices of the digital economy due to its mobility and the ability to accumulate capital [21]. The adaptability of the digital environment makes it possible to optimize the business processes in the most complex management models. The business task is to be properly integrated into these terms of the sharing economy and its prospects. The vector of sharing economy development is given in Fig. 5.

The sharing economy fields are quite wide:

1) financial

– trade in digital securities (confirmation of a share and transfer of ownership);
– currency exchange / conversion;
– housing and utilities sector;
– data storage;
– transactions between equal participants of the network;
– etc.

2) non-financial:

– protection of personal information of the consumers;
– confirmation of ownership rights;
– network infrastructure;
– etc.

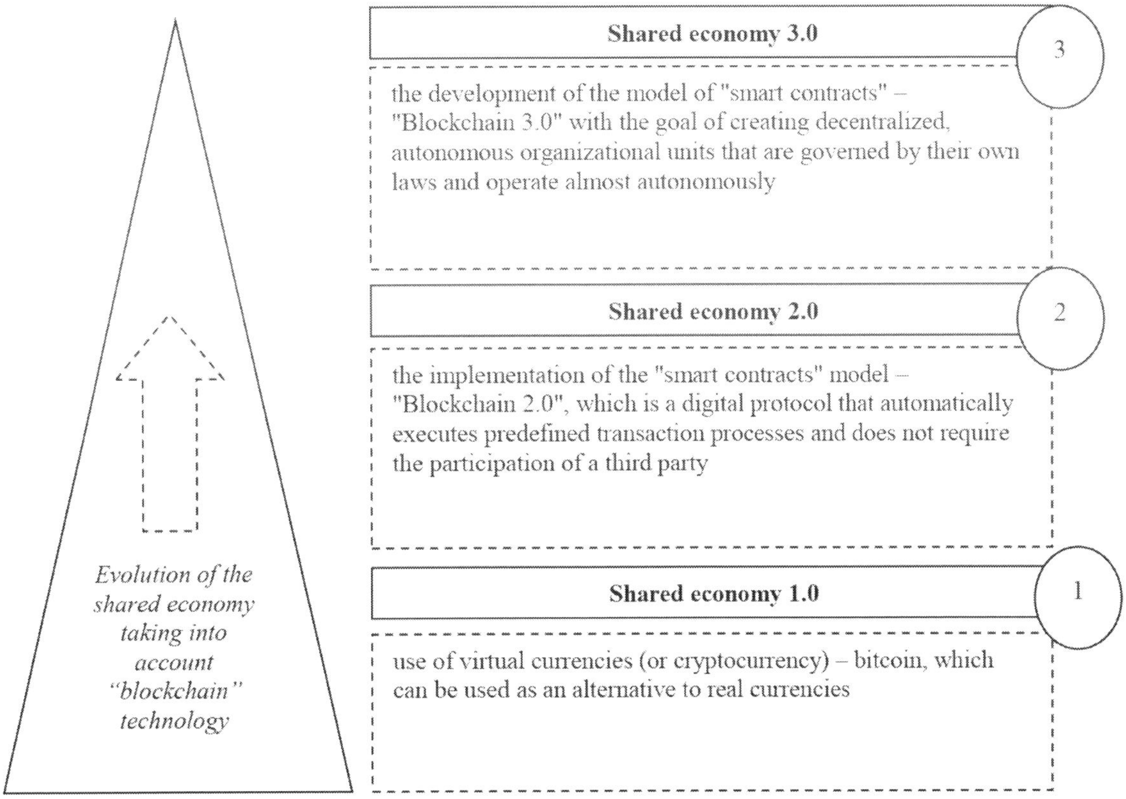

Fig. 5. The author's vision of the development of the shared economy, taking into account the "blockchain" technology.

This technology and various solutions on its basis have made significant progress, since the first blockchain-application "Bitcoin" was launched in 2009. Currently, two most important digital aspects in the financial field can be noted [21]:

– the tendency for creation of "smart contracts" applications based on the blockchain technology;

– programs for formation of closed chains of blocks.

We think that the scope of potential blockchain applications in the sharing economy due to these trends and programs.

The fundamental elements of the decentralized system of sharing economy are the following:

– transactions (selection of a suitable consumer/manufacturer) are carried out either fully automatically (based on the "smart contracts") or manually;

– transactions are reflected in the chain of blocks with the protection against extraneous interference;

– payments using crypto currency.

The authors indicated the following capabilities for using the "blockchain" technology by the Russian business in the time of digital economy:

– decentralized storage of transactions data to improve their protection level and to ensure the higher autonomy level from a single body that performs central administration;

– using the blocks chain to facilitate payments with crypto currencies, contracts digitization, digital content management, transactions verification, and trading operations performance.

The following branches: finance, investment, public sector, trading, health care, energy are the prospective for implementation and development of blockchain technologies in Russia.

The main aspects of subsequent proactive implementation of "blockchain" technologies into the digital model of sharing economy can be:

– issue of digital state currencies based on the blockchain;

– increase of a smart contracts share in the total volume of contracts up to 10%;

– full transfer of registers (recording of rights to real estate, registration of birth, marriage, death) to the "blockchain" technology;

– opening of the first sections of roads where autonomous cars driving will be performed through the blockchain;

– exchange of medical records between medical institutions based on the blockchain.

Thus, not only technologies but also new models for management of technologies and data become an important factor of success in the highly competitive and trans-border digital model of sharing economy, allowing for rapid response and modeling of subsequent challenges and problems.

The most difficult task that "blockchain" technology poses under development of the digital model of sharing economy is how to integrate the social concept, where there is no follow-up mechanism, into the sociotechnical system. These follow-up mechanisms appeared in the social concepts as a result of evolutionary cultural development. They led to the creation of a whole number of interrelated systems, each of which to a certain extent has the ability to adapt when it is necessary to deal with the improper or malicious behavior of individual participants. These interrelated systems can temporarily exclude participants and reintegrate them in case of correction, for example, using the social concept of forgiveness.

Social systems based on such collective interaction are relatively stable, true and fair. In contrast, process systems are based on deterministic, isolated concepts providing the adoption of operational decisions that can have serious consequences for individual participants. The digital economy is interfaced with the high-hume and high-tech epochs, that is, high humanitarian and technical technologies [12].

In order to create a carefully developed concept in terms of technology and to ensure that the potential benefits offered by the decentralized structure can be fully used, it will be necessary to implement the training procedure and continuous adjustment system based on the formation of a competence-based personnel model.

At the stage of development of the digital model of sharing economy, in the absence of sufficient practice to assess the practicability of implementing the certain restrictive measures, the restrictive regulation can lead to hindering the development of the new technological generation economy and, accordingly, to delaying Russia behind the leading economies of the world in modernization of traditional manufacturing industries and industries services, as well as modernization of management procedures. In this regard, in the nearest future, it is advisable to observe the non prohibitive legal regulation in this area. The legal regulation of the digital economy institutions shall be firstly aimed at providing the necessary conditions for their development including support for innovative developments, and to promote the technologies implementation and development including the "blockchain" technology.

Thus, the authors:

1. Showed that the new consumption economy model under the conditions of shared use of digitalization, big data concept, cyberphysical systems, Internet of things, etc., opens the global opportunities for effective development. Building the processes of interaction among

all digitalization participants will allow the business structures to combine the potential opportunities, harmonize process interests, and to reduce the risk level. And as a consequence, this will help to increase the level of their innovative activity and to create the prospecting base for the further economy development.

2. The features are reflected and the sharing economy characteristic is presented under the digitalization conditions.

3. The content, advantages, current state and prospects of the blockchain technology development are presented.

4. A transactional model of the economic system based on the blockchain technology is presented.

3 Conclusions

Mainstreaming of the "blockchain" technology with observance of all the laid principles will fundamentally change the way how the economy functions today and how financial transactions are carried out. The article specifies that the blockchain was developed to create a decentralized model for data exchange and storage, which is controlled with the decentralized operating system. The decentralized systems can not be controlled by a minority of participants or a single body that is responsible for the central management, and they are transparent for all participants, as well as self-controlled. The authors conclude that the "blockchain" technology allows creating a self-regulating and self-controlling sharing economy, in which transactions are performed through fulfilling digital contracts. This kind of decentralized management can lead to reduction in a number of inefficient operations and decreasing in the corruption level. Due to the fact that each individual network element processes each transaction, none of the elements control the database as a whole. From this point of view, decentralization also plays the role both in increasing the level of security and sustainability of the economic system.

The digital model of sharing economy provides free operations on own terms. This opens the prospects for development of innovative intermediary services in the future. Such services could allow a third party to approve or reject a transaction in case of disagreement between other parties that requires subsequent development of both regulatory and methodological support.

References

1. On approval of the program "Digital Economy of the Russian Federation". Regulation of the government of the Russian Federation No 1632 dated 28.07.2017. [online], Available at: http://base.consultant.ru (2017)
2. A. V. Babkin, D. D. Burkaltseva, D. G. Kosten, Yu. N. Vorobyov, Scientific and technical reports of the St. Petersburg State Polytechnic University. Economics, **10(3)** (2017)
3. On the Digital Economy of China. [online], Available at: http:// vsesovetnik.ru/archives/2205527.02.17 (2017)
4. Strategy for the development of the EAEU digital space, 2025. [online], Available at: http://d-russia.ru/wp-content/uploads/2016/10/strategy.pdf (2016)
5. In Japan the crypto currency has become an official means of payment. [online], Available at: http://www.rosbalt.ru/business/2017/04/01/1603901.html (2017)
6. D. Tapscott, *The electronic digital society: Pros and cons of the network intelligence epoch* (Kiev: INT Press; Moscow: Relf bull.1999)

7. A. Stephany, *The Business of Sharing: Making it in the New Sharing Economy* (Springer, 2015)
9. U. Huws, *Labor in the Global Digital Economy: The Cybertariat Comes of Age*. (NYU Press, New York, 2014)
8. M. Vidas-Bubanja, I. Bubanja, 39th International Convention on Information and Communication Technology, Electronics and Microelectronics (2016)
9. S. Asharaf, S. Adarsh, *Decentralized Computing Using Blockchain Technologies and Smart Contracts: Emerging Research and Opportunities*. (IRMA, Hershey: PA, USA: IGI Global 2017).
10. T. Issa, P. Kommers, Th. Issa, P. Isaías, *Smart Technology Applications in Business Environments*. (IRMA, Hershey: PA, USA: IGI Global 2017)
11. Yu. V. Vertakova, T. O. Tolstykh, E. V. Shkarupeta, V. V. Dmitrieva, *Transformation of management systems under the economy digitalization impact*. (Iugo-zapadnyi gos. un-t, Kursk, 2017)
12. World Development Report, 2016. Digital dividends. Overview. International Bank for Reconstruction and Development / World Bank. [online], Available at: http://wwwwds.worldbank.org/external/default/WDSContentServer/IB/2016/.pdf (2016)
13. R. Belk, Annals of the American Academy of Political and Social Science, **611** (2007)
14. R. Belk, Cambridge Journal of Regions Economy and Society, **10** (2017)
15. R. Botsman, R. Rogers, *What's Mine Is Yours: The Rise of Collaborative Consumption* (Harper Business, New York 2010)
16. A. Sundararajan, *The Sharing Economy: The End of Employment and the Rise of Crowd-Based Capitalism*. (MIT Press, Cambridge 2016).
17. T. A. Weber, Journal of Management Information Systems, **31** (2014)
18. C. P Lamberton, R. L. Rose, Journal of Marketing, **76** (2012)
19. M. Mohlmann, Journal of Consumer Behavior, **14** (2015)
20. A. V. Babkin, D. D. Burkaltseva, V. V. Pshenichnikov, A. S. Tyulin, Scientific and technical reports of the St. Petersburg State Polytechnic University. Economics. **10(5)** (2017) DOI: 10.18721/JE.10501
21. A. A. Aletdinova, et al. *Digital transformation of economy and industry: problems and prospects.* (Publishing House of Polytechnic University, Saint Petersburg, 2017) DOI 10.18720 / IEP/2017.4
22. IDACB: The market of crypto currency and blockchain technology increases 20 times larger. [online], Available at: https://www.if24.ru/rynok-kriptovalyut-vyros-v-20-raz/ (2018)
23. World Summit of Blockchain and Crypto-Currency. [online], Available at: http://blockchainhouse.media/vsemirnyj-sammit-blokchejna-i-kriptovalyut/ (2018)

The Analysis of industrial cooperation models in the context of forming digital economy[a]

Aleksandr Babkin [1*], *Vladimir* Plotnikov[2], and *Yulia* Vertakova[3]

[1] Peter the Great St. Petersburg Polytechnic University, 195251, Politechnicheskaya st., 29, Russian Federation
[2] Southwest State University, Kursk, 50 let Oktyabrya, 94, Russian Federation
[3] Saint Petersburg State University of Economics, 191023, 21, Sadovaya street, 21 Russian Federation

Abstract. Approaches which enable improving the efficiency of industrial enterprises functioning in the context of forming digital economy are discussed in the article. In contrast to the traditional analysis of this problem on macro- (national economy in general, creating a favorable institutional environment for industrial development and digitalizing of economy) or micro- (development of recommendations for implementing digital technologies in manufacturing and management subsystems of industrial enterprises) levels, the authors consider a meso-level. Studies undertaken have made it possible to come to a conclusion that current digitalization of both enterprises and industry in total determines the changes of industrial cooperation models. It has been indicated that significant opportunities for effective development of industry are connected with forming integrative groups of cooperation-interactive enterprises. Such models of interaction as outsourcing, cluster and strategic alliance have been considered and their pros and cons have been revealed. Recommendations on designing cooperation interaction between industrial enterprises have been formulated. The design is oriented on improving the effectiveness of using resources and reducing risks.

1 Introduction

Technological revolution of the contemporary world is closely related to digitalization of industry and its reorganization in accordance with new management principles [1, 2]. It is clearly seen that both developing and developed countries are eager to win technological leadership. The potential for that is formed not only at the micro- and macro- but also at the meso-level. At that, the indicated levels of industry management have their specific character and differ in the degree of development of competitive ability (technological leadership)

[a] This paper is an output of the science project of the government task of Ministry of education and science of the Russian Federation № 26.3546.2017/PCH "Development fundamentals of analysis and prediction of structural and dynamic parameters of the regional economy are based on the integration of the Russian and world experience of management of territorial development and modern scientific doctrines"
* Corresponding author: al-vas@mail.ru

forming instrumentarium.

At the micro-level we are talking about new technologies: their implementing can increase productivity of labor, quality of production, reduce costs; improve ecological characteristics of production activity of enterprises etc. The given range of problems is the focus of attention of a considerable number of foreign [3-5] and Russian specialists [6, 7] who investigate both merely technological and also organizational issues. The latter ones to a large extent are connected with the development of automated control systems for production processes and also with implementing digital management systems.

As a rule, issues of state regulation of innovative technological development of national economies are considered at the macro-level in the considered context. This theme is very popular not only in scientific studies [8] but it is also institutionally confirmed in the system of state administration documents. For instance, the program of "Digital Economy of the Russian Federation" is approved in Russia by the government executive order of July 28, 2017, No. 1632-r [9]. This document determines goals, objectives, directions and terms of realization of basic measures of state policy on creating necessary conditions for developing digital economy in the country. Variation of the suggested economic model from the existing one lies in the fact that data in digital form is considered to be the key factor of production.

The meso-level of forming competitive ability of industry in the new technological era and also forming technological leadership is less explored and investigated. What is it related to? Contemporary technologies are constantly complicating. As the result, division of labor is becoming more and more evident, as well as such phenomena as production specialization and cooperation of production units. Besides fundamental difference of new conditions connected with rapid development of digital technologies lies in the fact that the indicated cooperation becomes flexible. There appears an opportunity for reorganizing cooperation chains in real time scale. It enables improving industry efficiency. Technological opportunities appear that enable forming consortiums of "smart factories", dynamic optimization of production according to different criteria.

Issues of developing organization of interaction processes in industry at the meso-level are traditionally explored within the framework of development dealing with business networks [10-12]. But elaboration of contemporary digital technologies leads to the necessity of further investigation of the indicated subject area that determines its applicability.

2 Research aim

The aim of the undertaken research is analysis of organizational forms and industrial cooperation models in the context of forming digital economy.

3 Organizational forms of industrial cooperation of enterprises

Cooperation is an objective phenomenon. In modern industry, especially in high-tech one, implementation of engineering and manufacturing operations within the framework of one economical unit is not effective. It is related to such factors as scale effect, minimum effective scale of production, localization of resources, institutional environment, profits of localization and others. The study undertaken by the authors indicated that the most commonly available forms of cooperation are outsourcing, cluster and strategic alliance.

Outsourcing. The essence of outsourcing is in passing a variety of functions from a customer company to an executive (outsourcing agent) in order to concentrate the first function on key competencies and make secondary (outsourced) processes cheaper. Finally a situation is possible when the head company of such an outsourcing system is transformed into a management center and all production processes are passed to specialized performers. This model got widespread in electronic and telecommunication industry [13].

An illustrative example is production of iPhone. A mass consumer is sure (to a large extent influenced by advertisement) that it is a product of American industry. But it's not so. The Apple company office and development center are located in Cupertino, California. All manufacturing processes are being outsourced and they are implemented mostly in East Asia. At that, a model of double-level cooperation is being used. Production of component parts is implemented in Samsung enterprises (processors), LG enterprises (displays), etc. The final assembling of iPhone components is made at the Foxconn factory which is located in Shenzhen (China, Guangdong province).

In the context of globalization and distribution of informational and communicational technologies production outsourcing is becoming a global phenomenon. Elements of production process with high labor intensity and ecologically destructive companies of developing countries are being taken out abroad, in the countries with a low level of living and poor state regulation.

Clusters. The theory of cluster development was suggested by M. Porter [14]. According to him, clusters promote increasing competitive ability of enterprises thanks to the agglomerative effect which, in its turn, is governed by territorial concentration of industrial productions and organizations related to them (educational, scientific, engineering, logistic, etc.)

The activity in forming clusters of our epoch (beginning with 1970es) is specifically connected with processes of disintegration of vertically integrated companies and structures [15]. The basic reason for the processes was cardinal upgrade of complexity of production – first of all in machine engineering. The number and assortment of semi-finished products and components, used in final assembly of products, have increased manifold. In these conditions concentration of all production sites under the roof of one vertically integrated structure is no longer a realistic choice. The alternative variant is cooperation of independent producers on a mutually beneficial basis that is a cluster. Being an originator of the cluster approach M. Porter defines cluster as a "group of geographically neighboring interconnected companies and organizations related to their activity which function in a particular sphere and are characterized by the commonness of their activity and are mutually supportive" [14]. The given definition to the full extent reflects the essence of a cluster as an economic and geographic unit. The focus is that a cluster, as a rule, is not something isolated but a part of an integrated system. Here again, it is necessary to suggest that there is certain interconnection and interdependence between clusters within the limits of the system and that determines successful functioning of clusters.

Besides enabling cost saving and competitive advantage related to that, clusters also represent a powerful tool of innovative development. They have got widespread and their dynamics can be monitored by national regulators that support the business community in forming and developing clusters. Such projects as Cluster Mapping (USA, http://clustermapping.us), Cluster Observatory (EU, http://www.clusterobservatory.eu), Russian Cluster Observatory (Russia, http://cluster.hse.ru/clusters) and many other ones are focused on that. In particular, active creation of innovative territorial clusters in Russia is subject to the commission of the Chairman of the Government of the Russian Federation DM-P8-5060 of 28.08.2012. At the moment more than 90 innovative territorial clusters are created in Russia [16].

Organization of clusters is one of the forms of innovative development support including assistance in those branches and types of activity related to computerization and digital technologies.

Strategic alliances. A strategic alliance is association of companies for combined achievement of long-term goals and solving the problems of strategic development. It suggests close cooperation and may be completed with consolidation of companies, creating a joint enterprise or exchanging assets. As a rule, the motive for creating alliances in industry is obtaining new competencies by participants and a synergetic effect of their consolidating [12].

Companies in the alliance should complement each other and intensify competitive advantages. In this case there is a significant number of limitations for their creation both of organizational and legal nature and also of technological nature. It is a common practice that former competitors unite in an alliance. This leads to increased attention to procedures of their creation from antimonopoly services and other regulating authorities of the state and supernational level.

Each of the considered forms of cooperation of enterprises differs in its peculiarities. Comparison of outsourcing, cluster and strategic alliance characteristics is made in Table 1 on the basis of analysis [5-7]. While selecting a specific model for cooperation of enterprises it is necessary to take into account the specific nature of the considered organizational forms. In particular, for concrete projects hybrid forms of interaction organization can be constructed which take into account limitations and specific nature of these projects.

While selecting a form for cooperation of enterprises in contemporary conditions it is necessary to take into account the dependence of its model on the utilized system of informational exchange between them. Architecture and its constructions, composition, compatibility of separate elements and functional capacities are also important factors influencing the selection of the model of enterprise cooperation.

Table 1. Comparative analysis of outsourcing, cluster and strategic alliance.

Attribute	**Outsourcing**	**Cluster**	**Strategic alliance**
Subjects of cooperation	Technologically related enterprises	Enterprises localized in one territory	Enterprises-competitors
Industrial coverage	One branch	Different branches	One branch
Driver of efficiency of cooperative activity	Involvement of resources and competencies of a business partner, distribution of risks	Territorial proximity (reduction of logistic costs) and cooperative utilization of resources	Synergy of combining resources and competencies
Type of cooperation	Principal – agent	Different forms of cooperation	Partnership
Formal fixation of relations	Present	Absent	Present
Availability of a coordinating center	Present	Absent	Present
Scheme of creation	Goal-oriented organization	Self-organization, including that on the basis of external stimulation	Goal-oriented organization

4 Comparative analysis of models of production cooperation of enterprises

The studies undertaken [5-7] have indicated that in most cases for the analysis of production cooperation of enterprises such types and forms of activity are distinguished as outsourcing, cluster formations and strategic alliances.

Let us analyze outsourcing, clusters and strategic alliances from the perspective of their utilization efficiency in modern industry and taking the "digital revolution" into account. Development of informational and communicational technologies, blockchain technologies and processes of industrial digitalization related to them determine extensive application of these forms of cooperation and models of cooperation of enterprises. Such models in industry include a set of business characteristics defining the behavior of an economic entity on the market, the structure of property rights, mechanisms of management and control, forms of participating in the activity of every collaborative agent, etc.

Let us consider the basic advantages and disadvantages common to each model of cooperation.

Outsourcing. Relations that are defined by the model of "principal – agent" in economical theory take place in outsourcing. An agent (outsourcer), using its own resources, organizes performing of functions which can't be performed by a principal (customer). The reason for that is either lack of relevant competencies or a strategic decision to concentrate resources on those functions and processes that are considered to be the key ones.

Connections within the framework of this model can be very stable. This is shown, in particular, by the experience of world electronic industry where OEM-production has got widespread and, in fact, it has become an important factor of providing competitiveness. Specialized outsourcers that manufacture production for different customers under contracts, thanks to scale and training effects enable providing a high level of quality and low cost price. And their significant work and competency experience allows for providing flexibility of production program and low risks for a customer. Besides, trans-border outsourcing serves as a tool for legal optimization of tax burden.

Stability of cooperation guarantees that in the case of breach of relations it will be difficult for both the parties to find a new business partner. It is determined by the observed high level of specialization of enterprises which take part in outsourcing and are related to these competitive advantages. Within the framework of an outsourcing model, two connected elements of a production chain are formed and actively function. Guarantees of this functioning are of formal (contract obligations) and informal (mutual interest of parties in cooperation) nature.

Apart from merits outsourcing has also demerits. Interdependence of partners may result in a situation where one of them, who has a more significant market power, will take advantage of its position. In consequence of that the other partner will either incur losses or lose its key competencies and withdraw from the market. In the tumultuous economic environment (lack of stability in modern world grows) and in the presence of low credibility it is very likely that participants of potential outsourcing relations will be more concerned in the issues of their survival rather than in obtaining a mutual effect within the context of outsourcing. This risk needs special regulation and cooperative overcoming (with the participation of partners).

Clusters. An important distinguishing feature if a cluster is spontaneous character of its generation and functioning. Even in those cases when a major company or a state is demonstrating a cluster initiative it is not quite evident that this initiative will be successful. In any case, a cluster is formed and developed only in the presence of relevant stimuli. As a result, cooperation of enterprises inside a cluster is notable for its flexibility. Besides, thanks to importance of a cluster for regional development, government institutions and non-profit organizations are actively drawn into it (for example, universities). On the basis of the studies [15] advantages and disadvantages of clusters are represented in Table 2.

Table 2. Comparative analysis of advantages and disadvantages of clusters in industry.

Advantages	**Disadvantages**
Interbranch nature and, as a rule, complexity of relations, stability	Spontaneous nature of forming that generates risks of cluster initiatives
Favorable environment for diffusion of innovations and technologies transfer	Absence of formal regulation
Involvement of non-profit organizations and government institutions	Absence of centralized management or at least coordination of combined actions.
Network structure enables successful implementation of digital economy technologies and practicability of forming digital platforms	Risks of informational security

An important advantage of a cluster is that many elements of production and selling chains function in it and, what's interesting is that they often function in neighboring branches. At that, thanks to continuous cooperation, active diffusion of innovations and technologies transfer take place between enterprises of the cluster and it allows for increasing the efficiency of enterprises. At the same time one should keep in mind that it's impossible to create a cluster, it is possible only to enable its generation and development. The efforts of one enterprise or their consortium may be not enough for creating such conditions, support of the state may be also necessary. This peculiarity of clusters produces institutional limitations for their application.

Strategic alliances. The essence of a strategic alliance is partnership of independent enterprises-competitors in order to increase the competitive ability of each of them. At that, in contrast to a classical cartel, competitiveness for a customer is preserved. In an alliance competitors optimize the structure of their resources and also get the opportunity of implementing (using the partner's resources) those projects which it would be impossible to implement acting alone.

The important advantage of cooperation within the framework of a strategic alliance is the fact that it allows for increasing the efficiency of utilization of resources of the competitors while keeping competition between them, including that on the basis of forming integrated intellectual digital platforms. Both competitors (thanks to combining resources) and also consumers (competition for them is preserved) win, that is society on the whole. Nevertheless strategic alliances, as a rule, are under the spotlight of antimonopoly authorities and that generates risks for their successful functioning.

These risks are connected with the fact that there are no strict criteria which are regularized and would allow to clearly distinguishing a strategic alliance and a cartel. As a result the risk is very high that the alliance will be characterized by supervisory authorities as a cartel and its creation and functioning will be prohibited. Besides, both the government and competitors that are not in the alliance can take the initiative to introduce the ban. Therefore a strategic alliance can successfully function only if it is supported by the state.

5 Conclusions

Thus, according to the results of the analysis we can make the conclusion that in the context of forming digital economy the dependence of industry efficiency on organization of their cooperation interaction increases. This dependence is especially relevant to high-tech and innovative industries which are distinguished by high capital and knowledge costs. In this regard, their implementation by separate companies (even having significant resources and competencies) becomes impossible.

The studies undertaken by the authors [6, 7, 12] allowed concluding that digitalization of enterprises and industry on the whole that takes place at the present time determines changes of models of industrial cooperation. The most promising forms of cooperation of enterprises are outsourcing, clusters and strategic alliances. Each of these models has certain advantages and disadvantages therefore for organization of cooperation of enterprises in specific projects it is necessary to thoroughly develop and fix in a contract the interaction model every time in order to take the advantage for participants and manage risks. State regulation is meant to play an important part in solving these problems.

Besides, when selecting the model for cooperation interaction it is recommended to use hybrid organizational forms which combine the elements of outsourcing, clusters and strategic alliances. In the interaction design it is also important to take into account external and internal informational infrastructure of cooperating enterprises, its composition, functional capabilities and architecture. This will enable cooperating not only at the management but also at the technological level which will promote its efficiency and productivity.

References

1. B. M. Allen, Journal of Library Administration, **48(1)** (2008)
2. S. J. Andriole, *The 2nd Digital Revolution* (IGI Global 2005)
3. P. Tambe, L.M. Hitt, Management Science **60(2)** (2014)
4. J. A. Mañez, M. E. Rochina-Barrachina, A. Sanchis, J. A. Sanchis, Empirical Economics, **44(3)** (2013)
5. C. Ménard, Journal of Institutional and Theoretical Economics, **160** (2004)
6. A. Y. Karlick, V. D. Morozova, News of the Saint Petersburg State University of Economics, **2** (2001)
7. A.V. Babkin, V. A. Plotnikov, S. V. Muraveva, Proceedings of the 25th International Business Information Management Association Conference – Innovation Vision 2020: From Regional Development Sustainability to Global Economic Growth, IBIMA. (2015)
8. V. P. Vorobjev, N. N. Tikhomirov, News of the Saint Petersburg State University of Economics, **3 (99)** (2016)
9. On confirming the program "Digital economy of the Russian Federation". RF Government Executive Order, 28.07.2017, No. 1632-r. [online], Available at: http://base.consultant.ru (2017)
10. A. Grandori, G. Soda, Organization Science, **16(2)** (1995)
11. S. V. Starikov, *Organizing import-substituting production on the basis of network cooperation of industrial enterprises*: Thesis for a Candidate Degree of Economic Sciences. (Kursk 2017)
12. V. Plotnikov, Y. Vertakova, *Procedia Economics and Finance*, **24** (2015)

13. G. Kleyner, A. Babkin, Lecture Notes in Computer Science (including subseries Lecture Notes in Artificial Intelligence and Lecture Notes in Bioinformatics). **9247.** (2015)
14. M. E. Porter, Harvard business review. **76(6)** (1998)
15. A. V. Babkin, A. O. Novikov, Scientific and technological journal of the Saint Petersburg State University of Economics. Economic sciences. **1 (235)** (2016)
16. Russian Cluster Observatory [online] Available at: http://cluster.hse.ru/clusters (2018)

SHS Web of Conferences **44**, 00013 (2018) https://doi.org/10.1051/shsconf/20184400013
CC-TESC2018

Extracting features from laser scanning point cloud[a]

Vladimir Badenko[1*], *Alexander* Fedotov[1], and *Dmitry* Zotov[1]

[1] Peter the Great St. Petersburg Polytechnic University, High-performance hybrid geospatial data systems Centre, 195251, Polytechnicheskaya, 29, Russian Federation

Abstract. Analyses of gaps in processing of raw laser scanning data and results of bridging the gaps discovered on the basis of usage of laser scanning data for historic building information modelling are presented. Some results of the development of a unified hybrid technology for the processing, storage, access and visualization of combined laser scanning and photography data about historical buildings are analyzed. The first result of the technology application to historical building of St. Petersburg Polytechnic University shows the robustness of the approaches proposed.

1 Introduction

The laser scanning is the most up-to-date and actively developing type of the remote sounding technologies. Presently, these 3D technologies are used all over the world in a wide spectrum of applications: roads management, urban modeling, departmental investigations and cultural heritage preservation [1]. The corresponding types of data acquisition systems are as follows: ground, mobile and airborne laser scanning [2]. The laser scanning is one of the most active methods of remote sounding. The principle of laser scanners operation, irrespective of the type and purpose thereof, is based on measuring distance from the laser pulse source to an object. In the course of object surveying the required distance will be determined with respect to time delay (pulse-type method) or to phase shift (phase method) by a signal reflected by the object surface [3]. The laser scanning result will be a cloud of points, which is generally coupled with photos [4]. Thus, a user can have the following information for every point of a cloud: three coordinates, reflected signal intensity and color (R, G, B), which precisely describe an object under investigation. A geometrical accuracy and density of points of such clouds have significantly increased recently [5].

The purpose of this article consists in the analysis of some deficiencies in processing the unprocessed laser scanning data and presentation of some results of rectifying deficiencies revealed on the basis of using the laser scanning data for historic building information modelling. The article presents the results of processing a unified hybrid technology for

[a] The research was supported by Ministry of Education and Science of Russia within the framework of the Federal Program "Research and Development in Priority Areas for the Development of the Russian the Science and Technology Complex for 2014-2020" (project ID RFMEFI58417X0025).

* Corresponding author: vbadenko@gmail.com

processing, storage, access and visualization of combined data of laser scanning and photos of historic buildings.

2 Materials and Methods

An experience of architectural measurements of historic buildings with the use of laser scanning technologies has demonstrated that the measurement drawings of facades and interiors of buildings are being most efficiently built on the basis of raster ortho-images, which are obtained by means of projecting a cloud of laser points on the image plane. A similar approach is traditionally used in photographic survey [6]. The mobile laser scanning (MLS) is the most advanced and the least widespread technology in Russia. However, the number of MLS equipment in Russia has already exceeded the number of airborne laser scanners, while an amount of information per unit of time received by MLS scanner (up to 3-5 million points per second) several times exceeds the volume created during airborne scanning. There is a number of promising applications requiring collection of geospatial data with the use of MLS. In this case the processing of MLS data is developed insufficiently.

The analysis of the current state of investigations in this field has shown that there exists a great number of publications dedicated to the tasks of plotting digital models of buildings, detecting ground surface and reconstruction of road pavement, revealing and recognizing the road objects on the basis of MLS data [5, 7, 8].

In spite of the available successes, one can distinguish the following algorithms demanding more profound studying:

– for hierarchic processing of a great amount of data, which provide for hybrid processing and compression of data without loss of accuracy,

– for integration of scanning data received from different sources,

– for seamless combination of real-time data processing during shaping orthogonal image based on a single scanning and on the series scans received from different sources, for providing reduction of “dead zones” area.

The offered method corresponds to a complex problem solution through establishing an algorithmic support of hybrid data processing system received from all types of laser scanning (mobile, ground and airborne), as well as photos. A solution offered by the authors corresponds not to a general 3D modeling of urban districts or, for instance, historic buildings and structures. An offered approach provides for a method of automatic and semiautomatic processing and visualization of data on the basis of forming cylindrical scans for point clouds. In order to solve the problems of historic building information modeling (HBIM) [9], a method of big data volumes processing has been developed on the basis of laser scanning data. The method provides for more precise HBIM particularization, including a combination of scanning data for every scale and level of providing information of studies received by different scanning methods.

The determination of factors and assessment of indicators for factors influencing the accuracy are not analyzed in this method. Special approaches to compressing data without losing accuracy and reduction of “dead zones” area in ortho-images are used. A task of defining geometry of buildings is solved by the existing methods with the use of integrated information received by different methods with the use of interpolation and extrapolation of acquired data. However, an experimental investigation of efficiency of different methods of surface modeling has been carried out for providing an acceptable level of accuracy to support the suggested method.

3 Results

The investigation goal consists in the development of new algorithms of processing of cloud points (big data processing) received from the laser scanner. The creation of software for processing, visualization and vectorization of laser scanning data as well as data presentation via Internet, providing:

(1) increasing the efficiency and accuracy of processing laser scanning data (decoding and vectorization not less than 99.5%);

(2) provide the laser scanning customer (in the framework of engineering studies) with functionality of subsequent processing of scanning results on the basis of primary (unprocessed) information about the object (which is the most valuable information).

The investigations of offered technology have been tested in the course of creating 3D data for the buildings of Peter the Great St. Petersburg Polytechnic University (former Petersburg Polytechnic Institute). St. Petersburg Polytechnic Institute has been built by the example of Oxford and Cambridge as a complex with carefully designed and incorporated infrastructure. The construction of the main buildings of the Institute was performed according to a design of architectural engineer E. Virich, architectural engineer of the 1st degree, Academician of architecture since 1908, an outstanding representative of rationalistic architecture, one of the pioneers in using reinforced-concrete structures in 1900–1905.

The Polytechnic Institute complex is interesting as a coherent architectural ensemble, one of the few that has been preserved in the relatively unchanged form. The buildings correspond to unique architectural buildings of the boundary of XIX – XX centuries. A complex of buildings and a park is included into a "List of historical and cultural heritage sites of federal significance" approved by the decree of the President of the Russian Federation No. 176 dated February 20, 1995 and is an especially valuable cultural heritage site of the peoples of the Russian Federation as the complex historical, cultural, architectural ensemble and structures as well as a monument to the natural landscape representing a material, intellectual and decorative value. One of the oldest structures in the University building is a water supply tower built in 1905 (Fig. 1a), three years after PolytechnicInstitute opening. It is the highest point among two- and four-storied institute buildings, and it stands in contrast to the other structures due to its intricate and polygonal shapes. The height of water supply tower is 46 meters. Before 1953 it was used as an engineering structure for providing operation of water pipelines system. The built supply water tower became one of the educational buildings in the territory of the Institute. In 1905 the Laboratory of hydraulics was installed in the additional building close to the water supply tower.

There exists a multiplicity of variants of building digital models of big objects, including photographic survey and 3D laser scanning. The complexity of investigation has demanded utilization of both methods. In order to build 3D models for HBIM of historical heritage, the methods of 3D laser-scanning and photographic-survey data processing.

(a) (b) (c)

Fig. 1. (a) Water-Supply Tower in 1905; (b) Cloud of Points for Historic Building; (c) Result of Semiautomatic Triangulation.

A building of 3D model includes the following steps: selecting investigation object; collecting visual, technical and historical information; laser scanning and photographic survey for acquisition of a cloud of data points (Fig.1b); detection and extraction of segments of a dense cloud of points and a procedure of semiautomatic triangulation (Fig. 1b); obtaining external color models with the use of photos (Fig.2a); data export into applied architectural packages (Fig.2b, Fig.2c).

(a) (b) (c)

Fig. 2. (a) External Color Model; (b) 3D Grid for BIM; (c) Model of 3D BIM

A dense cloud of points has been built (Fig.1a) on the basis of comparing images with the use of OpenCV library [10]. A dense cloud of points is generally understood as a cloud featuring density of at least 1 point per 1 cm^2 in case of surveying big objects. In case of this object the cloud of points amounted to 32KK points. The processing of this number of points has no sense and is extremely expensive in terms of hardware resources. In order to do so, it is necessary to reduce a number of points. An optimal solution for big objects featuring intricate geometry is to reduce the number of points 10 times up to 3.2 KK

4 Discussion

The engineering study for the existing building is an activity, where the up-to-date high-tech laser scanners and equipment are used more and more frequently [11]. The corresponding methods are used for surveying different objects, beginning from historic buildings and ending with uninhabited territories for road construction [4, 12, 13]. The laser scanning systems acquired data more completely and effectively than the traditional survey methods do [14]. A future development of these systems provides for emergence of a compact, light and relatively inexpensive multipurpose of laser scanning, which shall be fast and simple for deployment and require minimal quantity of the existing equipment for operative support [1]. The known specific features of laser scanning data are as follows: high accuracy and density resulting in building big data volumes – spatial clouds of points [15]. A process of acquisition of the clouds of points for every type of laser scanning is well explored, and the corresponding software of acquisition of the cloud of points will be provided by a manufacturer [16].

An essential drawback of laser scanning technologies, which significantly restricts its use, is a permanent gap between quick development of technologies and capabilities of processing results (points cloud processing) [17]. The existing methods of geo-processing and analysis of images as well as high requirements to computation resources do not allow using the capabilities of technologies to the full extent [18]. Today the processing of laser scanning results (cloud of points) is frequently connected with equipment suppliers [19]. Though, the universal tools for processing and combining the clouds of points received from different sources are hardly available [9, 20].

The laser scanning clouds are presently collected and processed individually at the particular objects and territories according to process requirements (Xu et al., 2017). An automatic or semiautomatic segmentation and detection of objects in 3D laser scanning is the most resource-intensive step. There are also exist the special software packages developed for building particular types of models from the laser scanning data, such as Cyclone, RapidForm, 3Dipsos, all of them are intended for operation in 3D [4]. Besides, the suppliers of laser scanners offer to import the clouds of points to the most popular CAD systems, AutoCAD (Autodesk) and Microstation (Bentley). However, the processing of unprocessed data of 3D scanning in CAD environment is inconvenient, especially, if it is required to build 2D plans [21].

A complexity of historic buildings with an irregular geometry creates multiple problems in case of computer simulation and simulation of structural elements with different types of loads [22]. The people responsible shall take into account a number of possible and compatible solutions, which do not endanger the cultural significance of historic building [9]. Presently many publications offer to use the HBIM-based approach for solving the above problems. The first step of the modern HBIM is usually a remote acquisition of survey data with the use of laser scanner technologies in combination with digital photos [12, 22-24]. Therefore, there exist many examples of applications of laser scanning technologies for collecting data about historic buildings all over the world [9]. The scientific articles discuss the use of innovative laser scanning technologies for simulation and monitoring buildings of historic heritage, in order to forecast behavior thereof in the course of life cycle management.

5 Findings

A unified hybrid technology for processing, storage, and visualization of laser scanning data and photo surveying of historic buildings is offered on the basis of algorithms of decoding and vectorization. The informational structure for HBIM models of historic heritage in Saint-Petersburg (Russia) has been suggested. The first result of technology application demonstrated by the example of the historic building (water supply tower of Peter the Great St. Petersburg Polytechnic University) shows the robustness of the proposed technology. The developed technology can also be useful for processing the laser scanning data during engineering studies of roads and existing buildings.

References

1. H. Guan, J. Li, S. Cao, Y. Yu, *Int. J. of Image and Data Fusion,* **7(3)** (2016)
2. J. Heo, S. Jeong, H.-K. Park, J. Jung, S. Han, S. Hong, H.-G. Sohn, *Computers, Environment and Urban Systems*, **41** (2013)
3. C. Wang, Y.K. Cho, *Automat. Constr.*, **49** (2015)
4. P. Tang, D. Huber, B. Akinci, R Lipman, A. Lytle, *Automat. Constr.*, **19(7)** (2010)
5. B. Yang, Z. Dong, *ISPRS J Photogramm*, **81** (2013)
6. O. Risbøl, C. Briese, M. Doneus, A. Nesbakken, *J. Cult. Herit*, **16(2)** (2015)
7. M. Vaaja, J. Hyyppä, A. Kukko, H. Kaartinen, H. Hyyppä, P. Alho, *Remote Sens-Basel*, **3(3)** (2011)
8. C. Cabo, C. Ordoñez, S. García-Cortés, J. Martínez, *ISPRS J Photogramm*, **87** (2014)
9. C. Dore, M. Murphy, International Archives of the Photogrammetry, *Remote Sensing & Spatial Information Sciences*, **42(2W5)**, 185-192 (2017)
10. V. Badenko, D. Kurtener, V. Yakushev, A. Torbert, G. Badenko, *Lect. Notes Comput. Sc*, **9788**, 57-69 (2016)
11. L. Barazzetti, *Adv. Eng. Inform.*, **30(3)** (2016)
12. R. Volk, J. Stengel, F. Schultmann, *Automat. Constr.*, **38** (2014)
13. W. Mukupa, G.W. Roberts, C.M. Hancock, K. Al-Manasir, *Surv. Rev.*, **49 (353)** (2017)
14. A. Soni, S. Robson, B. Gleeson, *Applied Geomatics*, **7(2)** (2015)
15. B. Quintana, S.A Prieto., A. Adán, A.S Vázquez, *Adv. Eng. Inform.,* **30(4)** (2016)
16. V.V. Lehtola, H. Kaartinen, A. Nüchter, R. Kaijaluoto, A. Kukko, P. Litkey, E. Honkavaara, T. Rosnell, M.T. Vaaja, J.-P. Virtanen, M. Kurkela, A. El Issaoui, L. Zhu, A. Jaakkola, J. Hyyppä, *Remote Sensing*, **9** (2017)
17. N. Hichri, C. Stefani, L. De Luca, P. Veron, G. Hamon, International Archives of the Photogrammetry, Remote Sensing & Spatial Information Sciences, *ISPRS Archives*, **40(5W2)** (2013)
18. A. Kukko, H. Kaartinen, J. Hyyppä, Y. Chen, *Sensors,* **12(9)** (2012)
19. M. Lee, S. Lee, S. Kwon, S. Chin, *KSCE J. Civ. Eng.*, **21(6)** (2017)
20. X. Xiong, A. Adan, B. Akinci, D. Huber, *Automat. Constr.*, **31** (2013)
21. L. Barazzetti, F. Banfi, R. Brumana, G. Gusmeroli, M. Previtali, G. Schiantarelli, *Simul. Model Pract.*, **57**, 71-87 (2015)
22. M. Murphy, E. Mcgovern, S. Pavia, Structural Survey, **27(4)** (2009)
23. F. Chiabrando, M. Lo Turco, F. Rinaudo, International Archives of the Photogrammetry,

Remote Sensing & Spatial Information Sciences, *ISPRS Archives*, **42(2W5)** (2017)
24. V. Badenko, D. Zotov, A. Fedotov, E3S Web of Conferences – EDP Sciences, **33**, 01047 (2018)

Informational technologies and the prospects of personalization of food rations

Natalia Barsukova[1], *Elena* Moskvicheva[1*], *Irina* Timoshenkova[1], and *Evgeny* Tsopa[2]

[1] Peter the Great St. Petersburg Polytechnic University, Graduate School of Biotechnology and Food Technology, 194021 Novorossiyskaya st., 48, Russian Federation
[2] Saint Petersburg National Research University of Information Technologies, Mechanics and Optics, 197101 Kronverksky pr., 49, Russian Federation

Abstract: Among the main markets of the national technological initiative there is the platform of developing competitive projects of the food industry – FoodNet. The promising line of the market development is transition to personalized nutrition which takes into account a person's genetic traits, his or her physiological and biomedical needs and creation of digital platforms for its implementation. In the context of constant growth of the number of diagnosable genetic diseases, including alimentary-dependent ones, such an approach is very modern. Medical technological scheme of constructing personalized products is presented in the article and also its implementation as exemplified by gluten-free flour confectionery articles is considered. A program module for automatic calculation of the characteristics of developed products was realized on the basis of the suggested scheme and it represents a client-server application. The optimal parameters for the biscuit manufacturing technology were set on the basis of the program module operation which allows obtaining products for special use and enriched with mineral substances.

One of the key tasks of the Russian economy is implementation of the National Technological Initiative (NTI) – a complex of measures on forming principally new markets and creating conditions for global technological leadership of Russia by 2035. NTI will include system solutions on defining key technologies necessary for making changes in the sphere of norms and regulations, the working measures of financial and professional development, mechanisms of involvement and rewarding competency bearers. The choice will be made with due consideration of the main trends of global development based on the priority of network technologies focused on the human being as the end-consumer.

9 key directions for development within the framework of NTI were chosen: one of them is developing competitive projects of food industry – FoodNet – it embraces the market of manufacturing and realization of nutritive substances and food products of final types (personalized and general, on the basis of traditional primary products and their substitutes). The document also provides for development of auxiliary IT-decisions (e. g. those which provide for services on logistics and selecting individual nutrition). FoodNet is one of three markets aimed at security of the country and its system support with resources [1].

*Corresponding author: moskvicheva_ev@spbstu.ru

The strategic importance of the FoodNet market is confirmed by the provisions of

- The Food Security Doctrine of the Russian Federation approved by the Decree of the President of Russia No. 120 on January 30, 2010,
- The fundamentals of the national policy in the field of healthy nutrition for the population of the Russian Federation for the period to 2020 approved by the Russian Federation Government Executive Order No. 1873-p on October 25, 2010,
- The Concept on the Demographic Policy of the Russian Federation for the period to 2025 approved by the Decree of the President of the Russian Federation No. 1351 on October 9, 2007,
- The strategy of development of food and pharmaceutical processing industry of the Russian Federation for the period to 2020 approved by the Russian Federation Government Executive Order No. 559-p on April 17, 2012.

According to the United Nations estimates, the population of the Earth will increase up to 9-10 billion people by 2050. However, according to Yuan Tseh Lee, the President of the International Council for Science (ICSU), the Nobel prizewinner for Chemistry in 1986, food consumption will increase exceeding people's basic demands and not proportional to them; this will happen as a result of evolution of the consumption structure in the developing countries.

For example, animal protein consumption and also consumption of products with personalized properties will increase in the developed countries but consumption of the main food products will remain at a high level owing to the demand of under-privileged people. In the developing countries, the growth of income of the general public, population increase and outflow of working people into cities is expected. In those countries demand for products which have passed processing treatment and which possess healthy properties will increase [2]. Besides, individual rations which take into account physiological and biomedical needs of population will become more and more popular.

Today, in the integrated digital map of "The Common Image of Saint Petersburg in Future – 2035" we can see the prospects of developing food markets presented as "Future Nutrition: Personalization for Everyone" as one of strategic priorities. So, for example, there are services which offer preparing personal menu. For instance, services *ELEMENTAREE* and *REALFOOD* enable choosing one of the menu variants suggested on the sites according to one's goals and get a ready-made "constructor" for healthy and varied food: the menu is developed by a nutrition expert, high-quality products are thoroughly measured, the recipe is described in the manual in detail, and one has to spend some time in order to "gather" the obtained dishes. This service combines the two conceptions popular on the market: food delivery and individual selection of products [3, 4]. The idea is promising for future development in the field of creating individual menus on the basis of genetic analysis. Such an approach is based on the existing achievements in the sphere of nutrigenetics – the branch of science which task is to determine optimal variants of nutrition depending on genetic peculiarities of a person.

It is expected that in the nearest future, when forming rations and diets, the interconnection between the chemical food composition and the genetic profile of a person will be taken into account. This tendency in the nutrition science defines new approaches to creating specialized food products.

Currently, the growth of genetic diseases is observed, including alimentary-dependent ones, that is diseases which are precipitated by nutrition. Among these are: the entire group of cardiovascular diseases, osteoporosis, diabetes mellitus type 2, gluten enteropathy (celiac disease), obesity, some oncology diseases. A very important role for prophylaxis and treatment of such diseases is played by specialized diets which are meant for excluding precipitating factors from nutrition.

For instance, gluten enteropathy is precipitated by gluten – protein of grain varieties: wheat, rye, barley and oats. Celiac disease can be called "the disease of today". 150-200 years ago people didn't know about this disease. With regard to the human evolution, graminaceous plants have become the main part of the nutrition diet not long ago and in the course of several thousands years they contained almost no gluten. The majority of nations cultivated "gluten-free" plants such as rice, maize and panic. People began growing barley and wheat about 9000 years ago in Mesopotamia and in more then 5000 years cultivating these graminaceous plants expanded outside of the Mediterranean region and the Danube boundaries. In the course of time wheat became the most cultivated grain used for cooking dough and that significantly increased gluten "load" and the humanity didn't have enough time for adjusting to the new food and developing immune tolerance. That is why a number of people have the genetic disease – celiacia. Today approximately 1% of the Earth population suffers from this disease [5]. It is quite difficult to diagnose gluten enteropathy because there are almost no symptoms which 100% of people suffering from gluten intolerance have, and these symptoms can be expressed to different extents. Gluten-free diet for people suffering from celiacia which excludes products containing gluten from the nutrition ration is the only way to normalize the work of the digestive system without increasing the risk of oncology diseases. Gluten can be represented in two forms: distinct and hidden. Distinct gluten is contained in the products after processing wheat, rye, oats, barley, and hidden gluten can be found in sausage products, meat, fish and vegetable preserves, ice-cream, yogurts, cheese, oriental sweets, etc. [6].

The food market should take into account the demands of such a patient and provide him with the opportunity to obtain alternative food products with a modified chemical composition and given properties for forming an individual diet adjusted to the level and kind of metabolic disorders [7].

The strategy of developing such products is based on a medical technological algorithm which provides a cumulative result of monitoring nutritional status disorders and designing products with the address designation; their distinctive feature is scientifically based and proven effect aimed at complex correction of specific nutritional status disorders [8].

Successful solution of this problem is connected with two scientific approaches – digital modeling and constructing nutritional systems with the given chemical composition and properties which enables developing multicomponent products with the clearly defined complex of quality indicators.

Such methodology enables creating products with the determined (given) composition of necessary proteins, fats, carbohydrates, vitamins and dietary fibers, mineral and other substances. The selection of qualitative and quantitative composition of a product is done in three directions:

1. according to chemical composition and biological effectiveness,
2. according to stability of properties,
3. according to organoleptic indicators.

The determining step in such constructing is the selection of a product-prototype which is planned to be fully or partially modified. At this stage, the preliminary analysis of all positive and negative peculiarities of the primary product and also presupposed ways of its modification is made, main ingredients are chosen which will be probably included into the end-product, and also a system model is developed.

Then critical parameters are set for the end-product: the quantity and correlation of the key nutrients, organoleptic characteristics, ability to keep the qualitative and security factors, including biological effectiveness, throughout the entire period of consumption.

Technological compatibility of raw materials and ingredients which are planned to be used for constructing is estimated at the final stage of forming requirements to the product. As a result of the given estimation a conclusion is made about the possibility of using all the key nutrients in one product or about the necessity for creating a group of products for forming a complete and effective ration regarding alimentary therapy.

Calculation of composition of the personalized product is made on the basis of comparing its chemical composition with the correlation of separate nutrients with the values of the daily demand for nutrient materials and energy.

Then, using standard approaches, compliance of the product consumer properties with the primary prototype is estimated. In case it is necessary, the recipe is corrected for achieving the most acceptable consumer characteristics.

. The task-oriented personalized approach to the development of new alternative products is universal, it doesn't depend on the nature of nutritional status disorders being corrected and the type of designed products, and it can be used for alimentary therapy of various alimentary-dependent diseases.

A program module was implemented on the basis of the suggested algorithm; this module automatizes calculation of characteristics of designed products. The program module is represented by a client-server application. The architecture of the developed program module is in Fig. 1:

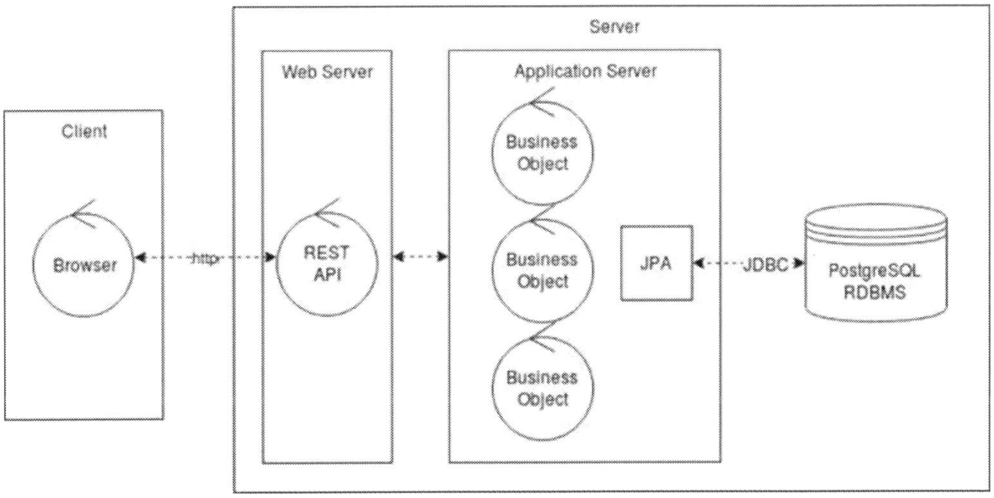

Fig. 2. The architecture of the developed program module.

As a repository for storing information on products, their characteristics, components and production technologies a relational database is used under the control of DBMS PostgreSQL 9.4. The server part of the module is a set of business-components EJB for Java EE platform operating under the control of the application server WildFly 11. Cooperation of the system with the database is carried out via JDBC with the use of Java Persistence API (JPA) 2.0 technology.

The user can cooperate with the developed module with the help of the web-interface built on the React+Redux platform. Cooperation with the server part of the system is carried out via REST API.

The suggested architecture of the program module has the following advantages:

1. All the applied program products and libraries are distributed under a license with the open source code which excludes any license restrictions including those for commercial use of the product.
2. The client part imposes minimum requirements on the client device (it can be, for example, a personal computer, a pad or a smart phone) and it doesn't require installing any additional program software: any modern web-browser is quite sufficient.
3. The server part is cross-platform and can be started in the infrastructure on the basis

of virtually any modern environment, for example, under the control of the Windows Server, Linux or FreeBSD.

4. If necessary, any modern relational DBMS of the enterprise level (for example, Oracle) can be used as a repository for storing information instead of PostgreSQL. At that, no changes in the architecture of application will be necessary.

The evaluation of the suggested approach and the developed module was carried out in the process of developing the assortment of new food products for alimentary therapy of gluten enteropathy patients [9-11]. As an example, the use of the program module in the process of constructing gluten-free biscuit on the basis of secondary products of processing pumpkin – pumpkin flour – will be considered.

As a prototype, general biscuit (recipe No. 1) [12] was chosen in the database; the biscuit is cooked according to the main method without heating. The given product can't be consumed by celiacia patients because it contains wheat flour rich in gluten. As modifying the given product, it is suggested to completely replace wheat flour with pumpkin seeds flour. Organoleptic indicators of the examined samples are the key characteristics according to which the product is chosen by the consumer. The combination of these indicators was determined according to GOST 50763 taking into account the weight coefficient [13]. All the characteristics of the examined samples are also stored in the common database; this enables making recalculation of the characteristics of the developed product in real-time mode.

As critical parameters of the end-product several organoleptic indicators were chosen in the database; they are represented in Table 1.

Table 1. Critical parameters for the end-product.

Indicator name	Characteristics
Surface appearance:	
form	Corresponding to the form in which bakery food is made, with a slightly raised up upper crust
surface	smooth, without large cracks and ripping
Crumb condition:	
baking thoroughly	well-baked, not wet by touch, elastic. After slight pressing the crumb must take the primary form
kneading	free of lumps and traces of improper kneading
crumb grain	developed, without cavities and firming

A prototype was created on the basis of the data from the base, and organoleptic analysis was carried out. As it follows from the analysis of the prototype and the biscuit based on pumpkin flour the examined sample was unsatisfying according to such indicators as texture, taste, shape and appearance at the cutting place. Consequently, the technology and recipe of biscuit production was changed on the basis of calculations made in the developed module:

1 Pumpkin seed flour was partially replaced by rice flour;

2 When whipping eggs sugar was added in the form of a syrup at a temperature of 114 °C thus providing a more stable and fine-pored foam.

For validating the parameters of biscuit technology with the use of pumpkin seeds flour and rice flour a central compositional plan of a complete factorial experiment with the use of additional points in the form of a "star" was realized. As particular factors of optimization, the correlation of pumpkin seeds flour and rice flour varying them from 0 to 100 % as output parameters – organoleptic qualitative indicators – were chosen. All the results of the experiments were introduced into the database of the developed module and that allowed to significantly reducing the cost of constructing regression plots and it also will enable reusing the obtained data in future.

Regression equations are received on the basis of experimental data, they characterize the dependence of the total organoleptic indicator (Y_1) of biscuit on the content of flour made from pumpkin seeds (x_1, %) and rice flour (x_2, %). The regression equation is represented as follows:

$$Y_1 = -284 + 9.81x_1 - 0.97\, x_2 - 0.06\, x_1^2 - 0.03\, x_1x_2 + 0.11\, x_2^2, \quad (1)$$

The coefficient of determination of the obtained regression equation R^2 is 0.96 which allows considering functional dependence of the total organoleptic indicator of biscuit on the content of flour made from pumpkin seeds and rice flour. The adjusted coefficient of determination R^2adj is 0.91 which confirms the importance of the chosen factors.

The graphical interpretations of the equation (1) formed in the developed program module as represented by the value curves and response surface are shown in Fig. 2 and 3.

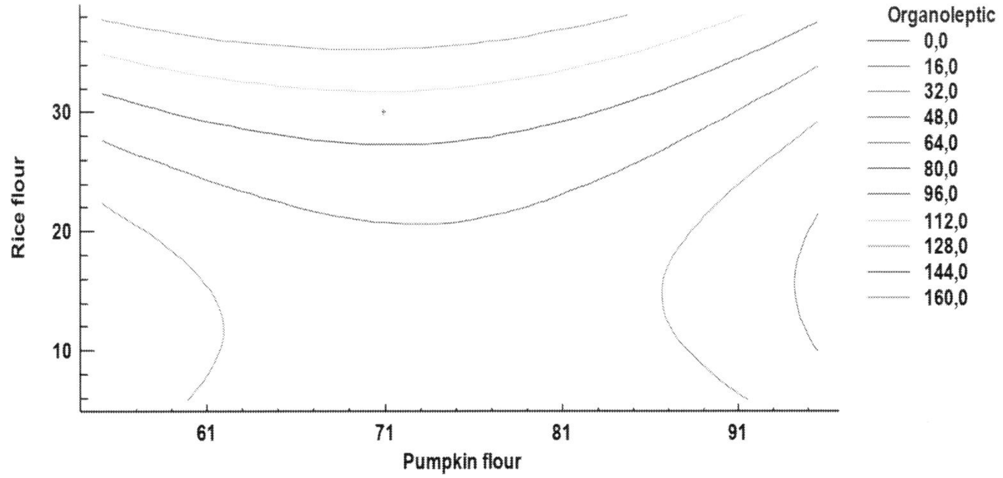

Fig. 2. The diagram of value curves of the total organoleptic indicator of biscuit semi finished product on the content of flour made from pumpkin seeds and rice flour.

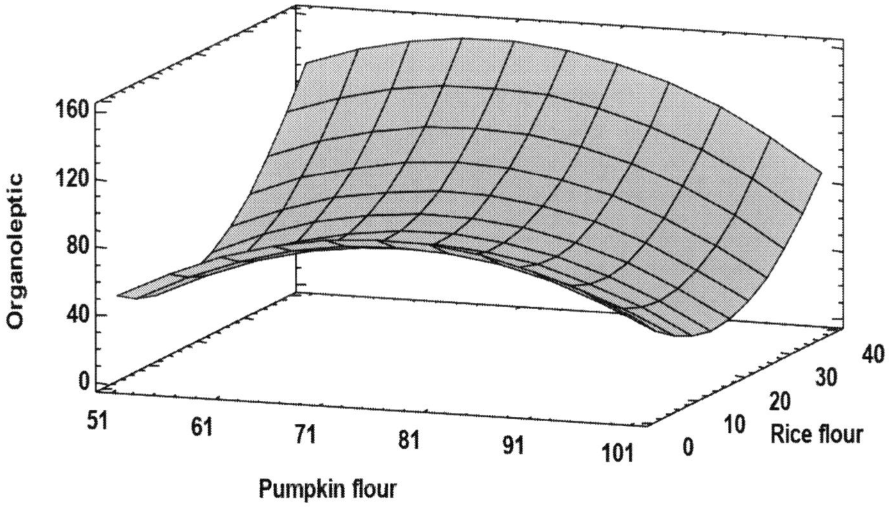

Fig. 3. The diagram of response surface of the total organoleptic indicator of biscuit semi finished product on the content of flour made from pumpkin seeds and rice flour.

The optimal content of flour made from pumpkin seeds and rice flour for producing biscuit with the best organoleptic indicators is 70±1% and 30±1% respectively of the mass of flour mixture.

The chemical composition of the worked out biscuit has been compared with the values of the daily demand of a person for food substances and energy (Table 3).

Table 3. Chemical composition of the worked out biscuit

Indicators	Indicator values in 100 g of the semi finished product in % of the daily intake		
	made of wheat flour	made of pumpkin flour	deviation
Carbohydrates	36.96	31.69	-5.28
Proteins	9.54	12.80	3.26
Fats	8.76	10.16	1.40
Dietary fibers	8.84	1.35	-7.49
Mineral substances, mg%			
Magnesium	6.86	20.79	13.93
Ferrum	9.73	6.93	-0.23
Zinc	3.57	9.24	8.98
Selenium	17.45	2.18	-15.27
Cuprum	0.68	1.92	1.25
Phosphorus	18.68	33.43	14.75
Manganese	32.80	36.30	3.50
Calcium	3.36	2.88	0.29
Potassium	4.62	2.59	3.11
Sodium	4.76	4.74	0.17

Conclusions

Modern conditions necessitate transition to personalization of nutrition which is based on medical technological scheme. The algorithm and the program module – which form the basis for the digital platform for optimizing the process of working out "clever" food rations – were developed by the authors within the framework of the given investigation. The considered principle of constructing food systems is successfully implemented for working out gluten-free flour confectionery. The obtained product made of pumpkin flour differs from its prototype product made of wheat flour in that it has higher concentration of protein and fat and besides it is enriched with such mineral substances as magnesium, phosphorus and manganese. Thus, we can speak of creating a "clever" product which provides up to 30% of the daily intake of important microelements and forms the basis of the balanced ration.

References

1. The products of the markets of the National technological initiative. Available at: http://asi.ru/nti/projects/ (2017)
2. FAO: by 2050 it is necessary to increase production of food stuff by 60%. Available at: http://milknews.ru/index/FAO_k_2050_proizvodstvo_produktov_nuzhno_uvelichit_na_60_percent.html (2017)
3. Simple. Tasty. Personally for you [online], Available at: http://elementaree.ru (2017)
4. Real Food – correct nutrition with delivery [online], Available at: http://www.realfood.pro (2017)
5. L. Greko, Life without gluten, **3** (2006)

6. S. A. Belmer. Doctor **5** (2011)
7. S. A. Eliseeva, N. P. Kotova, K. S. Chujkova, International scientific-research journal, **4-3 (58)** (2017)
8. E. A. Smirnova, V. A. Sarkisyan, A. A. Kochetkova, The questions of nutrition, **83 (S3)** (2014)
9. N. V. Barsukova, D. A. Reshetnikov, V. N. Krasilnikov, Scientific journal of SRU ITMO. Series "Processes and apparatus of food production" , **1** (2011)
10. V. N. Krasilnikov, V. S. Mehtiev, V. Y. Markina, Y. A. Timoshenko, Storing and processing agricultural supplies, **8** (2015)
11. E. V. Moskvicheva, E. E. Safonova, I. A. Timoshenkova International scientific-research journal, **3(62)** (2017)
12. A collection of recipes of flour confectionery and bun goods: Profi. **296** (2016)
13. N. V. Leiberova and others, Bread products **10** (2013)

Business model of construction organization management under conditions of new industrial basis

Nadezhda Belova[1*], and *Diana* Sbitneva[1]

[1] Saint Petersburg State University of Architecture and Civil Engineering, 190005 2-ya Krasnoarmeiskaya st. 4, Russian Federation

Abstract. The article gives consideration to modern trends of a new economical epoch, which results in transformations under conditions of running industrial and economic activity. In view of this fact substantiation has been provided on the necessity of changing principles of organizations' structure and functionality for successful long-standing development thereof. The authors pay special attention to the relevancy of suchlike changes in the sphere of construction production, since "new" is adopted comparatively slower there than in the other branches of industry. As a result, the investigations of indicators of a new industrial base in construction are distinguished by the authors and the characteristic features of building business model of construction organization management are described. The article provides a conclusion that the application of business model of construction organization management under consideration in conditions of new industrial base will help construction organizations to adapt its business system and strategy to modern transformations of industrial and economic sphere, select innovations and develop business processes, which will most fully implement goals of organizations proper and satisfy demands of their key partners.

The modern conditions of conducting economic activity feature speed and quality of changes taking place therein, which influence all spheres of human life. At present it is impossible to imagine successful functioning and long-standing development of at least a single organization without timely responding and preventing possible changes. In particular, the relevancy of such actions can be observed in the sphere of construction, which is fundamental in many respects for providing social and economic development, but is significantly inferior to other spheres of industry on incorporation and utilization of new technological and intellectual capabilities as a result of external and internal reasons (intricacy of selecting workforce able and prepared to generating and using innovations, insufficiency of knowledge exchange from project to project) [1].

The modern market conditions compel the construction organizations to fit into changing conditions permanently exercising a search for the new ways of selling their produce. The development of business model of construction organization management

* Corresponding author: bne0908@yandex.ru

aimed at providing its stable functioning for search of the sources of profit earning both in the internal and external environment under conditions of permanent changes can be referred to as one of the methods of solving this problem.

1 New economical epoch

Presently it is already an open secret that the world has entered a new economical epoch, which can be characterized by the following trends: 1) globalization of economical processes, 2) increasing speed of convergence of types of economic activity as well as 3) deregulation thereof for creating conditions of realizing free economics, 4) privatization of state property, 5) increasing intensity of competition between manufacturers of goods and 6) toughening of methods of competitive struggle, 7) transformation of retail trade and 8) tendency to an unmediated form of interaction with consumers, 9) increasing information awareness of buyers and 10) enhancement of market power thereof on the manufacturers as well as 11) all-around penetration of network information technologies and telecommunication systems into all spheres of social and economic activity.

The new economical epoch was marked by emergence of a concept "new economics". There exist two basic approaches to defining this concept, where each one reflects direction of future development of economical systems:

– the first approach contemplates identification of "new economics" with informational economics, which is understood as a complex of science-intensive types of activity realizing production and servicing of information and communication systems, creation and propagation of software products, development of communication networks as well as shaping, storage, information dissemination and acquisition. This complex implies to a greater extent building of information and communication system on Internet [2];

– the second approach is geared to understanding the "new economics" as the economics of buildings, which is understood as a combination of types of economic activity characterized by generation of knowledge as a source of economic growth and being guided by the technical implementation of received knowledge. The "new economics" includes in the above context a sphere of educational services, information and communication markets, production of innovations, rendering intellectual services (consulting, communication, analytics, marketing) [2].

These approaches help distinguish criteria to creating and developing economical systems oriented to efficient functioning in the long-standing perspective. The following can be attributed to the following criteria 1) possibility of involvement into global economic process, 2) system of independence and self-sustainability, 3) possibility of receiving authentic, complete and timely information, 4) possibility of permanent and continuous renovation of information and knowledge.

It should be noted that the recent main indicators and drivers of development of a new economical epoch are as follows:

1) globalization of innovative and scientific and technical systems, production system, monetary and financial system, information and communication systems, system of commodity-money relations, which result in opening and interpenetration of the economies, emergence of global hyper-competition and manifestation of interrelation of types of economic activity [3];

2) intellectual capital corresponding to knowledge as a production factor, main resource and infrastructure element, which results in changing conditions and channels of application knowledge. This transformation brings about provision of economic growth not through permanent increase of physical volumes of implementation of permanently upgraded products and services, but through increase of added value of sold goods, which

depends on innovations, alternative preferences of customers and speed of business reaction to qualitative change of these preferences [2];

3) global application of new information technologies resulting in the reduction of level of environment uncertainty and increase of efficiency of organization activity as a result of introducing information support of business processes, information online interaction with the organization external environment, creating information portals, remote rendering and receiving services, development of electronic business, electronic commerce and mobile commerce;

4) transition of character and structure of labor from the executory-reproductive to intellectual and innovative [2], the result of which is the change of requirements to the level of workers' competence. The modern market conditions produce higher requirements to personal and professional characteristics of personnel, viz. versatility and wide professional outlook, orientation to satisfying clients' needs, seeking permanent training and development of peculiar professional and personal qualities, demonstration of loyalty to occupation and organization, resistance to stress, capability of initiating and adopting changes, creative, innovative and flexible way of thinking, operational mindset;

5) innovations as the factor of economic growth, which dynamics and quality depend on the rate, scale, practicality and value of technological shifts, which introduction will entail an increase of value of goods for a consumer, orientation to permanent continuous improvement of goods to meet the changing consumers' preferences, involvement of personnel into a process value adding, provision and management.

Thus, the above indicators make it possible to define the "new economics" as a process of development of global economic system, in which framework the social and economic development is based on continuous renovation and utilization of knowledge without territorial and spatial reference to the location of economic entities.

2 New industrial base in construction

Proceeding from encyclopedic definition of the industrial base, which interprets it as a combination of industrial enterprises and production facilities, which can be used for production of this or the other commercial product or for rendering services [4], we can say that the structure of industrial base for the construction organization shall be represented by the following groups of economic entities: 1) production group is represented by the enterprises directly exercising a process of construction operations; 2) supporting group implies organizations providing the process of construction operations with necessary resources and directly engaged in the process of production of end construction produce; 3) auxiliary group corresponds to the enterprises and organization of market infrastructure, which are auxiliary with respect to the first two groups and satisfying the needs of these groups; and 4) regulating group includes a combination of physical persons and legal entities conducting monitoring and regulating activity in the process of construction and selling construction goods and services.

The new economic epoch changes a concept of business activity, its priorities and common factors. In this regard a transformation of requirements to industrial base takes place for implementation of construction operations. These requirements can be divided into four groups [1]:

1) development and use of new technologies, materials and tools, which include 1) up-to-date construction and finishing materials, 2) standardized modular or pre-fabricated components, 3) semi-automatic and automatic construction equipment, 4) new construction technologies (3D-printing, cross-breed robots), 5) "smart" equipment and equipment for optimizing life cycle, 6) digital technologies and application of "big data" in chain order of construction produce value adding;

2) optimization of business processes and operations by means of using 1) principles of economical production, 2) models of partners interaction with a uniform distribution of risks, 3) adaptive structure of project management, 4) models of management of subcontractors and suppliers, 5) economical and steady management of structure and operations, 6) stringent production process monitoring (volumes, time limits, expenditures);

3) development of flexible strategy of and innovative business model based on 1) differentiated business model, 2) targeted consolidation and partnership, 3) stable competitive products with optimal cycle of value, 4) entering foreign markets;

4) management of interaction of an individual, organization and culture in the way of 1) strategic planning of demand for personnel, 2) "smart" selection, 3) loyalty management, 4) continuous training and knowledge management, 5) forming highly-efficient organization structure, culture and motivation scheme.

It is necessary to pay attention under modern conditions of running business to the necessity of receiving maximum possible amount of trustworthy information about environment; it is conditional on the rate of changes going on in the preferences of consumers, activity of competitors and partners and the very conditions of exercising entrepreneurial activity. Thus, a significance of informational, innovative and, particularly, intellectual resources grows, they are able to pickup changes, adapt thereto and create conditions based thereupon for successful economic activity.

The sphere of construction activity belongs to that type of economic activity of entities, where decisions on the necessity of changes, development thereof, introduction and adaptation thereto are taken over quite a durable time period, this fact is conditioned by impossibility of quick incorporation of technological changes before the end of production process and duration of the construction process itself, which equals, as a rule, at least two years, great number of participants directly or indirectly engaged therein, as well as a wide circle of people concerned in its results. In this regard, a significance of entities of informational and innovative support of construction operations grows; the above entities carry out investigation and forecasting changes in the external environment (demands of consumers and community, activity of suppliers, partners and competitors) and internal environment (development of technologies of construction operations, emergence of new materials and structures) over a medium-term perspective and long-term perspective and development of innovations featuring a preemptive character. The, R&D establishments, HEIs, incubators, technological clusters, analytical-informational and marketing agencies can be attributed to such entities.

3 Business model of construction organization management under conditions of new industrial base

Presently, there exist many concepts, approaches and typologies to definition of business model concept, but this multiplicity can be divided into two groups: 1) the first group focuses attention of business model on the progress of technological and production processes and is aimed at the search of internal capabilities for gaining profit, 2) the second group is related to forming up mutual relations with the external environment of organization, which in the process of interaction help it, due to adding and providing value, generate new sources of deriving profit from the opportunities available and emerging in the market. In this case it should be mentioned that the value is understood as a unique, comprehensible and useful advantage from the relations with organization by the interrelation of advantages of interaction over its outgivings and in comparison with key competitors.

Under modern market conditions an approach gained the greatest widespread, within which framework the business model is presented as an analytical tool, which in graphical form provides a description of business structure and functioning, it reflects basic principles of creation, development and assessment of efficiency of all interrelated processes in organization and makes it possible to find the sources of gaining profit. The main purpose of business model development is a search for possible ways of developing organization, attaining goals of its activity. The main advantages of business model development as compared with compiling business plan, which in turn is also used for justification and reflection business processes implementation in organization, consist in the reflection of sense of business process existence, in describing the way the organization gains its cost (capital) from economic, social or cultural point of view at all stages of its life cycle unlike the business plan, which is limited by time boundaries of planning horizon.

One can distinguish many business models in the national and foreign literature, each of them helps have a look at business management from the positions of developing relations with clients, or business development as a whole. The most renowned and widespread of this number are the following models:

– business model of A. Osterwalder, Y. Pigneur "Business outline": it corresponds to nine blocks, such as consumer segments, value proposition, sale channels, relations with clients, incomes, key resources, basic processes, key partners, structure of expenses; the model purpose is a selection of business development directions [5];

– business model of M. Johnson "Seizure of clear space": it consists of three blocks, such as key resources, basic business processes, value proposition for consumers and formula of deriving profit, the model purpose is creation of formula of deriving profit for business [6];

– business model of H. Chesbrough, R. S. Rosenbloom "Open innovations": it corresponds to eight blocks, such as technological inputs, value proposition, market segment, structure of chain of value creation, income and profit rate, value-based network, competitive strategy and economic results; the model purpose is the use of new technologies [7];

– business model of D. Abell: it consists of three blocks, such as consumers, value proposition, key resources and capabilities; the model purpose is the development client-oriented strategy [8];

– business model of G. Linder and S. Cantrell: at first sight the model resembles a chain of adding value of M. Porter and includes ten blocks such as clients' needs, goods, value proposition, sales channel, interaction with clients, price formation, production, differences from competitors, financial structure, unique character of profit formula, but the purpose of this model is a creation of competitive advantages and forming significant differences from competitors [9].

Table 1 provides a comparison of the foregoing business models on the basis of compliance thereof with the guiding principles of building models and requirements of a new economic epoch.

Table 1. Comparative appraisal of modern business models*

Principles of business model presentation under conditions of new economic epoch	A. Osterwalder, Y. Pigneur	M. Johnson	H. Chesbrough, R. S. Rosenbloom	D. Abell	G. Linder and S. Cantrell
Clarity of information presentation on basic business elements	+	+	+/–	–	+/–
Availability of reflecting logic of adding and providing value for the parties interested in business	+	+	+/–	+	+
Explicit interrelation of model elements	+	+/–	+	+/–	+
Possibility of revealing and establishing a competitive advantage for business	+	+/–	+/–	+/–	+
Possibility of timely revealing and correcting bottlenecks in business processes	+	–	–	–	+/–
Comprehensible reflection of compatibility and complementarity of all elements	+	+/–	+	+/–	+
Model feasibility	+	+	+	+	+
Ability of taking into account capabilities and restrictions of business environment	+	+/–	+	+	+
Possibility of describing business differentiation and diversification	+	+/–	+/–	+	+
Availability of reflecting sources of getting income for business	+	+	+/–	–	+
Importance of reflecting business investment potential	+	+	–	–	+
Possibility and availability of reflecting business scale	+	+/–	+	+/–	+
Capability of adapting to changing environment conditions	+	+/–	+	+/–	+
Availability of describing transformation of information being received into new knowledge	+	–	+	+	+
Possibility of using new knowledge	+	+	+	+	+
Resulting number of points	15	9.5	10.5	8.5	14

*Appraisal scale: "+" – compliant (1 point), "+/–" – partially compliant (0.5 point), "–" – non compliant (0 point).

Proceeding from the Table data, one can arrive at a conclusion that the model "Business outline" proposed by A. Osterwalder, Y. Pigneur most fully comply with the present requirements produced to business models. It features availability and clarity of business processes taking place at organization, which help transform resources available with it into sources of profit on the basis of goods proposal, which will be valuable and demanded with target audience and relations with partners.

Every block of business model of A. Osterwalder, Y. Pigneur for construction organization shall answer a clearly raised question: 1) consumer segments – "whose and what problem is to be solved?"; 2) interaction with clients – "how to lay information against target group and get a feedback?"; 3) sales channels – "how to present value?"; 4) key processes – "what is to be done to meet requirements of consumers and attain organization's goals?"; 5) key resources – "what resources are to be possessed to meet requirements of consumers and attain organization's goals?"; 6) key partners – "who can help in to meeting requirements of consumers and attaining organization's goals?"; 7) income sources and structure of expenditures – "what will be the economic cost when to meeting requirements of consumers and attaining organization's goals?"; 8) value proposition – "what value will be provided to persons concerned?".

At the present stage of developing process of construction operations the logic of adding value consists in converting capital of construction organization expresses in the key resources via main business processes into resulting characteristics by means of selling goods with the aim of its capital gain. The authors are of the opinion that the construction organizations shall establish and develop competitive advantages based on 1) saving due to scale (owing to "economical production", 2) quick access to current assets (due to relations with partners), 3) high level of goods quality (due to using new technologies, materials and tools), 4) offering exclusive properties of goods or service (due to scientific investigations and innovations), and 5) improvement of data processing (due to using up-to-date information-communication systems) under conditions of a new industrial base for providing competitiveness in a long-standing perspective on the market. Proceeding from the above the authors have revealed the basic characteristics of business model of construction organization management provided in Table 2. These characteristics are based on opposing current limitations and possible environment risks and on using positive influence thereof on organization development.

Table 2. Basic characteristics of business model of construction organization management under conditions of new industrial base

Environment conditions: Limitations and risks	Business model characteristics	Key business processes of construction organization	Result for organization
Growing prices for resources required for production of construction produce	Providing independence, self-sustainability and autonomy of business model	1. Building inherent logistic and science-and-technology base; 2. Establishment of stable long-standing mutually-advantageous relations with partners	1. Reduction of expenses; 2. Use of new technologies, ideas, developments; 3. Disposal of produced intellectual property
Scantity of resources of suppliers in volume and in time			
High expenses of searching and changing over to new suppliers of resources			
Increasing requirements to quality of life, changing requirements to construction produce	Capability of business model to forecast environment changes and quickly adapt thereto	1. Building a system of collection and analysis of information about environment; 2. Development of system of using new knowledge	1. Increasing organization competitiveness; 2. Providing "survivability" of organization
High sensitivity to price with consumers			
Increasing intensity of competition and toughening methods of competitive practices			

Environment conditions: Limitations and risks	Business model characteristics	Key business processes of construction organization	Result for organization
Standardization of produce, absence of unique or significant characteristics for consumers therein	Possibility of providing value proposition in business model for parties concerned	1. Satisfying demands of different groups of consumers; 2. Development of unique trading proposition for each of them; 3. Creating competitive advantage	1. Increasing organization competitiveness; 2. Distancing organization and its goods from competitors; 3. Receiving intended and/or required profit
Low level of differentiation of construction produce in the market			
Reduction of investment activity and construction market attractiveness			
Availability of competitors with high level of knowledge and loyalty of consumers	Capability of business model to manage interaction with environment	1. Creative positive image of organization and its goods; 2. Increasing its popularity; 3. Forming loyalty of consumers	1. Increasing organization reputation; 2. Creating and using brand of organization and its goods
Liability of consumers to negative assessment of quality of construction produce, wide-spread opinion about its low quality			

A necessity of clear understanding of the needs and preferences of the partners for any organization of any sphere of activity increases at present, the consumers, suppliers, investors, intermediaries and employees of organization are understood in this case as partners, in whose activity the organization is interested. Therefore, the authors offer in the framework of business model development for construction organization to look for the partners on the basis of marketing tool – model "5W", which will help not only define their basic needs and interests thereof, which is the basis for value proposition for them, but also distinguish the main channels and methods of interaction with them. As a result, the construction organization will be able to find the market niche, for which its proposed value will surpass the value proposition of the competitors.

A necessity of building correct and efficient system of interaction with the external environment increases under present-day market conditions, it will help not only attract attention of the potential partners but support their interest, establish a necessity of long-standing cooperation. In this regard the authors suggest to develop a system of relations with the partners on the basis of 1) informing about organization's goods and activity by means of advertisement mainly on Internet, measures on stimulating sales and public relations, 2) arousing partners' interest through building channels of direct communication, which results in forming a concept of organization, its goods, differences of their goods from those of the competitors' and on the advantages (value) of interaction with it, 3) forming commitment of the partners to organization, which helps translate its positive image in the external environment. It also shall be noted that owing to organization of system of informing and communication with the external environment it will be possible to collect and analyze the opinions and needs of key partners, which get aggregated from their search requests in Internet, asked questions to employees during direct contact, discussions in forums and in social media, which will raise the level of organization awareness about their priorities and preferences, it will help get adjusted thereto, increasing by the same the value and forming the competitive advantage on this basis.

Due to development of information technologies the authors offer to pay attention to enabling implementation of interaction and necessary transactions not in the traditional, but in electronic form without direct personal contact by organization employees. The sphere of information technologies forges ahead, owing to this it is necessary to foresee in construction too a possibility of effecting activity both in the internal and internal environment by means of "block chain" technology, where the entire process of execution, coordination and approval of the required documents will be performed in electronic form with the use of digital signature and simultaneous entering into necessary registration documents without physical participation of individuals with the transactions being implemented. It will help reduce time for implementation of business processes, simplify understanding thereof and increase controllability thereof.

In order to sum up it may be said that the use of business model of construction organization management under conditions of new industrial base offered by the authors will make it possible for the construction organizations to adapt their business system and strategy to the latest transformations of industrial and economic sphere, select innovations and develop business processes, which will most comprehensively implement the goals of organizations proper and satisfy the needs of their key partners.

References

1. Shaping the Future of Construction: a Breakthrough in Mindset and Technology [online], Available at: http://www3.weforum.org/docs/WEF_Shaping_the_Future_of_Construction_report_020516.pdf (2016)
2. N.I. Bazylev, N.L. Gribanova, Problems of Modern Economics, **1(2)** (2006)
3. Yu. S. Ruleva, Bulletin of Ryazan Esenin State University, **23** (2009)
4. Economical Encyclopedia [online], Available at: http://www.m-economy.ru/art.php?nArtId=934 (2018)
5. A. Osterwalder, Y. Pigneur, *Business Model Generation: A Handbook for Visionaries, Game Changers, and Challengers* (John Wiley & Sons, New York, 2010)
6. M.W. Johnson, A.G. Lafley, *Seizing the White Space: Business Model Innovation for Growth and Renewal* (Harvard Business Review Press, Boston, 2010)
7. H. Chesbrough, R.S. Rosenbloom, *The Role of the Business Model in Capturing Value from Innovation* (Harvard Business School, Boston, 2000)
8. D.F. Abell, *Defining the Business: the Starting Point of Strategic Planning* (Prentice-Hall Englewood Cliffs, New Jersey, 1980)
9. D.J. Teece, Long Range Planning, **43** (2010)
10. A. Ovans, *What Is a Business Model?* (Harvard Business Review Press, Boston, 2015)
11. T. Gavrilova, A. Alsufyev, A.-S. Yanson, Foresight-Russia, **8 (2)** (2014)
12. M.S. Sabir, R.M. Hameed, K. Rehman, I. Rehman, Journal of Management Research, **4 (4)** (2012)

Application of methods of organizing complex expert examinations for increasing reliability and failure robustness of information systems and complexes[a]

Marina Bolsunovskaiya [1], *Aleksandra* Loginova[1*], and *Svetlana* Shirokova[2]

[1] Peter the Great St. Petersburg Polytechnic University, Institute of Computer Sciences and Technologies, 195251, Politechnicheskaya st., 29, Russian Federation
[2] Peter the Great St. Petersburg Polytechnic University, Institute of Industrial Management, Economics and Trade, 195251, Politechnicheskaya st., 29, Russian Federation

Abstract. The article provides a review of approaches and methods used by Russian and foreign authors for solving tasks of increasing reliability and failure robustness of information systems (IS) and hardware and software complexes. The methods of organizing complex expert examinations (MOCEE) are described and the possibility and necessity of MOCEE combined application for analyzing reliability and failure robustness of IS, their components and hardware and software complexes are proven. The following methods and models were used to perform a comprehensive assessment: PATTERN methodology, G.S. Pospelov's method of solving matrices, models based on the information approach of A. A. Denisov. A number of modifications of the above MOCEE is offered; methodology of system analysis for solving a task of assessing reliability of information system and its components has been developed; a conceptual model of methodology of developing new solutions in the field of IS and IT has been built.

1 Introduction

One of the most important characteristics of information systems, information complexes and its components are the reliability and failure robustness. A problem of increasing reliability and failure robustness has been solving for IS as a whole and for its particular components, such as software (SW), transmission medium, electrical support systems, data storage systems (DSS).

Special techniques and methods are used in up-to-date information systems and complexes for providing reliability and failure robustness, for instance, full or partial

---

[a] The research is carried out with the financial support of the Ministry of Education and Science of Russia within the framework of the Federal Program "Research and Development in Priority Areas for the Development of the Russian Science and Technology Complex for 2014-2020". Subsidy agreement No. 14.581.21.0023, 03.10.2017, The unique identifier is RFMEFI58117X0023
* Corresponding author: alexandra-lo@yandex.ru

backup of components, absence of single-point failure, etc. Besides, the devices of system status monitoring are used, including smart systems of monitoring and diagnostics of deficiencies. The development of suchlike diagnostic systems requires engagement of formalized methods.

The following groups of models are used when selecting mathematical tool for investigating systems failure robustness and reliability: Markovian chains [1-4]; models of queuing systems; models based on the graph theory [1, 5, 6]; methods of analysis and statistical estimation of distributions, theory of random labeled point processes, mathematical models of degradation failures [1-3]; differential equations [7]; logical networks, such as failure trees and functional integrity diagrams; logical equations [7]; models of multi-agent systems [8], etc. Based on the performed analysis one can come to a conclusion that presently there is no integrated solution in the field of providing DSS failure robustness, there are only individual solutions pertaining to the above sections. Thus, it should be recognized that a research problem of developing procedure of comprehensive evaluation of reliability and failure robustness of DSS as a IS component is actual.

The goal of this study is to develop methods of assessing reliability and failure robustness of DSS. It is offered to use the ideas of system-targeted approach and gradual formalization [9, 10] for building methods of assessing reliability and failure robustness of DSS, including convergence of methods of systems formalized presentation (methods of mathematical description of systems) with capabilities of methods of organizing complex expert examinations (MOCEE).

The important constraints in DSS development are the requirements of the system customer and capabilities of development tool infrastructure, as well as final equipment. It should be pointed out as well that the task of assessing future reliability and failure robustness of the system at the early stages of DSS life cycle, such as stage of designing, is the task featuring high degree of uncertainty. Therefore, MOCEE are used in this study for reliability evaluation of DSS; methods of this group make it possible to perform decision-making procedures with high level of uncertainty.

The work shows models built with the use of PATTERN methodology, G.S. Pospelov's method of solving matrices, information approach of A. A. Denisov.

2 Approaches and methods

2.1 PATTERN methodology

One of the simplest methods of assessing alternatives is the use of relative-importance values from PATTERN methodology [1, 11, 12].

It is suggested to use PATTERN methodology in this investigation for assessing development project and incorporation of hardware/software complex.

The criteria for assessing complex components and weight coefficients thereof are expertly determined at the first stage:

1. $K = \{k_1, ..., k_n\} = \{k_i | i \in \overline{1,n}\}$ – set of criteria used for assessing components of a hardware/software complex (such criteria as cost criterion; criterion of compliance with demands of future users; criterion of complementary dependence, etc. are traditionally used).

2. $Q = \{q_1, ..., q_n\} = \{q_i | i \in \overline{1,n}\}$ – set of criteria weight coefficients, for which the following requirement shall be met:

$$\sum_{i=1}^{n} q_i = 1 \tag{1}$$

3. $C=\{c_1,...,c_m\}=\{c_j \mid j \in \overline{1,m}\}$ – set of components (modules) of a hardware/software complex.

4. At the next stage every component will be assessed in accordance with i-criterion: S_{ij} – assessment of relative importance of j-component according to i-criterion.

The relative-importance values S_{ij} for every criterion can be calculated on the basis of experts' (or a single expert) appraisals using different methods depending on analysis peculiarities and formed group of experts. The methods of scaling, ranging, pair-wise comparisons, comparison on basis of linguistic scales, etc. can be used among others.

5. Combined value of j-component is calculated using its evaluation by each criterion and criteria weights:

$$S_j = \sum_{i=1}^{n} S_{ij} \times q_i . \tag{2}$$

2.2 G.S. Pospelov's method of solving matrices (MSM)

The method of solving matrices was offered by the Soviet scientist G. S. Pospelov in 1970-80s and corresponds to a tool of stratified representation of problem under investigation and step-by-step acquisition of assessments. The MSM has been used in the course of building complex production facilities, during implementation of unique capital-intensive projects (e.g., in the field of space exploration), etc. [9, 12]. The method is quite labor-intensive and produces high requirements to qualification of experts. Example of model of DSS assessment based on MSM is detailed in para.3.

2.3 Denisov Information Approach

The fundamentals of information approach to investigating systems were described by A.A. Denisov in 1970s; models built with the use of information approach elements have been utilized in control of technical systems and in social-and-economical systems management. An important peculiarity of these models consists in the fact that they include values of degree of alternatives compliance with the targets; as well as some models take into account dynamics of changes in the system under investigation; for assessing degree of compliance with targets a logarithmic regulation is used, which simplifies a procedure of processing acquired expert assessments [9].

This work gives examples of using information values of two types:

1) evaluation of alternatives (system elements) in static state with the use of expression:

$$H_i = -q_i \log(1 - p_i^{'}),\ i = 1,\ldots,n \tag{3}$$

where, H_i – information value of i-component (alternative); q_i – probability of achieving a selected goal with the use of i-component (alternative); p'_i – probability of using i-component (alternative) in the course of implementing a particular goal.

A cumulative significance of components (information value) can be calculated by the following formula:

$$H = -\sum_{i=1}^{n} q_i \log(1 - p_i^{'});\qquad(4)$$

2) assessment of the correspondence of alternatives (components) to system goals and probability of implementing different goals taking time factor into account.

3 Basic results

3.1 MSM modification for DSS assessment

It is proposed to use MSM at the first stage in the course of DSS project assessment in the following context (Fig. 1). Meaningfully, three levels presented in Fig. 1 are interpreted with regard to DSS assessment task, as follows:

1. $E = \{e_1,..., e_k\} = \{e_z | z \in \overline{1,k}\}$ – level of experts (engineers, project managers on building and incorporating DSS, etc.). The assessments of relative importance are allotted to experts (based on the level of their qualification, degree of involvement in project): α_1, α_2, …, α_z,…, α_k ($z \in \overline{1,k}$).

2. $K = \{k_1,..., k_n\} = \{k_i | i \in \overline{1,n}\}$ – level of criteria; every criterion also receives its assessment β_1, β_2, …, β_i,…, β_k, $i \in \overline{1,n}$ (to be calculated according to formula (7)).

3. $C = \{c_1,..., c_m\} = \{c_j | j \in \overline{1,m}\}$– level of alternatives (possible decisions on DSS organization), assessment of relative importance of these alternatives γ_1, γ_2, …, γ_j ,…, γ_m, ($j \in \overline{1,m}$) show, which alternative from the experts' point of view meets the specified list of criteria to the fullest extent possible.

The relations between elements of the neighboring levels are presented in the form of "solving matrix" with the number of columns equal to the number of elements at the upper level and number of lines equal to the number of elements of the lower level. The matrix elements in a general case are the assessments of significance of a link between two particular elements from the neighboring levels.

The algorithms of receiving evaluations for alternative DSS projects can be described in the following way:

1. The assessment of relative importance ("weight") α_z is allotted to every z-expert ($z \in \overline{1,k}$) at every step of working with model. The "weight" of experts is standardized:

$$\sum_{z=1}^{k} \alpha_z = 1.\qquad(5)$$

2. Every z-expert ($z \in \overline{1,k}$) at every step sets the values of assessing relations q_{iz} ($i = \overline{1,n}, z \in \overline{1,k}$), which reflect the ability of z-expert to perform assessment of alternatives by i-criterion (if $q_{iz} = 0$, then z-expert does not fulfill assessment by i-criterion).

The requirements of standardization are to be met for every z-expert:

$$\sum_{i=1}^{n} q_{iz} = 1. \quad (6)$$

3. Assessments of criteria β_i ($i = \overline{1,n}$) are calculated according to formula:

$$\beta_i = \sum_{z=1}^{k} \alpha_z q_{iz},\ i = \overline{1,n}, \quad (7)$$

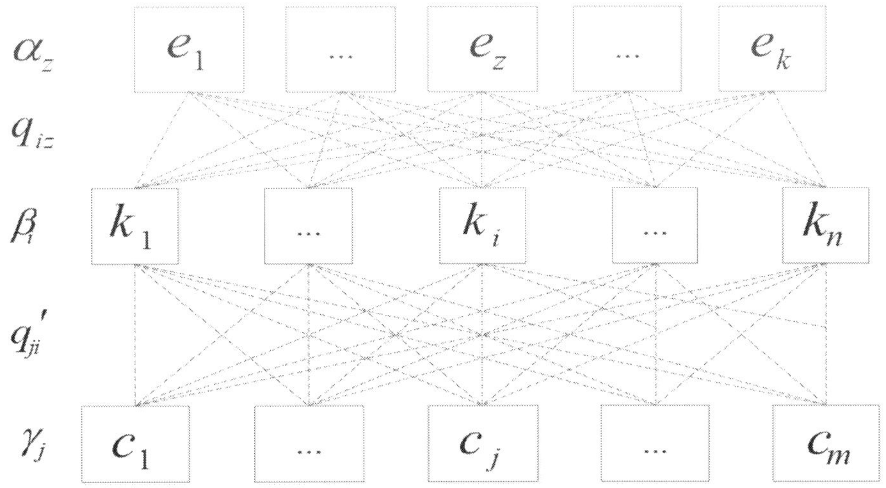

Fig. 1. Block diagram of model of calculating assessments of relative importance based on "solving matrices" method.

4. Assessments of relations between elements of the second and the third levels of the model q'_{ji} ($i = \overline{1,n}$, $j \in \overline{1,m}$) reflect a degree, in which the j-alternative satisfies i-criterion. If $q'_{ji} = 0$, then i-criterion is not met for j-alternative. The following standardization requirements shall be met for every i-criterion:

$$\sum_{j=1}^{m} q'_{ji} = 1. \quad (8)$$

5. Assessments of relative importance of alternatives will be calculated at the last stage of model handling (possible decisions on organization of DSS):

$$\gamma_j = \sum_{i=1}^{n} \beta_i q'_{ji},\ j = \overline{1,m}. \quad (9)$$

3.2 Building model of DSS assessment with the use of information approach

It is offered to build a model based on information approach of A. A. Denisov at the second stage for assessing variants of DSS building. Fig.2 shows an example illustrating the task of assessing variants of DSS implementation taking into account customer's requirements and capabilities of development organization. It shows possible variants of DSS implementation from the components, which are already available and can be used during projects implementation.

In order to assess the variants of DSS organization, the quantitative criteria are traditionally used. The model based on informational assessments of A. A. Denisov makes it possible to calculate a combined assessment of alternatives conjoining quantitative and qualitative criteria. In case of assessment by qualitative criteria, a degree p_i' of influence of i-variant of DSS project (or of inclusion of i-component (combination of components) into DSS) on implementation of requirements to IS as a whole ($0 \leq p_i' \leq 1$) is determined. These assessments will be converted into assessment of a potential of the corresponding project variant (corresponding DSS component) for convenience of further processing:

$$H_{ri} = - q_i \log(1 - p_i'), \quad (10)$$

where, p_i' – degree of influence of i-variant of DSS on reaching the goals (requirements) of the customer; q_i – probability of selecting this variant.

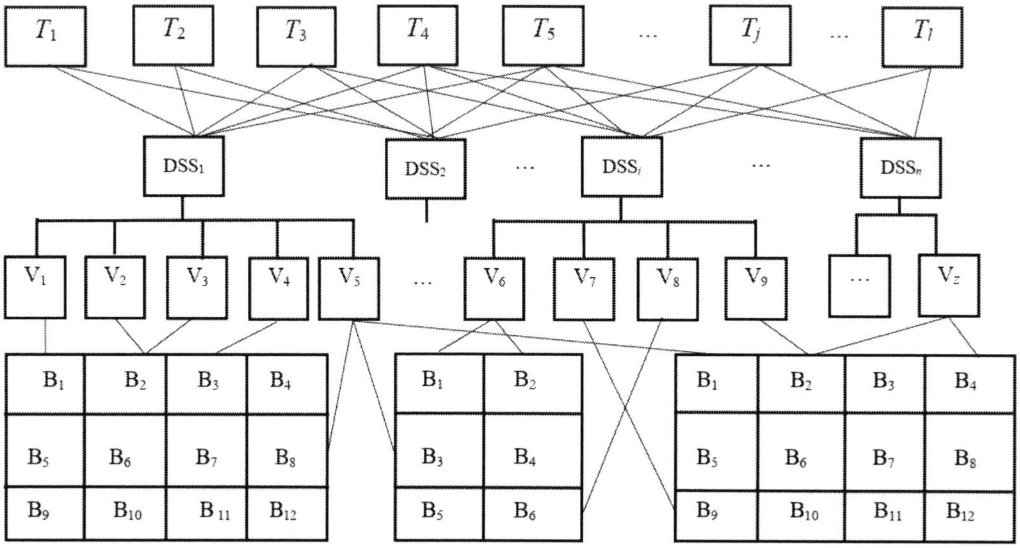

Fig. 2. Model of assessing variants of DSS implementation taking into account customer's requirements and capabilities of development organization.

Designations: $T_1, \ldots, T_l$ – customer's requirements to DSS (quantitative and qualitative); $V_1, \ldots, V_z$ – variants of DSS implementation, $B_1, \ldots, B_w$ – DSS components

The comprehensive evaluation of results $\sum H_{ri}$ includes both assessment of DSS variant acquired by means of assessing degree of influence on implementation of qualitative criteria, and the technical characteristics thereof corrected to informational values by means of calculating relative assessments p_{xi}. It is possible to use natural units of measurement together with cost units for assessing expenditures (e.g., labor-content of development of this or the other DSS component, necessary material costs, etc.), which get converted later into relative assessments p_{zi} and H_{zi} comparable with assessment of $\sum H_{ri}$ results.

Thus, the efficiency of every variant of DSS project can be expressed in the following way:

$$Э_{Bi} = \sum H_{ri} / \sum H_{zi}. \quad (11)$$

4 Directions of Further Investigations

It is possible to expand the proposed approach in the course of managing projects development and implementation, which envisage incorporation of an essential number of homogeneous components (e.g., software utilities) by appending with the models of assessing DSS development projects in dynamics [9]. The authors of this work offer to build a model of the process of DSS implementation as the model of development and incorporation of innovations with the use of the information values based on the A. A. Denisov's information theory.

The considered approach to assessing DSS projects on the stage of development and implementation can be used as a basis for creating decision-making tools in managing processes of IS and technical complexes design during development of new IT solutions.

Fig.3 shows a stratified conceptual model of the methods of developing new IT solutions.

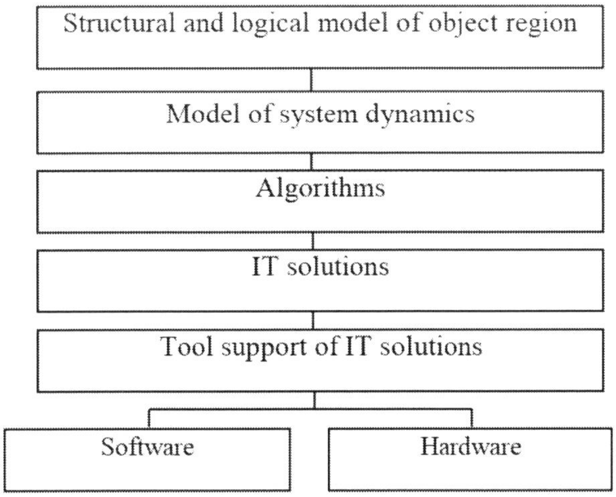

Fig. 3. Structure of the conceptual model of methods of designing and developing new IT solutions.

5. Conclusion

The article shows a necessity of using MOCEE in the course of solving tasks of enhancing reliability and failure robustness of a DSS as a component of information systems and complexes. The advantages of MOCEE are determined by the fact that they grant a possibility of fulfilling a decision making process in situations with high uncertainty. At the same time the number of studies where the MOCEE are used for designing and assessing serviceability of IS and information complexes is low at the present. This work offers a number of modifications of certain MOCEE. A methodology of system analysis for solving tasks of assessing reliability of IS and its components has been developed. A conceptual model of a new IT solutions development methodology has been designed.

References

1. F. Beichelt, P. Franken, Mathematical approach, **392** (1988)
2. V. Ya. Kopp, M. V. Zamoryonov, Yu. E. Obzherin, M. Yu. Larin, Scientific and technical journal of St. Petersburg Polytechnic University. Information science. Telecommunications. Management, **3 (247)** (2016).

3. V. Ya. Kopp, M. V. Zamoryonov, A. A. Selkin, O. V. Filipovich, Journal of up-to-date technologies, **1 (1)**, (2016)
4. B. Saghaie, R. Ragel, S. Parameswaran, A. Ignjatovic, Proceedings of the 23rd ACM international conference on Great Lakes Symposium on VLSI DOI: 10.1145/2483028.2483051 (2013)
5. I. V. Asharina, A. V. Lobanov, XII All-Russia meeting on management problems ARPMP-2014, 7387-7392 (Institute of management problems named after V.A. Trapeznikov, RAS, 2014)
6. K. Reinshke, I. A. Ushakov, *Assessing reliability of systems with the use of graphs*, (Radio I Svyaz 1988)
7. I.P. Simakov, P.V.Kholodnykh, Information technologies in management (ITM-2016) *Proceedings of the 9th conference on management problems* (2016)
8. S. E. Saradjishvili, A. V. Igumnov, Journal of Bauman Moscow State Technical University, **1** (2014)
9. V. N. Volkova, A. A. Denisov, *Theory of systems and system analysis* (YURAIT, Moscow, 2017)
10. V. N. Volkova, A. V. Loginova, S. V. Shirokova, E. A. Kozlovskay, Soft Computing and Measurements (SCM), 2016 XIX IEEE International Conference (2016)
11. M. M. Lopukhin, *PATTERN method of planning and forecasting scientific works*, **160** (1971)
12. E. M. Smolina, V. N. Volkova, A. A. Pirogova, Technological perspective in the context of Eurasian environment: new markets and points of economical growth. *Proceedings of the 2nd International Conference* (2016)

Formation of a given variable structure in detail by means of selective laser melting technology[a]

Evgeny Borisov*[1], *Dmitry* Masailo[1], *Igor* Polozov[1], and *Vera* Popovich[2]

[1] National Technological Initiative Center "New Production Technologies", Peter the Great St. Petersburg Polytechnic University, 195251, Polytechnicheskaya st., 29, Russian Federation
[2] Delft University of Technology, Mekelweg 2, 2628 CD Delft, Netherlands

Abstract. The issue for creation of products with functional properties adapted to working conditions is currently vital. The possibility of creating local areas with a specified microstructure and properties in the product is of special interest. This work covers the performed study of the structure and properties of the heat-resistant nickel alloy Inconel 718, depending on the process parameters used. The possibility for combination of different process modes during manufacture of one product to obtain its variable structure is shown. The specimens with areas of small equiaxed and large elongated grains were studied. The carried out EBSD analysis showed that the local change in the size and morphology of the material grain is possible by changing the layer thickness and process parameters of the selective laser melting process. It is shown that after the heat treatment and hot isostatic pressing, the differences in the structure and mechanical properties between the areas remain.

1 Introduction

In recent decades, a qualitative change in the nature of products manufactured by modern industry has taken place. Especially it concerns machine building, aviation, space industries, medicine (for example, in terms of implants manufacture), etc. The transition from manual design to digital, implementation of information technologies into the life cycles of products, automation of production processes contribute to formation of a new industrial base that will become the basis in case the future economy structure is formed.

One of the most important technologies to implement this concept is additive technologies. The additive technologies are of great interest for manufacturing metal products, as they allow creating complex-surface structures with increased mechanical characteristics.

Among the additive technologies, the selective laser melting (SLP) is currently considered as one of the most prospective for the manufacture of metal parts [1, 2]. The

[a] The work was carried out in the framework of the implementation of the federal target program "Study and development in priority aspects of development of Russian scientific and technological sector for 2014-2020", the unique identifier of the project is RFMEFI57817X0245.
* Corresponding author: evgenii.borisov@icloud.com

selective laser melting technology is already actively used for manufacturing metal products that relates to the possibility of manufacturing blanks which are as close to the final product as possible in terms of the geometry. The latter is especially vital in such areas as aviation and medicine [3-5]. In aviation, where titanium and nickel alloys are widely used, special requirements for products weight are used. The use of additive technologies makes it possible to create parts with a geometry that ensures the structure simplicity while maintaining high strength characteristics [6].

Among the nickel super-alloys, Inconel 718 attracts much attention of researchers due to its wide application in gas turbine components, aerospace unit parts, in petrochemical and nuclear industries thanks to its heat-, corrosion-resistant and high-temperature properties [4]. Traditionally, the parts are manufactured from this alloy by forging, rolling and casting. However, the modern industry development requires the production of products of complex shapes with high accuracy and high mechanical properties that sometimes are impossible to provide by conventional production methods.

In the literature, the works are used to study the selective laser melting process of Inconel 718 alloy, where the parameters impact on the relative density is considered, but, as a rule, they focus only on the laser power and the speed of its displacement, while remaining other values [7, 8]. To control the technical process, it is necessary to understand the influence patterns of one or another parameter on the final result. However, small data has been published on the possibility to use the features of the selective laser melting process to control the crystallographic texture and microstructure dispersion, and smaller data on the relationship between the preferred anisotropy, microstructure and mechanical properties of the alloy. In this regard, the purpose of this work is to establish patterns of structure formation depending on the initial process parameters and to develop a manufacturing method, and to study the properties of compact products with variable structure.

2 Materials and methods for research

Compact specimens were made on selective laser melting unit SLM280HL, manufactured by SLM Solutions GmbH. A powder of heat-resistant nickel alloy Inconel 718 obtained by gas atomization method was used as a basic material. The measured chemical composition of the alloy Inconel 718 powder is given in Table 1.

Table 1. Chemical composition of Inconel 718 powder particles (measured by energy dispersive spectroscopy)

Element	Ni	Cr	Fe	Nb	Mo	Ti	Al	Co	Mn
Content, mass %	51.4	19.4	18.5	5.3	3.4	1.0	0.7	0.1	0.1

Particle distribution in sizes was determined using a laser diffraction method with instrument Analysette 22 NanoTecPlus with a full scale range of 0.01-2000 μm. A flow rate of powder was evaluated using a hall flowmeter. Surface morphology, microstructure of particles and compact specimens, texture characteristics by electron backscatter diffraction (EBSD) were studied using scanning electron microscope TESCAN Mira 3 LMU (SEM) operated when increasing 4-106 at an accelerating voltage of 200V-30kV, the EBSD analysis was carried out at accelerating voltage of 20 kV at a pitch of 5 μm. The X-ray phase analysis was performed with multifunctional X-ray diffractometer Bruker D8 Advance. To determine the mechanical properties, the tests were carried out in accordance with ISO 6892-1 using test machine Zwick / Roell Z100 (Germany) with a maximum force of 99640 N. The relative density was measured using the metallographic method and hydrostatic weighing. The hot isostatic pressing (HIP) was carried out in gasostatic extruder Avure Quintus at a temperature of 1180 °C and a pressure of 150 MPa for 3 hours. The heat treatment was carried out in two stages: annealing at a temperature of 1065 °C for 1 hour with cooling in the air; aging was carried out in two stages, 1 – at a temperature of 760 °C for 10 hours, then cooling to 650 °C for 2 hours and curing at 650 °C for 8 hours, then cooling in the air.

3 Results of the work and their discussion

3.1 Study of basic material

Studies of the Inconel 718 powder with the scanning electron microscope (Fig. 1) showed that the powder particles have a round, nearly spherical shape. Some of the particles have growth-satellite (Fig. 1, a). These growths can affect the obtained filling density both by its increasing by filling small pores if they break away from large particles and by its reducing by preventing compaction if they are firmly fixed on the main particles. As well as these growths can affect the powder process properties, such as flow rate, degree of laser radiation absorption, etc. The studies of the particles surface morphology at high magnification showed that their surfaces have some irregularities reflecting the material cast microstructure and refer to cellular-dendritical crystallization (Fig. 1, b) [9]. From the results of the granulometric composition measurement, it is seen that the predominant particle size is about 37 μm. The difference is not very large; the sizes of more than 90% of the particles are within the range of 20 to 62 μm.

a)  b) 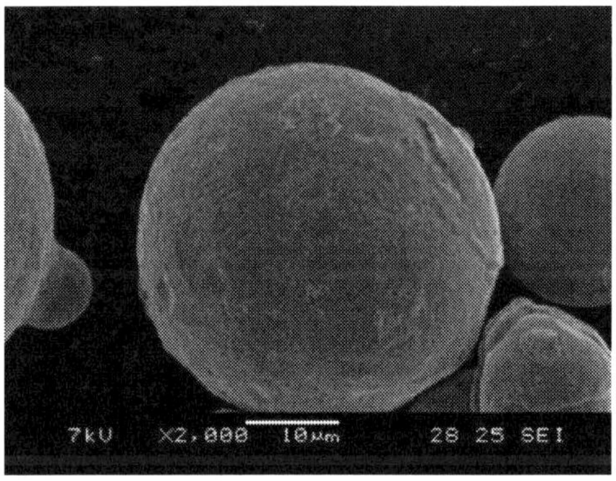

Fig. 1. SEM-images of super-alloy Inconel 718 particles obtained by gas atomization method.

3.2 Manufacture of specimens by selective laser melting

To obtain specimens for studying the microstructure, phase composition, and mechanical properties, the modes for layer thicknesses of 30, 50 and 100 μm were used. Due to rapid solidification during the SLM process (10^4-10^6 K/s), the initial microstructure consists of cellular dendrites. A solidification rate and the cells size, respectively, depend on the layer thickness and the process parameters used in the SLM.

It has been established that such parameters as a laser beam moving speed, its power and the distance between the individual passages have a greater effect on the specimens' porosity than on the structure parameters. Change in the construction layer thickness simultaneously with the change in the diameter of the laser spot makes it possible to significantly change the characteristics of the directed structure (Fig. 2). It is possible to obtain either a fine- or coarse-grained directed structure. The measurements showed that the average cell size at a layer thickness of 30 μm is 0.7-0.9 μm, at 50 μm it is 0.9-1.1 μm, and at 100 μm it is 1.3-2 μm.

 https://doi.org/10.1051/shsconf/20184400017

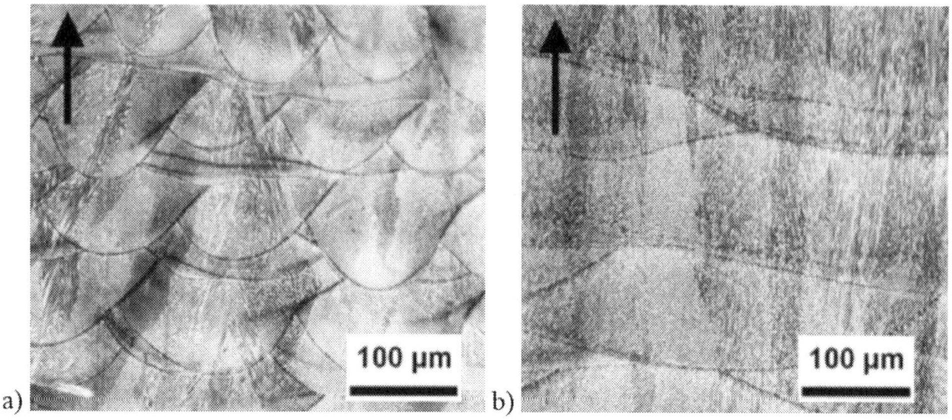

Fig. 2. The microstructure of specimens obtained by the SLM method using a layer thickness of 50 µm (a) and 100 µm (b)

Other differences in the microstructure formation with different layers thicknesses are shown in Fig. 3, where a texture study performed by the EBSD analysis is presented. The microstructure of the specimen made with a layer thickness of 50 µm has finely dispersed grains without a predominant orientation, whereas the microstructure of the specimen made at a layer thickness of 100 µm has columnar grains with a predominant orientation <001>.

Differences in the microstructure shall also affect the strength characteristics. To perform the rupture test, cylindrical specimens were prepared for testing in accordance with ISO 6892-1. The specimen yield strength, ultimate stress and elongation (given in Table 2) were determined from the tensile test results.

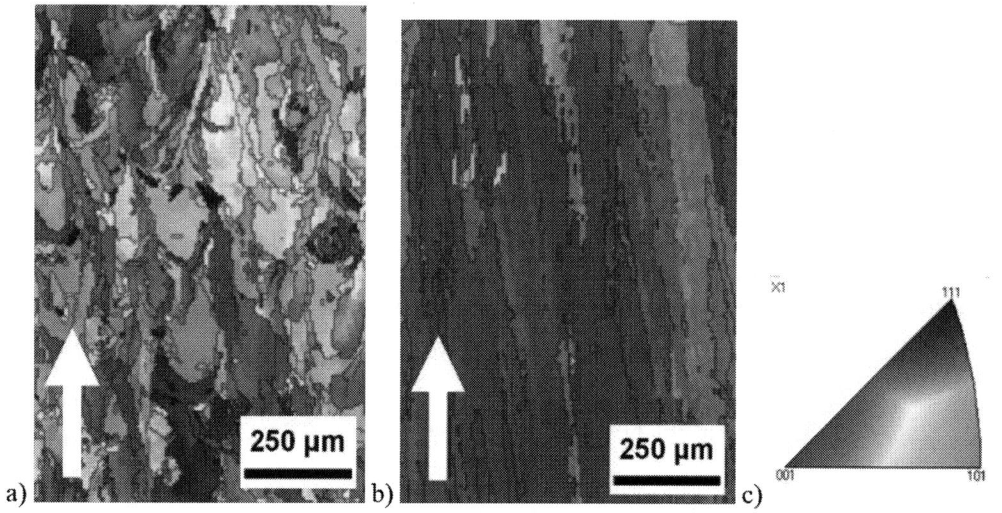

Fig. 3. The EBSD analysis of specimens made by SLM: a) crystal grains orientation map for a specimen with a layer thickness of 50 µm; b) crystal grains orientation map for a specimen with a layer thickness of 100 µm; c) an index map for figures a) and b). The specimens' growth orientation is indicated by arrow.

Table 2. The results of tensile tests of specimens of alloy Inconel 718 made by SLM method.

Layer thickness, μm	Yield strength, MPa	Ultimate strength, MPa	Percentage of elongation, %
Selective laser melting			
30	745 ± 9	1004 ± 8	25 ± 3
50	650 ± 11	845 ± 9	28 ± 4
100	543 ± 2	782 ± 6	31 ± 6
Selective laser melting + hot isostatic pressing			
50	645 ± 6	1025 ± 14	38 ± 1
100	481 ± 11	788 ± 12	34 ± 3
Selective laser melting + hot isostatic pressing + Annealing + Aging			
30	1157 ± 8	1363 ± 12	21 ± 1
50	1145 ± 16	1376 ± 14	19 ± 1
100	1065 ± 20	1272 ± 12	15 ± 4
Cast [10]	488	786	11
Hot rolling, grain is about 40 μm [11]	1245	1415	24
Hot rolling, grain is about 100 μm [11]	1145	1290	24

After annealing and aging, the mechanical properties have significantly higher values (see Table 2), this was due to changes in the material phase composition, separation of strengthening phase γ "-Ni3Nb. Mechanical properties after HIP decreased due to grain growth at an increased temperature, but the HIP significantly increased the percentage of elongation.

High-temperature properties are very important for super-alloys; the parts made of Inconel 718 are usually not used for a long time at temperatures over 650 °C. The results of studying the short-term tensile strength of tensile specimens before and after heat treatment and HIP carried out at 650 °C according to ISO 6892-2 are given in Table 3.

Table 3. Mechanical properties at 650 °C of specimens made with SLM and subsequent HIP and thermal treatments

Layer thickness, μm	Yield strength, MPa	Ultimate strength, MPa	Percentage of elongation, %
Selective laser melting			
30	716 ± 11	828 ± 9	27 ± 4
50	650 ± 11	845 ± 9	28 ± 4
100	543 ± 2	782 ± 6	31 ± 6
Selective laser melting + hot isostatic pressing			
50	626 ± 8	857 ± 14	29 ± 1
100	479 ± 5	665 ± 7	28 ± 2

Layer thickness, μm	Yield strength, MPa	Ultimate strength, MPa	Percentage of elongation, %
Selective laser melting + hot isostatic pressing + Annealing + Aging			
50	942 ± 11	1078 ± 8	20 ± 2
100	872 ± 13	1005 ± 12	17 ± 4

The results of mechanical tests at the increased temperature showed the stable strength properties with an elongation of about 30% for the conditions of SLM and SLM+ HIP. The specimens after HIP and subsequent annealing and aging have a lower value of the percentage of elongation, but the higher strength compared to other conditions.

While comparing the results of mechanical tests at the room and elevated temperatures of specimens made with different layer thicknesses and with different post-processing modes, it can be said that the smaller the layer thickness, the higher is the strength.

3.3 Manufacture of specimens with variable structure

A method for manufacturing the specimens with the specified structure in individual elements was developed at the next stage of the work. For manufacturing different areas of specimens, the modes for layer thickness values of 50 and 100 μm were used. The modes with a larger and smaller layer thickness were used successively in the specimens during the growth process. The specimens EBSD analysis shows (Fig. 4) that there is a mutual penetration of the coarse and fine grains at the boundary, i.e. there is a transition area. Its size is up to 500 μm, depending on the relative location of the coarse and fine grains areas.

a)

b)

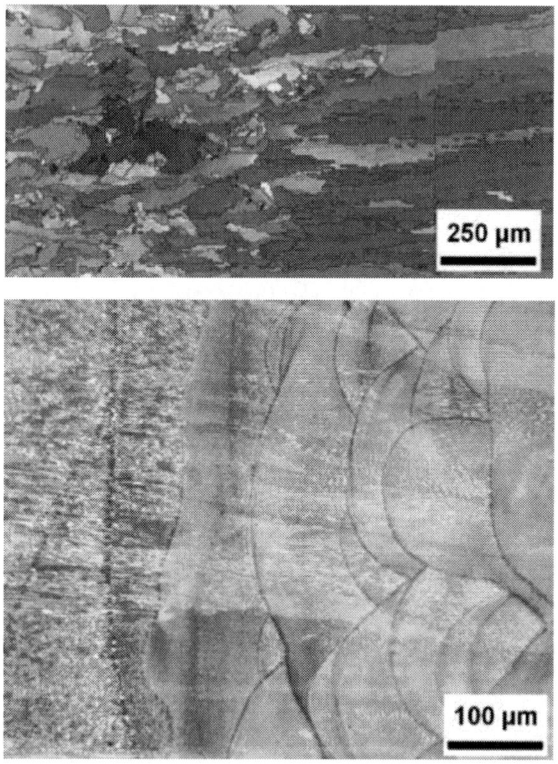

Fig. 4. The variable structure specimens manufacture procedure (a) and EBSD analysis of the transition area of 50 μm-100 μm (b).

High-temperature heating over the recrystallization temperature during hot isostatic pressing resulted in grains coarsening and formation of equiaxed grains in the area made at a layer thickness of 50 μm (Fig. 5). Thus, after the heat treatment, two areas are formed: an area of directed columnar grains and a fine-grained equiaxed area.

a)
b)
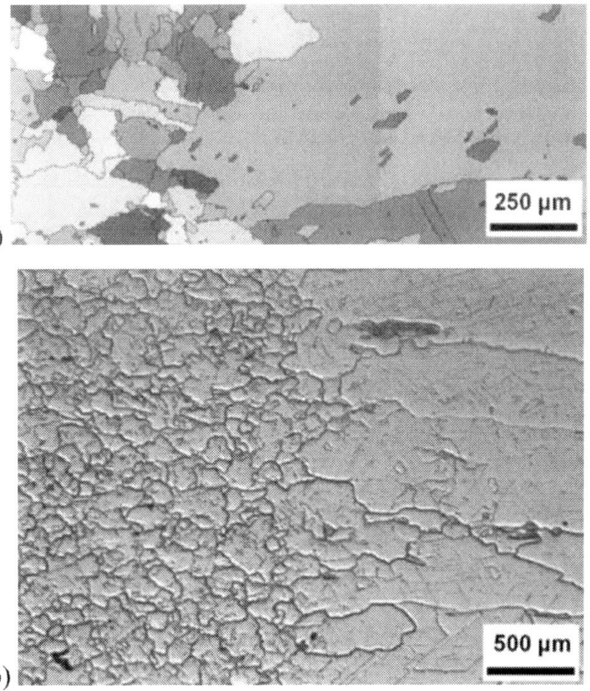

Fig. 5. The microstructure of the boundary area between the sections made at a layer thickness of 50 μm (left) and 100 μm (right) after SLM+HIP.

The results of measuring a hardness of specimens with variable structure after SLM are shown in Fig. 6.

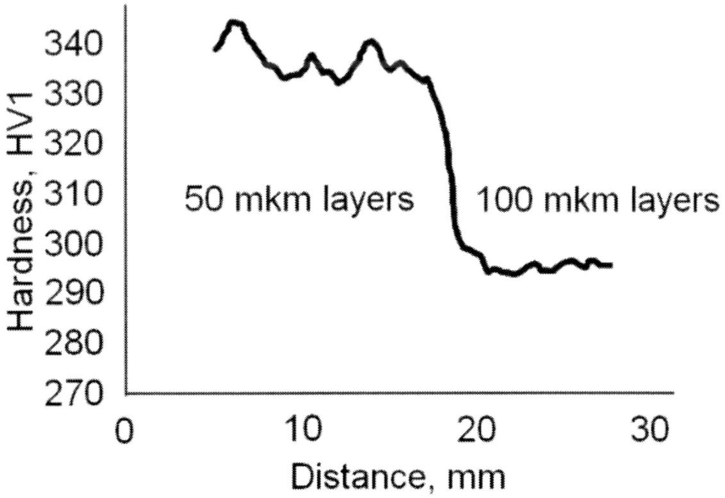

Fig. 6. Hardness of specimens with variable structure.

The analysis of the change in the hardness of specimens with variable structure showed that a difference in hardness values of about 20% is observed between the areas, the area of equiaxed fine grains has the higher hardness values.

4 Conclusions

The study for the process of selective laser melting of Inconel 718 powder is presented. It was shown that the greater is the layer thickness, the greater is the size of the dendritical cells in the structure, the EBSD analysis showed that the change in the layer thickness and process parameters leads to the change in the grains microstructure, as well as that using the large layer thickness, it is possible to implement the directional solidification mode with formation of columnar grains. The specimens' mechanical properties have a strong dependence on the layer thickness, the thinner is the layer, the higher is the strength of the specimens. The results of studying the microstructure of compact specimens made with alternating areas with coarse and fine grains are presented, and hardness measurements showed the change in the local mechanical characteristics. Based on the performed studies the concept for manufacturing products with the specified microstructure has been formed.

References

1. M. J. Holzweissig, et al. Metallurgical and Materials Transactions B. **46(2)** (2015)
2. A. Popovich, V. Sufiiarov, *New Trends in 3D Printing*, (InTech, 2016) DOI: 10.5772/63337
3. V. S. Sufiiarov, A. A. Popovich, E. V. Borisov, I. A. Polozov, Non-ferrous metals. **1** (2015)
4. D. F. Paulonis, J. J. Schirra, Superalloys. **718(625,706)** (2001)
5. A. K. Abraham, V. G. Sridhar, Trends in Biomaterials & Artificial Organs. **29(3)** (2015)
6. W. E. Frazier, Journal of Materials Engineering and Performance. **23(6)** (2014)
7. K. N. Amato, et al. Acta Materialia. **60(5)** (2012)
8. Q. Jia, D. Gu, Journal of Alloys and Compounds. **585** (2014)
9. V. M. Golod, V. S. Sufiiarov, IOP Conference Series: Materials Science and Engineering, **192 (1)** (2017) DOI: 10.1088/1757-899X/192/1/012009
10. B. Baufeld, Journal of materials engineering and performance. **21(7)** (2012)
11. J. P. Pedron, A. Pineau, Materials science and engineering. **56(2)** (1982)

New approaches to designing parts for digital additive production[a]

Evgeny Borisov[1], *Alexei* Orlov[1*], and *Nikolai* Razumov[1]

[1] Center of National Technological Initiative "New Production Technologies" of Peter the Great St.Petersburg Polytechnic University. 195251, Polytechnicheskaya st., 29, Russian Federation

Abstract. In accordance with a concept of additive technologies there occurs a necessity of applying new approaches to designing parts. One of the main tools to be operated is a numerical simulation, capable of providing a designer with the complex approach to the development of new articles in case of finesse. A preliminary simulation model of structurally-gradient materials in the software package ANSYS has been created in this work for predicting mechanical characteristics of compact samples of materials and structures. It provides the results of tensile calculations of stress strain behavior of samples obtained by finite-element simulation, as well as gives comparison thereof with the test data obtained after manufacturing using a method of selective laser melting.

1 Introduction

Digital data surround people already during long period of time permanently growing both quantitatively and qualitatively. Digital production is an integrated computer system including devices of numerical simulation, 3D visualization, engineering analysis and joint work intended for the development of structures of articles and production processes of manufacturing thereof. Digital production is a product of the fourth industrial revolution, the so-called "Industry 4.0". Digital production makes it possible to effect simulation modeling of production processes, receive a feedback from real process operations build it into a process article designing. One of the lines of production most suitable for changeover to a new industry level is the additive production.

The additive production is the process of manufacturing parts in the way of adding materials layer by layer. This technology makes it possible to produce finished articles with very intricate configuration, which is difficult or absolutely impossible to manufacture using traditional methods [1]. The additive technologies include such technologies as selective laser sintering (SLS), direct metal deposition (DED), electron-beam melting (EBM), selective laser melting (SLM). One of the most intensively developing technologies of additive production is the selective laser melting of metal powder materials, which is being widely incorporated into technological chains [1].

[a] The research was carried out in the context of implementing Federal Target Program "Research and development works on priority development fields of science and technology sector of Russia for 2014-2020", unique project identifier RFMEFI57817X0245

* Corresponding author: orlov_alexey88@mail.ru

In order to build digital infrastructure in the framework of additive technologies, it is necessary to solve many additional problems, for instance, such as predicting mechanical characteristics of compact samples of materials and structures of structurally-gradient materials [2]. In order to solve the set problem, it is necessary to work out a preliminary calculation model. The development of preliminary calculation model will be effected in the software package ANSYS. This software package makes it possible to build various calculation models with the use of a wide set of calculation modules, perform static, dynamic, hydrodynamic and other types of calculations [3]. It will be necessary to carry out simulation of sample expansion process in the framework of this work, hence, it will be necessary to use the calculation mechanics module. The samples will be manufactured using selective laser melting method with the use of metal powder Inconel 718 as the source material. In order to create the structurally-gradient samples, it is necessary to use different capabilities while manufacturing thereof.

2 Materials and investigation methods

The compact samples have been fabricated at the installation of selective laser melting SLM280HL of SLM Solutions GmbH. The powder of heat-resistant nickel alloy Inconel 718 produced by means of gas atomization has been used as the source material. The measured chemical composition of powder of alloy Inconel 718 is shown in Table 1.

Table 1. Chemical composition of particles of powder Inconel 718 (measured by means of energy dispersive spectroscopy)

Element	Ni	Cr	Fe	Nb	Mo	Ti	Al	Co	Mn
Content, % wt.	51.4	19.4	18.5	5.3	3.4	1.0	0.7	0.1	0.1

The tests for determining mechanical properties have been carried out in accordance with ISO 6892-1 at test machine Zwick/Roell Z100 (Germany) with maximum force of 99,640 N.

The development of preliminary calculation model has been performed in the software package ANSYS Workbench. This software package makes it possible to create different calculation models with the use of a wide set of calculation modules, perform static, dynamic, hydrodynamic and other types of calculations. The simulation of sample expansion process has been carried out in the framework of this work, hence, for which purpose the calculation mechanics module has been used [4]. First of all, the calculation models of homogeneous samples have been developed, the results have been compared with experimental data [5]. After that, the obtained results have been used for calculating strength characteristics of samples with variable structure.

3 Work results and discussion thereof

3.1 Investigation of mechanical characteristics of samples

Mechanical characteristics of heat-resistant nickel alloy Inconel 718 obtained after selective laser melting have been used in this work [6]. As it has been shown before, shaping of different structure [6] and, as a result, mechanical characteristics take place depending on the used technological parameters of the process of selective laser melting.

The investigations have been performed using homogeneous samples and samples with variable structure, which dimensions are shown in Fig. 1, a and 1, b, accordingly.

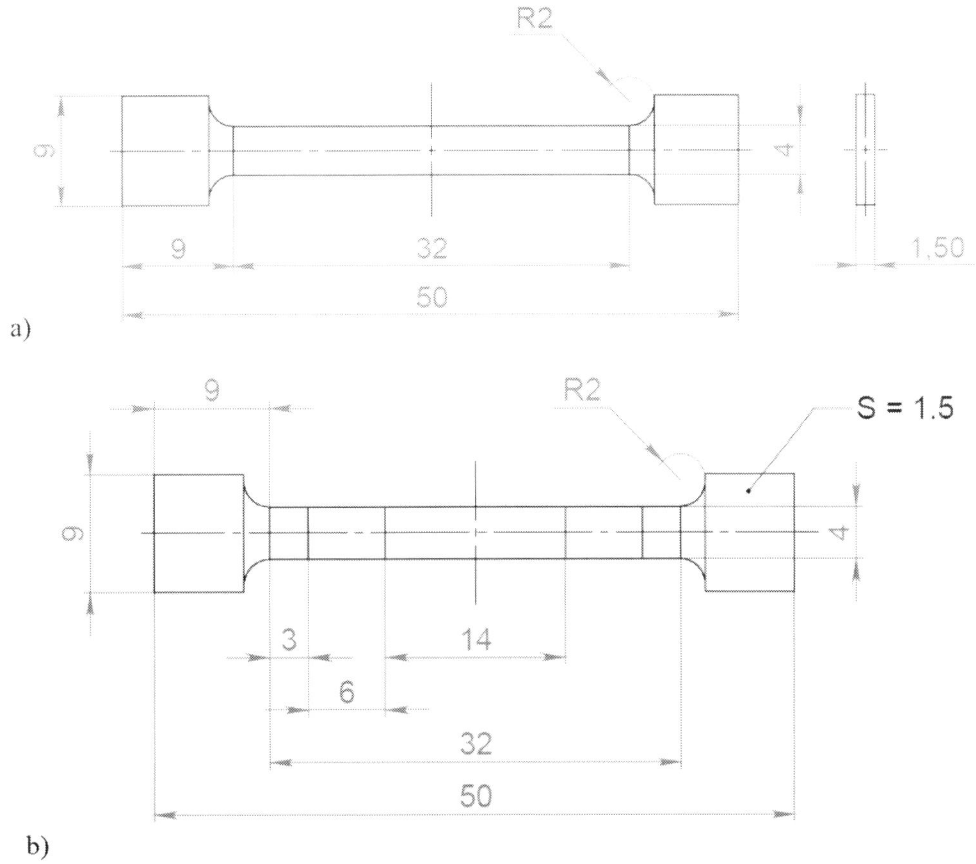

Fig. 1. Dimensions of homogeneous samples (a) and samples with variable structure (b).

The central inserts as wide as 6 mm in a sample with a variable structure have been fabricated with using layer thickness of 100 µm, when the rest part of the sample has a thickness of 50 µm.

The mechanical properties of homogeneous samples fabricated with the use of different technological parameters of the process of selective laser melting are shown in Table 2, and the samples with variable structure – in Table 3.

Table 2. Mechanical characteristics of samples made of Inconel 718 with two modes of lasers operation.

Layer thickness, µm	Proportional limit load, MPa	Young modulus, MPa	Ultimate tensile strength, MPa
50	645.1 ± 6.2	188.3 ± 8.1	1,024.9 ± 14.1
100	481.2 ± 11.9	184.9 ± 51.7	788.2 ± 12.2

Table 3. Mechanical characteristics of samples made of Inconel 718 with variable structure.

Proportional limit load, MPa	Young modulus, MPa	Ultimate tensile strength, MPa
500.2 ± 6.4	187.1 ± 8.6	816.9 ± 15.8

3.2 Building calculation model for analyzing mechanical characteristics and comparing calculation results with experimental data

According to data of results of investigating mechanical properties there are data for Young modulus. We select the first variant: Young modulus and Poisson factor. The value of Poisson factor is taken from Table and equals 0.29, Young modulus equals 1.9734e5 MPa. Modulus of volume elasticity and shear modulus get automatically calculated according to the known formulae (1):

$$K = \frac{E}{3(1-2\nu)}$$
$$G = \frac{E}{2(1+\nu)} \qquad (1)$$

where, K – modulus of volume elasticity, E – Young modulus, ν – Poisson factor, G – shear modulus.

Basic analysis settings are shown below:

- Number of Steps – 19;
- Auto Time Stepping – Off;
- Defined by –Substeps;
- Time Integration –On;
- Solver Type – Direct;
- Large Deflection –On.

According to the data of investigating mechanical properties of material time of finishing the last calculation stage equal to 520 s has been set, rate of grip transfer amounted to 1.5 mm/s.

Fig. 2 presents samples at the moment of shaping a neck of plastic strains with stress distribution as per sample 3D model.

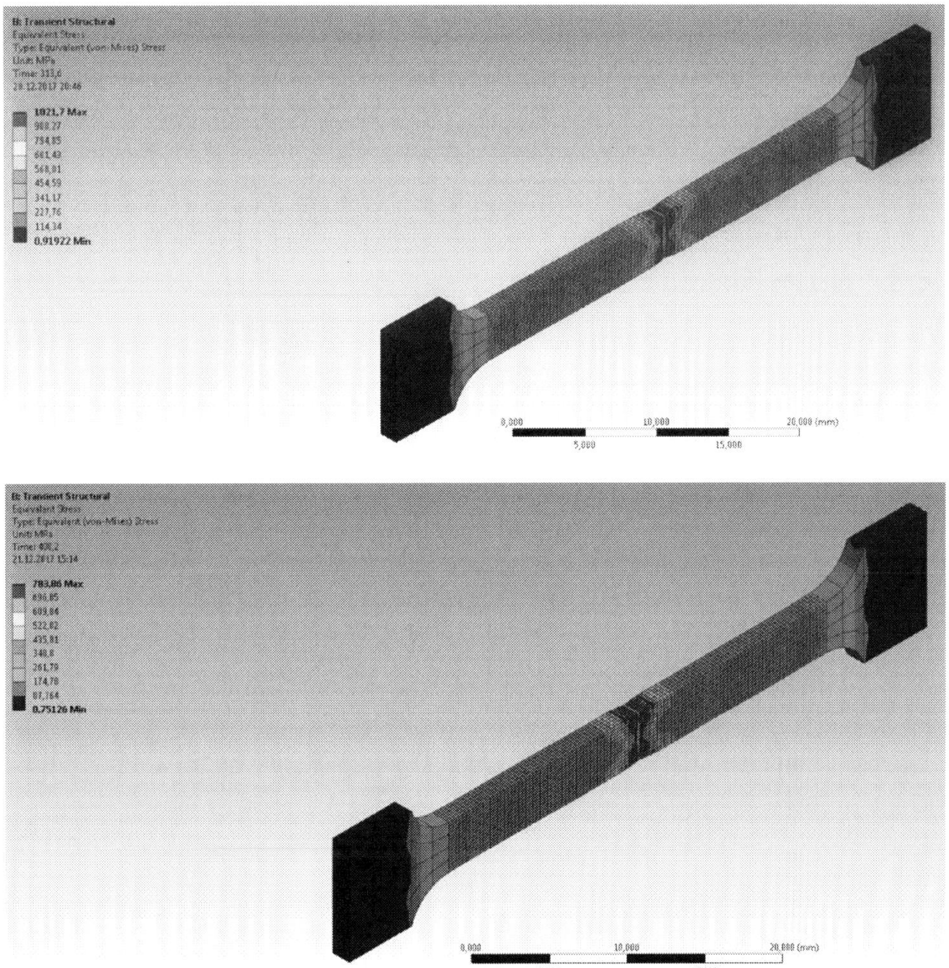

a)

b)

Fig. 2. Model of sample with displayed distribution of stresses. a – for Layer thickness of 50 μm, b – for layer thickness of 100 μm.

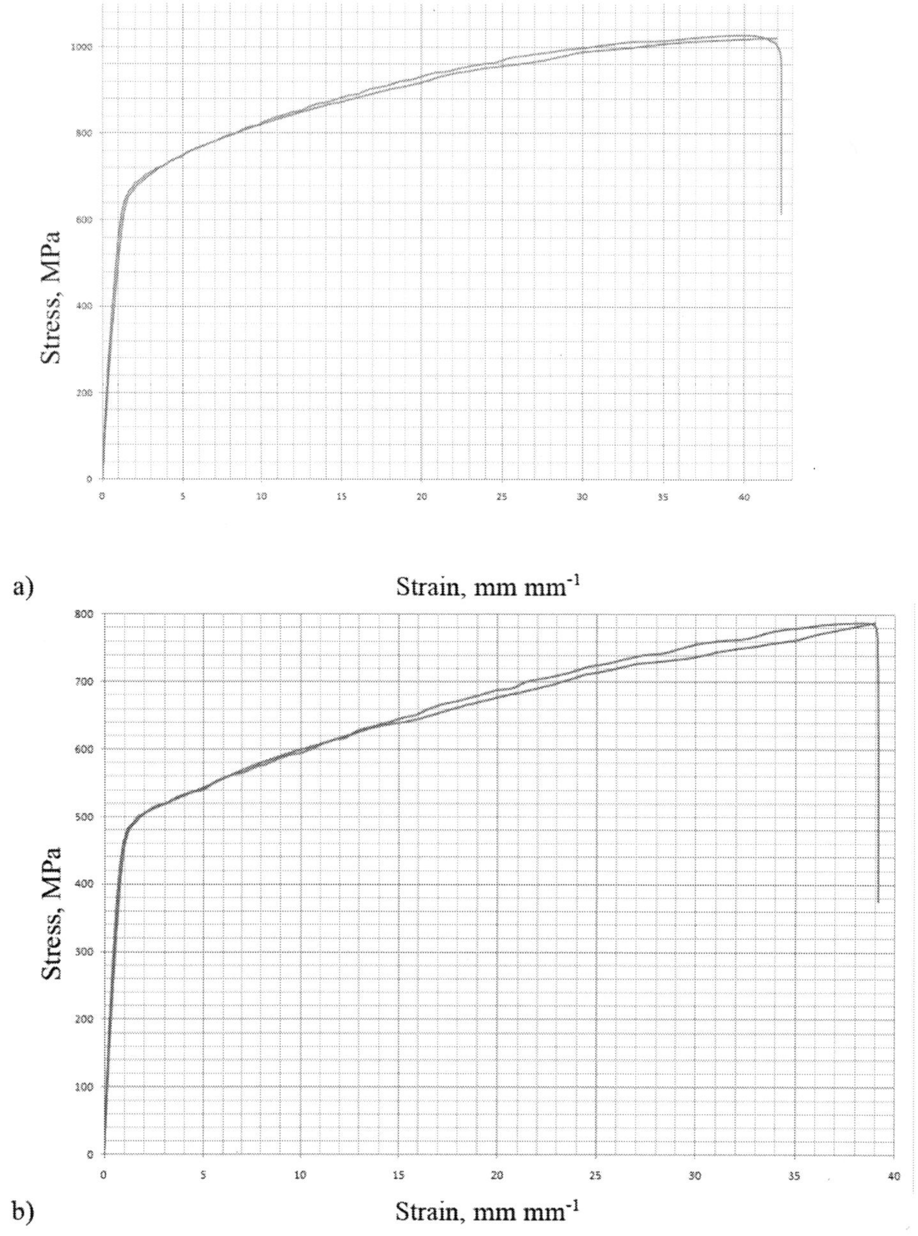

Fig. 3. Comparing graphs of dependencies of stresses vs. strains: data of investigating sample for mechanical properties are shown in blue; data of computer simulation results are shown in red. a – for layer thickness of 50 μm, b – for layer thickness of 100 μm.

Fig. 4 presents 3D model of structural-gradient sample with mesh and allocated properties of materials.

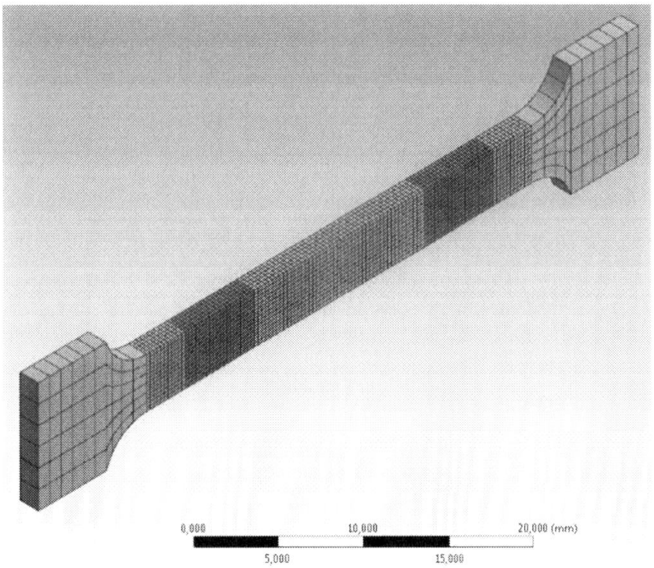

Fig. 4. Model of Structural-Gradient Sample with Mesh. Datum Made with Layer Thickness of 50 μm – Yellow Color; Inserts Made with Layer Thickness of 100 μm – Orange Color.

The computer simulation of process of sample extension resulted in obtaining a set of data, which have been compared with data of investigating samples for mechanical properties during stretching. Fig. 5 shows a sample with a variable structure at the moment of shaping a neck of plastic strains with stress distribution, Fig. 6 shows a comparison of calculated and experimental curve of stress dependence vs. strain during tensile test.

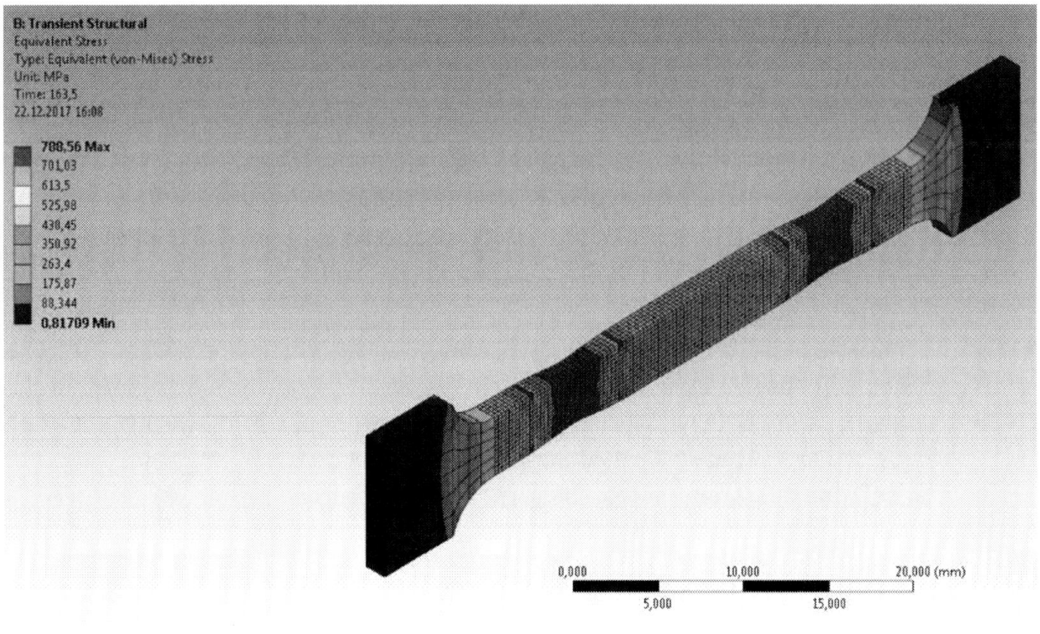

Fig. 5. Model of sample with variable structure with displayed distribution of stresses.

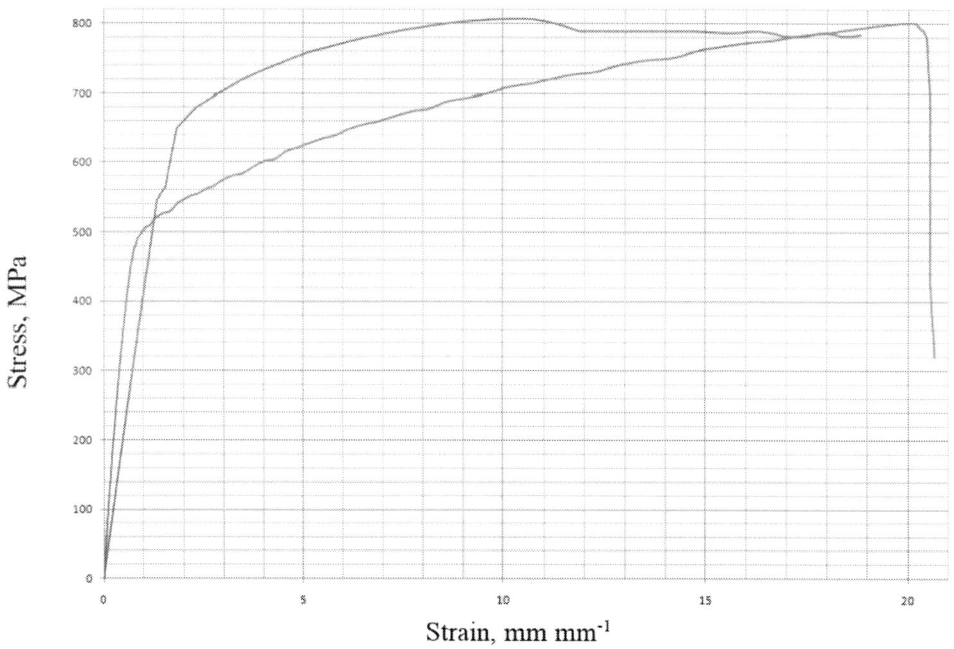

Fig. 6. Comparison of graphs of dependences of stresses vs. strains: data of investigating sample for mechanical properties are shown in blue; data of computer simulation results are shown in red.

4 Conclusions

The comparison of data has shown a discrepancy between experimental and calculated data. It is also shown in Fig. 5 that the neck of plastic deformations has formed immediately in two places, which is practically impossible. It testifies to the fact that the calculation model of structural-gradient samples is not absolutely correct and needs further improvement.

References

1. A. Popovich, V. Sufiiarov, Metal Powder Additive Manufacturing, *New Trends in 3D Printing*, Chapter 10, InTech, (2016) DOI: 10.5772/63337.
2. I. A. Roberts, et al. Int. J. of Machine Tools and Manufacture. **49** (2009)
3. D. V. Ivanov, A. V. Dol, *Introduction to the Ansys Workbench. Study guide* (Amirit, Saratov, 2016)
4. Post-Processing of Models Ansys Mechanical APDL by Means of Ansys Workbench. [online], Available at: http://www.ansys.soften.com.ua/blog/158-post-protsessing-modelej-ansys-mechanical-apdl-pri-pomoshchi-ansys-workbench.html (2018)
5. A. V. Gusarov, et al. Applied Surface Science **254** (2007)
6. V. A. Popovich, et al. Materials & Design. **114** (2017)

Parametric design as information modeling tool in dynamic architecture

Olga Bukunova[1*], and *Konstantin* Shumilov[1]

1 Saint Petersburg State University of Architecture and Civil Engineering, Faculty of Civil Engineering, 190005 2-ya Krasnoarmeiskaya st. 4, Russian Federation

Abstract. Dynamic architecture is a separate upcoming trend in educational process. The article gives examples of parametric software languages development built into graphic packages. The implementation is carried out within the framework of improving the educational process of training specialists in the construction profile with the aim of implementing the program of the digital economy and information modeling technology in construction. Visual programming allows you to create programs without directly writing code by means of graphical objects manipulation. At present, parametric design can be referred to a young and rapidly developing sphere. Essential condition for its further development is availability of trained specialists of respective qualification.

1 Introduction

"The new oil of economy is the data … Digital economy is about how we create, transmit, store, protect and process this data and make well thought out and high-quality decisions based on this data" [1]. The draft program contains nine branches: governing, data infrastructure, research and development, control system, personnel and training, data security, management, "Smart City" and digital healthcare [1]. The first experience with digital economy system development associated with information modeling knowledge technologies (Building Information Modeling – BIM) proved to be positive; it was possible to gain at once four positive parameters in the development of construction industry in Great Britain [2]. To create systems that can work in the real world, a new discipline has appeared – model engineering [3].

A separate perspective direction is a dynamic architecture in the design of buildings. Today, the dynamics in architecture can be used to give buildings a futuristic look and aesthetic properties. Such buildings are resistant to the effects of natural conditions and can perform functions uncommon for structures with a fixed structure. The architecture of the future shall comply with the demands of modern society and change dynamically with the change of its demands. One of these trends is the dynamic architecture that can comply with this demand.

Russia needs to update the process of construction specialists training accounting for modern demands. It is suggested to extend possibilities of information modeling of buildings by using parametric software languages built into graphic packages. For further

* Corresponding author: bukunovaolga@yandex.ru

development of parametric design it is necessary to have competent personnel capable of developing new technologies. Studying the possibilities of parametric programming in the learning process will provide benefits to graduates in the field of construction.

2 Revit as a Parametric Platform

Traditionally for buildings modeling geometry elements with known coordinate values were used. The process of editing manually is laborious, leading to numerous errors. Later parametric modeling supported systems appeared [4]. In this case a mathematical model of the object with adjustable parameters is created. Alteration of these parameters allows simplifying editing process and decreasing the number of errors.

Two main technologies are used in digital parametric modeling. One of them is based on saving of history of changes (repeating the actions for model and its components creation). The other one supports conditions for the possibility of geometry alteration and is called variational, or dimensional model [5].

When using variational parameterization, parametric connections and restraints which represent a system of equations setting dependencies between parameters are imposed on the object sketch. When using geometrical parameterization, the model is based on architecture components and display elements. In this technology, the object geometry is recalculated in case of its parameters and variables, as well as parent object position, alteration. As a result, geometric parameterization allows for a more flexible model editing mechanism [6].

Revit as a parametrical platform can become the main tool for future construction engineers. The essence of Revit design is generation of dependencies between building components and their implementation and introduction into model. Revit in future shall become as habitual for students as Word text editor or Excel electronic worksheets. That is why students shall study these software programs for a period of several terms. As of today there are two most common platforms for visual programming in design and architecture: Autodesk Dynamo and Grasshopper. Some others are also available in the market:

- Teklamo (allows transmitting data from a program created in Dynamo);
- Geometry Gym (allows transmitting data from Grasshopper to Tekla).

The use of such programs ensures closer connection between architecture and structure design processes and also allows more effective development of complex geometry structures, computerizing engineering design, transferring data bases between design engineers, working with data bases, automatic formatting of drawings, specifications and cost estimations [7, 8].

On the one hand, digital design simplifies design process and helps to avoid functional errors; on the other hand, it promotes the creation of avant-garde, innovative forms of buildings. It should be noted that building parametric model facilitates designing even in an educational project.

3 Studying the built-in graphical packages of parametric programming languages by students

Dynamic architecture is a separate upcoming trend in educational process. In order to make the building move, designers use bottom-up stitches of independent floors on a solid foundation, there are blades between them, through which the wind passes, this causes the floors to move and still generates energy. The facade of the building does not have a clear architecture; it constantly acquires various forms [9]. In this «moving» design it is important to employ super hard materials; for the framework metal columns and monolithic overlap are used. They are not only very strong and convenient in construction but also are not very expensive which is obviously important for even a project of 60 floors.

Despite the fact that this idea appeared in the twenties of the twentieth century, its popularity has grown in recent decades. This is due to development of computer technologies on the whole and visual programming in particular [10]. Visual programming practically needs no programming experience and allows after a short training to create user scripts for students of technical specialties with an analytical mindset. Visual programming allows creating programs without directly writing code by means of manipulation of graphical objects.

Dynamo (it is a Grasshopper analogue for its Rhino modeling tool) is an application on Revit for object modeling. Dynamo is provided with built-in Python which with the help of Revit API DataBase can receive any data on current object, properly process it (e.g., convert into Excel) and return it to Revit in a different form and with respect to other objects.

Thus, Dynamo is not only a small mechanization tool for Revit. Dynamo allows significant extending of standard software framework and increasing efficiency of its operation. With the help of Dynamo students can be taught new activities in Revit: build geometry, work with data, update properties and even send electronic letters. The application can import/export different data (Excel tables, raster displays, text files). Dynamo consists of two spaces combined in one window: programming space and that of geometry with the possibility of their mutual switching. Because of its novelty, Dynamo application is not yet widely spread but its high potential allows recommending this platform for study at the university.

Dynamo is a platform (a kind of ladder) that allows every engineer to transit from the user environment into that of developing own design tools. In some respect it is an analogue of VBA language built into MS Office, enabling to create macros to automate workstations and optimize and simplify user's life. Dynamo allows automation of practically all routine processes in geometry construction, formation of documentation, calculation and etc. The application is useful for all section designers. At the first level it is quite possible to use standard nodes (though their number increases rapidly with each new version and due to settings created by users). At the second level it is already possible to write codes in Design Script. At the third level it is possible to write codes in Python and get access to API, thus reaching the same level of those serious programmers who do not treat Dynamo as serious software.

4 Example of Use

Let us consider Dynamo application resources at the example of three-dimensional object construction with standard nodes as well as with DesignScript and Python.

I. Architectural object is a tower.

The object – tower – was constructed by writing code in Python language and partially nodes were used to borrow flooring type from Revit and demonstrate tower turning and narrowing.

Initial data: number of floors, storey height, side of flooring, number of columns, building angular sweep, coefficient of narrowing, side of core.

Two types of nodes were used to input initial data: Code Block (ensures possibility of DesignScript code direct creation), Integer Slider (regulator creating integer values).

The following values were calculated (Figure 1): tower height (*H*), radius of circle into which tower foundation will be entered (*x1*), coefficient for radius of circle alteration for building columns with tower narrowing (*s*), radius of circle to build core guidelines (*x2*) and data output array was specified (*arr*).

```
        H=(k-1)*h0-h0              /tower height/
        x1 = A/pow(2,0.5)          /radius of circle/
        s=x1-r*(k-1)               /radius of circle alteration for building columns/
        x2 = s/pow(2,0.5)-500      /radius of circle for guidelines construction/
        x3 = B*pow(2,0.5)
arr=[]
```

Fig. 1. Example of Calculation

Python is convenient for cycle operations, e.g., when setting points on the circle for columns construction (Fig. 2).

```
for i in range(0,k-1):
        x = (x1-r*i) * math.cos(0+w)
        y = (x1-r*i) * math.sin(0+w)
        p.append(Point.ByCoordinates(x,y,h0*i))
        x = (x1-r*i) * math.cos(math.pi/2+w)
        y = (x1-r*i) * math.sin(math.pi/2+w)
        p1.append(Point.ByCoordinates(x,y,h0*i))
        x = (x1-r*i) * math.cos(math.pi+w)
        y = (x1-r*i) * math.sin(math.pi+w)
        p2.append(Point.ByCoordinates(x,y,h0*i))
        x = (x1-r*i) * math.cos(3*math.pi/2+w)
        y = (x1-r*i) * math.sin(3*math.pi/2+w)
        p3.append(Point.ByCoordinates(x,y,h0*i))
        w=w+t
R.append(Rectangle.ByCornerPoints(p[i],p1[i],p2[i],p3[i]))
```

Fig. 2. Execution of Cycle Operations

The same way pairs of points were obtained for column guidelines construction.

```
for i in range(0,q):
        x = x2 * math.cos(0+w1)
        y = x2 * math.sin(0+w1)
        kol.append (Point.ByCoordinates(x,y,h0*0))
        kol1.append (Point.ByCoordinates(x,y,H))
        l9.append (Line.ByStartPointEndPoint(kol[i],kol1[i]))
        w1=w1+qq
```

Fig. 3. Column Guidelines Construction

Then initial data nodes were connected to PythonScript node (Fig. 4).

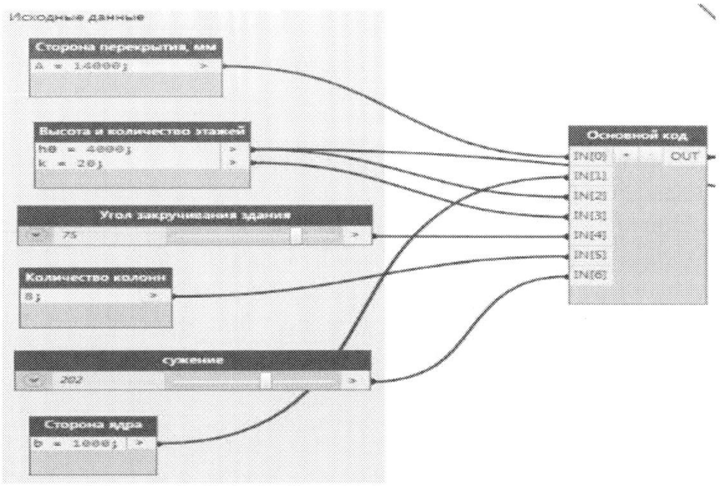

Fig. 4. Connection between Initial Data and Main Code Node

Then standard nodes *Levels* and *Structural Column Type* (obtaining supporting column level and type from Revit document) were used. With the help of *StructuralFraming.ColumnByCurve* node columns were constructed by the list of guidelines. To construct core, *Wall.ByCurveAndHeight* node was used. Floors were constructed with *Floor.ByOutlineTypeAndLevel* node for flooring creation by curve shape and level from Revit. Curve is obtained from initial code node by using Python Script node.

Alteration of sweep angle and tower narrowing coefficient allows online changing object geometric view to be used for further operations with walls, glazing etc.

Figure 5 shows tower view in Revit at sweep angle 0 and narrowing coefficient 0, and Figure 6 indicates the same at sweep angle 60 and narrowing coefficient 0.1.

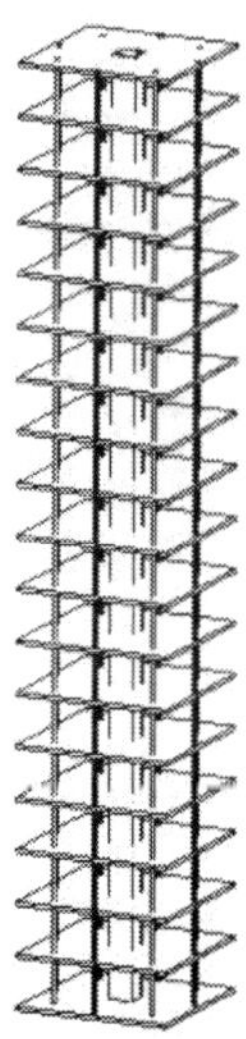

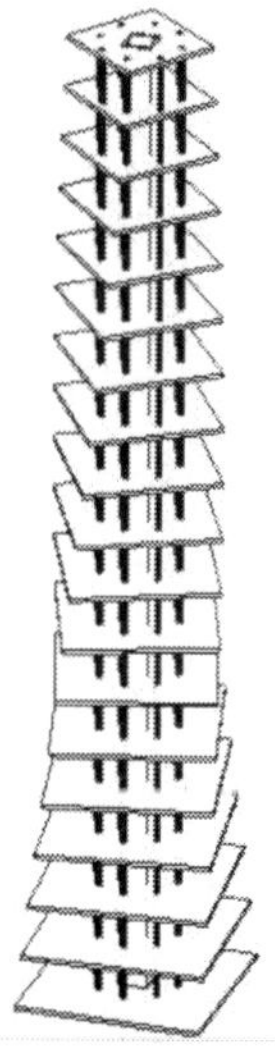

Fig. 5. Tower View at Sweep Angle 0 and Narrowing Coefficient 0

Fig. 6. Tower View in Revit at Sweep Angle 60 and Narrowing Coefficient 0.1.

II. The object is envelopment.

Construction of envelopment surface is considered with the help of Python Script node.

Surface was constructed with standard *PolySurface.ByLoft* function (surface construction by loft with curves).

As an example for the first curve *k,* z=Sin(y) function was used. With cycle *for* and library function *Point.ByCoordinates* a set of points was constructed (Fig. 7).

```
sur=[]
for i in range(0,a+1):
        x = 0
        y = i
        z= math.sin(i)
        sur.append(Point.ByCoordinates(x,y,z))
```

Fig. 7. Set of Points Construction for the First Curve

In a similar way a set of points was generated for the second curve construction z= 2*Cos(y/3) (Fig. 8).

```
sur1=[]
for i in range(0,a+1):
        x = b
        y = i
        z= 2*math.cos(i/3)
        sur1.append(Point.ByCoordinates(x,y,z))
```

Fig. 8. Set of Points Construction for the Second Curve

Then *NurbsCurve.ByPoints* function is used to construct two curves by obtained points and *Loft* surface (Fig. 9).

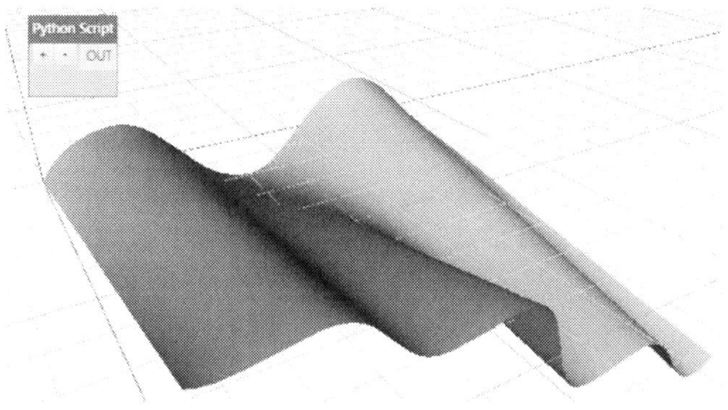

Fig. 9. *Loft* Surface

For comparison, spherical surface was constructed and on its example the combination of Python Script node and standard nodes from Dynamo library was considered. Two radii were given as initial data. The first one is the radius of surface base; the second is radius of surface convexity.

As in the previous example, surface was constructed with Python Script node. Python Script node body contains required libraries, initial data and required number of points is set (*q*).

Surface was constructed with *Surface.ByRevolve* function (surface creation by profile graph shifting around axis radius representing axis vector starting at the point start_angle in degrees and finishing at sweep_angle).

With *for* cycle and *Point.ByCoordinates* function, array *sur* of circle points was formed. Then with *NurbsCurve.ByPoints* function these points were joined into a circle (Fig. 10).

```
        for i in range(0,q+1):
                x = R1 * math.cos(0+w1)
                y = R1 * math.sin(0+w1)
                sur.append(Point.ByCoordinates(x,y,z))
                w1=w1+qq
k=NurbsCurve.ByPoints(sur)
```

Fig. 10. Surface Construction

Successively surface was constructed and displayed for different data variants (Fig. 11).

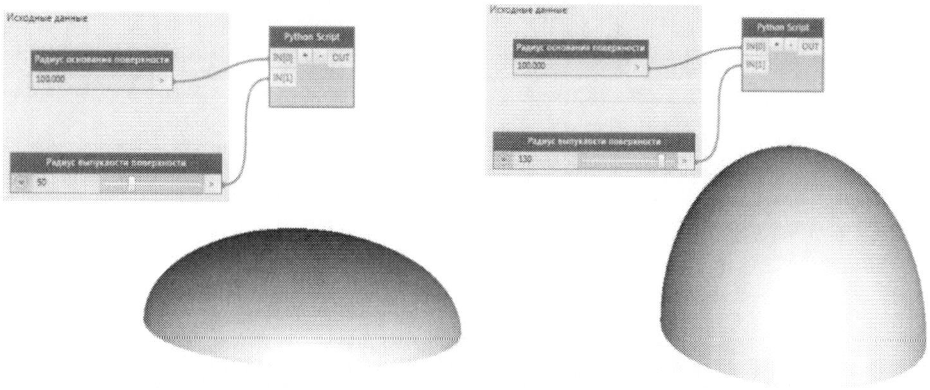

Fig. 11. Surfaces with radius of surface base 100, Radius of surface convexity 50 and 100

With the help of *Surface.Thicken* function, obtained surface thickness is set. With the help of *Surface.Area* and *Surface.Volume* surface area and volume are obtained.

Constructed envelopments are exported to Revit as well as special calculation packages for permissible loads analysis, structure reliability estimation, etc.

The above mentioned examples show how convenient and brief is the combination of standard nodes with Python Script node. Firstly, it is easy to alter initial data without disturbing the main code. Secondly, thanks to standard nodes Number and Integer Slider it is possible to visually follow object shape alteration at different values of initial data. Thirdly, as the main part of surface construction is written inside Python Script node body, there is no huge amount of nodes and their interconnections, script processing and complex phrase construction time decreases substantially.

As a result of executed work possibilities of drafting program Revit extension were analyzed with comparatively new tool – Dynamo customization code. An important feature of the tool is the possibility of creating and modeling of three-dimensional objects not only with standard node library but also by writing own code. Optimum solution is combination of standard nodes from Dynamo library and nodes with own code.

Use of Python Script is mostly advisable for complicated calculations, implementation of multiple cycle operations and object transformations (creation and rotation of floors, design elements, calculation of point coordinates during modeling of envelopments, etc).

Besides Python, there is also a programming language – Design Script, but it is not low-level, it operates only internal and only base nodes without access to external API, directly.

Rhino + Grasshopper is a more publicly available source, more established, has more textbooks and a lot of updates and plug-in software including physics imitation, evolutionary problem solver and other important tools. The combination is convenient for small projects with complicated parametrical detailing, sophisticated architectural design and imitation. It interacts with Grasshopper ArchiCAD.

Choice of software also depends on its demonstrativeness. There is no need to use graphical programming if it is possible not to parameterize elements. In the next few years all the three platforms (Dynamo + Revit, Rhino-Grasshopper + ArchiCAD, Marionette in Vector works) are expected to continue expanding their functionalities into respective solutions so as to cover as many BIM applications as possible. It will include reception and introduction of data on any element (implementer or documentation element), views and representations, histories, attributes, drawings, model sets, time-tables, publications. The main focus is on construction elements and then come all other program areas. In a few years it will be possible to produce all automated items in ArchiCAD with Grasshopper [11].

5 Conclusion

The design methods suggested support the new trend – dynamic architecture. Dynamic architecture has a number of features distinguishing it from common construction. The first peculiarity is connected with construction shape that permanently undergoes changes, adapting to weather conditions [9]. The second peculiarity is the dynamic construction method. Usually such structures are made up of pre-fabricated parts that are manufactured at plants and get to site pre-fabricated. The third feature of dynamic buildings is the fact that they combine modern technologies and preserve environment. Dynamic buildings are also capable of producing power for their independent power supply, e.g., from wind power. The next feature comprises functionalities, e.g., bridges in which central part can be lifted. This type can be attributed to the new stadium Krestovsky in St. Petersburg, which has a retractable roof, which is very convenient for bad weather, and the field of the stadium is pushing beyond its limits.

On the basis of dynamic architecture design and construction experience analysis carried out, a number of dynamic architecture advantages have been identified. First, it is the reduction of construction time. It takes about three weeks to construct a storey using common technique and it only takes three days for moving structure, entire building construction period will decrease up to 18 months (standard construction takes about 30 months). Second, in such a project the number of workers can be decreased. And at last expenditures can be saved on building machinery. It will be necessary at construction initial stage, during building core construction; no special machinery will be required during storey stringing.

That is why it is so important to use applications allowing construction objects modeling in training. At present, parametric design can be referred to as a new but rapidly developing sphere. Its employment in training process facilitates establishment of new architectural thinking, and it is made up on new information technologies. Essential condition for its further development is availability of trained specialists of respective qualification and innovation and software that will make it possible for all architects and builders using new technologies to study parametric design. Mastered new parametric design capabilities will give advantages to engineering students [5]. Dynamic trend is just beginning to actively develop and get implemented into construction. This is a new dawn in architecture. And if its active growth continues, in 20 years the world will change beyond recognition.

References

1. O. Pavlenko, E. Kazachenko, Digital Economy Programme will Turn Data into New Oil, Conclusions [online], Available at: http://tass.ru/ekonomika/4279297 (2017)
2. A. P. Dobrynin et al., International Journal of Open Information Technologies, **4 (1)** (2016)
3. V. P. Kupriyanovskiy, D. E. Namiot, S. A. Sinyagov, International Journal of Open Information Technologies, **(4) 2** (2016)
4. F. H. Abandaa, J. H. M. Taha, F. K. T. Cheungb, Journal of Building Engineering, **14** (2017)

5. O. V. Bukunova, A. S. Bukunov, Innovative Science: Collection of Articles on V International Research and Practice Conference Materials "MtsNO", **4(5)** (2017)
6. F. J. Sabongi, The Integration of BIM in the Undergraduate Curriculum: an Analysis of Undergraduate Courses [online], Available at: http://www.ascproc.asc-web.org (2009)
7. M. M Joannides, R. A. Issa, S. Olbina, Journal of Building Information Modeling (2011)
8. H. Abdirad, C.S. Dossick, Journal of Information Technology in Construction (ITcon), **21** (2016)
9. C. Salter, *Entangled: Technology and the Transformation of Performance* (The MIT Press, Cambridge, 2010)
10 Seok-Heon Yun, Ki-hyun Jun, Chang-baek Son, and Sang-chul Kim, Journal of Civil Engineering, **18 (2)** (2014)
11. I. Chikovskaya, Implementation of BIM – Experience, Scenarios, Errors, Conclusions [online], Available at: http://isicad.ru/ru/articles.php?article_num=16407 (2013)

Supporting connectivity of VANET/MANET network nodes and elastic software-configurable security services using blockchain with floating genesis block[a]

Alexey Busygin[1*], *Maxim* Kalinin[1], and *Artem* Konoplev[1]

[1] Peter the Great St. Petersburg Polytechnic University, Institute of Computer Science and Technologies, Department Information Security of Computer Systems, 195251 Polytechnicheskaya st. 29, Russian Federation

Abstract. This paper considers the tasks of supporting the connectivity of nodes in communication networks of unmanned transport (VANET/MANET-networks). High dynamics, decentralization and absence of hierarchy in the networks of this type actualize the task of supporting the connectivity of nodes with software-configurable security services, providing the network protection. It is offered to use a Blockchain technology based system for VANET/MANET network topologyand authentication data distribution and storage. The issue of unlimited blockchain growth preventing this method from being implemented in VANET/MANET networks is considered. The existing solutions of this issueare analyzed and drawbacks are identified. A notion of blockchain with floating genesis block is introduced and its advantages over similar ideas are demonstrated thus allowing it to be used to resolve the issue of continuously growing blockchain within the systems with stalingtransactions as a whole and in VANET/MANET networks in particular.

1 Introduction

The development of M2M (machine-to-machine) telecommunications, where wireless device systems transfer information from one device to another as well as informatization and cybernetization of vehicles has allowed network technologies to penetrate into the transport vehicle sphere and developed a new type of communication vehicular systems – VANET (vehicular ad hoc networks, in other words, peer-to-peer vehicular networks).

Along with that the mobility of VANET/MANET networks determines high dynamics in changes of network topology, its uncertain structure, unclear network perimeter, because

[a]With financial support from the Ministry of education and science of the Russian Federation as part of the Federal target program "Research and development of priority areas for Russia's research and process complex for 2014-2020" (Agreement No. 14.578.21.0224 dated 03.10.2016, unique identifier of this agreement RFMEFI57816X0224)
[*] Corresponding author: a.busygin@ibks.spbstu.ru

a high mobility of all interaction process participants is added to rerouting of links due to their breaks and enabling/disabling of nodes. In this connection, it is extremely important to maintain the connectivity of nodes with software-configurable security services that ensure their protection

For the networks of this type there are typical information security threats intended to disrupt the node connectivity such as routing attacks (forging, modification, blocking tramsmission of routing information, Hello flood, Sinkhole), selective transmission of packages (Black hole) and virtualization of network segments (Wormhole, Sybil) [1]. At the present moment there is a number of general protection methods offered against the abovementioned threats, for example in papers [1, 2]. However, for successful application of these methods it is necessary to know the network topology and have the node identification and authentication system in place. Meeting these requirements for self-organizing networks is a rather difficult task. In paper [3] a securemethod for network topology information and authentication data distribution and storage using the Blockchain technology is offered. The issue of using blockchain for VANET/MANET protection consists in a continuous increase in this data structure size resulting in quick depletion of disc space on the vehicular system networks nodes. Moreover, the time required to add new nodes into aunmanned vehiclenetwork increases significantly. This paper offers a solution to eliminate these drawbacks allowing connectivity of VANET/MANET nodes with program-configurable security services in conditions of directed cyberattacks.

2 Review of literature

S. Nakamoto has offered a method for reducing the blockchain data being stored on fully functional nodes by pruningthe old transactions, which are not needed for adding and verification of new blocks [4]. The disadvantage of this method is the need to load and verify the entire blockchain when adding new fully functional nodes. Without access to the full list of transactions being stored in blockchain these fully functional nodes cannot verify the current state of blockchain system

Another approach is to reduce the volume that is taken up by blockchain data by removing excessive data from the blocks, for example, by excluding some metadata and etc [5]. In a similar way in paper [6] it is offered to use the public keys in compressed form to cut down the size of transactions. This approach only slows down the rate of blockchain growth, but does not resolve the issue, which becomes critical in case of high transaction rate within the system.

Blockchain can also be used as a mechanism of synchronization between the nodes changing the system state[7, 8]. At a first step a transaction signaling that the time window starts is recorded to blockchain, during this period the system state ischanged. During this time the node exchange messages changing the system state, but these are not saved in blockchain (these messages are called off-chain transactions).When this time window is completed, a transaction with total result of all off-chain transactions execution is recorded to blockchain. This approach only slows down the blockchain growth, but does not resolve the issueas a whole.

Another approach [9-11] is known to be used in database control systems – horizontal scaling of data storage (sharding). In this approach it is proposed to divide data stored in blockchain between several nodes. In this situation the blockchain size is not reduced and the issueof its growthis not solved. Another solution with similar features consists in storing in blockchain data hashes only. The data itself is sharedbetween the distributed hash table nodes (Fig. 1) [12].

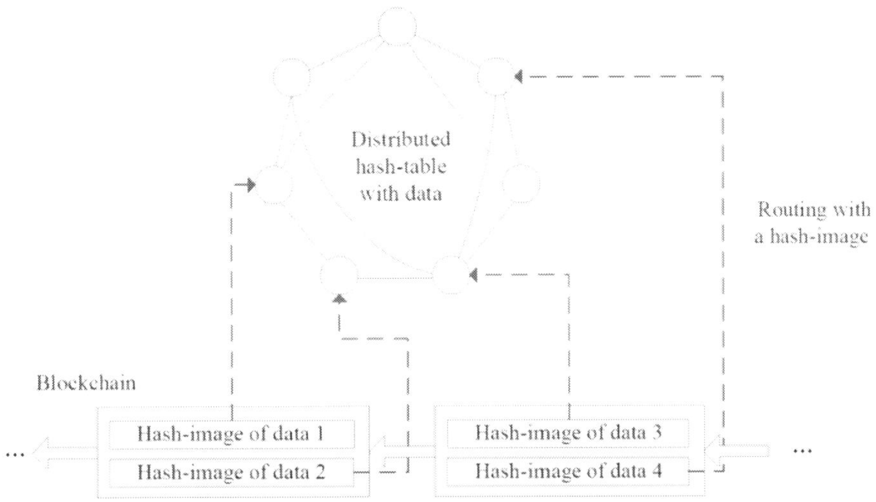

Fig. 1. Data storage diagram in distributed hash-table outside of the blockchain.

3 Using blockchain with a floating genesisblock

Let us consider the basic model of the blockchain. The blockchain is a ordered list of transactions changing the value of a set of variables from some data domain. For clarity let us consider the changed values of one variable *s* (Fig. 2).

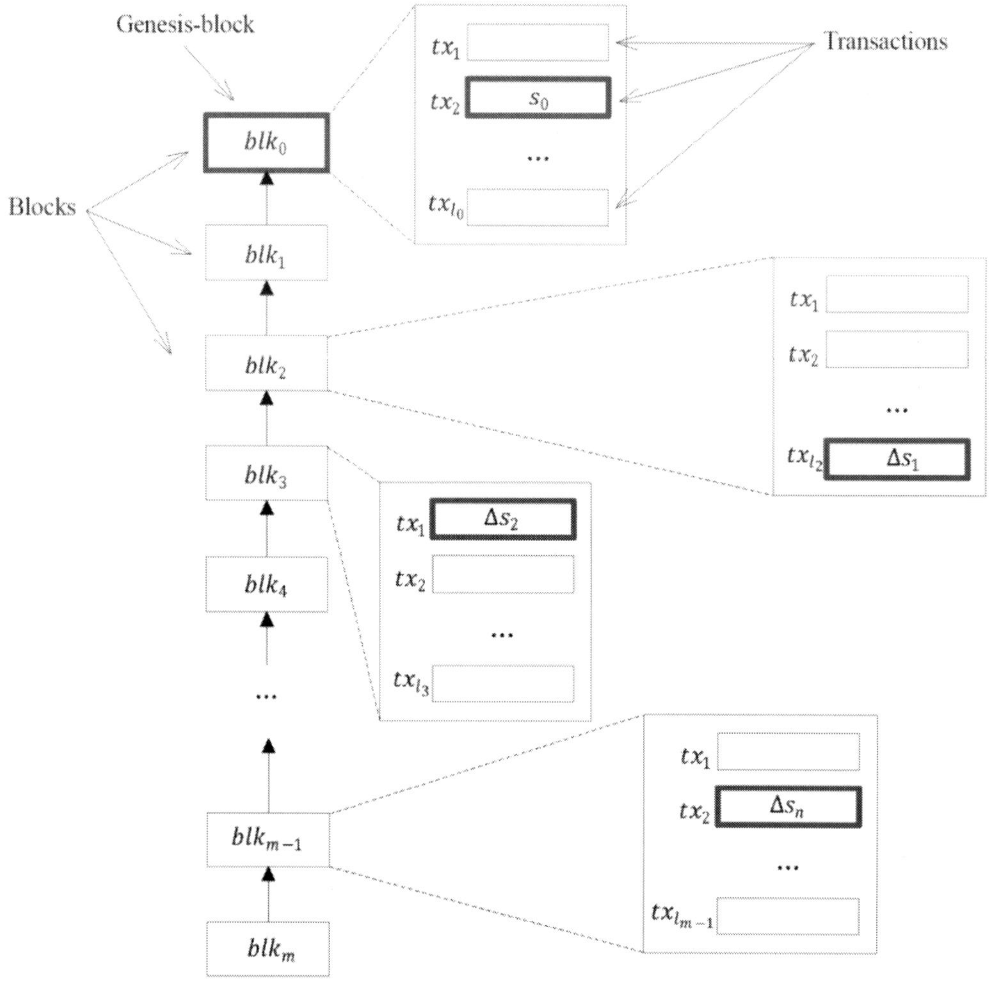

Fig. 2. Schematic block diagram of the blockchain base model.

The first transaction (transaction tx_2 of the block blk_0) sets the initial value of the variable s to be equal to s_0. Each next transaction (for example transaction tx_{l_2} of the block blk_2) changes the variable value relative to its last value. It is possible to obtain the current value of variable by implementing all transactions from the list. In other words, by summing up all changes made by every transaction:

$$s = s_0 + \sum_{i=1}^{n} \Delta s_i \tag{1}$$

The issueof this approach consists in uploading and processing the entire transaction list, whose size continuously increases. In order to resolve thisissuethe authors of this article proposeto fix(in Fig. 3 every $t = 2$ of blocks) the current value of the variable s on a regular basis in a special block. Let us call it a fixingblock.

This fixingblock does not store the changed values of variable, but its current values $s_0^{(k)}$ at the moment of recording block generation, which is similar to the block storing initial value of variable s_0 in the base model.

$$s_0^{(k)} = s_0^{(k-1)} + \sum_{i=1}^{n_{k-1}} \Delta s_i^{(k-1)} \tag{2}$$

n_{k-1} is the quantity of changes in the variable value between recording blocks $k-1$ and k.

Each fixingblock stores all required information about initial status of the system, therefore it can be used as a new genesisblock, which makes it possible to prune all the blocks that precede it. The fixingblock to be confirmed by a sufficient number of further blocks is selected as a new genesisblock. The genesisblock is not fixed and "floats further" with addition of new blocks.

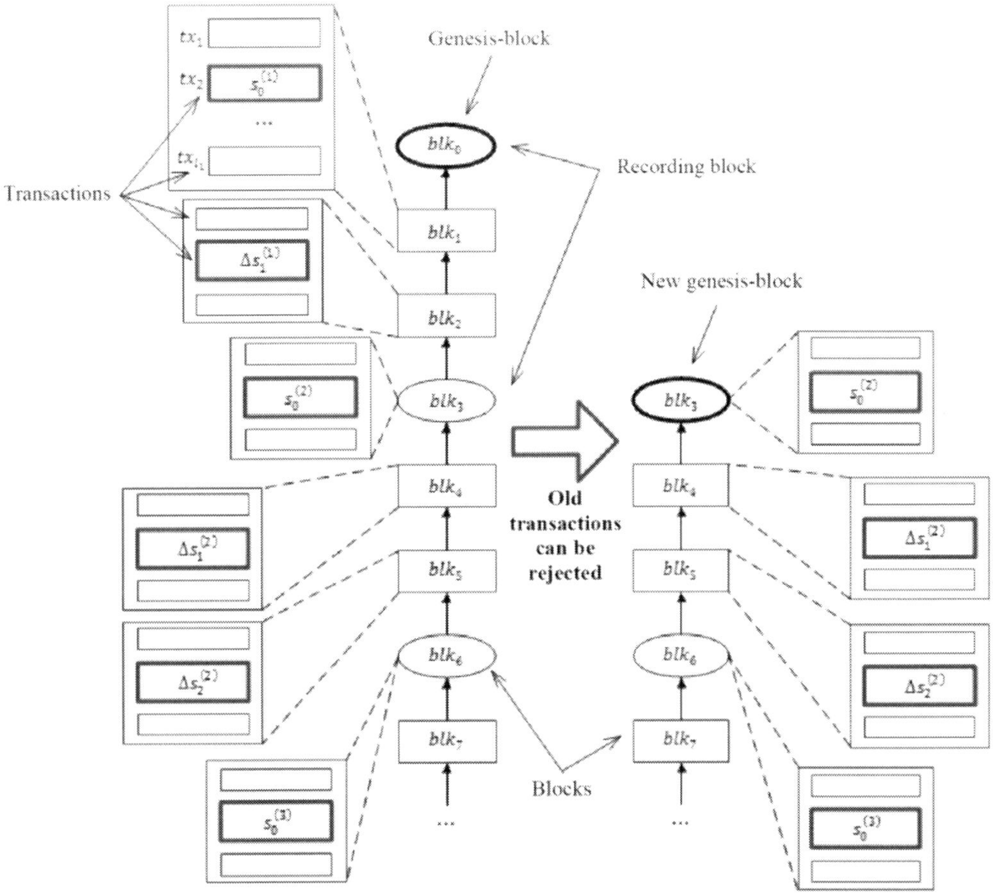

Fig. 3. Schematic block diagram of the blockchain with floating genesis-block.

It is possible to get the current value of variable s by implementing all transactions from the list in a successive order, starting from the fixingblock, which is a genesisblock:

$$s = s_0^{(k)} + \sum_{i=k}^{m} \sum_{j=1}^{n_i} \Delta s_j^{(i)} \tag{3}$$

m is the number of recording blocks after genesis block storing value $s_0^{(k)}$.

n_i is the number of changed variable values between fixing blocks i and $i+1$.

This proposed modification of the blockchain is vulnerable to an attack on new fully functional nodes and or those nodes that lost connection to the network for a long time (more than *t* blocks). While attacking the malicious node generates a fake blockchain beforehand and tries to send it on new nodes as a legitimate one.

An approach involving the blockchain download from trusted fully functional nodes is proposed for protection against this attack. In this case, the floating genesisblock will be protected by a digital signature of this trusted node. This approach allows avoiding storage of the block headers preceding the floating genesis-block by introducing a trust modeland decreasing the system decentralization.

Table 1 give the results of comparative analysis of existing methods for solving the blockchain growth issue with modification proposed in this paper. The number of variables, whose values are recorded in the blockchain as well as the transaction rateare assumed to be constant during this analysis.

Table 1. Comparative analysis of methods for continuously increasing of the blockchain.

	Necessity to download and verify of all blockchain transactions during startup of new fully functional node	**Blockchain size by time**	**Possible local access to blockchain**
S. Nakomoto's method	Yes	O(t)	Yes
Reduced size of serialized data	Yes	O(t)	Yes
Off-chain transactions	Yes	O(t)	Yes
Sharding	Yes	O(t)	No
Distributedhash-table	Yes	O(t)	No
Blockchain with floating genesis-block	No	O(1)	Yes

This comparative analysis shows that the blockchain with floating genesis block in distinction from earlier proposed fully functional nodes is worth considering. Considering that blocks are downloaded from trusted nodes this modification allows resolving the blockchain growth issue completely. This leads to reduced time required to add new nodes to the blockchain. However, the blockchain with floating genesis-block is applicable only to the cases when stale transactions can be deleted. The routing data of VANET/MANET networks features this property. At the end of a significant time interval the information about VANET/MANET networks and links between them lose its relevancy, which makes it possible to use the blockchain with floating genesis-block to protect the connectivity of networks of this type.

It should be noted that the solution proposedcan be used jointly with other methods considered in this article: reducing the blockchain serialized data, off-chain transactions and sharding.

4 Conclusion

The authors of this article have proposed a blockchain modification based on a floating genesisblock making it possible to resolve issuescaused by an unlimited growth of blockchain and apply secure routing protocols based on the Blockchain technology. Securerouting in its turn ensures that the VANET/MANETnetwork nodes connectionwith software defined security services as well as control the system as a whole.

References

1. C. Karlf, D. Wagner, Proc. 1st IEEE International Workshop on Sensor Network Protocols and Applications (2003)
2. W. Wang, B. Bhargava, M. Linderman, DNCMS (2009)
3. A.Busygin, A. Konoplev, Proc. of the 26th Research and technical conference on Methods and technical information security applications (2017)
4. S. Nakamoto, Bitcoin: A peer-to-Peer Electronic Cash System [online], Available at:https://bitcoin.org/bitcoin.pdf (2009)
5. ScaleChainblockchain compression[online], Available at:https://github.com/ScaleChain/scalechain/blob/master/data/docs/blockchain-compression.md(2016)
6. D. Bozhko, A. Troshichev, GOST N Blockchain: Compressed Signature and Public Key Recovery with GOST R 34.10-2012, Zero Nights [online], Available at: https://2017.zeronights.org/wp-content/uploads/materials/ZN17_Troshichev_GOST_COMPRESSED_SIGNATURE.pdf (2017)
7. J. Poon, T. Dryja, The Bitcoin Lightning Network: Scalable Off-Chain Instant Payments [online], Available at: https://lightning.network/lightning-network-paper.pdf (2016)
8. Raiden specification [online], Available at: https://raiden-network.readthedocs.io/en/stable/spec.html (2017)
9. L. Luu, V. Narayanan, C. Zheng, K. Baweja, S. Gilbert, P. Saxena, Proc. of the 2016 ACM SIGSAC Conference on Computer and Communications Security (2016)
10. A.E. Gencer, R. Renesse, E.G. Sirer, International Conference on Financial Cryptography and Data Security (2017)
11. Etheriumsharding specification [online], Available at: https://github.com/ethereum/sharding/blob /develop/docs/doc.md(2017)
12. M. Ali, J. Nelson, R. Shea, M.J. Freedman, USENIX ATC'16 (2016)

Homo Virtualis: existence in Internet space

Daria Bylieva[1*], *Victoria* Lobatyuk[1], and *Anna* Rubtsova[1]

[1] Peter the Great Saint Petersburg Polytechnic University, 195251 Polytechnicheskaya st. 29, Russian Federation

Abstract. The study of a person existence in Internet space is certainly an actual task, since the Internet is not only a source of innovation, but also the cause of society's transformations and the social and cultural problems that arise in connection with this. Computer network is global. It is used by people of different professions, age, level and nature of education, living around the world and belonging to different cultures. It complicates the problem of developing common standards of behavior, a system of norms and rules that could be widely accepted by all users. On the other hand, the Internet space can be viewed as a new form of existence where physical laws do not work, and in connection with this, social ones are often questioned. This paper focuses on how social norms regulate relations in Internet space. The authors represents the typology of deviant behavior in the network. The empirical basis of the research includes the sociological survey of students of the senior courses in the Institute of Computer Science and Technology of Peter the Great St. Petersburg Polytechnic University. Sociological survey allows to identify students' understanding of Internet space. The selection of students is conditioned by the fact that IT professionals are considered simultaneously as ordinary users of the network and as future professionals in this field.

Every day the number of internet users around the world is growing by tens of millions a month (at the beginning of 2018 it is already 4.1 billion [1]). The amount of time spent on the network is also rising today. Internet reality is becoming more important for a modern person. An increasing number of social processes are taking place in the network. E-commerce and online education, telemedicine, online public services are the most advanced areas of Internet technology. The qualitative nature of the changes associated with the widespread introduction of information technologies under the influence of Industry 4.0 and their impact on the social structure of society also lead to the emergence of new professions that are possible only in the Internet space. The rapid increase in time spent on the network is also associated with the pleasure obtained by one way or another (communication, playing, getting information of different kinds, creativity, etc.).

A huge variety of life spheres finds its application on the Internet. Every important thing for humanity is transferred there. The virtual space of the Internet aims to assemble the most complete reflection of physical space in the form of photo, audio, video and textual information.

*Corresponding author: bylieva_ds@spbstu.ru

On the one hand, expanding multimedia capabilities permit organizations to create virtual objects on the network that simulate the real presence. Virtual tours, three-dimensional panoramic images, maps with the effect of movement allow you to visit tourist attractions and museums. On the other hand, a large number of individuals are trying to put online the maximum number of photos of their environment. Not limited by reflection, the Internet space changes, complements and transforms reality.

Apparent similarity only misleads unsophisticated users. There is the space of mirages and simulacra, where the authentic and imaginary things have equal rights. In this sense, individuality becomes not identical to a person. V. Serkova,A. Pylkin, A. Safonova, J. Savitskaya prove: "the difference between reality and its reflection is included in the symbolic simulative game of the binary code with all attempts to "maintain" the reality resembling political economy or psychoanalysis. Reality is degenerated into the hyper reality, into "something that has been always reproduced" [2].

The Internet claims its rights as a new form of existence, not reducible to the particular case of physical space. The immateriality of the Internet allows us to interpret it within the framework of classical philosophical concepts. "Virtuality" can be viewed either as an objectively existing "world of ideas (Plato's Eidos)" or according to the Aristotelian line as "the mental state, operating the categories of actual and potential". According to this line, virtual reality presents some specific content of consciousness, short-term actualization of potential states of consciousness, which is excluded from the physical space of reality [3].

Internet reality is heterogeneous. It contains a lot of "worlds" and logics, sometimes contradicting each other. It is like a complex of imaginary individual products of many people The Internet can be filled with different discourses, objects and worlds. We know that M. Heidegger regarded imagination as the ability to contemplate without the subject [4].

O. Shipunova, I. Berezovskaya E. Gashkova suggest that the Internet produces a stream of texts and is perceived not as an ordered system, but as spontaneity in which everything originates spontaneously and the traditional limitations are removed. One of the essential features of the Internet space is the absence of obligatory general rules for the existence of virtual worlds and meanings [5]. The contradiction and the absence of unified rules make it possible to classify the Internet space as chaos (i.e. "oblivion of existence" as an ordered world).

The ideal (intangible) nature of the Internet generates advantages and complexities unaccustomed to the physical world. The most obvious example is the ability to share digital objects without losing them. The psychological consequence of this advantage is the intuitive rejection of the concept of property in the network. It leads, for example, to problems associated with illegal downloading music, films, games, programmes.

In the sphere of education, we see the cases when students copy other's intellectual property. Moreover, it is paradoxical for modern young people to complete the task themselves if the network has a solution. In the digital world, simple duplication is meaningless. The ability to find an answer in a network is recognized as a more valuable quality than the ability to solve the problem yourself. Teachers are faced with a situation where students prefer to spend a lot of time searching for a ready answer on the network than to decide it quickly on their own.

In addition, we should take into account the particular status of "presence" on the Internet. It would be very superficial to equate individual and someone who exists in the network. The difference is so great that it seems possible to introduce a new term describing the network manifestation of the person – Homo Virtualis. One individual can be represented on the network by several avatars / characters / communicators. A networked person may be presented not by one person but by several people or artificial intelligence. As Y. Shaev notes an individual tries to keep a distance between himself and the world of virtual narrative, to realize that all that happens to him in the virtual world – is an illusion [6]. "I" on the Internet is different from the real person, because a person plays a certain role. Accordingly, man sometimes perceives "life" on the Internet as a subjective reality occurring in his head or in a dream. A virtual person is the result of reconstruction in a network communicative space of a genuine or fictitious image, the ontology of whom is connected with the real subject. At the same time, Homo Virtualis does not have a material body and consists exclusively of signs and actions.

Z. Tufekci point out that the modern Internet, because of the growing popularity of social networks, has ceased to be a refuge for something without "the body, gender, race, and nationality, a place where we could evaluate each other as" ideas", approximately since 2004 "the "social" phase of the Internet came of age" [7].

However, the game element of the network has remained. Individuality existing on the network does not necessarily have to coincide with the personality outside the Internet. Today even such personality has been acquiring more certainty by having personal data and history of communication. Z. Tufekci notes that social networks do not hide, but disclose data about a person, even those which he does not want to be open to the audience: "have all combined to make the Internet productive of clashes between different social roles" [7].

New communication opportunities not only accelerate the processes of information exchange, they easily convert personal facts to public data. Any interpersonal or group communication can easily be shared with the public. Special pages on social networks (like "overheard") of various social groups and organizations reveal what they say behind closed doors, incidents and scandals instantly penetrate the network, often accompanied by photos, videos or screenshots of correspondence. Personal pages in social networks can be an excellent source of information if a person for some reason attracts attention.

On the other hand, there are "communicative tunnels", capable of tying people who could not meet and unite in real space. As K. E. Razlogov supposes "new latent identities" [8] are appearing connecting people with rare special interests that could never unite without information and communication technologies. Moreover, G. Karimova &A. Shirkhanbeik claim that it is even possibleto speak about "a community of things", which is defined as "any group of things that shares common goals or interests and creates a social universe with its own values, rules, and vocabulary that is in a constant transformation and communication within time/space matrix" [9].

E. E. Taratuta considers: "the subordinate status of virtual reality ("non-reality") means that it is not completely determined by the social rules and mechanisms. Therefore it is beyond the sphere of ontological responsibility" [10]. Physical laws do not operate in the Internet. Moreover, social rules are questioned. Virtual reality (regarded by us as a special kind of graphical user interface which presents a computer-generated immersive, three-dimensional, interactive environment) has its own logic, including the legal aspects (there may be hyper-realistic gambling murders, abductions, thefts, etc.). Very often perception of what is happening as an illusion or a game removes the limitations of the moral order.

If you turn into the communicative space of the network in the form of social networks, forums, etc., you will see that the boundaries of what is allowed are noticeably expanding. The severity of the discussions intensifies, deliberate provocations (trolling) and various types of fraud, including those related to the substitution of identity take place, etc. In the network space, the concept of deception loses its certainty. According to the prevailing views, it can not be considered a hoax if you try to hide in the network your true identity. However, there is the question: how to interpret the fact of appropriation of another's identity through photographs and / or names, even if there is no any economic gain. . The treatment of virtual characters in general seems to be a purely game area, not regulated by any social norms, until it turns out that, for example, the person being shot looks like a clearly recognizable man.L. Evseeva and others suppose that today the impossibility of virtual control and identification online swindlers, terrorist groups, religion sects, mentally disordered persons and charlatans frighten Society [11].

Any activity on the Internet is not only regulated by technical rules and capabilities, but can also be assessed in terms of compliance with legal and ethical standards. Moral law and moral responsibility are in a complex relationship with legal responsibility and with the legal rights of the user. While some researchers consider the implementation of the legal law to be a minimum requirement of morality, others question the ethical validity of certain laws, which in practice are often violated by computer users. Not only ordinary users, but also a number of representatives of the scientific community, defend the view that copying programs for non-commercial purposes can be morally permissible, even if it contradicts the law.

For example, in 2011 the site "Sci-Hub" was created to enable scientists to get acquainted with scientific research without having to pay expensive subscriptions. The creator of the site believes that laws on copyright close access to knowledge for most people, bringing enormous economic benefits to some individuals. When a request is made on the site, it is checked whether there is a required scientific work in the database. If there is no such scientific work, then the algorithm bypasses the paywall on the website of the publisher or the necessary journal. In May 2017 Sci-Hub's offerings included 56,246,220 articles from the corpus of scholarly literature, equating to 68.9% of all articles [13]. Studies show that this resource is used by the scientific community around the world, and the leaders in the number of downloads were Iran, China, India, Russia and the United States [13].

Today, many communication platforms of the network establish ethical rules or codes, which administrators or moderators can follow, and in practical user guides one can find information about "network etiquette". The opportunities of the global computer network are used by people of various professions, age, level and education, living in different countries and belonging to different cultures. All these facts complicate the problem of developing common standards of behavior, a system of ethical norms that could be widely accepted throughout the world. However, many researchers insist on the relevance of such a system today, infusing that understandable and feasible "traffic rules" are required for both amateurs and professionals working in the network.

Let's look at the process of regulating relations according to social norms in the Internet space. It is also important to find out the borderline between modern legislative regulation and the area of morality roughly. In the suggested scheme, two types of actions in the network that damage society are identified: misappropriation or attack (damage). The most law-governed types of misdeed in the network are economic crimes (fraud with bank cards (carding), notifications sent by quasi administrators of payment systems or from the bank, from quasi mail servers or from social networks for the purpose of obtaining passwords (phishing), and other methods of stealing electronic money). The object of the crime may not be money, but confidential information, which is a trade secret, personal information, including passwords and user data.

Particularly controversial is the issue of restrictions on the dissemination of information. On the one hand, the value of the Internet is evident as a space most adapted for an open exchange of views among a multitude of interested parties. On the other hand, there is information that can cause harm. For example, an Internet crime is the creation, distribution, and in some countries, viewing information related to child pornography. The most difficult problem is the question of political wars in the network, when the Internet is used for misinformation, manipulation, inciting conflicts, creating extremist groups. The government in this case resorts to various forms of censorship, up to blocking the Internet and arrests of users. However, modern software allows you to bypass network locks. Use of "fake news", automated "bot" accounts has been acting for many years. However, over the last few years, the practice has become significantly more widespread and technically sophisticated, with bots, propaganda producers, and fake news outlets exploiting social media and search algorithms to ensure high visibility and seamless integration with trusted content [14]. However, information wars in the network can not be evaluated from the standpoint of ordinary social norms, as actions during the war can not be estimated from the point of view of the legislation and morality of peacetime.

Consider the results of the sociological survey conducted by the authors in September-November 2017. The goal was to find out students' view of the Internet space in the Institute of Computer Science and Technology of Peter the Great St. Petersburg Polytechnic University. An interesting part of the study is about the students' attitude to the future professions in the IT sector, presented in the Atlas of new professions. [14] According to the forecasts of researchers, in the next 10 years there will be technologies of very accurate recognition of Internet users online. It will be possible to track almost every click. Technologies from spyware and science fiction films can become a reality. It will be possible to identify the user of the device not only by scanning fingerprints or retina, but also by DNA analysis. Thus, this can lead to the fact that the boundaries between virtuality and the physical world will be blurred. It means that society in the digital space will be organized according to the same principles as the real society including state borders and government control. At the same time, a "digital gap" between people (in the level of computer literacy) will create a new kind of social stratification. Following this logic, there will be the legislation regulating cyberspace. "Electronic governments" will begin to work in full force and become much more interactive. However, are young specialists ready for such changes and how do they see the future in IT sphere. Already today, N-Tech. Lab has developed technology that allows you to find a profile in a social network in less than a second with an accuracy of 70%, which creates opportunities not only for dating but also for police investigations.

Respondents were the students of the senior courses of the Institute of Computer Science and Technology of Peter the Great St. Petersburg Polytechnic University. The choice of respondents' data was due to the possibility of considering IT specialists simultaneously as ordinary users of the network and future professionals in this field.

The sample set for the questionnaire survey of students was formed on the basis of a quota sample (N = 300 respondents). The sample of the survey was proportional to the specialties presented in the institute: fundamental informatics and information technologies, software and administration of information systems, computer science and computer technology, information systems and technologies, software engineering, applied informatics, information security, computer security, information security of automated systems, information-analytical security systems, instrumentation, quality management, system analysis and management, management in technical systems, innovation. In most cases, students were interviewed individually. In terms of quality, this survey approached a standardized interview. This provided a high degree of representativeness of the collected information. The socio-demographic and professional characteristics of the interviewed students are as follows: among the respondents 62% have a permanent job in their speciality, 13% have a part time job in their speciality (freelancers) and 25% – do not work. The gender composition of the respondents: men – 68%, women – 32%. Age structure: 20-22 years – 88%, 23-25 years – 12%.

Respondents were asked to choose the most interesting and least realistic profession in their opinion from the Atlas. [12] According to the results of the survey, such professions as the curator of information security, the IT-auditor, the developer of Big data models and the architect of information systems became popular. Particularly it is interesting that 95% of respondents claimed a cyber-researcher i.e. an expert in the investigation of cybercrime the least realistic profession. Giving reasons to their position, the students referred either to the professional level (a stable view of the possibility to hide any of their actions on the Internet), or to the division of responsibility between the real and virtual worlds (punishment for action in the network can not go beyond it), or to the impossibility to organize society in the digital space on the same principles as in realness (the Internet as a zone of freedom). Thus, we see that young people do not believe that the virtual space of the network can be subject to legislative regulation.

This study also confirms the hypothesis that the virtual world is perceived by most users as not existing in the material world, hence the problem of the norms of existence in this reality arises. The less the connection of a particular area of the Internet with the physical world, the less rigid norms there are. There is a desire not to transfer the laws and morals of society to the Internet, leave this space free of sanctions for any actions and penalties from the state. It seems that a real person is not identical with a virtual person and therefore should not be punished for his actions outside the virtual framework. Separately, it is worth paying attention to the very concept of a virtual person, who is he? We imagine him without a material body; the "I" exists only in the virtual space of the network. However, this concept needs a more detailed study in the scientific world and the constant improvement of the definition in accordance with the development of the Internet, virtual reality, robotics, machine learning and artificial intelligence.

References

1. Internet World Stats Internet usage statistics [online], Available at: http://www.internetworldstats.com/stats.htm (2018)
2. V. Serkova, A. Pylkin, A. Safonova, J. Savitskaya, EpSBS, **35** (2018)
3. E. Gashkova, I.Berezovskaya, O. Shipunova, EpSBS, **35** (2018)
4. A.A. Shadov, St. Petersburg State Polytechnical University Journal. Humanities and Social Sciences, **8 (2)**(2017)
5. O.D. Shipunova, I.P. Berezovskaya, E.M. Gashkova, St. Petersburg State Polytechnical University Journal. Humanities and Social Sciences, **8 (3)**(2017)
6. Y. Shaev, Logos Universality Mentality Education Novelty: Philosophy and Humanistic Sciences, **3 (1)** (2015)
7. Z. Tufekci, Public culture,**26 (1)** (2014)
8. K.E. Razlogov, Voprosy Filosofii, **7** (2015)
9. G. Karimova, A. Shirkhanbeik, Cogent Social Sciences, **1** (2015)
10. E.E. Taratuta,*The philosophy of virtual reality* (St Petersburg State University, St Petersburg,2007)
11. L. Evseeva, J. Obukhova, A. Tanova, SGEM, **1** (2017)
12. D. S. Himmelstein, A. R. Romero, S. R. McLaughlin, B. G. Tzovaras, C. S.eLife; **7**(2018)
13. J. Bohannon, Science, **352 (6285)** (2016)
14. Manipulating Social Media to Undermine Democracy. Freedom on the Net 2017 [online], Available at:https://freedomhouse.org/report/freedom-net/freedom-net-2017 (2017)
15. Atlas of Emerging Jobs [online], Available at: http://atlas100.ru/ (2018)

Factories of the future: operation and perspectives of development

Paul Chang[1], *Diana* Kaledina[2], *Anatoly* Popovich[3], and *Andrey* Volkov[3*]

[1] Buffalo Machinery Co., Ltd. 428-46, 56, Lane 318, Desheng Road, Daya District, Taiwan
[2] JSC "Baltic Industrial Company", 188660, Leningrad region, Vsevolozhsk region, building 1, office 212, street of 28th km of Ring highway, Russian Federation
[3] National Technological Initiatives Center "New Industrial Technologies" of Peter the Great St. Petersburg Polytechnic University, 195251, Polytechnicheskaya st., 29, Russian Federation

Abstract. The role of automation in industrial development was highlighted. We discussed the significance of automation for creating the factory of the future. We presented the basic criteria of efficiency of automated factories. We analyzed the experience of creating automated factories, indicated the basic scientific-technical problems related to automation of production and suggested the ways to overcome them. We listed the basic factors of scientific-technical progress that should be the basis for automation of production and indicated its basic elements. We showed the role of technological equipment, tools and accessories. We analyzed the results of state support of industry.

Creating the "factory of the future" is primarily characterized by a high level of automation of production and has been a popular idea throughout the entire history of industrial development [1].

The idea of automation was especially popular during the last three decades of the USSR. It would be a major mistake to discard the experience accumulated in that sphere. Automation of production is primarily based of the theory of productivity of machines and labor presented in the works by professor G. A. Shaumian in 1946 [1]. The keystone of this theory is the notion of the growth rate in the productivity of social labor that was used as the basic index in all the directives of the communist party of the USSR. The expression "social labor" implied considering all the costs for manufacturing the commodity, including the cost of creating the equipment and constructing production facilities. This theoretical criterion of efficiency of automation, which was used throughout the period of the developed socialism, is unquestionable.

The notion of the "factory of the future" is close to the notions "FAP" (Flexible Automated Production), FPS (Flexible Production System), FMS (Flexible Manufacturing System) and CAM (Computer-Aided Manufacturing) introduced during the late XX century [2]. The keyword here is the term "flexibility". Creating a modern automated production system is time-consuming and costly, whereas the "period of usefulness" of many commodities is conditioned by fashion and scientific-technical progress. In most cases, a new factory has to be created before the particular image of the object of manufacturing can be

* Corresponding author: volkov-and-1@yandex.ru

detailed. It is this property of flexibility makes it possible to adapt the production system to quickly-changing situations. At the same time, the rate of change in the conditions tends to increase.

The fundamental basis of the "factory of the future" is a universal digital control platform for all the stages of creating the product: from R&D to testing the ready product. Undoubtedly, it is an important direction in creating modern factories, but it is not the key factor in developing up-to-date industry. For the first time, the basic scientific provisions for automation on the basis of all-through computerization of designing and production in the USSR were formulated in the research made under supervision of S. A. Mayorov and G. V. Orlovsky and published in 1983 in the Leningrad branch of "Mashinostroyeniye" publishing house [3].

For the first time in our country, the attempts to implement this concept were made within the framework of an ambitious "Targeted complex territorial-industrial development program for Leningrad and Leningrad district on the basis of automation with the wide use of computer technologies for the period 1984–1985 and up to 1990" that was named "Intensification-90" [4]. The experience of creating FPS in the USSR within the framework of this program that was spread throughout the country without proper consideration was quite negative for most industries. Erroneous and dogmatic financial and material investment into industry thoroughly undermined the economic potential of the country. The reasons for failure were the following: firstly, the ill-considered selection of technological processes for implementation in FPS, whereas the efficiency of their automation could vary tenfold depending on their physical essence, with similar costs; secondly, the type of production was not taken into consideration (mass, serial or single-item production), which affects the degree of flexibility of the equipment, and, therefore, its cost; thirdly, the level of automation was raised without good reason, even though specialists have known for a long time that each next stage of automation is less efficient than the previous one; fourthly, creating sophisticated technical systems was done in one stage, which unreasonably extended the period required for the FPS to reach the full production capacity or, sometimes, due to low reliability of particular sub-systems, it was not achieved at all.

For example, an FPS with a high level of automation for manufacturing printed circuit boards is efficient with any type of production. Circuit boards can easily be universalized, the production is highly fail-safe and the components are highly standardized. On the other hand, creating a highly-automated FPS (in one stage only) for small-series mechanic processing of cast billets is problematic. The main particular feature of such production is a wide or weakly predictable nomenclature of products, the ratio between the cost of automation of the main and secondary processes, as well as a significant difference between the input of the of the main and secondary processes in the overall labor consumption and, therefore, in the cost of a particular product.

The analysis of the accumulated experience shows that, during creation of modern production systems, the following provisions should be considered:

Firstly, the nomenclature of production should be thoroughly examined with consideration of the possible variability of technological processes and perspectives of scientific-technical development of the particular industry.

Secondly, the introduction of the equipment into operation should be stage-wise so as to ensure the adequate increase in the level of automation. For example, for metal processing, the following sequence of commissioning can be proposed: the basic technological equipment – computer-controlled machine tools, automated storage spaces system, automated dispatching system, automated transport, automated accumulation storage systems, industrial robots. Stage-wise implementation of the project makes it possible to adjust production technologies one after another as well as significantly cut down the single-investment amount while preserving high economic efficiency (productivity of the social labor). For this example, the main problem is selection of the nomenclature and the amount of the processing equipment units. The basis for approaching the above problem was given in the works by professor A. P. Sokolovsky on classifying the machine parts and typification of the corresponding technological processes for mass production during 1939-1955 [5]. The final stage of this process – automation of transportation and cargo handling – can be quite costly, but with little decrease in the production cost (the growth of productivity of the social labor).

Analyzing the state of domestic machine engineering, we cannot ignore the key issue of the modern tools and technological accessories. For example, the industrial magazine "Stankoinstrument" published an editor's comment stating the advent of the long-awaited industrial revolution in metal processing" symbolized by development of the platform CoroPlus manufactured by Sandvik Coromand, the world leader in metal processing. The authors of the concept think that it will ensure unprecedented progress. The system CoroPlus implies integration of all the tools sensors, algorithms, analytical capabilities and cloud technologies in one system and it does not pay a lot of attention to tools proper, its design and material. One of the leading specialists in the theory of cutting, professor of Michigan university V. P. Astakhov states that the reserve for increasing the durability of tools and the productivity of processing is determined by its design. In his works, he indicated the significant errors in the theory of processing by cutting that have been confirmed by experiments and are still relevant [3, 6].

The significance of creating high-quality tools and accessories to increase the productivity of labor and efficiency of machine-tools were brilliantly reflected in the report of the people's commissary of heavy machinery engineering V. A. Malyshev in the XIX congress of VKPb in 1939 [7]. However, the issue with Russian-made tools and accessories still remains unsolved. So it seems that a very important problem of diagnosing the state of the cutting surfaces has suddenly become prevalent over the tool itself, its design and material.

Another issue regards the problems of automated designing of technological processes. In most cases, they are not related to the problems of automation of the production processes and can be easily implemented in a stage-wise manner, with consideration of nomenclature and type of production. It is easy to purchase a complete software set for the design-technological department, but ensuring its efficient use is often very problematic because of the functional redundancy or a stage-wise manner of implementation.

Creating the "smart factories", as they are called, is very interesting and perspective in the scientific aspect, but their economic efficiency in the RF at the present moment is doubtful. The industry requires factories with a balanced set of technological equipment and accessories to manufacture competitive product for the Russian market that should greatly exceed the share of the export. The basis for the industry of the present and the future is still using the metal processing machine-tools and technological accessories. During the latest years, the Ministry of Industry and Trade has been attempting to change the tide and ensure a steady growth in productivity of modern machine-tools and equipment. The schemes of state support have not been sufficiently elaborated for this task to be solved.

At the present time, "smart factories" are a scientific "hi-tech" rather than the actual necessity for the Russian economy. Development of this concept is undoubtedly important, but it should not substitute the actual market demands for industrial development. So, the attention to the overall "computerization and cloud technologies in production" can be given after the factory itself has been created. It is no good to provide unconditional state financial support of such "high-tech" directions in the amounts exceeding the support of the actual, not virtual equipment, tools and accessories, so as to avoid the mistakes made by the program "Intensification-90" that were spread throughout the country and contributed to the collapse of the soviet economy.

Separate attention should be paid to the foreign experience and equipment. Industrial development requires significant modernization of the existing technologies, as well as creating new ones. Additive technologies play a significant role here.

Additive technologies (AT), or technologies of layer-wise synthesis, are currently one of the perspective production processes that have been actively developing. They provide engineers with an innovative approach to designing and manufacturing, as compared to the traditional methods of casting and metal-cutting.

In many cases, using additive technologies provides more flexibility in selecting the configuration of the article, which makes it possible to optimize the weight and functionality of the article due to using complex 3D shapes, designing thinner walls, as well as combining several functional parts so as to manufacture them as a single article [8]. It is noteworthy that the time required to manufacture the pilot articles is much shorter (the R&D stage is shorter), and the material consumption is smaller.

Additive technologies is a generic name for the technologies of manufacture by the data of the digital model (a CAD model) by the method of layer-wise adding of the material (whence the name, "additive").

The article is created in the layer-wise manner by forming one after another layer of some or other material that is hardened or fixed in accordance with the configuration of the CAD model and joining each subsequent layer to the previous one [9, 10].

The companies manufacturing the equipment for using additive methods have given various names to these technologies [9]. Due to this, there is some uncertainty in the literature as to the names of various technologies. In order to solve this question, the American organization ASTM International (American Society for Testing and Materials) dealing in development of technical standards for a wide range of materials, articles, systems and services, recommended two basic terms – Additive Fabrication (AF) and Additive Manufacturing (AM), as well as their "legitimate" synonyms, such as "additive processes", "additive techniques", "additive layer manufacturing", "layer manufacturing" and "freeform fabrication". They all have the Russian equivalents "additive technologies", "additive manufacturing", as well as the "technologies of layer-wise synthesis".

AT can be classified according to the following characteristics: the model materials selected (liquid, granular, sheets, threads); the method of forming the layer; the method of hardening or fixing the layer etc.

Attention to additive technologies, "direct build-up" of metal articles, as an alternative to the traditional technological methods of manufacture, was first drawn in the aircraft, spacecraft and power-generating engineering industry. The motive was economic plausibility. Additive technologies are often less costly than the traditional technologies, and they often provide new capabilities for manufacturing. For example, it can allow manufacturing parts and die mold having complex 3D shapes, with cooling channels of arbitrary configuration, which cannot be done with the traditional methods of mechanical processing [11].

Additive technologies have some limitations and drawbacks of their own [12]:

- currently, they can only be used with a limited range of materials;
- in some cases, supporting structures are required, and they need to be removed from the finished item afterwards;
- the size of the manufactured article is limited to the size of the working chamber of the particular manufacturing installation.

At the present time, the convenience of additive technologies is a confirmed fact. Besides the lower costs of manufacture, additive technologies make it possible to significantly shorten the period for obtaining the final product. Manufacturing can be started immediately upon completion of the design stage. No rigging is necessary. Therefore, the period from designing to obtaining the final product can be shortened from several weeks to several days [12].

Currently, large foreign companies dealing in aircraft manufacturing are actively developing and implementing additive technologies into their technological processes. In particular, the company Boeing has created a large R&D facility for additive technologies in St.-Louis. It deals in manufacturing prototypes from polymeric materials, as well as the ready parts of gas-turbine engines. For example, this company uses additive technologies for manufacturing inlet channels for engines of high-altitude aircraft. This made it possible to manufacture and dispatch the parts to the customer in two hours after receiving the order.

The company Airbus uses the technology of selective laser melting to reduce the weight of a swivel joint by using strong but lightweight meshed structures (Fig. 1) [13].

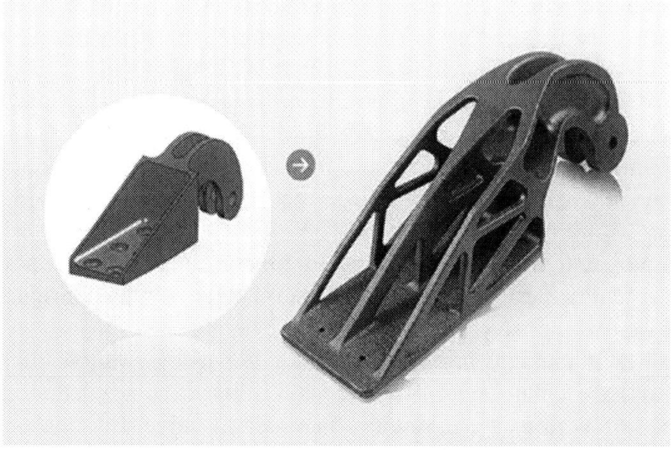

Fig. 1. A swivel joint before and after optimizing the design for additive manufacturing [13]

At the moment, GE Aviation have completely transferred the process of manufacturing nozzles of gas-turbine engines to additive technologies. The company GE uses 300 installations, and is planning to manufacture more than 100 thousand parts using additive technologies by the year 2020 [14].

The California-based company SpaceX widely used additive technologies to build their "Super Draco" engine for the next-generation spacecraft Dragon V2. In particular, the combustion chamber was manufactured using 3D printing methods [15]. The American agency (NASA) is pioneering the use of additive technologies for manufacturing parts for the space truck Space Launch System [16].

Fundamental research in the leading countries to develop methods and algorithms to use the capabilities provided by additive technologies have brought about a new class of systems – named "hybrid systems" – that use the advantages of both the additive and the subtractive technologies (machining, drilling, milling etc.) requiring no labor-consuming post-processing.

For example, a Japanese-German company DMG-MORI (the Japanese machine-building company MORI SEIKI CO. and the German machine-tool manufacturer Gildemeister AG) created a hybrid installation LASERTEC 65 3D (Fig. 2) [17].

Fig. 2. A hybrid installation DMG MORI LASERTEC 65 3D [17].

At the present time, many companies worldwide are developing their own models of production equipment to use similar technological principles.

This type of installations can fully utilize the idea of the "factories of the future" from the technological viewpoint, and it completely complies with the concept "Industry 4.0".

References

1. G. A. Shaumyn (ed.), *Autamatization of production processes* (High school Publ., Moscow, 1967)
2. S. A. Maiorova, G. V. Orlovskiy (eds), *Flexible autoamatic production* (Mashinostroenie, Leningrad, 1983)
3. V. P. Astakhov, Izvestiya TulGU. Technical sciences. **8** (2016)
4. S.G. Lagushkin, Scientific and technical news SPBPU. St. Petersburg State Polytechnical University Journal. Humanities and Social Sciences **4 (208)** (2014)
5. G. P. Sokolovskiy, *Scientific fundamentals of the technology of machinery manufacturing*. (State scientific-technical publishing house machinery manufacturing literature, Moscow, 1955)
6. Hill R, Journal of the Mechanics and Physics of Solids. **3** (1954)
7. Verbatim report. XVIII Congress of the Communist Party. March 10-21, 1939 (OGIZ, Moscow, 1939)
8. S. Hashmi, *ComprehensiveMaterialsProcessing*. (Newnes, 2014)
9. M. Zlenko, A. A. Popovich, I. N. Mutylina, *Additive technologies in machinery manufacturing*. (Publishing Politech. University, Saint Petersburg, 2013)
10. E. C. Santos, et al. Int. J. Mach. Tools Manuf. **46(12-13)** (2006)
11. V. M. Dovbysh, P. V. Zabednov, M. A. Zlenko, *Additive technologies and goods made of metal* (FGUP "NAMI", Moscow, 2014)
12. E. Atzeni, A. Salmi, Int. J. Adv. Manuf. Technol. **62(9-12)** (2012)

13. TCT Magazine [online], Available at: http://www.tctmagazine.com/additive-manufacturing/eos-and-airbus-group-innovations-join-forces-on-study-for-3d/ (2018)
14. GE [online], Available at: http://www.ge.com/stories/advanced-manufacturing (2018)
15. SpaceX [online], Available at: http://www.spacex.com/press/2014/05/27/spacex-completes-qualification-testing-superdraco-thruster (2014)
16. NASA [online], Available at: http://www.nasa.gov/exploration/systems/sls/selective_melting.html (2018)
17. DMG-MORI [online], Available at: http://en.dmgmori.com/ (2018)

Model of the omni-channel Interaction in the Web 4.0 environment

Anna Chernikova[1] , *Sergey* Krasnov[1*], and *Sergey* Sergeyev[1]

[1] Peter the Great St. Petersburg Polytechnic University, Institute of Industrial Management, Economics and Trade, 195251, Politechnicheskaya st., 29, Russian Federation

Abstract. The practical implementation of the concept "Industry 4.0" entirely depends on the level of coordination between businesses, organizations and the entire group of consumers. The dominating comprehension of such interaction as a net of complex topology where nodes act as objects that have an interface a surface for contacts, results in a neuro-net-concept or the Web 4.0. Within the framework of the Russian national program "National Technological Initiative", the development of this direction is considered as one of the main priorities. The quality of implementation of the system interaction in this paradigm is greatly influenced by algorithms used in the cloud servers of the nodes included into the structure of the Web 4.0. Besides, operation of businesses in the conditions of global markets will take place in the situation of strict competition and solutions forming the basis of the software have to be based on the scientific approach with the use of the methods of optimization and mathematical models. As the competition in the commercial sphere turned into the contest between the economic efficiency of on-line platforms, this work proposes a particular implementation of the algorithm of omni-channel interaction formed on the basis of a mathematical model.

Interaction with the outer environment of every economical subject including both industrial plants and service organizations [1], as well as commercial wholesale and retail networks, can be evaluated using a lot of various reference values. The primary task of managers of these organizations consists in finding ways of the most efficient use of their business' potential, as well as covering the maximum number of consumers. The omni-channel interaction implements the front-edge technologies [2] of the digital economy. First of all, we should note the intrinsic possibility to work with large numbers of customers sometimes even with exact personality. Besides, we should take into consideration the possibility to use the entire history of the customer's preferences and purchases. This issue, as well as implementation of the technologies of targeted approach [3, 4], make it possible to formalize the process of mutual influence of the basic indexes of the business performance and use a well-developed set of mathematical methods to take optimal decisions [5].

* Corresponding author: hsm.krasnov@gmail.com

While selecting the strategy of interaction of the business in the Web 4.0 environment [6], it is, first of all, necessary to rely upon the development of information technologies, Internet networks, XaaS solutions [7], SIM solutions, search engines co-operation with advertising providers, aggregators' sites. Besides, we need to take into consideration the domination of integrated digital systems in the market. At the same time, online processing of any kinds of interactions [8], including payments, led to deep changes in the architecture of business in all the spheres. This was primarily made possible due to system integration of interaction models of corporative systems of CRM (Customer Relationship Management), ERP (Enterprise Resource Planning), as well as the operation [9] in the mode M2M (Machine-to-Machine). The growing role of online sales, the increased use of virtual sites has brought about the paradigm of omni-channel interaction. At the same time, the growing competition in the large network business environment puts forward the task to use all the management tools with maximum efficiency to communicate with the customers. Such activity is made still more difficult due to instability of the business environment [10]. Planning even for a period as short as 2-3 years ahead has become a serious task [11] that would require employing a DEA (Data Envelopment Analysis) method. This forms a basis for improving business processes, optimizing the corresponding surfaces of digital data, transform the methods of communication with the customers.

The proper transition to omni-channel interaction was only made possible due to development of both the Web 3.0 technologies and the combination of alternative channels making it possible to interact with the identified customers with consideration of their locations. The main part in this process was played by mobile applications having the maximum degree of convertibility and promotional activity. Today, in various business spheres, impressive results have been achieved in using omni-channel communication. In particular [12], the company Walt Disney Parks and Resorts Worldwide, Inc. specializing in tourism and recreation controls hotels, entertainment parks and sports complexes was able to integrate all the different communication channels into one digital system to communicate with both the existing and the prospective customers. At the same time, they also use the capabilities of customers' smartphones, the data of GPS-tracking, customers' authorization and other components [13] aimed at both loyalty enforcement and new customers' acquisition. Due to the fact that, at the current stage of business development, aimed at maximizing the number of customers [14], there is no alternative to omni-channel technology; methods need to be developed [15] that would make it possible to evaluate the economic efficiency of the created virtual platform [16] and the loyalty level of the identified customer. This will also make it possible to optimize the operating format and services matrix.

In this work we modelled the business segment and offered three variants of interaction with customers: advertising, presentations, market monitoring. Even though these kinds of activities were chosen conditionally, to a large extent, they reflect the largest expenditures in reality. As all the mathematical formulas are scalable, it is easy to increase the scale of the equations in the model [17] as defined through the number of arguments. Let us set the task, define the basic descriptors and introduce the corresponding notation.

Let us introduce formalism for the model of commercial activity comprising S nodes (business branches). Before the beginning of the reporting period, the top managers approve the plans for the budget. It is necessary to consider all the possible investment variants. Basing on the analysis of the reports from the previous period and the statistics of the reports for similar commercial networks, it is known that, if an amount of money v_j was invested in advertising or in the network branch with number j, where $j = 1, 2, ..., s$, the profit from such activity can be described by function $P_j(v_j)$. If an amount w_j was invested into the relevant branches for presentations, the expected profit will be $Q_j(w_j)$.

Monitoring of customers' market preferences, depending on the location of the branch j as a network component, with the amount of investment x_j will, in accordance with our investigation results, bring the future profit during the next reporting period according to the function $R_j(x_j)$. The budget of a branch depends on its size, turnover, distinctive matrix, the level of post-sale service. Correspondingly, the amount of financing for improving the interaction with customers is limited to the sum L_j, where $j=1,2,...,s$. The consolidated budget for the entire set of measures for all the branches is also limited to the total sum N.

It is necessary to distribute the investment in the optimal way [18] between the branches of the network and calculate their values for all the three directions. The criterion here is the maximum of the total profit of the commercial network. The marker limits are the maximum allowable expenditures L_j and N.

In the formal way, this task can be recorded as the search for the maximum of the composite function of the kind: $\sum_{j=1}^{s}\left[P_j(v_j)+Q_j(w_j)+R_j(x_j)\right]$ in the presence of the set levels of the total amount of finance for the measures

$$\sum_{j=1}^{s}(v_j+w_j+x_j)\le N \tag{1}$$

and the budget limit for branch number j of the commercial network:

$$(v_j+w_j+x_j)\le L_j,\ j=1,2,...,s. \tag{2}$$

It also should be considered that the values v_j, w_j, x_j have to fit the inequalities (the non-negativeness condition):

$$v_j\ge 0\quad, w_j\ge 0\quad, x_j\ge 0\qquad \text{for all the values } j=1,2,...,s \tag{3}$$

While solving the equation, it is necessary to determine and formalize the uncertainty of functioning [19] of such complex economical object as a commercial network. This will make it possible to form algorithms to take managerial decisions, with the efficiency criteria [20] being the profit maximization.

This task belongs to the class of problems of discreet optimization [21]. One of the most universal methods of their solving is the dynamic programming method. In this particular case, completely plausible are both Bellman's principle and the possibility for consecutive analysis. Let us present the problem of budget selection as a concept of a discreet controllable system [22] and let us formulate the corresponding recurrent relations. The advantage of such approach to the problem is also the possibility to insert the obtained algorithm for searching the optimal solution into the well-spread CRM and ERP solutions that are the basis for the concept [23] "The Industry 4.0".

During the analysis of the formalized formulation of the problem, we can note that the limit (1) is imposed as a whole on all the arguments of the model, and the inequality (2) relates to the local sums of finance of the branch number j of the commercial network.

To formulate the task in the terms of the dynamic programming, it is necessary to introduce notation $g_j(n)$ – the function of the profit maximum with the optimal distribution of the sum n among $j=1,2,...,s$ brunches in the network. Then we can record the recurrent relation of the dynamic programming as follows:

$$g_j(n)=\max\left[P_j(v_j)+Q_j(w_j)+R_j(x_j)+g_{j-1}(n-v_j-w_j-x_j)\right] \tag{4}$$

where $j=1,2,...,s$ and the notation $n=0,1,2,....,N$ is adopted, and only non-negative integer values v_j,w_j,x_j participate the optimization, and they correspond the limiting inequality $(v_j+w_j+x_j)\le\min(L_j,n)$.

Further on, to solve the multidimensional optimization task [24], we will transform the obtained equations of the mathematical models. We can present these equations as a search for the maximum of the sum:

$$P_j(v_j)+Q_j(w_j)+R_j(x_j) \tag{5}$$

On condition that the following limitation is observed:

$$(v_j+w_j+x_j)\le y \tag{6}$$

and the non-negativeness v_j,w_j,x_j among the values of the natural row of numbers.

We will search for the solution for each value of the auxiliary variable y that can take values: $y=0,1,....,L_j$. Then we can introduce the function

$$p_j(y)=P_y(y_j),\ y=0,1,....,L_j \tag{7}$$

and apply the recurrent method to the task (5, 6). We will transform (4) into the form:

$$g_j(y)=\max_{w_j}\left[Q_j(w_j)+p_j(y-w_j)\right],\ y=0,1,....,L_j \tag{8}$$

where the search of the optimal solution will be carried out only by the values $w_j\le y$, and the condition:

$$r_j(y)=\max_{x_j}\left[R_j(x_j)+q_j(y-x_j)\right],\ y=0,1,....,L_j \tag{9}$$

The result will be the value $p_j(y)$ from (7) and (8) for each j in the process of the search for $q_j(y)$. Accordingly, for the values $r_j(y)$ under $y=0,1,....,L_j$, the search will be carried out by the values of the functions $q_j(y)$ and the condition (9). We will transform (4) and the result will be obtained from the solution of the ratio: $g_j(n)=\max_y\left[r_j(y)+g_{j-1}(n-y)\right]$, $j=1,2,...,s$, where $n=,1,...,N$. The additional condition is that: $y\le\min(L_j,n)$ under $j=1,2,...,s$.

The obtained solution to the task can be spread over a wider class of problems arising in the actual commercial activity [25]. For example, one can register the seasonal character of such parameters as the demand, the revenue and the profitability. The described method pf dynamic programming will entirely apply also for the case when the limiting function is non-linear [26].

Despite that the above-listed equations are complex, the practical use of the described algorithm is pretty simple. It is only necessary to insert the budget limitations taken from the previous reports [27] and the influence of expenditures on the basic indexes of branches' profitability in the commercial network. Other calculations are carried out on computers using wide-spread sets of applications [28]. For solving non-linear tasks we also need the data on the demand for the product depending on the season and the data on the social-demographic landscape and specialization [29] of the branches and enterprises in the network.

Operation of the enterprises with the use of the concept "The Industry 4.0" requires transition to the new way of thinking based on the synthesis of artificial intelligence systems, machine-to-machine interaction with the use of all the available digital platforms. The criterion remains to be the economic efficiency, but the target will be achieved by using complex algorithms based on mathematical models and scientific methods of optimization. This paradigm brings about new tactics of interaction with customers, when modern approaches of incremental influence of large numbers of customers replace the old tactics of downward communication. Integration of business with social networks, geotargetting, cross-functional management and work with identified customers – these are merely a part of the entire digital environment. Even this simple example of omni-channel interaction makes it possible to state that, if there is a critical mass of customers incorporated in the Web 4.0 network, the classical "Sales funnel" can get a negative decrement, which is highly impossible without using digital economy methods.

Russia, as an influential participant of the world industry, has all the capabilities to promote the concept "The Industry 4.0" using such advantage as availability of scientific personnel in various branches of industry. It is necessary to employ innovative principles of work with the customers. The highly increased role of digital interaction conditioned by penetration of online portals and social networks requires accumulation of innovations.

Virtual presence in Internet applications, presence of ratings based on customers' feedback will inevitably lead to solving the task of optimizing economic indexes. The newly developed mathematical model can be especially well employed in the environment of the network commerce as it is easily scalable. At the same time, such important marketing parameters of omni-channel interaction as customer identification, customer's location consideration, the data set on the relationships history, are actually formalized only within the framework of program algorithms superimposed on the capabilities of the Web 4.0. It is the scientifically substantiated calculations based on stochastic algorithms that will make it possible to obtain a competitive advantage and optimize the basic economic indexes.

References

1. V. V. Glukhov, E. Balashova, Lecture Notes in Computer Science (including subseries Lecture Notes in Artificial Intelligence and Lecture Notes in Bioinformatics), **9247** (2015)
2. A. N. Tsatsulin, A. V. Babkin, N. I. Babkina, *Proceedings of the 28th International Business Information Management Association Conference – Vision 2020: Innovation Management, Development Sustainability, and Competitive Economic Growth* (2016)
3. S. M. Sergeev, *Proceedings of the VIII International Conference* (2015)
4. S. G. Bozhuk, A. S. Krasnov, *International Conference "Quality Management, Transport and Information Security, Information Technologies", (IT&QM&IS-2017)* DOI: 10.1109/ITMQIS.2017.8085790 (2017)
5. A. V. Babkin, T. J. Kudryavtseva, Modern Applied Science, **9(1)** DOI: 10.5539/mas.v9n1p109 (2015)
6. Neuroweb [online] Available at: http://www.globalneuroweb.org/ru/ (2018)
7. T. Shchukin Neuronet: the next generation communication environment, Technowars. **5**, (2014)
8. S. M. Sergeev, News of the Institute of Mathematics and Informatics, Udmurt State

University, **1**, 73 (2012)

9. A brief history of digital marketing technology,kapost.com, Retrieved 8 February (2017)
10. A. V. Babkin, V. A. Plotnikov, S. V. Muraveva, Proceedings of the 25th International Business Information Management Association Conference – Innovation Vision 2020: From Regional Development Sustainability to Global Economic Growth, IBIMA 2015 (2015)
11. Juha Karvanen, Ari Rantanen, Lasse Luoma, Survey data and Bayesian analysis: a cost-efficient way to estimate customer equity, Quantitative Marketing and Economics, **12 (3)** (2014)
12. The Walt Disney Company [online] Available at: http://disneyparks.disney.go.com (2017)
13. B. Park, L. Simar and V. Zelenyuk, Categorical data in local maximum likelihood: theory and applications to productivity analysis, Journal of Productivity Analysis, **43 (2)** (2015)
14. S. M. Sergeev, Innovations, **3(173)** (2013)
15. S. M. Sergeev, *Proceedings of the VII International Conference, Voronezh* (2014)
16. Hermann, Pentek, Otto: Design Principles for Industrie 4.0 Scenarios (accessed on 4 May 2016) (2016)
17. S. M. Sergeev, *Selected Papers of the International Scientific School "Paradigma" Winter-2016 (Varna, Bulgaria)* (Yelm, WA, USA, 2016)
18. S. V. Krasnov, S. M. Sergeev, N. V. Mukhanova, A. N. Grushkin, Infocom Technologies and Optimization (Trends and Future Directions) 6th International Conference ICRITO, (2017)
19. "CRM in Customer Service", CRM Magazine, (Retrieved 22 November 2015)
20. E. Abushova, E. Burova, S. Suloeva, Lecture Notes in Computer Science (including subseries Lecture Notes in Artificial Intelligence and Lecture Notes in Bioinformatics), **9870** LNCS DOI: 10.1007/978-3-319-46301-8_7 (2016)
21. B. Wahba, The Fluff Cycle (And How to End It By Solving Real Sales and Marketing Problems), Strategy Science, Inc., (2012)
22. S. M. Sergeev, Cross-functional management in stochastic planning, Economics and management of control systems, **8(2.1)** (2013)
23. D. Lavrova, A. Pechenkin, V. Gluhov. Applying correlation analysis methods to control flow violation detection in the internet of things, Source of the Document Automatic Control and Computer Sciences, **49 (8)**, DOI: 10.3103/S0146411615080283 (2015)
24. S. M. Sergeev Expansion of DEA methodology on the multimodal conception for the 3PL , Proceedings of the XXIII-the International Open Science Conference (Yelm, WA, USA, January 2018). Science Book Publishing House. Yelm, WA, USA, (2018)
25. G. Kleyner, A. Babkin, Lecture Notes in Artificial Intelligence and Lecture Notes in Bioinformatics), **9247**. DOI: 10.1007/978-3-319-23126-6_50 (2015)
26. S. M. Sergeev, Selected Papers of the International Scientific School "Paradigma" (Summer-2015, Varna, Bulgaria) Compiling Editor Dr.Sc., Prof. E.Sibirskaya. Yelm, WA, USA, 38-41 (2015)
27. H. Kagermann, W. Wahlster and J. Helbig, (eds.),: *Recommendations for implementing the strategic initiative Industrie 4.0, Final report of the Industrie 4.0 Working Group*

(2013)

28. V. V. Glukhov, I. V. Ilin, A. I. Levina , Lecture Notes in Computer Science (including subseries Lecture Notes in Artificial Intelligence and Lecture Notes in Bioinformatics), **9247**, DOI: 10.1007/978-3-319-23126-6_47 (2015)
29. T. Malinina, V. Murina, *Proceedings of the 8th International Scientific Symposium on Electrical Power Engineering, Electroenergetika* (2015)

Graphic programming by elements of nonstandard structural forms

Vsevolod Chugreyev[1], *Vadim* Kaikov[1], and *Tatiana* Kapitonova[1*]

[1] Saint Petersburg State University of Architecture and Civil Engineering, Faculty of Economics and Management, 190005 2-ya Krasnoarmeiskaya st. 4, Russia

Abstract. The article describes one of the variants for solving the actual practical problem on information building modeling with application of several computer programs. The authors showed the relationship between graphic programming and model parameterization using specifications. The main purpose of the work was to show the algorithm for designing an architectural and construction object from the choice of the conceptual form to obtaining the information required for the industrial production of parts. The authors note the importance of studying similar problems in the framework of training courses of architecture and civil engineering universities.

Good design methods are in desperate need of processes automation. Hand labor facilitation by computers allows creating more and more geometrically complex forms. However, as we know, it is not enough to create a new form, it is required to form its cutting, to provided with the necessary information, to bring it to the machine. The relationship between project and production is a very important BIM component in the world practice. [1] The only way to keep up with the times is to learn, perfect and create new automation technologies [2].

One of such tasks is the implementation of architectural design solutions with complex glazing. An incredibly defused environment of professionals in this field takes place despite of the great interest in these forms in the Russian-language information space.

In Saint Petersburg, the Lakhta-Center is an example of the Russian specialists' achievement presenting the complex shell cutting that is shown in Fig. 1 [3].

* Corresponding author: t.r@bk.ru

Fig. 1. A fragment of the Lakhta-Center glazing (ZAO GORPROJECT, Revit and Grasshopper units) [4]

We are interested in non-standard (non-rectangular) cutting of panels in one of the modern buildings constructed based on the project of bureau Zaha Hadid Architects (Fig.2).

Fig. 2. Port Authority Building in Antwerp (Zaha Hadid Architects) (http://clipgoo.com/daut/as/f/t/the-wonderful-zaha-hadid-architect-buildings-cool-design-ideas-3369_amazing-interior-architectural-buildings-images_interior-design_interior-design-salary-designer-san-antonio-job-description-internsh.jpg)

The upper part of the building is a free form glazed with triangular panels, the tangible embodiment of which is associated with a large number of similar elements (glazing panels and imposts) with geometric differences, and thus requiring the process design flexibility. The existence of such projects basically became possible due to the programming of graphic objects with receiving the specifications sent to an automated production.

The development of computer hardware and software at the present stage creates the need to organize the fullest possible use of these resources, and requires establishing the relations between the original idea and the ultimate embodiment of the plan. In addition, the computer model can identify in advance the inconsistencies and deviations of the project, investigate the object behavior in different conditions (seismic, weather, etc.), identify the impact on the environment and people habitat, and make corrections with minimal financial costs.

The purpose of programming is the compilation of such algorithms that could be used for solving various problems, in this case architectural design.

Not every architect should and can be a graphic programmer. This is absolutely not necessary. As applied to our task, it is sufficient for him to know that the form to be designed as glazed can be implemented using the ready algorithm. The graphic programmers are a special type of modern architects who have a set towards mathematics and can shift hand labor to the computer systems.

The design of structural glazing of complex forms is a chain of actions for creating and cutting a surface, forming a points array, creating an adaptive element, and adapting each element to the points array. This chain of actions can take various forms, extending and shortening depending on the task complexity.

The factor ensuring a significant part of the success is the right choice of software. For the wide distribution of graphic programming, it is important that software products are not only available, but also available to different layers of users.

The software choice is determined for us by the following requirements:

- The form-designing geometry format: if the exact proportions of the object do not fully "fit" or are dependent on each other, then it is necessary to refer to the method of visual programming, otherwise, when the form-designing elements are unambiguous and unchangeable, it is possible not to parametrize the form-designing element;
- A variety of form-designing tools and visibility of their operation.

After the available computer resources have been analyzed, we fixed on the software shown in Fig.3.

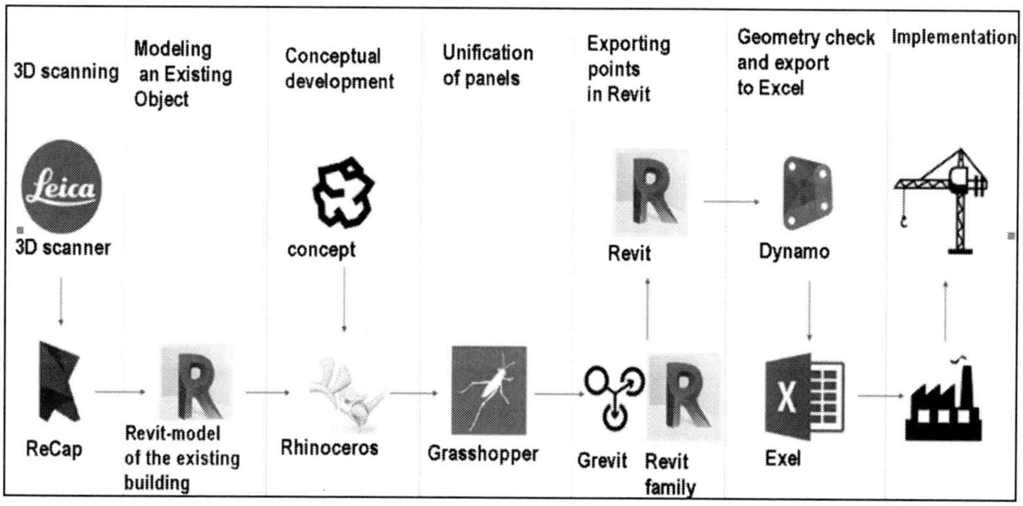

Fig. 3. Interrelations of the selected software.

Then we will present a program that automates the process of dividing the surface into structural elements (triangles) and drawing up specifications for their glazing and imposts.

Lets choose a surface formed by lofting through three profiles of open curves of different curvature as the simplest curvilinear form. Upon completion of the form development, it is necessary to place it in the Revit environment from other ones. The imported form must have an extension of sat.

The simplest partitioning of the form into a grid in Revit is done in the mode of editing the form-designing element or in the form-designing families (Fig. 4). The non-standard partitioning can be formed in Dynamo or Grasshopper. The exact sequence of operations is impossible but there is the final result – the double points array a [i][k], where i is a number of the structural element, and k is a number of the adaptive element point. Thus, to cover the form with ten panels, each of which will be based on six points, we will have to get a list of ten lists for six elements, each of which will be the coordinates of the adaptive point of the structural element [5].

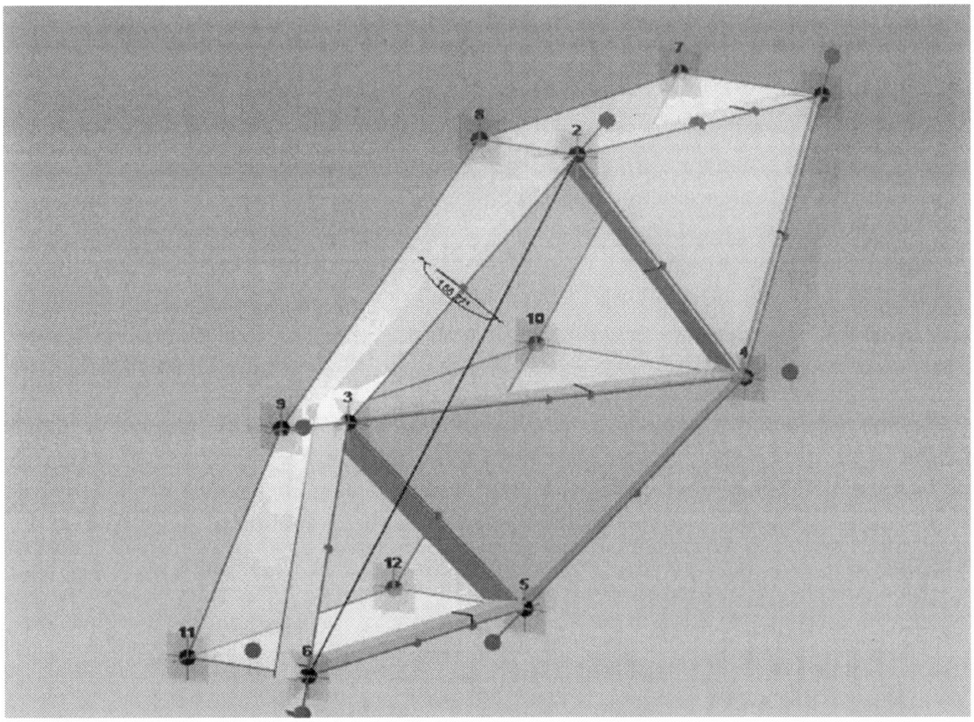

Fig. 4. The simplest partitioning of a test form in the Revit.

In case of Dynamo, the points grid reference is transmitted directly through the node "adaptive component by points", to which the list of these points will be provided, and in case of Grasshopper, the list of points will have to be transmitted via the Grevit plug-in, which will be installed both on the Grasshopper and on Revit.

A general parameters file is created in the project to create the specifications for the structural system elements. Adaptive points are created in the family file. The geometry is parametrized based on these adaptive points. It is recommended that all the set parameters are common, so that they can be read and marked. As much as possible, it is recommended to express the parameters through each other using the mathematical formulas. This will result in the more correct calculation and the possibility for complete exclusion of physical geometry to facilitate the model.

For further parameterization, it is necessary to create the specifications for materials and elements by selecting the adaptive families through the category "generalized models". The created specifications will allow reducing all the parameters generated by the structural elements to a single list that will be exported to Excel for further processing or linked to Excel by means of Dynamo or Flux.

It should be understood that the above method is very conditional and does not disclose all the design fundamentals. Any problem is complicated when a number of input data increases. Sometimes there are cases when the slightest missed condition that is not taken into account in the script will require its complete replacement.

However, in general, the factors that complicate the problem solution can be classified according to the following points:

a) Computing – increasing an amount of computation which can cause complications in the geometry calculation. Problems of this kind may require the optimization of the script structure.

b) The form composite character when the form is created from several surfaces which can not be represented as a single solid one. The form composite character can significantly complicate the process of form division since the cases of mismatching the breakdown grids are possible, and they can disturb the aesthetics and function of the structure to be formed.

c) The nature of the starting form. An improper format of the starting form can significantly complicate the breakdown process since it will require data conversion or even make a correct breakdown impossible in no circumstances.

d) Increasing the details of the adaptive structural element. This parameter can significantly affect the problem complexity since it will require more time both to develop the structural element itself and to develop a script controlling its location.

e) Application of unofficial "combined" nodes in the script body can complicate the problem, as it does not guarantee its correct operation.

The problem contains a complex form, the volume of which shall necessarily be adaptive. This means that it is not enough to use only the Revit and Dynamo environments to solve the problem. It is required to apply the Rhinosceros and Grasshopper.

The historical part of the building was exported to the Rhino environment. It should be noted that the export shall be configured in the DWG format so that Revit does not convert the original NURBS geometry to the MESH format and also does not export excess parts of the building which do not influence the aesthetics of the formation of the global volume of the building.

A sketch form design is to work with the standard Rhino tools (Fig. 5). After the form is found, it is necessary to think in advance the principle of its programming and division.

Fig. 5. A sketch form design in the Rhino.

The sequence of basic geometry formation:

1. A point with three variable coordinates will be the basis of the studied form;
2. Formation of other three points of the rectangle by adding an additional value of x and y coordinates to the starting X and Y coordinates;
3. Rectangle formation by connecting the points with straight lines;
4. Parametrization of six points by three parameters on a rectangle forming a hexagonal building profile: two points on two opposite sides of the rectangle and other four points on the other two opposite sides, the result is a profile symmetric about its center;

5. Parametrization of the automatic rotation of points through an angle formed by two opposite points and the X axis, and it provides automatic alignment of the form so that with changing its dimensions one pair of opposite points is always able to form a segment parallel to the orthogonal axis of the building;
6. Formation of a closed polyline by successively joining points and formation of a surface that lies within the closed polyline;
7. Surface extrusion along the vector.

Thus, we obtain the simplest form, further actions with which can be compared with faceting that means successive cutting of the form parts by planes based on three points, each of which is parametrized on the form edges. Here it is necessary to track the direction of the plane normal line that shall always be fixed toward the form part to be cut.

It should be noted that the grid is continuous on the form bends. This continuity is achieved through the interaction of an inclined forms and three rows of sectional planes. Three uniform rows of sectional planes – 0, 45 and 90 degrees form a triangle with the intersection of any edge.

The next action is used to break the grid by the resulting continuous lines onto three-, four- and five-sided surfaces. For this purpose, it is necessary to check the surface grid interaction by selecting the lines as per the belonging of a certain surface. For this action, the Surface Closest Point node was used that determined a distance from the point lying in the middle of the curve to the planes, and then by the filtering method, that is zero values selection from non-zero ones was done using the Dispatch node. Thus, we compared all grid lines with all edges and filtered the lists so that the surface indices coincided with the line ones belonging to this surface.

After obtaining the correspondence of the indices of both lists, it is necessary to bring both lists to the Surface Split node that will separate certain planes with the corresponding lines. The result will be the formation of separated surfaces which are the basis for the panels (Fig. 6).

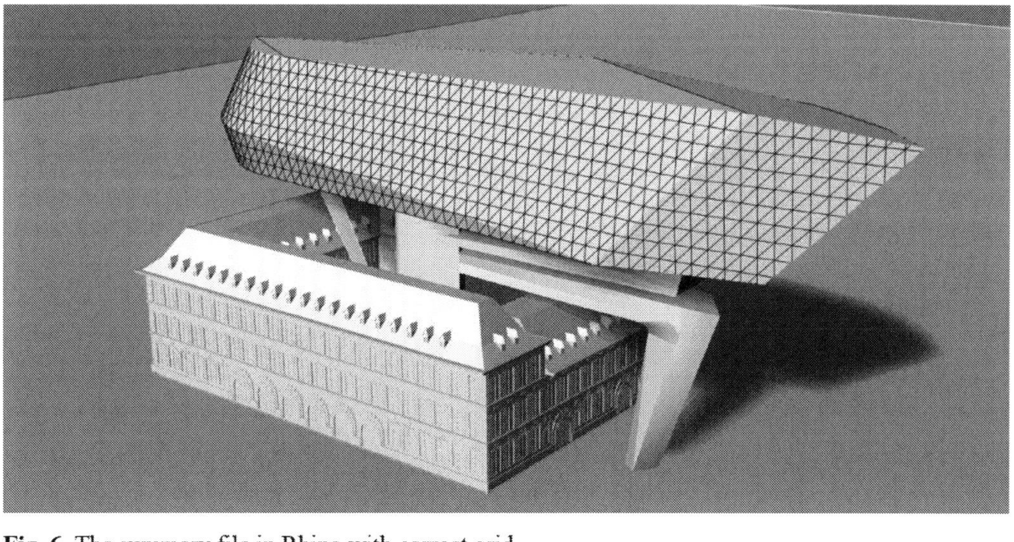

Fig. 6. The summary file in Rhino with correct grid.

It is necessary to consider the boundary points from the resulting surfaces. For this purpose the Deconstruct Brep node, shall be used that allows obtaining the geometry apexes. Now it is required to consistently perform three operations:
1. Unify the geometry and delete the matching points, that is, if a distance between points is less than a certain value, then several points become one with the averaged coordinate.
2. Classify the geometry from three, four and five points in different lists.

3. Change the numbering of points in a single order (clockwise or counter-clockwise) and, possibly, divide the staggered panels into different lists.

Then these data shall be sent to the Grevit plug-in node, having converted the dimensions before. Three nodes will be in total, each node will be responsible for one of the three elements. The names of the respective families shall be provided at the entrance to these nodes.

The adaptive component programming in Revit is reduced to three families, one for each of the resulting types of glazing.

The adaptive framework creation means the formation of three adaptive points and the lines reference to them. These lines will be a peculiar axes. The geometry of the imposts and glasses will be referenced to these lines (Fig. 7).

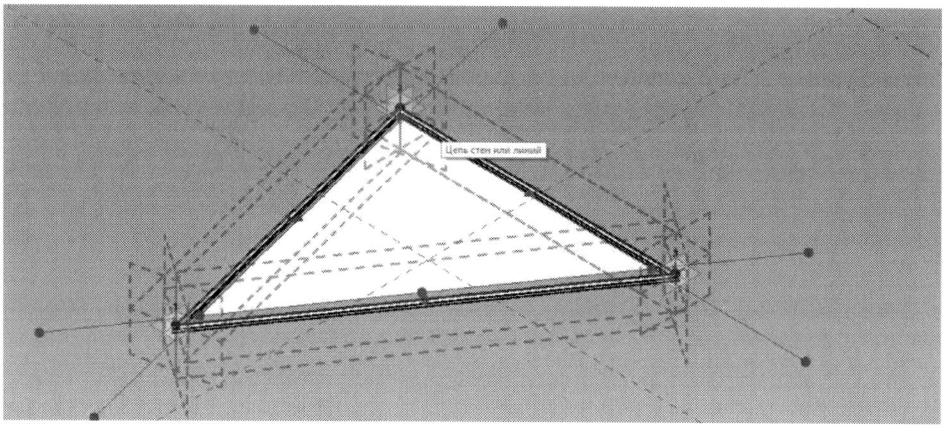

Fig. 7. An example of the family based on three points.

It is recommended to make the imposts profile by a separate family developed and based on the template "Metric system. The family based on an edge." The glass plane like the imposts profile shall be referenced to the axial lines shifted to the center by a certain indent. This is resulted from the peculiarity of the modular glazing [6]. For the reason that the impost profile will be formed by an nested family, it should also be remembered that the parameters of the nested family shall be repeatedly referenced to the parameters of the main family.

The specifications shall be common to provide reading the family parameters by the Revit specifications. For this purpose, create a general parameters file in the project menu; the file contains the names of all the required parameters.

Most parameters are preferable to be determined not by the method of filling up the parameters for reports on the object geometry, but by the method of formulas creation in the menu of family sizes. Formulas creation helps to avoid deleting the parameter marks when errors occur [7].

The next step is location of the geometry with the Grevit plug-in, the feature of which is that it forms a unique link of two programs allowing to implement forms in the Revit without the Dynamo. The plug-in is simultaneously installed on both software – the Grevit plug-in activation key is pressed in the Revit. Further, after pressing the activation key that is suitable for the Grevit node, the data from Grasshopper is sent to the Grevit nodes and on their basis the Grevit builds the geometry in the Revit.

We created a file of common parameters in order to be able to reduce them to the specification as per the category "Generalized models".

There are several disadvantages of the methods to be used:

- The absence of a single design software.

There is nothing paradoxical that the environment of form-designing in the Revit is well suited for the formation and parametrization of a structural element, but it is not suitable for rapid and free form-designing. Visual objects parameterization requires the sequence and logic for object creation, and this fact, in turn, is very contrary to the problem of quick and free generation of any free form. The transition from one modeling environment to another is always very abnormal since it requires good knowledge of the interface of both environments.

- The absence of the required nodes.

The nodes limitation in the programming language results in an inefficient, stretched script form. Here it can be noted that there are ways to add the nodes in different programming languages.

- Resource efficiency of the node programming.

A way to form the grid by splitting the geometry by the Surface Split node is very functional and user-friendly, however, it is quite resource-consuming for the computer. However, these parametric objects would be impossible in principle to create usual methods of "manual" modeling.

- Human factor.

Despite the fact that parametric shaping has been existing for several decades, people who are at the intersection of programming and design remain very few. A consequence of this fact is the slow development of tools and functionality of software application.

Globally, the applied methods are out of date together with the outdated programs through which we address them. The most important thing is to understand the program operation principles which will lead to complete success, or limitation at any stage.

The modeling by means of the nodes has one essential feature: being between the programming and the design, it completely blurs the framework between these concepts, increasingly expands the thinking space, deviating an architect from the primary task of "creating the quality object" to the more primary task of "developing the method for creating the quality object" or even "developing the qualitative method for creating the quality object". This violation of the primary meaning creates serious psychological discomfort for a designer. However, this is only a prelude to the problems of the future world, and only a few of people can predict them.

The authors are convinced that if the paper is competently popularized with these methods, in the future we will be able to get professionals of a new level who will be able to understand the BIM both in terms of the tools and the holistic way of thinking [8]. These professionals will be able to bring the market of Russian architecture to a new digital level as they will never have the question "how can this be created?"

The market requires more specialists at the intersection of programming and design. Now these competences can no longer be based on personal contacts and ambitions. The state itself shall take the BIM-training initiative. The new opportunities [9] that will be provided by these technologies will help create career benefits [10] for university students, reinforcing their interest in the BIM-technologies development. This problem exists not only in Russian, but also in foreign practice [11], and it shall be solved comprehensively starting from the school bench – wide application of graphic design methods to form the required way of thinking and applied skills.

References

1. F. H. Abandaa, J. H. M. Taha, F. K. T. Cheungb, Journal of Building Engineering, **14** (2017)

2. Seok-heon Yun, Ki-hyun Jun, Chang-baek Son, and Sang-chul Kim, Journal of Civil Engineering, **18 (2)** (2014)
3. Lakhta Center [online], Available at: https://www.youtube.com/channel/UCHFGjNnME5T8w1zEKzchdZQ (2018)
4. Albert Sumin from Gosprojekt on Grasshopper and Dynamo [online], Available at: https://digitalgipsy.org/2016/01/11/albert-sumin/ (2016)
5. The website of the multi-field research and consulting agency Bureau Bouwtechniek that specializes in building technologies [online], Available at: http://b-b.be/en/portfolio/new-port-house/ (2018)
6. Geektimes [online]. Available at: https://geektimes.ru/company/lakhtacenter/blog/284082/ (2018)
7. Autodesk official website [online], Available at: https://www.autodesk.ru/campaigns/aec-building-design-bds-new-seats/landing-page (2018)
8. P. Matejkaa, A. Tomeka, Procedia Engineering, **196** (2017)
9. Z. Pezeshki, S. A. S. Ivari, Arch Computat Methods Eng (2016)
10. P. Smith, Procedia - Social and Behavioral Sciences, **226** (2016)
11. J. Ferrandiz, A. Banawi, E. Pena, Univ Access Inf Soc, **2** (2017)

Economic model of an innovative enterprise in the digital economy[a]

Daniil Demidenko[1], *Julia* Dubolazova[1], and *Ekaterina* Malevskaya-Malevich[1*]

1 Peter the Great Saint Petersburg Polytechnic University,Higher Engineering-Economical School, Institute of Industrial Management, Economics and Trade, 195251 Polytechnicheskaya st. 29, Russian Federation

Abstract. Currently, the innovation vector is a necessary condition for development of high-tech and high-efficiency industries, a competitiveness factor of enterprise products in market conditions in any economic activity forms. In conditions of transfer to the digital economy, the innovation process – as an incentive for technological modernization of production, increasing of its efficiency and development of new competitive products – allows generating relatively high value added that in terms of corporate finance is a key factor in increasing the company market value that in turn is a generally accepted criterion of the economic efficiency of the enterprise activity as a whole.
The article specifies the concept of the economic model of the enterprise that performs innovative activities in conditions of the digital economy. A comparative analysis of the economic model of the enterprise that does not implement innovation and the innovative enterprise is carried out. The economic model of the innovative enterprise proposes a gradual transition from the production of simple goods to science-intensive and high-technology products by increasing in the level of production development, technologies and skills of employees. The process for formation of the economic model of the enterprise is a mechanism that is a set of elements unified by the system of direct and back links between them and intended to create value added. Based on the performed analysis, it was detected that the innovation enterprise has a number of preferences that compensates for the innovative risk and increases the value added. The model of the value added of the enterprise that performs innovative activity is formulated.

1 Introduction

In the Russian economic science, the interest in the problems of economic growth is actual based on the introduction of innovations in all areas of activity. Based on these conditions, the development of economic management methods in organizations is primarily aimed at saving all the production factors used to achieve the desired result. The achieved savings are subsequently directed to production expansion and to economic growth with a relatively

[a]The study was carried out with the support of the Grant Council of the President of the Russian Federation (draft NSH – 3792.2018.6)
[*]Corresponding author: malevskaia@spbstu.ru

lower cost per unit of the obtained result.

In conditions of a new "digital" economy, the concept of economic growth was replaced with the concept of economic development associated with the process of introducing innovations in all areas of activity. In this case, provision for the "innovation" of industrial development and identification of drivers for growth of high-tech and competitive products step forward, and the "classical" methods, tools, criteria of economics lose their practical importance, and their actualization is necessary taking into account the requirements of economy digitalization.

Today, the economics has the most topical issue of innovation; the works of economics classicists are devoted to studies in this field, both at the macro and micro levels [1, 2]. Thus, Joseph Schumpeter, in the fundamental work "The Theory of Economic Development" [3] introduced the distinction between the concepts of economic growth and economic development into the economics. Economic growth is the increase in the production and consumption of the same goods and services over time, and economic development is the updating of products and production methods, in other words, it means the innovation. According to the definition of Schumpeter, the innovation is a concept that includes five elements: (1) Creation of a new product that is not yet known for the consumer, or a new product quality. (2) Creation of new production methods which have not yet been applied in this industry, which is not necessarily based on scientific discovery and can consist in a new form of commercial commodity circulation. (3) Opening of a new market where this industry has not yet been represented, whether or not the market has existed before. (4) Opening of a new source of production factors, whether or not this source has existed before or was created anew. (5) Creation of a new industry organization, for example, achievement or dissolution of a monopoly position. Thus, the wide concept for innovativeness of any element of the production process is presented.

The actuality of economy "digitalization" is confirmed by the topic of the latest publications of Russian economists. Thus, the work of G.B. Dvas [4] proposes the methodical approach to the development of the regional program for digital economy development combining regional approach to the control with aspects and measures of the program "Digital Economy of the Russian Federation", initialization of aspects and measures reflecting the structure and features of the regional economy.

The latest works of S. D. Bodrunov [5] are devoted to the analysis for the deindustrialization of the Russian economy and foundations for formation of a new industrial society in the framework of the 4th Industrial Revolution. The author deems it appropriate direction to reindustrialization as an instrument for the revival of Russian industry in the context of the need to ensure economic security. It is the author's opinion that the most important component of industrial reinstitutionalization is a new industrial policy at the formal and legislative level of the federal and regional management.

R.S. Grinberg in the work [6], summarizing the system changes in Russia, shows that the existing and predicted economy reforming mechanism often "encourages" the consolidation of trends in the primary economy structure. The author states the approaches to solving the problems of the Russian economy reindustrialization among which the special role is assigned to the "Concept of Economic Sociodynamics" that most adequately reflects modern socioeconomic terms.

The known risk management mechanisms shall be actualized, since innovation activity belongs to a high risk category. The main aspects of innovation activities risks management in the context of globalization are considered in the works of modern authors [7, 8, 9], as well as issues of practical application of risk management mechanisms known in principle with reference to innovation-active enterprises. [10, 11, 12]

The transition to a digital economy enters upon the question of finding adequate criteria for assessment of economic efficiency of enterprises in a changeable business environment.

Wealth maximization of shareholders, owners of the enterprise has become a paradigm of corporate management in recent years. The digitization of the economy is based on the approach to the enterprise value-based management. The shareholders wealth is measured by the enterprise activities internal rate of return. In this case, the shareholder's income can be manifested both in dividend payments, and in the growth of the company's market value of stock that is in the growth of equity value or enterprise "capitalization". Information about the company capitalization dynamics is used by the owners to assess the current enterprise economic situation and to predict. [13, 14]

Economic Value Added (EVA) is traditionally considered the best available measure of company value [15, 16, 17]. EVA is recognized by many economists as the most important company performance indicator – the company's management is effective provided that the economic value added increases.

2 Study target setting

In the market-economy countries there is the saying: "Economists know the prices of all assets in the world, but they do not know the value of any of them". In a sense, the saying is true – the asset value is the price at which an asset purchase and sale transaction is made in the market. In this case, the question of why the asset value may be below its market price, economists usually redirect to philosophers. If the value is a synonym for the market transaction, then the best indicator of the company's value will be the aggregate price at which its own capital and debts are sold in the financial market. However, in many cases, the use of market prices is unacceptable, it is necessary to have a more accurate and reliable assessment of the market value of assets and the company as a whole.

The reasons for this situation are as follows: firstly, equity is in the hands of shareholders or public companies and is exchanged in this environment, so the market prices may not exist. In addition, company securities are negotiated in the market, but irregularly and in insignificant volumes, therefore, it is impossible to obtain adequate assessments of the market value based on the analysis of purchase/sale prices. As previously stated, the companies' securities are negotiated well, but with a view to obtain commercial benefits from purchase/sale. In practice, independent comparisons of value and market price often reveal a significant number of undervalued assets. The analysts forcedly use the activity control to detect the presence (or absence) of market value growth and, therefore, to evaluate correctness of the economic strategy used by the company.

It follows the need to use special methods to determine the market value or companies' capitalization; this explains the existence of this specific aspect of economic and financial analysis in companies – assessment of their value.

To determine the company market capitalization, there are, as you know, several methods that provide for different accuracy of the assessment results. To compensate for potential risks of unreliable assessment, it is usually performed using different methods according to the applicable standards. The acceptable proximity of the obtained results point to their sufficiency and reliability. All methods are grouped into three approaches which are known based on the appraisal practice – extravagant – a set of methods based on the determination of costs required to restore or replace an object taking into account its wear. Comparative is a set of methods based on the comparison of the object with similar objects in relation to which there is information on the relevant transaction prices. Profitable is a set of methods based on the definition of expected revenues from the facility.

In practice, the most common method for assessment of company capitalization value is precisely the "profitable" method, according to which the current value (at the time of assessment) of future/predicted company income is taken as a capitalization assessment. Pretax or net profit, net cash flow, company's sales value, and other "volumetric" indicators featuring the performance of activities can be used as an income indicator. Application of this approach based on the use of forecast data poses risks of unreliable forecasts, but this is currently the only way to obtain an assessment that is not based on previously obtained results. The company's capitalization value is assessed by means of a profitable approach under the following conditions: in every period of activity a normally functioning company can receive revenues from selling the beneficial results of its activities in the market, or from selling the company at the price of capitalization (market value).

Let's consider the relationship between the indicator of the company's economic value added and the efficiency of its activities. The model of economic value added (Value, V) with the relevant required additions to the already known provisions on the formation of the indicator of "economic value added" or "economic profit" can be taken for the economic model of the enterprise (or asset).

The economic model of value added is an economic mechanism, i.e. a set of elements unified by the system of direct and back links between them and intended to create value added as a result of unequivocal use in accordance with the functional purpose (direction of production activity).

As you know, the value added received as a result of investments is:

$$V = I * (r - i), \tag{1}$$

where V (Value) is the cost, I is investment, r is the return on invested capital, i is the interest rate or the actual price of money in the financial market.

As is known, the latter is a "risk-free" interest rate identical for all assets "i_0" plus an individual risk premium for each asset, or $i = i_0 + \Delta$. The premium increases the price of purchasing investment and financial resources for investment, while reducing the value added. In the absence of risks (in a perfect competitive market), the purchasing price is equal to the risk-free interest rate, and the risk premium will be zero. When determining the capitalization value, equity market assessment, accounting of faulty assessment risks and other risks by income-based method is of great importance. As it was stated, in case of financial and economic analysis, risks exposure in discounting of cash flows is taken into account through the use of a risk premium relative to the risk-free interest rate. Risk exposure in each period can be determined by different methods of statistics, but it can be assumed that the estimated period is further from the assessment time, the larger risk premium will correspond to it.

The presented economic model of value added includes the elements with nature of both random variables that are realized with a certain probability, and nonrandom elements:

$$V = I * (r - (i_0 + \Delta)), \tag{2}$$

Here random elements are "r" and "Δ", as they are realized with a risk which probability is $0 \le p \le 1$. If the risk is realized, then $p = 1$, a value of risk premium "Δ" is actual, but in this case income from investments will not be obtained, their profitability is zero "$r = 0$", since this event comes with a probability of "1-p", with realization of risk $p = 1$. Taking into account that the mathematical expectation of a nonrandom value is the value itself, the mathematical expectation of a random value of the economic value added is:

$$V = I \times \big((1 - p) \times r - (i + p \times \Delta)\big) = I \times (r - p \times r - i - p \times \Delta), \tag{3}$$

The condition for the significance of the mathematical expectation, the values of the economic model of value added, is its non-negativity ($V \geq 0$), from which the limit value of the risk premium can be obtained (obvious algebraic transformations are not given):

$$\Delta \leq \frac{r * (1 - p) - i}{p}, \tag{4}$$

For example, if $r = 0.2$; p = 0.1; $i = 0.15$, then the risk loading shall not exceed 0.2.

3 Research results

Therefore, let's state the concept of the economic model of the enterprise that performs innovative activities in conditions of the digital economy. Innovations are traditionally associated with the greater risk. Compensation for the risk is expressed in the risk premium value when calculating the discount rate. It is possible to present the following economic model of a risk premium " $\Delta = \Delta(V_n)$ ".

If we imagine that investment and financial resources are purchased to ensure their asset value, then the higher the value of asset/value added, the lower the risk premium.

$$V_n = I_n * (r_n - (i_0 + \Delta(V_n))), \tag{5}$$

The simplest linear model of the risk premium:

$$\Delta = \frac{V}{V_0} \times \Delta_0, \quad 0 \leq V \leq V_0, \quad 0 \leq \Delta \leq \Delta_0, \tag{6}$$

And the corresponding economic model of value added:

$$V_n = I_n * (r_n - (i_0 + \frac{V_n}{V_0} \Delta_0)), \tag{7}$$

Having determined the value of V_n from this condition, we obtain:

$$V_n = \frac{I(r_n - i_0)}{1 + I * \frac{\Delta_0}{V_0}}, \tag{8}$$

Obviously, the presence of a risk premium reduces the economic value added (the formula denominator always has a positive value and over 1).

Summarizing the above, it is possible to schematically depict the economic model of the enterprise conducting innovation activity (Fig. 1). In this case, the specific character of "innovation" is the introduction of specific financing sources such as government support and innovative financing sources which in turn are the elements of the enterprise innovative mechanism.

Now we understand that the innovative financing sources, for example, are ICO, Initial Coin Offering – the issue of shares or tokens intended to pay for the project's services in the future, as a financing source appeared relatively recently, however, as judged by the volumes of external investments (in 2017, blockchain-projects around the world purchased about $ 1.5 billion during the ICO), it should be taken into account when analyzing alternatives to purchase capital to high-risk projects along with venture capital funding.The process is also compared with crowd-funding. The ICO allows you to purchase significant crypto-investment in the economy.

A separate issue may be selected as the "innovations commercialization" block that is the creation of demand for innovative products. In the research formulation, as previously stated, the innovations are any element of the production process, or several elements, or the entire production cycle. In this case, it is obvious that a "new" product does not yet have its consumer when entering into the market. Hence, the need to create demand for the product of the enterprise that conducts innovation activities, as an element of the enterprise economic model.

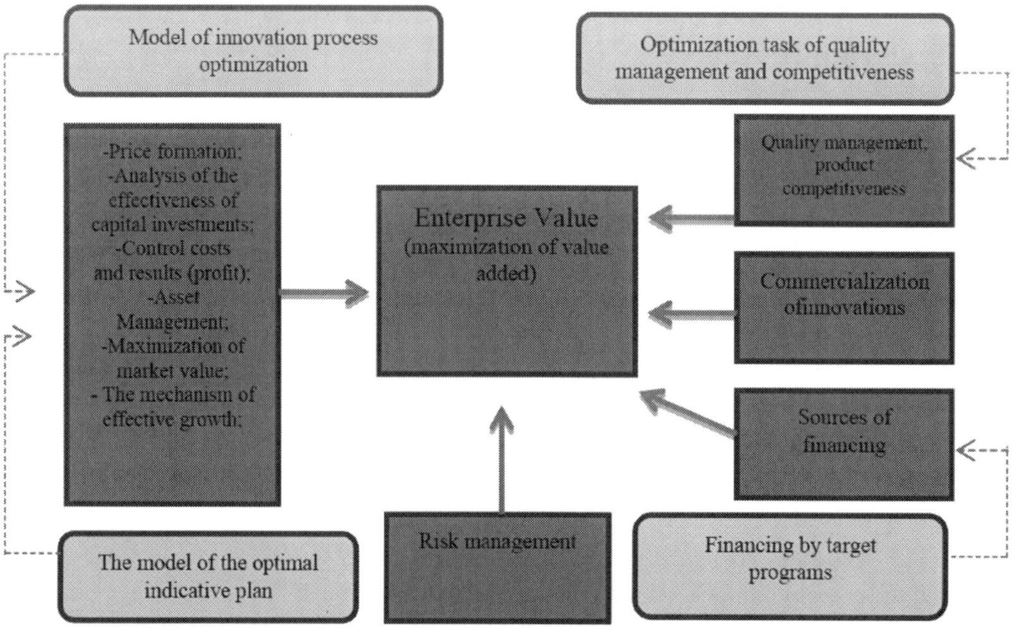

Fig. 1. The economic model of the enterprise that carries out innovative activities.

If the assets belong to the enterprise (which produces innovative products using innovative factors of production – technologies, materials, labor processes), then in the framework of the economic mechanism model it can be assumed that this enterprise has certain preferences (subsidies, concessional lending, etc.). This reduces a risk premium value and prevents the reduction of economic value added in conditions of increased risks associated with innovation. These preferences are absent for "ordinary" non-innovative enterprises and assets that determines the specific nature of the economic mechanism of innovation activity.

4 Conclusion

Based on the performed comparative analysis for the model of the economic value added of the enterprise that does not implement innovation, and the innovative enterprise, it can be concluded that the economic model of the innovative enterprise operating in the digital economy is the economic mechanism, i.e. a set of elements unified by the system of direct and back links between them and intended to create value added as the main economic efficiency of the enterprise. In this case, it was detected that the innovation enterprise has a number of preferences that compensates for the innovative risk and increases the value added. The model of the value added of the enterprise that performs innovative activity is formulated.

As well as, we note that currently the use of processes to assess the market capitalization of companies as the study results significance is a practical aspect of economic analysis and has no serious scientific basis, so the use of optimization principles in the process of assessing the market capitalization value can contribute to improving the scientific level of this aspect.

The study was carried out with the support of Peter the Great St. Petersburg Polytechnic University. We also would like to thank our colleagues, employees of the Engineering and Economical Higher School, Industrial Management, Economy and Trade Institute, who acted as experts that helped to significantly improve the work.

References

1. R. R. Nelson, *National innovation systems: a comparative analysis* (Oxford university press, Oxford, 1993)
2. T. E. Burns, G. M. Stalker, *The management of innovation* (Tavistock publications, London, 1961)
3. J. Schumpeter, *The Theory of Economic Development* (Direct media Publishing, Moscow, 2008)
4. G.V. Dvas, *Formation of regional programs of digital economy development* (Saint Petersburg scientific center RAS, Saint Petersburg, 2017)
5. S.D. Bodrunov, Economic recovery of Russia, **1**(2017)
6. R. Grinberg,Problems of management theory and practice, **7** (2017)
7. R. Raja, M. B. Sarkar, StrategicManagementJournal, **37.5** (2016)
8. L. V.Nikolova,J.J.Kuporov, D. G. Rodionov, International Journal of Economics and Financial Issues, **5.3S** (2015)
9. D. G.Rodionov, L. A. Guzikova, I. A. Rudskaya, Actual economy problems, **8** (2014)
10. D. G.Rodionov, et al., Procedia-Social an dBehavioral Sciences, **207**(2015)
11. M. Habermann, M.Swink, A. W. Mackelprang, Journal of Operations Management, **38** (2015)
12. A. Hyytinen, M.Pajarinen, P. Rouvinen, Journal of Business Venturing, **30 (4)** (2015)
13. S. D. Young, S. F. O'byrne, D. S. Young, S. Young, Stephen O'Byrne, *EVA and value-based management* (McGraw-Hill Professional Publishing, New York, 2000)
14. D. Kyriazis, C. Anastassis, European Financial Management, **13(1)** (2007)
15. A. K.Sharma, S.Kumar, International JournalofEconomics and Finance, **2(2)** (2010)
16. G.B.Stewart, Journal of Applied Corporate Finance, **7(2)** (1994)
17. S.F. O'Byrne, Journal of Applied Corporate Finance, **9(1)** (1996)

Modern-day Russia and the problems of the "silver" generation in the digital millennium

Larisa Desfonteines[1], and *Elena* Korchagina[1*]

[1]Peter the Great St. Petersburg Polytechnic University, Institute of Industrial Management, Economics and Trade, Higher School of Economics and Trade, 195251 Polytechnicheskaya st. 29, Russian Federation

Abstract. An important peculiarity of the future economy is principal change in the labor market structure determined by demographic factors one of which is significant increase of pension aged population. This age group becomes the key potential resource of increasing the number of employed people in all the developed and in some developing countries. Population with graying hair becomes a powerful resource for development of economy of a new type which has received a poetic name – "silver" economy. Studying the problems and prospects of developing the "silver" economy is one of the most actual scientific tasks of the modern time. The second important tendency of the modern era is vigorous development of technologies and transition to digital economy. Successful involvement in the changing labor market requires confident mastering of modern informational communicational technologies. However, this task is a certain challenge for representatives of the "silver generation". A review of foreign studies on the problems of the influence of demographic changes at the labor market of developed countries on the structure and quality of labor force is represented in the article; a dynamics of using modern digital technologies by representatives of the "silver generation" is described; the instruments of stimulating the use of modern information technologies in older age groups are distinguished. The analysis of demographic tendencies in Russia is conducted; the necessity of involving employable representatives of older age groups in the labor market is justified. On the basis of the empirical study undertaken by the authors, the peculiarities of value orientations at work places of representatives of different age groups are distinguished and characterized, and also key psychological characteristics of representatives of the elder generations of employees as members of work collectives are described.

The problem of the silver economy may be considered from the point of view of different aspects. The first one of them is focused on statistic analysis of the demographic changes that take place and also on studying various opportunities which appear as a result, such as introduction of new market segments and products adjusted to their demands, estimation of sales prospects and innovations. The second one aims at estimating the influence of demographic changes on national labor markets, estimating and forecasting the quality of

* Corresponding author: elena.korchagina@mail.ru

labor force. Finally, the third aspect is connected with the questions of developing mechanisms of involving representatives of older generations in work activity, studying psychological peculiarities of representatives of different age groups, exploring the questions of their cooperation at workplaces, estimating efficiency of the leadership system taking into account this cooperation.

The represented study deals with the second and the third aspects mentioned above. A review of foreign studies on the problem of demographic changes at the labor market of developed countries influencing the structure and quality of labor force is represented in this study; dynamics of using modern digital technologies by representatives of the older age groups are revealed. Also analysis of demographic tendencies in Russia is carried out; the necessity of involving employable representatives of older age groups in the labor market is justified; on the basis of empirical study, the peculiarities of core values at workplaces of representatives of different age groups are revealed and characterized; key psychological characteristics of representatives of the older generation workers as members of labor collectives are described.

Demographic changes reduce the number of people of the employable age of the entire population size in all the developed and many developing countries which negatively influences the economic growth. From the economic point of view it is very important to divide population into three main groups: people younger than the employable age (as a rule, from 0 to 15 years old inclusively), people of the employable age (from 16 to the pension age accepted in the country) and people older than the employable age. Representatives of the first and the third groups are economically dependent. People of the employable age are, vice versa, economically active and take part in the production of goods and services. The dependent groups of population rely on material support for implementing demands in consuming goods and services. Changes in the age structure of population will influence the relation of economically active people and economically dependent people with potentially negative consequences for economic growth [1].

However, this negative tendency can be compensated, at least partially, by the way of increasing the level of employment especially in the older age group. The study carried out for the OECD countries has shown that most of them have serious possibilities for increasing the degree of using labor force including people from the older age groups [2]. The increase of the degree of involvement of older generations' representatives in labor market can become a serious instrument for opposing negative demographic tendencies.

At the same time, for using the resource of older generations it is necessary to change the existing institutions which regulate the labor market [3-5] and also improve the system of employment assistance and re-education of elderly people [6]. It is important to use a system approach to solving the problem of attracting and refraining representatives of older generations at the labor market. Simple changing of one indicator can't automatically improve the employment coefficients. In order to raise the efficiency of reforms, changes in the institute of employment should be accompanied by reforms in the institutes of professional education, pension support, etc.

An important issue in increasing social activity and life quality of the elderly is using digital technologies. Modern digital technologies assist social integration and enable access to commercial and state services. Introduction of digital technologies has changed life and worldview of the elderly. In April 2012, the Pew Study Center proved that more than half of the elderly (in the age of 65 and older) are the Internet-users. This indicator increased to 59% in 2014. The number of the Internet-users among the elderly has increased by 6% during the year, besides, 47% of the elderly have high broadband connection at home [7]. At the same time, representatives of the older generation experience certain difficulties in the process of mastering information and communication technologies.

The study by L. Damodaran confirms the fact that more and more representatives of the older generation become users of modern information and communication technologies [8]. The results of the study show that representatives of older age groups very much appreciate the advantages and independence they possess owing to using computers and the Internet network. It helps them to keep in touch with their family and friends, to find useful information; it simplifies everyday life (Internet shopping with delivery, online-banking, access to social services, etc.). However, at the same time, representatives of the given age category experience certain problems more often including those connected with understanding of the technical "slang" and the lack of necessary abilities for solving technical problems especially in the issues of computer security. In this regard, the demand for studying educating programs of computer competence and also getting respective technical support is very high in this age category. Besides, support for stimulating elderly people to use modern information and communication technologies is very important both on the part of family members and also on the part of local communities. Thus, organizing special training courses in local schools, libraries and consultation centers is an important instrument for decreasing the so called "digital divide" that is, reducing the break between people who use and those who don't use information-communication technologies especially in the older age groups.

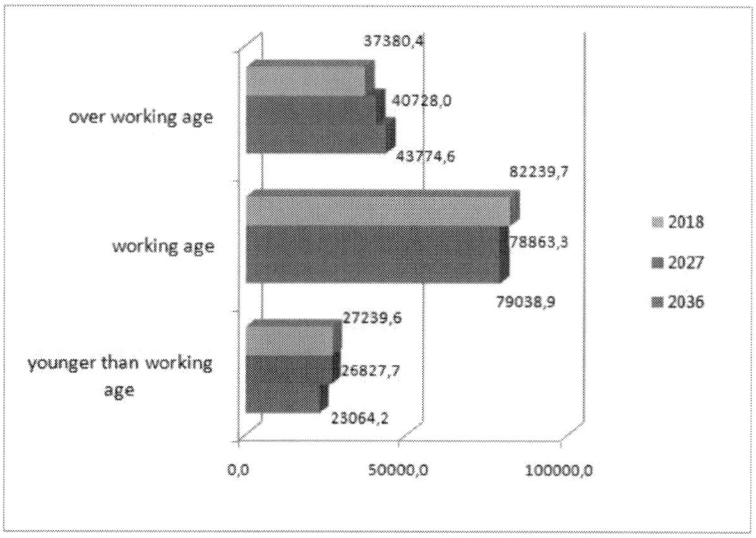

Fig. 1. The number of people of the Russian Federation on separate age groups in thousands of people. Source: The estimation of the Federal State Statistics Service of the Russian Federation.

Let us analyze the current demographic situation and the prospects of its development in the Russian Federation. According to the data of the Federal State Statistics Service, the part of population of the Russian Federation younger than the employable age in 2018 is 18.5%, the employable age – 56%, older than the employable age – 25.5% (Fig. 1). By 2036 the proportions between the data of the population groups according to the average variant of the forecast by the Statistics Service will significantly change: the part of the population younger than the employable age will reduce to 15.8%, the part of the population of the employable age will insignificantly increase to 54.2% (that in absolute values corresponds to reducing from 82239.7 to 79038,9 thousand people), the part of the population older than the employable age will increase to 30% (in absolute values it means the growth from 37380.4 to 43774.6 thousand people or by more than 17%) [9].

According to the data of the average variant of the Statistic Service forecast, the general number of people in Russia will not significantly change in the following 20 years (decrease by 2036 will make about 982 thousand people or 0.67%). At the same time, structural changes in different age groups will be serious enough as we can see on the demographic pyramids built for 2018 and 2036 (Fig. 2). According to the average variant of the forecast, the number of children and teenagers younger than 15 years old will decrease by 15.3%, from 27.2 to 23.1 mln people in 2036 in comparison with 2018, the number of people aged 16-59 will decrease by 4.3% from 88.3 to 84.5 mln people. The structure of the older age groups will also change. The number of people aged 60-69 will slightly reduce regarding other categories: from 17.7 mln people to 16.7 mln people (by 6%). At the same time, the number of people aged 70-79 will seriously grow from 8.4 mln people to 14.5 mln people (by 72%) and the number of people aged 80 and older will increase from 5.1 mln to 7.1 mln people (by 38%). In general, the number of people aged 60 and older will increase from 31.3 mln to 38.3 mln people (by 22.4%), the number of people of the oldest age category of those observed by the Statistics Service – aged 85 and older – will also increase from 2.2 mln to 2.7 mln people (by 20.6%) [9].

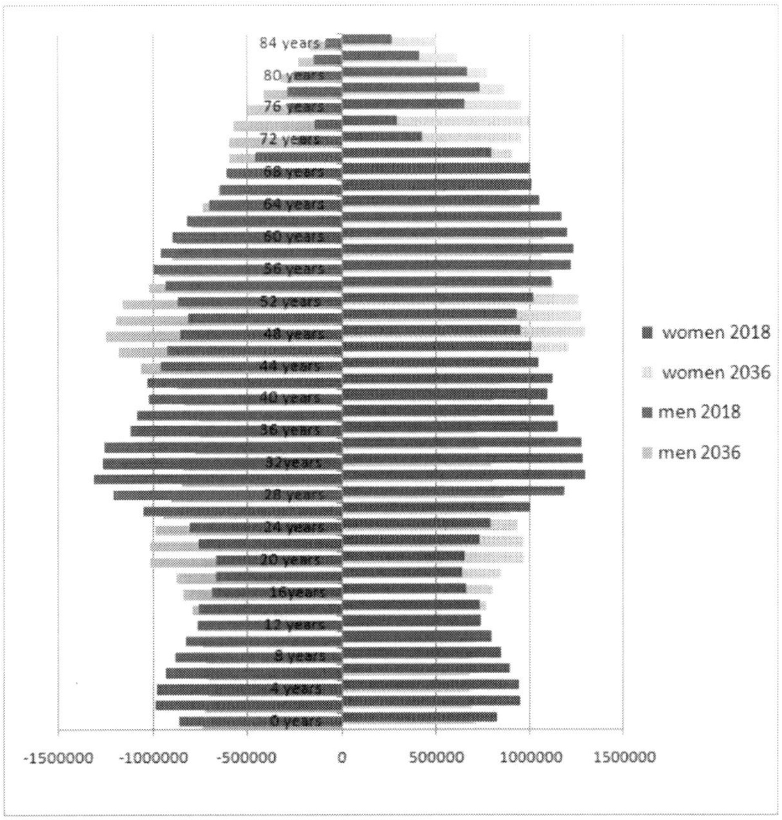

Fig. 2. The supposed number of people in the Russian Federation for 2018 and 2036 (by the beginning of the year, people). Source: The estimation of the Federal State Statistics Service of the Russian Federation.

Thus, according to the analyzed average variant of the forecast, the number of people in Russia who belong to one of the most employable categories out of the older categories (younger than 69 inclusively) will slightly decrease and the general growth will be observed in the groups of people aged 70 and older. It is evident that these changes will significantly influence the structure of the Russian labor market. In this regard, the task of increasing the involvement of people aged 60-69 in labor resources of the RF becomes extremely urgent.

The analysis of the demographic tendencies leads to one more interesting conclusion connected with labor market. The predictable prospects show that the group of older employees (aged 50-65) may become a large subgroup of work force. It will be reflected in the growth of the number of aged workers in companies and organizations and, consequently, it will lead to the growth of age variety at work places. On the one side the increase of age variety may precipitate the appearance of psychological tension and even conflicts at work places. On the other hand its influence may be positive for organizations-employers. This positive influence refers to the growth of informational quality, variety and significance for taking management decisions [10]. The importance of the information which circulates in the organization is connected with cognitive resources of its employees which increase together with the growth of demographic variety. Besides, people with different life and professional experience may have different outer and inner social networks and that leads to the growth of additional value of information [11]. Such informational variety may be especially useful for working with unstandardized problems and for searching creative decisions [12]. Thus, aged employees, as a rule, have knowledge and experience which are useful for increasing the efficiency of the group work. However, such human capital may be effectively used only in the environment where friendly and respectful relations between members of the collective are present [13].

An important demographic factor which is also characteristic of Russia is the growth of the number of women in older age groups. Such characteristics as emotionality, compassion, caring for other people, etc. are often distinguished among the other gender peculiarities of women at work places. These characteristics especially brightly become evident among representatives of older generations, the period of personal development of which was significantly influenced by traditional gender models of behavior [14]. On the other hand, together with development of the service sector the growth of the number of work places is observed that require having not only deep professionalism (or the so called hard skills) but also abilities that are traditionally related to women (sociability, amiability, empathy) which makes women-representatives of older age groups popular in certain professional spheres. Organizations-employers can gain benefits from rich experience and accumulated knowledge of older employees. "Soft skills" that are characteristic of this category are the key factors of success for many work places. Work is very important for representatives of all age groups, however, especially in the older age it takes on core-type significance which "structures peoples' way of life, forms methods for their cooperation with the material and social reality, defines their social status and self-respect" [15]. Thanks to the presence of such "soft" skills older employees are, on the average, as productive as younger ones.

Fast ageing of population connected with birth-rate falling and life-time increase requires special studying of personalities of aged people, their motivation and purposefulness of their interests. The suggestion that aged people wouldn't work, perform socially beneficial activities, express interest in social events is indefensible because in any age a person seeks to obtain new information, informational deprivation negatively influences their well-being. Any age is characterized with avoidance of hunger for information; pursuit of expanding information field is a natural need of a living organism's intellect. It is confirmed by the fact that elderly people actively master internet technologies, the Internet. Olga Golodets noted that in the period of 2011-2015, the years of computer competence, more than 500 thousand of elderly people studied this subject in Russia [16]. In 2012, the founder member of "Kommersant" and "Snob", Vladimir Yakovlev, started a project "The age of Happiness" in Russia which is devoted to active maturity. Stories of people who find themselves once again after 50 are presented on the site – they get new professions, get married, make business, set sporting records [17].

The generation of the 1960-es enters the "silver" age in the contemporary Russia; this generation has managed to reveal itself in new economic conditions and has achieved certain success. These people has mastered modern information technologies, gained foreign professional experience, got used to using creative approach to solving complex social situations. This generation is not characterized by habitual, traditional for the Russia mentality model of behavior. It's most likely that this generation won't stop taking active part in social life after retiring. They will seek to keep the habitual consumption level, keep physical and intellectual activity and increase the quality of their life.

Interests, aptitude, peculiarities of a person, the ways of realizing his social activity are defined by many parameters, however, his age is the biologic axis that generalizes and directs all the personality's characteristics. Speaking about distinguish ability in selecting forms of professional and social activity it is necessary to take the peculiarities of value orientations of the elderly into account. In 2010-12, the authors conducted social research on the structure of value orientations of employees who work at the enterprise which transports gas in the Southern Urals region. The purpose of the study was revealing value orientations and social potential of employees of the pre-retirement and pensionable age who work in enterprises for a more productive use of their professional experience. The study of the structure of the employees' value orientations enabled determining leading values of older people and their level of social activity. 452 people took part in the social research: out of them – 175 (39%) aged 56-62; 258 (57%) aged 46-55 and 19 aged 62 and older (4%). The research was carried out anonymously, in a group and individually.

A questionnaire for estimating the factors of labor attraction adjusted to the conditions of the field was selected as the main methodical material for studying value orientations; the questionnaire contained 68 questions [18]. The methodology was modified according to the purpose of the research, names of a number of value orientations were changed and values were added that correspond to the age group. The term of value orientations as a factor that determines attractiveness of professional activity was used in this methodology. Value orientations in psychical organization of a person are intertwined with cognitive and will processes and make substantive component of a person, the basis of attitude to reality, the source of conscious selection of professional engagement and the form of social activity. In social psychology a person's values are considered from the point of view of forming a unity of a work collective, the value-oriented unity ensures solidarity of the work collective, its manageability and, as a consequence, it increases the efficiency of its activity.

The list of value orientations is approximately the same for people of different age and those having different professional interests. However, the hierarchy of values and ranks of significance differ depending on a person's age. Forming a hierarchy of values is connected with the peculiarities of a person's life journey, age, social roles. The priorities of value orientations enable selectivity in choosing ways and kinds of social activity by a person, the direction of his or her development and reactions in complex social situations. The values hierarchy of older people is already formed. But it doesn't mean that this formation of a person is static and constant. The main function of value orientations is coordination and adjustment of all psychical processes. Top-priority values ensure the basic vector of direction of a person's psychical activity.

The following factors of labor attractiveness were used as the main parameters of values in the conducted research: a creative and interesting job; favorable labor conditions; positive relations with employees; recognition from colleagues; developing one's own abilities; material and social procurement; integrity and perfectionism in working relations; developing every member of the collective; an active life position; rational organization of work; general success; health; achieving personal goals; difference in life positions of the members of the collective. As a result of statistic processing, the following indicators were calculated: aggregate score for each of the value orientations and the rank of each of the values for men and women.

A special methodology was used for estimating social potential [19]. Evaluating unrealized social potential enables predicting success of a person in the social sphere. The social potential of a person is determined as a combination of all the person's possibilities, hidden and и distinct, necessary for any social actions. The social potential of a person enables creating motive power for his or her career in professional sphere. It is an integrated indicator of a person and makes multiple connections with other person's characteristics (intelligence level, motivation, values). The quantity indicator estimating the level of the unrealized social potential reflects also the ability of the test person to build a career in this or that social sphere. The hierarchy of value orientations, as an indicator of a person's focus, makes direct connection with social activity and realizing the person's social potential. That is why two indicators were evaluated in the study: top-priority values and social potential separately for men and women aged 46 and older.

The conducted social research enabled obtaining the following results which describe peculiarities of values of older people and their social potential. The structure of value ranks of women of pre-retirement and pensionable age enables distinguishing the following values most significant for the given group (arranged in accordance with preferences): positive relations with employees; material and social procurement; health. Such value orientations as achieving personal goals, developing every member of the collective; differences in life positions of the members of the work collective; general success, have the lowest positions in the structure.

The conducted qualitative analysis of answers on each of the questions showed that women aged 46-62 strive for positive relations in any work collective; for material and social procurement and programs for health support. The need for warm friendly relations and favorable psychological climate in a work collective may be distinguished as the most important values. Duration and persistence of work in a certain team leads to an increase in the importance of the psychological climate in this work collective, which leads to a great deal of attention to the system of interpersonal relations at work. Age peculiarities are characterized by the inclination for keeping positive, stable relations, creating favorable basis for social contacts. The low rank of the "general success" value can be explained by the peculiarity of performed social roles of older women.

The structure of the ranks of men aged 46-62 enables distinguishing the following significant value orientations (arranged in accordance with preferences): recognition from colleagues; positive relations with employees; a creative and interesting job; developing one's own abilities; health. The following values have low ranks: achieving personal goals; differences in life positions of the members of the collective; developing every member of the collective. The conducted qualitative analysis of selections on each of the questions showed that men-employees aged 46-62 strive for favorable psychological climate in the collective; for developing one's own abilities, they want to upgrade their skills/qualification and professional competence. A strive for recognition from colleagues and a strive for warm, friendly relations can be distinguished as the most important values.

Comparative analysis of value orientations of outermost age groups of men and women aged 46-48 and 58-62 showed that the following values in the ranks has changed: a creative and interesting job; general success; active life position; health; material and social procurement. Increase in employee's age, changes in social status and retirement change the hierarchy of values: significance of creative and interesting jobs, general success and an active life position increases. It is interesting that the rank of values of material and social procurement and health decreases. It may be explained by the fact that material stability and social security has been achieved. Decrease in the rank of health importance is, probably, connected with stabilization of aged people's physical condition and understanding the finiteness of life. The revealed tendency of changes in values hierarchy is confirmed by the structure of value orientations of men and women aged 62 and older, which significantly differs from values of younger employees. The following values have the greatest significance in professional activity (arranged in accordance with preferences): a creative and interesting job; recognition from colleagues; an active life positions; positive relations with employees; general success. The most insignificant value for the given age category is achieving personal goals.

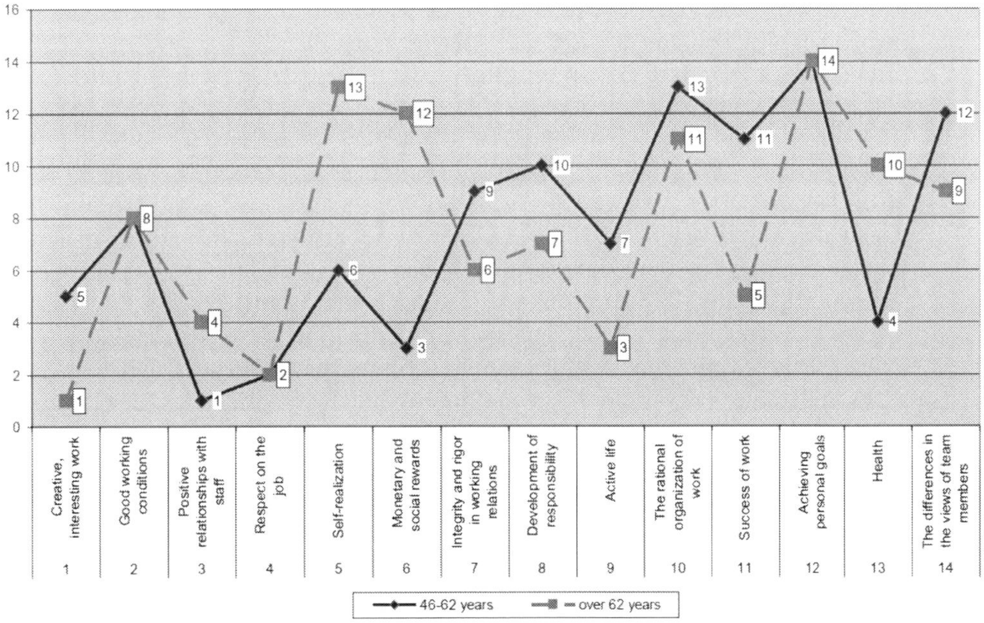

Fig. 3 – Ranks of values of all the surveyed people of different ages (the lower the rank position, the greater the significance of the value having a corresponding rank).

Comparing the ranks of values of two groups of different ages (46-62 and older than 62) is represented in Fig. 3. The analysis carried out showed that employees older than 62 have an active social position in life. They aim at having creative and interesting jobs; recognition from their colleagues; increasing their personal authority; favorable psychological climate in their collective. It should be noted that general success of a work collective has great significance in the lives of these people which refers to a developed feeling of team spirit and mutual aid. Material and social security, health, rational organization of work is valued less than by people of other age groups.

Older generations demonstrated changes in the hierarchy of values; they refer to positive relation to others, activity in achieving collective goals and quite strong altruism in relation to labor – they are less interested in gaining material values and more interested in achieving general success. Such distribution of value ranks in the group may be explained by great life experience and wisdom of employees of older ages. The information revealed may initiate using older employees as mentors for young people.

Special attention should be paid to the fact that the younger employees are, the higher they estimated material and social security and the lower they estimate principality and perfectionism in labor relations. This fact is interesting from the point of view of using professional potential of people of older ages. The analysis of the distribution of value ranks in the entire set enabled revealing psychological regularity: the older the age, the fewer employees are afraid of hardships in their activity and they display more personal responsibility.

Exploring social potential of employees of pre-retirement and pensionable age showed the following results. In the set of women of 46-62 years old: the average indicator of unrealized social potential is 51.2 st. points. In the group of men this indicator is 48.7 st. points. The difference is not statistically important. It is interesting to note that this indicator has greatly increased for the group of people older than 62. Unrealized social potential of older employees is 61.8 st. points. This fact enables predicting high social activity in the group of employees older than 62.

Generalizing the results we can make the following conclusions:

- The revealed mechanism of increase of personal responsibility, reducing fear of hardships in work together with increase in employees' age, both for men and women, is a hidden potential for the "silver economy".
- The older generation of employees may reveal its unrealized potential as specialists-consultants, mentors of young people.
- Unrealized social potential of employees is the basis of activity for people of this age in public and social directions with a significant part of taking creative decisions.
- Generalization of one's own life experience, wise relation to life and understanding its finiteness lead to a more active life position, increasing interest in creative labor aspects and positive and altruistic relations with other people.
- Fixation of employees of older ages on trustworthy interpersonal relations in a collective gives opportunities for forming favorable psychological climate in the work collective, a new opinion on conflict resolution and principles of creating a team.

The results of the study carried out reveal positive sides of aging of the population. Many production enterprises already actively use the potential of the older generation. However, in general, modern society is still focused on the values of young age, considering aging as an inevitable restriction of social activity. Appeal to "silver economy" is inevitably connected with the use of unrevealed potential of the older generation and attracting a significant layer of society to its enrichment and development. If earlier the aging labor force could cause problems for national labor markets in connection with the supposed decline in productivity – today the results of social economic development enable (at least in developed economies) not only reducing demographic risks of performance degradation but also benefit from the qualities connected with the characteristics of today labor force. Modern companies should transfer their thinking from the position "how can we reduce the inefficiency of the human capital caused by demographic changes" to the position "how can we use the rich human resources which are offered by the modern generation to maximum effect".

References

1. D. N. Weil, The American Economic Review, **89(2)** (1999)
2. G. Henseke, *Demographic change and the economically active populations of OECD countries – Could older workers compensate for the decline? From Grey to Silver. Managing the Demographic Change Successfully* (Springer-Verlag, Berlin, 2011)
3. R. B. Freeman, International Economic Journal, **19(2)** (2005)
4. D. R. Howell, D. Baker, A. Glyn, J. Schmitt, Capitalism and Society, **2 (1)** (2007)
5. S. Nickell, L. Nunziata, W. Ochel, The Economic Journal, **115** (2005)
6. H. P. Blossfeld, D.Hofaecker, S. Buchholz, S. Pollnerova, *Late careers and retirement under globalization: Becoming retired in times of accelerating social change* (American Sociological Association, Boston, 2010)
7. Older Adults and Technology Use. Pew Research Center, April [online] Available at: http://www.pewinternet.org/2014/04/03/older-adults-and-technology-use/ (2014)
8. L. Damodaran, W. Olphert, S. Phipps, Working with older people, **17 (1)** (2013)
9. The official site of the Federal State Statistics Service. Demography [online] Available at:

http://www.gks.ru/wps/wcm/connect/rosstat_main/rosstat/ru/statistics/population/demography/ (2017)
10. D. L. Van Knippenberg, M. C. Schippers, Annual Review of Psychology, **58** (2007)
11. C. M. Beckman, P. R. Haunschild, Administrative Science Quarterly, **47 (1)** (2002)
12. R. S. Burt, Social Networks, **24 (4)** (2002)
13. L. M. Shore, B. G. Chung-Herrera, M. A. Dean, K. H. Erhart, D. I. Jung, A. E. Randel, G. Singh, Human Resource Management Review, **19(2)** (2009)
14. L. Von Rosenstiel, *Grundlagen der Organisationspsychologie* (Schäffer-Poeschel, Stuttgart, 2000)
15. H. Applebaum, *The concept of work: Ancient, medieval, and modern* (State University of New York Press, New York, 1992)
16. Silver economy: how can we improve the life of the elderly and make money from that [online], Available at: https://rb.ru/longread/silver-economy-in-russia/ (2017)
17. The official site of the project "The Age of Happiness" [online], Available at: http//theageofhappiness.com (2017)
18. G. S.Nikiforov, M. A.Dmitriyeva, V. M.Snetkov, *Practical course on management psychology and professional activity* (SPb, 2003)
19. The best psychological tests (Petrokom, Saint Petersburg, 1992)

Labor management and social and labor relations in the digital economy[a]

Dmitry Desyatko[1*], *Boris* Genkin[1] , and *Viktoriya* Rapgof[2]

[1] Saint Petersburg State University of Economics, Economics and Finance Faculty, 191023 Sadovaya st. 21, Russian Federation
[2]Saint Petersburg State University of Architecture and Civil Engineering, Faculty of economics and management, 190005 2-ya Krasnoarmeiskaya st. 4, Russian Federation

Abstract. Social partnership is the most important type of social and labor relations in the modern economy, which is based on the active participation of trade unions in the enterprises management, payroll rate determination, and improvement of its conditions. In addition, in the framework of the conditions of extensive application of digital technologies the employees being outside the premises of the employer's organization began to perform a significant part of the functions of many organizations, and for a certain category of employees, the possibility of their replacement with intelligent machine systems will become the reality in the near future. The paper shows that one of the optimality criteria for the parameters of the social system is the country's living standards. The proposed criterion takes into account GDP per capita, the Gini ratio and the crime rate. The paper also shows that in the digital economy one of the main factors of the living standards growth is the application of new scientific results. The specific measures are proposed to create new forms of social and labor relations in the digital economy.

1 Special aspects of labor management in the automated productions and management data processing systems

Labor management systems are determined by the following basic concepts:
- human activity;
- workplace;
- labor rating.

Human activity is characterized by three components:
- regulated;
- creative;
- ethical [1].

---

[a] This article was prepared under financial support of the Russian Science Foundation (Grant No. 18-18-00099)
[*] Corresponding author: ddesyatko@yandex.ru

The regulated component in the production systems is particularly presented on car assembly lines. Despite the use of robots, a part of the operations is performed by workers. In these productions, the need for automation based on the digital technologies is determined by economic and social factors.

The creative component is the basis for everybody who creates new scientific, technical, and entrepreneurial ideas. The human creativity becomes the main economic resource in the modern economy.

The ethical component of human activity in the production systems is especially important for managers at all levels. The teamwork effectiveness depends largely on them. The ethical aspects for using the digital technologies are largely based on the human employment prospects.

The concept of "**workplace**" has two aspects. The first aspect features a set of elements (equipment, tools, means of communication) that are necessary to perform a certain part of the production process. In this respect, the workplace can be individual or collective. The second aspect of the concept of "workplace" features a field of one employee. This aspect is used in the employment management systems and the labor market analysis.

In the framework of the conditions of extensive application of digital technologies the employees being outside the premises of the employer's organization began to perform a significant part of the functions of many organizations. To denote such employment, the terms "free", "remote", "home", "distance", etc. are used.

A considerable number of publications have been devoted to the problems of "remote" workplaces over recent years. It should be noted the paper [2], the authors of which pay attention to the importance of legally accurate definition of the nature of work on electronic platforms, so that working platforms will be provided with a special protection similar to part-time regulations, fixed conditions or agency work. In cases they are not qualified as employees, they should be protected as self-employed ones. Studies conducted under the auspices of the Eurofound 2015 [3] have showed that nine new forms of employment appeared from the beginning of the 21st century, three of which are a direct consequence of the rapid development of digital technologies: ICT-based mobile operations where workers do not use their employer's premises as their main workplace and spend the most part of their time working with information and information technologies; employees can be hired or self-employed on the online platforms ("crowdsourcing of work"), which allows organizations or individuals to access to an uncertain and unknown group of other organizations (for example, PeoplePerHour, ClickWorker or Amazon Mechanical Turk) via the Internet; call-type work is characterized by continuous labor relations without continuous work, when the employer signs an employment agreement with the employee, but does not undertake to provide the work continuously (a zero contract is the most famous example of this phenomenon). The importance of changing the labor nature and the possibility of its replacement with intelligent machine systems is investigated in the papers [4, 5, 6, 7].

Labor rating is the most important part of labor management and remuneration. The paper [1] presents the importance and necessity of correct economic use of expenditure rates and results, duration rates and labor intensity of operations, other rate.

The process of comprehensive substantiation of labor standards, taking into account the interrelation of technical, economic and social factors, is implemented as the choice of the optimal variant of the rate and the relevant parameters of the technical and labor processes.

The main objects of labor rating are the rates of duration and labor (operations) intensity:

$$N_T = N_D \times N_N \tag{1}$$

Where

N_T – labor rate,

N_D –duration rate,

N_N –a rate of workers performing this operation.

The process operations duration rates are usually calculated using the formula:

$$N_D = (t_o + t_b)(1 + \frac{K_o + K_r}{100}) + \frac{T_e}{n} \tag{2}$$

where t_0 is the main (process) time; t_b is an auxiliary time for parts installation and removal; K_o is a workplace service time, K_r is a rest and personal needs time factor; T_e is an equipment setup time; n is a size of the parts batch.

The process time (t_0) is calculated based on the choice of a rational equipment operating mode. All other formula elements are determined by rates, which, as a rule, are established according to the statistics and do not have sufficient justification for the particular workshop conditions.

In the conditions of automated manufactures using computerized numerical control equipment, the operations duration calculation shall take into account, first of all, the planned level of automatic operation of equipment. This level determines the abilities to implement the output program.

If the direct costs of products include only the costs of the main (machine, hardware) time, then:

$$N_d = t_o \frac{T_s}{T_s - T_b} \tag{3}$$

where t_0 is a machine (hardware) time per a product unit; T_s is a working shift duration; T_b is a scheduled and accident[b] breaks in equipment operation per shift.

A rate for a number of employees maintaining the automated equipment shall be calculated based on the standards of labour intensity of the scheduled breaks for equipment repair and setup. When calculating the rates for a number of employees maintaining the automated equipment, the probability of accidental equipment failures shall also be taken into account. The tables based on the queuing theory [1] are proposed for practical calculations.

2 Special aspects of social and labor relations in the digital economy

The social and labor relations feature the economic, psychological and legal interrelationships between individuals and social groups based on the labor activity

Social partnership is the most important type of social and labor relations in the modern economy, which is based on the active participation of trade unions in the enterprises management, payroll rate determination, and improvement of its conditions. The main ideas

[b] Caused by equipment failure

of social partnership were developed and implemented by a group of German economists under the guidance of L. Erhard [8].

The social system, where private ownership of the production means and market pricing remains, is commonly called a socially oriented market economy [9].

The progressive scale of personal taxes that allows significantly reduce the economic inequality of the country's population plays an important role in this system of public relations. Health care and pension system management also contributes the reduction of inequality.

The elements of capitalism and socialism are combined in the socially oriented market economy.

This confirms the validity of the Hegel's triads: thesis→ antithesis→ synthesis. In this case, this triad is specified in the form: capitalism → socialism → market economy and social partnership.

Based on the idea of social partnership, which is the basis of social and labor relations in the modern economy, we can formulate the task to choose the optimal structure of the social system parameters.

The criterion of optimality in this task is the country's living standards. The constraint system includes the characteristics of the country's resources and the conditions for their most effective use.

Thus, the following parameters shall be determined:

$$X = \{x_1, x_2 \dots x_n\}, \tag{4}$$

under which

$$K_x = \frac{\textit{Actual levels of goods consumption}}{\textit{Needs of the population}} \to \max \tag{5}$$

and the following limits are observed:

- legal rules;
- available resources;
- personal income differentiation degree;
- environmental standards;
- other parameters.

where $X = \{x_1, x_2 \dots x_n\}$, – the set of analyzed parameters of the social system; K_x – the living standards depending on X.

In the digital economy one of the main factors of the living standards growth is the application of new scientific results.

In modern Russia, a share of GDP research costs is a little higher than 1%, which is significantly less than in developed and many developing countries. Therefore, one of the conditions (limits) of the problem under consideration shall be the following relationship:

$$R \,\&\, D(X) \geq 0.02GDP \tag{6}$$

where R&D(X) is a share of science costs in GDP.

As shown in [8], the main indicators of the country's living standard are the following:

- GDP per capita (G_p);
- Level of income differentiation (D);
- Crime rate (C).

Therefore, the objective functions that meet the criteria for the optimality of the social system parameters are:

$G_p(X) \rightarrow max$;

$D(X) \rightarrow min$;

$C(X) \rightarrow min$.

where $G_p(X)$ – gross domestic product per capita; $D(X)$ – income differences factor; $C(X)$ – crime rates.

Our earlier studies [9] allowed us to determine the living standard indicators for developed and some developing countries. The highest living standard indicators are in countries where the idea of the socially-oriented market economy has been implemented (Iceland, Sweden, Finland, Denmark, Netherlands, Japan, Germany), where the average rating for the three above-mentioned indicators ranges from 9.7 to 22.3 points. Indicators of the US and Russia are significantly worse because of high levels of income and crime differentiation (69.7 and 78.3, respectively).

In the same study, it was shown that for a sample that includes the developed countries of Europe, the United States and Russia, a correlation number between the income and crime differentiation rates is more than 0.95. High levels of crime in the US and Russia are largely due to the fact that income differentiation rates in these countries are 2 times higher than in developed countries of Europe, including Sweden, Norway, Denmark and Germany.

One of the most important aspects of social and labor relations is the ratio of productivity and wage, taking into account the personal income differentiation.

As seen from Fig. 1, 2, the dynamics of wage levels in developed countries generally corresponds to the dynamics of productivity.

When analyzing the ratio of productivity and wage, it is necessary to proceed from the fact that the growth rates of wage of farmers, workers, engineers, artists, writers can not objectively outstrips the growth rates of their labor productivity.

The higher is the hierarchy level, the less noticeable is the relationship between the levels of productivity and wage. This fact is illustrated in Fig. 5 which combines the information of Fig. 3 and 4.

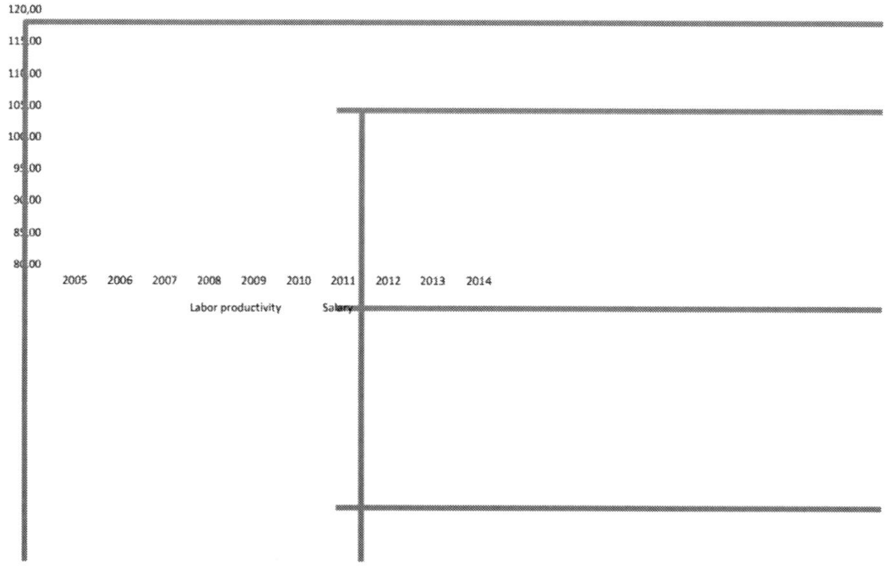

Fig. 1. The dynamics of labor productivity and wage in France, 2005-2014.

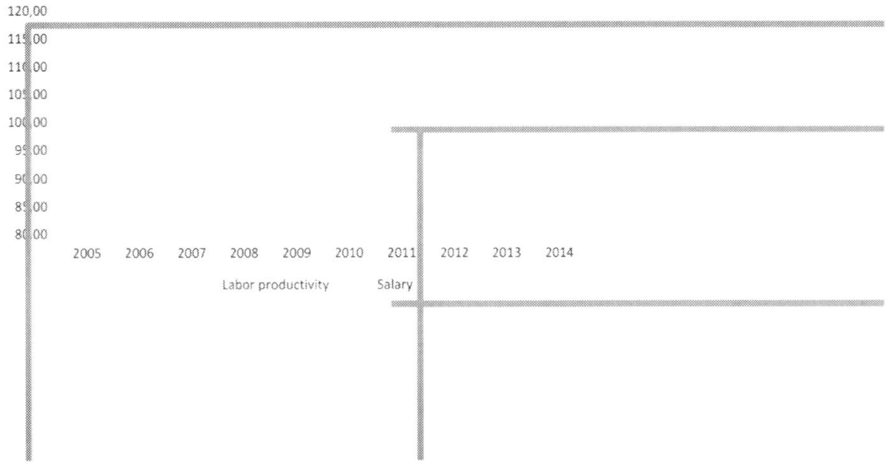

Fig. 2. Dynamics of labor productivity and wage in Finland, 2005-2014.

The growth rate of wage in Russia outstrips the growth rates of labor productivity (Fig. 3). The main reasons for this ratio are the following:

- Russia's lag in productivity of labor from developed countries is 2-3 times [10];
- a high degree of personal income differentiation.

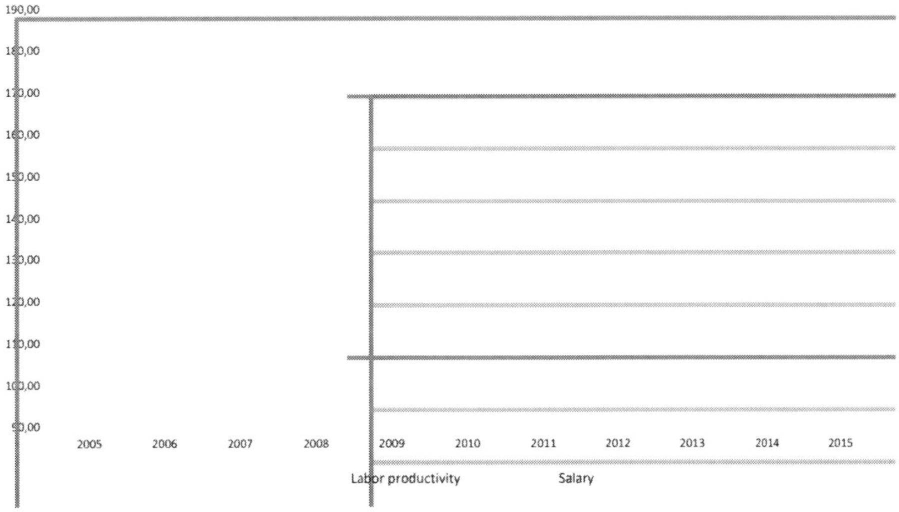

Fig. 3. Dynamics of labor productivity and wage in Russia, 2005-2015.

Fig. 4 shows the dynamics of personal income levels in five groups (quintiles).

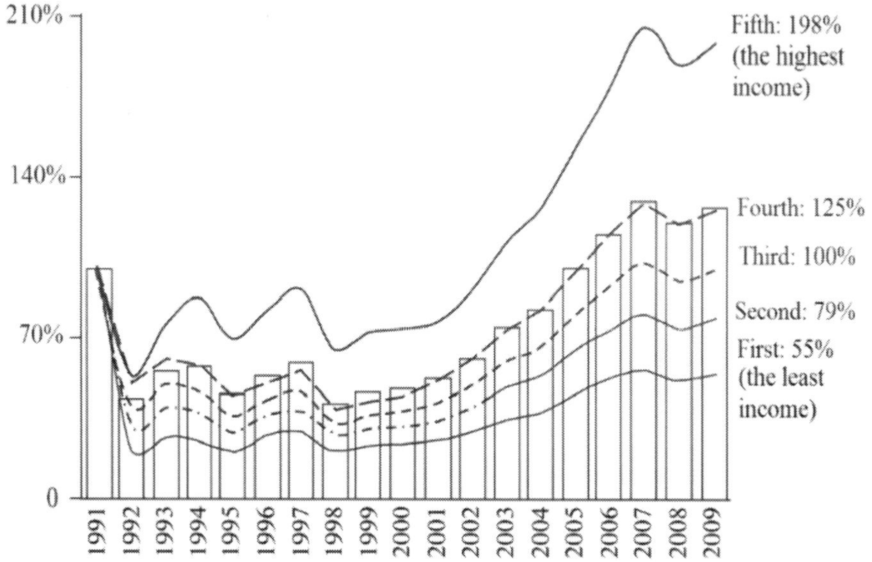

Fig. 4. Dynamics of real money personal income in Russia by 20% income groups [11].

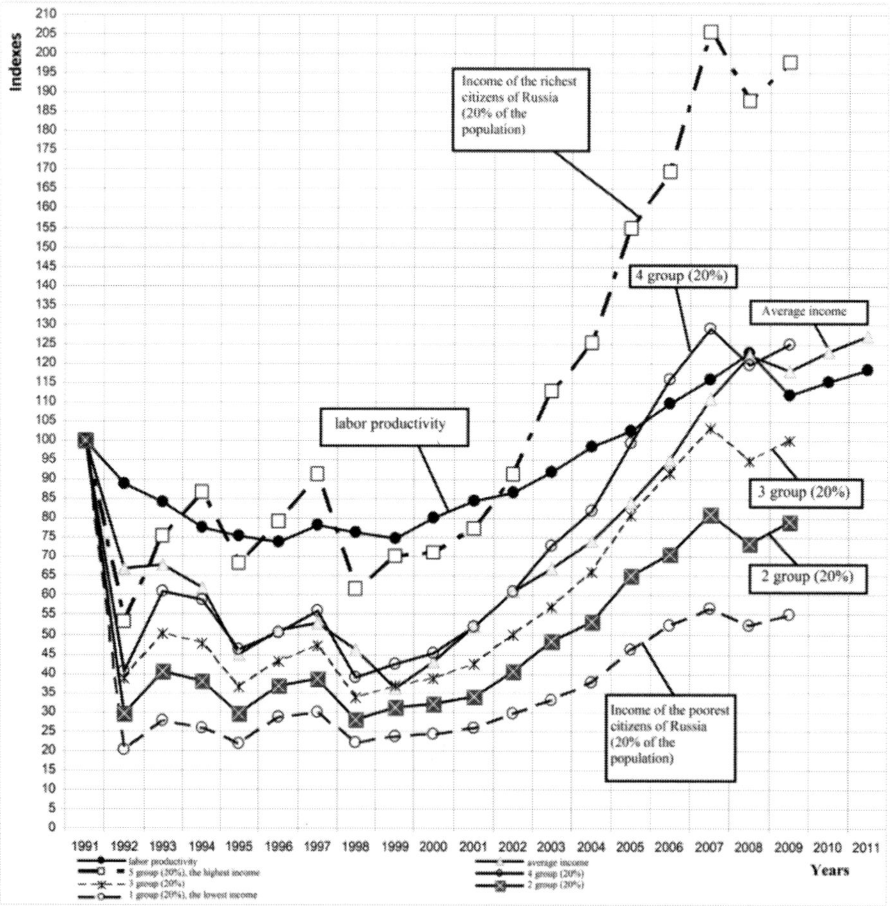

Fig. 5. Dynamics of labor productivity and real money personal income in Russia by 20% income groups [11].

As seen from Fig. 5, for the richest 20% of the Russian population, the income growth rate is much higher than the growth rate of labor productivity.

We fully admit that among the richest citizens of Russia (5th quintiles) there are outstanding inventors and businessmen, whose incomes correspond to the results of their labor. But it is clear that such representatives of business are not very many.

More than three years ago, a system of performance-based contracts was introduced in the budgetary organizations of Russia (schools, universities, regulatory bodies), which establish the relationship between the employees performance of the organization and the bonuses level.

Accounting of officials' performance is much more difficult than assessing the importance of publications by an associate professor or professor. An objective assessment of management efficiency of economic and social processes at various levels of the administrative hierarchy shall be based on the assessment of a large amount of statistical information. This supposes the use of modern means of data collection and processing, which allow arranging the accounting of personal incomes for all sources.

To improve social and labor relations in modern Russia, we introduced a proposal on the adoption of the Law "On the motivation of productivity growth and remuneration based on innovation and social partnership" [1]:

1. The motivation of labor productivity and wage growth is carried out by regions and sectors of the economy.
2. The minimum wage in a region shall be no less than the regional subsistence minimum wage.
3. In all organizations of the region's commercial sector, the minimum wage (MW) shall increase annually in accordance with the growth rate of labor productivity in the relevant sector of the region and the level of inflation in the past year.
4. The average wage of workers and employees of enterprises (without the income of members of the boards of directors) shall be no less than three times the minimum wage at the enterprise.
5. The relationship between the growth rates of productivity and the minimum wage is established as a result of negotiations between representatives of employers, trade unions and the government of the region.
6. In the non-profit sector and regional authorities, the growth of the minimum wage shall correspond to the average growth in labor productivity in the region and the level of inflation in the past year.

The proposed scheme for managing productivity and wages does not use any internal information of enterprises. They are considered as "black boxes" and transmit to the management bodies only the usual statistical information on the products output and a personnel number. On the basis of these data, the indicator of the average labor productivity in the economy branch and on the region as a whole is determined.

Similar ideas are expressed in those countries of Western Europe, where the processes of economy digitalization are very fast. Therefore, one of the largest German trade union amalgamation IG Metall [4] deserves attention: they are aimed at guaranteeing the social rights of workers in the digital world: development of new coding forms for the digital world, adaptation and protection of cognitive law; development and implementation of comprehensive rules for mobile workers; definition of the rights to participate and protect when working on the basis of electronic platforms; increase the level of employees' data protection; development of approaches based on the concept of humane digital workplace; development of the competence of officials working part-time; encouraging public debate that influences research policy; development of standards for occupational safety and health; more active efforts to promote learning at the company level; use of new methods of training in the ICT workplace and certification of skills acquired at the workplace.

Adoption of the proposed law and proposals from German trade unions fully corresponds to the ideology of social partnership, which is the basis of social and labor relations.

References

1. B.M. Genkin, *Arrangement, rating and remuneration of labor at industrial enterprises*, (Norma, Moscow, 2014)
2. J. Drahokoupil, B. Fabo, European Economic, Employment and Social Policy, **5, 6** (2016)
3. Eurofound, *New forms of employment* (Publication Office of the European Union, Luxembourg, 2015)
4. E. Brynjolfsson, A. McAfee, *The second machine age. Work, progress and prosperity in a time of brilliant technologies* (W. W. Norton & Company, New York, 2015)
5. C. Degryse, *Digitalization of the economy and its impact on labour markets* (ETUI, Brussels, 2016)
6. EU-OSHA, *A review of the future of work: robotics* (European Agency for Safety and Health at Work, Bilbo, 2015)
7. C. Fuchs, E. Fisher, *Reconsidering value and labour in the digital age (dynamics of virtual work series* (Palgrave Macmillan, Basingstoke, 2015)
8. L. Erhard, *Half a Century of Reflection* (Russiko, Moscow, 1993)
9. B.M. Genkin, D.N. Desyatko, E.A. Ekimova, Living standard in Russian regions, **4** (2016)
10. S.Yu. Glaziev, *Russia is on the way to the innovative economy* (RAS Report, 2014)
11. E.G. Yasin, *The level and lifestyle of the population of Russia in 1989-2009* (Publ. House VShE, Moscow, 2011)

Socio-cyberphysical systems and intellectual space in the development of the Arctic zone of the Russian Federation[a]

Nikolay Didenko[1*], and *Djamilia* Skripnuk[1]

[1] Peter the Great St. Petersburg Polytechnic University, Institute of Industrial Management, Economics and Trade, 195251 Polytechnicheskaya st. 29, Russian Federation

Abstract. The article states the new technical basis of production, which is socio-cyberphysical systems and intellectual space, and also analyzes the current state of studies on the problem regarding the development of socio-cyberphysical systems and intellectual space. The concepts definition is described – socio-cyberphysical systems and intellectual space. The paper proposes to take the target subspaces of the Arctic territory of the Russian Federation as a territory for application of socio-cyberphysical systems and intellectual space. There are seven types of target subspaces for the Arctic development as the targets for the ideology of socio-cyberphysical systems and intellectual space: base cities, mobile filed camps, territories for mineral resources extraction, recreational areas, fishing grounds, northern sea route, safe existence protection infrastructure. The article outlines the concept of building socio-cyberphysical systems and intellectual space. The global conceptual goal of the Russian Arctic development is stated as a transition to the functioning of the Arctic zone in the mode of sustainable development on the basis of socio-cyberphysical systems and intellectual space. The targeted integrated programs have been conceptually selected as a tool for arrangement and management of the socio-cyberphysical systems and intellectual space development in the target sub-spaces of the Arctic zone of the Russian Federation.

1 Introduction

The term Cyber Physical System (CPS) appeared in 2006 and is a promising innovation line. The socio-cyberphysical systems are an information technology concept that implies the integration of various technical systems including Cyber Physical Systems into the integral part with person involvement in this system and able to adapt to environment changes.

The intellectual space is the cumulative result of human activity and idea complex. The cumulative result of human activity is associated with the territory, where people live and which is developed. The idea complex is associated with the probable transformation of the

[a] The paper is based on research carried out with the financial support of the grant of the Russian Science Foundation (Project No. 14-38-00009)
[*] Corresponding author: didenko.nikolay@mail.ru

territory. The intellectual space can exist in the form of data banks, databases, knowledge bases, technologies for their maintenance and application, information telecommunications systems. The intellectual space is a data representation of the essential properties and states, as well as the relationship with the external world of the territory where people live and which is developed.

The problems discussed in this article are unique from the point of scientific research in the world science, as, firstly, the whole complex of problems in the socio-cyberphysical systems and intellectual space requires a continuous refinement of the properties and nature of the objects in question for their correct description. Secondly, as in any multi scale system, the very approach to solving emerging problems fundamentally excludes the classic approaches with centuries-old traditions of "physical" experiment. The approach to solving emerging problems assumes extensive application of mathematical modeling and the methods of "Computational Economics" as a new field of analysis of this research of the socio-cyberphysical systems and intellectual space. In the part of the "Computational Economics", which studies the economic processes of dynamic systems of interacting active rational agents, a widely recognized tool for studying such systems is computer agent-based modeling. The main researchers in this area shall be considered companies and developers of simulation platforms.

The current state of research on the problem of the socio-cyberphysical systems and intellectual space development is characterized by the fact that the approaches to individual sub-areas for the territory development on the basis of socio-cyberphysical systems and intellectual space are actively developing in a number of countries. The socio-cyberphysical systems are the types of systems that shall firstly be conceived and developed taking into account both technological and organizational aspects from the earliest stages. In fact, the design of such systems requires a suitable combination of beneficial technologies in the operational structure, integrating and coordinating the set of processes managed by complex organizations, each of which consists of independent and autonomous units. Along here the problems in the identification and development of adaptation systems for technical networks for smart spaces are discussed which are selected to focus, in particular, on (a) the social and technical model and process, (b) a multilevel integration structure, and (c) systems analysis methods for adaptation at runtime. Perspective robotic technology systems, socio-cyberphysical systems can not exist without artificial intelligence, which in turn depends on computational capability.

Significant scales in solving particular problems related to socio-cyberphysical systems and intellectual space are performed at the National Institute of Standards and Technology (NIST), where the higher priority is given as a whole to the problem of socio-cyberphysical and intellectual systems. The NIST philosophy presents the examples of cyber-physical systems: robots, smart buildings, medical implants, autonomous cars and drone aircraft. One of the most important challenges in the area of design, development and management of these cyber-physical systems is the issue of combined action of cyber-physical systems and people.

The issues that play an important role in the analysis and design of cyber-physical systems are the definition and modeling of the "situational understanding" (in other words, to be aware of what's going on around) of the human experience in interaction with these systems and the environment, as well as change in general circumstances and / or separate parameters created by these systems. The cyber physical systems in the NIST vision form the basis for the development of production, in particular, in the following areas: smart production, smart healthcare, smart grid infrastructure, smart buildings and infrastructure, smart cars, mobile systems and defense systems.

From the development of the software for intelligent systems, the world's leading research centers are the research universities specializing in engineering and technology:

Eindhoven University of Technology (TU / e); the University of Science and Technology Beijing, China; Inria – Institute for Research in Computer Science and Automation, France; The National Center for Scientific Research (CNRS), France. Studies of socio-cyberphysical systems (SCPS) in relation to production networks are actively performed in Brazil (Federal University of Santa Catarina, Brazil) and Germany (University of Bremen, Bremen, Germany).

The authors who study various aspects of socio-cyberphysical systems can be identified.

So Giacomo Cabri Massimo Cossentino et al study adaptive social and technical systems for intellectual spaces [1]. A group of Chinese scientists (Tao Zhang, Qing Li, Chang-shui Zhang et al) classify the technologies used for intelligent autonomous systems [2]. Intellectual unmanned autonomous systems are one of the most important applications of socio-cyberphysical systems. The development of such systems can significantly contribute to innovations in artificial intelligence technologies. The studies of Chinese scientists include the trends in the development of intelligent autonomous systems by summarizing the main achievements of each technological platform. The classification is applied to the appropriate technologies including artificial intelligence ones, unmanned vehicles, drone aircraft, service robots, space robots, marine robots and intelligent plants.

G. W. Gabrielsen [3], Enzo Morosini Frazzon, Jens Hartmann et al. are actively engaged in the design of adaptive social and technical systems for intellectual spaces. [4].

The socio-cyberphysical systems are studied from the point of various production, transport and trade operations, using the potential of the cyber physical system to determine human behavior using large data analytics [5]. In this case, contextual variables are identified that determine the cultural, administrative (or institutional), geographic and economic (including the infrastructure) environment, where these operations are planned. The importance of socio-cyberphysical systems in logistics [6], energy [7] is noted, as they significantly rely on the complex and dynamic interactions with the environment.

The study of socio-cyberphysical systems from the interaction between the physical and cyber world allows considering the socio-cyberphysical systems as the most effective and stabling systems in the process of their implementation [8]. In this case, a new challenges class arises, a new field of studies related to the modeling, design and testing of socio-cyberphysical systems prior to their implementation is opened [9], [10]. The methods and tools associated with the physical and cyber space are not suitable for the socio-cyberphysical systems.

2 The target subspaces of the Arctic territory of the Russian Federation – the areas for application of socio-cyberphysical systems and intellectual space

The general feature of this region being unique by geographical location, natural resources and military-strategic importance is: insufficient population of the territories, insufficient labor force for development, urbanization, severe climate and uncomfortable living conditions, the need to preserve the territory ecosystems, the presence of waste and pollution from human activity [11].

In terms of actual technological achievements and trends, the global conceptual goal of the Russian Arctic development can be stated as a transition to the functioning of the Arctic zone in the mode of sustainable development on the basis of socio-cyberphysical systems and intellectual space. Representation of the Arctic space of the Russian Federation as a set of target subspaces is a general conceptual idea of the organization and management of the development of the Arctic space of the Russian Federation.

The subspace is a part of the Arctic space, which has a number of distinctive features (attributes) that allow for the functional division of the Arctic territory also characterized by a special development goal. The subspace as a part of space has physical boundaries, but the sub-spaces do not require to be set by boundaries of the administrative-territorial entities of the regions.

The objective for arrangement of the Arctic territories development currently facing the government requires the cooperation of various participants in the process to achieve a synergistic effect. The physical unification of regions and municipalities to ensure effective development of the Russian Arctic is undoubtedly impossible (or, at least, difficult) for administrative and legal reasons: this may require both a change in the territorial division of the country and the transformation of the regulatory bodies. At the same time, the Arctic subspaces as target management objects can be more flexibly integrated into a network of interactions.

The next argument in favor of applying the principle of dividing the Arctic space into target components is the relative homogeneity of different types of subspaces in comparison with municipalities that allows more adequate aggregation and modeling of the necessary processes. Indeed, the municipalities that form the Russian Arctic space differ in a number of indicators, and to arrange the reclamation and development of their territories, an individual account of all the features of these regions is required. At the same time, the target subspaces (within a separate type) are quite similar in their key characteristics (the main reason is that the target subspaces are not the complex entities as the Arctic regions). In other words, each separate region (not necessarily the Arctic one) can be represented as the target subspaces, but the subspaces need not be limited to the administrative-territorial division of regions.

Among the possible types of target subspaces that compose the Arctic zone of the Russian Federation, there are [12, 13]:

a) The base cities are large and medium populated and production points, which are presently not so much in the Arctic space of the Russian Federation. The base city means a territorial unit with a mixed building and a population of at least one thousand people in the territory of which there are industrial organizations, construction sites, railway terminals and other industrial infrastructure facilities, as well as commercial, domestic, medical, cultural, educational and administrative facilities. As examples of subspaces, of the "basic city" type, we can name such settlements as Murmansk, Apatity, Severomorsk, Monchegorsk, Kandalaksha, Naryan-Mar, Iskateley settlement, Anadyr, Bilibino, Pevek, Novy Urengoy, Noyabrsk, Salekhard, Nadym, Muravlenko, Labytnangi, Chokurdakh, Saskylakh, Tiksi, Chersky, Deputatsky, Vorkuta, Norilsk, Dudinka, Igarka, Arkhangelsk, Novodvinsk, Severodvinsk, Mezen, Kamenka, Onega, etc.

b) Mobile field camps are one of the ways to develop the Arctic territories, where arrangement of permanent household, cultural, educational and other types of infrastructure is difficult and economically unprofitable. Mobile field camps are usually located near deposits of mineral resources or within the areas of infrastructure facilities construction and maintenance.

The main criterion of this sub-space type is its "project" focus: the field camp is created to perform a specific objective (mining operations in harsh environment, construction, etc.), after which it can be moved, demolished or converted in a complete basic city.

c) Territories of mineral resources extraction. These areas mean deposits and industrial facilities constructed for extraction of minerals. Let us emphasize once again that the concept of "the territory of mineral resources extraction" is not limited only to the definition of the resource field (i.e., minerals accumulation); the explored or suspected deposits, where direct extraction of resources has not yet begun, do not belong to the category of this target sub-space [13].

d) Recreational areas. These areas include such objects of tourist interest as reserves, national parks, zones of eco-, ethno- and extreme tourism and other attractions of the Arctic space that form a network of Arctic tourism. A. Kajan [14], J. Dawson, M.E. Johnston, E.J. Stewart [15], N. Didenko, D. Skripnuk, and O. Krasulina [12] present the prospects for the development of polar tourism and its impact on the welfare of the indigenous population. As examples of recreational areas, it is possible to identify the natural-ethnic park "Beringia" in the Chukotka Autonomous District, the geological natural monument of regional importance "Kharberiysky" in the Yamal-Nenets Autonomous District and the Lapland Reserve in the Murmansk Region.

e) Fishing grounds. Similarly, as in the case of mining areas, this concept does not exclusively include the variety of fish resources available for catching; this target sub-space includes the means and infrastructure for commercial fishing. Arctic fishing is a special economy branch the development of which requires an extremely circumspective approach because of the fragility of the Arctic ecosystem and its susceptibility to climate change [16]. As examples of fishing grounds, it is possible to distinguish water areas of the Murmansk Region (included in the Barents-Belomorsk Territorial Administration of the Federal Agency for Fishery) and the Yamal-Nenets Autonomous District (included in the Nizhneobsk Territorial Administration of the Federal Agency for Fishery).

f) Northern Sea Route. According to the legislation of the Russian Federation, the water area adjacent to the Northern Sea Route of the Russian Federation covering the internal sea waters, territorial sea, the adjacent zone and the exclusive economic zone of the Russian Federation and bounded at the east by the line of separation of sea areas with the United States of America and parallel to Cape Dezhnev in the Bering Strait, at the west – by the meridian of Cape Zhelaniya to the Novaya Zemlya Archipelago, the eastern coastline Novaya Zemlya Archipelago and western boundaries of straits Matochkin Shar, Kara Strait, Yugorski Shar [17 - 19].

This target subspace differs from all the other ones listed above both by its size (extension), and its complexity, as well as by the variety of connections with other subspaces. The Northern Sea Route is allocated as a separate target sub-space, primarily because of its geo-economic importance (other transport corridors of the Arctic zone, which are a part of the infrastructure providing the interaction of sub-spaces in network formations have no similar strategic importance for the development of the country's economy) [18, 19].

The Northern Sea Route comprises not only a possible shipping route, but also port and service institutions that make up its sub-space [20].

g) The infrastructure for protection of safe existence is a target sub-space that performs the functions for protection of safe existence and development of the Arctic space. The Arctic security system shall consist of various defense establishments and facilities, threat detection and prevention services, means for security of communications and information, customs, ecology, reconnaissance satellites, etc. Military settlements, bases, educational formations shall also be assigned to this type of subspaces [21 - 23].

Thus, the Arctic space division into the sub-spaces is of a functional nature: each type of sub-space performs various functions in accordance with its inherent attributes – integral and necessary properties.

3 The concept of building socio-cyberphysical systems and intellectual space

The concept includes a methodology for classification of processes that are developed based on the principles of key technological trends underlying the socio-cyberphysical systems in the framework of the concept of development of the Arctic zone of the Russian

Federation.

The concept includes the main manifestations of technological mega-trends that are crucial in the innovative and technological development of the Arctic zone of the Russian Federation and are based on the possibility for creation of the socio-cyberphysical systems: power supply technologies for the Arctic territories based on mobile nuclear power plants and renewable sources; subsea hydrocarbon production on the shelf; use of unmanned vehicles; additive technologies and 3D printing; advanced robotics; new materials; the Internet of Things; radio relay – tropospheric communication; use of space technologies in the development of the Arctic (a system of satellites in the Highly Elliptical Orbit); automated complexes that can be used for underwater (ice) operations on the Arctic shelf for monitoring the environmental situation, minerals exploration; digital technologies in economic activity; natural gas aircraft; telemedicine and mobile health systems in the Arctic; sanitary drone aircraft; systems of distance production training at enterprises operating within the regions of the Arctic.

The concept includes the structure of the intellectual space of the Arctic zone of the Russian Federation: (a) conceptual models of the Arctic zone of the Russian Federation presenting the activity of agents in the Arctic zone of the Russian Federation by mathematical and logical tools; (b) a set of databases being the initial information for building a set of conceptual models of the Arctic zone of the Russian Federation; (c) a combination of ideas, tools, models and devices for analyzing and comparing the conceptual models of the Arctic zone of the Russian Federation; (d) a set of technological driver bases and technological mega-trends, developing technological revolution for the use in the innovation and technological development of the Arctic zone of the Russian Federation.

The use of socio-cyberphysical systems and intellectual space for the development of target subspaces of the Arctic zone of the Russian Federation is based on the following provisions:

(1) Development of the content and structure of the intellectual space of the Arctic zone of the Russian Federation.

(2) Development of the method for studying the intellectual space of the Arctic zone of the Russian Federation.

(3) The choice of a conceptual model for development of the Arctic zone of the Russian Federation, i.e. a set of key provisions that determine the lines, architectonics and various approaches to performance of economic activity in the Arctic zone of the Russian Federation.

(4) Development of the processes concept for each type of target sub-spaces based on the principles of key process trends that underlay the socio-cyberphysical systems for the Arctic zone of the Russian Federation.

(5) The analysis of collections of process driver bases and technological mega-trends, developing fourth industrial revolution, for use in innovation and technological development of each type of target sub-spaces.

(6) Formation of the socio-cyberphysical systems "database" for application in the innovation and technological development of each type of target subspaces and analytical methods for on-line data assessment.

(7) Orientations to real objects – the target sub-spaces of the Arctic development in the extension and use of the socio-cyberphysical systems and the intellectual space of the Arctic zone of the Russian Federation, which are replaced with their simpler, safer and more accessible models which properties are similar to ones of the real objects under study in a certain substantial part.

The concept contains the methodological tools for forecasting the social and economic boundaries and assessing the risks of using the processes developing based on the principles of the socio-cyberphysical systems and the intellectual space for the development of the target sub-spaces of the Arctic of the Russian Federation, and assessment of risks to life under global changes taking place in the Arctic.

The targeted integrated programs have been conceptually selected as a tool for arrangement and management of the social and cyber physical systems and intellectual space development in the target sub-spaces of the Arctic zone of the Russian Federation. The target program is a set of research, production, design and experimental, socio-economic, business management and other activities aimed at achieving the set goals, and coordinated by contractors, terms, resources and objectives.

The concept provides for the analysis of the problem, as well as the compilation of a possible forecast of situation development. At the preliminary stage of creating the target program, there are the following operations: problem identification, current situation assessment, forecast of its further development, and decision on the application of the program-target method. At the stage of creating the target program, its objectives are identified and structured. Such method as building the goals tree – the decision tree is used. The general goal is chosen and hierarchically divided into subgoals. The decision tree reflects the trends of long-term prospective study to a greater extent it shall be used to establish the hypothesis of the development of scientific trends, rather than to display target programs.

In the Concept, the study of socio-cyberphysical systems and intellectual space for the target sub-spaces of the Arctic zone is represented by an alternative structure graph under certainty, risk and uncertainty.

References

1. C. Giacomo, C. Massimo, D. Enrico, IEEE 25TH International Conference on enabling technologies: infrastructure for collaborative enterprises (WETICE) (2016)
2. T. Zhang, Q. Li, C.-S. Zhang, Frontiers of information technology & electronic engineering, **18 (1)** (2017)
3. G.W. Gabrielsen, Journal of Toxicology and Environmental Health, **77 (9-11)** (2014)
4. E. M. Frazzon, J. Hartmann, T. Makuschewitz, B. Scholz-Reiter, Procedia CIRP, **7** (2013)
5. A. Awais, B. Muhammad, D. Sadia, K. Shehzad, M.-A. Nasro, Future Generation Computer Systems (2018)
6. E. M. Frazzon, S. Loureiro, Jr. O.F. Lima,B. Scholz-Reiter, Proceedings of 44th CIRP Conference on Manufacturing Systems (2011)
7. S. Poudel, Z. Ni, N. Malla, International Journal of Electrical Power & Energy Systems, **90** (2017)
8. R. A. Rojas, E. Rauch, R. Vidoni, D. T. Matt, Procedia Manufacturing, **11** (2017)
9. J. Miranda, R. P.-Rodríguez, V. Borja, P.K. Wright, A. Molina, IFAC-PapersOnLine, **50 (1)** (2017)
10. H. Zhuge, Artificial Intelligence, **175 (5-6)** (2011)
11. D. Rudenko, N. Didenko, WELLSO 2015 – II International Scientific Symposium on Lifelong Wellbeing in the World, European Proceedings of Social and Behavioral Sciences, 7 (2015)
12. N. Didenko, D. Skripnuk, O. Krasulina, International Multidisciplinary Scientific Conference on Social Sciences and Arts, SGEM2016, V (2016)

13. N. Didenko, D. Rudenko, D. Skripnuk, International Multidisciplinary Scientific GeoConference Surveying Geology and Mining Ecology Management, SGEM2015, III (2015)
14. A. Kajan, Scandinavian Journal of Hospitality and Tourism, **14 (1)** (2014)
15. J. Dawson, M.E. Johnston, E.J. Stewart, Ocean & Coastal Management, **89** (2014)
16. M. M. McBride, P. Dalpadado, K.F. Drinkwater, ICES Journal of Marine Science, **71 (7)** (2014)
17. M. Blunden, International Affairs, **88 (1)** (2012)
18. D. R. Rothwell, Ocean Development and International Law, **43 (3)** (2012)
19. L. C. Smith, S. R. Stephenson, Proceedings of the National Academy of Sciences of the United States of America, **110 (3)** (2013)
20. G. B. Stenson, M. O. Hammill, ICES Journal of Marine Science, **71 (7)** (2014)
21. N. Hong, Journal of World Energy Law & Business, **5 (1)** (2012)
22. G. Backus, Bulletin of the Atomic Scientists, **68 (4)** (2012)
23. N. H. Nicol, L. Heininen, Polar Record, **50 (1)** (2014)

SHS Web of Conferences **44**, 00029 (2018) https://doi.org/10.1051/shsconf/20184400029
CC-TESC2018

Digital technologies and higher education in Russia: new tools of development

Tatiana Dmitrieva[1*], *Elena* German[2], and *Tatiana* Khvatova[1]

[1] Peter the Great St. Petersburg Polytechnic University, Institute of Industrial Management, Economics and Trade, International College of Management, 195251, Politechnicheskaya st., 29, Russian Federation
[2] Peter the Great St. Petersburg Polytechnic University, Institute of Computer Sciences and Technologies, Higher School of Cyber-Physical Systems and Management, 195251, Politechnicheskaya st., 29, Russian Federation

Abstract. The article gives consideration to the main trends of development of the system of higher education under conditions of economics digitization. The influence of technological revolution on the social sphere of society (education, employment) and public services has been analyzed. Characteristics have been given to the state and basic problems of development of higher education under conditions of digital economics; the main tasks and the ways of solving them in the area of focus: human resources and education of the program "Digital economics" have been enumerated. Consideration has been given to the project of the new network University of National Technical Initiative for training in professions associated with the use of advanced production technologies, intellectualization and robotization of production; its basic goals, objectives and specific features: short life cycle and network principle of functioning have been described. A concept of open educational resources – a modern social technology of training has been disclosed.

1 Community digitization under conditions of technological revolution

An explosive development at the turn of 21 century and propagation of new technologies, penetration thereof into all spheres of human activity bring about nowadays quick and deep changes of global markets, structure and character of the present-day industrial production, economics and social sphere. These changes get assessed as "technological revolution" based on the changeover from mass production of standardized produce to a flexible high-performance production manufacturing individualized produce. At that, the automation and robotization as well as intellectualization of production processes become the "flow-through" manufacturing processes for all production types. Particularly these technologies shall provide a fundamentally different quality of economic growth.

*Corresponding author: DmitrievaTatAl@gmail.com

Significant changes are expected in the nearest future in the labor market, especially in the traditional industries and occupations:

- change of labor market structure towards production facilities robotization will have consequences for employment in the segment of blue-collar occupations. According to forecasts the robots will replace to do jobs fulfilled by the people in 25–30% types of professional activity in the developed countries by 2035 [1];
- change of employment structure towards using artificial intellect will have consequences for "white-collar workers" - managers, analysts, and in some cases for top professional managers too. It is expected that up to 30% of corporate audit checks will be done by 2025 with the use of artificial-intellect technologies. Full robotization is possible in some segments of bank activity, business accounting, legal services, complex analytics [1];
- quick change of qualification requirements to employees make them change their attitude to professional career and selection of trades: the employees shall be ready and willing to establish work for themselves and take care of its economic efficiency;
- simultaneous formation of a demand for new occupations and trades in the labor market related to the use of advance production technologies, intellectualization, robotization of production.

The serious changes take place in the sphere of education, public health services, security and other services traditionally rendered by the state:

- practically all the spectrum of state services becomes electronic;
- monitoring of legally significant actions and financial operations begins to get implemented by means of intellectual robotized systems;
- a number of non-cash financial arrangements increases which is provided by the unlimited access to Internet;
- digital services in the social sphere related to real-time monitoring facilities (e.g., "smart" home, telemedicine) become more and more widely used;
- computer-aided education formats, including remote ones get developed. For instance, the digital educational platform Coursera declared in March 2016 that the number of its students had reached 18 mln., a number of passed courses had amounted to 3.6 mln., while a cumulative traffic of video reviews of courses had amounted to 17 thousand years. The number of students registered at edX platform reaches 7 mln. people. The Spanish massive open online courses (MOOC) platform Miriada X has attained a figure of 2 mln. students. All-India Counsel for Technical Education (AICTE) has decided that 10% of the curriculum in 10.8 thousand of technical institutions of the country are to be based on MOOC platform [1]. The number of students to pass the online courses shall amount to 11 mln. persons in Russia by 2026 [2].

The quality of services will rearrange itself in the sphere of education under conditions of technological revolution:

- professional education will encounter a growing competition on the part of non-academic sphere. A changeover from a design-oriented education to the experimental-oriented one will take place. A transfer of practical skills will be provided not only through traineeships, but due to specifically established university laboratories too. The use of digital technologies in education will bring about the emergence of new methods of rendering educational services;
- the transformations will take place in science and scientific activity associated with the use of artificial intellect, "big data" and digitization of investigations. The full-scale experiments will be replaced with digital simulation; the use of digital means of information acquisition, processing and storage grows.

2 Convergence of education and economics of knowledge

Improvement of educational system as the basis of the community social development and its economic growth is an important condition for the development of innovative economics.

The following trends are decisive at this stage of shaping the economics of knowledge:

- Education and training as the basis of the economics of knowledge.
- Creation and development of scientific potential – an important component of technological development.
- Process of convergence and integration of intradiscipline sciences.
- Building easy-to-access, prompt, portable, demanded sources of knowledge comparable with the biggest modern informational resources with respect to information volumes.
- Knowledge engineering (knowledge management).
- Promotion of automation into the sphere of knowledge production and rendering intellectual services [3, 4].

Development of higher education (HE) shall be oriented to increasing the quality of education and its accessibility, as well as training skilled personnel capable of quick integration into new labor markets, as well as continuously increase the level of their qualification and use knowledge, skills and competences acquired in the process of training.

The following basic directions are envisaged in the sphere of higher education in Russia, for example, in the framework of state program "Education development": modernization of structure of programs of higher education for providing flexibility and efficiency thereof; modernization of HE contents and technologies for providing compliance thereof with the requirements of modern economics and varying people's inquiries; forming a system of continuous education, which helps plot flexible (modular) trajectory of mastering new competencies; transformation of part of programs of secondary vocational education into programs of applied bachelor degree course; internationalization of Russian HE and expansion of export of Russian educational services.

In case of higher education modernization it is necessary to increase the quality of management and professional development of managers and qualification of scientific and pedagogical staff.

According to the forecasts of long-term social and economical development of the RF for a period up to 2030 developed by the Ministry of Economic Development and Trade of the Russian Federation the following results are expected [3]:

- specific weight of a number of students being educated in the leading HEI increases from 5% (2011) to 20% (2020);
- by 2020 the variation of number of students being educated according to the programs of higher education from a total number of students being educated according to the programs of vocational education will equal according to programs: applied bachelor degree course - 11%, bachelor degree course - 40%, specialists - 8%, master's degree program - 10%;
- specific weight of employed population that has passed the refresher training course and continuing education course at the age of 25-56 years will increase by 2020 from 2% to 55%;
- specific weight of a number of students of HEI that have passed training abroad within academic year for at least 1 semester (except HEI of CIS) will increase from 0.1% (2011) to 6% (2020);
- at least five Russian Universities will join the top hundred of the leading world Universities according to the world rating;

- increase of a number of students up to 30% that get educated according to priority and capital-intensive directions, who will get education in HEI with big volume of contractual developments and investigations;
- increase of quantity of federal state HEI performing international recruiting of scientific and pedagogical personnel (during 5 years – 15 pers.).

3 Digital economics and education

A concept of electronic economics has been articulated for the first time more than twenty years ago by Nicolas Negroponte, Head of UN Program "One Laptop Per Child". Later the concepts of Internet (or Web) economics have appeared; now a term Digital economics is used more frequently, which is understood as the economical activity, based on digital technologies.

The scientists of Tufts University conducted investigation in 2017 in cooperation with MasterCard Inc., in the framework of which a rating of 60 countries was compiled by the level of digital economics development [5]. At that, more than 170 indicators were used, e.g., availability of broadband network of mobile communication, laws on intellectual property, etc. As a result, Digital Evolution Index was assessed to indicate a proportion between demand and offer in the framework of digital economics, level of support on the part of the government and state institutions, rate of innovations development. In the course of investigation the countries were divided into four groups: "leaders", "promising", "with decelerating rate of growth" and "problematic".

Proceeding from investigation results, the leading countries featuring the most developed digital economies are as follows: Norway (broadband communication), Sweden (information technologies), Switzerland (technological development), Denmark (technological development), Finland (broadband communication), Singapore (technological development), South Korea (advanced technologies), Great Britain (technologies and innovations), Hong Kong (information technologies), USA (at that, many rural country regions have no broadband communication and suffer deficit of digital technologies), Australia, Canada, the Netherlands, New Zealand (Chairman of group Digital 5).

Russia has joined a rating of "promising" together with such countries as: China, Kenya, India, Malaysia, Philippines, Indonesia, Brazil, Columbia, Chile and Mexico. According to the report these are the countries possessing a "potential, which can help them occupy the leading positions" [6]. The following countries have been recognized as "problematic": SAR, Peru, Egypt, Greece and Pakistan.

According to calculations of BCG (Boston Consulting Group), Russia lags behind the leading countries approximately by 5-8 years [7]. Therefore, in order to increase the rate of digitization, it is necessary to actively develop the baseline technologies of a new pattern – robotics technology, Internet of things, cloud services, additive production.

Russia has essentially advanced in the market of cloud services only, outpacing the markets of the leading countries with respect to the rate of development. There are certain barriers in the other spheres. For instance, the participants of the robotics technology market "are disturbed by the lack of personnel, insufficient experience of developments commercialization and high entry threshold alongside with weak competencies in marketing and industrial design according to investigation of the Russian venture company. The development of additive technologies is impeded by high dependence from the import equipment and consumption materials becoming more expensive, while in the sphere of Internet of things a slow response of the users is a hindrance" [8].

In August 2017 the Government of the Russian Federation approved the state program "Digital economics of the Russian Federation" designed up to 2024. The program has defined five basic directions of digital economics development: "regulatory control; personnel and education; forming investigation competencies and technical capacities; informational infrastructure; informational security" [9].

Giving consideration to the direction of personnel and education it is apparent that its tasks are as follows: "creating key conditions for training personnel of digital economics; improvement of education system, which shall provide the digital economics with competent personnel; establishment of the labor market, which is to be supported by the requirements of digital economics; building a system of motivation on mastering necessary competencies and participation of personnel in the development of digital economics of Russia" [9].

Director of Center on electrochemical energy storage and electric power systems of SkolTech, professor Keith Stevenson, staff expert of the Institute on the problems of digital generation reckons that the modern system of higher education is to be built on the principles of interdisciplinary and decentralization, which will result in the formation of a new system built according to an "apportioned" principle. The scientist underlines that an immediate access to any knowledge relevant at the age of information technologies is the main prerequisite for the establishment of information community aimed at receiving practical knowledge and skills, cross-cultural communication, self-learning capability and an ability to make several things simultaneously – multitasking [10].

In order to solve the main tasks of the direction "personnel and education", the investigation centers in the field of digital economics are being established in the leading Russian HEI. A National center of digital economics, which main task is the scientific and scientific-and-methodological support of digital economics in the RF as well as training of the respective personnel, has been established at Lomonosov Moscow State University. The Center has prepared proposals on establishing digital environment of the Eurasian Economic Union (EEU), conducting International conferences devoted to digital technologies.

The National Research University "Higher School of Economics" has presented a research and education project "Digital economics" to be implemented by the Department of world economics. The project has been established for the sake of studying: influence of the growing digitization of economics on the industrial, social, institutional and environmental aspects of economical activity in the world; development of digital transition in Russia and its integration into international environment of digital economics.

Bonch-Bruevich St. Petersburg State University of telecommunications as the leading industry HEI subject to general jurisdiction of the Federal Agency of Communication has taken an active part since September 2017 in establishing the centers of competence of "Digital economics" program in the direction "Investigations and developments".

4 Network University of National Technical Initiative as a new approach to higher education development

A project of the new network University of National Technical Initiative (NTI) on training specialists for work under conditions of digital economics and a concept of educational program of a new format oriented to professional development were introduced in Saint-Petersburg in autumn 2017 in the framework of BarCamp[1] "National technological revolution 20.35".

[1] BarCamp – International network of conferences set up by its participants and takes place in the format of discussion sessions and presentations. The main topics are as follows: new media, social media, blogs, Web 2.0, startups, open-sources, etc.

The Network University will be oriented to training leaders of the companies implementing a concept of national technological initiative and operating in the new global markets. Every trainee will get a chance to analyze the prospects of its career progress in a company as well as acquire necessary knowledge and experience. A profile of competences reflecting its real achievements and can be a guarantee of success in a particular role and in a particular project will be formed for every graduate instead of the diploma.

The leading HEI of the country will participate in NTI University "20.35": Moscow Institute of Physics and Technology, Peter the Great St. Petersburg Polytechnic University, Saint Petersburg National Research University of Information Technology, Mechanics and Optics, Novosibirsk State University, Tomsk State University, Far Eastern Federal University, as well as Federal Agency for Scientific Organizations, commercial companies. The work of the University will be intended for a short life cycle – since 2020 till 2035.

The key University's specific feature is the network principle of functioning with the use of capabilities of educational organizations and digital educational platforms, the best course and models of training, which are available in different HEI. The main task of the University is to build a platform by 2035, consisting of goal-oriented occupations, profiles and suppliers of competencies, which will help build a personal trajectory of trainee's development. At that, it is planned in the nearest ten years to train 10 thous. technological leaders, 100 thous. players of the new markets and 1 bln. digital profiles of competencies.

New social technologies of education, including open educational resources[2] (OER) will be used in educative process at NTI University "20.35" [11]. Let us note that OER are actively developing and are being used at the federal and regional levels in Russia. They include: websites of HEI and subdivisions thereof, personal websites, websites of topical scientific and educational projects and systems of remote education, open electronic libraries of HEI, topical educational portals, Internet University of information technologies, educational video portal UniverTV.ru, portal "Unified window of access to educational resources" [12].

The recommendations of UNESCO Institute say that the "student organizations shall take an active part in providing OER quality in the framework of social media as well as it is necessary to encourage participation of students in measures aimed at supporting OER development" [13]. Taking it into account in the framework of BarCamp, the organizers have conducted a forum on the development of IT tasks on building new and refinement of the existing platforms for the network University. The presentation of NTI University "20.35" model has taken place at the forum and simultaneously hackathon[3] has taken place in five Russian cities (Moscow, Saint-Petersburg, Vladivostok, Tomsk, Novosibirsk) "Gather University" that has gathered more than 1,000 participants – students, postgraduate students and young specialists.

The main task of hackathon was the establishment of services, applications, modules and platform solutions for NTI "20.35". As a result the participants of hackathon have prepared the following products: new types of digital educational content; smart systems of building individual trajectories of human-being development; artificial agents and digital counterparts; game characters accompanying the process of training; biometrical technologies of personal identification and assessing the trainee's state; virtual tutors; digital track analysis tools; competence profile management system. The issue of motivation and readiness of teachers to use new educational technologies is relevant for

---

[2] UNESCO Institute on information technologies has developed "Recommendations for cooperation with open educational resources in the sphere of higher education", which are designed for governmental structures, higher educational institutions, higher-education teaching personnel, student's organizations and establishments responsible for providing quality and accreditation [13].

[3] Hackathon – a forum of development agencies, when the experts from different fields of software development (software specialists, managers, designers) work jointly on solving a certain problem.

Russian system of education. Thus, there exists a necessity of training teachers on the new educational technologies based on application of information and communications technologies. Let us note that an additional impetus for OER development in Russia is the enactment of the fourth generation educational standards envisaging application of new requirements and approaches to organization of educational process.

Today the world is on the brink of the next wave of innovations, which can seriously transform an established approach to education. The key changes will consist in the means of information transmission and storage, which makes education more approachable expanding the network of students all over the world. In this case, the academic activity will become more flexible and client-oriented, while a consumer of educational services will be able to shape the inquiries for receiving practical knowledge in the way convenient for it and within the shortest time possible.

References

1. V. N. Knyaginina. Expert and Analytical Report. **136** (2017)
2. Identification Document of Priority Project "Modern Digital Educational Environment in the Russian Federation". [online], Available at: http://static.government.ru/media/files/8SiLmMBgjAN89vZbUUtmuF5lZYfTvOAG.pdf (2016)
3. Forecast of Long-term Social and Economical Development of the RF for a Period up to 2030 (the Ministry of Economic Development and Trade of the Russian Federation) [online], Available at: http://economy.gov.ru/minec/activity/sections/macro/prognoz/doc20130325_06 (2013)
4. J. Lichy, M. Kachur, T. Khvatova, *Journal of Marketing Management*, **33 (9-10)** (2017)
5. B. Chakravorti, R. S. Chaturvedi. *Digital planet 2017. How competitiveness and trust in digital economies vary across the world.* (The Fletcher School, Tufts University July 2017)
6. T. Kelly, A. Liaplina, S. Tan, H. Winkler. *Reaping Digital Dividends: Leveraging the Internet for Development in Europe and Central Asia. Washington, DC.* (World Bank, 2017)
7. B. Banke, V. Butenko, I. Kotov, et alii. *Russia Online? It is not Possible to Catch up with. Falling Behind (Catching up with. It is not Possible to Fall Behind)* (2017)
8. K. Kurkin, *Expert Severo-Zapad.* **9-11 (746)** (2017)
9. Resolution of the Government of the Russian Federation" No.1632-p dated 28.07.2017. Program "Digital Economics of the Russian Federation" [online], Available at: http://static.government.ru/media/files/9gFM4FHj4PsB79I5v7yLVuPgu4bvR7M0.pdf (2017)
10. L. Stein, Anthology Digital Economics. Skolkovo Foundation, **35-40** (2017)
11. A. V. Markeyeva. *Economics.* **8 (9)** (2014)
12. A. Sigalov, A. Skuratov. Educational Portals and Open Educational Resources in the Russian Federation (2012) – [online], Available at: http://iite.unesco.org/pics/publications/en/files/3214704.pdf
13. Recommendations on Work with Open Educational Resources (OER) in the Sphere of Higher Education. UNESCO Institute on Information Technologies in Education. Education Association. (2011)

On the way to driverless road-train: Digital technologies in modeling of movement, calculation and design of a road-train with hybrid propulsion unit

Roman Dobretsov[1], *Matvey* Gubachev[1], *Ivan* Naletov [1*] and *Alexey Vasiliev*[1]

[1] Peter the Great Saint Petersburg Polytechnic University, Institute of Energy and Transport Systems, 195251 Polytechnicheskaya st. 29, Russian Federation

Abstract. Today, road-trains are one of the most widely-spread and multi-tonnage transport vehicles on road arteries interconnecting countries and cities. The concept of hybrid road-trains mostly meets the widely-spread policy for stepping up the rates of exhaust gas emissions and reducing specific hydrocarbon fuel costs but only an intermediate link in the development of more significant and important design – a driverless road-train. This article considers active trailers and their models with different design options for heavy tractor truck propulsion unit drive. The influence of trailer link drive on turning has been studied in "Universal gear" software. Special attention has been given to an electrical drive of active semi-trailer wheels as the most advanced one at the present moment. We have obtained the data intended to be used in design of active trailer chassis and identified the weight and size characteristics of energy accumulators required for movement of a road-train with active trailer. The efficiency factor for different semitrailer drives has been analyzed and calculated, in particular: Low EF of electrical drive. The relevancy of active trailer concept including that for driverless road-trains has been determined on the basis of received data.

1 Introduction

At the beginning of 1950th of the last century Soviet designer B.M. Fitterman offered a concept of active trailers. This idea consisted in supplying power from the tractor truck propulsion unit to the trailer or semitrailer wheels with by means of power mechanical drive. Thus, the first experimental model based on GAZ-63D chassis with additional power take-off box was built. Torque was transmitted by means of gearboxes and universal joint shafts. After tests it was possible to identify the weaknesses in design and standard assemblies in relation to high loads [1]. Road-trains with mechanically driven semitrailers were designed with success later, for example: GAZ-66K with single-axle semitrailers with mechanically driven wheels, tractor truck ZIL-157KV-1 with semitrailer PAU-3 for transport vehicle 9T22, truck-tractor MAZ-502V with single-axle active semitrailers,

*Corresponding author: pimon-kora@mail.ru

URAL-380 with active semitrailer Ural-862, KrAZ-E259 with active sided semitrailer E834, ZIL-157KV-1 with mechanically driven semitrailer wheels, NAMI-058S and semitrailer Ural-862, active semitrailer MMZ-881, KrAZ-260D and semitrailer MAZ-9382 with mechanical drive [1,2,3].

Apart from mechanical drive, a hydraulic drive was also used in road trains with active trailers, the power was transmitted as follows: Through the power take-off box some torque is transmitted to the hydraulic pump, from there some fluid through branch pipes goes to the hydraulic engine, then torque from this hydraulic engine through reducing gearbox or universal joint shaft is transmitted to the trailer driving axles. Examples of train roads with hydraulic drives: Special-purpose tractor truck ZIL-157V with hydraulically driven wheels of semitrailer MMZ-584, ZIL-137 with hydrostatic drive [1].

The book [1] mentions a road train with electrical drive of driving wheels:

"The first road train with electrical drive of driving wheels was designed in 1959 in the USSR under the supervision of G.I. Bazylenko, no less original design with hydraulic came to light the next year. The authors of this article could not find any photographs or additional information about this road train with electrical drive. The options of operation with electrical drive are described in papers [4] and [5]. Paper [4] offers a self-contained propulsion system to be used as an option or simple engine power take-off by means of power take-off and generator. The authors have shown a hybrid drive scheme in paper [5].

Today, the concept of active road train acquires a new life as part of design basis to develop a national driverless road train. Road trains with active trailers or semitrailers, apart from anything, are provided with high cross-country capacity and can be used in both in the Far North conditions and in the timber and oil and gas processing industries.

The purpose of this work is to calculate parameters (weight and size) of power storage units to allow an active trailer run in continuous mode (for further consideration of their influence on the characteristics of road train), EF analysis for different drives of active semitrailers and the influence of an active trailer on the whole road train movement by means of up-to-date software.

The research methodology consists of: theoretical part (a comparative analysis of technical solutions on the basis of system-wide approach), analytical approach to identify design features for active trailers with electrical drive, studies and comparisons of stability when a road train with passive and active trailer links making a turn in "Universal mechanism" software complex.

The use of an active trailer link will make it possible to enhance the cross-country capacity of a road train in heavy road conditions and increase an average traffic speed over general purpose roads and make it more self-sustained, which is relevant for the concept of off-road driverless road trains. The negative side of this approach is that the road train design (in particular –a trailer) is made more complex and its weight and production costs are increased. Therefore, it seems to be important that apart from a comprehensive analysis of technical usage aspects of active trailers [5], it is necessary to get a conclusion from logistics experts in this region on the practicability of these machines give the local features of road networks.

The cross-country capacity is improved by increasing the road train's adhesive weight and the average speed is increased by reducing the risk of drifting during maneuvers. The last property to the full extent makes it possible to implement an active trailer with traction electric motor drive (TEM) controlled by an electronic control system. The aspects of improving the road train's efficiency and reducing harmful emissions are of concern as well [5].

2 Selection of parameters for energy accumulators of road train with active trailer

Let us calculate the energy costs and evaluate power spent to overcome external obstacle trailer movement within a road train. A timber road train based on tractor truck Ural 43204-1111-41 and double-axle timber drag trailer 904712 designed to transport clean wood and logs up to 23 m long over all types of roads and terrain was taken as a prototype. The loaded trailer's maximum weight is 4500 kg, the timber drag trailer's lifting capacity is 7200 kg and the weight of transported cargo is 16000 kg [6]. Engine YaMZ-236 installed on the trailer provides the traction forces required to make the road train move.

The resistance forces are calculated only with due consideration of weight acting on the road train's trailed link being equal to:m_{tr}=11700 kg.

The speed effect on the factor of rolling resistance is taken into account according to formula 1 [7]:

$$f = f_0\left[1+(0.0216\cdot v)^2\right], \tag{1}$$

Where f_0 is the factor of rolling resistance at low speeds; v is the road train's speed, m/s.

These resistance forces are calculated without a road slope that is why dependence 2 has been used:

$$P = f\cdot m_{tr}\cdot g\ , \tag{2}$$

Where m_{tr} is the trailer's weight, f is the factor of rolling resistance with speed.

When the road train moves at a low speed the influence of aerodynamic forces can be neglected. In transport mode the effects of aerodynamic forces are already significant, that is why let us calculate the aerodynamic forces according to dependence 3 [7]:

$$P_w = c\rho F v^2/2\ , \tag{3}$$

Where c is the factor of aerodynamic resistance; ρ is air density kg/m^3; F is the vehicle's frontage area, m^2; v– is the road train speed, m/s.

In order to find the required energy (and consequently, travel resistance power), let us make an evaluative calculation for typical road conditions. ThecalculationresultsaregiveninTable 1. The received data are used to select a traction electric motor, the parameters of energy accumulators and to resolve the issues of equipment layout on the trailer.

Table 1. Power, energy characteristics of travel resistance.

Road conditions	Travelspeed , m/s	Travel resistance force, kN	Specificenergy, MJ/h	Specificpower, kW/h
Systematic travel: earth road (f_0 = 0.025)	5	6.71	120.72	33.53
Heavy conditions: water-logged unpaved run (f_0 = 0.25)	2	34.01	244.90	68.03
Transportmode:asphalt (f_0 = 0.01)	12	6.68	288.74	80.21

Using the received calculation data on the road train travel resistance forces, let us select the parameters for energy accumulators determining the peculiarities of its layout on a transport vehicle.

The traction electric motor (TEM) and energy accumulators fitted on the trailer will require a more powerful generator. It is also expedient to consider the issue of increasing the on-board voltage at least within the TEM feed system, which will make it possible to significantly reduce the weight and size characteristics of these electrical machines. In addition, for further reduction of TEM sizes, it is expedient to provide a double-mode reducing gearbox with automatic control.

The most advanced type of energy accumulators now is electric double-layer capacitor (capacitors with double electrical layers), because this type of electrical device can handle high amounts of stored energy and discharge power with relatively high EF value (at the present moment, electric double-layer capacitor fed buses are manufactured by HyundaiMotor,Trolza, Belkommunmash [8]).

For the purpose of calculation we have used the energy accumulators with electric double-layer capacitors K58-20. Specific discharge power of electric double-layer capacitors K58-20 with matched load is 1.0 kW/kg, 1.5 kW/dm^3 [9].

Based on the need to provide power input equal to33.53 kW/h (without wiring resistance), let us to evaluate the accumulator's weight [9]:

$$m_{acc} = \frac{W_{з}}{W_{\text{mp.dlc.}} \cdot \eta_{н} \cdot \eta_{TEM}}, \tag{4}$$

Where η_{acc}=0.85 *is the accumulator's EF*; η_{tem}=0.9 *is the traction electric motor's EF*; W_s is the spent specific power kW/h; $W_{\text{mp.dlc.}}$is the specific discharge power of electric double-layer capacitors, kW/kg.

Accordingly the accumulator's volume (approximately) [9] is calculated as per dependence 5:

$$V_{acc} = \frac{W_S}{W_{Vp.dlc.} \cdot \eta_{acc} \cdot \eta_{TEM}}, \tag{5}$$

Where η_{acc}=0.85 *is the accumulator's EF*; η_{tem}=0.9 *is the traction electric motor's EF*; W_s is the spent specific power kW/h; $W_{\text{mp.dlc.}}$is the specific discharge power of electric double-layer capacitors, kW/dm^3.

In such a manner, in order to overcome the trailer's rolling resistance over an earth road (most typical conditions for timber industry) at a speed of 5 m/s (18 km/h) it is necessary to ensure that a capacitor battery unit up to 43.8 kg in weight and 29.3 dm^3 (0.028 m^3) in area is installed.

According to the labor safety and driver's rest regulations and working hours allowed for them (not more than nine hours) let us evaluate the weight and volume of accumulator to be equal to 394.2 kg and V=0.260 m^3 in an approximate way.

It should be noted that the trailed link activation is not intended for continuous operation. The trailer's drive should be activated in heavy road conditions requiring this, during uphill movement etc. Moreover, the TEM can be used en-route to stabilize the trailer during maneuvers.

The first option for accumulator layout seems to be safer. The second option for accumulator layout is more favorable in terms of active trailer's reliable operation (loss of accumulator-to-generator connection is less critical than that of TEM-to-accumulator connection).

Thus, when the accumulator and TEM are located on the trailer the spring-suspended weight of the latter will increase by 400 kg approximately. The received data is intended to be used in design of trailer's chassis, the concept of which is considered in detail in paper [5].

3 Calculation of efficiency factor for active trailer drives

It is necessary to analyze the active trailer drive for efficiency factor. A mechanical drive is simple in design and has low weight and a universal-joint drive is used for power transmission. The drive's EF reduces due to a bigger length of this universal-joint drive.

The mechanical drive's EF is calculated for the accepted scheme as per dependence 6:

$$\eta_{м} = \eta_{de} \cdot \eta_{sgb} \cdot \eta_{tgb} \cdot \eta_{b}^{4} \cdot \eta_{ujd}^{2}, \tag{6}$$

Where e $\eta_{de} = 0.35$ is the diesel engine's EF; $\eta_{gb} = 0.85$ is the speed change gearbox's EF; $\eta_{tgb} = 0.99$ is the transfer gearbox's EF; $\eta_{p} = 0.97$ is the bevel gear's EF (4 gearboxes); $\eta_{к} = 0.95$ is the universal-joint drive's EF with a big distance between the gearbox and drive axles taken into account. Thus, $\eta_{м} = 0.235$.

It should be noted that when such road train turns the kinematic incompatibility of drives has a negative effect on the whole road train's movement .The issue of this kinematic incompatibility is still open [1, 10, 11].

The use of hydrostatic drive makes it possible to get rid of geared and universal-joint drives. The trailers with hydrostatic drive are designed using the "hydraulic shaft" or "hydraulic motor-wheel" principle [10].

Hydraulic units make it possible to run at low RPM. The hydraulic motor-wheel's RPM based on a limit speed is equal to [10] as per dependence 7:

$$n = \frac{v_{rt.}}{0.377 r_0}, \tag{7}$$

Where *n is* revolutions, r/s; *v* is the road train's speed, m/s; r_0 is the tire radius along its central part, m.

Here we get to know that when unit 11MNo20 with maximum permissible shaft revolutions equal to 1440 RPM is used (this hydraulic unit was used on road train ZIL-137), the maximum travel speed with a radius of tires equal to 0.6 m is 5.4 m/s with hydraulic drive used without an extra step-up gearbox.

The trailed link drive is on road train ZIL-137 is turned on only when heavy road sections are to be negotiated with hill-climbing, first and second gears engaged [1, 10].

The hydraulic drive's EF with the parameters of other drives was not compared as there is an acute shortage of information about hydraulic drive systems and their application is limited and intermittent in trailers due to the above-mentioned reasons.

The trailer's electrical drive is the most promising one at this moment [5].The electrical drive has a number of advantages: simple power feed, good traction performance, possible power flow redistribution depending on travel resistance [10].

According to the accepted scheme as per dependence 8 the following results are received

$$\eta_{e} = \eta_{de} \cdot \eta_{tgb} \cdot \eta_{a} \cdot \eta_{tem} \cdot \eta_{rec} \cdot \eta_{drive} \cdot \eta_{gen}, \tag{8}$$

Where $\eta_{de} = 0.35$ is the diesel engine's EF; $\eta_{tgb} = 0.99$ is the transfer gearbox's EF; $\eta_{a} = 0.85$ – is the accumulator's EF during charge/discharge; $\eta_{tem} = 0.9$ is the traction electric motors' EF; $\eta_{gen} = 0.9$ is the generator's EF; $\eta_{drive} = 0.99$ is the drives' EF;

η_{rec} = 0.93 is the rectifiers' EF [12]. Numeric value of the electrical drive's EF η_e = 0.22.

It is possible to call this option for evaluating the electrical drive's EF pessimistic: While calculating the electrical drive's EF it has not been taken into account that some energy is recovered; the minimum EF values of serial units and devices have been used. Due to an electric double-layer capacitor the electrical drive's EF may turn out to be slightly less than the mechanical drive, however, due to the electrical drive's capabilities make it possible to control the active trailer's wheel in an individual manner. Statistical and experimental data are required to calculate and estimate the drives for efficiency.

4 Road train motion analysis

Two road trains with active and passive trailed links have been compared in "Universal mechanism" software using a special automotive modeling module "Automative" (Fig. 2, 3) show time-based turn side-slip angle dependence.

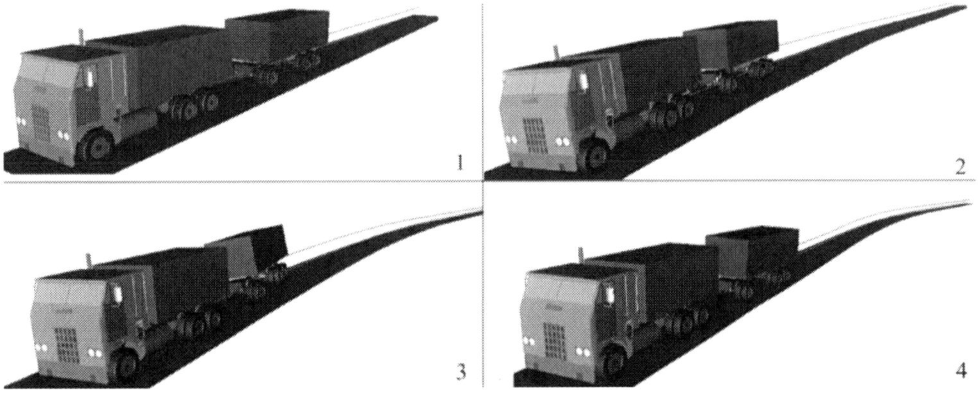

Fig. 1. 3D visualization of a turn:1 – direct movement, 2- fast turn of a tractor truck, 3- swinging of a trailer, 4 – stabilization of a trailer

The context of this simulated experiment is that the road train at selected speed V_0 then a sharp jerk of the steering wheel occurs, which results in swinging of the trailer (Fig.1). Fig. 2 and 3 show that the road train with active drive has higher slide-slip angles during turn, which should have a negative effect on this road train's stability.Also, within an interval of 4.7-5 s on the chart it is possible to see a sharp decrease in sideslip angles down to zero with a further increase (see Fig.2).

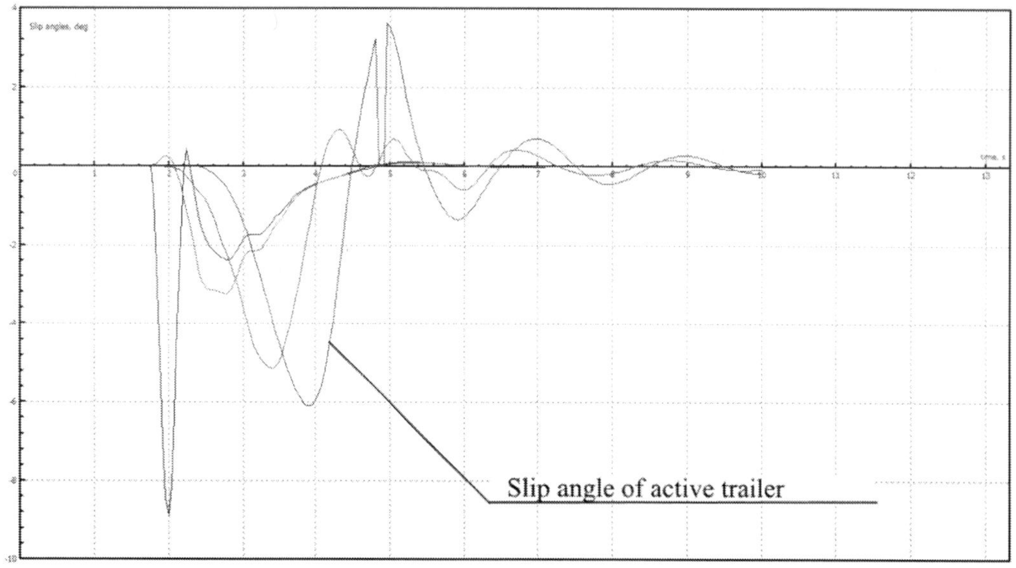

Fig. 2. Time-based sideslip angle dependence: turning of road train with active trailer.

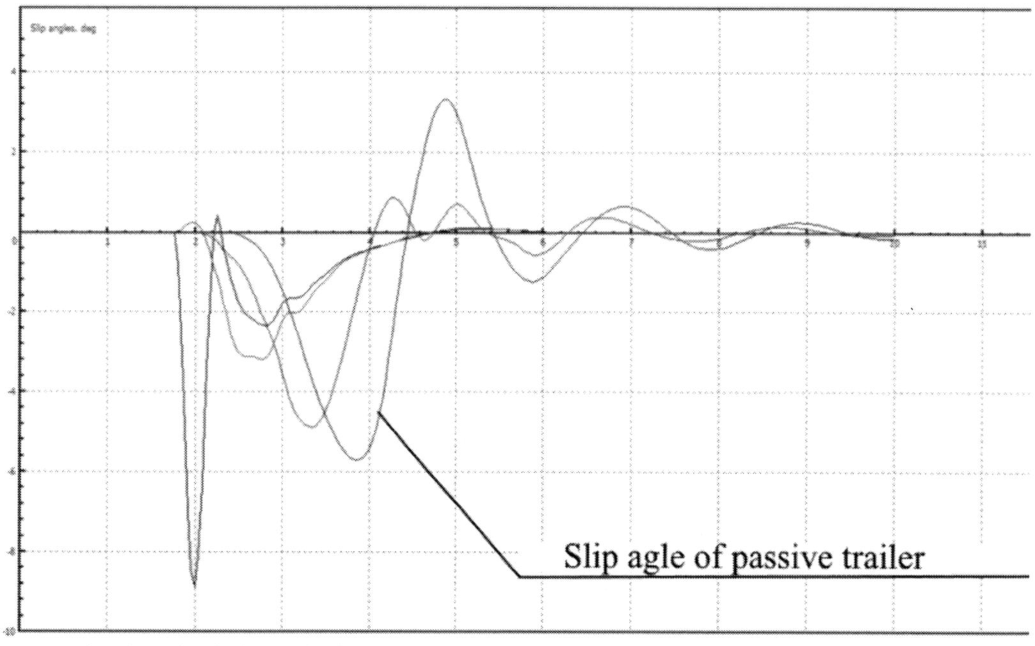

Fig 3. Time-based sideslip angle dependence: turning of road train with passive trailer.

A break on the chart is related to lift-off of the active trailer's wheels from the surface. Probably the wheels lift off due to power feed to the wheels. At the same speed within the given time interval the road train with passive trailer has no loss of stability (see Fig.2, 3).

Time-based roll and yaw angle dependencies of the trailers with active and passive trailed links are close in shape and differ slightly in amplitude values.

5 Conclusions

The data received as a result of calculations and digital modeling bring us to a conclusion on how it is important to conduct a more serious software-aided and digital modeling, which will form a basis for practical experiments and help to develop a full process picture of how the road train with active and passive trailer, which is expedient to be used as a basis for the development of driverless road trains, moves. The analysis of results shows that it is required to increase the roll stiffness of suspension for trailers with electrical drive, which is important to consider in design of this type transport means.

We have indentified the need to develop an automatic TEM control system, which will make it possible to counteract the above-mentioned sideslips of trailer's wheels, reduce the road train's yaw angles as a whole; it is expected that this system can be used as a road train stabilization system and provide kinematic compatibility of links.

Modern technologies allow going back to the concepts of a road train with active and passive wheels; in this case it is possible to make design structures, whose operation is justified in a great number of life activities.

At this moment, the design of active trailers is a very interesting task that needs to be resolved, first of all, in electronic format, because the modern design capabilities make it possible to a greater extent of accuracy to simulate any structure, mechanism or design as well as different events involving them, which will greatly reduce capital costs during design of equipment and simplify the development and testing process for invented equipment. The use of hybrid schemes with possible energy recovery on vehicles is the most challenging and has a huge potential to save fuel saving and reduce atmospheric emissions with keeping and even increasing the vehicle's self-sustainability as a transport means [12].

The principle of hybrid drive with a "motor-semi-axle" pattern for driving the trailer's drive wheels from an electric motor [14] is the bases of the concept. The development of more perfect wheel drives remain to be important and relevant issues [11] to allow road trains [15] to have a more improved cross-country capacity and maneuverability. One of the possible forms for developing the concept of hybrid road trains with proposed scheme can be a driverless road train, whose design basis will be formed by the results of conducted research, calculations and modeling.

References

1. E. Kochnev, *Secrete motor vehicles of the Soviet Army* (Yauza, Eskmo, Moscow, 2001)
2. KrAZ-260D History of the vehicle development [online]. Available at: http://zazsila.ru/news/2012-08-23-155 (2018)
3. Mytichinsky machine-building plant MMZ-881 [online], Available at: http://denisovets.ru/mmz/mmzpages/mmz881.html (2018)
4. V. Gorelovet al., N.E.Bauman, MSTU. Digital magazine, **12** (2016)
5. A. Vasiliev et al., Proceedings of scientific conference with international participation. (Publishing house of Polytechnic University,Saint Petersburg, 2017)
6. Timber truck Ural with self-loading trailer[online], Available at:http://www.sibpromtrans.ru/les/les_samopogruz.php (2018)
7. V. Tarasik, *A theory of vehicle movement* (BXV-Petersburg, Saint Petersburg, 2006)
8. Electrobuses [online], Available at: https://bkm.by/catalog/elektrobusy (2018)

9. Electric double-layer capacitors (ionistores)[online], Available at: http://www.elecond.ru/kondensatory_ionistory.php (2018)
10. M. Zapryagaev et al., *Army vehicles. Design and calculation* (Voenizdat, Moscow,1970)
11. Ya. Zakinet al., *Designs and calculation of road trains*(Publishing house "Machine building", Leningrad, 1968)
12. V. Gaevsky, I. Odinokova, Scientific and technical magazine "Automotive industry"(2017)
13. R. Dobretsov et al., Proceedings of scientific and practical conference "Development and usage of electrical transmission systems for military equipment (JSC VNIITransmash) (Publication of JSC VNIITransmash, Saint Petersburg, 2016)
14. A. Vasiliev et al., Proceedings of scientific conference with international participation. Publishing house of Polytechnic University(2017)
15. A. Vasiliev et al., Proceedings of scientific conference with international participation (Publishing house of Polytechnic University, Saint Petersburg, 2017)

World practice and Russian experience of housing and utilities sector digitization

Irina Drozdova[1*], and *Aleksandr* Petrov[1]

[1] Saint Petersburg State University of Architecture and Civil Engineering, Faculty of economics and management, 190005 2-ya Krasnoarmeiskaya st. 4, Russian Federation

Abstract. The housing and utilities infrastructure is a socially significant branch of economy for life support of population and satisfactory of their demands for adequate housing and utilities services. Implementation of digital technologies in the housing and utilities infrastructure is justified under the program "Digital economy of the Russian Federation" and the concept "Russian smart cities". It was found out that using the technology of Internet of Things in the housing and utilities infrastructure allows to increase efficiency of business-process, reduce costs for maintenance and operation of housing facilities, and to optimize the payment system of the housing and utilities services. It is established that the driver for development of housing and utilities infrastructure digitization shall be implementation of intelligent devices for metering all types of resources and power consumption in dwelling houses which will be gradually unified in the intelligence system of settlement for recourses consumption based on SIM-cards.

1 Introduction

In conditions of globalization of international economics and social transformation of population which provide for transfer to the forth industrial revolution (Industry 4.0), paradigm shift of its economic development based on digitization of economy and society, blockchain technology, Internet of Things (IoT) market development become actual for Russia.

In terms of technology, the digital economy is defined by four trends: mobile technologies, business analytics, cloud computing and social media; globally – social networks.

According to the McKinsey's report "Digital Russia: new reality" in terms of a number of Internet users, in 2016 Russia took the first place in Europe and the sixth one in the world (87 million people). According to data of Rosstat, in the period from 2010 to 2016, a number of households in Russia with access to the Internet increased from 48.4% to 74.8% [1]. In this case, Russia takes second place by the lowest prices for the Internet and mobile communications in the world. According to the World Bank, an increase in a number of high-speed Internet users by 10% increases the annual GDP growth from 0.4 to 1.4% [1].

* Corresponding author: drozdova@lan.spbgasu.ru

Currently, a share of the digital economy in the GDP of economically developed countries averages 7% (the highest indicator in Great Britain is 12%), in Russia – 2.8% [1].

According to forecasts, 65-70% of the world population (about 6.4 billion people) will live in cities by 2045. Mass migration to cities will have a significant impact on city transport systems, food and water supply, energy infrastructure, sanitation and public safety.

Information and communication technologies promote the growth of "smart cities" using digital technologies to improve the efficiency and sustainability of urban centers.

2 Current state of the sector

Housing and utilities infrastructure (HUI) is one of the largest fields of Russian economics which establish an economy development and social well-being of country population. The main purpose of the housing and utilities infrastructure is stable and qualitative provision of population with housing and utilities services required for life activity of each citizen. The share of the domestic housing and utilities complex is about 6% of GDP, more than 30 thousand enterprises operate in the industry, a total number of personnel exceeds 2 million people [2].

Housing and utilities infrastructure is one of the most important areas where, according to experts, the digital transformation of the Russian economy is to begin.

The process of housing and utilities infrastructure digitalization began with the creation and implementation of the state information system (GIS GKH) in 2016 as information storage on all housing and utilities enterprises within the Russian Federation. Its activities are regulated by the Federal Law No. 209-FZ dated July 21, 2014 "On the state information system of housing and utilities infrastructure". The system contains the information on public utility services, performed works, communication systems, housing facilities stock, etc. The service providers shall publish the reports on their activities in the SIS of the housing and utilities infrastructure, data on tariffs for residential rental payment, list of debtors for public utility services, etc. Consumers of housing and utilities services can monitor the quality and scope of performed operations and provided services, monitor the costs of their Condominium Partnerships, send complaints and appeals to housing supervisors, resource providers, homeowners' association, Condominium Partnership, and hold residents' meeting in electronic form on a real-time basis.

Thus, SIS of housing and utilities infrastructure is a strategic infrastructure project that allows optimizing the interaction between authorities, citizens and organizations providing housing and utilities services.

Currently, 74 thousand organizations of the housing and utilities infrastructure are registered in the system including 75% of Condominium Partnerships (TSZh), 88% of utility providers, 100% of homeowners' association and state housing inspectorates, the information on 0.5 billion payment for housing and utilities services, 33 million personal accounts of citizens, 10.8 million homes have published. 1945 IT systems are integrated with the SIS of housing and utilities infrastructure including more than 500 banking solutions to make on-line payments [1].

Automation of business processes in housing and utilities infrastructure is based on the use of Internet technologies, in particular, a comprehensive billing system is developed for the housing and utilities infrastructure and cloud computing SaaS-platform energy. Utilities providers, homeowners' association of housing and utilities infrastructure, and united information-computing center use the system "On-line Billing". The platform is based on a comprehensive functionality for charging housing and utilities infrastructure for individuals and legal entities, recalculations taking into account the communal consumption, distribution of payments for services and suppliers. The SIS of the housing and utilities infrastructure and services "Subscriber Profile" are integrated with the billing system, which allow monitoring tariffs and rates, looking through calculations for rent, controlling own utility payments, keeping records of meter readings, printing copies of receipts for payment of housing and utilities services, making payments for services using a bank card (Internet-acquiring).

One of the smart technologies used in the housing and utilities infrastructure based on the modern IT solutions is the blockchain [3, 4, 5]. This is a database built based on complex mathematical calculations with cryptographic protection of the information transmitted in the chain. In this case, the blockchain technology can ensure full transparency of payments in the housing and utilities infrastructure featuring low payment discipline and a chain of intermediaries between the population and resource providers. Blockchain technology implementation allows the resource provider to track payment for the utility service of each consumer at any time. This will exclude the possibility for concealment and misuse of collected funds by an unscrupulous intermediary.

The transition to intellectual commercial accounting with the use of the blockchain technology also limits the losses of electric and heat energy in the networks, which are 30% according to the Ministry of Energy of the Russian Federation. The blockchain technology will allow managing the energy system, entering into smart contracts and conducting financial calculations, however, the technology itself is only functional if there are smart revenue metering devices (SRM) integrated via the Internet and allowing the use of real-time information. According to the iKS-Consulting study, in early 2017 the total number of apartments in Russia was 65.2 million, and the number of houses – 3.7 million. The total indicator of households' probability with conventional hour meters in Russia is about 99%. The total potential of the smart meters market within Russia in the segment of private utility power and water consumption is more than 206 million smart meters according to the analysts' estimation data. According to the estimates of the Ministry of Energy, installation of smart hour meters throughout the Russian Federation will cost about 400 billion rubles [1].

It should be noted that the blockchain technology has only just begun to spread in the electric power industry of the economically developed countries. Currently, there are two scenarios for the blockchain technology in the electric power industry. The first allows small power producers, utilities and users themselves to sell electricity surplus. The second scenario involves the use of tokens for electricity payment. Smart contracts also provide new opportunities for all market participants. Thanks to the blockchain technology an "Electricity Internet" is formed that helps to save and changes the approach to power production.

The Russian venture company together with the scientists of the Ural Federal University (UFU) developed the startup accelerator GenerationS as a blockchain-platform. The platform records data by volumes of power production and consumption and provides automatic invoices. Using this technology, consumers will be able to make automatic payment for electricity that will avoid filling up paper receipts and on-line forms manually. In addition, the need for payment service providers will be excluded.

Currently, the technologies based on the Internet of things (IoT) are actively introduced in the housing and utilities infrastructure. This is commercial accounting with remote data collection from individual meters, and electronic schemes for waste handling, etc. One of the most popular and actual fields of the Internet of things ("smart house"), directly relates to buildings erection and operation. An important aspect is the prospect of integrating SIS of housing utilities infrastructure with existing IoT technologies.

The Internet of things is popular among breakthrough technologies that can change the business model of companies and entire industries, and advances, for example, artificial intelligence, robotics, virtual and augmented reality, blockchain. The Internet of things has a number of important advantages including readiness for direct implementation and scale of application.

The Internet of things represents a system of integrated computer networks and connected physical objects with built-in sensors and software for data collection and exchange with the possibility of remote control and control without human participation. According to various estimates, a number of connected meters will be within the range of 20 to 50 billion by 2020 [6, 7].

The successful examples of the Internet of things introduction based on the initiative of both the state and business are known in the foreign practice. In the EU countries, South Korea, China and India, the smart city technologies are introduced that improve the management of power consumption and transport flows. The UK and the USA have implemented the large-scale programs to introduce "smart meters" for remote monitoring of power consumption in households [3].

The concept for development of 50 smart cities of Russia is implemented in Russia based on the integration of information and communication technologies and the Internet of things, the priority fields of which are transport, housing and utilities infrastructure, energy, industry and E-government.

The technologies based on the Internet of things are already beginning to be massively implemented in the Russian megacities (Moscow, Saint Petersburg), improving the management of the transport system, urban infrastructure and housing and utilities infrastructure facilities.

Streetlights equipment with motion sensors allows to automatically turning on and off lighting of streets and local areas. The dimming technology allows you to adjust lighting brightness depending on the day time and weather conditions. "Smart lighting" is also used in the entrance halls. The street lighting management has already been centralized in Moscow, but motion sensors and dimming technologies are implemented in the framework of isolated projects. In addition, the integrated information and control system of outdoor lighting (IICSOL) provides automation of the entire life cycle of outdoor lighting facilities. The system is designed to store information about accidents, work plans, repairs, maintenance and planned construction. The controlled lighting in the entrance halls is implemented in accordance with the initiative of citizens.

The monitoring of garbage cans filling capacity allows optimizing the graphs of garbage disposal: the garbage truck approaches when the containers are filled. As well as the technologies have been developed which allow delivering garbage from containers to garbage disposal points by pneumatic pipes. To dispose garbage, two technologies have been developed: cans filling capacity tracking and disposal after they are filled and analyzing the data by the weight of the garbage disposed in vehicles to provide subsequent building a model that optimizes the export schedules.

The sensors installed on the communal engineering, with which the streets are cleaned, allow real-time monitoring of movement route and speed, fuel consumption and operation mode, ensuring control over task performance by drivers.

Monitoring for the condition of electric networks and water pipes allows to avoid emergency situations and to pass to the maintenance according to the condition.

Pilot projects in the field of housing and utilities infrastructure are being implemented in Moscow. In particular, in the area of Lublino 16 mixed-use buildings are selected to create a "smart quarter", where the technology of "smart city": lighting, garbage collection, automated access to entrance halls and yard, smoke control, etc. will be tested.

The automated resources usage system (ARUS) in Moscow includes pressure gages which monitor the condition of pipes and help to avoid emergencies. Pilot installation of water leakage sensors in apartments and common areas (basement and apparatus floor) is planned to monitor leaks in water supply networks, as well as installation of CO_2, CH_4, temperature, humidity sensors in apartments and common areas. It is expected that this will reduce the risk of fire, gas leakage and increased relative humidity as a result of roof leakage, water breakthrough in water supply or heating systems.

The Department of Information Technologies of Moscow implements the IoT technologies in the housing and utilities infrastructure, in particular, IICSOL and ARUS systems.

Since 2018, mass adoption of "smart meters" in Moscow households is planned that will allow energy suppliers to introduce flexible tariffs, for example, for peak and night hours.

All utility equipment in Moscow is equipped with devices that allow monitoring speed, route, fuel consumption and operation mode (for example, asphalt cleaning or not). As a result, fuel economy reached 4%.

3 Main world trends

Currently, the following smart systems are used for the cities management in the world and Russian practice [8].

Smart Metering. The smart metering technology of energy consumption (electricity, gas, water, heat), in addition to installing smart metering devices, involves the creation of information networks for data transmission. This solution is one of the types of intercomputer communication M2M and, therefore, blends with the IoT concept. The effect from the implementing the smart meters and their data collection networks according to experts will reduce the required amount of new power capacity by 20%. Due to the intellectualization of maintenance and technological operations, it is possible to connect more consumers to the already available facilities, to reduce losses from energy theft by 95%, and technical losses by 50%, to reduce consumer debt by 50-70% [4]. Each of these parameters is critically important for the Russian energy supply market.

Smart Home This is one of the most relevant solutions of IoT as residents have access to integrated management of the home or apartment life support systems. This smart home management allows coordinating the operation of heating and ventilation systems, security and fire alarms, video surveillance, communications and telephone, lighting, power supply, etc. It is possible to remotely control the home premises situation that prevents or significantly reduces the risk of accidents caused by water or gas leakage, electric devices connected to the mains, etc. However, the main advantage of IoT solutions in the smart home is the ability to reduce the power and heat costs. The smart home management system with gages, sensors, meters and household appliances connected to the single IoT network automatically maintains the optimal mode of power and heat consumption in the premises, informs about the left lighting, opens windows and selects the appropriate mode for switching on electrical devices based on time of day and current tariffs.

Smart Grid The energy industry is a typical example of new technologies could solve many problems of urban economy, in this case, the problems of transportation and consumption of energy resources. The Smart Grid provides on-line monitoring and managing the energy networks, as well as it implements communications between consumers and energy suppliers. Thus, it means not just smart meters and network devices – the Internet of things will connect electric car, home batteries, solar panels, thermostats and consumer electronics devices, such as TVs and air conditioners, to the Smart Grid. Constant on-line monitoring of energy consumption provides, if necessary, to direct energy flow in the opposite direction, from the consumer to the grid, and include it into accounts with the consumer. This will help to plan the power supply and consumption and to simplify the process of customer service. In the future, the principles of Smart Grid can be distributed to the networks of heat, gas and water supply, water disposal and sewerage.

Smart City The citizen needs grow: one day there was enough food, shelter and relative safety, but now, in order to make the city attractive and comfortable for people, it shall satisfy much more serious and complex requirements. The focus in urban management shifts to the good transport and utilities infrastructure, normal environmental conditions, effective security system, competent facilities operation, etc. The Internet of things makes it possible to improve the life quality. Thus, the IoT technologies will provide economical and ecological use of city systems of life support and utilities infrastructure (water supply, heating, electric power supply, lifting mechanisms, communications, etc.) by combining city services and organizations into smart distributed applications. This will allow them to interact quickly based on the modern IT both in daily work and in emergency situation.

Thus, the use of Internet of things technologies allows managing business processes in the housing and utilities infrastructure in a comprehensive, efficient and high-quality manner.

4 New vectors of development

With the implementation of the Internet of things technology in the sphere of housing and utilities infrastructure, new participants – service providers, operators of information network and systems appear which provide the necessary infrastructure support. The network or platform provider functions can be performed by the communication network operators using their infrastructure and network capabilities (data centers, call centers, communication channels and lines, access networks, etc.). This approach maintains qualitatively new requirements for automated and information systems in the housing and utilities infrastructure. The gage or sensor itself is, in fact, only a registrar of certain changes with the ability to transmit the collected information. The problem is that these data shall be correctly transmitted and meaningfully interpreted. Therefore, the mass implementation of smart meters initiates appearing new information systems with enhanced capabilities for information collecting, transmitting, processing, ensuring information security, billing and analytics of collected data. As a result, large integral systems appear in the housing and utilities sector, which provide a complete information life cycle – from the initial registration of a certain parameter change to its meaningful interpretation and making decision on the management of appliances, facility or the housing and utilities sector as a whole.

The Smart Metering subsystem is responsible for collecting, processing and storing information received from meters. It allows arranging the management of utility network elements in order to control the energy resources consumption and the dispatch services organization. The subsystem of personal services includes a set of applications implementing a number of services together with the smart metering subsystem that provide comfortable and safe living (control of smoke, leakage, unauthorized access to home, etc.).

The billing subsystem provides a full cycle of settlements for housing and utilities services including consumers accounting, energy consumption data processing, services invoicing, receipt of payments monitoring, work with debtors, etc.

Calculation of energy balances for homeowners' associations, executors, energy providers, resource providers is performed by the balance calculation subsystem that controls over unauthorized use of energy resources, losses accounting at various sections of utility networks. The monitoring and control subsystem interacts with SCADA/APCS systems of resource providers.

The subsystem of citizens' registration is used to register citizens permanently or temporarily residing within the municipal formation territory. Consumer affairs subsystem CRM performs the functions of information and reference services, registration and processing of applications of housing and utilities services' consumers. The analytical subsystem allows to perform multi-dimensional analysis of data related to the population, housing stock and energy consumption, and to present these data in a convenient graphical form for statistical and analytical reports.

The information portal provides the consumers access to the regulatory reference and calculation information and to energy consumption statistics, receipt of invoices, energy saving expert advice, filing requests, complaints and claims, other information services related to housing and utilities infrastructure through the personal profiles. As well as other subjects of the housing and communal services sector has the access to the Internet portal for disclosing information via the Internet in accordance with the current standards and rules.

The databases are ordered set of registries, log books and regulatory and reference information about suppliers and consumers of housing and utilities services, information on the housing stock status, service agreements, services tariffs, benefits and subsidies, regulations for interaction of organizations during services rendering, The information system of public utilities is the most important functional component and source of information for SIS of the housing and utilities infrastructure.

The use of the Internet of things technologies contributes to saving resources. The foreign experience shows that water resources and power consumption can be reduced by 15-30% [3]. In Russia, the first experiments in this direction are just launched, and one example is the implementation of the Smart Grid project in Tyumen. The system measures pressure, temperature, flow and leakage in the surrounding areas of the heating network, provides dynamically to monitor failures. The system based on a comprehensive monitoring, accounting and control of data allows reducing the network operating costs and improving the operating efficiency in case of emergency. It should be noted that the project is implemented based on the domestic software developments and equipment, and is fully adapted to the conditions and standards of the Russian housing and utilities infrastructure complex. The equipment allows to quickly monitoring all changes in the heat network. This is required to eliminate leaks, problems with thermal insulation, to perform network balancing ensuring uniform heat supply to consumers that significantly saves funds of the energy providers. Currently, over 200 control points have been installed in Tyumen, information from which enters the information system. Their number will subsequently increase. It is planned to establish 4.5 thousand points to account dwelling consumption.

One of the ultimate goals of implementing such systems is differential pricing: in the course of time, each person will be able to manage his expenses for housing and utilities infrastructure, knowing where he can save. At the first stage about 30 million rubles were invested in the system, which were required to organize communication channels and purchase server equipment. The next steps may be already more expensive, but all investments in the Smart Grid system should pay off within a year.

The transition to Internet of things technologies in the housing and utilities infrastructure enters into new opportunities based on formation of the single information space of the industry, allows creating IT systems to inform customers and process their data, implementing mobile and cloud solutions including large data analytics.

However, according to data of Rosstat, the level of information and communication solutions penetration in the housing and utilities infrastructure is still low. For example, only 65% of resource providers used basic information technologies in 2016 including local networks, electronic document management systems, and other similar solutions – no more than 5% [2].

Resource providers do not strive to the widespread use of digital technologies, partly due to a lack of funds, partly due to the desire to receive more favorable payment for them based on the rates. As well as homeowners' associations, for which increase in the level of automation and transparency could bring quite certain benefits, do not interest in improving the infrastructure against the talks about the possible direct interaction of resources providers and consumers.

Thus, the main driver for the development of housing and utilities infrastructure in the near future will be the active implementation of smart meters for all types of resource and energy consumption in dwellings, which will gradually be combined into a smart metering system, digital system of mutual settlements for resources consumption based on SIM cards using the Internet of things technologies that will allow to lower expenses on payment of housing and utilities infrastructure, expenses of resource and energy providers, and to increase efficiency and quality of these services.

References

1. Digital Russia: new reality [online], Available at: https://www.mckinsey.com/~/media/McKinsey/Locations/Europe%20and%20Middle%20East/Russia/Our%20Insights/Digital%20Russia/Digital-Russia-report.ashx (2018)
2. A. Parshkov, Technologies. Engineering, **1 (7)** (2018)
3. World experience and prospect of development of industrial Internet of things in Russia [online], Available at: https://www.crn.ru/news/detail.php?ID=113441 (2016)
4. M. Samsonov, A. Roslyakov, S. Vanyashin, A. Grebenkov, *Internet of things in a smart city* (Asgard, Samara, 2016).
5. N. Kemaykin, Society: Politics, Economics, Law, **11** (2017)
6. B. Panshin, Science and innovation, **3 (157)** (2016)
7. Internet of Things (IoT) in Russia. Currently available future technology [online], Available at: https://www.pwc.ru/ru/publications/iot/IoT-inRussia-research_rus.pdf (2016)
8. A. Pidzhukov, Tele-satellite, **4 (258)** (2017)
9. A. Petrov, I. Drozdova, World Applied Sciences Journal, **23** (2013)
10. L. Primak, L. Chernyshov, *Energy saving in the housing and utilities infrastructure* (Akademicheskij proekt, Moscow, 2011)
11. K. Gulin, V. Uskov, Problems of territory development, **4 (90)** (2017)
12. P. Nielsen, Energy Efficiency in the Public Sector: Lessons Learnt, Presentation given at the meeting of the Working Group on Energy Efficiency and Related Environmental Aspects [online], Available at: https://energycharter.org/fileadmin/DocumentsMedia/Thematic/Public_Sector_EE_2008_en.pdf (2008)
13. J.M.L. Prado, I.M.G. Sanchez, Journal of Productivity Analysis, **27 (3)** (2007)
14. V. Komkov, N. Timakhova, *Energy saving in the housing and utilities infrastructure* (INFRA-M, Moscow, 2010)
15. J. Magyar, Energy Efficiency in the Public Sector (Slovak Republic), Presentation given at the meeting of the Working Group on Energy Efficiency and Related Environmental Aspects [online], Available at: https://www.edgebuildings.com/wp-content/uploads/2017/10/EBRD.pdf (2007)

Foundation architecture of telemedicine system services based on Health 4.0 concept

Alisa Dubgorn[1], *Olga* Kalinina[1], *Anastasia* Lyovina[1*], and *Oksana* Rotar[2]

[1] Peter the Great St.Petersburg Polytechnic University, Institute of Industrial Management, Economics and Trade, Higher School of Business Management, 195251, Polytechnicheskaya st., 29, Russian Federation
[2] Federal State Budgetary Establishment "National Medical Research Center of V.A. Almazov" of the Ministry of Health of the Russian Federation, 197341, Akkuratova st., 2, Russian Federation.

Abstract. Telemedicine as an application area of the modern medicine is flourishing supported by the corresponding technologies development. Development of telemedicine technologies is one of the main trends in digitalization of health care service put into practice within the Health 4.0 concept. Implementation of telemedicine systems is particularly topical for countries possessing a great territory, due to which the problem occurs to provide equal access to specialized and hi-tech medical aid for all inhabitants in the country. Creation of the effective telemedicine system for rendering medical aid to patients in remote locations requires a system approach to engineering and implementation of such system. Represented in the article is a structure of the telemedicine system engineering and implementation project with the use of service-oriented approach to simulation of social-economic systems, as well as requirements to upper level services of such system within the first stage of the project.

1 Introduction

One of the factors characterizing health care services in a country is its availability, including hi-tech and specialized medical aid. The character of territorial distribution of centers, providing hi-tech and special medical aid, on the one hand, puts forward a problem to ensure availability of such medical aid for patients from remote locations, on the other hand – a problem of effective use of resources by centers rendering such aid. It is impossible to solve these problems without application of modern telemedicine technologies – computer and telecommunication technologies for acquisition and exchange of medical information.

Routing of patients in the process of detection, monitoring and rendering hi-tech and specialized medical service is not a linear motion from one point to the other. Since there is a tendency towards personalized medicine it is necessary to provide a possibility to process, store, and analyze large volumes of patient personal data. Since there is a complicated combination of factors (not only medical ones) determining the patient readiness for certain treatment it is necessary to make definite decisions (medical and administrative) after each

* Corresponding author: alyovina@gmail.com

process stage, which shall influence the further patient pathway. The hi-tech and specialized system of medical services features as follows [1]:

- Complexity and dynamics of processes;
- Uncertainty in demand and availability of resources;
- Patient-oriented approach;
- High speed and flexibility of decision making;
- Necessity in balancing the medical and economical efficiency.

Similar to many spheres of activity the modern health care becomes more and more technological; the advanced medical knowledge turns out to be concentrated in the special medical centers. The consequence of such centralization is the increase in a distance between such centers and potential patients who need the medical aid. As a result, many patients have no opportunity to get the precise diagnosis and the corresponding treatment. This problem is particularly acute for countries possessing the significant territory (for example, Russia, India, China, Brazil). The patient monitoring and routing process at rendering the specialized medical service to patients from remote locations requires a number of factors to be accounted (not only medical ones), which determine the patient readiness for certain treatment. Besides, after each process stage it is necessary to make definite decisions (medical and administrative) which influence the further patient pathway. Representation of specialized medical service to patients in remote locations is a very information-intensive process, since it requires proper acquisition, transmission, processing and analysis of large amount of data on patients and effective system of decision making on its base. Since the development of capital-intensive technological health care is to be continued, the actual task is development of technological and organizational principles of telemedicine system creation which shall provide data acquisition, storage, transmission, processing and analysis, as well as medical and administrative decision support in the process of rendering specialized medical aid to the territorially remote patients.

Due to development of technologies, including information-communication ones, at the present time the tendencies to digitalization are observed in many spheres of economical activity. The most known digitalization concept is the Industry 4.0 [2]. This concept means transition to completely automated digital production controlled by the intellectual systems in real-time mode with constant interaction with external environment, going beyond one enterprise, with a prospective of integration into the global industrial network of Things and Services[3]. The Health 4.0 concept being an "industry-specific interpretation" of the Industry 4.0 concept in medicine is aimed at increase of efficiency, decrease in expenditures and transition to customized services for patients. By using such technologies as Big Data, IoT, M2M, cloud computing the medical organization can increase availability and economical efficiency of medical aid, thus improving the patients' life quality [4]. Development of telemedicine systems is impossible without application of modern technologies in the sphere of data acquisition, processing, transmission, storage and analysis, as well as other modern technologies.

Allotted in the article is a task of setting requirements to the telemedicine system services developed according to the Health 4.0 concept and making it possible to provide an access to specialized and hi-tech medical assistance for remotely located patients.

2 Methodology

The Health 4.0 is a strategic concept for the health care field based on the Industry 4.0 concept. The purpose of the Health 4.0 is to ensure digital transformation of the field in order to make the health care system more customized and to provide patients health care in real-time mode thanks to the wide use of CPS (cyber-physical systems), cloud computing, Internet of Everything, including things, services and people, as well as mobile networks under development (5G). With the help of cyber-physical systems, visualized software blocks and modern data processing technologies the patients can be "virtualized" to make it possible to receive and analyze data on patients' health in any place in real-time mode. This will create prerequisites for development of personalized and precision medicine.

At the present time, the leading medical organizations in the country which attract a large number of scientific & research organizations and commercial enterprises develop approaches, methods and the corresponding material-and-technical infrastructure to detect and monitor the patients of pathological condition. In order to solve this task the use is made of such technologies as telemedicine, Internet of Things (IoT), mobile and electronic health care (mHealth and eHealth), cloud computing, Big Data, predictive analytical systems[5]. At the present time there is a great number of the described examples for modern technologies application in medicine (e.g., [6-10]). So, significant results are achieved in the sphere of development and practical implementation of the detection and monitoring system for patients with heart conditions, using:

- mobile applications for acquisition and transmission of patients condition parameters;
- telemedicine technologies for remote communication between patients and doctors;
- processing and analysis technologies of Big Data received from patients;
- predictive analytical systems for forecasting of patient condition dynamics.

Many works are dedicated to the issues concerning improvement of individual medical aid types rendering with the use of telemedicine technologies [10-12]. However, not many works could be found concerning the issues of a complex telemedicine system architecture development. Considered in [13] are approaches to increase availability and improve quality of medical assistance for the hard-to-reach and remote inhabited localities of the Russian Federation, implemented with the use of mobile telemedicine complexes (MTC) within the project on creation of telemedicine systems (TMS). The authors have analyzed the possible TMS architectures, have revealed deficiencies of the two-segment TMS the main of which is the system disintegration from a network of the ambulatory prevention and treatment facilities (PTF) existing in the RF regions, have proposed the use of three-segment TMS architecture which includes the existing ambulatory treatment facilities into the scheme of informational interaction besides mobile telemedicine complexes and TMS in-patient clinics. Absence of full-fledged legal environment for rendering medical assistance in such a format is also mentioned in publications dedicated to organization of telemedicine systems [14]. The analysis of international experience of developments in the sphere of telemedicine solutions has shown that there is a demand in investigation aimed at development of a complex solution on rendering medical assistance in the remote locations with the use of telemedicine concept, including the elaborated managerial, information-and-technological and hardware components.

At creation of the efficient telemedicine system it is necessary to use a complex approach which makes it possible to consider all various components in their interrelation and interdependence. In the present management such approach is an enterprise architecture which allows creating the efficient control systems consisting of the business-process systems, organizational structure, information systems, applications, technological infrastructure [15]. Described in [16, 17] is the elaborated service-oriented approach to analysis and re-engineering of the enterprise architecture and its elements. Such approach allows efficient formation and re-formation of the management system of enterprises and other social-economical systems by considering interrelation and interdependence of various elements of the control system. Application of such approach in the project of development and implementation of the data acquisition, transmission, processing and analysis system for patients in the remote locations shall make it possible to develop an effective complex solution taking into account a great number of various components of rendering the remote medical assistance. Such approach in development and re-engineering of the system architecture assumes the initial determination of requirements to the system services on the basis of which the whole system will be established.

Structure of the project on development and implementation of the telemedicine system was created in the article, and requirements to services of such system within the first stage of the developed structure of the project were established.

3 Results

In the present work the requirements to services of the telemedicine system created within the Health 4.0 concept are established. The developed telemedicine system must have the following characteristics:

- Reach the most remote and / or limited resource;
- Develop the qualified resource pool in the territorially remote points;
- Provide quick access of patients to experts and resources;
- Help in rendering proper patient care in conditions of constant monitoring, emergency assistance and personal injury, as well as in rehabilitation;
- Be self-supporting thanks to synergetic interaction between the concerned parties in the system of medical aid rendering;
- Include elements of computer-assisted training providing a system of medical decision making support.

Implementation of telemedicine system for rendering assistance to patients in remote locations is intended to provide the following advantages:

- Increase in patient satisfaction. In individual cases there is no longer any necessity in personal meetings with doctors from the territorially remote regions, the time of patient waiting in queue and the time required for document management can be decreased, the risk of errors and delays connected with writing disposals, prescriptions, registration of patients can be reduced. Besides, the main attention will be drawn to expansion of rights and possibilities of patients through patient training, extension of interaction with patients and implementation of educational and prevention programs.
- Increase in quality of medical assistance. The higher level of patient servicing is provided, among other things, by means of complete and accurate electronic arrangement of patients which shall reduce a number of errors, omissions or duplication of information and actions based thereon.
- Increase in work performance of medical stuff. Doctors and other medical stuff will devote more time to patients thanks to significant automation, in particular concerning the document management process. This will make it possible for medical stuff to devote more time to patients, to service more patients or to devote the saved time to other productive types of activity.
- Increase in operational efficiency of medical establishments engaged in the system of medical aid rendering to patients from the remote locations. Health care

organization can eliminate duplication of functions and administrative delays by means of automation and effective data exchange. The risk of errors decreases due to reduction in the volume of manual information input.

The main stages of the telemedicine system implementation project are given below:

1. Creation of requirements to telemedicine system services on detection and monitoring of pathological condition patients in the remote locations;
2. Creation of management architecture for telemedicine system on detection and monitoring of pathological condition patients in the remote locations;
3. Creation of a model for processes of detection and monitoring of pathological condition patients with the use of telemedicine technologies;
4. Establishment of requirements to:
    a. data processing and analysis model for telemedicine system;
    b. business-analysis system;
    c. hardware components (technological infrastructure) of the telemedicine system developed, including analysis of requirements for deployment of communication infrastructure;
    d. mobile applications and personalized data acquisition and transmission system for patient management implemented with the use of "Internet of Things" technology;
5. Development of:
    a. data models for detection and monitoring of pathological condition patients with the use of telemedicine technologies;
    b. data processing and analysis, including a platform for data storage and exchange, business-analysis system;
    c. technological infrastructure of telemedicine system;
6. Development of:
    a. a platform for data storage and exchange;
    b. mathematical, simulation and statistical models for decision making support within the detection and monitoring system of pathological condition patients with the use of telemedicine technologies;
    c. methodology of computer-based education for the data exchange and storage platform;
    d. BI-systems;
    e. mobile applications for acquisition and transmission of personalized patient monitoring data;
7. Complete set, construction and installation works, startup and adjustment works to create the technological infrastructure;
8. Integration of:
    a. developed business-analysis system and data exchange and storage platform;
    b. developed mobile application and data exchange and storage platform;
    c. patient management personalized data acquisition and transmission devices implemented with the use of "Internet of things" technology, mobile application and data exchange and storage platform
9. Creation of the test database for pilot tests of the data processing and analysis model being developed;
10. Pilot tests of individual components and the whole telemedicine system,

The first stage of the telemedicine system development project – creation of requirements to the system services – is considered in the present article. Proposed in [18] is classification of Smart Hospital services with subdivision into longtermness of their implementation perspectives. Similar to the proposed classification the following list of the necessary telemedicine system services has been developed (Table 1). It should be explained that this list relates just to telemedicine system and stipulates availability of general services of medical aid rendering system (according to [18]).

Table 1. Upper level services of telemedicine system.

Upper level services	Service description	Technologies used at service implementation
Mobile telemedicine complex	Represents the hardware at the location of medicine services rendering, is intended for acquisition of initial data from patients, including application of diagnostic equipment.	IoT Technologies of data transmission Cyber-physical systems (CPS) M2M connectivity
Communication channels	Set of means or methods for improvement of medical service, health care and provision of education in the field of health care with the use of telecommunication technologies, covering a wide spectrum of technologies and tactics for rendering virtual medical and educational services	Technologies of data transmission Cloud technologies
Video-communication and remote communication	A set of telecommunication technologies which allow for two or more points communication through simultaneous two-way video and audio transmission	Videoconferencing Channels of data transmission
Electronic clinical chart	Systematic acquisition of information on patient and population health in electronic digital format. This makes the exchange of medical information between medical establishments possible. This service is an integral part of not only the telemedicine system, but the whole system of medical assistance rendering within the Health 4.0 concept. Included in a list of telemedicine services in order to emphasize its critical importance at organization of telemedicine system	eHealth Data storage Cloud technologies

Upper level services	Service description	Technologies used at service implementation
Possibility of patient participation	Involvement of patients in the process of their own health support to achieve the best result. This service involves a wide spectrum of possibilities – from patient portals to strategies in social networks, from tracking the vital functions with the help of portable devices for patients actively participating in the health-improving programs	mHealth Social Media Marketing (SMM) Internet of Things (IoT)
Data management	Development and implementation of architectures, policies, practices and procedures for effective control over the enterprise information lifecycle	Business-analyses Big Data Cloud technologies
Data storage	Data storage is created on the basis of different sources, provides storage of the current and historical data used for creation of analytical reports	Business-analyses Big Data Cloud technologies
Decision making support system	Allows for substantiation of decision making by processing the various accumulated data	Business-analyses Big Data Computer-based education Mathematical, simulation modeling, statistical analysis
Determination of position in real-time mode	The position determination system in real-time mode automatically identifies and tracks position of objects or people in real time with the use of tags and sensors	IoT Geoinformation systems (GIS)
Monitoring of patients' state	Wide spectrum of services rendered at a distance to patients with detected chronic illnesses or having passed certain treatment. Includes the condition control and public awareness campaign carried out by specialists for patients' care management	eLearning IoT Cyber-physical systems (CPS) M2M connectivity

In order to implement the listed telemedicine system services it is supposed to use the following methods, approaches and technologies:

- telemedicine technologies. The character of the territorial distribution of centers rendering hi-tech and specialized medical assistance in Russia, as well as peculiarities of patient routing processes in the course of such assistance rendering stipulate the necessity in implementation of modern telemedicine technologies which make it possible to remotely exercise individual constituents of the medical assistance rendering process. At that, efficient resource use of centers rendering such assistance is provided;
- Big Data management technologies. Medical assistance rendering in the territorially distributed locations is connected with a necessity in personalized acquisition, processing and analysis of data on patients within the region and even the country.

Management of such big volumes of information is possible thanks to the use of modern technologies of big data management;

- Internet of Things technology. Management and control of patients' condition before and after rendering the hi-tech and specialized medical assistance must be of personalized and continuous character. Technical implementation of such monitoring of patients condition is possible by the use of "Internet of Things" technology that means acquisition of information from the object (patient) with the use of special devices and transmission of information through Internet for subsequent processing (including the use of Big Data management technologies);
- M2M connectivity. The technology is directly connected with "Internet of Things", provides data exchange between machines (including cyber-physical systems) without human participation;
- predictive analytical systems. Acquisition and analysis of data on patient condition for forecasting thereof, performed with the use of predictive analytical systems, make it possible to increase efficiency of the made medical and managerial decisions in the system of rendering hi-tech and specialized medical assistance;
- computer-based education. The use of computer-based education at operation with big volumes of patient data is aimed at support of making managerial decisions in medicine concerning development of individual paths of patients routing, evaluation of risks and classification of patients, as well as diagnostics in real-time mode;
- mobile networks 5G. Provides a possibility of multi-frequency connection and multi-modality, including NB-IoT and mobile service in order to provide information exchange between physical and virtual worlds [4];
- cyber-physical systems (CPS). Represent integration of computer-based and physical processes where embedded computers and networks perform monitoring and control of physical processes with feedback cycles, as a rule. The specific applications for health care can be connection of Body Area Networks systems and sensors to disease control platforms with the use of feedback auto-regulation cycles or feedback with the help of devices (e.g., smart phones) [4];
- mathematical modeling, simulation modeling and statistical analysis. Operation with big data requires elaboration of models on their processing and analysis. Mathematical, simulation and statistical models of data processing are planned to be implemented in the developed business-analysis system.

4 Conclusions

Telemedicine as an applied sphere of the modern medicine is flourishing now which is conditioned both by internal and external reasons. On the one hand, the tendency towards value-based medicine is observed in the health care field that means a growth of patient role at creation of requirements to the quality of medical services. On the other hand, the rapid development of technologies makes implementation of new services in the health care field principally possible. Thus, favorable conditions for development of value-based medicine are created, in particular to provide equal access to the services of specialized and hi-tech medical assistance for all patients in the country.

The telemedicine system providing detection, control, medical assistance and condition monitoring of patients in remote locations represents a complex of different control objects. Creation of such system requires complex approach to its engineering and implementation. Represented in the article is a structure of the project on engineering and implementation of telemedicine system with the use of service-oriented approach to modeling of social-economic systems from establishment of requirements to pilot tests. Service-oriented engineering of telemedicine system is aimed at creation of the efficient, flexible and evolutionary system by taking into account the interrelation and interdependence of system components at its creation. Formulated in the article are requirements to upper level services of such system which represents the first stage of the telemedicine system development and implementation project. Besides, a potential of the modern digital technologies at implementation of the required services is determined. Implementation of the proposed architecture of services is intended to ensure high medical and economic efficiency of rendering specialized and hi-tech assistance to patients in the remote locations by far-sighted use of resources of both medical organizations in situ and specialized medical centers of federal importance.

The topic of the present article can be developed by elaboration of the telemedicine system IT-architecture according to the established requirements to services, as well as investigation of implementation methods for individual telemedicine system services, including the use of key technologies of the Health 4.0 concept.

References

1. E. A. Ryngach, T. V. Treshkur, A. A. Tatarinova, E.V. Shlyakhto, Terapevticheskii Arkhiv (2017)
2. M. Herman, T. Pentek, B. Otto. Design principles for Industrie 4.0 scenarios. Technical University of Dortmund, Faculty of Engineering, Audi Endowment Chair Supply Net Order Management [online], Available at: http://www.leorobotics.nl/sites/leorobotics.nl/files/bestanden/2015%20-%20Hermann%20Pentek%20%26%20Otto%20-%20Design%20Principles%20for%20Industrie%204%20Scenarios.pdf (2017)
3. The Fourth Industrial Revolution. Popular about the main technological trend of the XXI century. Available at: http://www.tadviser.ru/index.php/Article:Forth_industrial_revolution_(Industry_4.0). (2017)
4. C. Thuemmler, C. Bai, (eds.) *Health 4.0: How Virtualization and Big Data are Revolutionizing Healthcare*, DOI 10.1007/978-3-319-47617-9_2 (2017)
5. I. V. Ilin, O. Yu. Iliashenko, A. I. Levina. *Proceedings of the 29th IBIMA Conference – Sustainable Economic Growth, Education Excellence, and Innovation Management through Vision 2020* (2017)
6. J.M.L.P. Caldeira, J.J.P.C. Rodrigues, P. Lorenz, IEEE Communications Magazine **50 (5)** (2012)
7. J.J.P.C. Rodrigues, I. De La Torre, G. Fernández, M. López-Coronado, Journal of medical Internet research **15(8)** (2013)
8. V. Arun, S.K. Padma, V. Shyam, Med Med Sci Res **4(189)** (2015)
9. J. Santos, J.J.P.C. Rodrigues, B.M.C. Silva, J. Casal, K. Saleem, V. Denisov, Journal of Network and Computer Applications **71** (2016)
10. V. Arun, V. Shyam, S.K. Padma, Primary Health Care **5 (210)** (2015)
11. V. N. Rostovtsev, T. I. Terekhovich Organizational-technological system of telemedicine clinical examination [online] Available at: http://minzdrav.gov.by/dadvfiles/001079_754732_2_5_rostovc.pdf (2017)
12. T. S. Smal, V. D. Zavadovskaya, I. A. Deyev. Use of telemedicine technology for expert evaluation of X-ray examination quality for osteo-articular system in conditions of remote regions [online] Available at: http://www.rejr.ru/volume/26/11.pdf (2017)

13. G. Ya. Ilyushin, V. I. Limansky. Rendering medical assistance to population with the use of mobile telemedicine systems [online] Available at: http://www.mathnet.ru/links/5c7df673fd59c0a7d674df4be31b7b0c/ssi507.pdf (2017).
14. A. O. Lositsky, E. L. Borshchuk, A. D. Chuprov. Legal issues of telemedicine treatment-diagnostic services implementation into the state finance system at the present time [online] Available at: http://www.eyepress.ru/article.aspx?24747. (2017)
15. M. Lankhorst, et al. *Enterprise Architecture at Work. Modelling, Communication and Analysis* (2017)
16. I. V. Ilin, O. Yu. Iliashenko, A. I. Levina, *Proceedings of the 28th IBIMA Conference – Vision 2020: Innovation Management, Development Sustainability, and Competitive Economic Growth*. (2016)
17. I. V. Ilin, K. V. Frolov, A. A Lepekhin, *Proceedings of the 29th IBIMA – Sustainable Economic Growth, Education Excellence, and Innovation Management through Vision 2020* (2017)
18. Smart hospital services catalogue. Available at: http://awtg.co.uk/white-paper/smart-hospitals-service-catalogue/ (2017)

Information technologies and construction sector: Why construction loses competition for innovations to other industries?

Rudolf Faltinsky[1], and *Galina* Tokunova[1*]

[1] Saint Petersburg State University of Architecture and Civil Engineering, Faculty of economics and management, 190005 2nd Krasnoarmeiskaya st. 4, Russian Federation

Abstract. Over the last 10 years investments into innovation made at the beginning of 2000s resulted in significant growth not only in separate industries but in global economy as a whole. The development of digital technologies significantly reduced the costs of advance technologies, which made them affordable to a wide range of consumers. Using new tools and methods for interaction of social and economic subjects became a real accelerator of rapid growth for some industries such as media, information and communication technologies or finances. However, no significant innovative changes occur in the construction sector despite a generally acknowledged important role in the economy of both separate countries and in global economic processes. The article considers the factors that have an effect on the digital transformation of construction industry, the peculiarities and problems of this process.

Construction makes a substantial contribution to different economic and social processes. Construction business presumes cooperation among organizations from various industries encompassing a wide spectrum of society life. In the USA, for example, people on average spend almost 90% [1] of time within a room. Thus, a building and materials used to construct and finish it have a significant effect on its inhabitants' health and well-being. Moreover, today about 100 million people work in the construction industry worldwide [2]. Housing construction is 38% of global construction, transport infrastructure and power engineering projects are 32%, commercial premises and buildings are 18% and industrial facilities are 13% [3]. It is worth noting the state's role in construction industry, not only as a regulator but as a participant of economic relations. Public procurement amounts to 31% of the construction market sales in England, 44% in Germany and massive 57% in the United States of America [3]. Construction industry is the largest global consumer of resources and raw materials. This branch of economy annually consumes around 50 of global steel production and 3 bln tons of other raw materials [4]. As far as electric power consumption is concerned, 25-40% of its global generation is consumed within and by buildings [5].

In such countries as USA, Italy, France the construction sector amounts to about 4-5% GNP, in developing countries such as China its share is about 7-8% [6]. It is expected that in

* Corresponding author: tgf_1608@mail.ru

the nearest years the sector will significantly grow and the total income of construction companies will amount to 15 trillion $ by 2025 [2].

Despite an important role played by construction in the global economy, at present there are no innovative digital technologies implemented in the construction sector, requiring upfront investments. The R&D investments in construction leg behind those made in the other global economy sectors: less than 1% of companies' revenue. In automotive and aerospace industries this indicator amounts to 3.5% and 4.5% respectively [7]. Part of the technologies being implemented in construction comes from other sectors from technological and processing industries and as a result is not accounted for the construction industry. For example, innovations in the timber and wood processing industries, surely, have direct advantages for construction but their R&D costs are seldom referred to them. If you look at research data by McKinsey&Company [7] the lack of financing is one of the reasons for low rates of digital transformation within the construction industry. The penetration of digital technology into construction industry as a whole remains at a relatively low level (Fig. 1).

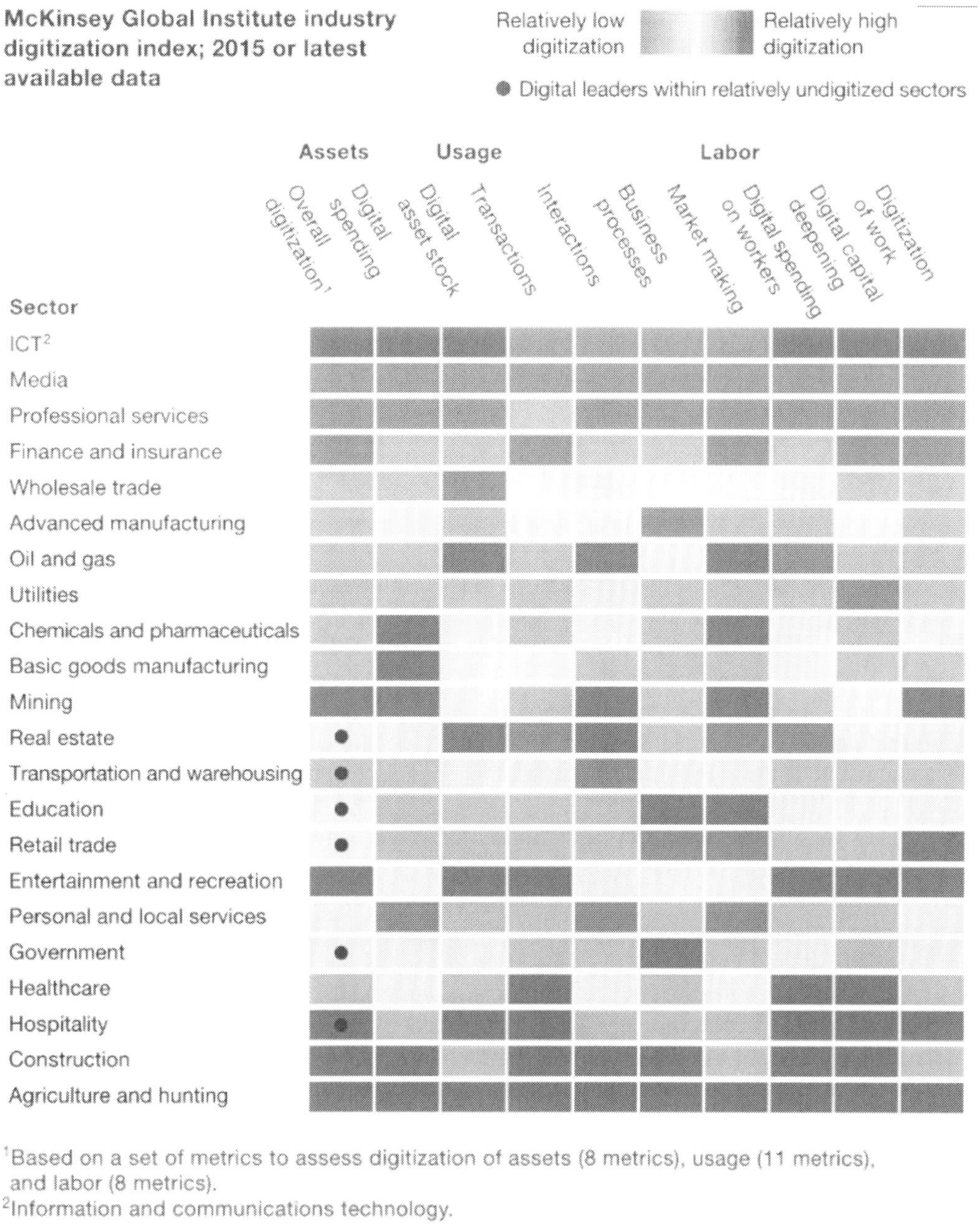

Fig. 1. Level of penetration of digital technologies into different sectors of global economy [7].

Now then most industrial branches have gone through enormous changes over the last several decades and gained from digital and process innovations, the construction sector has not practically utilized the available potential of these transformations. It is one of the reasons why 20% of construction projects are not completed within timeframes and 80% of projects exceed their budget [7]. One more indicator of this backlog for innovative transformations in the construction sector that even in such developed countries such as the United Kingdom and Germany there has not been practically labor productivity growth in the construction sector since 1990, however, the GNP shows stable growth in general (Fig. 2).

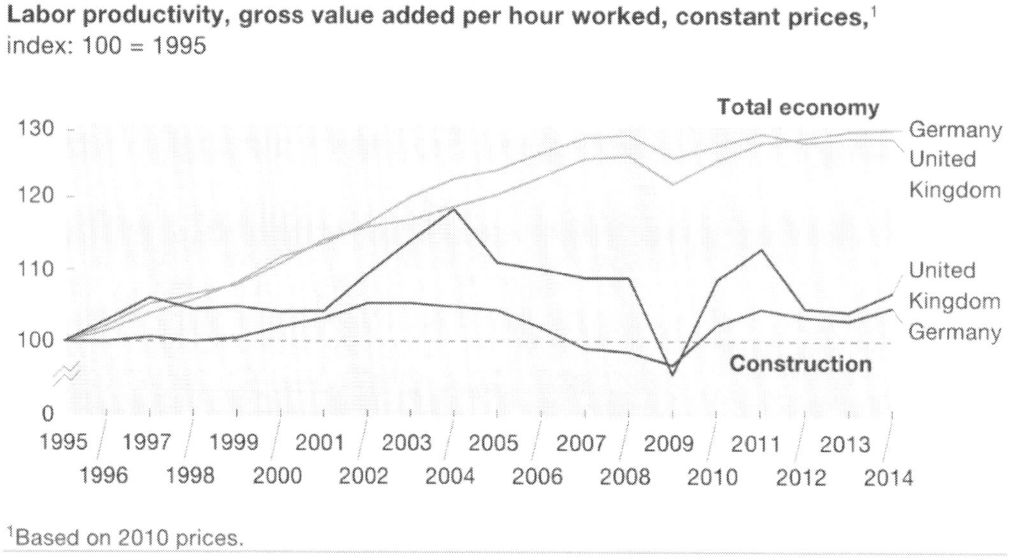

Fig. 2. Growth rates of economy and labor productivity in construction [7].

If data from different research works on the level of penetration of digital technologies is compared, for example, conducted by McKinsey&Company and International comparisons of labor productivity by industry: for 2014, then it is possible to make a conclusion that those sectors, which have implemented advance digital tools and technologies, show much higher relative and absolute indicators of labor productivity. In insurance and financial sectors, information and communications sectors in Italy, Germany and France productivity is 50-60 euro/hour but at the same time this indicator amounts to 20/30 euro/hour in the sphere of construction.

It is impossible to change this situation in the construction sector by introducing several key innovations such as, for example, new high-speed data transmission channels in the telecommunications sector, due to the fact there is a very complicated structure of cross-industry relationships. Integrated digital transformations of all principles, systems and tools of the sector are required.

According to evaluation of the European commission 70% of innovations in all the industrial sectors are new materials or improved existing ones. Construction materials account for one-third of construction costs that is why they are a rather upcoming trend for development and implementation of innovations. For example, Canadian company Carbon Cure Technologies has developed an innovative technology to enhance the concrete strength by bonding carbon dioxide.This technology will also reduce the amount of harmful emissions into the atmosphere; these emissions are caused by refineries.

Industrial sectors of the global economy, for example, the automotive industry have already reached a breakthrough moment in automation of their manufacturing processes [11], however, the construction industry still has a very low level of automation.At the same time, a significant reduction in costs of key process developments (for example, the cost of unmanned aerial vehicles has dropped by more than 100 times [3]) has become a significant driver for innovations in construction machinery [12]. Equipment has gained a central role in increased productivity, reduced construction costs, reduced lead time, improved quality and reduced risks.The construction of a 57-story building by Broad Group China to innovations implemented in production 90% of construction work processes have been carried out at the factory, which made it possible to construct the building for 19 days [3].

One the key technologies, that can change the construction sector in the future is 3D-printing. According to specialists of Chinese company WinSun the additive construction methods allowed reducing the material consumption twice as much in comparison with the quantities that are usually required during construction of a residential building and the construction time was only the third of what was required during classical approach. All together, the labor costs reduced by 80%, which makes it possible not only to reduce costs and imply lower risk of injury among workers [13].

The development and implementation of digital technologies and processes for operation with big data takes on a central place in transforming the construction industry. These innovations make it possible to create new functional possibility throughout the entire construction project life cycle. According to research conducted by The Boston Consulting Group the large-scale implementation of BIG-data technologies will allow the global economy to save 13-21% within 10 years annually during construction and 10-17% during operation of non-residential buildings, which amounts to 0.7-1.2 trillion $ and 0.3-0.5 trillion $ respectively [14]. Deep implementation of BIG-data technologies entails the infrastructure to be developed for acquisition and transmission of data for processing. The "smart house" or "smart city" ideas become not only the declared principles but practically implemented solutions, which gets to be more affordable due to reduced costs of transmitters, data processing and storage technology as well as information transmission speed. One of the leaders is Singapore that has launched a web-site [15], which can be used by citizens to view some monitoring data and the state authorities, for example, can develop the models of influence exerted by high-rise building being constructed on the wind-flow pattern. A variety of received data makes it possible to enhance the reliability level of reports on current status of objects and forecasts concerning their parameter changes.

Developing tools and technologies for collection, processing and transmission of big data allow building interaction between all construction project participants based on BIM (building information modeling). BIM is a process in which digital information is generated, collected, analyzed and transmitted to all participants accurately and consistently throughout the entire project life cycle starting from survey to dismantling and site return to original state. BIM is a central element of digital transformation of the industry, reflect advantages of all implemented innovations and makes it possible to:

- Control construction process in real time, monitor contractors, trace key indicators and timeframes in any required scale - from strategic level to a certain worker within selected work section;
- Control all design changes, carry out operational recalculation of all indicators while editing a model, including the amount of required materials, labor costs, work completion timeframes, budget.
- Automate all construction machinery control up to automatic adjustment of an operating component (blade, bucket etc) based on design data uploaded in a machine and practically without operator's involvement;
- Simulate different construction scenarios; select an optimal one out of them at pre-design stage.
- Receive operational, analytical information providing the customer with relevant data for strategic monitoring and planning at all project implementation stages;
- Calculate site operation and maintenance costs based on collected and combined information received from different sources and data at all construction stages;
- Create contractors database, manage contracts, accounting documentation, construction development programs.

According to research conducted by University of Maryland BIM is capable of reducing costs of design and construction stages by 30% and 10% respectively due to implemented innovations. In this case, design costs will decrease by 8% and construction budget saving will amount to 3%.

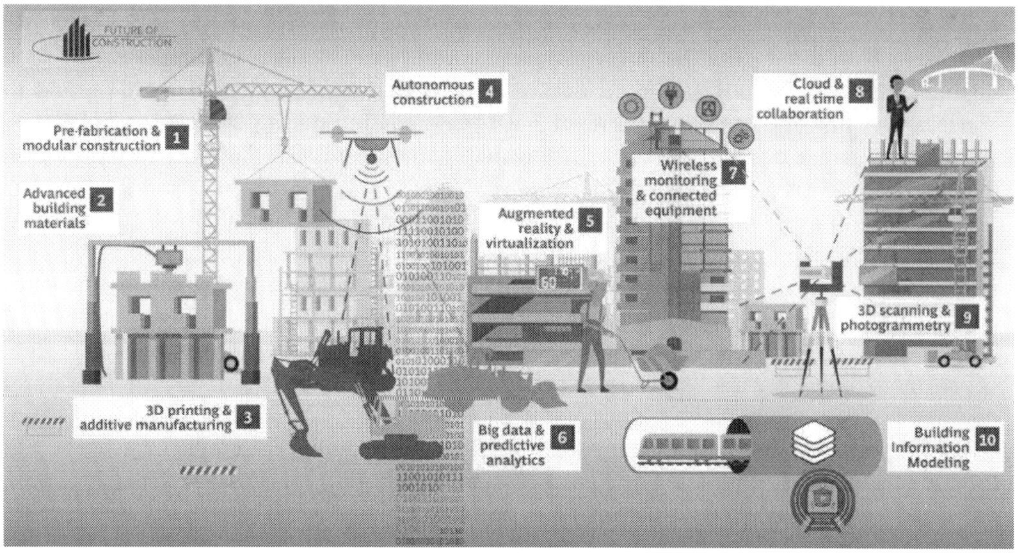

Fig. 3. Key technologies applied in BIM [17].

BIM was originally used only for construction of building but with development of digital technologies and capabilities to process big data at present it is also used in other areas.For example, in the United Kingdom a famous British BIM was launched during implementation of a railway project, which is being implemented in the old part of London and has a complex infrastructure [18]. Finland started implemented its BIM project practically at the same time with the United Kingdom and its experience quickly spread all over Scandinavia and in some time all over Europe. For example, in December 2015 the Federal Ministry of Transport and Digital Infrastructure of Germany published a "road map" for implementation of BIM according to which the information modeling will become an integral part of future government-run infrastructural projects [19]. China should be mentioned in terms of BIM implementation. An average global growth rate of architectures and contractors, who use BIM to run 30% of their projects amounts to 95%.In China this indicator amounts to 108%. China is among five quick-growing BIM regions along with the United Kingdom, South Korea, Australia and Germany [20]. In Russia the plan for phased implementation of information modeling technologies in the area of industrial and civilian construction was adopted on December 29, 2014 [21] and a "road map" for implementing BIM technologies was approved in April 2017. However, the terms of mandatory information modeling application in implementing state-run projects are not approved yet due to unavailability of digital infrastructure and insufficient human resourcing for its full-scale implementation.

Today the sphere, coverage and geography of projects, which are implemented both with separate innovations, digital tools and with BIM technologies is quite versatile. An increasing technological gap of the construction sector and other branches is a threat for the future development of not only some countries but global economy as a whole. An annual increase in population worldwide, development of global infrastructure will require new large-scale construction projects to be implemented. In this situation the cost and quality parameter requirements will be more demanding due to limited resources. Innovations in construction are not yet widely spread and a gap between innovative leaders and other companies is increasing. Every region and country has its individual peculiarities which have an effect on the level of implementing digital economy elements. In this case it is possible to mention global problems in the construction sector, which force the construction sector to lose completion for innovations to other areas of global economy.

Branch-wise. Construction companies jointly run projects, which have various parameters and properties or jointly implement single projects. Applicable innovative solutions are difficult to adapt and use for other projects, which does not contribute to exchange of knowledge, experience and joint developments. The system of tender procedures is not suitable for innovations either. The construction sector is perceived as a production process that runs in accordance with predetermined detailed parameters in implementing a project. Implementing innovations, in other words, changing a project is difficult to put in practice and virtually impossible.

Engineering. Implementing innovative solutions in construction is related with technological risks, which arise both during use of a new material or a technology with historical short-term level of appraisal and during interaction of an innovation with traditional processes and materials [22]. It is quite reasonable that project participants do not want to take construction risks related to engineering solutions that have not been sufficiently time-tested and case-recorded.

Market. The key factor of competitive strength in mass consumption segment is price. New properties or improved quality brought by innovations remain to be the secondary factor in demand and quite often not balanced in relation to price. Advance developments are mainly applied in "high" and "elite" construction segments with a relatively small turnover in the construction economy, which does not allow innovative products to be developed from economic point of view [23, 24].

Economic. Innovations often require much higher initial investments, in this case profits are observed throughout the entire project life cycle. For example, most costs to develop a BIM model are incurred during design, whole most advantages from BIM use are obtained by project participants at further stages.

Human resources. Demographic shifts in developed countries lead to an increase in workers' average age within the construction sector. The skill and knowledge requirements tend to be higher, while the education system allowing a sufficient number of specialists to be trained is not implemented.

Legislative. Construction sites and structures form an integral part of society and should provide comfort and what is most important, safe operation. The possible use of innovation, especially in the area of construction materials must be confirmed by appropriate and sometimes many legislative acts, which with an average construction project period equal to 5 years [25] significantly increases the period of their massive implementation.

Due to high capital intensity digital innovations are not the factor forming competitive environment in the construction sector. Innovative activity is perceived as costs but not as required investments into company's development and competitive strength. Problems need to be identified to form a combination of organizational and economic tools to solve these problems and to integrate digital tools or engineering solutions with the investment and construction process.

References

1. N. E. Klepeis, W. C. Nelson, W. R. Ott, J. P. Robinson, A. M. Tsang, P. Switzer, The National Human Activity Pattern Survey (NHAPS): A resource for assessing exposure to environmental pollutants. *Journal of Exposure Analysis and Environmental Epidemiology,* **11(3)**, 231-252 (2001) [online], Available at: [https://www.nature.com/articles/7500165.pdf, date of referencing 01.02.2018]
2. Global Construction Perspectives and Oxford Economics, *Global Construction 2025* (2013)
3. World Economic Forum, The Boston Consulting Group, *Shaping the Future of Construction. A Breakthrough in Mindset and Technology* (2016) [online], Available at:

[http://www3.weforum.org/docs/WEF_Shaping_the_Future_of_Construction_full_report__.pdf, date of referencing 29.01.2018]

4. World Steel Association, *World Steel in Figures 2015* (2015) [online], Available at: [https://aceroplatea.es/docs/WorldSteelFigures2015.pdf, date of referencing 29.01.2018]
5. United Nations Environment Programme, *Buildings and Climate Change: Status, Challenges and Opportunities* (2007) [online], Available at: [http://hdl.handle.net/20.500.11822/7783, date of referencing 30.01.2018]
6. M. Ishkenova, *A brief review of construction sector in the USA, Turkey and EU states* (2016) [online], Available at: [http://rfcaratings.kz/wp-content/uploads/2015/11/Stroitelnyj-sektor-RK-_okt.2016-g..pdf, date of referencing 31.01.2018]
7. R. Agarwal, S. Chandrasekaran, M. Sridhar, *Imaginingconstruction'sdigitalfuture* (2016) [online], Available at: [https://www.mckinsey.com/industries/capital-projects-and-infrastructure/our-insights/imagining-constructions-digital-future, date of referencing 01.02.2018]
8. A. Ward, A. Kirchherr, P Wales, *International comparisons of labour productivity by industry: 2014* (2017) [online], Available at: [https://www.ons.gov.uk/economy/economicoutputandproductivity/productivitymeasures/articles/internationalcomparisonsoflabourproductivitybyindustry/2014#results. date of referencing 01.01.2018]
9. L. Probst, E. Monfardini, L. Frideres, S. Moujahid, P. Luxembourg, *Smart Living: Advanced building materials (2014)*
10. http://info.carboncure.com/xprize-team
11. K. Schwab, *The Fourth Industrial Revolution* (2017)
12. P. Gerbert, M. Lorenz , M. Rüßmann, M. Waldner, J. Justus, P. Engel, M. Harnisch, *Industry 4.0: The Future of Productivity and Growth in Manufacturing Industries* (2015) [online], Available at: [http://image-src.bcg.com/Images/Industry_40_Future_of_Productivity_April_2015_tcm9-61694.pdf, date of referencing 01.02.2018]
13. Case Study prepared by the Boston Consulting Group as part of the Future of Construction Project at the World Economic Forum *Demonstrating the Viability of 3D Printing at Construction Scale* (2016)
14. P. Gerbert, S. Castagnino, C. Rothballer, A. Renz, R. Filitz, *Digitalin Engineering and Construction. The Transformative Power of Building Information Modeling* (2016) [online], Available at: http://futureofconstruction.org/content/uploads/2016/09/BCG-Digital-in-Engineering-and-Construction-Mar-2016.pdf (2018)
15. https://www.onemap.sg/main/v2/ (2018)
16. K. Parvan, *Estimating the Impact of BIM Utilization on Building Project Performance* [online] Available at: http://hdl.handle.net/1903/13063 (2012)
17. World Economic Forum, The Boston Consulting Group, *Shaping the Future of Construction. An Action Plan to Accelerate Building Information Modeling (BIM) Adoption* [online], Available at: http://www3.weforum.org/docs/WEF_Accelerating_BIM_Adoption_Action_Plan.pdf (2018)
18. Standard BS 1192:2007+A2:2016,*Collaborative production of architectural, engineering and construction information – Code of practice* (2007)

19. Federal Ministry of Transport and Digital Infrastructure: Road Map for Digital Design and Construction - Introduction of modern, IT-based processes and technologies for the design, construction and operation of assets in the built environment (2015) [online], Available at: [https://www.bmvi.de/SharedDocs/EN/publications/road-map-for-digital-design-and-construction.pdf?__blob=publicationFile, date of referencing 01.02.2018]
20. Dodge Data & Analytics, *The Business Value of BIM in China* http://images.marketing.construction.com/Web/DDA/%7B43cf3d41-46b5-4413-8aea-40d30e7ac57f%7D_EN_Business_Value_of_BIM_In_China_SMR.pdf (2015)
21. Implementation plan of staged information modeling technologies in the area of industrial and civil construction approved by order of the Ministry of construction and housing and utilities infrastructure of the Russian Federation N 926/пр dated December 29, 2014 (2014)
22. E. U. Elkina, West Irkutsk State Technical University, *Latent risks in innovative development and reduction in quality control during investment projects in housing construction*, **9 (92)** (2014)
23. F. M. Bass, T. V. Krishnan, D. Jain, Marketing Science, *Why the Bass Model Fits Without Decision Variables*, **13 (Summer)** (1994)
24. A. A. Alexeev, Economy and National economy management, *Engineering innovation mechanisms in construction* **10(131)** (2015)
25. Information-analytical agency INFOLine,*200 largest construction projects of shopping centers in RF. 2015-2018 projects* (2015)

Basic principles of constructing a convergence model for managing innovative development of the economic and social system

Inna Geraskina[1*], and *Alexander* Petrov[1]

[1] Saint Petersburg State University of Architecture and Civil Engineering, Faculty of Economics and Management, 190005 2-ya Krasnoarmeiskaya st. 4, Russian Federation

Abstract. Basic principles of constructing a convergence model for managing innovative development of the economic and social system are presented in the paper. The conceptual feature is accounting of system regularities and basic properties of the controlled object. The convergence model is focused on forming a synergetic potential of the economic and social system creating the sensitivity and its adequate reaction to synchronous and multiway managerial influence for development as per the special innovation vector. The model proposed by the authors is based on the collective effect of components (organized, information, production and intellectual) of the management system, determination of spatial-time position of the studied object, affected areas, control parameters and an interference value for stability and ability for changing of social and economic system over to the innovation trend. It was detected that its evolutionary dynamics is determined by the key factors: the existence of limits, the constant striving for the growth and hysteresis. High-priority problems of establishment were designed, and they consist in the modeling and forecasting the organization and management innovations and in arrangement of conditions for transfer to a qualitatively new trend that meets the requirements of the strategic plan.

The study of principal trends for development of the social and economic system (SES) and the environment being subject to systemic changes points to the necessity to improve the management model and system, arrangement of new requirements and approaches to the management. The key features for transformation of the economy and society actuating the activities on modernization of the existing management system are the following:

– scientific and technical progress and the necessity to form the intellectually creative, innovative type of the economy;

– objective globalization processes for creation of unified global system of management and public relations;

– limitation and degradation of resources aimed at finding ways to transition to the energy-resource efficient processes and technologies (sustainable development);

– hyper competition in the world market and high rate of renewal of product assortments, product differentiation where marketing and service functions make the greatest contribution to the creation of new cost and value;

– a high level of system consistency and exponential growth in data amount required for analysis and adoption of constructive managerial decisions;

*Corresponding author: geraskina82@mail.ru

– system dynamics, complication of the business environment and processes in terms of technical improvement of production, organization of labor and management.

The interconnectedness of these factors significantly influences the strategic benchmarks of economic entities. Against this background, the underlying theories are ineffective, and the conventional models that previously allowed predicting and controlling the business require the replacement with more systematic lateral thinking. The investigations of endogenous regularities, sensitivity zones and structural dynamics effects on the SES development trends are actualized. The application of synergetics and dissipative structure theories to the management of complex systems allows determining a degree of human impact on the SES development as from the points of certain parameters of order, force, magnitude and time of control actions [1, 2].

The conservative approaches that do not take into account the natural ways of evolution (attractors) immanently inherent in the managed system are ineffective from the point of the dialogue of innovative SES development. The V.D. Ayurov's point of view impresses; he believes that it is not inadvisable to control dissipative systems subjectively, since the control actions when imposing the functioning modes being not peculiar to it harm it only, and they are rejected [3].

The opinion of Professor B.L. Kuznetsov is interesting. He considers that the local subsystems of synergetic management are fundamentally different from classical analogues, since they use autocatalysis, auto regression, autocorrelation, coherence, amplification combinatorics of system-forming factors so that the process of innovation origin from the flicker quantum of scientific idea to the technological cluster is a single process, coordinated in space and time, combined by the single functional – efficiency and a single business mechanism [4].

The analysis of the long-term success of American companies ("Sony", "3M", "Wal Mart", "Walt Disney", "Boeing", "Hewlett-Parkard", etc.) given by D. Collins and D. Porras in the paper "Constructed forever" (2002) allowed to draw the following conclusion: deep development mechanisms in the absence of systemic exposition of the concept of advanced corporations prosperity have a fabulous similarity in the principles of management that have formed over a long period of time and have become the basis for progress stimulation: a) it is necessary to start a business with the desire to build a company but not to earn money; b) the driving force is aiming for a set of goals, including profit; c) to recede from a reasoned strategic plan for the benefit of non-standard solutions; d) move cautiously forward, catching and using special opportunities; e) a development benchmark is ideology reflecting the goals and causes of the organization existence [5].

The managers should understand the impossibility of accounting all options to predict the SES behavior. In case of failures, it is necessary to use a crisis bailout plan to try to direct the process in the right direction with convergence of the management system elements.

Currently, not all leaders have synergistic thinking to consider the SES as a living organism capable of homeossatis and self-organization. This understanding gradually comes to researchers of complex systems, in whatever field of knowledge they work. In this respect Professor G. Haken is sure that the time for synergetic formation has come [6, 7].

The system-synergetic thinking, to our opinion, is identified with arguments about the complexity of the world order, responsibility and ambiguity of the results of managerial decisions, modeling and the relative unpredictability of innovations in the system, choice problems. The presupposition of convergence SES management is conceptualized in saving its liveness and achieving strategic indicators, which management systems shall be oriented at, irrespective of their organizational level.

The management system is determined by the subsystem of the larger system that ensures achieving the goals of the managed system (subsystem) by influencing the structure, processes, relationships and relationships between entities under conditions that are acceptable for the existence of the managed system. The convergence model of managing the SES innovative development is aimed at increasing the effectiveness of management impacts, integrity control, homeostasis, synergistic potential. The latter creates the sensitivity and adequate reaction of the SES under investigation to synchronous, multi-position managerial influences for the goals system development according to a certain vector. It is important to take into account the rate of development dynamics which is increasing while moving from the global development to the local one (the smaller the social and economic system scale and the sphere of activities under consideration are, the more fluctuations in the rates of their innovative development are). Accelerating innovative development leads to an adequate growth of the synergetic potential that is a system attribute formed as a result of intersubjective interactions and structural-institutional dynamics mainly due to intangible assets and complementary effects accompanied by increasing the system activity and entropy.

An important characteristic of SES is the combination of order and chaos, the synthesis of which in the concept of a dissipative structure is considered in two aspects: 1) the system "order" exists only due to the chaos introduced into the environment; the existence is maintained by the constant exchange of matter, energy and data with it; 2) due to the "order", the SES gains the ability to adequately respond to chaotic environmental impacts, while maintaining stability. As viewed from the synergetics, the chaos can generate a new order that arises spontaneously, "not forced" by some exogenous force. The fluctuations occurring in the SES can be amplified instead of attenuation, and the system self-organizes.

The convergence model of managing the SES innovative development is aimed at achieving self-regulation, self-management and self-organization. It is assumed that the state has the critical role in creating a positive environment for the SES innovative development (institutional conditions that mean the standards and rules that contribute to either surge or paralysis and decline in the synergistic potential of the system). On being the management entity, it objectifies the development goals and objectives, ensures their achievement and solution. The state in this status positively determines the direction, rates, business and financial support for innovative development. On the one hand, the conditions completeness of the latter is ensured by hysteresis, historical, cultural, technological and managerial experience and, on the other hand, by the existing mechanism that to the maximum liberates the creative potential of the SES.

Since the intellectual sphere is the main source of innovations, it is possible to influence the SES entities by introducing negative entropy, taking into account the basic properties to the maximum, which are revealed when monitoring the environment and the structure to implement reflexive control. The order parameters and the set of control variables for the purpose of the synergistic potential required for increasing the SES activity, achieving the bifurcation state and synergetic effects in the context of path dependency control can be identified in case of economic and mathematical modeling [8, 9].

Effective models of managing the SES innovative development shall be compared with the features of a country and territory, national economy state, specific goals and objectives solved at certain intervals, resource supply opportunities and industry specificity [10]. In this regard, the detailed understanding of the general regularities and features of development of the SES and its entities is actualized. The structure of this system shall include the basic components and interacting subsystems: organizational, information, production and intellectual. They are sensitive to the production perception by end users whose reactions are accounted in accordance with its content. The decision on transformation is formed only based on the set of the SES state characteristics and the processes occurring in the management system.

The specialized tools and subsystems that provide real-time monitoring the state of the processes occurring in them, their analysis and identification of the prerequisites for innovative development shall be created as part of the SES management system. In particular, the information subsystem as a basic process platform provides the collection and regulation of primary data, ranking, assessment of their significance, utility and scope of application. The technological basis will be composed by the network information technologies without which the convergence management processes are not effective in the organizational subsystem that reflects the structure of SES elements interaction in terms of composition and capacity fixed in the form of structure-forming relations and documents. The problems in such priority areas as: innovative solutions, the quality of management processes, fluctuation signs identification, bifurcations and other synergetic effects will be erased in the intellectual subsystem, the set of computer knowledge engineering elements (artificial intelligence), professional knowledge and personnel experience on the basis of its intellectual properties. Due to the fact that the decisive role shall be given to the information technologies in all subsystems, the processes of self-organization foremost belong to the competence area of information management.

The convergence of the management system components means impossibility of their independent existence, configuration and formation: each version of one of them most effectively corresponds to certain versions of others; a change in one of them will require the reconfiguration of the others. Otherwise, the management system will be ineffective. Therefore, when formulating the tasks of self-organization, the SES shall take into account the interrelations between the subsystems and the nature of their interdependence (Table 1).

Table 1. The content of relations between subsystems of the system for managing the SES innovative development

Relation	Function
"Intelligence – Information"	Updating the data content with more complete and valuable information arising from the analysis of the existing experience.
"Information – Intelligence"	Formation of the information space, provision of personnel with the information that increases in a level of its competence, development of intelligence and accumulation of organization knowledge
"Intelligence – Organization"	Increase in the level of intellectuality (conciseness) of employees interaction in the process of labor activity, management self-organization
"Organization – Intelligence"	Organization of processes for collective analysis of problem situations and information comprehension, assurance of group decision making on the basis of knowledge exchange and raising the level of individual and collective intellectual potential of the organization on this basis
"Intelligence – Production"	Transfer of accumulated knowledge or intellectual potential to the level of the main production and thereby increasing its efficiency, competitiveness, openness and negative entropy of the production subsystem
"Production – Intelligence"	Reflection of identified innovative production solutions in the form of professional knowledge leading to an increase in the knowledge based capital of the organization in the field of primary activity
"Information – Organization"	Filling of communication processes between the personnel, system and environment, which allows forming efficient internal and external organizational structures both exogenously and in the order of self-organization

"Organization – Information"	Addition of the information domain of the organization by presentation in the information structures (databases) of the organizational solutions with assessments of their effectiveness in the form of appropriate organizational records
"Information – Production"	Provision of the production with all the completeness of information required for its effective operation and innovative development
"Production – Information"	Representation of indicators featuring the production process and the conditions for its existence in the information structures of the management system (databases)
"Organization – Production"	Formation of organization bases of production (organizational and management documentation) taking into account specificity and changing operation environment
"Production – Organization"	Reflection in the organization provisions of the activity status (organizational and management documentation) of peculiarities and specific features of the production

Modification of the state of any element(s) violates the settings of the entire system and requires managerial influence towards the formation of their new harmonious coordination (combination). A value of the quantitative elements (subsystems) transformations of the system and the relations between them can become a prerequisite for a synergistic effect provided that they are harmoniously combined. If the dynamics deteriorates the quality and exceeds a certain permissible limit, then the system properties change in principle and the previous settings no longer solve the above mentioned problems. Accordingly, it is necessary to make a decision to change the composition, structure and organization of the components of the SES management system.

The convergence model of managing the SES innovative development changes the management nature: from coercion of the management object to a new state, before creating favorable conditions for achieving a natural, targeted order. It is important to take into account that system imbalances can destroy the system integrity provided that: 1) at extreme nonlinearity, a hard resonance breaks it, while unlimited openness dissolves it in the external environment according to the entropic equilibrium principle; 2) when the nonlinearity is softened, the feedback is weakened, and its excessive closeness leads to entropy increase. That is, the organization and management innovations shall be aimed not only at the management improvement, but also at creation of favorable conditions for the possibility of achieving an innovative development trajectory.

During the discussion of any modernization project, the following questions: "Where to start?" and "What shall be the priority steps for modernization?" always take place. If there is no well-defined algorithm for obtaining the synergistic effects, many researchers propose a "trial and error" method based on extrapolation of actions, forecasting, experience and synergetic thinking of the leader who sets the rational goals for the organization.

In this case, the process of understanding the strategic goals and objectives for the SES striving for self-organization, stability and innovation is fundamental. Short-term benefits (for example, welfare and high profits from productive activities) in the long term may result in SES functioning deterioration. Many of the well-known global problems (climate change, depletion of oil resources, exponential population growth, agricultural land degradation, freshwater deficit, etc.) and their consequences have already been evident. According to D. Medouz and J. Randers, the environmental load continues to grow despite the development of technologies and the efforts of public organizations. The scientists described this in the report "Limits of Growth" (1972) prepared under the project of the Club of Rome "Problems of Humanity". Even then they noted that humanity "has gone beyond the limits and is in an unstable field" due to the consumer attitude to the nature. To reduce the impact on the environment and return to an acceptable level, personal and social values shall be changed and that will take a long time [11].

According to the concept of sustainable development, the main problem lies in ensuring the balanced SES development with the imperative to prevent a catastrophe and society orientation towards self-maintenance based on the convergence models and approaches to management. Technical advance, innovations, sustainable development, formation of competitiveness and marketing management are certainly necessary, but not sufficient, since the development is the result of non-linear interactions.

The convergence model of managing the SES innovative development can serve as a powerful management foundation to search and support the self-organizing trends. In practice, this is associated with risks caused not only by the desire to get into the future that is absent in the possibilities spectrum, but also by the inability to detect the development path in the presence of the possibilities spectrum. In the first case, there is the danger of aggressive management when the goal is achieved by reorganizing the managed system that involves a continuous flow of significant costs and efforts to keep the SES on an unstable way. The balanced management supposes an impact on the social and economic system to achieve the desired and immanently inherent states with the synergistic effects through the consistent implementation of the functions and mechanisms in the SES to form the organizational survival basis in turbulence, as well as institutional forms and relationships that stimulate and develop the ability to an innovate component.

Therefore, the methodological provisions of the convergence model of managing the SES innovative development are as follows:

– its heterogeneous structure covers heterogeneous elements – technology, organization, ecology, mentality, psychology, politics, security, all kinds of resources and their interrelations;

– it is focused on a positive synergistic effect through the principles and influence the control parameters for analyzing the phase space and identifying inherently inherent development paths;

– its fixed management parameters established in the space-time and resource coordinates take into account the boundaries of the balanced approach, adequate to the mission, goals, potential, opportunities and threats of the environment;

– its unique architecture (due to the absence of the standard algorithm of actions and orientation to a creative approach) is specified by a set of development elements – investment, intellectual, technological and product resources forming the synergetic potential;

– the task of SES management structures is the modeling and forecasting of development trends that form the positive feedbacks and create the prerequisites for its transition to a new quality meeting the requirements and the image of the "future";

– the SES development path can be set by the systems of differential equations with the aim of predicting and scientific substantiating the programs to be developed which shall be realistic and realizable. In a number of scientific papers, the authors demonstrated the practice of modeling the trend for development of the most important subsystems of the national economy based on the second- and third-order differential equations [9].

First of all, the stable innovative SES development shall focus on its internal intrinsically characterized self-organization and its own laws of evolution which shall be taken into account and improved in the proper focus. A development vector cannot be imposed on the complex systems, firstly, it is necessary to understand their own trends (natural attractors), and then output them with resonant, topologically verified effects to the path of evolutionary formation.

An important factor in the SES self-organization is the national idea that expresses the symbolic capital of the culture in the information space. Activation of the innovative development of Russia's economy is possible in conditions of coherent management due to the positive synergetic effects in the systems aimed at a large-scale innovative breakthrough and development of resources of the new technological order. However, the following dilemma arises: "How to manage "without managing"?", "How to force the SES to one of the own and favorable development paths with a small resonant impact?", "How to ensure self-controlled and sustainable development?". The implementation of the principles, approaches, tools and the business mechanism of the balanced SES development system will allow full using the existing system potential and obtaining the positive synergetic effect.

Finally, the following important conclusions shall be drawn.

Sustainable innovative development of the SES assumes the formation of a synergistic potential represented by a systemic property formed as a result of inter-entity interactions and structural-institutional dynamics, mainly, due to intangible assets and complementary effects accompanied by increasing the level of its activity and entropy which provide the sensitivity and adequate reaction of its subjects and relations in the system to small exogenous (mainly, management) and endogenous effects to develop the economic system by a specific vector of goals and achievement of strategic indicators.

To provide the appearance of the system-synergetic effects in SES and its subsystems, it is required to have the following basic conditions: nonlinearity, openness, dynamism, organization, heterogeneity, freedom of economic activity, coherence, working feedback and functional correspondence of elements, synchronization of flowing processes and processes, efficacy of system response to signals from the environment. The synergistic effect in SES is the result of the coherent action of its heterogeneous composite components that causes endogenous transformations and qualitative changes in the system state under resonant exogenous effects [2, 9].

The management of SES innovative development means modeling and timely response to transformation of external and internal conditions which means identification of resonant zones where the consequences scale is determined by the force of their impact and consistency with the endogenous properties. Innovative development is determined by the basic parameters – the degree of internal ordering and the strength of the external control action. A synergetic effect occurs when the positive feedbacks operates within the economic system and directed to it from the outside.

Thus, the meaning of the stated prerogative of actions is not to replace the concept and model, but in the harmonious, peak effective use of raw and innovative factors available in the national SES. It is required to change the concepts in the evolution. Movement to the adopted social model shall be step-by-step, synchronous and parallel-sequential. This methodological approach in the light of the strategy of SES transfer to the innovative development path is determined, firstly, by the interrelations, interdependence and interpenetration of social phenomena, and, secondly, by the need of accounting the inertness of the system itself, i.e., time during which the desired state is achieved.

References

1. I.N. Geraskina, Economic analysis: theory and practices, **16 (2)**(2017)
2. I.N. Geraskina, *Management of innovative development of economic and social systems* (Research Institute of the Humanities by the Government of the Republic of Mordovia, Saransk, 2017)
3. V.D. Ayurov, *Economy synergetics* (Publishing House of Moscow State Mining University, Moscow, 2005)

4. B.L. Kuznetsov, S.B. Kuznetsova, *Theory of synergistic market* (Publishing House of Kama State Academy of Engineering and Economics, Naberezhnye Chelny, 2006)
5. J.C. Collins, J.I. Porras, *Built to Last. Successful Habits of Visionary Companies*(Harper Collins Publishers, New York, 2002)
6. G.Haken, *The secrets of nature. Synergetics: Theory of interaction* (Institute of Computer Sciences, Izhevsk-Moscow, 2003)
7. G.Haken, *Hierarchy of variabilities in self-organizing systems and devices* (Mir, Moscow, 1985)
8. G.G. Malinetsky, *To build reality from fairytale... High technologies – Russia's way to the future* (Publishing House URSS, Moscow, 2015)
9. I.N. Geraskina, A.V. Zatonskiy, A.A. Petrov, International Journal of Civil Engineering and Technology (IJCIET), **8 (10)** (2017)
10. A.A. Akaev, S.Yu. Rumyantseva, A.I. Sarygulov, V.N. Sokolov, *Structural-cyclic processes of economic dynamics* (Publishing House of Polytechnic University, St. Petersburg, 2016)
11. D. Medouz, J. Randers, *Growth limits. 30 years later* (BINOM. Laboratory of Knowledge, Moscow, 2012)

Computer modelling of fire resistant solutions for structures in high-rise buildings with using of new fire-retardant materials

Marina Gravit[1] , *Eliza* Gumerova[1*], and *Vladimir* Lulıkov[1]

[1] Peter the Great St. Petersburg Polytechnic University, 195251, Politechnicheskaya st., 29, Russian Federation

Abstract. The article describes possibilities of computer modeling of fire resistance for structures in high-rise buildings, which include new fire-resistant plaster compositions. As an example of program complex, "Sofistik" (Germany) was chosen for the calculation of reinforced concrete structures of tier buildings. The characteristics of fire protection compounds and their regulation, which are usually used, also are shown. According to the new code "Highrise buildings and complexes. Fire safety requirements", limits of fire resistance for walls of not less than 240 minutes. Skyscraper "Lakhta center" with a height of 462 m and limits of fire resistance of load-bearing reinforced concrete structures 180 and 240 minutes is built up in Russia. The article investigates the means of fire protection in the business center. Moreover, modern form of cladding in Mada Residences building (Dubai, UAE) is concerned to make some conclusions about future fire resistant solutions.

1 Introduction

High-rise buildings and multifunctional complexes are divided into fire compartments by their functional purpose, floor area, and the total height of the building. The boundaries of fire compartments are fire barriers: fire walls and floors with the normative limits of fire resistance. The required parameters of fire resistance of building structures are defined depending on its purpose, height, and value of the combustible load. So, in the above-mentioned objects, the fire resistance rating varies from 3 to 4 h [1].

The construction of tall buildings requires a heightened fire safety. One of the most important tasks is to protect bearing structures from the effects of dangerous factors of a fire to prevent their premature collapse. In this regard, the theme of ways of improving the fire resistance of structures is relevant, for example, by using the plaster compositions on the supporting part of the building.

Building structures are characterized by fire resistance and fire hazard [2]. The fire resistance of the structure is a time for the construction to fulfill its design purpose in fire conditions [1].

* Corresponding author: eliza_gumerova@mail.ru

There are no unified criteria for the classification of buildings by number of storeys in Russia, therefore it is considered in this work that high-rise building – 6 floors and above. The practice of multi-storey massive construction focused on the height of buildings which value is not more than 75 m [3]. These buildings have a great degree of potential fire danger and greatly hampered evacuation [4, 5].

To provide the required evacuation, modern software systems are used increasingly in order to calculate the factors, project evacuation routes in different fire cases according to normative documents. Scenery of the development of pores and pore risk calculation by normative methodical. Such programs also calculate blocking time of escape ways by dangerous fire factors using some mathematic simulations. These programs, mainly, are based on international development "Fire Dynamic Simulation" (USA, Finland), in which the models for computation of smoke spread time and heat transition value. These program complexes can be used for calculating the thermal gradient in various building areas in order to define the heat degree of building constructions.

The reliability of high-rise buildings is determined by the ability of supporting structures to resist the effects of high temperatures [6]. Nowadays the following limit values of fire resistance for buildings to 100 m – 150 min, from 100 m to 150 m – 180 min, for buildings higher than 150 m – 240 min [7]. In Russian Federation the new document new code "Highrise buildings and complexes. Fire safety requirements" is drafted.

It is possible to apply the various program complexes solving the corresponding problems, for calculation of the fire resistance, using the finite-element method. For example, the American program complex "Ansys" can calculate a full-fledged model of the structure, based on fire resistance parameter, at any point of the building. Since this software package is considered to be one of the most expensive and difficult to use, for simpler tasks (such as calculating the fire resistance of individual load-bearing elements) it is more rational to use such a program as "Abaqus", "Cype", "Elcat", "Sofistik", etc. The calculation of a typical concrete slab in this software package is shown on Fig. 1.

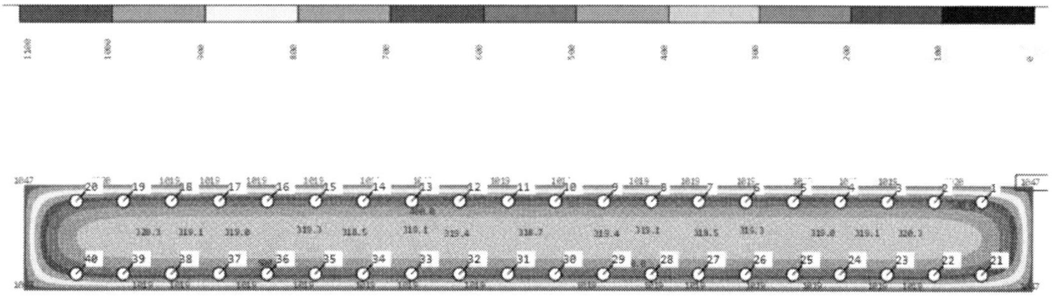

Fig. 1. Thermal gradient in calculation report in "Sofistik".

Since the software "Sofistik" uses a hypothesis Dupee for transition to the simplified task, it is necessary to set the geometric properties of structural section, materials and loads, acting on the element. Thickness is adopted 0.2 m, width 2 m and compressive load 300Kn for the plate. According to the calculation, the fire resistance limit of the structural element is equal to R120.

According to the thermal gradient (Fig. 1), it is possible to determine the fire resistance limit of the reinforced concrete slab: the loss of bearing capacity will occur at the time of heating to 700 degrees of the reinforcement, which is under the thin protective concrete layer. On Fig. 2 there is an example of calculation of a reinforced concrete column without fire protection and with fire protection plaster composition "Fendolite" with its fire resistance limits to 180 min.

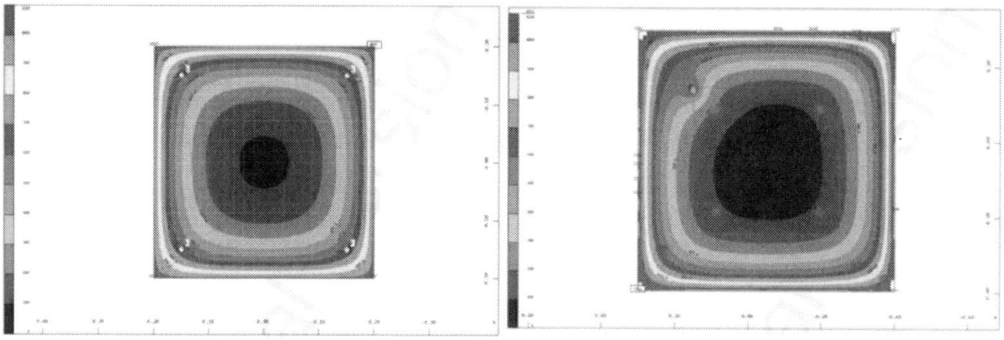

Fig. 2. Example of calculation of reinforced column 400x400 taking into account fire resistance on the left and on the right side.

Reinforced concrete high-rise buildings have considerable weight, which causes significant loads on the ground. Concrete constructions in the form of columns have high fire resistance, however, as the steel, they also prone to almost instant collapse in terms of limit loads [9, 10].

If the outer layers of the concrete are heated above t > 600 degrees, the limit of their strength goes below the stress from the external load, and these layers in the column cease to participate in the perception of external loads. Therefore, only the central part of column section carries the load, i.e. it can be considered concrete, not reinforced.

The most basic ways in implementation are the methods for increasing the fire resistance of building constructions and elements of internal furnish by impregnating the protected surfaces with special flame retardants (impregnation, paints and varnishes) and protection by fire-resistant plasters [3, 11]. It is especially important to be careful while using fire retardant coating in view of its special challenges and responsibilities [8].

Due to the normatives of Russian Federation [2, 7, 19] there is no possibility to evaluate the value of time resistance of the object before the onset of progressive collapse. Skyscraper "Lakhta center" with a height of 462 m and limits of fire resistance of load-bearing reinforced concrete structures 180 and 240 minutes is built up in Russia.

2 Fire resistance for structures in "Lakhta Center"

Fig. 3. Lakhta Center, Saint-Petersburg, Russia.

Progressive fire extinguishing systems and traditional solutions are used fort fire safety in "Lakhta Center" (Fig. 3). The aim of fire protection system is to prevent case of fire, ensure the safety of people and protect the property. The evacuation of people from the floors of building Tower is provided by several variants:

- Safety corridors – corridor (station passage), the walling of which is made with the limits of fire resistance not less than 120 minutes, protected by system of smoke ventilation. Such corridors are aimed at the safe movement of people from the premises to the stair enclosures in case of fire,
- Two smokeproof stairways, equipped with air boosting device and entrance through pressurized lobby,
- Two emergency exits to the evacuation stairwell of the building. Evacuation is from the upper level of observation deck – on a curved ramp with a slope, or by internal open staircase to the lower level,
- All escape routes have such width that it could easily carry a stretcher.

2.1 The degree of fire resistance

The degree of fire resistance with increased limits up to R/REI 240, i.e. 240 minutes (4 hours) is foreseen for the building of Tower.

Reinforced concrete bearing elements of the parts of the building under and above the ground, the ceiling elements have protective layers of concrete until the adapter fitting not less than 45-70 mm.

Steel bearing elements of the building frame and the secondary beam of ceilings are paved with fire-retardant materials (flame retardants, board materials).

Steel bearing elements of operated and decommissioned coatings, elements of stairwells and staircases have a fire-retardant treatment by intumescent paints or paved with fire resistant materials.

2.2 Plastering

We will consider the most effective and easy-to-use method of fireproofing – plastering [12]. There are many available technologies that can be used depending on the particular type of building. The main indicator of the plaster materials is the cohesion that means bond strength. A threshold value is 1000 psf = 47,88025 kPa for buildings taller than 420 feet (128 m) [13]. Boundary value of the bond strength is 430 psf = 20,597 kPa for buildings with height below 420 ft (128 m). According to American standards fire resistant means of similar bulk density (up to 240 kg/m^3) and the method of applying, for example, marks Monokote MK-6 GF, Monokote MK-6/HY, Monokote Z-106/G (manufacturer: Grace, USA) are not allowed for use in high-rise construction (above 128 m) [14, 15].

Sand-cement plaster with thickness 25-60 mm, which is applied on the steel mesh, is used to increase fire resistance limit of metal structures up to 2 hours or more. Plaster with the thickness of 40-60 mm is reinforced with double mesh, which protects it from premature collapse in case of fire.

The most important properties of the plasters can be easily changed by putting additives in mixture [16, 17]. As tests show, samples of vermiculite solution with volumetric weight from 500 to 800 kg/m^3, which are heated to temperature of 900-1000 °C and placed in water, do not crack and retain sufficient strength, while samples of cellular concrete under the same conditions are completely destroyed. Fire-retardant efficiency of vermiculite solutions is in 4 times higher than of the sand. Thus, the limit of fire resistance of roofs and ceilings, which is equal to 1.5 h, is provided at a thickness of a layer of vermiculite fireproofing solution of 8 mm (table 1).

Expanded vermiculite is a loose, porous material in the form of scaly particles, which are produced by rapid firing of vermiculite concentrate – hydromica, which contains bound water between elementary layers. Steam, which is generated from this water, pushes the plates of mica and increases the initial volume of grains in the 6-15 times or more [18, 19]. Unique technical features of it are temperature resistance, fire resistance, reflectivity, and chemical inertness. It does not emit any gases, which is an important advantage in comparison with other known materials of organic origin at increased temperatures.

Table 1. Fire resistance of building finishing materials.

Type of insulation	Density, [kg/m^3]	Width, [mm]	Fire resistance limit, [min]
Cement slab	250-300	40	110
Cement slab with plaster	250 – 300	50	155
Loam brick	1500	120	325
Loam brick with plaster	1500	120	360
Cement and vermiculite plaster	500	15	600

Table 2. Characteristics of compounds of fire-retandant vermiculite building solutions.

Composition (by volume)	Density, [kg/m^3]	Strength, [kg/cm^2]		Width of layer, [mm]
		Compressive	Bend	
Cement and vermiculite (1:4)	500	12.5	8.2	13.5
Cement and vermiculite (1:6)	450	16.8	11.5	31.2
Cement and vermiculite (1:7)	400	10.8	7.8	13.4
Gypsum-vermiculite (1:3)	350	2.5	-	20

Portland cement with grade, which is not lower than M-400, plaster with grade not lower than G5 and vermiculite 0.6 – 2 mm are used for the preparation of these compounds.

The plaster mix which on the basis of exfoliated vermiculite and calcium aluminate cement (M-400) with the addition of asbestos has the most effective flame retardant properties.

Such plaster coating is related to group of heat-resistant and can withstand temperatures over 800 °C (table 3).

Table 3. Fire resistance of building finishing materials.

Composit Cement/vermiculite/ asbestos	Density, [kg/m³]	Width of layer, [mm]
1 / 2 / (3-4% from weight of cement)	800 – 900	10 – 13
1 / 1 / (15% from weight of cement)	1100 – 1200	12 – 15

Plasters on cement can be applied indoors and outside. The compositions and paint compositions on liquid glass and the plaster are only for interior use in areas with humidity no more than 85%. The most popular plasters for improving the fire resistance of bearing structures are in table 4, 5.

Table 4. Comparative properties of plaster compositions [15].

	Composition	Fire resistance limit	Durability, years	Density [kg/m³]	Required thickness of layer [mm]
Cafco Fendolite ®	Vermiculite and portlandcement	REI240	50	-	10
Neospray	Vermiculite and portlandcement and additives	REI240	25	490	22
Sosh-1	Perlite and organic additives	REI180	20	450	30
Krilak	Binding with additives	REI240	50	690-850	18
Vimark	Gypsum	REI 120	-	750	15
ByProc	Cement	REI240	40	750	15
Fassa KF 4	Perlite	REI180	50	700-820	10
Knauf Italia FP120	Portlandcement	REI200	-	650	20

Table 5. Fire resistance of building finishing materials.

Product	Density [kg/m^3]	<75 feet	>75 feet <420 feet	>420 feet	Garage Parking	Pools	External impression
Monokote MK-6/HY, MK-6 GF[(a)]	15	▪					
Monokote MK-10/HB	15	▪	▪				
Monokote MK-1000/HB	18	▪	▪	▪			
Monokote Z-106/G	22	▪	▪				
Monokote Z-106/HY	22	▪	▪	▪	▪	▪	
Monokote Z-146	40	▪	▪	▪	▪	▪	▪
Monokote Z-156	50	▪	▪	▪	▪	▪	▪

3 Modern plaster composition in UAE

Developed in Spain and made from extruded porcelain, it has been specified by Artar Real Estate Development for the 36-storey Mada Residences building, which will be completed in the second quarter in 2018 rapidly taking shape at the heart of Dubai's Downtown district (Fig. 4).

Artar Real Estate also said that Mada Residences is "the first residential tower in Dubai built using specially developed cladding that can resist temperatures of up to 1200 °C".

The company said it decided to the use the new cladding after inspecting its fire resistant qualities at the manufacturing facility in Spain. The insulation powers of the new cladding panels also reduce AC consumption in the summer to produce energy savings of up to 30 per cent, it added.

The project's scope of work consist of a 39-storey residential tower offers intelligently designed and spacious luxury 2, 3 and 4-bed apartments located in Downtown Dubai, Dubai. The project includes spacious layouts ranging from 2,852 square feet to 3,234 square feet, the luxury residences come with Bianco Venus marble floors, generous European designed kitchens and some of the largest terraces.

Each apartment has been crafted with family-centric livability for those who love their spacious spaces. With floor to ceiling glass, balconies in every apartment and well thought-out amenities designed in a way that elevates the usability of space and achieves enduring value.

The intelligent use of space becomes evident from the moment you enter the reception, all the way to the apartments, where every bedroom comes with an en-suite bathroom. Spacious walk-in closets and balconies are core features and benefits resulting from adhering to the concept of livability.

Fig. 4. a) Construction, July 2017 b) Project of Mada Residences

Progressive fire extinguishing systems and traditional solutions are used fort fire safety in "Lakhta Center". The aim of fire protection system is to prevent case of fire, ensure the safety of people and protect the property. The evacuation of people from the floors of building Tower is provided by several variants:

- Safety corridors – corridor (station passage), the walling of which is made with the limits of fire resistance not less than 120 minutes, protected by system of smoke ventilation. Such corridors are aimed at the safe movement of people from the premises to the stair enclosures in case of fire,
- Two smokeproof stairways, equipped with air boosting device and entrance through pressurized lobby,
- Two emergency exits to the evacuation stairwell of the building. Evacuation is from the upper level of observation deck – on a curved ramp with a slope, or by internal open staircase to the lower level,
- All escape routes have such width that it could easily carry a stretcher.

4 Prospects for the development of fire-resistant plaster compositions

- The creation of materials with low density that form a light coating and do not have a significant additional load on the bearing structures,
- Development of methods for the determination of coating thickness depending on the thickness of the metal and the required fire resistance of steel structures, which will allow to calculate quickly and accurately the development of the project of fire protection of structures,
- Increase of the adhesion and cohesion of the plaster. In compliance with the regulatory requirements the material shall not crack and does not flake off. The formation of the coating without joints and thermal bridges.

It is need to consider the probability of occurrence of emergency situations, during which the building will be experienced the multiple loads. Hence there is necessity of using some special regulations. In contrast to the normative documents of the Russian Federation, a part of which is the translation of relevant foreign, there is a positive experience of application of regulations in international practice.

In the standards, these regulations are embodied in the form of special features of fire resistance of structures and buildings as the ability of these facilities for a certain period of time to resist the combined special effects of working loads on the structure and high-temperature fire. Rules, which describe the bond strength in the USA, have been taken primarily as anti-terrorist. Light plaster will be blown or damaged in case of intensive fire exposure convection and the shock wave.

In this regard, fire resistant plasters should possess improved adhesion and cohesion.

In the rules of there is a note that special technical conditions should be developed for specific buildings and reflect the specifics of their fire protection, including additional technical and organizational measures. Specific technical specifications must be supported by necessary calculations.

Fire resistance limits of load-bearing structures should be at least 4 hours and building structures must resist to temperature of 1100°C for buildings with height more than 100 m. Consequently, it is necessary to tighten all of the requirements for the fire resistance of the buildings.

The methods which are established by the standard should be applied while establishing the fire resistance limits of structures to determine their applicability. Due to the international experience, the fire resistance limits of building structures above: R120 for load-bearing elements of the building; REI60 for ceilings between the floors and over basements; REI120 for stairwells, should be provided in high-rise buildings.

References

1. Federal Law of the Russian Federation FL-123. *Technical Regulations on fire safety requirements* (2008)
2. MA Qian-li, Huang Ting-lin,. Procedia Engineering, **11** (2011)
3. O. Halyavin, M. Gravit, A. Pryanikova. Saint Petersburg State Polytechnic University Science Week (2015)
4. P. Kolarkar, M. Mahendran. Fire Saf. J. **53**, 85-104 (2012)
5. A. Ulybin, N. Vatin. Journal of the unique construction of buildings and structures. **10 (25)** (2014)
6. B. Schafer. Steel Constr. **4(3)** (2011)
7. Project of Russian normative document. *Highrise buildings and complexes. Fire safety requirements*.
8. Roger G. Morse. *Fireproofing at the WTC towers*. Fire Engineering 10/01/2002
9. V. Roitman. *Rationing protect tall buildings from the progressive destruction at the combined special therapeutic effects.* Fire and explosion safety part. **16 (2)** (2007)
10. V. M. Roitman. Construction Security, **871** (2006)
11. V. Roitman. Global Security, **871** (2006)
12. G. Craighead. *High-Rise Security and Fire Life Safety* (2009)
13. J. Lataille. *Fire Protection Engineering in Building Design* (2002)
14. L. Huanga, T. Chen, H. Yuan, Transportation Research Procedia, **2**, 518-523 (2014)
15. *International Building Code, Section 403, High-rise Building* (2009)
16. M. Gravit, E. Mikhailov, S. Svintsov, A. Kolobzarov, I. Popovych. Materials Science Forum, **871** (2016)
17. P.Stephenson, Institution of Fire Engineers in the Middle East [online] Available at: https://gulffire.mdmpublishing.com/fire-engineering-in-the-middle-east/ (2018)

18. Construction updates – Mada residences [online], Available at: http://www.mada-residences.ae/construction-updates.html (2017)
19. Construction updates of Dubai's Mada Residences revealed [online], Available at: http://www.constructionweekonline.com/article-46829-construction-updates-of-dubais-mada-residences-revealed/ (2017)
20. Lakhta-center. [online], Available at: http://lakhta.center/ru/ (2018)

Development of digital simulation on the basis of technologies of virtual and augmented reality[a]

Alexander Gren[1], *Benjamin* Jamarillo[2], *Vladislav* Kiev[2], *Nikolai* Shabrov[2*], and *Dmitry* Vasiliev[2]

[1] Emuge-Franken, 91207 Nürnberger Straße 96-100, Germany
[2] Peter the Great St. Petersburg Polytechnic University, 195251 Polytechnicheskaya st. 29, Russian Federation

Abstract. The world scientific and industrial community enters presently a new phase of its development. Suffice to mention such key developments as the strategy of development of "Industry 4.0" for German manufacturers [1], two American concepts: "Industrial Internet" [2] and "Internet of things" [3]. The work on artificial intellect [4] released in 2003 laid the bases for industrial development of systems with artificial intellect, while a wide discussion on the Fourth industrial revolution [5] as a continuation of the concept of "The second industrial era" [6] was initiated in 2016 at the World economical forum. The implementation of these industrial concepts brings about a high level of competition and, as a result, searching new technologies of manufacturing competitive produce. The manufacture of competitive produce is closely connected with the problems of apprehension a great volume of information connected with the results of designing, simulation, marketing and sales of the factories' produce. The program Industry 4.0 implies a wide use of the cutting-edge digital technologies and, particularly, the technologies of virtual and augmented reality.

The point at issue is the expansion of technologies of digital engineering in the direction of technologies of virtual engineering with an active application of multi-screen systems of virtual environment CAVE 3D (Computer Aided Virtual Environment) and technologies of augmented reality (Fig. 1).

[a] The authors express their gratitude to Russian Science Foundation (RSF) for supporting investigations in the framework of grant No.18-11-00245
* Corresponding author: shabrov@rwwws.ru

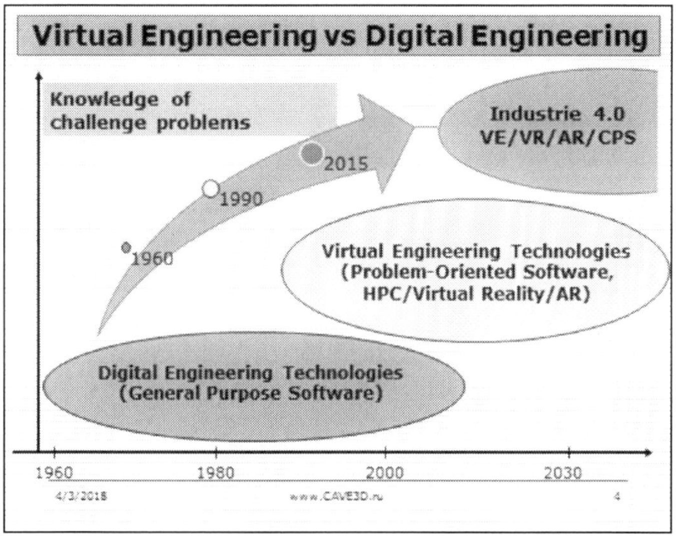

Fig. 1. Stages of engineering technologies development.

There are two types of predictive simulation problems: ordinary and extraordinary. There is a guarantee of getting solution by means of commercial multi-purpose software code for ordinary problems, which is perfectly well provided by the set of models and numerical diagrams of this code. This type of simulation is characteristic for the stage of development of the industrial revolution Industry 3.0. The present time demands solving call problems for creating the breakthrough technologies to provide development of the present-day industry. This means that the solution of science extraordinary problems is on the agenda, which demands the new approaches at all stages of solution simulation.

However, the latest versions of commercial software code are in arrears of the advanced frontiers of science by 10+ years immediately after release. In view of this fact it is impossible to provide solution of extraordinary problems by the set of physical and mathematical models of commercial multi-purpose code owing to inadequacy of the used or due to ineffective scaling of calculations (Fig.2). In order to solve the extraordinary problems, it is necessary to develop the unique physical models and equations of the object state, development of numerical diagrams of solving equations and, as a result, building the problem-oriented in-house dedicated software system with all attributes appropriate of the modern system, including pre- and post-processor, on-line help, means of forming online report and analyzing simulation results in in-situ mode on the basis of virtual environment systems.

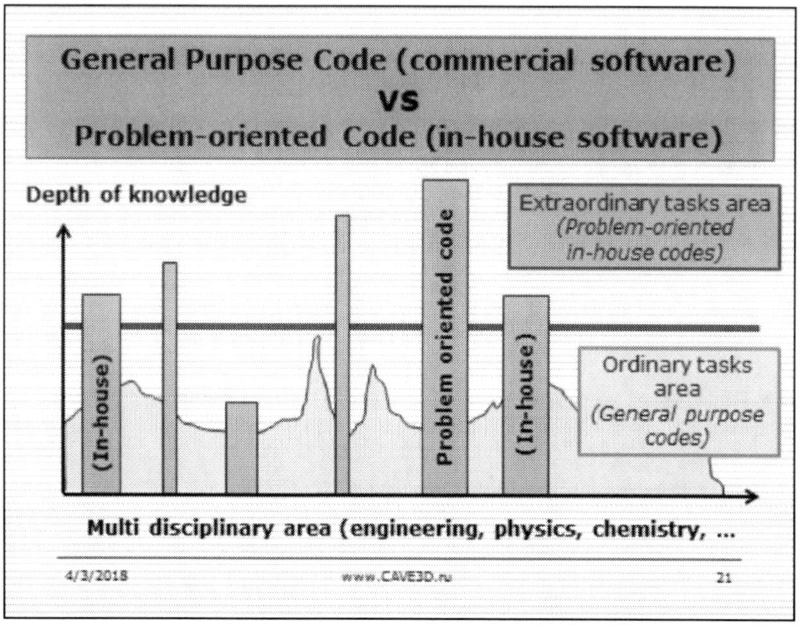

Fig. 2. Level of depth of jumping into problem for commercial code and problem-oriented in-house code.

The stage of development of engineering technologies in the program Industry 4.0 is characterized by conducting analysis of results of predictive simulation using the means of systems CAVE 3D [7], which are the decision-making centers in the context of analysis of results (Fig. 3).

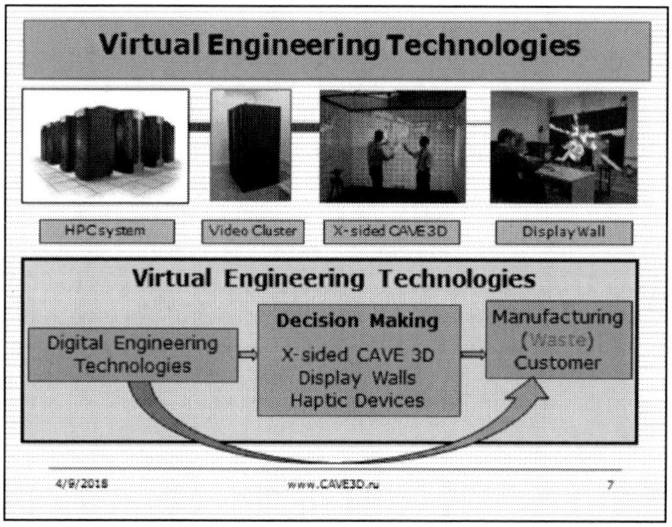

Fig. 3. Place of decisions-making center in general procedure of virtual engineering technologies.

Recently, reasonable attention is paid to the problem of analyzing results of predictive simulation in HPC systems in in-situ (on-the-fly) mode. Two circumstances contribute thereto. First of all, the emergence of hardware in the market, which helps obtain a high-quality image and, secondly, an acute necessity of "on-the-fly" analyzing results with the aim of monitoring and correcting the progress of making calculations in HPC systems. Particularly, it is applicable to the problems based on multi-scale and interdisciplinary models (turbulent combustion processes, etc.), which demand extensive resources of HPC systems. Thus, a chance has appeared recently to adequately improve the process of analyzing results of predictive simulation in HPC systems in "on-the-fly" mode with the use of virtual environment systems.

The technologies of virtual engineering feature significant advantages over digital engineering technologies, which dominated prior to beginning of the industrial revolution Industry 4.0 stage. The main advantage consists in a significant shortage of industrial waste since a comprehensive control of results of 3D model simulation in virtual environment system CAVE 3D takes place prior to beginning the article production (Fig. 4).

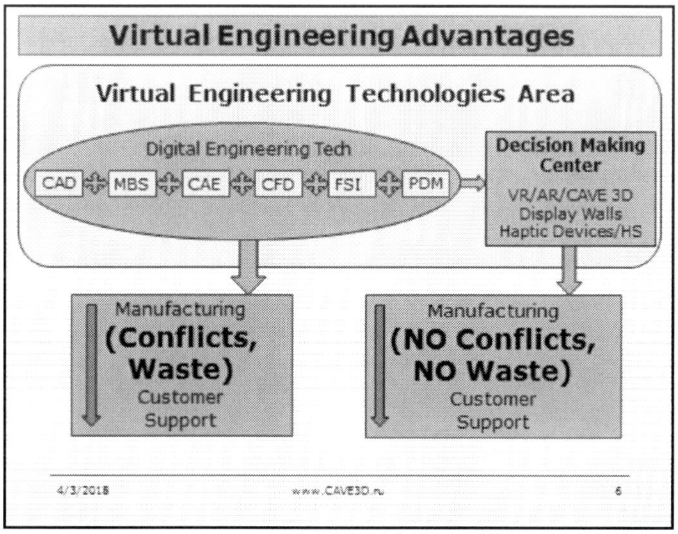

Fig. 4. Advantages of virtual engineering technologies against digital engineering technologies.

At the same time the growing level of high competition in the industry stimulates the development agencies and manufactures of the machine-building produce get across the advantages of a particular product to a buyer of the machine-building produce quickly and in an understandable fashion. Therefore, a growing interest is observable presently to the developments of virtual technical manuals on the basis of augmented-reality technologies.

A virtual technical manual has been created together by EMUGE-FRANKEN (Germany) and Peter the Great St. Petersburg Polytechnic University at the chair of "Computer technologies in machine-building". EMUGE-FRANKEN, the German company boasting more than 90 years of experience, develops and manufactures the precision tools as well as high-accuracy высокоточную tooling equipment for fastening the parts to be machined during machining at the industrial enterprises. Creation of such tooling-related solutions in the technology of cutting and milling thread makes a basis of the business.

An animated model of screwed-shank chuck HF20 assembly has been selected as an "augmented reality" (Fig.5). The company's experience shows that this product is needed by the companies on the Russian market dealing with metals processing by drilling and threads generation.

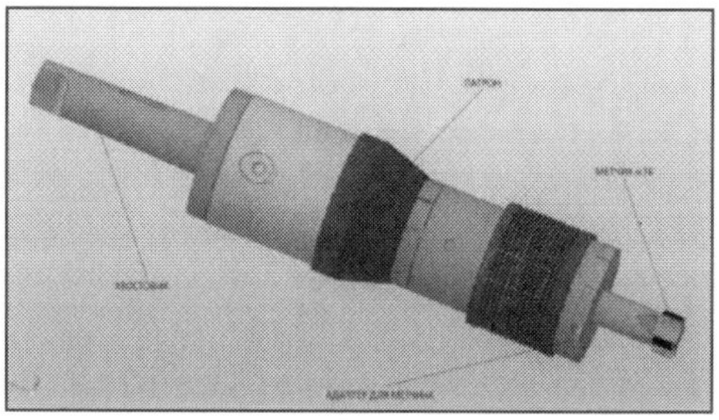

Fig. 4. Building 3D model of chuck holder in CAD system KOMPAS 3D.

The augmented reality makes it possible to better understand such advantages of the product as: possibility of shank replacement with the shank of the required shape (standard and size) and adapt the screwed-shank chuck to different variants of machine-tool spindle, possibility of changing adapter for a required task, e.g., drilling hole or cutting thread. The 3D interactive models and augmented-reality animations provide for a new level of training, understanding documents by the experts or users.

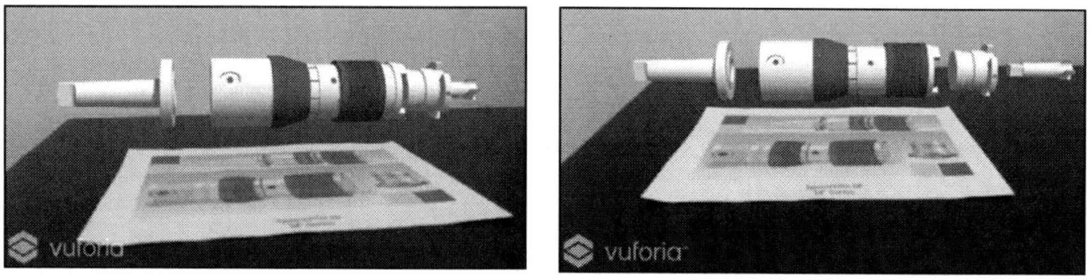

(a) (b)

Fig. 6. Final view of process of assembly (a) – disassembly (b) of CAD model of chuck holder. Reproduction is made from application for mobile phones android.

An image of the screwed-shank chuck in the catalog is used as "Target". In case the image comes in view of the camera of tablet or Smartphone the animation of sequence of assembly of the screwed-shank chuck, adapter and tap will be output to the screen of a device (Fig. 7).

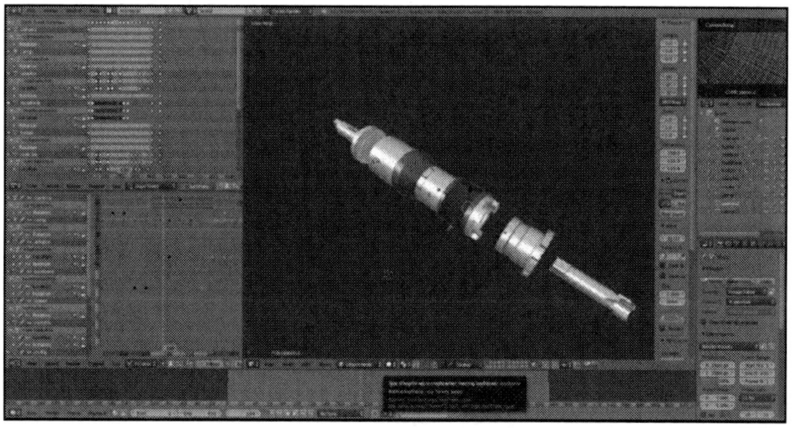

Fig. 7. Development of scenario of animation of process of assembly – disassembly of CAD model of chuck holder.

The "Unity" software with its extension "Vuforia" is used for augmented reality, where the brand for chuck reproduction from telephone application has been developed for the first time. The chuck has been imported from "Blender" software with the required corrections made (chuck size, color, etc.). An application for the telephone and tablet has been made in the final process by means of "Android studio" software. In case of directing a tablet to the brand an animated 3D model of the chuck holder will appear on the screen. The model has been thoroughly elaborated and optimized for real-time demonstration in mobile devices, moving around the brand it is possible to visualize the chuck from different sides of viewing.

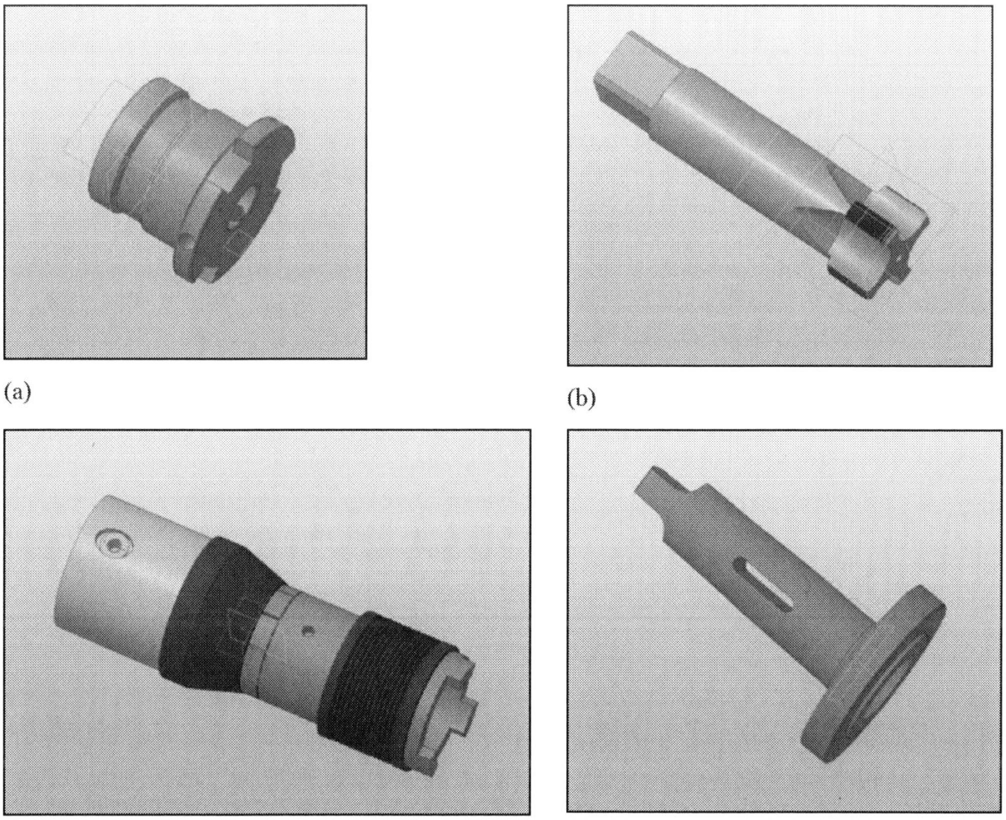

(a) (b) (c) (d)

Fig. 8. Chuck holder components: a – adapter for tap, b – tap, c – chuck body, d – shank.

The augmented reality in this project makes it possible to show the sequence of assembly from the chuck parts (Fig. 8) and show operation of the screwed-shank chuck making it in the way customary and comprehensible for human-being having a Smartphone or a tablet and the company's catalog at hand only.

It should be noted that the growing application of technologies of virtual and augmented reality in modern engineering at all stages of designing and analysis is a world-wide trend of development of the modern digital technologies.

References

1. H. Kagermann, W. Wahlster, J. Helbig, Recommendations for implementing the strategic initiative INDUSTRIE 4.0., Industrie 4.0. Working Group [online], Available at: http://www.acatech.de/fileadmin/user_upload/Baumstruktur_nach_Website/Acatech/root/de/Material_fuer_Sonderseiten/Industrie_4.0/Final_report__Industrie_4.0_accessible.pdf (2013)

2. P. C. Evans, M. Annunziata, Industrial Internet: Pushing the Boundaries of Minds and Machines [online], Available at: https://www.ge.com/docs/chapters/Industrial_Internet.pdf (2012)

3. M. Swan, J. Sens. Actuator Netw., **1** (2012)

4. S. J. Russel, P. Norvig, *Artificial Intelligence: A Modern Approach* (Prentice Hall, New Jersey, 2003)

5. K. Schwab, The Fourth Industrial Revolution: what it means, how to respond, World Economic Forum [online], Available at: https://www.weforum.org/agenda/2016/01/the-fourth-industrial-revolution-what-it-means-and-how-to-respond/ (2016)

6. E. Brynjolfsson, A. McAfee, *The Second Machine Age: Work, Progress and Prosperity in a Time of Brilliant Technologies* (W.W. Norton & Company, New York, 2014)

7. The High-Performance Computing Center Stuttgart [online], Available at: http://hlrs.de (2018)

Application of additive technologies for synthesis of titanium alloys of Ti-Al, Ti-Al-Nb systems of elemental powders[a]

Alexey Grigoryev[1], *Igor* Polozov[2*], *Anatoliy* Popovich[2], and *Vadim* Sufiyarov[2]

[1] JSC "ODK-Klimov", 194100, Kantemirovskaya st., 11, Russian Federation
[2] The Center of the National Technology Initiative (NTI) "New Production Technologies", Peter the Great St. Petersburg Polytechnic University, 195251, Polytechnicheskaya st., 29, Russian Federation

Abstract. Additive technologies are one of the drivers for development of new industrial revolution. For developing additive production it is necessary to expand the nomenclature of materials used in the form of powders. One of the ways for synthesizing new alloys in additive technologies is applying a mixture of powders as primary components; the powders correspond in their composition to the given alloy. The technology of selective laser melting enables synthesizing the necessary alloy by means of layer by layer melting of a powder mixture. A study of the process of Ti-5Al and Ti-6Al-7Nb titanium alloys synthesis of elemental powders by means of selective laser melting was undertaken in this work. Microstructure, chemical composition, mechanical properties of the synthesized alloys were studied and also the influence of thermal processing on the microstructure of the Ti-6Al-7Nb alloy obtained of elemental powders was explored.

1 Introduction

Modern rate of industrial development requires implementing progressive methods of producing metal ware. One of them is additive technologies which combine using digital projecting for creating a computer model of the future workpiece and manufacturing the piece itself by means of adding the material layer by layer on special equipment [1]. Additive production is one of drivers which has an impact on developing the concept "Industry 4.0" and which is now actively used for making the products. Nevertheless, for full implementation of the new production concept it is necessary to further improve additive technologies. One of the directions for development is expanding the nomenclature of materials used in additive production.

Selective laser melting of powders is one of the most widespread and promising methods for producing metal ware by means of adding the material layer by layer. Metal powders are used as primary materials in the technology of selective laser melting. Powders for additive technologies, as a rule, are produced with the help of gas and plasma atomization of melt

[a] The research was carried out with financial support of the Russian Science Foundation (grant project No. 18-13-00111)
[*] Corresponding author: polozov_ia@spbstu.ru

mass. In connection with difficulties in producing powders of complex alloys for additive technologies the nomenclature of commercially available powders for additive production is significantly limited at the moment.

The decision for this problem can be found while applying alternative methods for producing items of titanium alloys with the help of additive technologies. One of such directions is using a mechanical mixture of powders of separate elements of the alloy for producing items by means of layer synthesis, as the result of which in-situ synthesis of the required alloy will be made. At present there are works which describe the results of studies devoted to layer synthesis of alloys of such systems as Ti-Nb [2], Al-Si [3], Mg-Al [4]. The presented works as a rule demonstrate that the selective laser melting (SLM) method may be successfully used for in-situ synthesis of alloys that are unavailable in the form of prealloyed powder.

Titanium alloys are widely used in various branches of industry, for example, for manufacturing aviation equipment parts thanks to their high strength-to-weight ratio, corrosion stability and ability to be used at relatively high temperatures. Over the last years the tendency for increasing the titanium parts percent as compared with the total mass of a gas turbine engine. In connection with that using additive technologies for synthesizing titanium alloys is of great interest for industry.

The goal of the present work was to undertake a study and evaluate the possibility of layer by layer synthesis of titanium alloys of different types of elemental powders by means of selective laser melting. With the use of powder mixtures the composition of which corresponds to Ti-5Al and Ti-6Al-7Nb alloys, compact samples were synthesized, a study was undertaken including the microstructure, phase composition as a primary material and the material after thermal processing, and also mechanical properties of the synthesized alloys were estimated.

2 Materials and working procedure

For studying the process of in-situ synthesis of titanium alloys of elemental powders three alloys were chosen: Ti-5Al (%, mass.) and Ti-6Al-7Nb (%, mass.). Titanium powders (CP Ti Grade 2, analogue of BT1-0), aluminum powders (99.9% purity) and niobium powders (NBP-1a grade, 99.7% purity) were used as primary powder materials for preparing powder mixtures. Ti and Al powder particles have a spherical shape, while Nb powder particles have a comminuted shape. Grain fineness of metal powders was determined by method of laser diffraction on the particle size measurement instrument Analysette 22 NanoTec plus (Fig. 2.2) with the total measurement range 0.01 – 2000 μm. Data on the grain fineness of primary powders are given in Table 1.

Table 1. Grain fineness of primary powders.

Powder	d_{10}, μm	d_{50}, μm	d_{90}, μm
Ti	23.8	44.6	76.1
Al	8.5	21.2	41.1
Nb	15.1	32.9	65.1

Powder mixtures were prepared of primary powder components with the use of the laboratory gravity mixer in the course of 12 hours. The time for mixing the powder components was selected in such a way as to provide for equal distribution of separate components in the powder mixture.

For synthesizing the samples by means of laser melting a SLM 280HL set was used manufactured by SLM Solutions GmbH. Synthesis of compact samples is implemented on the main platform. A thin layer of powder material is applied to it. The layer is applied with the help of a special moving block which is filled with powder. This block batches the powder material while moving over the platform surface and the powder layer is distributed and leveled over the surface with the use of a silicone squeegee. Then the layer is processed with laser emission. The laser beam is focused on the surface of the powder layer creating a spot of a small diameter. With the help of a mirror system the laser beam is deflected and moved over the layer surface in accordance with the file created earlier. By means of laser emission the powder material is melted and then a solid phase structure is formed and at the same time the current layer is alloyed with the previous one. After that the platform is lowered to the height equal to the thickness of the powder layer, a new layer of the powder is applied and the process is repeated until all the layers have been processed. Synthesis of the samples was implemented in argon atmosphere.

The SLM 280HL set has two ytterbium fiber lasers with the wave length equal to 1.07 μm and the maximum power of 400 W and 1 kW. The laser with the maximum power of 400 W has a focusing spot with the diameter of 80 μm and Gaussian distribution of power over the spot, and the laser with the maximum power of 1 kW has a focusing spot with the diameter of 700 μm with equal distribution of power.

For studying the microstructure, phase composition of the synthesized material samples with the size of 10x10x10 mm were made. For running mechanical tests cylindrical blanks were made with the diameter of 12 mm and height of 90 mm, then samples for tensile tests were ground out them by means of mechanical processing according to GOST 1497–84 "Metals. Methods of tensile tests". The meanings of the basic parameters of the SLM process used for sample synthesis are in table 2

Table 2. Parameter values of the SLM process used for the synthesis of compact samples.

Laser profile	**Laser power, W**	**Scanning speed, mm/s**	**Distance between laser passes, μm**	**Layer thickness, μm**	**Laser spot diameter, μm**
Gaussian	245–305	755-855	90-150	50	~80
equal	650-950	250-350	450-550	100	~700

A study of the microstructure of compact samples was undertaken on a scanning electronic microscope (SEM) TESCAN Mira 3 LMU both in secondary electrons and in backward scattered electrons. This microscope has an attachment for performing energy dispersive X-ray spectroscopy (EDS) which was used for the spot analysis of chemical composition of compact samples and for obtaining data on distribution of chemical elements in the sample.

The analysis of phase composition of the samples was made with the use of a Bruker D8 Advance diffractometer on which X-ray patterns of the samples on CuKα (λ = 1,5418 Å) emission were obtained.

Testing of mechanical properties of the samples for tensile breakage at ambient and elevated temperatures was performed in accordance with GOST 1497-84 (ISO 6892 "Metallic materials – Tensile testing") and GOST 9651-84 (ISO 783 "Metals. Methods of tension tests at elevated temperature") on the Zwick/Roell Z050 testing machine.

Thermal processing of the synthesized samples of Ti-5Al alloy was implemented in a MTI VBF-1200X vacuum furnace. Annealing at 750 °C and 1 hour equalizing was implemented with further after cooling with the furnace to the ambient temperature. Thermal processing of synthesized samples of Ti-6Al-7Nb alloy was made in the KJ-1700X muffle furnace. The samples were previously placed in quartz tubes where high vacuum was prepared. The samples annealing was implemented at temperatures from 1050 °C to 1350 °C with equalizing from 1 to 3.5 hours and after cooling in a furnace.

3 Results and discussions

Powder mixture of Ti-5Al alloy after mixing for 12 hours is displayed in Fig. 1. Particles of titanium and aluminum powders have preserved spherical shape after mixing that is important for plasticity of a powder mixture. Aluminum particles are smaller in comparison with titanium powder particles and are equally distributed in the powder mixture. At that, in some places there is coagulation of separate finely dispersed aluminum particles.

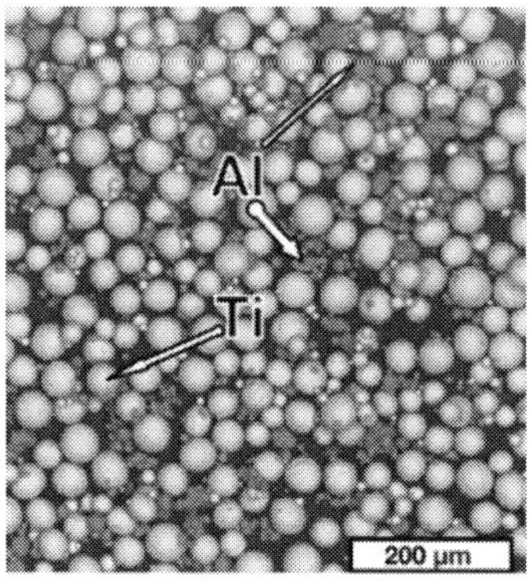

Fig. 1. An image of powder mixture of Ti-5Al alloy.

Images of etched grinding surface of compact samples of Ti-5Al alloy made on the scanning electronic microscope (SEM) in backward scattered electrons are presented in Fig. 2. There are no sections with unmelted particles of Ti or Al elements. Relative density of the compact material measured by means of hydrostatic weighing is 98.97±0.07%. EDS analysis of the sample along the line (Fig. 2, b) (and in separate points of the sample (table 3), specified in Fig. 2, a, indicates that complete decomposition of Al in Ti matrix has taken place. Chemical composition of synthesized samples corresponds to the required one.

(a)
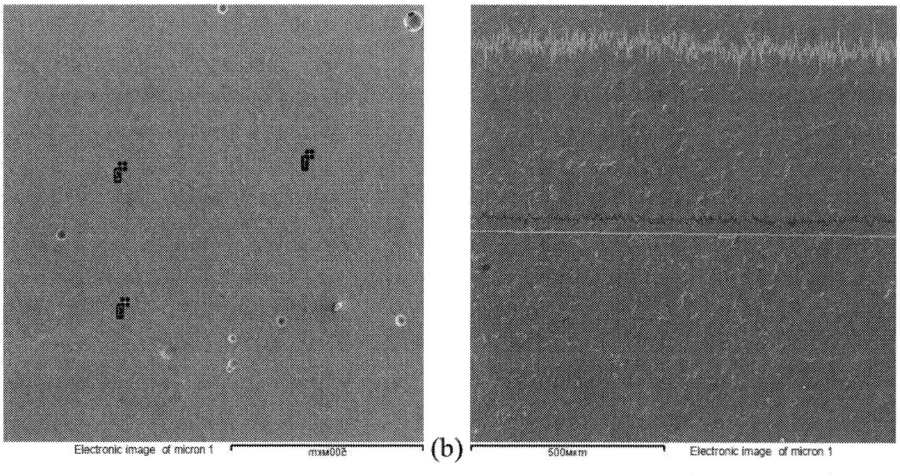

Fig. 2. SEM-images of the etched grinding surface of samples made of Ti-5Al alloy powder mixture at laser power 275 W (a) and 950 W (b).

Table 3. Results of the analysis of chemical composition by means of energy dispersive X-ray spectroscopy of Ti-5Al samples made by means of SLM in separate points of the samples.

Laser power, W	Point	Al, mass. %	Ti, mass. %
275	1	4.9	95.1
	2	4.9	95.1
	3	5.0	95.0
950	1	4.4	95.6
	2	4.5	95.50
	3	4.2	95.8

After having been mixed in gravity mixer the powder mixture of Ti-6Al-7Nb alloy was used for synthesis of compact samples by means of SLM. In the process of SLM of Ti-6Al-7Nb powder mixture titanium, aluminum particles were melted and niobium particles were partially melted (Fig. 3). The structure of synthesized material is solid solution of alloying elements in titanium with separate niobium particles. EDX analysis results (table 4) in different points of the sample indicated that composition of the areas where there are no separate Nb particles includes both Al and Nb in the quantity close to the composition of the initial mixture, white areas correspond to niobium. Maximum relative density of the synthesized material is 98.9%.

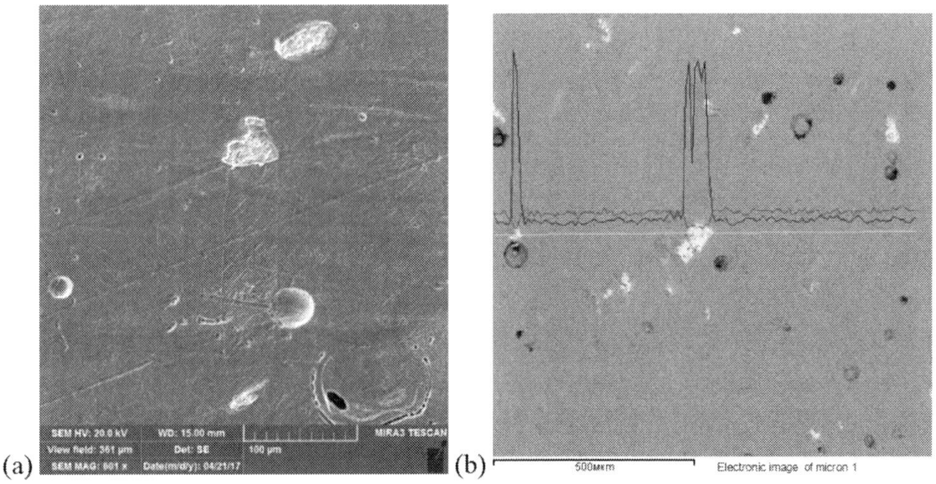

Fig. 3. SEM-images of the etched grinding surface of a sample made of Ti-6Al-7Nb alloy powder mixture at laser power 950 W.

Table 4. Results of the analysis of chemical composition by means of energy dispersive X-ray spectroscopy of a Ti-6Al-7Nb sample made by means of SLM in various points of the sample.

Point	Nb, %	Al, %	Ti, %
1	98.23	0.23	1.54
2	94.19	0.53	5.29
3	7.21	6.53	86.26
4	5.43	5.92	88.64

For dissolving Nb particles and obtaining a more equal chemical composition in the synthesized material thermal processing was performed in the form of annealing in different modes. Microstructure of the material after annealing is shown in Fig. 4. At the annealing temperature lower than 1350 °C Nb particles haven't dissolved in the matrix. At 1350 °C and 3.5 hours equalizing separate Nb particles are not present. The material has (α+β)-platelike microstructure. Presence of these phases is confirmed by the results of X-ray phase analysis (Fig. 4). When thermal processing temperature is increased volume fraction of the beta-phase and average thickness of alpha-phase plates is also increased.

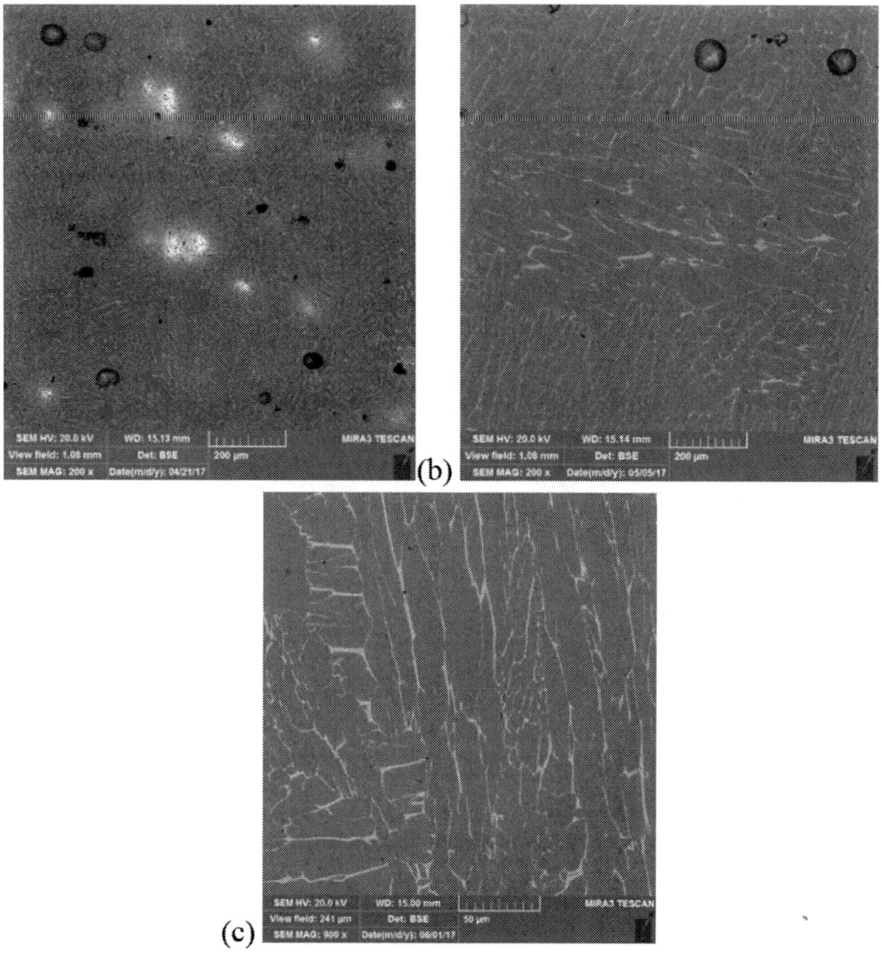

Fig. 4. Microstructure of samples made of Ti-6Al-7Nb alloy after annealing: (a) 1050 °C, 1 hour; (b) 1350 °C, 2.5 hours; (c) 1350 °C, 3.5 hours

Results of mechanical tests of the Ti-5Al and Ti-6Al-7Nb alloy samples are given in table 5. At ambient temperature, strength limit of samples of Ti-5Al alloy after annealing at 750 °C for 1 hour is 897 ± 7 MPa with percentage extension – 5.0 ± 1.2 %, and that is compatible with properties of the samples made according to traditional methods. Strength limit at 400 °C is 521 ± 12 MPa exceeding strength limit of a cast sample and is at the level of a deformable sample of BT5 alloy. In the case of Ti-6Al-7Nb alloy yield tensile strength and strength limit of samples after annealing is 770 and 850 MPa respectively at 2% tensile elongation. These values are lower than those of the material made by means of selective laser melting of prealloyed powder of this alloy. Reduced mechanical characteristics may be connected with a large amount of cavities in the material.

Table 5. Mechanical properties of Ti-5Al and Ti-6Al-7Nb alloys synthesized by means of selective laser melting of elemental powders and comparing them with the properties of samples made according to other technologies.

Testing temperature, °C	Alloy	Yield tensile strength, MPa	Strength limit, MPa	Percentage extension, %	Source of data
20	Ti+5Al (selective laser melting and annealing)	855 ± 15	897 ± 7	5.0 ± 1.2	The given study
	BT5Л	-	800	6	[5]
	BT5 deformable annealed	-	685-735	6-8	[6]
400	Ti+5Al (selective laser melting and annealing)	412 ± 10	521 ± 12	9.7 ± 1.1	The given study
	BT5 deformable annealed	-	520	-	[5]
20	Ti+6Al+7Nb (selective laser melting of powder mixture and annealing)	774 ± 10	850 ± 10	2.0 ± 0.2	The given study
	Ti-6Al-7Nb (selective laser melting of prealloyed powder and annealing)	1360 ± 30	1480 ± 26	1.4 ± 0.6	[7]
	BT6 (fritting)	740	830	5	[5]

4 Conclusions

4.1 By means of SLM it is possible to synthesize α-titanium alloy (BT5) of elemental Ti and Al powders with homogeneous distribution of chemical elements and high mechanical properties. Microstructure of the obtained alloy consists of α-Ti equiaxial grains of various sizes. Strength limit is 897 ± 7 MPa, percentage extension – 5.0 ± 1.2 %.

4.2 With the help of the SLM method it is possible to synthesize Ti-6Al-7Nb alloy of elemental powders, however in the initial state there are separate unmelted Nb particles in the material inside the areas with equal distribution of Ti, Al, Nb of the specified composition.

4.3 In the initial state Ti-6Al-7Nb alloy microstructure has the form of finely dispersed precipitation of needle-shaped martensite with separate Nb particles. After H/T (α+β)-plate like structure is formed. Nb particles dissolving takes place at 1350 °C annealing. Strength limit of the samples is 850 Mpa at percentage extension equal to 2%.

References

1. H. Gaub, Reinforced Plastics, **60(6)** (2016)
2. M. Fischer, et al. Materials Science and Engineering, **(62)** (2016)
3. P. Vora, et al. Additive manufacturing, **7** (2015)

4. E. O. Olakanmi, Journal of Materials Processing Technology **213(8)** (2013)
5. B. N. Arzamasov, T. V. Solovyeva, S. A. *Gerasimov, Spravochnik po konstruktsionnym materialam [Handbook of structural materials]* (MGTU Baumana Publ., Moscow 2005)
6. Federal Standard GOST 26492-85 "Titanium and titanium alloys rolled bars".
7. E. Chlebus, et al. Materials Characterization **62(5)** (2011)

Digital simulation of physical processes in vehicles engine power units[a]

Sergey Hoodorozhkov[1], *Andrey* Krasilnikov[1*], *Evgeney* Zakhlebayev[1]

[1] Peter the Great St. Petersburg Polytechnic University, 195251 Polytechnicheskaya st. 29, Russian Federation

Abstract. This article studies the issues of digital simulation of physical operating processes in vehicles transmission. Simulation of dynamic processes is carried out in power transmissions at the design stage. The procedure for using the digital packages such as MATLab – Simulink and Simscape was considered for the numerical simulation of dynamic processes in mechanical systems based on the example of the theoretical calculation of K-744 tractor transmission dynamics. A digital model of K-744 tractor transmission is constructed, its calculation scheme is given, the initial characteristics are determined. A digital model of the tractor engine was created by means of the Simulink package. A nature of change in tractor engine torqueis determined by it. The calculated analysis of normal transmission frequencies is performed. Forced torsional vibrations are calculated in the tractor change gearbox generated by the vehicle engine operation. The conditions of resonance in the transmission are analyzed. The unfavorable modes of joint operation of the engine and the gearbox are determined for K-744 tractor.

1 Introduction

The appearance of torsional vibrations in the vehicles transmission is provided by the presence of inertial-elastic linkages including yielding shafts, gears, engine flywheel, etc. A disturbance external effect is applied to these systems from the motor side, the torque of which periodically varies. In certain modes of the transmission operation, resonance oscillations may be generated in it. To study such phenomena, dynamic calculations are performed, which generally includes the synthesis of the kinematic scheme, calculation of stiffnesses and moments of parts inertia. In this case, the system simplifies by placing the concentrated masses on the same shaft. Then the system of differential equations is formed, free frequencies is numerically determined, system torsional vibrations are calculated under the action of the engine torque from forces of gases

[a] The present research work has been carried out with financial support from the Ministry of Education and Science of the Russian Federation in the frames of the federal targeted program "Research and Development in the Priority Areas for the Development of Science and Technology Sector of the Russian Federation for 2014-2020" pursuant to the project: "The Design Of The New Model Series Of Automated Boxes Change Gears For Agricultural And Road-Building Equipment In The Range Of 140-440 kW, Adapted For Use In Complex Systems Unmanned Tractor"(Unique Project Identifier RFMEFI57816X0213)
* Corresponding author: a_kr36@mail.ru

pressure in cylinders and from engine inertia forces. The frequency diagram is made and resonant modes are determined [1, 2]. In this case, as a result of the multimass system simplification, the calculations accuracy decreases.

2 Purpose

The purpose of this study was to develop the algorithm for numerical study of dynamic processes in vehicles transmissions using modern digital software packages. The solution of this task will allow providing the adoption of justified effective technical solutions at development of new models of equipment, and reducing a time of their creation.

3 Problem solution mode

For digital simulation of dynamic processes in vehicles transmission, it is proposed to use modern software tools for engineering calculations, in particular, the applications of MATLab package – Simulink and Simscape [3, 4]. This method provides for substantial simplification of dynamic calculations for power transmissions. The MATLab packages – Simulink and Simscape provide fundamental blocks that can be used to create models of physical components – such as an internal combustion engine, friction clutch, gear reduction unit, flexible shafts, damping devices and other components of the power transmission. The Simscape automatically derives the differential equations featuring system behavior from a model which form is close to the kinematic scheme, [5, 6].

This paper, as an example of the simulation of torsional vibrations in a perspective automated K-744 tractor gearbox, considers the algorithm and results of this mathematical application usage.

Based on the known kinematic, inertial-elastic and damping parameters of the gearbox, a Simscape model is developed (Fig. 1) to simulate dynamic processes, in particular torsion vibrations under the action of the engine torque. As an example, the Simscape-model of the gearbox with the engine is displayed in the following state – the first gear, the first range, the bench mode of output shaft load.

The figure shows the gearbox shafts in the form of typical library blocks "Flexible Shaft_1 ... 11" describing the elastic-damping and inertia features by the sections broken at the connection points of blocks "Inertia_5 ... 17" featuring a response time of the driven and drive masses of friction clutches, and gear wheels fixed on shafts. The gearbox properties are described by means of blocks "Simple Gear": R1…R8.

When simulating, real values are given for the inertia moments of gearbox rotating masses, values of torsion stiffness of shaft sections, gear ratios of gear pairs.

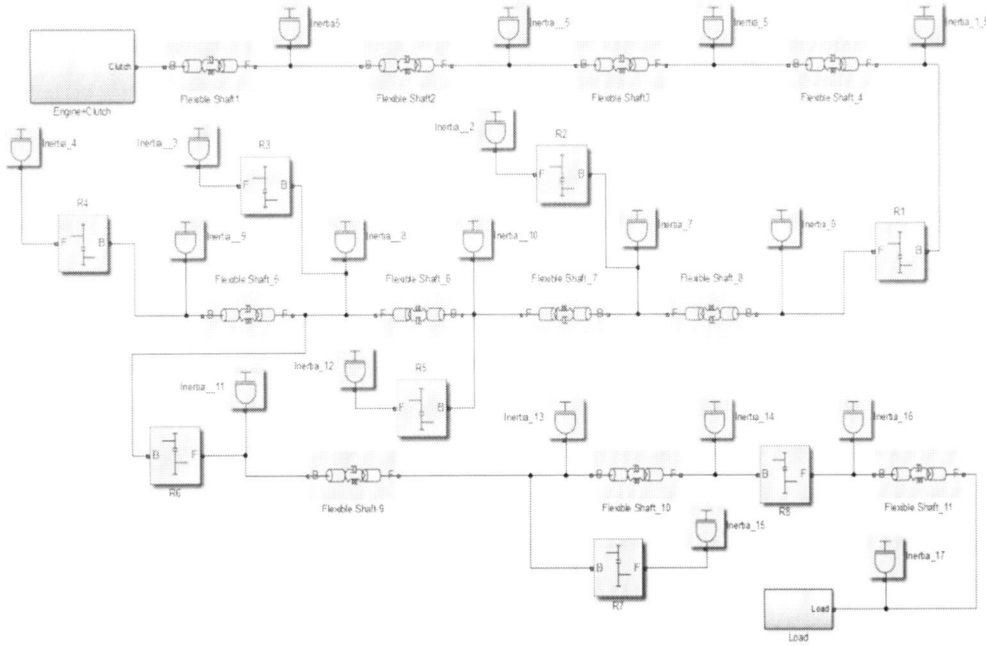

Fig. 1. Simscape-model of K-744 tractor gearbox (1st gear, 1st mode).

K-744 tractor gearbox is mated to engine ЯМЗ-5362 [7]. In the model shown in Fig. 1 the engine block with the gearbox is represented by the subsystem "Engine + Clutch", which is a 6-cylinder internal combustion engine with a reciprocating duty cycle. The reciprocating internal combustion engine model calculates the current torque transmitted by the engine crankshaft, and allows simulating transmission vibration. As an example, the total engine torques for the duty cycle at the external speed characteristic at revolutions $n_{eng.}$equal to 2000 rpm are shown in Fig. 2. Torqueses are determined by the results of thermal, kinematic and dynamic calculations of the engine.

The control actions for fuel supply (Throttle) and the rate of friction clutch actuation are formed in the block "Signal Builder". The load device on the output shaft of the gearbox is represented by the block "Load", a braking torque specified by the block "Signal Builder" is 3000 Nm.

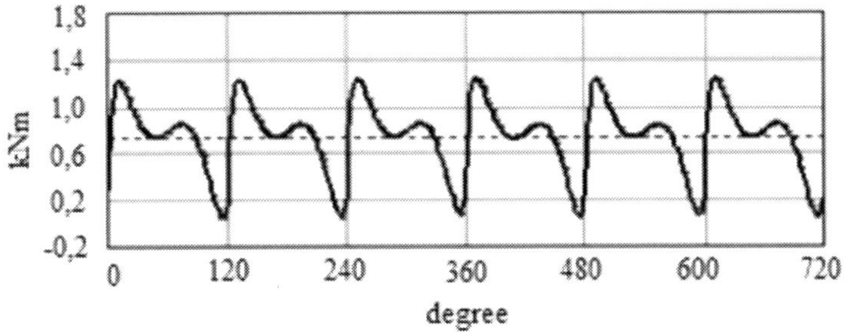

Fig. 2. The total and average engine torques (kNm) corresponding to the external speed characteristic at $n_{eng.}$=2000 rpm.

The results of simulating the torsion vibrations in the tractor transmission gearbox at the 1st gear and the first mode in the bench loading conditions are shown in Fig. 3. The braking mode of the gearbox output shaft and the rate of the first transmission clutch actuation are adopted to simulate the start-up and acceleration mode with equalizing the speeds of the drive and driven masses of friction clutch (see Fig. 3, a).

The curves of torque on the input "Flexible Shaft_1" and output "Flexible Shaft_4" sections of the input shaft (Fig. 1) when the engine rpm corresponding to Fig. 3, a are shown in Fig. 3, b, as an example.

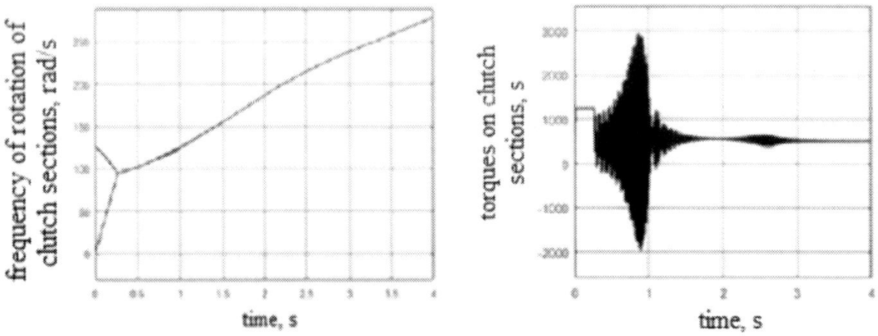

a) b)

Fig. 3. A speed of drive ω_1 and driven ω_2 masses of the friction clutch (a) and torques at the shaft sections "Flexible Shaft_1...4" (b).

It follows from the graphs that, at the end of the transient process associated with the equalization of speed of drive and driven masses of the friction clutch, the stationary torque components on the shafts correspond to resistance moment at the gearbox output shaft taking into account the reducing steps. In this case, at t=0.9(it corresponds to the engine speed ω = 115 rad/s, see Fig. 3a), a resonance of torsional vibrations is observed at the input and intermediate shafts – Fig. 3b caused by coincidence of free and forced frequencies of gearbox inertia-elastic links. At t=2.7s (corresponding to the engine speed ω = 217 rad/s), the second resonance is observed on the same shafts – Fig. 3, b.

To test the conditions for the existence of resonance effects, it is necessary to determine the spectra of gearbox natural oscillations and forced oscillations due to the action of the engine torque. In the first case, it is advisable to use the *Linear Time-Invariant models (LTI)* in the MATLab programming environment using a logarithmic amplitude-frequency response (Bode diagram).

When constructing the Bode diagram, input and output points (Open-Loop Input, Open-Loop Output) shall be set on the input and output shafts of the gearbox of the Simscape model, and start the *"Analysis-Control Design-Linear Analysis" procedure*. The results of Bode diagram construction is given in Fig. 4.

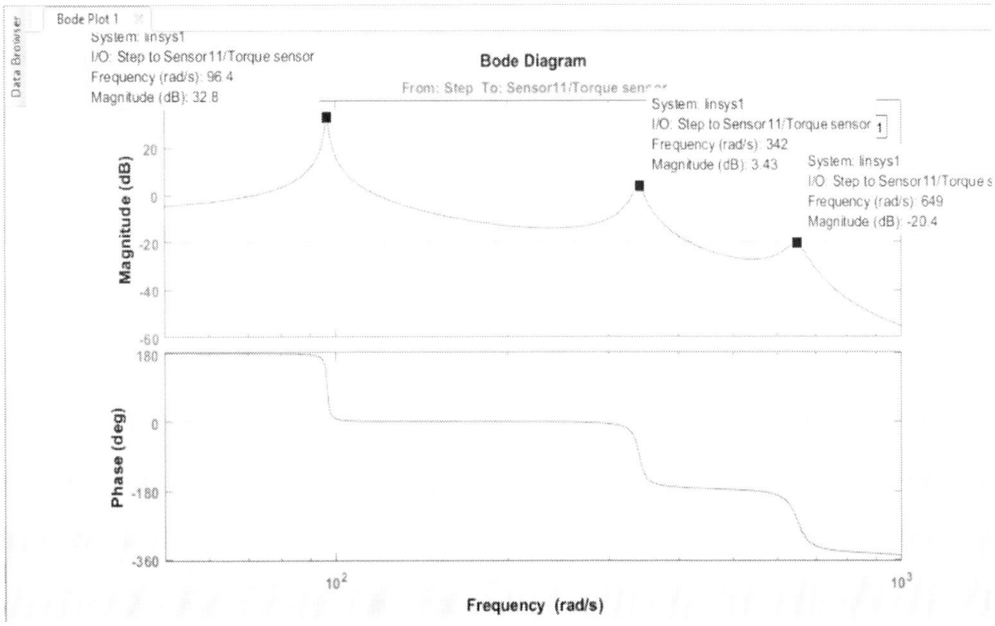

Fig. 4. The Bode diagram of the gearbox (Simscape-model, 1st gear)

Maximum resonance amplitudes on the graph correspond to free frequencies of the system – 96.4, 342 and 649 rad/s. Other free frequencies are insignificant (by amplitude).

For frequency analysis of external disturbance of the gearbox input shaft caused by an engine torque, it is advisable to use the fast Fourier transform:

$$A = fft(M_{sum}) \tag{1}$$

where: A – frequency-domain representation of engine torque;

M_{sum} – summary engine torque in terms of crank angle within an interval of 0 to 720 deg. (see Fig. 3), kN·m;

fft – standard function of the fast Fourier transform.

Torque spectrum amplitudes are determined using the formula

$$Ms_l = \sqrt{Re(A_l)^2 + Im(A_l)^2} \tag{2}$$

where: $Re(A_l)$ – real part of the spectrum;

$Im(A_l)$ – imaginary part of the spectrum;

l – number of harmonics for torque synthesis.

Synthesis harmonics spectrum phases

$$Q_l = \arg(A_l) \tag{3}$$

Synthesis harmonics amplitudes

$$\frac{Ms_l}{\sqrt{length(M_{sum})}};\; M_0 = \frac{Ms_0}{c} \tag{4}$$

where: c=2 – torque function periodicity factor:

length(M_{sum}) – a size of torque reference points array;

The results of the frequency analysis of engine torque at the speed $n_{eng.}$, 2000 rpm are given in Fig. 5.

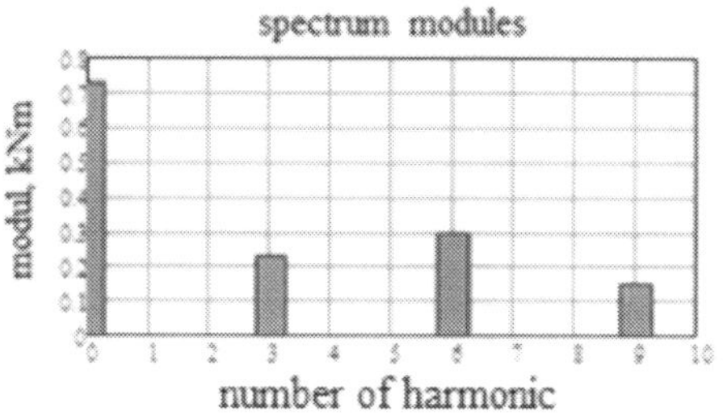

Fig. 5. Engine torque spectrum modules at speeds $n_{eng.}$=2000 rpm at full-load curve

Inverse Fourier transform domain into torque recovery curves is represented as synthesized expression

$$M(t) = \sum_{l} M_{c \cdot l} \cdot \cos(l \cdot \omega \cdot t + Q_{c \cdot l}) \quad (5)$$

Torque frequency analysis suggests that, in addition to the constant component with zero frequency M_0, the frequency spectrum with maximum amplitudes includes 3rd, 6th and 9th order harmonics. With increasing crank speed from 1200 to 2300 rpm, the 3rd harmonics amplitude $M_{3 c}$decreases approximately 6 times (from 0.66 to 0.099 kN·m), the remaining components of the amplitude spectrum remain practically unchanged.

It is possible to determine engine speeds based on the known frequencies of free torsional oscillations and engine torque spectrum, which will force torsion resonance frequency in the tractor transmission gearbox.

The diagram for frequencies of free torsional vibrations of the tractor transmission gearbox: ω_{c1}=96.4 rad/s, ω_{c2}=342 rad/s, ω_{c3}=649 rad/s allows to determine resonance frequencies $\omega_r$of engine rotation: on basic harmonics n _eng: ω_{r_1} =96 rad/s, on overtone of 3rd order external frequency ω_{r_2}=115 rad/s, and ω_{r_3} =217 rad/s.

The above data confirm the adequacy of the results obtained during computer simulation of the Simscape model: the presence of resonant effects at torsional vibrations of shafts in the gearbox on the overtone of the 3rd order engine external frequency. Engine fundamental harmonic resonance is not recorded, since the initial speed of the gearbox input shaft upon completion of friction clutch slipping in case of simulation of the process for starting and acceleration in the 1st gear and the 1st mode is over 96 rad/s.

4 Conclusions

As a result of theoretical study, the following has been defined:

1. Application of the engineering environment MATHWORKS SIMSCAPE in the digital simulation of dynamic processes in vehicles transmissions provides for significant reduction in calculations volume and complexity.

2. The MATHWORKS SIMSCAPE package includes the library of necessary model blocks to simulate transmission elements including the internal combustion engine with setting the required characteristics.

3. Application of the engineering environment MATHWORKS SIMSCAPE provides for the modern interface when receiving, processing, visualization of calculation results

including directly in the simulation process, as well as large data arrays recording and storing.

The obtained results allow effective using the presented algorithms during virtual simulation of dynamic systems of vehicle transmissions, particularly during calculation of torsional vibrations in transmission gearboxes.

References

1. S. Timoshenko, D. H. Young, W. Weaver Jr., *Vibration problems in engineering* (John Wiley & SONS, Inc., New York, 1974)
2. G.S. Maslov, *Calculations of shafts* (Engineering, Moscow, 1980)
3. Simscape™ User's Guide. Copyright 2007, by The Math Works, Inc. [online], Available at: https://www.mathworks.com/help/physmod/simscape/ (2013)
4. Using SIMULINK. Copyright 1990, by The Math Works, Inc. [online], Available at: http://aer.ual.es/docencia_es/sr/archivos/simulink.pdf (1996)
5. S. I. Hoodorozhkov, *Theory and automated control systems. Simulink Transport systems ACS analysis and synthesis* (Publishing House of Polytechnic University, St. Petersburg, 2014)
6. S. Hoodorozhkov, E. Zakhlebaev, Scientific and technical statements of SPbSPU, **231** (2015)
7. Engines YAMZ-536, YAMZ -5361, YAMZ -5362, YAMZ -5363, YAMZ -5364 Operation Manual 536.3902150 RA [online], Available at: http://izh-maz.ru/data/documents/536.3902150-RE.pdf (2011)

Technological development and income inequality: a role of financial market[a]

Yuri Ichkitidze[1,2*], *Anton* Lushkin[1], *Laslo*Ungvari[1,3], and *Sadat* Akaeva[4]

[1] National Research University Higher School of Economics, 194100 Kantemirovskaya st. 3, Russian Federation
[2] LETI University, Proffesor Popov st. 5, Russian Federation
[3] University of Applied Science Wildau, 15745,Hochschulring 1, Germany
[4] Peter the Great St.Petersburg Polytechnic University, 195251 Polytechnicheskaya st. 29, Russian Federation

Abstract. In this paper we study the effects of financial markets on an increase in income inequity. The notion, which is employed as a working hypothesis that the market equilibrium around the fair price and unbiased changes in prices has a neutral effect on inequity while the systematic underreaction accompanied by time trends contributes to its growth, has been considered. In order to check this hypothesis we have studied the long-term cycles in dynamics of the US stock index and income inequity and shown that the stock market growth observed in 1980-2017 is correlated to an increase in income inequity. The presence of causality in this relationship has been found through the evidence of systematic underreaction given by the share prices of fast-growing companies to the information about the diffusion of technological innovations. The research results prove that the free financial markets with technological development in progress contribute to instability, as they while enhancing income inequality increase the unemployment growth risks and require additional efforts from the state to redistribute income.

1 Introduction

The growing income inequality in the period after 1980th is a subject of research by many authors. It is well-known that the income inequity indexes including the capital gains are higher that the inequity indexes taking into account only the salary and wages growth [1]. This reflects the fact of capital concentration in the hands of more wealthy people and explains a favorable effect of inequity on the development of economics as a whole. However, much too high inequity of incomes can also be a depressive factor for economic development [2-4]. Against this background it remains an open question how the stock markets affect the income inequity. On the one hand, if the markets are efficient, in other words, if the stock prices fairly reflect the fundamental information then the fact of propertyconcentration should have no effect on an increase in inequity and there is no volatility. On the other hand, the presence of time trends and the systematic underreaction of prices to the fundamental information [5-7] develop conditions for wealth multiplication in hands of a small circle of persons, therefore the financial market with the fact of property concentration turns out to be in the situation of unstable equilibrium, in which further technological development goes along with a permanent increase in inequity. Researching this issue will make it possible to substantiate additional state control of inequity as well as proactively prevent unemployment and support stable development.

2 Research hypothesis and methodology

A hypothesis for neutral effects of financial markets on the income inequity is closely related to possible market self-control. The supporters of neoclassical synthesis adhere to an opinion that the policy of minimum state interference in the issues of inequity control is optimal, as long as the market mechanisms aid in optimal distribution of resources including the ability of financial markets to provide credit (financial assets in a more comprehensive sense) from redundant economic sectors to more deficient sectors thus making it possible to reduce inequity. These market mechanisms should be supplemented by necessary institutional environment, namely, the protection of civil rights and freedoms, equal access of society members to public information, developed competitive environment etc., and then the financial system will be able to control inequity in the society by itself. However, at the present time this hypothesis can be placed in doubt. A striking example of how the financial system actually controlled

[a] The article was prepared with the financial support of the Russian Science Foundation (Grant No. 18-18-00099)
* Corresponding author: yichkitidze@hse.ru

inequity was a crisis in 2008 when a temporary decrease in inequity was provided by illusively supplying credit to the disadvantaged population. Another evidence of how the financial system is unable to self-control are the facts of time series in stock prices and systematic deviations from market efficiency, which imply profitable investment opportunities made accessible to a small circle of persons by the asset market and therefore contributing to a systematic increase in income inequity.

Our empiric study consists of two parts. In the first part we show the presence of relationship between the price cycles in the US stock market expressed in the terms of switching model and in the level of income inequity within the USA. The main discussion is about whether these cycles and identified relationship between them are fictitious, in other words, result from a mere concurrence of circumstances or this relationship is of system-based nature. For the purpose of analysis we have employed such tools as the Markov switching model [8-14], that means that the evidence of market efficiency based on the independency of consecutive price increments is not an indisputable proof; it is restricted by the assumption of the autoregression model linearity, and ignores the case where non-linear laws exist in the real world. Taking into account this alternative, namely, the fact that the Markov switching model may be considered as a competitive alternative for the random walk model, we draw attention to the fact that there are four approximately 30-year cycles in the dynamics of the S&P500 index in constant prices and it has a significant threshold correlation with the income inequality.

In the second parts of this study we disclose the indentified relationship between the stock market cycles and inequity at a micro level, drawing attention to the role of technological development in creating the stock market cycles and generating the income inequity growth respectively. We study in detail the systematic underreaction of innovative companies' stock prices to the information about diffusion of innovations and demonstrate that the influence of financial markets on inequity is related to the deviations from market efficiency, which allows some society sectors to make systematic profits due to this underestimate and thus contributes to the inequity growth.

3 Cycles in income inequity and dynamics of US stock indexes

3.1 Long cycles in US stock price indexes

Since the ARIMA model [15] has become the standard model of the time-series analysis in economics, the majority of researchers abandoned the use of the Fourier analysis [16, 17]. However, in case of the model of Markov process switching, the Fourier analysis remains a tool that allows for describing the historically established temporal trends (cycles) and for assessing the model's parameters. For this reason, in order to characterize the cyclicality in the S&P500 series during the period from 1889 to 2010, let us conduct en elementary harmonic analysis, using the following cyclical model:

$$y = a \cdot \sin(T) + b \cdot \cos(T) + c \quad (1)$$

Let us build a series of chain growth rate with regard to real values of S&P500 for 10 years from the Shiller database. Let us then define cycles of the first order. The maximum value of the determination coefficient is observed with the cycles of the period of 32 years (R^2=0.38). Let us define the cyclical component in the obtained series of remainders under the additive model once again. Now the maximum value of the determination coefficient is observed with the cycles of the period of 40 years (R^2=0.13). Finally, one more type of cycles (65 years) can be defined in the series of third remainders (after removal of two previous cycles). Its determination coefficient equals to 0.09.

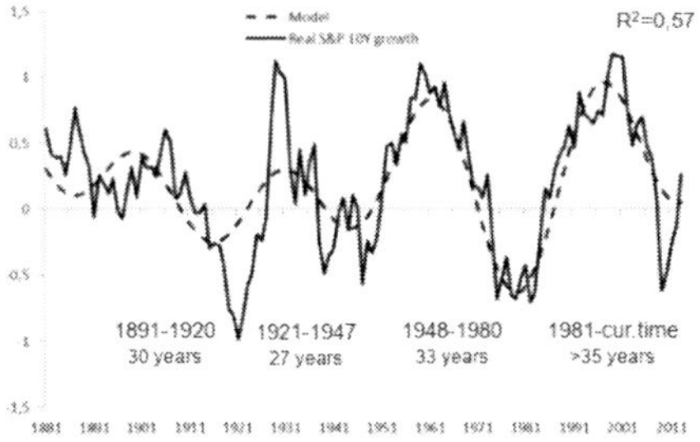

Fig. 1. Kuznets cycle in stock prices.

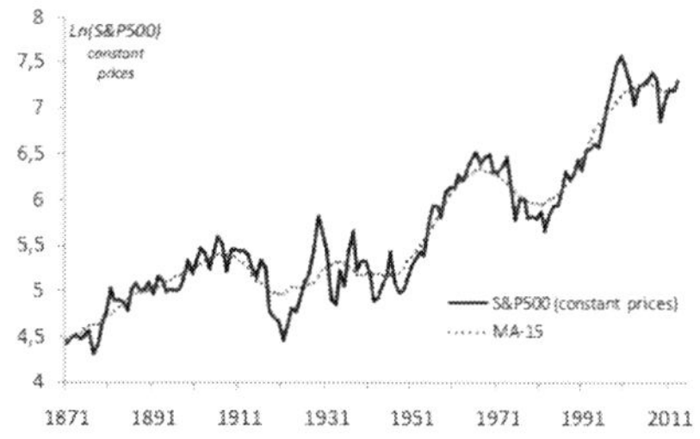

Fig. 2. Cycles of the stock market represented by the moving average.

The general cyclicality model with regard to the studied indicator is represented in Fig. 1. In dynamics of stock prices, we can observe four cycles with the period of approximately 30 years. The growth phase of the first cycle corresponded to growth of the stock market in 1897-1906. The second cycle (1921-1947) had the clear growth phase falling in 1921-1929. The third cycle (1948-1980) was characterized by growth in 1949-1965. Finally, the fourth cycle observed from 1981 had the growth phase falling in 1982-1999. It is obvious that these 30-year cycles can be classified as Kuznets cycles in dynamics of stock prices. They do not disappear upon analysis of nominal return.

Let us use the obtained result to assess the parameters of the Markov switching model. Fig. 2 shows the S&P500 dynamics in constant prices (annual data); the above found cycles are represented using moving average with a smoothing period of 15. Let us calculate the average duration of the growth/recession. We find that the average duration of the growth periods is 23.25 years, which corresponds to average annual possibility of switching equal to 0.0430, and the average duration of recession periods is 14.3 years, which corresponds to the average annual possibility of switching equal to 0.0698. The assessment of the average trend rate at the growth stage is 4.15 pct per annum, at the decline stage, 2.16 pct per annum. Residuals after the removal of the trend have an autocorrelation equal to 0.59 and are stationary. White noise is characterized by a zero average and a standard deviation of 0.15. Thus, the final model of the price logarithm may be represented as follows (2):

$$p_t = p_0 + \sum_{i=1}^{t} \lambda_i \mu_i + \sum_{i=1}^{t} \omega^{t-i} \cdot \varepsilon_i \tag{2}$$

Where λ_i is the trend rate;

$\mu_i = \{-\mu_{i-1}, p; \mu_{i-1}, 1-p\}$, $\mu_0 = \{1, 0.5; -1, 0.5\}$ is the parameter characterizing the trend direction, with a switching possibility p;

ω – is the coefficient of residuals autocorrelation after removal of the trend;

E_i – is white noise with the given standard deviation.

Because of mathematical specifics, this model, as well as the pure random walk, creates the independency of consecutive price increments, that is why, based on the statistical analysis, it is easy to erroneously conclude about the absence of systematic trends. At the same time, unlike the pure random walk, this model means that stock prices are predictable based on the retrospective values, particularly, not only on the basis of the information about the previous prices, but also on the basis of other observed values. This casts some doubt on the market efficiency, which denies existence of cyclicality in stock prices, because, if a cycle existed, then actions of rational market participants would remove the correlation caused by such cycle, i.e. make increments of market prices independent.Therefore, market efficiency concludes that all cycles observed in the economic reality would be cycles of random nature, which do not correlate with other economic indicators. Hence, there is no sense in discussion of cyclicality in stock markets. Along with this there are doubts in the ability of financial markets to control inequity; however, this statement requires additional empirical verification.

3.2 LongcyclesinUSincomeinequality

Now let us study the long cycles in such income inequity index in the USA as income share of 1 of the wealthiest people (see Fig.3). One huge cycle can be observed in it, which is related to a decrease in inequity in the period from 1935 to 1978 and then to an increase in inequity from 1980 up to now. Let us eliminate this cycle by means of centered moving average and let us proceed to a row of additive remainders (Y_t). The main period of inequity growth can be visually observed from 1920 to 1929, from 1950 to 1969, from 1979, from 1986 to 1995 and to 2000 and from 2003 to 2007 (see Fig. 4). Let us check the hypothesis for correlation of observed cycles in the US income inequity with the cycles observed in the stock market dynamics. By employing the logarithmic profitability indexes of income of 1% of the wealthiest people and SP500 in constant prices it possible to calculate regression, which has a correlation factor of 0.21 (see Fig.5). In other words, the dependence between the stock market profitability and the inequity level is present; it is positive but quite weak. At the same time, using the trending stationary mode, namely the correlation analysis between the remainders of both indexes after detrending by means of centered moving average makes it possible to draw a conclusion about a closer relationship between two indexes (see Fig. 3-4).

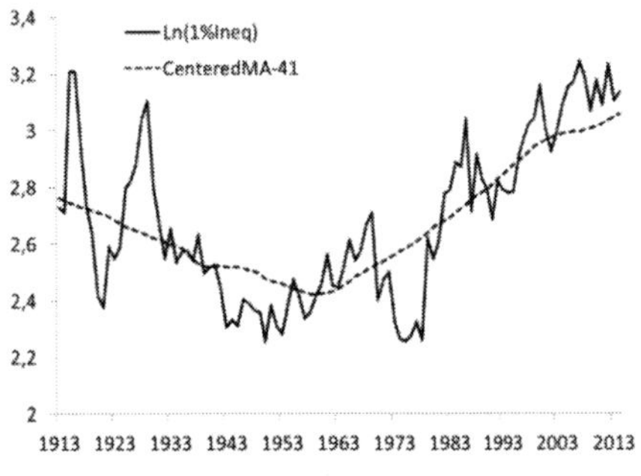

Fig. 3. Income share of 1% the wealthiest people (1%Ineq)

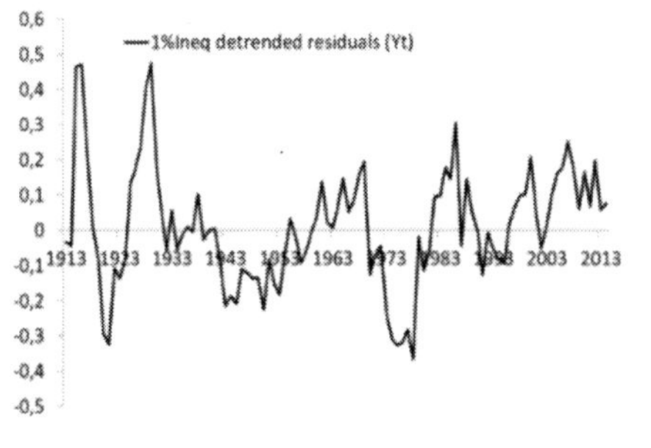

Fig. 4. Detrended remainders (Y_t) for income inequity

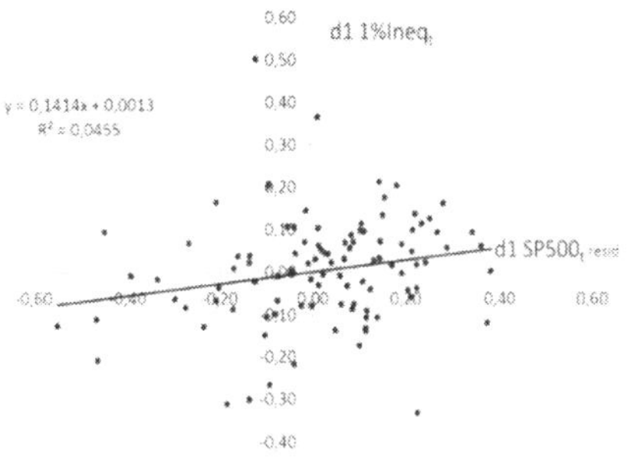

Fig. 5. Regression between the first inequity differences and SP500 in constant prices

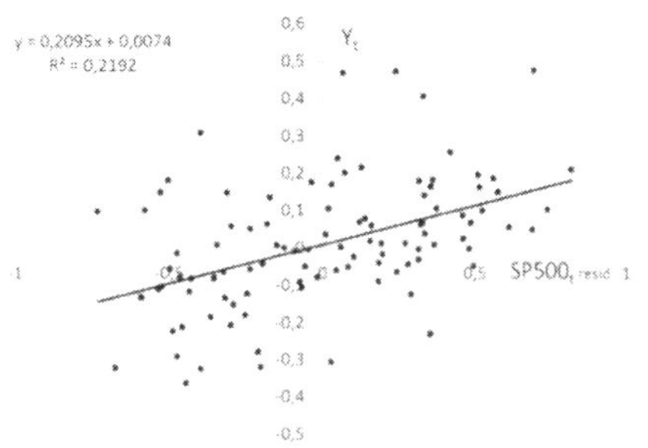

Fig. 6. Regression between detrended inequity remainders and SP500 in constant prices

These results prove that there is a positive relationship between the stock market earning power and income inequity; however, its mechanism is yet to be studied. It is possible that there is an external factor that determines the established correlation between both indexes, at the same time we are interested in particular how the stock market affects the inflation growth. This question needs to be clarified in more detail.

4 Evidence of underreaction of fast-growing companies' stock prices

The key question in generating time-series in stock prices is the processes of over and underreaction. [18] correctly indicated that the market efficiency remains to be an incontrovertible concept until the over and underreaction periods are unsystematic on the market. However, the theories developed over the last years consider the domination of underreaction in generating time-series in stock prices [5-7]. In this section we empirically check these theories while studying the fair cost of innovative (fast-growing) companies. Our hypothesis is that the underreaction of stock prices is originated by the long-term diffusion of information about innovative processes.

As the basis of fair stock price calculation we use the dividend discounting model, see [19] with a forecast period of 15 years. In particular, we use formula 3.

$$P_f = \sum_{t=1}^{T} \frac{k_d \cdot ROS_t \cdot S_t}{(1+r_e)^t} + \frac{\left(P/S\right)_T \cdot S_T}{(1+r_e)^T} \quad (3)$$

Where

S_t is the predicted value of profit per 1 share

$\left(P/S\right)_t$ is the predicted value of multiplier $\left(P/S\right)$,

ROS, k_d, r_e are the predeicted values of sale profit margin,devedent payout coefficientand current profit marign rate per stock capital estimated by the CAPM model.

We predict revenues based on the autocatalytic curve extrapolation in accordance with a hypothesis for diffusion of innovations [20, 21] and predict the remaining indexes at the level of average values over the last several years. The results are presented in Fig. 7-10. In the 1990s the market stock price was underestimated for all high-tech companies under consideration (exceptfor McDonalds) in the 2000s there ware underestimation even for McDonalds. At the same time, the fair price calculations for Apple company in the period from 1998 to 2007 show a significant underestimate in comparison with the market price. Partially, it is connected to the fact that the company went back to developing a new product in the period from 2001 to 2005.

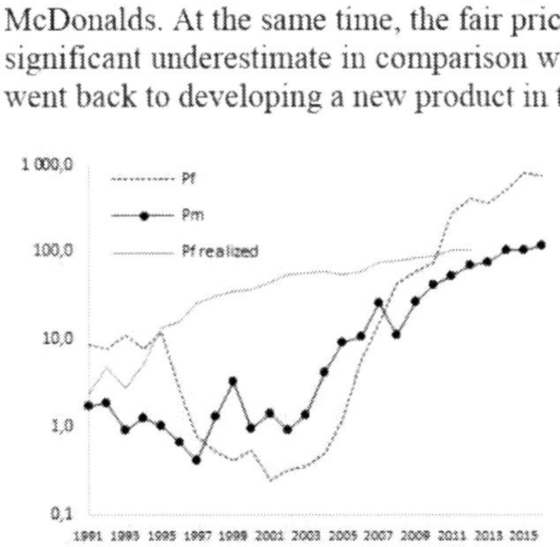

Fig. 7. Fair price and market price of Apple's share

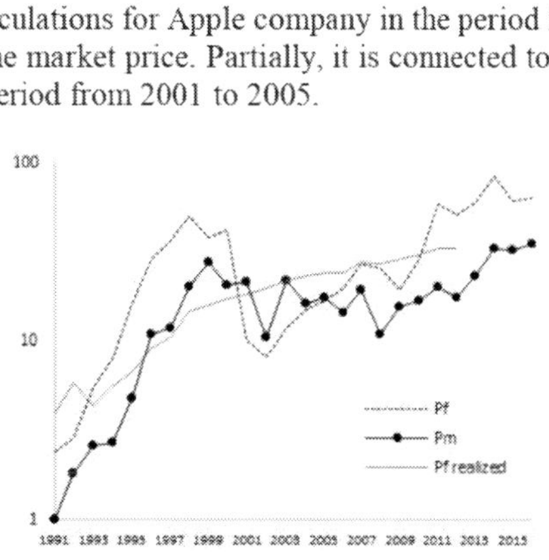

Fig. 8. Fair price and market price of Intel's share

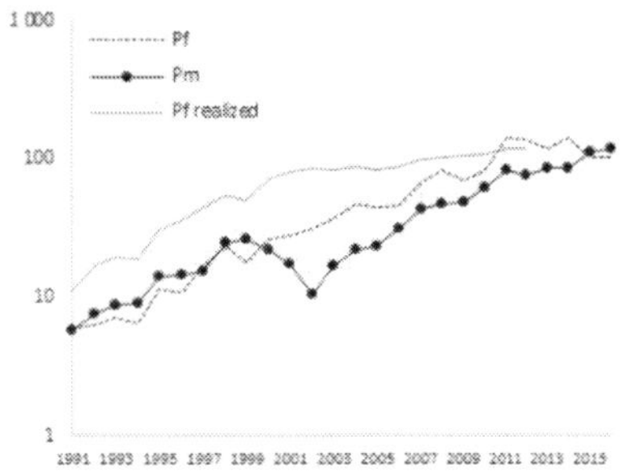

Fig. 9. Fair price and market price of McDonalds's share

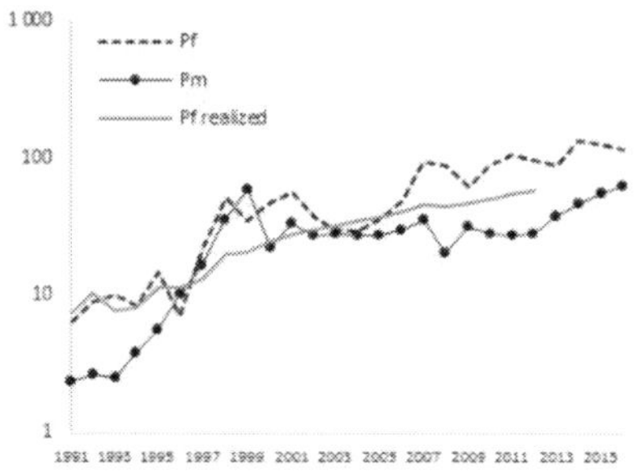

Fig. 10. Fair price and market price of Microsoft's share

5 Conclusions

Taking into account the abovementioned proofs of dependency in the cycles between the income inequity and the stock market dynamics as well as the demonstrated empirical underreaction of stock prices to the diffusion of fundamental information, the hypothesis for the stock market effects on an increase in income inequity seems to be reasonable. This result is backed up by proofs [22] in terms of trends in the global system development and fleshes out the reasons contributing to an increase in income inequity. Further studies are required to strengthen the evidence base, however, already now it is clear intuitively the global financial system operates to the benefits of its major beneficiaries but not to the needs of society. Paul Krugman has phrased this conclusion as follows: "Even when financial magnates earn money for investors, in most cases they do not create value for the society, but, in fact, they expropriate it from other market players" [23].

References

1. T. Piketty,E.Saez, American economic review, **96(2)** (2006)
2. R. G. Rajan, *Fault lines: How hidden fractures still threaten the world economy* (Princeton University Press, New Jersey, 2010)
3. R. Frank, *The Darwin Economy: Liberty, Competition, and the Common Good*(Princeton University Press, Princeton, 2011)
4. J. E. Stiglitz, *The price of inequality: How today's divided society endangers our future* (WW Norton &Company,New York, 2012)
5. H. Hong, J. C. Stein, Journal of Finance, **54(6)** (1999)
6. A. Frazzini, Journal of Finance,**61(4)** (2006)
7. Y. R. Ichkitidze, The Quarterly Review of Economics and Finance, **68** (2018)
8. J. B. Hamilton, Econometrica, **57**(1989)
9. J. B. Hamilton,Journal of Econometrics, **70** (1996)
10. J. B. Hamilton, *Regime-Switching Models, New Palgrave Dictionary of Economics* (Palgrave McMillan Ltd, Basingstoke, 2008)
11. H. M. Krolzig, *Markov switching vector autoregressions* (Springer, Berlin, 1997)
12. A. Timmermann, Journal of Econometrics, **96** (2000)
13. S. J. Taylor, *Modeling financial time series* (World Scientific, New Jersey,2008)
14. R. S. Mamon, R. J. Elliott,*Hidden Markov models in finance: further developments and applications* (Springer,Berlin, 2014)
15. G. Box, G. Jenkins, *Time series analysis: Forecasting and control* (Holdenday, San Francisco, 1976)
16. K. H. Chan, J. C.Hayya, J. K. Ord, Econometrica, **45**, (1977)
17. C. R. Nelson, H. Kang, Econometrica, **49**(1981)
18. E. F. Fama, Journal of financial economics, **49(3)** (1998)
19. A. Damodaran, *Investment Valuation: Tools and Techniques for Determining the Value of Any Asset* (Wiley, New Jersey, 2002)
20. E. M. Rogers, *Diffusion of Innovations* (Simon and Shuster Inc, New York, 1995)
21. M. Hirooka, *Innovation Dynamism and Economic Growth* (Edward Elgar Publishing, Cheltenham, 2006)

22. Y. R. Ichkitidze, *2017 XX IEEE International Conference, On certain trends of world economy's development*, In Soft Computing and Measurements (SCM) (2017)
23. P. Krugman, *End this depression now!* (W. W. Norton & Company, New York, 2013)

Smart Hospital concept and its implementation capabilities based on the incentive extension

Oksana Ilyashenko[1*], *Igor* Ilin[1], and *Dmitry* Kurapeev[2]

[1] Peter the Great St. Petersburg Polytechnic University, Institute of Industrial Management, Economics and Trade, Higher School of Business Management, 195251 Politekhnicheskaya st. 29, Russian Federation
[2] National Medical Research Center of V.A., 197341 Akkuratova st. 2, Russian Federation

Abstract. Currently, the health care as one of the priority development areas for the state requires special attention in the transition to the innovative management models based on the use of advanced medical concepts and digital technologies. Therefore, the transition to the SmartHospital model and the formation of an appropriate architectural solution become actual for health organizations which strategic task is the transition to the digital space and strengthening their positions in the medical services market. Prior to starting the development of the Smart Hospital architectural model as applied to the specific health organization, it is advisable to use a reference model that will take into account the basic business and IT requirements of the organization, limits and used technologies. The creation of the reference SmartHospital architectural solution is preceded by a preparatory stage that allows revealing the architecture and limit requirements. The article proposes the incentive extension on the basis of which the requirements and limits are formulated for the reference model of the SmartHospital architectural solution.

1 Target setting

The exponential potential growth and increase in capabilities of new technologies in medicine, the rapid IT development, development and implementation of the ideas of the 4th Industrial Revolution over the past few years have marked the prospect for formation of a completely different health care model.

Currently, the health care is considered as one of the priority spheres of development in many countries of the world. A key trend is search for promising opportunities in the social and economic fields. The social sphere mainly focuses on reducing mortality and a proportion of complex disease patients. The development of the health care system in the economic sphere proposes the creation of health organizations management system. Their strategic task is the transition to the digital space and strengthening their positions in the medical services market.

According to the Federal State Statistics Service, an average life expectancy increased by six months from January to May 2017 in Russia compared to 2016, and for the first time

* Corresponding author: ioy120878@gmail.com

it exceeded 72 years and is 72.4 years. Mortality decreased by 3% in 2017 compared with 2016 [1]. According to Deputy Prime Minister of the Russian Federation O. Yu. Golodets, the health and demographic development issues are the absolute priority of the Government [2].

One of the reasons for mortality reduction is the timely and quality provision of medical care based on the current medical concepts. Despite the decrease in the mortality rate, there is a number of trends in society that require increased attention to the solution of issues related to the treatment and prevention of diseases that are the main mortality factors (blood circulatory system diseases, cancerous diseases, infectious diseases, etc.). These trends include an increase in the average age of the population as a whole, an increase in life expectancy, an increase in the proportion of people over 65, and a reduction in the number of young specialists graduating universities. As a result, there is a danger of growth of diseases, an increase in a proportion of complex disease patients in the population against the shortage of staff capable of providing highly skilled medical care. In this case, the health care delivery cost is steadily increasing at the moment. The problems solution all over the world is based on the use of the personalized medicine concept [3], achievements in biomedicine. These concepts and medicine technologies are implemented by means of the actual IT in the framework of the Health 4.0 concept [4]: IoT and IoS - Internet of Things and Internet of Services; cloud computing and Big Data; predictive analytics; block chain technologies; artificial intelligence and machine learning; developed mobile networks (5G).

The implementation of the above tasks requires the health organizations to transit to a completely different model of health care delivery that in turn requires changing in the management model of the health organization, namely, the transition to the Smart Hospital model. According to the European Union Agency for Network and Information Security (ENISA), the Smart Hospital is a health organization that provides health care and is based on optimized and automated processes built using the actual IT in accordance with the Health 4.0 concept to improve the existing procedure for patient care and to implement the advanced medical technologies [5]. The strategic objectives of the Smart Hospital are to provide extended patient care including remote medical services, to ensure efficient stream of patients and medical information, to increase diagnostic, surgical and organizational capabilities while maintaining the required level of patient information protection.

The Smart Hospital model introduction affects all levels of health organization management and requires re-engineering the health organization architecture as a whole or its separate components [6]. To create the target Smart Hospital model, it is advisable to use some reference model that will allow taking into account the main business and IT requirements of the organization, limits and the used technologies [7]. The formation of the reference Smart Hospital architectural solution is preceded by the preparatory stage associated with the incentive extension development that will provide the requirements for the architecture and limits. This study proposes the incentive extension on the basis of which it is possible to state the requirements and limits for the reference Smart Hospital architectural solution.

2. Methods of research

The development of the incentive extension of the reference architecture solution of the Smart Hospital model is based on the researchof M. Lankhorst [8]. The incentive concepts are used to simulate the motives or reasons underlying a design or a change of the enterprise architecture. They arrange and limit the design process, thereby affecting the result of the enterprise architecture design. These concepts are based on research for the development of the target requirements [9] and the architecture principles [10]. The result of incentive concept implementation is the incentive extension including concerned parties simulation, change factors, business objectives, principles, requirements and results. Let's consider each of the specified components of the incentive extension in more details with reference to the health organization implementing the Smart Hospital model.

3. Research results

Using the methodology for building the incentive concept proposed by M. Lankhorst and its graphic representation as the incentive extension, we will form the latter for the reference model of the Smart Hospital architectural solution.

First of all, we will define the stakeholders of the health organization implementing the SmartHospital model. In our opinion, for the health organization, the stakeholders interested in the organization development are:

- top management of the health organization represented by the head;
- The Ministry of Healthcare of the Russian Federation that is an economic and legal mechanism for control for the development of the entire health care system and individual health clinics. The Ministry of Healthcare of the Russian Federation controls for an amount of financing health clinics, the development strategy of the entire health care system, taking into account the social and economic situation in the country, the world healthcare development trends, etc ;
- the Suppliers of medical equipment and drugs interested in implementation of value- and actual IT based personalized medicine concepts by health clinics.
- insurance companies interested in developing partnerships with health clinics to implement various health insurance routes.

The main drivers of the health organization that encourage the organization to implement the Smart Hospital model and perform the corresponding architecture re-engineering are:

- using a new medical and information technologies [11];
- changes in the legislation, namely, the law on telemedicine effective from January 1, 2018 [12], the strategy for development of the healthcare of the Russian Federation for the long-term period 2015-2030 [13]. Implementation of telemedicine technologies capability qualitatively changes the system of organization at interaction with patients and, as a result, the system of business processes and IT support of health clinics;
- the increasing cost of medical services delivery takes up the matter with health clinics to revise the patient stream management system, personnel capacity, etc.;
- population aging and a change in the diseases spectrum, high mortality and incidents of certain types of diseases, such as cardiovascular diseases (CVD), cancerous diseases. This leads to the need to change the medical services system in terms of development of the prevention and early disease detection system.

The analysis of the situation in health clinics from the point of view of the listed drivers allowed stating the following assessments: presently, in the most clinics there is no corresponding management model and IT infrastructure that would allow meeting the above social challenges to modern medicine. Another important assessment of the health clinics activity as a result of the stated factors being the reason of changes in architecture is the ineffectiveness of the resource allocation system, especially with regard to patient stream management and the use of human resources. This allowed to state the goals facing health clinics. Taking into account the existing social problems, world trends in medical and information technologies, the identified management problems in health clinics, the goals of the clinics architecture development are increasing the efficiency of health organizations, on the one hand, with a steady increase in the medical care quality, on the other hand. The achievement result of the stated goals will be the Smart Hospital model implementation based on the Health 4.0 concept and the implementation of the "4P" medicine principles [14]. The use of the Health 4.0 technologies-cloud computing, IoT, Big data, predictive analytics, machine learning and artificial intelligence, block chain technologies and mobile technologies - combined with the "4P" concept [15] - value-based, personalized, predictive and participatory medicine - are the key requirements for the reference architectural solution functionality and allow implementing a number of intermediate results, which integrated combination will provide a transition to the Smart Hospital model: the dominant position of the health organization in the market of monitoring and treatment of remote patients; implementation of services providing the Health 4.0 concept implementation; automation of business and operational processes; transition from disease-oriented effectiveness criteria to patient-oriented ones [16].

It should be noted that the achievement of these results is possible only when observing a number of requirements both for a Smart Hospital architectural solution functional and personnel training mentioned above. To solve the tasks for automation of business and operational processes, implementation of remote monitoring, transition to patient-oriented effectiveness criteria, it is required to extend the specialists competence in obtaining interdisciplinary knowledge by health workers. The necessary condition of the successful subdivisions management for employees performing administrative functions is the formation of management competencies, which vector is directed towards the digital health clinic transformation.

When implementing this clinic architecture functionality, it is necessary to take into account a number of limits. First, the activities digitizing proposes the use of cloud computing. In this case, it is necessary to take into account the limits associated with the use of patient personal data. The use of block chain technologies is required to arrange the required level of information security and access to data in accordance with the implemented security policy in the health clinic. Secondly, considering the import substitution concept, there are recommendations for the software use including domestic information systems [17].

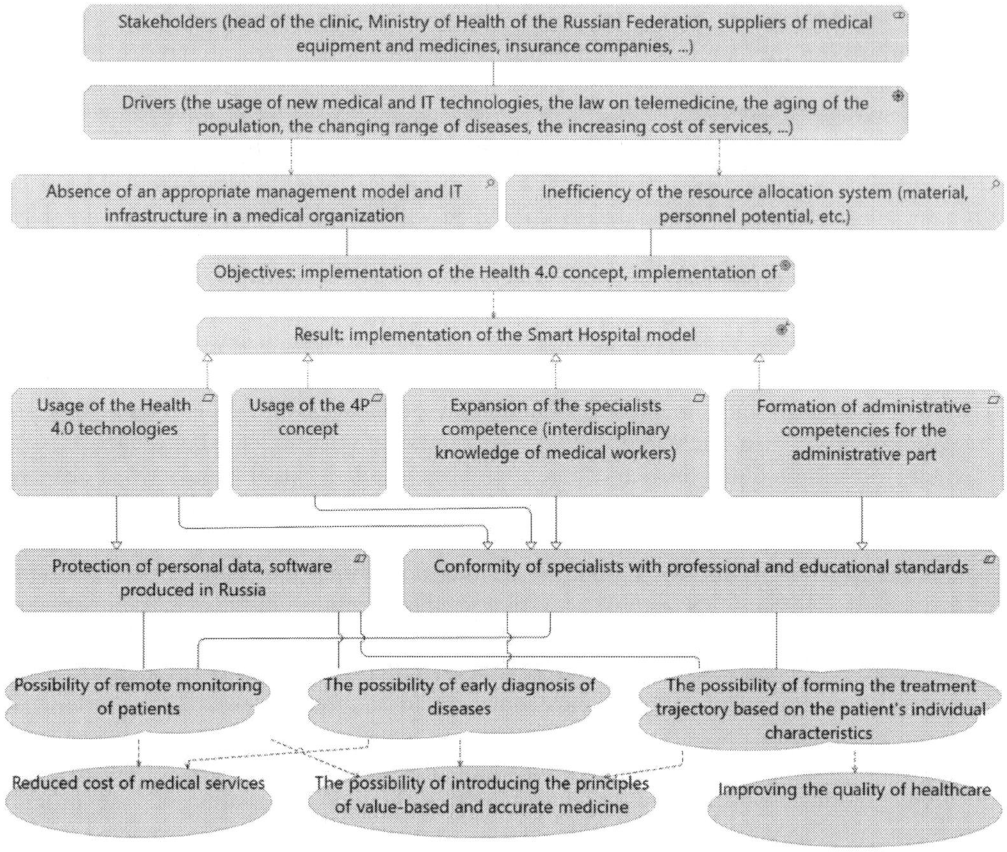

Fig. 1. The enlarged scheme of the incentive extension of the reference architectural solution of the health organization implementing the Smart Hospital concept.

To fulfill the requirements regarding the development of the competence of the medical organization personnel, it is necessary to pay attention to the personnel training in accordance with the changing professional and educational standards of medical education [18]. Employees holding managerial positions (at the department chief level and higher) must have managerial competencies. To this end, it is required to form a specialist model who manages the structural subdivisions of the health organization or the organization as a whole that has not only the professional doctor competencies but also has a set of management competencies that will promptly respond to changes in the requirements of the external and internal environment and take appropriate decisions in terms of managing development of the organization as a whole or its separate components.

The incentive extension result is formation of the simulated architectural solution value and its value for the health organization as a whole or for its separate components. The main values for the health organization implementing the Smart Hospital model are remote patients monitoring that is especially important for such a territorially extended country as the Russian Federation; early diseases detection that will allow implementing actual medicine strategies: early diseases detection in combination with risk factors control; the possibility for arranging a treatment ways based on the individual patient characteristics. This will allow a health clinic to implement the value-based and personalized medicine principles while reducing the medical services cost. This incentive extension value is an actual problem of the modern health care system, as medical services cost is now growing exponentially. As a result of the description of the main components of the incentive extension in accordance with the M. Lankhorst's methodology, the incentive extension was formed for the reference architectural solution of the health organization implementing the Smart Hospital concept (Fig. 1).

4. Conclusions

As a result of the study, the existing socioeconomic problems are described, which as a whole the health system and health organizations being the main health care providers deal with. The paper considers the medical concepts that require the support of actual digital technologies, justifies the feasibility of creating the reference model of the Smart Hospital architectural solution. The model building proposes a preliminary description of the relevant requirements and limits. A methodology for creating the incentive extension proposed by M. Lankhorst was used as a method for creating the upper-level requirements and limits for the reference model of the Smart Hospital architectural solution. In the future, it is planned to propose the reference Smart Hospital architectural solution taking into account the identified requirements and limits.

References

1. Federal State Statistics Service [online] Available at: www.gks.ru/free_doc/2017/demo/t3_3.xls (2018).
2. Delovoy Peterburg [online] Available at: https://www.dp.ru/a/2017/08/14/Srednjaja_prodolzhitelnost (2018).
3. V. A. Stepanov, *Personalized medicine: challenges and solutions* [online] Available at: http://www.sbras.ru/files/files/prezidium20171221/ 5_stepanov-persmed-pressoran-nsk-dec2017.pdf (2017).
4. By 2020 the Smart Hospital will be a reality [online] Available at: https://www.futurehealthindex.com/2017/06/13/by-2020-the-smart-hospital-will-be-a-reality/ (2018).
5. European Union Agency for Network and Information Security [online] Available at: file:///C:/Users/User/Downloads/Smart%20Hospitals%20(1).pdf (2018).
6. I. V. Ilin, O. Yu. Iliashenko, A. I. Levina, Reengineering of high-tech and specialized Medical care delivery process for telemedicine system implementation. *Proceedings of the 29th International Business Information Management Association Conference – Sustainable Economic Growth, Education Excellence, and Innovation Management through Vision* **2020**,1822-1831.
7. I. V. Ilin, K. V. Frolov, A. A. Lepekhin, From Business Processes Model of the Company to Software Development: MDA Business Extension. *Proceedings of the 29th International Business Information Management Association Conference – Sustainable Economic Growth, Education Excellence, and Innovation Management through Vision* **2020**, 1157-1164 (2017)
8. M. Lankhorst et al. Enterprise Architecture at Work. Modeling, Communication and Analysis (2017)
9. A. V. Lamsweerde, Goal-oriented requirements engineering: A roundtrip from research to practice. 12th IEEE Joint International Requirements Engineering Conference. RE'04. Kyoto, Japan (2004)
10. D. Greefhorst, Proper, E. Architecture Principles. The Cornerstones of Enterprise Architecture. *Springer* (2011)

11. JC Hsieh, AH Li, CC Yang. Mobile, cloud, and big data computing: contributions, challenges, and new directions in telecardiology. *Int J Environ Res Public Health* **10(11),** 6131–53 (2013)
12. Federal Law No. 242-FZ dd. 29.07.2017 "On introduction of changes to some legislative acts of the Russian Federation regarding application of information technologies in health care" [online] Available at: http://publication.pravo.gov.ru/Document/View/0001201707300032 (2017)
13. The Russian Federation Health Development Strategy for the Long-term Period of 2015-2030 [online] Available at: https://old2015.rosminzdrav.ru/ministry/61/22/stranitsa-979/strategiya-razvitiya-zdravoohraneniya-rossiyskoy-federatsii-na-dolgosrochnyy-period (2017)
14. L. Hood. *Systems Biology and P4 Medicine: Past, Present, and Future*. Rambam Maimonides Med J. **4(2),** (2013) [online] Available at: https://www.ncbi.nlm.nih.gov/pmc/articles/PMC3678833/ (2017)
15. Jong-Myon Bae Value-based medicine: concepts and application. *Epidemiol Health.* **37** (2015)
16. Cardiovascular risk factors in hypothyroidism in the populations of the Russian Federation and the USA.
V. G. Vilkov, S. A. Shalnova, A. O. Konradi, Yu. V.Zhernakova, S. A. Boytsov, Profilakticheskaya Meditsina (2016)
17. Round table "Import substitution in IT equipment: requirements of Customers and ways of their implementation" [online] Available at: http://sipower.ru/novosti/item/256-kruglyj-stol-importozameshchenie-v-it-oborudovanii.html (2017)
18. E. A. Ryngach, T. V. Treshkur, A. A. Tatarinova, E. V. Shlyakhto, Algorithm for the management of patients with stable coronary artery disease and high-grade ventricular arrhythmias *Terapevticheskii Arkhiv* (2017)

Business model for Smart Hospital health organization

Igor Ilin[1], *Oksana* Iliyaschenko[1*], and *Alexandra* Konradi[2]

[1] Peter the Great St. Petersburg Polytechnic University, Institute of Industrial Management, Economics and Trade, Higher School of Business Management, 195251, Polytechnicheskaya st., 29, Russian Federation
[2] Federal State Budgetary Establishment "National Medical Research Center of V.A. Almazov" of the Ministry of Health of the Russian Federation, 197341, Akkuratova st., 2, Russian Federation

Abstract. Modern trends in the society development such as population growth, increase of longevity, development of medical technologies and trend of business digitalization require adaptation of the services offered by health organizations to the new conditions. The health organizations management shall form a development strategy, and therefore, form and continuously improve the business model taking into account the dynamically changing environment, new technologies, legislation, etc. for successful positioning in the market, saving and developing the value of the services offered in the health care sector. The article provides a reference business model of a health organization based on the Smart Hospital concept. While implementing this concept, the health organization relies on a new computing infrastructure based on mobile and cloud technologies, large data and analytics, Internet of things (IoT), new achievements in machine learning. These revolutionary technologies enable the health organization to drastically change the business models and create new products and services in the health care.

1 Target setting

The exponential potential growth and increase in capabilities of new technologies in the medicine, the rapid IT development, development and implementation of the ideas of the 4th Industrial Revolution over the past few years have marked the prospect for formation of a completely different health care model.

Let's consider the main current trends in the medicine field. Currently, the "4P" medicine and the value-based medicine concept are most significant. The "4P" medicine concept consists of the following components [1]: preventive medicine, participation medicine, predictive medicine [2, 3], personalized medicine [4]. The value medicine [5] adds the "4P" concept. The medical trends and concepts can be successfully implemented based on the actual digital technologies only. The Health 4.0 is a strategic health care concept based on the Industry 4.0 concept. The Health 4.0 objective is to ensure the implementation of value-based and personalized medicine ideas through the mass use of actual IT: Internet of Things

* Corresponding author: ioy120878@gmail.com

and Internet of Services, capabilities for processing and using a big amount of data (Big Data) [6], cloud computing [7], Machine Learning [8], block chain technology, developed mobile networks (5G), etc. The use of these technologies makes it possible to create "smart" infrastructure of health organizations, developing the Artificial Intelligence based solutions to provide expert knowledge and analysis of great amount of medical data at a relatively low cost.

The implementation of these concepts and technologies is already transforming the health care sector. In the near future the large-scale introduction of technologies that ensure the implementation of ideas of value-based and personalized medicine will provide an opportunity to implement the Smart Hospital concept. According to the experts in the field of digitalization of health care, the Smart Hospital concept is based on optimized and automated processes supported by the actual IT focused on improving the existing procedures and implementing new opportunities for patient treatment and care [9]. The implementation of the solutions that support the Smart Hospital concept is one of the priorities for large companies offering the relevant IT solutions including SAP, IBM, Siemens, Google, etc., as it is an important component for the business and can help to solve problems regarding reduction of costs in the health care system while maintaining the required health care quality level.

The introduction of such solutions requires the management of health organizations to understand the development strategy and the developed business model. The successful health care business models increase customer loyalty, consumer benefits and can contribute to the creation of a competitive cost structure, taking into account the choice of the appropriate automation option and health organization processes digitization. It is obviously that the business model may have certain characteristics depending on the specific activities of the health organization, environmental conditions, etc. However, regardless of the health organizations specifics, the implementation of the Smart Hospital concept involves the formation of client-oriented business models. They expand the capabilities of drivers, strategies and tools for analyzing, modeling and implementing innovative business models. We offer a service-oriented business model in this article to develop a health organization that is going to implement the Smart Hospital concept.

2 Methods of research

To solve the problems, it is necessary to form a health organization business model as mentioned above. We will consider that the business model is an analytical tool for "... description of the basic principles for organization creation, development and successful operation" [10]. The business model is similar to the strategic plan that is later implemented through the organizational structures, processes and systems of the organization.

There are a large number of approaches to the business model formation that have created and evolved in accordance with the needs and changing market conditions: the "closed innovation" business model (Closed R & D business model) [11], Henry Chesborough's "open innovation" business model [12], D. Debelac's model. [13], A. Osterwalder and Y. Pigneur's approach [10], L. Schwarzer's approach of [14], Chan Kim and Rene Moborn's concept who developed the blue ocean strategy [15], etc.

Having analyzed all the abve approaches to creating the business model, it can be concluded that all the proposed variants of the organization business models are based on 4 key elements that determine its content: a proposal in the form of value for customers that is proposed by the organization based on the produced goods and services; interaction with the consumer, the infrastructure that the enterprise uses to create the value; organization financial efficiency.

The A. Osterwalder's model advantage is a clear segmentation of all key parameters that reflect the logic of the organization activities and aimed at making a profit. In addition, this model has a tool support, wide practical application and it is used in the activities of a large number of successful concerns and corporations. According to these provisions, we concluded that it is advisable to carry out the research based on the use of A. Osterwalder and Y. Pigneur's business model template. Alexander Osterwalder in cooperation with Yves Pigneur developed a methodology for creating a business model based on the business model template that consists of 9 structural blocks [10]: consumer segments, value proposals, basic activities, key resources, key partners, customer relations, sales channels, revenue streams, and cost structure. Each of the considered blocks has its own description and structure. The practical approach to creating the innovative business models proposed by A. Osterwalder is used in the TOGAF standard of the Open Group industrial consortium, has the Archi tooling, is used in many industries around the world, in particular, by 3M, Ericsson, Capgemini, Deloitte, Telenor, etc.

3 Research results

Based on the A. Osterwalder and Y. Pigneur's methodology the following description of the reference Smart Hospital business model is proposed.

Consumer segments. The business model development begins from the definition of consumer segments. In our case, the consumer segments are patients which can be classified according to the different reasons. The patients' classification will be the basis for creating the consumer segments for the health organization. The health organization implementing the Smart Hospital concept renders all types of medical assistance provided by Federal Law No. 323-FZ dd. 21.11.2011 "Basic principles of health care of Citizens of the Russian Federation" (Article 32) [16]. All patients may be classified according to the types of care to be delivered:

- at-risk patients;
- primary care patients;
- specialized and high-tech care patients;
- ambulance and ambulance secondary care patients;
- patients who need postsurgical health monitoring and/or care (including palliative care)

As well as to individuals the health organization can render services to corporate clients. Patients can live directly in the region of the health organization location or be within remote regions including hard-to-reach areas.

The next version of the patients' classification is according to the sources of care funding: CHI (compulsory health insurance), quotas of the Ministry of Health of the Russian Federation, VHI (voluntary health insurance) and direct patient's services payment.

The considered variety of patients in different classifications has some intersections. For example, a corporate client, – a large oil and gas company engaged in the production and processing of petroleum products, has oil derricks within remote, hard-to-reach regions. The company should monitor the health of employees working at remote locations. In this regard, the company is interested in proposals for corporate clients with regard to identifying at- risk and remote health monitoring patients. In this case, the financial interaction is arranged through the VHI.

Another example is arrangement of the postsurgical health monitoring and care. This kind of services should be arranged using the IoT opportunities. For example, the postsurgical health monitoring of apoplectic consists not only in care, but also in rehabilitation course arrangement. The IoT opportunities play an important role in this point. The sensors attached to the patient's body allow to obtain information about the patient's condition, the motor activity capabilities, and, if necessary, to promptly adjust the rehabilitation process.

Value-based proposals. The identified consumer segments allow creating a number of value-based proposals supported by appropriate medical and IT in the framework of the Health 4.0 concept:

- services for continuous patients health monitoring;
- services for early diseases detection that is especially important for diseases with high mortality rate [17];
- selection of treatment methods taking into account the patient's genome, life environment features, etc.;
- patients rehabilitation services;
- patients care services (any time and anywhere);
- comprehensive services based on a combination of different value-based proposals. For example, when rendering services for early diseases detection, the patient receives a set of services related to treatment and the need for rehabilitation under special conditions in the framework of the comprehensive proposal;
- services for corporate clients depending on their activities specifics.

Basic activities. All value-based proposals are created in the framework of key activities which the health organization renders in accordance with Federal Law No. 323-FZ dd. 21.11.2011 "Basic principles of health care of Citizens of the Russian Federation" (Article 32) [16]:

- medical care (primary, specialized, etc.);
- disease prevention;
- early diseases diagnostics;
- monitoring of patients who received medical care, and at-risk patients;
- implementation of comprehensive medical services from early diseases detection, medical care with subsequent monitoring health condition of at-risk patients or ones who received medical care.

Key resources. Medical concepts and IT are a component of key resources. The main key resources of the health organization implementing the Smart Hospital concept are both the conventional resources, and the resources required for the concept implementation:

1. Material resources – resources that ensure the institution functioning in terms of financial security. The material resources include medical equipment, drugs, buildings and structures, transport resources, utilities (including water and power supply, ventilation systems) and communication channels (telephony, telecommunications, etc.).
2. Staff – human resources providing the health organization activity (doctors, nurses, management personnel, technicians, drivers, IT staff, accountants, personnel department, statistics department).
3. Intellectual resources including scientific developments in the field of biomedicine, genetic engineering, and IT.
4. Information technology resources:
   4.1. The Health 4.0 technologies (IoT, Big Data, cloud computation, mobile technologies, machine learning, artificial intelligence, predictive analytics, telemedicine);
   4.2. IT solutions of large companies for the medical industry (SAP, IBM, Microsoft);
   4.3. "4P" technologies and value-based medicine (VBM).
5. Financial resources assume the definition of all sources of organization activities funding. In case of health organizations, funding sources are insurance, state quotas, off-budget revenues.

Key partners. Key partners include a network of suppliers and partners thanks to which the business model functions. There are two types of partnerships for the health organization:

1. Strategic cooperation between complementary companies. This type includes the Federal Health System Institutions of the Russian Federation, insurance companies, public organizations, funds, research institutes and universities.
2. The manufacturer's relationship with the suppliers to ensure receiving the quality components. The Suppliers of medical equipment, pharmaceutical companies and suppliers of IT solutions for health organizations support these relations.

Customer relations. The value-based proposals are focused on the identified consumer segments and are implemented through the relationships with Customers. To implement the created value-based proposals, it is necessary to create a patient base, arrangement of the feedback system with patients through mobile applications and social media. The patients should be involved in the process for satisfaction assessment of the services provided. Thus, for example, to implement the patient rehabilitation services, specialists' on-line consultation is necessary. Early detection supposes the use of cloud services to download research results when fixing an appointment. It is also advisable to set up a system for informing the patients about the specialists' on-line timetable, the possibility for fixing an appointment (on-line, by phone, automatically in the event of preventive examination, etc.), open lectures, actions, etc.

Sales channels. Value-based proposals come to the consumer through the information networks allowing to increase the level of consumer awareness of the services to be implemented and present the value-based proposals for the potential patients. There are 2 types of sales channels for the health organization – partner and own. The partner channels include the portal of the Ministry of Health of the Russian Federation, the portals of health organizations of other regions, insurance companies. The own channel is the health organization site providing the information about the services rendered, the possibility of on-line fixing, as well as the information about the automatic patient fixing of an appointment with the specialists when the scheduled time for the examination is reached.

Revenue streams include the material profit that the company receives from each consumer segment. The health organization, when rendering services to individuals, earns income based on rendering the services for CHI, quotas (HTMC, HTMC as part of CHI), VHI or based on rendering the paid services. Receipt of income when rendering services to legal entities is carried out under the VHI.

Cost structure. Creating and implementing value-based proposals, maintaining relationships with Customers, making profits – all these processes are associated with any costs. Let's consider the most significant costs associated with functioning of the health organization business model which is implementing the Smart Hospital concept. Fixed and variable costs may generally be identified in the health organization. The feature of the health organization implementing the Smart Hospital concept is an addition of the list of fixed costs for personnel training and retraining taking into account the new requirements for personnel in the conditions of activities digitalization, medicine research and development costs and health organization activities and IT support costs including costs for activities digitization.

4 Conclusions

As a result of the study, the existing medical trends and concepts that can be implemented based on the actual technologies are described. Based on the analysis of the existing approaches to creating the business models, the A. Osterwalder's model was chosen. As a result of the business model main components analysis, a description of the reference health organization business model implementing the Smart Hospital concept was developed that allows creating a specific health organization business model, forecasting its development and successful introducing the innovations. Further, it is planned to continue research in the development of the reference architectural Smart Hospital solution based on the presented reference business model.

References

1. L. Hood, Rambam Maimonides Med J **4(2)** DOI: 10.5041/RMMJ.10112 (2013)
2. V. S. Baranov, Medical genetics **16(5)** (2017)
3. Ye. Malyshev V. Shlyakhto, A. O. Konradi, Hyperpiesis. **8(3)** (2002)
4. V. A. Stepanov. Personalized medicine: challenges and solutions [online] Available at: http://www.sbras.ru/files/files/prezidium20171221/ 5_stepanov-persmed-pressoran-nsk-dec2017.pdf (2017)
5. B. Jong-Myon, Epidemiol Health. **37** (2015)
6. I. V. Ilin, O. Yu. Ilyashenko, S. V. Shirokova, , Levina, O. Hamalainen. *Big Data for business analytics* (Saint Petersburg 2016)
7. I. V. Ilin, O Yu. Ilyashynko, A.D. Borremans, Science and Education. **12(87)** (2016)
8. R. Kohavi, F. Provost, Glossary of terms, **30(2-3)** (1998)
9. By 2020 the Smart Hospital will be a reality [online] Available at: https://www.futurehealthindex.com/2017/06/13/by-2020-the-smart-hospital-will-be-a-reality/ (2017)
10. A. Osterwalder, Y. Pigneur. Business models development. **288** (Alpina Publisher Skolkovo Series, Moscow 2013)
11. D. Denisov. Open innovations model. "Business-magazine", **6**. (2011) [online]Available at: http://www.cfin.ru/investor/venture/ open_innovation.shtml (2017)
12. T. Oganesyan, D. Medovnikov. The dog is still on the hay **8**, 742. (2011) [online] Available at: http://expert.ru/expert/2011/08 /sobaka-poka-na-sene. (2017)
13. D. Debelak, *Business Models: The principles for creating a prosperous organization* (Grebennikov Publishing House, Moscow 2009)
14. L. Schweizer. The concept and evolution of business models (2007) [online] Available at: http://www.research.by/webroot/delivery/files/2007n2r01.pdf. (2017)
15. Kim W. Chan, R. Moborn, *Blue ocean strategy* (Mann, Ivanov and Ferber, Moscow 2013).
16. Federal Law No. 323-FZ dd 21.11.2011 "Basic principles of health care of Citizens of the Russian Federation" (Article 32) [online] Available at: http://www.consultant.ru/document/cons_doc_LAW_121895/. (2017)
17. Ye. Malyshev V. Shlyakhto, A. O. Konradi, O. P. Rotar, et al. Preventive medicine. **17 (5)** (2014)

Electronic platforms as a new ecosystem of the organization and the conduct of business[a]

Roman Jaque [1*], *Marat* Sarygulov[2], and *Joao* Leitao[3]

[1] Saint-Petersburg State University, Economics dept., 199034 University emb. 7/9, Russian Federation
[2] Saint-Petersburg University of Technologies of Management and Economy, Institute of Economy, Management and Information Technologies, 190103, Lermontov pr. 44A, Russian Federation
[3] Universidade da Beira Interior (UBI), P-6200-001, Portugal

Abstract. At the present moment, leading industrial countries and such new and quickly growing economies as China and India that also actively use the possibilities provided by new technological platforms, form a new type economy known as "digital economy" or "economy of joint use". As the new technological platform is based on information technologies, the best synergetic effect is achieved through using electronic platforms, with their number and variety quickly growing, so they are actually creating a new infrastructure for communication between the primary economic agents. A new ecosystem also provides new possibilities, including instrumental ones, for conduct of business, searching for jobs and developing the business environment. This article analyzes new trends in development of business in the conditions of a newly forming digital economy.

1 Introduction

Since the beginning of this century, a particular feature of technological development is quick industrial implementation of micro-level technologies. This offered such possibilities as: firstly, creating digital infrastructure (the Internet, cell phones, smartphones) that is, practically, affordable for every customer and, secondly, the actual timely and addressed answer to customers' requirements. For example, such leaders of the digital industry as Facebook, YouTube and WhatsApp had, respectively, 1.59 billion and 1.0 billion active users in March 2016 [1], whereas as soon as in June 2017, this number grew to 2.0, 1.5 and 1.2 billion users, respectively [2]. Another spectacular example is quick growth in the volume of electronic (on-line) trade that was only made possible in the conditions of the widely-spread Internet. Starting from 1995, the volume of the world trade has been constantly growing and had reached USD 50 billion by 2000; by 2010, this volume had reached USD 250 billion [3]. The latest research showed that, in 2017, this figure was USD 2.3 trillion, and by 2021 the volume of the world electronic trade is expected to reach the

* Corresponding author: zhak55@ya.ru
[a] This article was prepared with financial support from the Russian Scientific Fund (Grant No. 18-18-00099)

level of USD 4.5 trillion [4]. A constituent part of this process is development of on-line banking. For example, in the USA in 2000, this service was used by 16 million homes, and 10 years later this figure was 52 million homes [3]. A research carried out in 2015 in Europe showed that two-thirds of customers make purchases using a PC or a notebook, and 15% use smartphones [5]. Such wide coverage of customers and a very quick growth in the number of users means that digital technologies create radically new possibilities for commercial communication and meeting customers' demands, which is most important for conduct of business.

At the same time, electronic platforms, while quickly reacting to customers' needs, create conditions (on the competition basis) for removing separate professional groups from the market. A classic example is the company Uber who deal in transportation – not possessing a single vehicle of their own or employing a single driver, in 2014 it provided jobs for 160 thousand drivers, and the volume of capitalization of the company was evaluated as USD 41 billion [6]. In 2016, the company already had 50 million users in 450 cities and 78 countries, and cooperated with 7 million partner-drivers who provided 50-60 million journeys per month, with the net yearly profit of the company reaching USD 6.5 billion and capitalization of USD 48 billion [7]. Having a flexible time-schedule, drivers working with this company provide cheaper services with a better quality, while receiving higher income than the taxi drivers employed on the permanent basis. As the research of the activity of the company Uber in the USA showed, the average hourly pay for the drivers with the company is USD 19, as compared to USD 13 for professional taxi drivers [8]. Such significant difference in the level of income causes changes in the structure of the jobs market, especially considering that, in every segment, companies are formed who follow the ideology of Uber. To name a few, there are such companies as TaskRabbit and Handy (personal and household services), Freelancer and Upwork (business services), Instacart and Postmates (delivery services), Heal and Pager (medical services).

One of the significant consequences of the wide use of digital technologies is the change in the character of work and the structure of employment. The process of "digitalization" not only allows accelerating various processes in the economy as a whole but also provides new possibilities to select the form of organizing own work for representatives of many professions without being tied to the classic scheme "employer-employee". An analysis of the American jobs market showed a significant growth in the number of workers using alternative forms of employment – during the period 2005 to 2015, this share in the total number of employees had grown from 10.1% to 15.8% (14.2 million to 23.6 million employees) [9]. Speaking of the "contingent" workers segment (partially employed, self-employed, freelancers, temporary and unqualified workers), their share in the total number of workers is evaluated at the present as about 40% and is expected to become 50% by 2030 [10]. Obviously, such changes should be considered by businessmen and will affect business activities.

2 Electronic platforms

Quick development of the Internet and the electronic trade stimulated economic research to achieve a better understanding of the economic essence of these processes. In this regard, it should be noted that electronic platforms were found to be the primary element of the forming new system. Despite that economic literature offers various definitions for the term "electronic platform", we will highlight those few that, in our opinion, best describe this new element of the economic system. Firstly, the "two-sided" platforms were examined, whose purpose is ensuring that both parties reduce their expenditures for finding partners and communicating in the process of obtaining profit from trade [11]. In the evolution plane, this definition further developed the approaches previously adopted in the economic literature [12]. Further development of two-sided platforms showed that such basic functions of theirs as minimizing expenses, creating "public sites" and finding business partners tend to expand. As a result of such development, more complicated multi-scale platforms were created, with two basic characteristics: to enable direct communication between two or more parties, with each party having a direct connection with the platform [13]. In 2015, the European Commission gave the following definition for multi-scale platforms (citation): "the Commission proposes a definition of online platforms: an undertaking operating in two (or multi)-sided markets , which uses the Internet to enable interactions between two or more distinct but interdependent groups of users so as to generate value for at least one of the groups. Certain platforms also qualify as intermediary service providers" [14]. As the latest definition for the term "electronic platform" is a result of a certain consensus in the international expert community, we will base of this definition.

At the present moment, there is a wide variety of on-line platforms in the market, differing in the intensity of their activity, the chosen sector of business and the business models they use. For example, we can highlight platforms dealing in joint economic activity (Crowdcube, AirBnB, Uber, BlaBlaCar) or market interactions on-line (eBay, Booking.com, Asos, Allegro, Amazon). There are also search engines (Google, Yahoo, Bing) and social networks (Facebook, Twitter), platforms to exchange video (Dailymotion, Vimeo, YouTube), music and video platforms (Deezer, Spotify, Netflix, Canal Play), on-line gaming (Steam). A legitimate result of such growing variety of platforms is changing the business models for companies, which caused some scholars to characterize such transformation as "platform-based companies" and, according to an evaluation for 2016, there were 135 companies with the capitalization above USD 1 billion and the total volume of capitalization USD 3.7 trillion [15]. A particular feature of the companies who chose electronic platforms to be the basic drivers of their business is quite a fast speed of capitalization, which is confirmed by the data presented in Table 1.

Table 1. Comparative dynamics of indexes for the companies that use E-platforms and those that do not [15]

Company	Founded in	Number of employees	Market capitalization, USD billion
BMW	1916	116,000	53.0
Uber	2009	7,000	60.0
Marriott	1927	200,000	17.0
Airbnb	2008	5,000	21.0
Walt Disney	1923	185,000	165.0
Facebook	2004	12,691	315.0
Kodak	1888	145 000	30.0
Instagram	2010	13	1.0

It is noteworthy, that in this table the capitalization for the company Kodak is indicated for its best period, and this company no longer exists. For Instagram its capitalization is for 2012, when it was sold for USD 1 billion; according to the latest data, its capitalization for the year 2017 was evaluated as USD 50 billion [16].

The Organization for Economic Co-operation & Development (OECD) listed the following basic economic functions of electronic platforms [17]:

– providing the infrastructure for customers and businesses to promote communication and decrease the cost of transactions;

– collecting, classifying and evaluating information – both for business and customers to decrease the cost of searching;

– promoting social communication and information exchange – to provide customer feed-back;

– ensuring the offer-demand balance – to ensure availability of a wider variety of more relevant goods and better access to the market;

– promoting market processes for better competition between offers due to a wider choice, a better relevance or lower price.

In a recent research prepared for Google, one of the key characteristic of platforms is highlighted – decreasing the asymmetry of information and the possibility to eliminate the price discrimination [18].

Electronic platforms are becoming a more and more important element of the world economy covering more and more sectors – from trade and industry to medical services, culture and education. For example, one of the largest market participants who created possibilities for direct exchange of commodities and information for 35 million legal entities, the company Alibaba Group, in 2012 alone, carried out trade transactions amounting to USD 170 billion. Another company – Dhgate, who also operates on electronic platforms only, trades in 30 million items of commodities in 227 countries for 5 million customers. The company TradeKey exclusively specializes in "connecting" suppliers and customers from 200 countries [19]. Wide possibilities for business are provided by the platforms using block-chain technologies, especially in the bank sector and trade of Crypto currency [20]. The possibilities of platform will be growing, especially considering development of new and innovative technologies – cloud calculations, methods of collecting and processing large volumes of data, quantum calculations.

3 Electronic platforms and jobs markets

A wide variety of platforms provides possibilities for diversifying not only the forms of business but also new forms of communication between employers and workers. The most important qualitative change is the possibility for self-employment, like, for example, for driver-partners with the company Uber; another example is the Italian company CoContest specializing in design of interiors [21]. A special review prepared by the European Trade Unions Institute highlights the following cardinal changes that can greatly influence the situation in the jobs market in the conditions of a wide use of electronic platforms [22]:

– flexible possibilities provided by platforms in respect of adapting and re-organizing traditional relationships between employers and workers, for example, in such form as self-employment;

– remote services, which can potentially lead to off-shoring such services and changing local jobs markets;

– possibility to increase competition due to eliminating barriers, which will definitely affect the conditions of work and payment;

– decreased entrance barriers promote weakening physical barriers between the working and home environment, which can bring risks for health and the moral climate;

– reputation mechanisms used by platforms promote development of the jobs market itself;

– platforms can promote differentiation between types of works depending on their character, to separate between the creative and skilled works and the unskilled works;

– platforms can introduce instability due to non-standard or fake employment.

In a recently published research by Oxford Internet Institute [23] there is a summary of the experience gained by some companies on the Fortune 500 list on hiring freelancers through electronic platforms. It is noted that the primary reasons why companies turn to the services provided by platforms are as follows:

– a relatively easy access to a wide jobs market;

– lower cost of transaction;

– shorter time to make contracts at reasonable prices and with good quality of works.

The research also notes that, during 2016 and 2017, the number of projects obtained through these platforms has grown by 26%, the most of them being for such works as: software development, design, texts writing and editing.

Electronic platforms as a new element of the economic system is differently comprehended by new businesses and those who have a long history of work in traditional markets. This, in particular, was confirmed by a research dealing with development of platforms and businesses [24]. It notes the importance to support co-ordination between information systems of the companies and the electronic platforms. As this co-ordination requires certain investment, the companies using traditional forms of doing business are very reluctant in taking such solutions. On the other hand, new companies devote less attention to financial risks, with the focus on finding new and reliable partners.

4 Conclusion

Electronic platforms greatly accelerate economic processes and can ensure high de-centralization of decision-making on the part of customers and manufacturers. Essentially, a new type economy is being born to function on new architectural principles. As yet, electronic platforms are mainly directed towards service providing, but it can be expected that processing industry will undergo significant structural changes as the platforms are developed. In this regard, finding new forms of co-operation between business and employees is becoming a topical scientific and practical task. The approaches described in this article summarize the accumulated experience. However, more complicated tasks still remain to be solved, including these two key tasks:

– decreasing the asymmetry of information and price discrimination can promote quicker development of business;

– creating a new type of employer-employee relations based on digital platforms and directed not only to development of business but also to protection of social and economic interests of employees.

References

1. McKinsey Global Institute, Digital Globalization: The New Era Of Global Flows [online], Available at: http://www.mckinsey.com/business-functions/digital-mckinsey/our-insights/digital-globalization-the-new-era-of-global-flows (2016)
2. J. Constine, Facebook now has 2 billion monthly users…and responsibility [online], Available at: https://techcrunch.com/2017/06/27/facebook-2-billion-users/ (2017)
3. K.C. Laudon, The Future of Global and North American E-commerce 2006-2011 [online], Available at: https://www.cti.gov.br/sites/default/files/slides_the_future_of_global_and_north_american_e-commerce.pdf (2006)
4. Worldwide Retail and Ecommerce Sales: eMarketer's Estimates for 2016–2021. eMarketer Report eMarketer [online], Available at: https://www.emarketer.com/Report/Worldwide-Retail-Ecommerce-Sales-eMarketers-Estimates-20162021/2002090 (2017)

5. UPS Pulse of the Online Shopper. A customer experience. A UPS Consultation paper. Europe Study. [online], Available at: https://www.ups.com/media/en/gb/OnlineComScoreWhitepaper.pdf (2015)
6. G. Petropoulos, Policy Contribution, **5** (2017)
7. 90 Amazing Uber statistics [online], Available at: https://expandedramblings.com/index.php/uber-statistics/
8. J.V. Hall, A. B. Krueger, An Analysis of the Labor Market for Uber's Driver-Partners in the United States [online], Available at: https://s3.amazonaws.com/uber-static/comms/PDF/Uber_Driver-Partners_Hall_Kreuger_2015.pdf (2015)
9. L.F. Katz, A.B. Krueger, The Rise and Nature of Alternative Work Arrangements in the United States, 1995-2015 [online], Available at: http://www.nber.org/papers/w22667.pdf (2016)
10. C. Vollmer, Network Technology Revolution [online], Available at: http://jobenomicsblog.com/wp-content/uploads/2014/11/Network-Technology-Revolution-7-Nov-20141.pdf (2014)
11. D. S. Evans, R. Schmalensee, Competition Policy International, **3(1)** (2007)
12. J.C. Rochet, J. Tirole, Two-Sided Markets: An Overview [online], Available at: http://web.mit.edu/14.271/www/rochet_tirole.pdf (2004)
13. A. Hagiu, J. Wright, *Multi-Sided Platforms* (Harvard Business School, Harvard, 2015)
14. Consultation on Regulatory environment for platforms, online intermediaries, data and cloud computing and the collaborative economy'. European Commission [online], Available at: https://ec.europa.eu/digital-single-market/en/news/results-public-consultation-regulatory-environment-platforms-online-intermediaries-data-and (2015)
15. M. Van Alstyne, Platform Shift: How New Biz Models Are Changing the Shape of Industry [online], Available at: http://chairgovreg.fondation-dauphine.fr/sites/chairgovreg.fondation-dauphine.fr/files/attachments/161103_Van%20Alstyne_Marshall.pdf (2015)
16. V. S. Chauhan, FB Stock: Facebook Inc. (FB) Owned Instagram Could Be Worth Over $50 Billion [online], Available at: https://amigobulls.com/articles/2017-04-18-fb-stock-facebook-inc-fb-owned-instagram-could-be-worth-over-50-billion (2017)
17. The economic and social role of Internet intermediaries. OECD [online], Available at: https://www.oecd.org/internet/ieconomy/44949023.pdf (2010)
18. Benefits of online platforms. www.oxera.com [online], Available at: https://www.oxera.com/getmedia/84df70f3-8fe0-4ad1-b4ba-d235ee50cb30/The-benefits-of-online-platforms-main-findings-(October-2015).pdf.aspx?ext=.pdf (2015)
19. S. Sharif, Top 10 B2B Platforms to Help your Business Grow Worldwide [online], Available at: https://www.digitaldoughnut.com/articles/2017/july/b2b-platforms-to-help-your-business-grow-globally (2017)
20. K. Shiba, Newsletter, **3** (2017)
21. I. Maselli., B. Fabo, Digital workers by design? An example from the on-demand economy, CEPS Working Document 414, Brussels, Centre for European Policy Studies [online], Available at: https://ideas.repec.org/p/eps/cepswp/11030.html (2015)
22. J. Drahokoupil, B. Fabo, ETUI Policy Brief, **5** (2016)
23. G. F. Corporaal, V. Lehdonvirta, Platform Sourcing. How Fortune 500 Firms Are Adopting Online Freelancing Platforms. Oxford Internet Institute. University of Oxford [online], Available at: https://www.oii.ox.ac.uk/publications/platform-sourcing.pdf (2017)

24. D. Truong, M. Bhuiyan, Journal of Entrepreneurship, **13** (2009)

Simulating combustion processes based on digital technologies

Marsel Kadyrov[1], *Maria* Khabarova[1], *Alexander* Khabarov[1], and *Alexei* Trinchenko[1*],

[1] Peter the Great St. Petersburg Polytechnic University, Institute of Power Engineering and Transportation Systems, 195251, Politechnicheskaya st., 29, Russian Federation

Abstract. The thermal power plants (TPP) make a basis of power-generation industry of the majority of countries. The global growth of power consumption and the policy of energy-saving demand to increase the efficiency of plants operation, which is, among others, determined by the technical level of steam-generating units. The up-to-date digital technologies make it possible to assess the efficiency of boiler furnace operation at the stage of boiler unit designing, its reconstruction or retrofitting and upgrading. Developed in the article are the algorithm, mathematic model and computer program of calculating diffusion-kinetic process of combustion of D-grade Donetsk coal in the coal-dust flame of boiler E-230-14,0-520. The assigned tasks have been solved by using theoretical methods of analysis, the capabilities of devices of computer-aided calculations have utilized for visualization of results. The considered digital approach to solving technical tasks makes it possible to meet the current and future challenges.

1 Introduction

The goal of the energy policy of country according to the energy strategy of Russia for the period up to 2030 is the maximum efficient use of natural energy resources and potential of the energy sector for steady economic growth, increase of quality of life of the country's population and contribution to strengthening its foreign-economic solutions.

The thermal power plants (TPP) make a basis of power-generation industry of Russia with the share in the structure of the installed power of the industry as of 2017 equal to 58.6 %. The share of TPP operated on coal equals 27.5 %. The efficiency of TPP operation depends to a great extent on the technical level of the main equipment, to which the steam boilers belong too.

One of the priority principles of building the power industry of future is the concept of Internet of Energy (EnergyNet), which is on the agenda of the National Technological Initiative of Russia (NTI). The new capabilities of the power industry of future are determined, among others, by such NTI direction as digital designing and simulation. It is necessary to secure the efficient energy generation apart from building reliable and flexible networks. Building of design calculations for plants equipment with the use of exclusively standard methods downloads a definite uncertainty into result of designing, when

* Corresponding author: trinchenko@spbstu.ru

simulation with the use of digital technologies makes it possible to more accurately predict the efficiency of units operation. Most frequently the description of some physical processes is replaced with a number of correction factors. The insufficient consideration of the problem of fuel combustion process in polifraction flame of the steam power-generating boiler at the stage of designing can bring about in practice an excessive consumption of fuel, for instance, caused by mechanical underburning and, as a result, it entails the price growth for electric energy for consumers. Otherwise, the uprating of heat losses from mechanical underburning will cause a growth of capital expenditures.

The burning process will be determined by complex physical and chemical phenomena [1, 2] related to fuel burning in the furnace chamber of steam boiler. A process of forming a mixture of fuel and oxidizer is attributed to the main physical processes accompanying conversion of fuel internal energy into heat. The temperature and concentration of reacting substances belong to chemical factors exercising key influence on the fuel burning parameters. The complex fields of velocities, concentrations and temperatures can be observed in the furnace devices of steam, which determine in combination the kinetics of chemical transformations.

The purpose of the work is the investigation of process of combustion of particles of D-grade Donetsk coal in the coal-dust flame of boiler E-230-14.0-520.

The following problems have been considered and solved in the process of investigation:

• Model and methods of determining velocities of gas and air flows in the steam boiler furnace chamber have been developed. The characteristic flow zones and the resulting field of velocities have been determined, which utilization is possible for calculating paths of movement of burning coke particles of a variable mass. The model helps obtain vector $\vec{W}$ in any point of furnace chamber and close the balance of flow rates in the cross sections of along coordinate axes.

• Taking into account the process stage character, the burning of coal particles of polifraction fuel moving in the flow of gases has been calculated, the paths of movement thereof in the furnace have been acquired;

• Dependences of changing size, density and mass of coal particles vs. time have been determined;

• Assessments of fuel mechanical underburning have been carried out.

2 Model of flame burning in boiler furnace

A model of burning process based on the diffusion and kinetic theory of burning is capable of changing quality (solid fuel type and composition, its grind, etc.) and quantity characteristics of the process (fuel consumption, velocity of burner air, etc.) making it possible to perform analysis of duration of individual stages of combustion process as well as quantitative evaluation of mechanical incompleteness of fuel burning in the furnace chamber.

A profound understanding of burning processes in power-generating units is required for practical calculations of the burning process at its different stages. In order to solve the problem of solid fuel particle burning, a definite process schematization has been adopted. The process is broken into relatively independent stages: particle heating until volatile matter yields or gets ignited, combustion of volatile matter around particle and combustion of residual coke consisting of carbon and ash. The stage of coke carbon burning is the most durable for coal dust and makes up to 90% of total time of particle burning.

The duration of initial stages is determined with respect to empirical-formula dependences suggested by V. I. Babiy [3]:

$$\tau_{пр} = -0.384 \cdot \frac{c_ч \cdot \rho_ч \cdot \delta^2}{\mathrm{Nu} \cdot \lambda_г} \cdot \lg\left(1 - Q/Q_{max}\right)$$
$$\tau_{в.л.} = k_{в.л.} \cdot 5.3 \cdot 10^{14} \cdot T_г^{-4} \delta^{0.8} \quad , \qquad (1)$$
$$\tau_{г.л.} = k_{г.л.} \cdot 0.5 \cdot 10^6 \cdot \delta^2$$

where, $c_ч$ – specific heat capacity of fuel dry mass, kJ/(kg·K); $\rho_ч$ – initial particle density, kg/m^3; δ – size of particle of fraction under consideration, m; Nu – thermal Nusselt criterion; $\lambda_г$ – heat conductivity, kW/(m·K); Q/Q_{max} – ratio of amount of heat absorbed by a particle to the amount maximum possible at this gas temperature; $T_г$ – gas flow temperature, K; $k_{в.л.}$, $k_{г.л.}$ – trial coefficients.

Determination of gas temperature level by height of the boiler furnace chamber E-230-14.0-520 (Fig. 1) has been carried out with the use of dependence suggested by A. M. Gurvich and A. G. Blokh. The temperature level variation by furnace height features a characteristic view (Fig. 2), and is described by the following dependence:

$$\theta(z) = \frac{\alpha}{\beta - \alpha}\left(e^{-\alpha z} - e^{-\beta z}\right), \qquad (2)$$

where, z – relative distance from fuel inlet point; α = 22.78, β = 0.85 – calculated parameters characterizing, accordingly, the intensity of heat radiation in case of fuel burning out and intensity of heat transfer to heating surfaces [4].

The combustion of coke carbon is a heterogeneous process determined by both kinetics of carbon particle burning and diffusion transfer of oxygen and combustion products. The result of simultaneous character of these processes is a definite distribution of concentrations of oxygen and combustion products at the burning surface.

In order to solve the problem of carbon particle burning, a concept of "reduced film", an area of strongly pronounced gradients of concentrations has been applied. The main types of gas reacting with the coke carbon include oxygen (O_2), carbon dioxide (CO) and water steam (H_2O). According to [5] the following basic resultant reactions take place at the particle external surface and at the surface of pores (thermal effect in kJ/mole):

heterogeneous

with "dry" gasification	with "wet" gasification
1.	3′.
$C+O_2=CO_2+394.6$	$C+H_2O=CO+H_2-130.4$
2.	3″.
$2C+O_2=2CO+219.6$	$C+2H_2O=CO_2+2H_2-132$
3.	3‴.
$C+CO_2=2CO-175.6$	$C+2H_2=CH_4-74.8$

homogeneous

4.	4′.
$CO+O_2=2CO_2+570.2$	$2H_2+O_2=2H_2O+231.5$
	4″.
	$CH_4+2O_2=CO_2+2H_2O+891$
	4‴.
	$CO+H_2O=CO_2+H_2+40.4$

A scheme with the non-burning boundary layer is characteristic for the coal-dust fuel burning, when the diffusion processes only take place within the limits of a given film, while the oxide of carbon and hydrogen being generated as a result of carbon interaction with water steam and oxygen go beyond the boundaries of the given film and burn in the gas flow. A characteristic pattern of distribution of concentrations of reacting components at the surface of burning carbon particle is shown in Fig. 3.

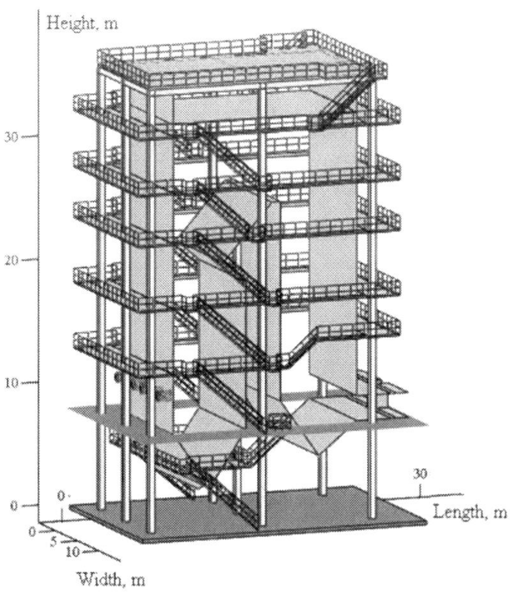

Fig. 1. Design model of boiler E-230-14.0-520

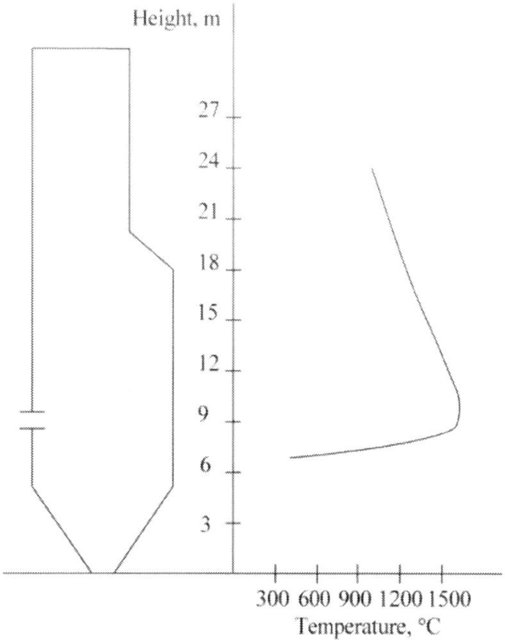

Fig. 2. Distribution of temperature (T) by height of furnace chamber (H)

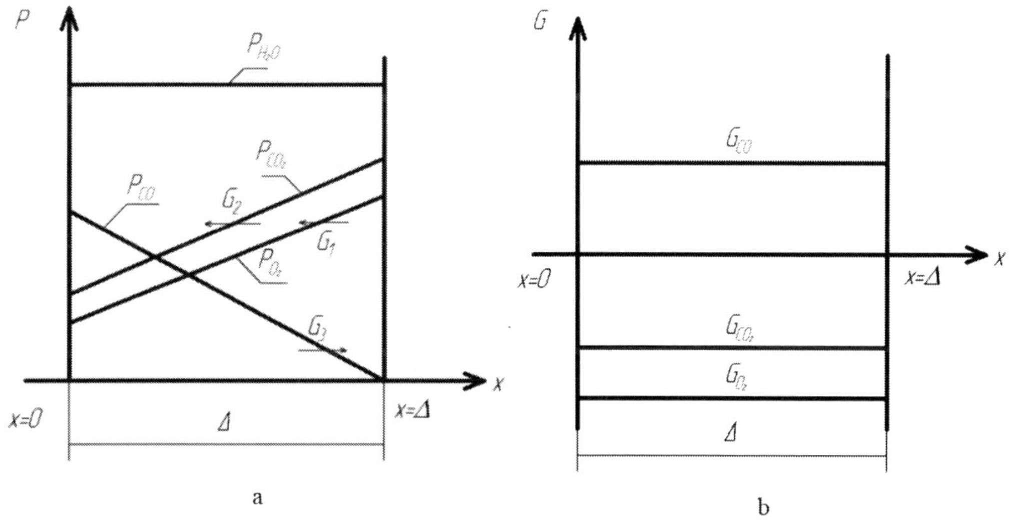

Fig. 3. Distribution of partial pressures (a) and flows (b) of components in a given film

The rate of carbon burning out taking into consideration the stoichiometric relationships (actual reactions):

$$G_c = 1/(RT)[(k_1 + 2k_2)p_{10} + k_3 p_{20} + k_{3'} p_{50}], \tag{3}$$

where, R = 8.31 J/(kmole·K) – universal gas constant value; T – temperature by height of furnace chamber, K; k_i– constant rate of i-reaction, p_{i0} – pressure of i-component at particle surface, kPa.

The variation of constant values of chemical reactions rate vs. temperature conforms to Arrhenius dependence:

$$k_i = k_{0i} \cdot exp[-E_i/(RT)], \tag{4}$$

where, k_0 – pre-exponential factor of Arrhenius dependence (in m/s for heterogeneous and 1/s for homogeneous reactions); E – apparent activation energy, J/mole.

In order to calculate a link of activation and pre-exponential factor, a “pole” suggested by S.M. Shestakov was used:

$$lgk_{0i} = 0.2 \cdot 10^{-4} \cdot E_i + 2. \tag{5}$$

The consideration of combustion process from the diffusion-kinetic positions helped compile a system of differential equations, which solution are the sought-for values in the expression for carbon flow from the fuel particle surface (G_c):

$$\begin{cases} dG_1 = -k_{4'}/(RT)p_1 dx \\ dG_1 = -D/(RT)d^2 p_1/(dx^2)dx, \\ dG_4 = dG_1 = -2dG_5 \end{cases} \tag{6}$$

where, G_i – flow of i-component, kmole/(m^2/s); $k_{4'}$ – constant value of reaction rate 4'; p_i – pressure of i-component, kPa; D – diffusion coefficient, m^2/s.

Variation of particle size in time (burning out) will be determined by formula [6]:

$$\frac{d\delta_1}{d\tau} = -\frac{2 \cdot M}{\rho_\kappa} \cdot G_c, \tag{7}$$

where, M = 12 kg/kmole – carbon molar mass; ρ_κ = 900 kg/m^3 – coke density.

Processing of screening curve of design fuel (Fig. 4) has helped acquire sizes of particles, quality thereof, mass and initial surface area for every fraction. The distribution of particles between fractions is determined according to formula of Rosin-Rammler:

$$R_{0i} = exp(-b \cdot \delta_{0i}^n), \tag{8}$$

where, b – experimental factor characterizing the grind fineness; n – polydispersity indicator characterizing uniformity of grain distribution.

In the process of combustion of fuel particles, in addition to changing the size, the density changes and, as a consequence, the mass changes too. The mass changes due to the changed density of particle at the stages of particle heating (before yield and ignition of volatile matter) and burning of volatile matter near particle. After beginning of particle burning out the density is considered permanent and equal to the density of coke, while the mass change takes place due to changing size of coal dust particle. The described character of changing characteristics for particles with size of 300 μm is shown in Fig. 5.

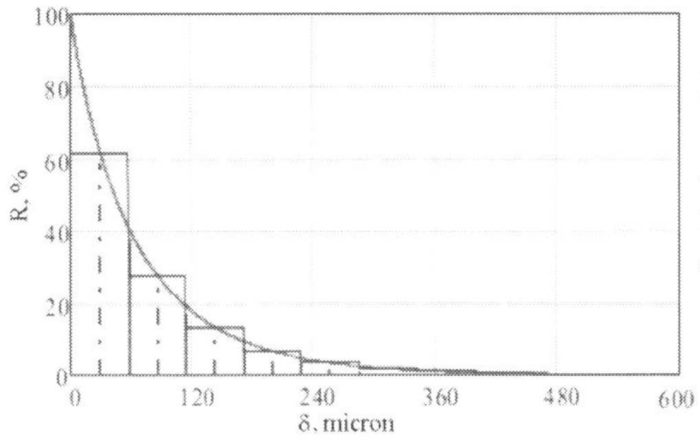

Fig. 4. Results of processing dust grain-size characteristic

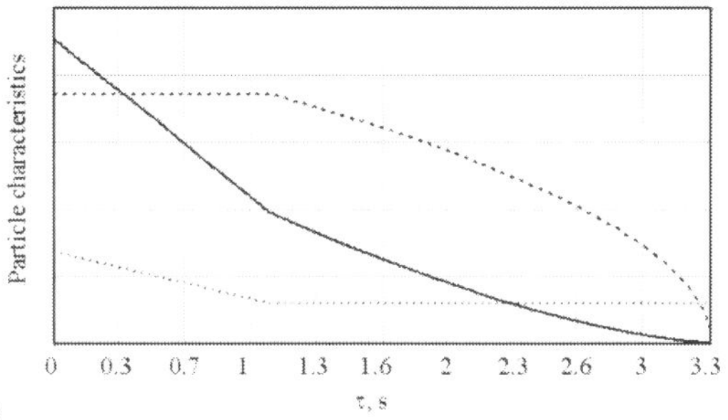

Fig. 5. Variation of mass (—), density (·····), size (-----) of particle in time (δ_0 = 300 μm)

In order to calculate paths of motion of coal reacting particles, it is necessary to define the vector field of velocities of gas and air mixture in the steam boiler furnace chamber. The aerodynamics of combustion process determines conditions of fuel interaction with oxidizer. The purpose of calculating burning process is quite complex. A plane flow pattern has been adopted in this work with introduction of random distortion along the third coordinate. The initial area is being considered as a free immersed jet, its design dependences are shown in [5]. The upflow axis is S-shaped. As a result of uniting areas the vector field of velocities of gas and air flows in the section of furnace chamber has been obtained (Fig. 6).

In the course of particles moving in the gas flow it is customary to single out individual, the most significant factors: force of aerodynamic drag and gravity force of a particle [7-9]. Taking into account the variable mass for the flat pattern, it is possible to put down the equation of reacting particles movement in projections on the axis of 2D rectangular coordinate system [5]:

$$\begin{cases} \dfrac{dmv_x}{d\tau} = \dfrac{c \cdot f \cdot \rho_г}{2} \cdot (w_x - v_x) \cdot \sqrt{(w_x - v_x)^2 + (w_y - v_y)^2} \\ \dfrac{dmv_y}{d\tau} = \dfrac{c \cdot f \cdot \rho_г}{2} \cdot (w_y - v_y) \cdot \sqrt{(w_x - v_x)^2 + (w_y - v_y)^2} - m \cdot g \end{cases} \quad (9)$$

where, V and W – velocity of particle and gas flow, m/s; m, f – accordingly, mass and frontal area of a particle, kg and m^2; $\rho_г$ – gas flow density, kg/m^3; $c = f(\mathrm{Re})$ – coefficient of resistance of burning particles is calculated according to expression:

$$c(\mathrm{Re}) = \begin{cases} 24/\mathrm{Re} & when\ \mathrm{Re}<1 \\ 24/\mathrm{Re} + 4/\sqrt[3]{\mathrm{Re}} & when\ 1 \le \mathrm{Re} \le 10^3 \\ 0,48 & when\ 2 \cdot 10^4 \le \mathrm{Re} \le 2 \cdot 10^5 \end{cases} \quad (10)$$

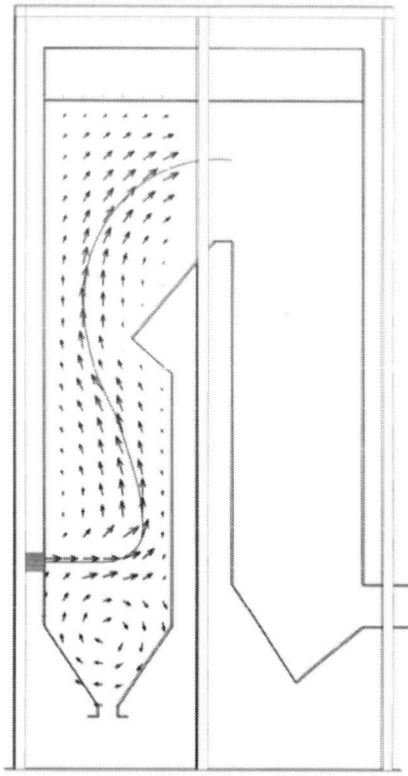

Fig. 6. Velocity vectors in boiler furnace E-230-14.0-520

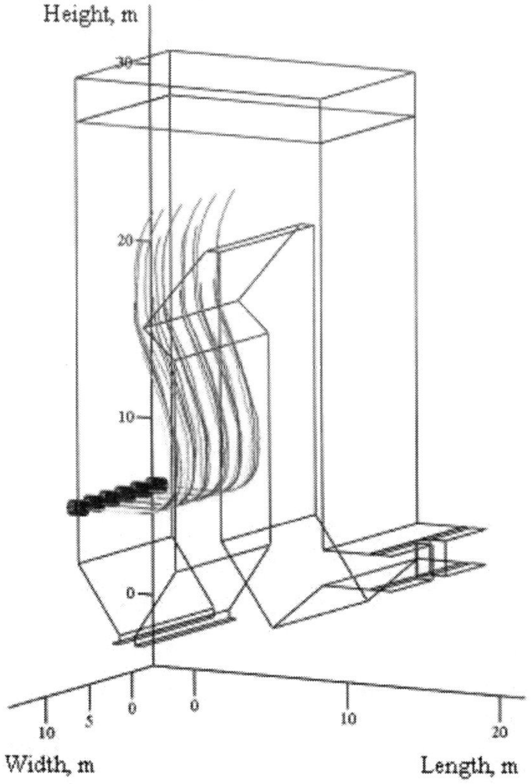

Fig. 7. Paths of motion of burning particles in boiler furnace E-230-14.0-520

System (9) with the known field of velocities is solved by means of a numerical method implemented in the environment of computer mathematic simulation. The paths of motion of reacting particles of characteristic sizes have been obtained as a result of calculations (Fig. 7).

3 Digital designing of burning process

The technologies utilizing computation equipment make it possible to give consideration to power engineering problems in more profound detailed manner with the use of a significant volume of iteration calculations. The detailed review of production processes at the stage of designing provides for a possibility of more precise (as compared with the use of absolutely standard methods) prediction of plant equipment operation indicators and, as a result, reduces capital investments, in future it will provide for reliable power supply of the consumers.

The economical efficiency of TPP operation, as the generating basis of the present-day power engineering of the world, determines macro scale conditions for full-scale permanent development of production facilities. The variable plant's expenditures get determined by fuel consumption and directly influence the economic indicators of its operation. When making thermal calculations of the boiler unit, a loss of heat from fuel mechanical underburning (q_4) is adopted according to standard method of thermal design of boiler units. The value q_4 = 1% has been adopted for the case under consideration.

The numerical determination of q_4 can be performed with the use of dependences to calculate coal particle burning out. The coke mechanical underburning calculated for 1 kg of fuel (G) can be determined for pulverized-coal flame according to formula:

$$G = \frac{q_4}{100} \cdot \frac{Q_н^р}{Q_к}, \tag{11}$$

where, $Q_к = 8100$ kCal/kg – coke combustion heat.

On the other hand G can be presented as:

$$G = K^p \cdot \int_{(\delta_{0i})_\tau}^{\delta_{01}} b \cdot n \cdot \delta_{0i}^{n-1} \cdot e^{-b \cdot \delta_{0i}^n} \left(\delta_i / \delta_{0i}\right)^3 d\delta_{0i}, \tag{12}$$

where, $K^р$ – relative contents of coke in as-received fuel; δ_{0i} and δ_i – initial and current size of particle of i-fraction, m; δ_{01} – initial size of the most coarse particle, m; $(\delta_{0i})_\tau$ – initial size of particle fully burnt by the moment of time τ, at the end of which the particles continue to burn with the initial size exceeding $(\delta_{0i})_\tau$, m; R_{0i} – relative mass content (balance on a sieve) of particles with size equal or exceeding δ_{0i}, in the initial dust.

Thus, the value of q_4 will be determined according to dependence:

$$q_4 = K^p \cdot \int_{(\delta_{0i})_\tau}^{\delta_{01}} b \cdot n \cdot \delta_{01}^{n-1} \cdot e^{-b \cdot \delta_{01}^n} \left(\frac{\delta_1}{\delta_{01}}\right)^3 d\delta_{0i} \cdot \frac{Q_к}{Q_н^р} \cdot 100. \tag{13}$$

Integral (12) s admissible with respect to the initial size of the biggest particle, which according to [5] can be determined by the formula:

$$\delta_{01} = (6.9 / b)^{1/n}. \tag{14}$$

The value δ_{01} corresponds to mesh size of such a sieve, where the balance equals 0.1% of the mass of pulverized coal, i.e. when $R_{01} = 0.1\%$.

In order to determine q_4 according to provided algorithm, a computer program has been developed, which helps perform numerical evaluations of the amount of fuel mechanical underburning.

4 Conclusive provisions and findings

The up-to-date digital approaches to solving technical problems due to application of significant computational facilities make it possible to expand, deepen the spectrum of problem consideration. The results acquired by means of simulation reveal a more precise process pattern. Suchlike methods of investigation contribute to building a new generation of facilities bringing the human resources and, as a result, a possibility of occurrence of random errors to minimum at the stage of equipment designing. In this case, the accuracy of calculation results increases as much as the processes get studied with more details.

The simulation of polifractional solid fuel burning in the furnace chamber of boiler E-230-14.0-520 has shown that the value of mechanical underburning adopted when making thermal design exceeds the design value by 0.5%. It determines an increased fuel consumption and reduction of efficiency in the design boiler calculation. With the adopted value of mechanical underburning: $\eta = 92.33$ %, $B = 38.2$ t/h; with calculated: $\eta = 92.83$ %, $B = 38.0$ t/h.

Thus, the developed model makes it possible to define more exactly the unit design characteristics and can be used both in the course of building new boilers, and during reconstruction and retrofitting, and upgrading thereof too. The calculation results conform properly to experimental data, which helps use the presented model for investigating the process of burning of hard organic fuel in case of its flame combustion.

References

1. A. Vasilyev, V. Lozhkin , D. Tarkhov , O. Lozhkina, V. Timofeev, IOP Conf. Ser.: J. Phys.: Conf. Ser., **919** (2017)
2. J. Kaikko, A. Mankonen, E. Vakkilainen, V. Sergeev, Energy Procedia, **120** (2017)
3. V. Babiy, V. Kuvaev, *Combustion of coal dust and calculation of coal-fired torch* (1986)
4. M. Khabarova, A. Trinchenko, Proc."Science week SPbSPU", **1** (2016)
5. V. Pomerantsev, K. Arefyev, D. Akhmedov, *Basis of the practical theory of burning* (1986)
6. M. Khabarova, M. Kadyrov, A. Trinchenko, Proc. "Science and innovations in technical universities" (2017)
7. A. Trinchenko, A. Paramonov, M. Kadyrov, A. Koryabkin, IOP Conf. Ser.: Earth Environ. Sci., **90** (2017)
8. A. Trinchenko, A. Paramonov, IOP Conf. Ser.: Earth Environ. Sci., **90** (2017)
9. A. Trinchenko, A. Paramonov, V. Skouditskiy, R. Anoshin, IOP Conf. Ser.: J. Phys.: Conf. Ser., **891** (2017)

Estimation of applicability of modern neural network methods for preventing cyberthreats to self-organizing network infrastructures of digital economy platforms [a,b]

Maxim Kalinin[1*], *Vasiliy* Krundyshev[1], and *Evgeny* Zubkov[1]

[1] Peter the Great St.Petersburg Polytechnic University, Department of Information security of computer systems, 195251, Politechnicheskaya st., 29, Russian Federation

Abstract. The problems of applying neural network methods for solving problems of preventing cyberthreats to flexible self-organizing network infrastructures of digital economy platforms: vehicle adhoc networks, wireless sensor networks, industrial IoT, "smart buildings" and "smart cities" are considered. The applicability of the classic perceptron neural network, recurrent, deep, LSTM neural networks and neural networks ensembles in the restricting conditions of fast training and big data processing are estimated. The use of neural networks with a complex architecture– recurrent and LSTM neural networks – is experimentally justified for building a system of intrusion detection for self-organizing network infrastructures.

1 Introduction

Digitalization and Internetization of economy have specified a new problem – the problem of cyberthreats having active and destructive impact on automated and connected cyberphysical systems and, through them, on entire network infrastructure. The object of protection previously understood as a combination of data with limited access obtains new representation as an element of cyberspace where traditional operations of reading/writing have physical consequences. Cyberthreats impacting the modern infrastructure of digital economy platforms – communications of unmanned transport, wireless sensor networks of digital industry, industrial IoT, "smart buildings", and "smart cities" – are dangerous because

[a] With financial support from the Ministry of Education and Science of the Russian Federation within the framework of the Federal Special Purpose Program "Studies and projects in the priority fields of development of the scientific technological complex of Russia for 2014-2020" (Agreement 14.575.21.0131 of September 26, 2017, 09.2017, unique identifier RFMEFI57517X0131).
[b] The results of the work were obtained with the use of computing resources of the super-computer center of Peter the Great St. Petersburg Polytechnic University – Super-Computer Center "Politekhnichesky" (http://www.spbstu.ru).
[*] Corresponding author: sci@ibks.spbstu.ru

they carry a threat not so much for data as for the work of devices, executive subsystems, physical processes and, further, for resources, finances, ecology. and people life.

Self-organizing network infrastructures (for example, VANET – a network among connected cars, FANET – a network between flighting facilities, MARINET – a network between floating crafts, WSN – wireless sensor networks, IIoT – industrial Internet of Things) have peer-to-peer architecture, support multiple links between hosts and dynamic control of routing at each network node that determines their advantages over traditional networks, that is the possibility of multi-line transfer of data to large distances without stationary retranslators, immunity to spacial variations in network topology, dynamic reconfiguration of a network under the conditions of distorting actions and faults [1]. The revealed opportunities have created new conditions for implementing new cyberthreats including bringing equipment out of operation, traps to cyberphysical systems, cyberterrorism on transport and in industry, organizing large-scaled megabotnets of sensor networks, organizing massive failures of unmanned vehicles, digital fabrics, intellectual industrial and smart city systems.

Distribution of cyberthreats to vehicular and industrial network infrastructures is temporarily restrained by minor penetration of inter-machine communications but there are already incidents with industrial networks and autonomous cars which demonstrate their complete unsafety against occured threats (for example, [2]). As introduction of security means into inter-computer network is a complicated procedure due to the peculiarities of networks of such a type (decentralization, dynamics, peer-to-peer character, etc.) and the limitations of computational resources on hosts, active demand for methods of aprior protection is formed. These methods should provide for timely determining of cyberthreats and, therefore, increasing level of protection without interfering network infrastructure. The basis for solving the specified problem is made of different types of artificial neural networks (ANN) which have appeared last decade; including deep ANN, recurrent networks, LSTM networks, and their ensembles.

2 The related works in the field of preventing cyberthreats to self-organizing network infrastructures

The task of any intrusion detection systems (IDS) is detecting a cyberattack according to some indicators [3]. In contemporary self-organizing network infrastructures, the volume of data to be processed rapidly increases; this information should be processed by IDS in real-time. For example, a network consisting of 1000 cyberobjects of digital factory (there is a control bus and about 20 controllers in each cyberobject) generates about 4 million of data sets per minute, which can influent the undercontrolled processes. Big data significantly complicates the task of developing new IDS – so the task of providing their effectiveness and, primarily, their productivity becomes the essential one.

Different approaches to solve the problem of cyberthreats detection are known:

a) statistical approach [3, 4] (a pattern profile of the system is created, then it is being averaged in the process of training, any deviation from the pattern profile is considered to be an intrusion). The disadvantage of this approach is that the intruder may train the system gradually putting the system into the condition that IDS doesn't detect any anomalies;

b) forecasting of the patterns [3, 5] (IDS approximates the profile and predicts the future events basing on the previous ones). However, many of the modern cyberattacks cannot be described by those rules and they will be missed by the detector;

c) artificial neural networks (ANN) [3, 6-8]. The ANN apparatus gives opportunities for parallel processing of data and revealing hidden dependencies and deviations. The process of searching for anomalies consists in selecting significant properties, preparing parameters and training the neural network, at that, a profile of normal activity is formed. During the work, real data is conveyed to the ANN input and the ANN determines their belonging to this or that class. For the ANN ability for training and generalizing, there is an opportunity for predicting and searching for anomalies information about which did not take part in training.

Though neural network methods have been already actively developed for many years, the interest in this field has been lately increasing and this is coused by progress in IT and demand for fast processing of big data which has appeared. ANN provide significant advantages against other methods of adaptive data processing: accounting hidden dependencies in datasets, automatic selection and optimization of significant attributes for object classification that reduces time for developing and implementing methods of data analysis, solving intellectual tasks by approximation of arbitrary functions. Alternative methods of machine learning and data mining don not work with the dependencies directly and have to use heuristic control. The ANN apparatus solves this problem initially by means of parallel distribution of signals. Only ANNs possess the two last features which enable focusing specifically on ANN methods and that makes developments in this field scientifically and practically significant.

3 Investigation of modern neural networks for intrusion detection in self-organizing network infrastructures

Uncertainty of security perimeter of network infrastructure, absence of security means for protecting self-organizing networks, unsuitability of the traditional methods of network protection created for stationary computer networks confirm the necessity of developing special methods and means for objects of the given type on the basis of the approach of detecting cyberthreats.

Traditional ANNs are multilayer perceptrons with logical transferring functions [7], module ANNs of direct and back signal propagation [7]. Being universal and flexible, they still do not satisfy the increased requirements to the volume of training data sets (the problem of saturation on "big data"), have a low coefficient of effectiveness (not higher than 95% in most cases), the time of training is very long, and they are not able to build dependencies of great complexity. Classic ANNs are characterized by extreme redundancy (width and depth of an ANN) and resource intensity (growth of requirements to the volume of the memory and CPU capacity) [8]. For operative control of security of self-organizing network infrastructures compact and fast ANNs are needed.

The classic perceptron of direct signal distribution and actively developing ANNs have been selected for estimation of applicability and correlation of modern ANNs in comparison with traditional ones for solving the problem of detecting cyberthreats aimed at flexible network infrastructures: recurrent ANN [9], deep ANN [10], LSTM neural network [11], and ensemble of neural networks [12]. Program modeling has been carried out for them with the use of the computing capacities of the supercomputer center of Peter the Great St.Petersburg Polytechnic University – SCC "Polytechnichesky". A typical cyberattack was chosen as a test one: "Black Hole" [12] which is aimed at dynamic routing in self-organizing networks, exploits their specific features and there are no solutions for its detection with traditional IDS. The results obtained in the course of training the investigated ANNs are listed in table 1.

Table 1. The results of training the investigated ANNs.

Neural network model	Error (for the training set)	Size of the training/ working set	Training time, s
Perceptron	0.002	22/11	3.9
Recurrent ANN	0.04	4500/1500	44.5
Deep ANN	0.001	22/11	2.2

Neural network model	Error (for the training set)	Size of the training/ working set	Training time, s
LSTM-network	0.04	4500/1500	50.6

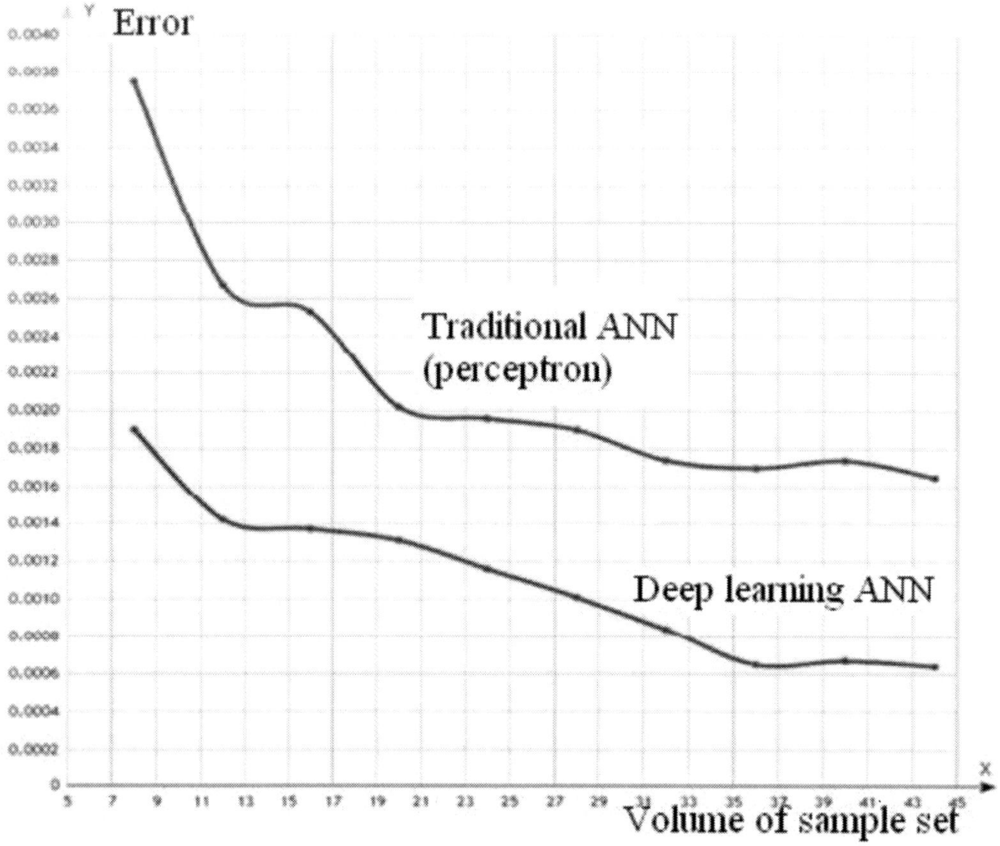

Fig. 1. Dependencies of the error coefficient on the volume of a sample set for perceptron and deep ANN.

ANNs with a simple architecture (perceptron and deep ANN) get a win against modern ANNs with a complex architecture. Parameters of an ANN ensemble were defined as the maximum value of the training time, the maximum value of the error coefficient and the largest set of data which is necessary for training the components of an ANN. Perceptron is not adapted to working with "big data", a recurrent ANN and a deep ANN are not sensitive to "big data" while training. According to the results of modeling, a similarity between the behavior of perceptron and a deep ANN is noted (Fig. 1). When using a set of an analogous size, a deep ANN is trained with a smaller error coefficient, at this, a sharp drop when increasing the set is not observed. Comparing the characteristics of a recurrent ANN and a LSTM network (Fig. 2) demonstrates their similarity, however, a recurrent ANN has a series of drops in the process of training which are missing in the analogous process in an ANN with memory because the latter uses the optimization mechanism – the memory enables locking the result through a feed-back and remembering the conclusions made.

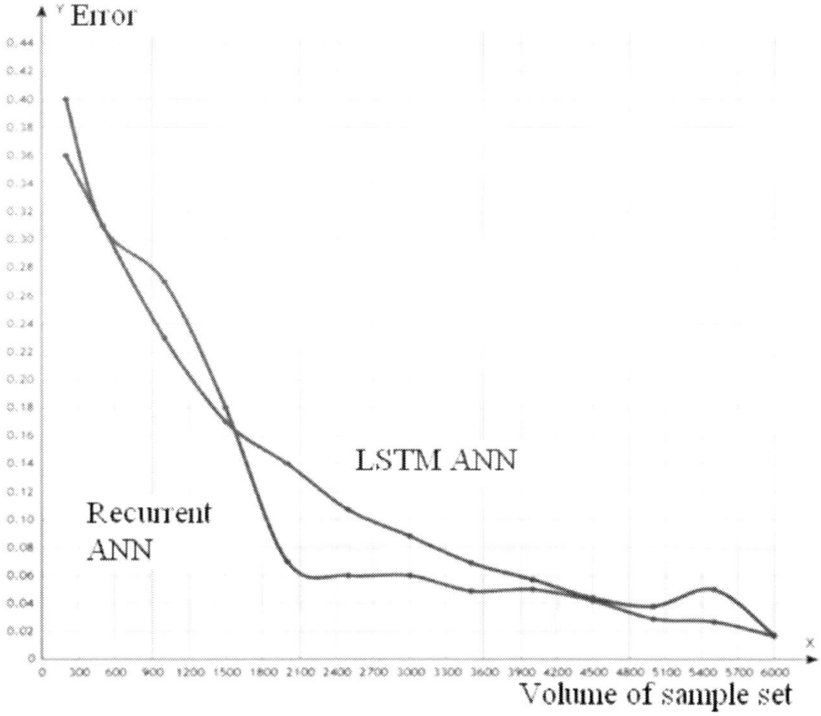

Fig. 2. Dependencies of the error coefficient on the volume of a sample set for recurrent and LSTMnetworks.

Taking into account the sensibility of an ANN to the volume of a sample set during training and taking into account the fact that self-organizing network infrastructures according to their characteristics are the objects in which "big data" about the security of nods will be constantly generated and it is necessary to process them while solving the tasks of detecting cyberthreats, it is necessary to validate ANNs with respect to their readiness to process large datasets because it is one of the main advantages of modern ANNs over traditional ANNs and other detection models. In order to understand how well networks function with a big datasets, for exact comparison, three formulas of calculating the error coefficient are distinguished [13]:

mean squared error (MSE): $\frac{(R_{O_1}-R_{\Pi_1})^2+(R_{O_2}-R_{\Pi_2})^2+\dots+(R_{O_N}-R_{\Pi_N})^2}{N}$;

root mean squared error (Root MSE): $\sqrt{\frac{(R_{O_1}-R_{\Pi_1})^2+(R_{O_2}-R_{\Pi_2})^2+\dots+(R_{O_N}-R_{\Pi_N})^2}{N}}$;

squared arctangent (Arctan): $\frac{\arctan^2(R_{O_1}-R_{\Pi_1})+\arctan^2(R_{O_2}-R_{\Pi_2})+\dots+\arctan^2(R_{O_N}-R_{\Pi_N})}{N}$.

where R_{O/Π_i} is the relation of expected/obtained result, where i is an index, $i = 1, 2, \dots, N$; N is the volume of data which is processed in the ANN. In Table 2 it is shown how ANNs are able to process "big data" (the volume is 4 mln attributes).

Perceptron demonstrates short time of processing but its error on a big dataset is quite large comparing with other ANNs. It is also unstable at the stage of training. A deep ANN is void of this problem at the training stage but at the stage of processing it demonstrates unsatisfactory results as well because ANNs with such architecture are more suitable for the tasks where many resulting responses are predetermined. It is recommended to use modern ANNs with a complicated architecture, recurrent ANNs and their ensembles, for solving the task.

Table 2. Comparison of ANNs for processing "big data".

Neural network model	Error (for the working set)			Processing time, s
	MSE	*Root MSE*	*Arctan*	
Perceptron	0.37	0.61	0.23	2.1
Recurrent ANN	0.01	0.13	0.01	28.8
LSTM-network	0.02	0.14	0.01	27.2
Deep ANN	0.50	0.71	0.31	3.0

4 Conclusion

The experimental results of investigation demonstrate inapplicability of traditional approaches to solving the task . The traditional neural network becomes useless for big data processing in time and resource limitations.. Validating recurrent ANN and LSTM networks shows that complicated modern ANN are able to cope with the task because they apply the mechanisms which optimize their operation (for example, memorization). Efficiency of solving the task can be raised by simultaneous application of several polytypical ANNs forming heterogeneous ensembles of neural networks.

Using new neural network methods will enable building modern systems for detecting intrusions for the first time; they will make it possible to block unauthorized activities in time in flexible self-organizing network infrastructures of digital economy.

Project is financially supported by Ministry of Education and Science of Russian Federation, Federal Program "Researching and Development in Priority Directions of Scientific and Technological Sphere in Russia within 2014-2020" (Contract No. 14.575.21.0131, September 26, 2017, the unique identifier of the agreement RFMEFI57517X0131).

Project results are achieved using the resources of supercomputer center of Peter the Great St.Petersburg Polytechnic University – SCC "Polytechnichesky" (www.spbstu.ru).

References

1. B. Krishna, International Journals of Advanced Research in Computer Science and Software Engineering, **7(7)** (2017)
2. R. Langer. To Kill a Centrifuge [online] Available at: www.langner.com/wp-content/uploads/2017/03/to-kill-a-centrifuge.pdf (2018)
3. M. Erritali, B. El Ouahidi, International Journal of Engineering and Technology, **5(2)** (2013)
4. K. R. Karthikeyan, A. Indra. Intrusion Detection Tools and Techniques – A Survey. International Journal of Computer Theory and Engineering, **2(6)** (2010)
5. X. Li. Probabilistic techniques for intrusion detection based on computer audit data. *IEEE* Transactions on Systems Man and Cybernetics. Part A: Systems and Humans, **31(4)** (2001)
6. S. Sodiya, O. A. Ojesanmi, O. C. Akinola, O. Aborisade, International Journal of Computer Applications, **106 (18)** (2014)
7. M. A. Widrow, Proceedings of the IEEE, **78(9)** (1990)
8. S. Nikolenko, A. Kadurin, E. Arkhangelskaya, *Deep education. Immersion into the world of neural networks (*"Piter" Publishing House, Saint Petersburg, 2018)
9. A. Mallya. *Introduction to RNNs* [online] Available at: *http://slazebni.cs.illinois.edu/spring17/lec02_rnn.pdf* (2018)
10. V. Sze, Y. H. Chen, T. J. Yang, J. S. Emer, Proceedings of the IEEE, **105(12)** (2017)

11. R. Adhikari, R. K. Agrawal, International Journal of Computer Applications, **32 (7)** (2011)
12. N. K. Chaubey, International Journal of Security and Its Applications, **10(5)** (2016)
13. M. V. Shcherbakov, A. Brebels, N. L. Shcherbakova, A. P. Tyukov, T. A. Janovsky, V. A. Kamaev, A Survey of Forecast Error Measures [online] Available at: www.researchgate.net/publication/281718517_A_survey_of_forecast_error_measures (2018)

A fuzzy set model for assessment of a perspectives level for integration of new materials in industrial enterprise processes[a]

Elena Kasianenko[1], *Evgenii* Konnikov[1*], and *Nikita* Lukashevich[1]

[1] Peter the Great St. Petersburg Polytechnic University, Institute of Industrial Management, Economics and Trade, 195251 Politekhnicheskaya st. 29, Russian Federation

Abstract. The definition of effective improvement vectors is currently one of the most pressing challenges facing the industry representatives. The transition to the sixth technological mode effectively contributes to competition intensification in all markets of industrial products. This is largely due to the fact that existing process systems are at the peak of their effectiveness. Further development requires qualitative changes. However, the principal improvement is a long-term and high-risk process. For this reason the issue of creating effective models for assessment of the strategic lines of processes improvement becomes increasingly important for industrial enterprises. This article considers in details the vector of industrial enterprise processes improvement based on the integration of new materials. As a result, a model allowing to assess a perspectives level for integration of new materials in industrial enterprise processes is created.

1 Introduction

At present, the process of transition to the sixth technological mode has become evident to everyone. The existing process systems achieve an optimization peak that in conditions of a competitive environment generates the need for their qualitative change (principal improvement). This problem is especially actual for industry representatives as investments in this case are more long-term. Therefore, in terms of the qualitative changes in processes at an industrial enterprise, we mean the formation of a new industry, "the Industry 4.0".

---

[a] The research results were published in the framework of the project "Development of a forecast for implementing the scientific and technological advancement priority defined in item 20a of the Scientific and Technological Development Strategy of the Russian Federation (transition to the advanced digital, intelligent production technologies, robotic systems, new materials and design methods, big data, machine learning and artificial intelligence)" is funded by the Ministry of Education and Science of the Russian Federation from the grant funds in the framework of the Federal Program "Research and Development in Priority Fields for Advancement of the Scientific and Technological Sector of Russia for 2014-2020", Event 1.1, Granting Agreement No. 14.572.21.0008 dated October 23, 2017, the unique identifier: RFMEFI57217X0006
* Corresponding author: konnikov.evgeniy@gmail.com

Among the topics of scientific publications on this subject, there are several main trends. Some authors focus their attention at the development of new production technologies, for example, additive technologies, computer engineering, laser material technologies, etc. Gressa & Kalafsky [1] study the influence of additive technologies on the global structure of demand and consumption, that is, the study subject is the long-term economic effect resulted from the introduction of additive technologies in production. Cozmei & Caloian [2] emphasize the capital capacity of additive productions concluding that the additive technologies development will invariably lead to the global improvement of the taxation system. Gebler, Schoot Uiterkamp & Visser [3] agree with them, they see the purpose of additive technologies in increasing the company's profit through the use of consumer surpluses, thanks to the construction of a flexible production system that implies the custom orders production. The consequences of the additive technologies integration into the real economic sector, in particular, the increasing level of different types of risks, were the subject of Mellor, Hao & Zhang' study [4], who stated that one of the significant risks is almost unlimited capabilities in the field of final product use.

Another study line in the area of the sixth technological mode is a wide range of topics related to sustainable development, sustainable production and consumption, that is, the approval of new, sustainable consumer values. Leiserowitz [5] wrote about the relationship between sustainable production and consumption, and achievement of the corresponding long-term economic, social and environmental result. Thogersen [6], Peattie & Collins [7] noted the risks and dissonances of this process, while revealing contradictions between the values and their implementation declared by the companies. Garetti and Taisch [8] studied the factors affecting the industry stability and macroeconomic balance.

Finally, new production technologies and new sustainable values inevitably lead to appearance of new materials, such as metamaterials, aerogels, self-healing materials, foamed metal, bio-ceramics, etc. Although the markets for these materials are only at the stage of implementation according to the life cycle model, they are already the subject of detailed study of scientist-economists. In particular, Menshutina and Lebedev [9] focus their attention to capitalization of enterprises of high-tech industries which deal with developments in the field of new materials. Slyusar [10], Lapshin [11] study the field of the future long-term effect from the implementation of such materials in the production structure, etc.

The whole set of the existing particular solutions of the challenge can be represented as a universal scheme (see Fig. 1).

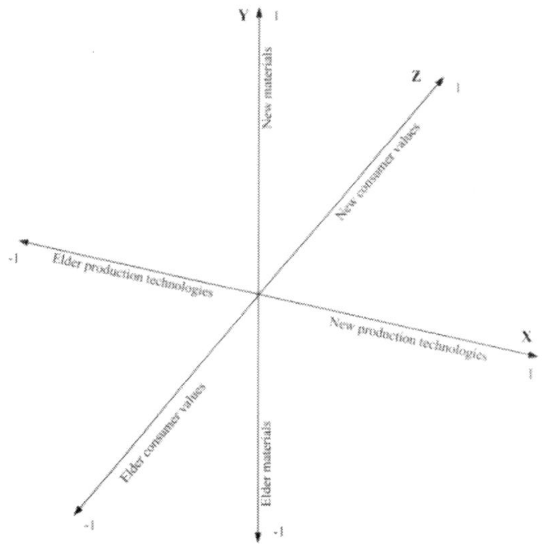

Fig. 1. Process improvement octant.

This octant consists of 8 sectors due to its geometry. Each axis features one of 3 highlighted improvement lines, and has 2 opposite states. Thus, each of the sectors is featured by the state of three main lines of process improvement. The description of these fields is given in Table 1.

Table 1. Description of process improvement octant fields.

Item No.	Field	Field description
1	"A fundamentally new process"	X=1; Y=1; Z=1.
2	"Integration of new materials to meet the new needs"	X=-1; Y=1; Z=1.
3	"Integration of new materials to better meet the existing needs"	X=-1; Y=1; Z=-1.
4	"A new way to meet the existing needs"	X=1; Y=1; Z=-1.
5	"New technologies to meet new needs"	X=1; Y=-1; Z=1.
6	"Meeting the new needs by using old ways"	X=-1; Y=-1; Z=1.
7	"New technologies to meet old needs"	X=1; Y=-1; Z=-1.
8	"Insignificant improvement"	X=-1; Y=-1; Z=-1.

Based on the content analysis results, it was established that one of three listed lines or their combination was laid down in the basis of the solutions proposed by the scientists-researchers. The effectiveness of each of the described improvement lines can be significantly different depending on many factors. However, an industrial enterprise can use each of them at the strategic planning level. These lines can be compared based on three criteria: capital capacity; risk level; long-term economic effect. The expert comparison of the described lines based on the above criteria is shown in Fig. 2. This comparison is made based on a ten-point scale, where 10 is the maximum value of the criterion, and 1 is the minimum one. The expert group consisted of 10 leading scientists-researchers in this field representing the profile academic departments of SPbPU and SPbGEU. An expert review was made based on the Delphi method.

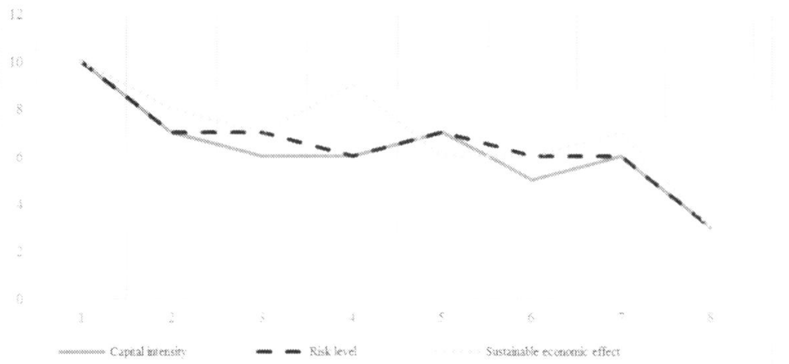

Fig. 2. Expert comparative study of the process improvement.

According to the presented data, we can conclude that the long-term economic effect is provided to a greater extent in case of new materials integration. This is due to the fact that only the use of new materials will form fundamentally new properties of the final product, which, in turn, will create a new consumer value, while maintaining the already formed material and technical base of the industrial enterprise. In this case, the risk level shows insignificant deviations for most states (boundary (1 and 8) states can be neglected, as they imply either, in fact, the formation of a new activity line, or a minor improvement that more is of additional). Capital capacity shows the lowest results in the case of lines which do not involve the new materials integration. First of all, this is due to the fact that the markets for new materials are unsaturated, and the manufacturers of new materials are not able to create a scale effect. However, the most potentially effective line is 4 – "A new way to meet the existing needs", and 2 – "Integration of new materials to meet the new needs". This statement is based on the fact that with a relatively low risk level these lines are featured by a relatively higher long-term economic effect exceeding their capital capacity. Therefore, the advanced field for industrial enterprises as part of transition to the new technological mode is the processes improvement through the new materials integration.

According to the study – Transparency Market Research, the capacity of the world market for new materials will grow by an average of 10.4% per year, and will reach 102.48 billion dollars by 2024, against only 42.76 billion dollars in 2015 [12]. Based on the analysis of the statistics presented in the company's reports -Transparency Market Research, Markets and Markets and Grand View Research, the following new materials most relevant and prospective for industry development were identified: metamaterials; aerogels; bioceramics; graphene; foamed metal; self-healing materials. The market for each of the presented materials is rapidly growing, and a lack of experimental experience of their application in the industry indicates an increased risk level of their integration into the processes. However, these are the industrial enterprises that will be able to successfully integrate these materials, be competitive in the long term. Therefore, the model building to assess the prospects for integrating these materials into the processes of industrial enterprises is an extremely critical task.

2 Assessment model and results

The research subject specificity does not allow using one of the most common assessment methods as is, since a sufficiently accurate and adaptive prospects assessment model can not be based on statistical or exclusively expert methods only. The solution for the problem of increasing the results accuracy of assessing such phenomena lies in the methods application based on the fuzzy sets theory. Methods based on the fuzzy sets theory are based on an expert assessments system; however, as against the statistical and expert estimation methods, they provide the possibility to take into account the uncertainty level by using the membership functions (μ (x) ∈ [0; 1]) of a subset to a given set [13].

The prospects are assessed based on a system of indicators built as per the hierarchical principle, and defined in different units of measurement. At the first system level there are extended criteria, the aggregate interaction of which synergistically affects the level of integration prospects. The second system level is represented by specific indicators affecting one or another criterion. These indicators describe the state of both the external and internal environment of an industrial enterprise. The system of these indicators is given in Table 2.

Table 2. The indicators featuring the prospects level for integration of new materials into industrial enterprise processes.

Item No.	First level indicators	Second level indicators	The line of influence on the final result
1	Capital capacity	Average integration cost	↑=>↓
2		Possibility for integration with the existing processing technologies	↑=>↑
3		Human resources cost	↑=>↓
4		Cost of additional research	↑=>↓
5	Risk level	Level of process imperfection of the material	↑=>↓
6		Degree of differentiation of the world distribution of manufacturers	↑=>↑
7		Degree of differentiation of application areas	↑=>↑
8		Level of application areas adjacency	↑=>↑
9	Long-term economic effect	Current market capacity	↑=>↑
10		Growth rate of market capacity	↑=>↑
11		Current capacity of main consumer markets	↑=>↑
12		Level of process development of application areas	↑=>↑

The formed model has 2 linguistic variables: the prospects level for integration of new materials and the level of each specific indicator under consideration (12 indicators in total). The term-set of each linguistic variable consists of 5 subsets:

- Linguistic variable X is the prospects level for integration of new materials;
- The linguistic variable Y is the values of the specific indicators.

Its own level of significance r_i is assigned to each indicator. In accordance with the system hierarchy, it was found that the first level indicators are of equal importance. The second level indicators, in turn, are equally important for the first level ones.

The standard five-level 01-classifier developed by A. O. Nedosekin and most commonly used, where the membership functions are trapezoidal triangular numbers [14] is applied as a classifier for the prospects level for integration of new materials. This classifier has 5 node points, where a membership function value is equal to one (0.1, 0.3, 0.5, 0.7, 0.9).

Based on the results of calculation of each of the specific indicators, their values are recognized by the criterion λij∈[0;1]. This indicator correlates the specific indicators with the values of the 01-carrier:

$$\lambda_{iJ} = 1 - \frac{X_i - \alpha_3^*}{\alpha_4^* - \alpha_3^*}, \quad (1)$$

where α_3^* and α_4^* are the T-numbers of the i-th subset of the term-set.

Based on the results of recognition of the specific indicator values, the integral indicator of the prospects level for new materials integration (X) is calculated:

$$X = \sum_{j=1}^{5} p_j \sum_{i=1}^{n=12} r_i \times \lambda_{iJ}, \quad (2)$$

where p_j is node points of the 01-carrier

The obtained integral indicator of the prospects level for new materials integration is linguistically interpreted in the same manner as the specific indicators.

The fuzzy set model for assessment of the prospects level for new materials integration into the industrial enterprise processes is proposed. This model compensates for the disadvantages of other models by integrating both statistical and expert indicators which have a synergistic effect on the final result. Further research will be devoted to approbation and improvement of the generated model.

References

1. D.R. Gressa, R.V. Kalafsky, *Geographies of production in 3D: Theoretical and research implications stemming from additive manufacturing*(Geoforum, 2015)
2. C. Cozmei, F. Caloian, Procedia Economics and Finance, **3** (2012)
3. M. Gebler, Schoot Uiterkamp A.J.M., Visser C, Energy Policy, **74** (2014)
4. S. Mellor, L. Hao & D. Zhang, International Journal of Production Economics, **149** (2014)
5. A.A. Leiserowitz, Annual Review of Environment and Resources, **31** (2006)
6. J. Thogersen A, Journal of Environmental Psychology, **1** (2004)
7. K.J. Peattie, A.J. Collins, International Journal of Consumer Studies, **2** (2009)
8. M. Garetti, M. Taisch, Production Planning & Control, The Management of Operations, **23 (2-3)** (2012)
9. N.V. Menshutina, E.A. Lebedev, Vestnik khimichesloy promyshlennosti (2016)
10. V. Slyusar, Electronics: Science, Technology, Business, **7** (2009)
11. R.V. Lapshin, Applied Surface Science, **360** (2016)
12. Advanced Materials Market ,Transparency Market Research [online], Available at: https://www.transparencymarketresearch.com/advanced-materials-market.html (2017)
13. O.S. Igolnikova, B.Kh. Sanzhapov, *A fuzzy set model for assessment of financial component of the innovative potential of a construction organization* (VolgGASU, Volgograd, 2010)
14. Z.I. Abdulayeva, A.O. Nedosekin, *Strategic Analysis of Innovative Risks* (Polytech Publishing House, St. Petersburg, 2013)

Convergence and divergence in biology and medicine[a]

Vadim Korablev[1*], *Sergei* Kozyrev[2], and *Pavel* Yakutseni[2]

[1] Peter the Great St. Petersburg Polytechnic University, Institute of Physics, Nanotechnologies and Telecommunications, 195251 Polytechnicheskaya st. 29, Russian Federation
[2] Peter the Great St. Petersburg Polytechnic University, Advanced Research Center, 195251 Polytechnicheskaya st. 29, Russian Federation

Abstract. A convergence of digital and physical worlds shapes capabilities of attaining a fundamentally new level of knowledge about molecular and system-level principles of functioning of both individual elements of living world matter, and the entire biosphere. Accordingly, there appear those growing points, which change the traditional types of specialists' employment beginning to get oriented to solving the key problems of ecological and food-supply security, problems of biologically renewable sources of energy and materials, biotechnologies and bionic applications in engineering and industry, and ultimately to the challenges of public health services and healthcare. The basic changes of labor market in the fields related to biology and medicine have been shown. The directions of application of computational methods for searching biologically inspired breakthroughs for engineering and industry have been given consideration. The presented data can be interesting for analyzing negative, neutral and positive scenarios of development of universities and other education research communities.

Beginning from mid-1990s a new situation has been formed – the basic social mandate consists in researches and developments associated with biosciences and medicine. It appears that after scientific revolution of early new time, industrial revolution of 18-19th centuries, development of industrial society in the 20th century, and resultantly, reaching the unbelievable standards of technical comfort, the major challenge of our epoch is a lengthy and healthy life.

1 Development of biology and medicine as a major trend of our time

An impressive specific feature of development of present-time biology is the shift of this science from a descriptive paradigm to the sphere of exact sciences – physics and mathematics. The result of development of new generations of instruments, methods of

[a] The work has been supported by project No.16.7002.2017/БЧ of the Ministry of Education and Science of the Russian Federation
* Corresponding author: korablev@spbstu.ru

investigating the living world is a generation of knowledge changing the world of public health services and healthcare, bio-oriented engineering and industry. An important peculiarity of the process is as follows: long-term trend of increasing expenditures in the field of biosciences and medicine; extensive establishment of interdisciplinary associations of specialists in the field of physics, biology, medicine, chemistry, engineering, management and industry accompanied by an intensive involvement of digital technologies.

The data shown in Fig. 1 are quite indicative for characterizing the trends of expenditures for development of biosciences and medicine. Apparently, that for more than ten years already the federal budgeting in terms of a system of national institutes of public health services of the USA exceeds $25 bln., budgeting of all fundamental and applied works on engineering hardly reaches $12 bln., while the budgeting fluctuates in the limits of $6÷4 bln. for the sectors of physics, environmental protection, computer science [1]. The amounts of governmental and private investments in the European Union in the same period were equal to: pharmaceuticals and biotechnologies, equipment and services for public health service – $114 bln., process equipment – $95 bln., automotive branch – $84 bln., software and computer services – $39 bln., electronic and electric equipment – $38 bln., materials and chemicals – $26 bln., aerospace and defense complex – $24 bln. and further in descending order [2]. Thus, it is necessary to ascertain the fact that biology, bio-inspired industry and medicine become the main customers and consumers of R&D in XXI century instead of space and defense programs and electronics.

The other manifestation of dominating bio-oriented development is the bibliometric data from the countries of European Union and the USA. For instance, the analysis of Internet base SCImago Journal & Country Rank (http://www.scimagojr.com) shows that the share of quoted documents, predominantly, the scientific articles in the field of medicine, biochemistry and molecular biology is nearly 38%. This indicator equals 20% and decreases from 28% and 26% during 1996 and 2002, accordingly, for the domains of physics and engineering.

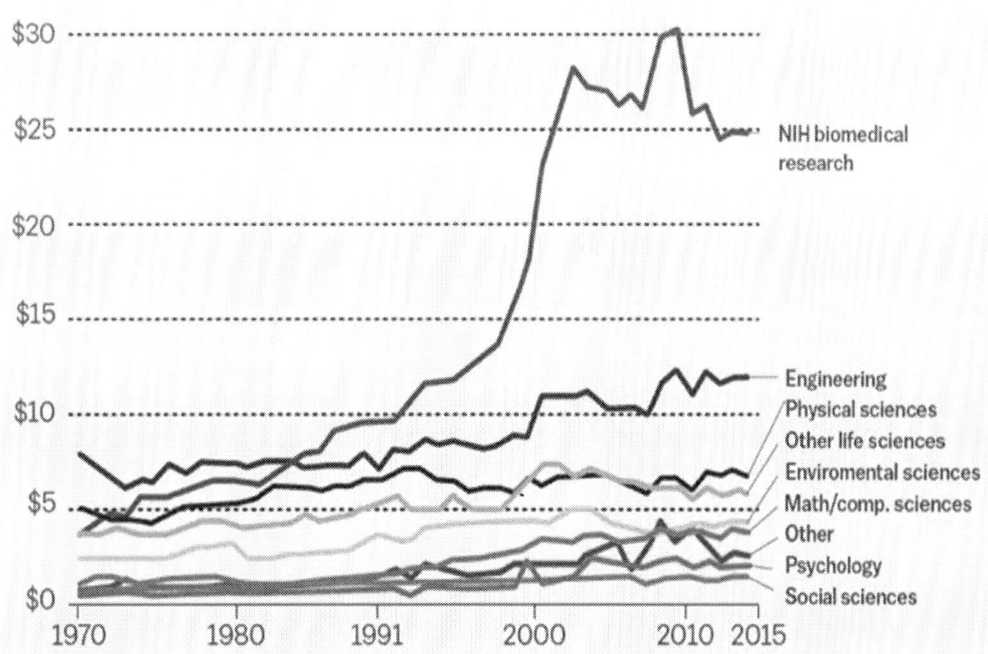

Fig. 1. Dynamics of federal expenses of the USA for scientific research and development by lines of activity. Data have been received from sources referred to in the work [2].

Without doubt, the emergence of the above trends is accompanied by structural changes in the leading Universities, even those, which positioned themselves as purely technical earlier. The Internet data in the majority of world higher educational institutions, including Russia, testify to a permanent drift to the field of medicine, biology and its applications. ARWU, THE and QS pertaining to biology and medicine occupy the first positions of divisions of the world ratings, Massachusetts Institute of Technology (MIT), California Institute of Technology, Zurich Institute of Technology and Federal School of Technology of Lausanne appear regularly on the charts. So, cumulative proceeds from the main activity of MIT in 2012 amounted to about $3 bln., whereof the medical and biological works sponsored by the Government of the USA have already provided 23% of total financial turnover of MIT with 16%, 15% and 14% of orders associated with defense, industry and power engineering, accordingly. The share of sector of life science and medicine reaches 40÷50% for 2017 in the top-rated technical HEI of the advanced economies of the world. The department of natural sciences and mathematics of the Federal Institute of Technologies of Zurich consists of four divisions: biology, chemistry and applied biosciences, mathematics, physics. Technical University of Munich has its own hospital (34 clinical units for 1,100 beds) providing clinical investigations and translation of scientific discoveries into medical practice. Such practices are characteristic for the Universities of other countries of technological nucleus, China, region of Southeast Asia. During the last three years the leading Universities of Russia, first of all those that take part in the program of improving competitiveness "5-100-2020" set up bio-oriented research divisions and departments in their structure.

It is expected that the development of the line of activity will preserve the dominating character for decades in future and will be accompanied by intensive incorporation of those methods of computational data analysis, predictive simulation and virtual testing, which similarly to the systems of computer-aided design (CAD) will be able to provide the next interdisciplinary level of convergent creation of prototypes and technologies of bio-inspired prototypes and technologies of bio-inspired industry and medicine the same as half a century ago in engineering. Unfortunately, the present situation in the field of biology and medicine is extremely disengaged.

2 Divergence in biology and medicine

In comparison with the world of inanimate and technical systems, the hierarchical structure of biological objects is more than complex. Different levels are distinguished quite frequently in biology: atoms and molecules (1); simple bimolecular complexes (2); atom and molecular clusters and nanosystems (3); functional ensembles of atom and molecular clusters and nanostructures (4); subcellular formations and organelles (5); individual cell and cellular ensembles (6, 7); clusters of interacting cellular ensembles and tissues (8, 9); individual organs (10); systems of interrelated organs (11); organisms (12), groups thereof further to populations, biomes and right up to integral concepts of biosphere. At that, the poorly interacting cohorts of specialists get developed and resumed around every level. They get divided in turn both by the objects of research (proteins, nucleic acids, mitochondrions, lungs or other), and from the point of view of properties under investigation, like structure, biochemistry, functions and so on and so forth. After that differentiation of collectives and groups by applications begins: pharma industry, biotechnologies, medical equipment and so on.

The upside of such a situation is an unprecedented stream of emerging investigation technologies and data on split-level phenomena and processes of the world of biosystems, shaping revolutionary ideas, generating new sectors of markets of bioeconomics, employment and medical services.

Unfortunately, today, when the flow of reports about biomedical breakthroughs has become almost daily, yesterday's seemingly most remarkable sensations turn out to be in the basket of past hopes. The enhancing crisis of hyperspecialization, increasing barriers of interdisciplinary communications and, hence, the accompanying destruction of systems of substantial financing and administration of science and education appear to be a negative side of the process of development of biosciences. There emerges a picture of associations, where the steady and directed development is replaced with the personal interests of the groups under conditions of multidimensional branch of human knowledge – bioscience and medicine. A sector encompassing the army of biologists, health professionals, physicists, engineers and computer experts falls to isolated detachments generating omnidirectional growth points, which under conditions of absence of comparative criterion are frequently deemed as consensuses of professionals. Here, at the frontier of breakthroughs we impersonally face a wide spectrum of ideas with limitedness of general resource of investigations and developments.

In general, facing a situation of almost the so-called "black box" we always see more than a multiplicity of development points: some are attracted by proteomics, the other are attracted by regenerative medicine and cell technologies, the third deal with metaanalysis or "BigData", and all together they are looking for those common factors, which will be able to predict general mechanisms of biosystems and a human being under normal conditions, in situations of illness and medical interventions. An important goal is the implementation of that approach, when "deliberation" of ideas is effected at the level of quantitative calculation, reaching that "growth superpoint", which existing in physics and engineering sciences makes it possible to combine knowledge of different specialists, substantiate prospects of projects, articles or structures.

3 Digital and real experiment

The models of objects and technologies are developed, expected properties are calculated and after that only the prototypes get created, which help assess the result in the course of real (full-scale) experiment in exact and engineering sciences in case of existing sufficient theory after appearance of the original idea.

In the life sciences we face a more complex reality. The depth processes of functioning biosystems still frequently remain in the field of vision of researchers, while the available models most frequently feature too much a primitive character. Therefore, generally, in biology and medicine one has to solve a problem of experiment interpretation, i.e. restoration of internal unobservable subject matter of events by their external manifestations. In the exact and engineering sciences such situation corresponds to a case of so called problems of diagnostics, "black box" approaches and other inverse problems. At that, the suchlike inverse problems in mathematics always belong to a class of ill-posed ones, and the solution thereof is either absent, or produces unstable or non-sole result. The cost of absence of predictive a priori models in biology is high today more than ever, since the volumes of works in the field of biology and medicine reach hundreds billions of dollars, the accumulated data arrays are counted in petabytes, the number of people involved in this sector grows by millions.

In scientific articles published in the field of exact sciences, typically, an opposite combination of approaches is used: theoretical simulation – real experiment. The simulation in modern physics and engineering provides for the following since long:

- exhaustive information capacity of data about multiple properties of systems under consideration, including those invariably unavailable for real observation;
- visualization of different-scale scenes of virtual reality;

- consideration of external conditions unattainable in setting up a full-scale experiment and safety of investigations;
- predictive simulation providing for capabilities of directed designing and testing technologies and prototypes, substantiation of viability of the scheduled works;
- sharp reduction (reaching the orders of magnitude) of volumes, time limits and cost of works due to replacement of full-scale testing with digital experiments.

The methodology of bio-oriented investigations also begins to change. A triad customary to application-oriented physicists and engineers begins to be translated instead of traditional, extremely resource-intensive, and in view of the above peculiarities, solution of inverse problem and knowingly unreliable cascades of checks and re-checks: theoretical models; calculations according to these models; minimal test experiment. At that, the development of special methods of molecular and system-level simulation of split-level elements of a live world is required for biology and branches of medicine related thereto.

At the level of atoms and molecules we gradually transfer to considering ever more complex supermolecular structure, which makes it possible to obtain atomistically exact data about structure and interaction of both individual biologically important molecules, and complex ensembles of these substances, including molecules of water and ions of biometals. As a result we get not only ultimately detailed data on the position and motion of atoms and molecules in space and time, but also the data on energy jumps, thermodynamic, spectral properties and other easily measurable systems' properties, which makes it possible to supervise the authenticity of calculation. Practice shows that the accuracies of simulating small molecules appear to be higher than the errors of real experiment, while for macromolecules and nanobiostructures they are frequently comparable therewith [2].

Apparently, that the methods of system-level simulation acquire precedence in supermolecular hierarchically higher levels of organization of biosystems. For instance, the systems of differential levels connecting parameters characterizing the properties of systems/subsystems of the live world and variables reflecting current concentrations of different substances and intensity of processes of functioning of a separate organ or organism are given consideration. [2]

Acquisition of high-accuracy molecular pictures can determine the values of parameters of system-level models unknown in advance, which sharply increases the reliability of solutions. It should be noted that the present-day tools of molecular mechanics, semiempirical quantum mechanics, density functional and post Hartree-Fock metods make it possible to get exhaustive and reliable data, which can be used for building system-defined higher models of recognition and biomechanics of cells, organs and hydrodynamic streams in biophase of living organisms, etc.

The cumulative application of methods of system-level and molecular simulation promise ever more split-level models of bioprocesses taking part on a spatial scale from atoms and molecules, cells and tissues to organisms and populations and time dynamics from picoseconds to days and years.

The successes of calculation approach have already brightly proven effective in investigating the level of nanomolecules and nanobiosystems. It is quite sufficient to mention here a field of molecular engineering and biocatalysts, materials and nanoprocesses *de novo* or designing medicines. Whereon the chemists have for years synthesized thousands of compounds, while the health professionals and biologists have tested these compounds for the role of new medicinal products, virtual models of the required biotargets appear, which make it possible to multiply reduce the volumes and time limits of experimental works, save up to $1 mln. per year for a project. Unfortunately, the fields of biology and medicine belong to a case, when direct simulation of the required multiscale objects (models of "digital" cell type, digital organ and digital man) is still inaccessible. Developing medicines, we fairly well forecast peculiarities of its absorption from the injection place, penetration to the place of action and molecular action on its target tissues, but further a complex reaction of different parts of tissues and organism arrives, most frequently predetermining a fuzzy, unexpected or unwanted result.

Presently, a direct simulation of biosystems using the methods of quantum or molecular mechanics is actually restricted by the levels of individual atom and molecular structures up to combinations thereof with the use of supercomputers. Further, a gap appears somewhere at the levels of cellular components, where are already unable to offer a substantial digital model and return to searching for empirical common factors of the "black box". There appears a necessity of solving two opposite problems. This, first of all, implies further development of methods of direct molecular simulation of more and more complex structures following a principle of emulation "bottom-upwards". Secondly, it implies a system-level (simulation) modeling of macroscopically observable systems and components thereof with the aim of combining the obtained results in the direction "top downwards".

4 Convergence of competences

The construction of individual proteins, deoxyribonucleic acid (DNA)/ ribonucleic acid (RNA), lipids, saccharides staying in isolated state or in liquid medium is being intensively investigated for many decades already. Consideration is given to biologically important micromolecules and complexes of micro- and macro-molecules, e.g., of ligand receptor or protein-protein type. The urge is there to distinguish one of the objects for simulation as one of the promising and undeveloped directions for development, viz., saccharides, frequently also referred to as carbohydrates, carbohydrates, polysaccharides or glycans. Glycans in line with proteins, lipids and nucleic acids correspond to one of four fundamental types of biomacromolecules and feature an individual spectrum of key functions associated with power-engineering, identification, structure formation and other processes of the living world [3]. They make about 66% of dry weight of the entire biosphere and accumulate about 70% of energy reserved thereby and are considered as a source alternative to oil for production of new materials and nanotechnologies of different purpose [4]. An unusual peculiarity of glycans is an outstanding structural versatility determining new orders in terms of density of information recording as compared with biopolymers of proteins, DNA/RNA. These substances make an important component of man's nutrition, but infrequently they interfere with the immune system functioning being a source of a number of other threats for health. It is supposed frequently with reference of an assemblage of the mentioned data that many functions of glycation remain yet undisclosed, while further development of glycobiology, in particular, simulation and investigation of molecular structures belonging to glycation can result in one of new scientific revolutions of our century, which is stated even in official documents prepared for the governments of the developed countries [4]. Simultaneously, during the last years, unlike genomics and proteomics, glycomics still remains to be the field of activity of comparatively narrow circle of professionals having published about 5 thousand articles against more than 200 thousand works dedicated to proteins, DNA/RNA, as it is indicated by our analysis of bibliographical base of PubMed for 2017. Supposedly, we defend the next position of convergent development of molecular biosciences. It is really so, It is not very easy for any physics university in this niche, but is comparatively simpler to attain a considerable breakthrough. Though, in the event it is just an example. It is important that glycans are always present in DNA/RNA, in more than a half of proteins and frequently in lipids. A differentiation of biomolecules by types, the same as any differentiations, appears to be quite conventional, while a combination of different implications gives frequently an unexpected result.

In terms of convergence, apparently, more reasonable is the consolidated investigation of biomolecular systems not uniform in structure, integral nanobiostructures. The experimental data on the structure and functional properties of such systems are not numerous, indirect and inaccurate. The emulation procedures of atomistically exact simulation describing detailed state of such complex functional systems as "bottom-upwards" quickly encounters the limited power of the used computers. The simulation models making it possible to describe behavior without simulating "top downwards" conditions provide for the use of multiplicities of knowingly undefined, poorly controlled parameters.

A similar situation can be observed also at the other levels of hierarchy of knowledge (Ref. items 1-12, first paragraphs, section 2). In general in the system-level biology and medicine we frequently make out the systems of complex differential equations, but we face not only big quantities of variables, like concentration of substances, time, etc., and a great number of unknown parameters such as constant of rate of substances transfer or reactions, etc.

It appears that the exit from the existing situation is quite evident and this is rather a preparation of goal-oriented projects and convergent specialists capable of consolidating experimental knowledge received *in vitro, in vivo,* plan and carry out digital experiments *in silico* based on the opposite methods of emulations/simulations than divergent development of biosciences following a principle of seed financings. In other words, to work in the framework of multiscale modellinge, where, for instance, it is possible at atomistical level of molecular subsystems to calculate primary constants of speed or affinity, build models of complex supermolecular systems and even more hierarchically high systems/super systems of different types, which promises basic changes of our perceptions of fundamental mechanisms of functioning living world, development of diseases, methods of searching for means of diagnostics and therapy, directions of developing nanobionics, biotechnologies and bioengineering of the nearest and long-term future.

5 Scenarios of changing employment of scientific society

According to official sources of the USA in the field of life science (science and engineering only) 286, 400 specialists have been employed as of 2016 [5], while the total number of people employed in the leading biomedical clusters of the country only exceeded one mln. people. According to the data of British statistics 86,900 researchers and development experts have been employed as of 2014 in London alone [6], in this case it is considered that every specialist of the sector is provided with an advanced financing and provides today the employment of about two and half specialists of allied professions (clinical medicine, physics, engineering, computer technologies, mathematics, etc.). In dynamics it means that if during a decade the number of sector's specialists increases by 34 % or 64 % (big or medium and small companies of London accordingly), then in the other sectors of science and engineering rather significant re-orientation of scientific and engineering services will be observed in the rest sectors of science and engineering, which denotes a global shift of 25-30 % in the sector of employment of 5-6 mln. of scientists of the world.

Probably that the main social mandate, raised before scientists and development experts in the field of biomedical investigations is associated to a great extent with the increase of lifespan. The emergence of ageing contingents of population denotes a growing number of patients suffering of two-three chronic diseases simultaneously, at a time when pharmacotherapy of a single disease gives a positive result in less than 60% of cases even for a non-aged diseased person [7], which implies a practical impossibility to help. At that, in Russia [8] the same as in the other countries of the world due to a problem the load on clinics increases permanently, which only aggravates the social and economical situation of the majority of countries.

It appears that this situation will exercise further pressure on the groups, which continue to use methods of intuitive trials and errors traditional for the sector, unfortunately, still capable of providing maximum possible durability, number and financing of employees engaged in fulfillment of any project. It is expected that the same as in computational physics and engineering of the past ages, the snowballing process of forming digital biology and medicine will develop, when every success attracts tens and then thousands of allied scientists and development experts, which will require solution of the whole number of scientific and educational problems related to the emergence of required for still divergent today biosciences and developments of convergent specialists accumulating capabilities of convergence and translation of technology of different applied and fundamental sciences.

References

1. Survey of Federal Funds for Research and Development (National Center for Science and Engineering Statistics, Alexandria, 2017)
2. A. Rudskoi, S. Kozyrev, P. Yakutseni, Proceedings of the II-nd international scientific conference "Technological Prospects in the Framework of the Eurasian Space: New Markets and Economical Growth Points" (2016)
3. A. Varki et al., *Essentials of glycobiology* (Cold Spring Harbor Laboratory Press, New York, 2017)
4. Transforming Glycoscience: A Roadmap for the Future. (Committee on Assessing the Importance and Impact of Glycomics and Glycosciences, Board on Chemical Sciences and Technology, Board on Life Sciences, Division on Earth and Life Studies, National Research Council, 2012)
5. J. F. Sargent, *CRS Report R43061* (Congressional Research Service, Washington, D.C., 2017)
6. Numbers of workplaces and of employees in Life Sciences and Healthcare in London, 2001-2014 [online], Available at: (https://www.ons.gov.uk/employmentandlabourmarket/peopleinwork/employmentandemployeetypes/adhocs/numbersofworkplacesandofemployeesinlifesciencesandhealthcareinlondon20012014 (2015)
7. N. J. Schork, Nature, **350** (2015)
8. M. B. Denisenko, E. Ya. Varshavskaya, Economical Journal of the Higher School of Economics, **21** (2017)

Space IT platforms: challenges of the XXI century

Vadim Korablyov[1*], *and Alexander* Zheleznyakov[2]

[1] Peter the Great St. Petersburg Polytechnic University, 195251 Polytechnicheskaya st. 29, Russian Federation
[2] Russia State Scientific Center for Robotics and Technical cybernetics, 194064 Tikhoretsky Prospect 21, Russian Federation

Abstract. More than half a century of man-in-space exploration not only demonstrated the new manufacturing capabilities of the countries involved in the study of distant and near space, but also presented the main challenges that humanity will face in the exploration of the space in the first half of the 21st century. One of these challenges is the rapid growth in a number of satellites used not only by government structures, but also by private sector. This problem gives rise to another one – ensuring the safety of the satellites flights and contamination of the earth orbit by man-made objects. A particular problem is the growing militarization of the space. There is another natural challenge such as a cometary-asteroid hazard. In the near future, humanity has to answer these challenges. This is important for two reasons. Firstly, only overcoming them, we will be able to continue our expansion in the space. And, secondly, only by solving the encountered problems, we will be able to maintain the stability on the Earth. An important factor for a successful response to the challenges is international cooperation in space, which allows combining the resources of space powers including intellectual potential. In this case, we can rely on the soonest achievement of the set goals. Of course, this will mark new frontiers, which will be a challenge for the next generations.

1 Introduction

The farther humanity enters the depths of the Universe, the more challenges it has to face. We obtain some of them from the Nature, but most of them are due to the development of human civilization itself. In other words, every man sets the tasks, which he himself intends to solve. And it largely depends on us ourselves how adequate the answer to the challenges will be.

If we reject the political and philosophical aspects of the space exploration, and focus only on science and technology, then now we can formulate the following challenges which humanity has to response not to stop in its development:

1. Creation of new space technology that will allow us to live and work confidently in the space, being of benefit for all earthlings, regardless of their national, social, religious and gender identity.

* Corresponding author: korablev@spbstu.ru

2. The beginning of the Moon and planets development of not only scientific research, but also with the intention to obtain practical benefits.

3. Sending of research probes to the solar system outskirts and into the interstellar space.

4. Non-admission of the space militarization.

5. Earth protection against comets and asteroids.

6. Clearing of the near Earth space from the man-made objects.

These are just the main challenges, but their solution is impossible without creating a new generation of space technology platforms.

2 Road map

The main leading players in space exploration have already been identified; they are the United States, China, Russia, the European Union, the UK, India and Japan. All these countries have adopted long-term space programs that are aimed both at supporting national security and substantially promoting private companies in the implementation of space programs.

Today, the space-related programs are an important part of the national economies. For example, the European Union in the period of 2012-2020 plans to invest €12 biln. in the space programs, having increased a number of its satellites from 18 to 30 pcs. in the period until 2035. In 2014, with employed 230,000 persons, the aerospace industry provided the output of products and services amounting to €45-54 biln. that makes 21% of the world market [1]. The UK estimates its aerospace industry at a level of £11.8 biln, with 35,000 employees, and has ambitious plans to bring the output of the sector up to £40 biln. by 2030 [2]. According to the Federal Aviation Service of the United States, only in 2009, space transportation generated the contribution to the US economy at a level of US$208.3 biln. [3]. In 2015, the world market of the space services was estimated at US$323 biln, of which 76% was for commercial infrastructure and systems [4].

The wide involvement of the economy in the implementation of the space programs is primarily due to the need to create **a new space technology**.

For more than 60 years in the space exploration, humanity has been using technical solutions that were adopted in the early years of the space age. Changes are insignificant – the measuring and computing systems became more powerful, new materials began to be used. However, the space technology has conceptually changed little.

As a result, by today, we have almost reached the limit of our capabilities in space exploration.

We can confidently launch satellites and spacecraft into low-earth orbit. We can send people to the same orbit. It is guaranteed to return them to the Earth.

We have developed the geostationary orbit and have learned to send scientific stations to the libration points.

We can send automatic interplanetary stations to almost any celestial body. Truly speaking, in some cases the flights will take many years before the research vehicle approaches the concern heavenly body. And the mass of these probes is not large.

But today this is not enough for humanity. It is necessary to flight to the planets not only for their study, but also for development. It is necessary to deliver not hundreds of kilograms but hundreds of tons of cargoes to the space depths. And it shall be performed not for long years, but in a few weeks or several months.

To solve these problems, it is necessary to create new models of space technology, first of all, new rocket engines, which will ensure the forward movement. If this does not happen, then we will "circle over the Earth" for a long time.

Since during interplanetary flights we often mean the presence of a man on the spacecraft, then it is necessary to create such crafts which will protect people against space radiation and against the adverse effects of long space flight factors [5].

The only acceptable way out from this situation may be a nuclear rocket engine. According to the calculations, its application will significantly shorten the time of interplanetary expeditions that minimizes the risks for manned flights.

The use of nuclear energy will also allow us to enter the interstellar space that is a vital necessity for humanity in the long term [6].

The creation of new models of space technology will make it possible to response the second challenge we formulated. Namely, to start **development of the Moon and planets from the practical point of view.**

Until today, all interplanetary expeditions were exclusively cognitive. We studied the Moon and planets with a view to obtain new information as much as possible: their structure, the presence of organic substances on them, the history of their origin and development.

Now, man is not enough to have knowledge only. He became interested in practical aspects of the development of other worlds – whether there are minerals there, whether it is possible to extract them at low cost, whether there is a sense to transport them to the Earth or to use them for long-range space flights.

And the nature of scientific research has undergone significant changes. If we studied the only celestial bodies in the XX century, now we intend to use them to study even more remote areas of the Universe.

Why should we develop the Moon and other celestial bodies of the solar system.

Firstly, they are unique scientific bases, where research and experiments impossible on the Earth and in near space can be carried out.

Secondly, they will become excellent test areas for new models of space technology, which we can use to reach remote corners of the solar system and exit into interstellar space.

Thirdly, they are ideal "intermediate spaceports", which make it possible to move forward more effectively when studying distant natural objects.

Fourthly, it is possible they will become a huge source of natural resources and will provide earthlings with raw materials for many and many years.

Fifthly, only by exploring the planets, we can really, and not in words, expand the range of humanity habitat.

Table 1. Possible periods for manned expeditions to other celestial bodies (assessment).

Celestial body	Moon	Mars	Venus	Asteroids	Jupiter's moons
Flight periods	2025-2028	not until 2040	not until 2100	About 2050	After 2150

In addition, the development of the Moon and the planets, primarily the natural satellite of the Earth, also means humanitarian activity. How so the psychology of humanity has changed after the first human flight into the space, so as it will change after we have moved from single landings to the constant presence of people on the Moon and Mars bases. Many already now perceive the earthlings as a galactic race. And after Moon and Mars are developed, they only "harden" to their view [7].

The third challenge considered in the paper, on the one hand, reechoes the first two ones – **sending of research probes to the outskirts of the solar system and to interstellar space** is possible only with the availability of new space technology and intermediate bases on the celestial bodies closest to the Earth. On the other hand, these works will be performed separately, but in parallel with the development of the Moon and the planets, since they have a more philosophical nature, rather than the hope of quick practical results.

We have not yet fully studied the structure of the solar system. Our vision of it constantly changes. Moreover, the more we learn, the more questions that require an answer arise.

Table 2. Spacecraft in flight.

Name of the craft (date of launch)	Pioneer-10 (March 3, 1972)	Pioneer-11 (April 6, 1973)	Voyager-1 (September 6, 1977)	Voyager-2 (August 20, 1977)
Distance from the Sun at present	18.3 biln. km	17.3 biln. km	21 biln. km	17.7 biln. km

More recently, we believed that interstellar space begins somewhere at a distance of 30-40 billion kilometers from the Sun. Now these estimates have grown by a factor of two or three. And there is no guarantee that the solar system does not extend even farther [8].

Notwithstanding we intend to break away interstellar spaces. This desire has deep historical roots. This is evidenced by mythology, literature of antiquity, the Middle Ages and modernity. Truly speaking, it is fantastic for the most part [9].

Man has always wanted to subdue faraway worlds, not always wondering how he can do it. Now we practically approach the frontier, which overcoming we can not only dream, but also begin to put our dreams in place [10].

Apparently, it will not be easy to do. And this event will require a very impressive cost. However, this must be done to lay the foundation for the future [11].

The first three challenges, which were mentioned in the paper, have a pronounced technogenic overtone and entirely depend on the level of science and technology development. In contrast, the fourth challenge is a result and a consequence of relations between states. It is about the intention of some countries to use the space for military purposes. The immediate task of humanity is to prevent the **militarization of the cosmic space**.

The political and military circles of the world's major powers began to consider the space, as a battlefield, even before the beginning of the space age. The first space launches, the first spacecraft launched into the earth orbit, only confirmed in their opinion.

In the 1960s military use of astronautics achievements was considered almost as a mandatory application to any space program. It was in those years that anti-satellite systems, survey and detailed photographic reconnaissance systems, partial orbital bombing system (in the USSR) were created and adopted, and the development of manned interceptor and combat orbital stations began [12].

Fortunately, common sense even then prevailed over the desire to gain space supremacy. The international agreement – the Treaty Banning Nuclear Weapon Tests in Three Environments (including the space) was signed in 1963, and the treaty on principles governing the activities of states in the exploration and use of outer space, including the Moon and other celestial bodies – in 1967, which prohibited to deploy the nuclear and other types of mass destruction weapons in the space. The agreement on restrictions on anti-satellite systems was signed between the USSR and the USA a little later [13].

Truly speaking, the availability of these agreements only limited the military activities of the space powers. For example, there were never any restrictions on the creation and deployment of reconnaissance and auxiliary military systems. However, the ban on strike combat systems played a big role in the international tension detente.

Today the situation has not improved. Appearance of new space powers, consolidation of China's role in space exploration force once again to make efforts to prevent the space militarization. Initiatives with which Russia and other countries periodically advance in the UN and other international organizations are aimed at those aspects [14].

Nevertheless, the threat of space militarization remains high. Including and by means of the appearance of new technologies that allow to place weapons in the space virtually by stealth. This is the challenge that can be solved only by political means, only by agreements between the countries participating in the process of space exploration. And although we put this problem on the fourth place, full responses to the first three challenges are impossible without overcoming this one.

In recent years, the challenge of **Earth protection against comets and asteroids** has become very urgent. Awareness of the life's fragility on Earth, its high dependence on those processes that occur in the space made humanity to take the comet-asteroids hazard more seriously and to actively engage in the development of protection measures against it.

Meteorites have recently fallen to Earth as rarely as it was before. However, now we know more about the solar system structure and could more realistically assess the danger that small celestial bodies "roaming" through the great spaces.

Table 3. The probability of Earth collision with comets and asteroids in the next 100 years (assessment).

Body size	> 3 km	1-3 km	0.5-1 km	0.1-0.5 km	0.05-0.1 km	< 0.05 km
Probability	10^{-8}	10^{-7}	10^{-6}	10^{-5}	10^{-2}	1
Disaster scales	global	regional	local	local	regional	no consequences

In addition, the humanity technical potential has reached such a level when we can not only talk about confronting such a danger, but also develop a set of protection measures that reduce a probability of humanity destruction in case of natural disasters.

Now a probability of the human civilization disaster due to falling of asteroid with a size of several kilometers to the Earth is very low. Solar system spaces have been substantially "cleared" for billion years of its development. Everything that could fall has already fallen. Nevertheless, even though theoretically, but such a danger exists. If there is a collision threat, humanity will have no more than three years to respond to it. It's too little to have time to develop technologies that will allow protecting our planet against a space impact [15].

There is an insignificant probability, although it is much higher than the probability of global catastrophe, falling the celestial bodies of smaller sizes, about 1 km in diameter, to the Earth which are capable of causing the destruction of some countries or countries group, and creating significant problems for the "survivors". Parrying this danger also requires the development of new technologies.

However the probability of falling small meteorites of up to several tens of meters in diameter is significant. The example of the "Chelyabinsk meteorite" still sounds familiar.

And although a local catastrophe is only possible in case of falling the bodies of these sizes, the protection against them is also required. This protection is even more necessary than the one against hypothetical giant asteroids.

Moreover, technical means already exist for these purposes. Truly specking, their full deployment will require significant material costs, to which no country in the world is ready to go yet [16].

Protection from comet-asteroid danger is the only global challenge that the Nature has thrown down. Unless, the overcoming the vast spaces separating planets and stars are considered in such aspect.

The comet-asteroid danger is reechoed with another challenge being generated by every man – with the **space pollution by artificial objects**.

According to NASA estimates, there are more than 500,000 artificial objects in the Earth orbit [17]. These are operational and nonoperational satellites, booster stages, nose fairing half, fragments of space vehicles and other space debris. And this is only what we can see from the Earth or from the specialized satellites.

Many more artificial objects have smaller linear dimensions and can not be traced from the Earth. It is believed that fragments of 2 to 10 cm in the earth orbit are more than 250,000, and fragments of even smaller sizes are from 700,000 to 1 million [18]. The dynamics and forecast of space debris is shown in Fig. 1.

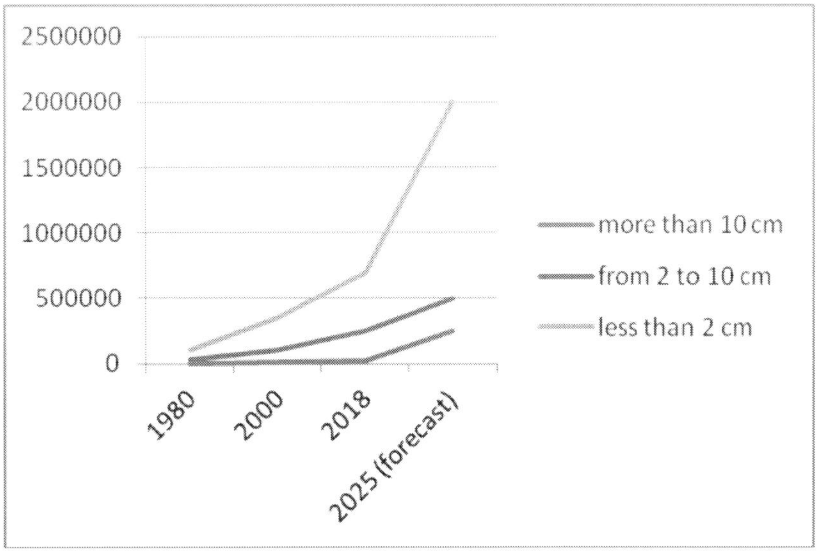

Fig. 1. Dynamics of space debris fragments growth by years.

Such a space contamination has already led to difficulties in space activities. For example, the International Space Station has regularly to maneuver to avoid probable approaching dangerous fragments approximately once every two months. Unmanned vehicles have to maneuver similarly.

For the past 25 years, at least 10 incidents related to space debris have been recorded in the space. In this case, space vehicles were seriously damaged and could not function properly, and sometimes they are completely failed.

Some experts also associate a number of incidents which have led to the loss of satellites with space debris. However, it was not possible to detect the real cause.

The most serious incident is the collision of Russian and American communications satellites, which occurred on February 10, 2009. This incident led to the appearance of several thousand fragments larger than 10 cm and, possibly, several tens of thousands of smaller fragments in the earth orbit [19].

The activation of military activities in the space, especially the testing of anti-satellite systems, could theoretically lead to more contamination of the Earth space. In this case, a threat of man exits into the space.

Now there are no approved methods for protection against space debris. The leading operators of launch services are recently trying to exclude the existence of booster stages in the low orbit, de-orbiting them after the task has been carried out and burning them in the terrestrial atmosphere. However, when the apparatus is put in the geostationary earth orbit, this technique is not used.

Rather exotic methods (laser guns, nets, harpoons – see Table 4) for cleaning the earth orbit are considered as perspective. But none of them is currently used and is considered only as a prospective one [20].

Table 4. Prospective methods for cleaning of the earth orbit.

Method description	Operating Principle	Note
ElectroDynamic Debris Eliminator	Satellites capture using harpoon and network.	Low efficiency. It can only be used to recycle large objects.
Gossamer Orbit Lowering Device	Increase of satellite aerodynamic drag due to the inflatable shell.	It is applicable only for large objects.
CleanSpaceOne	Robotic system using a jet tug.	High price. It is applicable only for large objects.
HybridSail	Satellites moving to other orbits using a light sail.	Difficulties with sail installation on unappropriated objects.
Low orbit rebooting with tungsten dust	Creation of tungsten dust cloud (no more than 30 mm particles) in the low orbit, increasing of aerodynamic braking of satellites.	It works only for small objects.
Laser Orbital Debris Removal	Using powerful pulse lasers to push satellites from the orbit.	Technical implementation complexity.

At the same time, the space debris problem requires its immediate solution, if we intend to continue using the astronautics in our life.

One last thing to be said about. As previously stated, all the challenges discussed in the paper are of a global nature. That is, it is a challenge for all humanity. Not only one country but the whole humanity has to response these challenges.

Thus, international cooperation is a fundamental factor in the space development. The cooperative efforts of the space powers will allow not only to unite their intellectual potential, but also to reduce each cost loading, as well as rationally to distribute the work in the selected aspects, to eliminate duplication in the development of space technology samples and when addressing the global challenges.

The practice of recent years has shown the possibility and justification of such cooperation even with escalating the tension in interstate relations. And this process does not and should not have an alternative.

On responding to all these "cosmic" challenges, humanity will be able not only to preserve the potential that has been acquired over the years of the space age, but also to reach new frontiers, the overcoming of which is a vital necessity for us. In addition, we will be able to save the peace on our planet and to solve many economic and social problems.

References

1. Space Strategy for Europe. COM(2016) 705 final. Brussels [online], Available at: https://ec.europa.eu/transparency/regdoc/rep/1/2016/EN/COM-2016-705-F1-EN-MAIN.PDF (2016)
2. National Space Policy. HM Government [online], Available at: https://assets.publishing.service.gov.uk/government/uploads/system/uploads/attachment_data/file/484865/NSP_-_Final.pdf (2014)
3. The Economic Impact of Commercial Space Transportation on the U.S. economy in 2009 [online], Available at:

https://www.faa.gov/news/updates/media/Economic%20Impact%20Study%20September%202010_20101026_PS.pdf (2010)

4. The Space Foundation, "The Space Report: 2016," 2016 [online], Available at: http://www.spacefoundation.org/sites/default/files/downloads/The_Space_Report_2016_OVERVIEW.pdf (2016)
5. I. I. Khamits, I. M. Filippov, L. S. Burylov, S. M. Tanenbaum, A. V. Perfiliev, D. I. Gusak, Space equipment and technology, **1 (16)** (2017)
6. V. P. Legostaev, V. A. Lopota, V. V. Sinyavsky, Space equipment and technology, **1** (2013)
7. V. P. Legostaeva, V. A. Lopot, *The Moon – a step towards the technologies of solar system development* (RSC Energia, Moscow, 2011)
8. G. G. Raikunova, *Fundamental space research. Book 2 Solar* system (Fizmatlit, Moscow, 2014)
9. A. V. Volkova, *White spots of the solar system* (Niola-Press, Moscow, 2008)
10. E. Landau, NASA.gov, **1** (2017)
11. P. Luzin, New Defense Order, **4 (46)** (2017)
12. A. I. Antonov, Bulletin of MGIMO, **4 (25)** (2012)
13. E. K. Zvedre, IMI yearbook, **2 (8)** (2014)
14. E. S. Ascheulova, E. L. Farafontova, Actual problems of aviation and astronautics (2015)
15. Yu. D. Medvedev at al., *Asteroid and cometary hazard* (International Institute of Asteroid Hazard, Saint Petersburg, 1999)
16. A. V. Zaitsev, Earth and Universe, **2** (2003)
17. P. De Selding, Space Insurers warn that current low rates are not sustainable, SpaceNews [online], Available at: http://spacenews.com/space-insurers-warn-that-current-low-rates-are-not-sustainable/ (2016)
18. S. S. Veniaminov, A. M. Chervonov, *Space debris is threat to humanity* (Institute of Space Research, Moscow, 2012)
19. National Aeronautics and Space Administration, Orbital Debris Quarterly News, **13 (2)** (2009)
20. V. S. Aslanov, A. S. Ledkov Attitude Motion of Cylindrical Space Debris during Its Removal by Ion Beam // Mathematical Problems Engineering. – 2017. – Article ID 1986374.

Technological and economic perspectives for development and manufacturing of cathode materials for lithium-ion batteries for transport industry

Yuri Koshtyal[1,2], *Maxim* Maximov[1,2*], *Denis* Nazarov[1,2], *Alexander* Rumyantsev[1], and *Qing Sheng* Wang[3]

[1] R&D laboratory "Functional Materials", Peter the Great St. Petersburg Polytechnic University, 195251 Polytechnicheskaya st. 29, Russian Federation
[2] Center for National Technological Initiative "New Manufacturing Technologies", Peter the Great St. Petersburg Polytechnic University, 195251 Polytechnicheskaya st. 29, Russian Federation
[3] ENV (Zheijang) New Energy Material Technology Research Institute, 313100 Mingzhu Road 1278, China

Abstract. Energy accumulators are one of the key directions of research and applied development in the spheres of power generation, saving and efficiency. Lithium-ion batteries (LIB) are widely used in portable power sources for modern electronics. However, currently the most perspective sphere of their use is transport industry. In this article we discuss the perspectives of using LIB in road vehicles manufacturing, as well as the main trends development of new cathode materials for LIB. In the medium-term perspective, the issue that is the closest to commercial use is related to nano-technologies and new materials (including nano-materials in LIB components (cathode, anode, electrolyte fluid, separator) that can raise the characteristics of these accumulators to a new level of quality and efficiency.

For the first time, the Lithium-ion battery (LIB) was used as a widely used power source by Sony in 1991. Due to its characteristics, such as high energy density, slow rate of self-discharge, sustaining its capacity during the discharging and recharging cycles, lack of the memory effect etc. Lithium-ion batteries are widely used as a power source for various types of electronic devices [1]. In particular, they are used as a power source in such devices as smartphones, notebooks, electric vehicles, digital photographic and video cameras etc.

Lately, we can see steady growth in the market volume for Lithium-ion batteries. The largest relative growth is seen for to segments of LIB use – road vehicles (hybrid and electric cars, buses and trolleybuses) and power accumulators for industrial use (uninterrupted power sources, electric power storage in power generation and distribution systems) [2].

* Corresponding author: maximspbstu@mail.ru

According to the forecasts from analysts of Credit Suisse, it is expected that, by 2030, sales of electric and hybrid vehicles will reach USD 400 billion, and the revenue from sales of batteries will exceed USD 100 billion [2]. Many vehicle manufacturers, such as Tesla, Nissan, General Motors, Mitsubishi etc. have already entered the market with a few generations of electric and hybrid vehicles. Considering the requirements for decreasing pollution from exhaust gases, as well as changes in demand, analysts from Berenberg expect that the demand for LIB for vehicles industry can become dominant as early as by 2021 (Fig. 1).

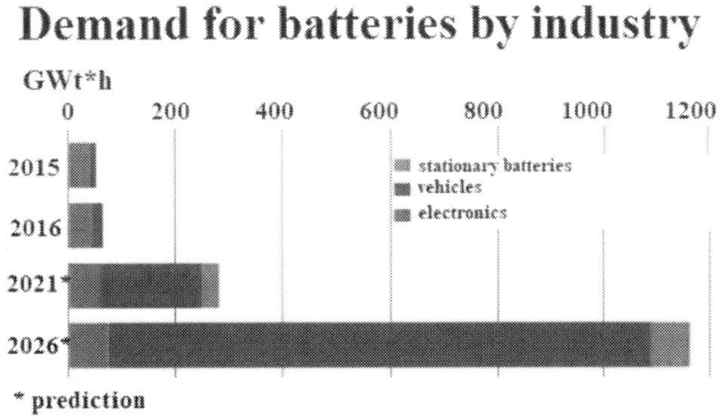

Fig. 1. Demand for LIB by industries, according to the data from Berenberg [3].

One example of a very successful commercialization of LIB is Tesla Motors that built a batteries manufacturing plant (Tesla Gigafactory) in 2016 in the Industrial Center in Tahoe Reno, in Storey County, Nevada, USA. According to the evaluation of the consulting company Benchmark, in the near future, more than 20 gigafactories will be manufacturing Lithium-ion batteries worldwide. Some of them are already operational; others will start manufacturing by 2021. Despite the success of Tesla Motors, manufacturing Lithium power sources is mainly based in Asia [4]. However, at the moment, Russia can already compete with China in respect of labor costs, which is a component in the cost of manufacturing, including manufacturing of Lithium-ion batteries. Therefore, if this trend remains, manufacturers may turn to stimulating development of LIB manufacturing in Russia.

The primary influence onto the price and characteristics of batteries is from the materials used – on average, about 74% (Fig. 2), with cathode materials being the main contribution to the cost [2].

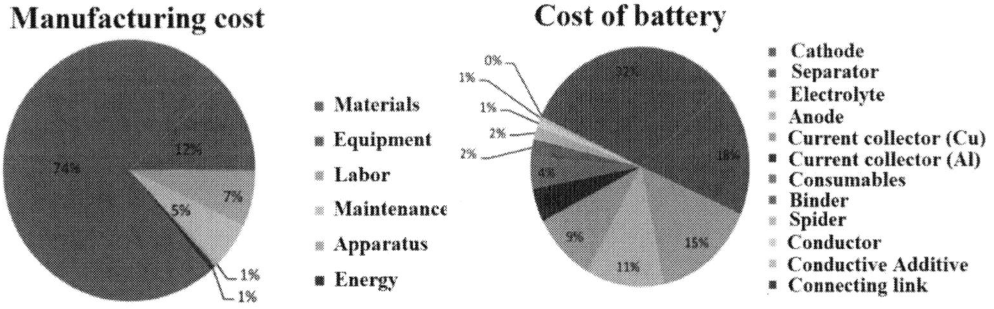

Fig. 2. Cost of LIB manufacturing and materials.

The low level of competition in the Russian market of manufacturing cathode materials for Lithium-ion batteries, as well as a number of state programs for import substitution, opens wide perspectives for developing this industry. At the moment, manufacturing cathode materials in the territory of Russia is carried out by OJSC "CATHODE MATERIALS" based in Novosibirsk. At the same time, there are no large capacities for manufacturing cathode materials for LIB, and the growth in the volume of manufacturing can cause a significant decrease in the manufacturing cost. Besides, growing domestic competition will promote improvement of the product quality and the manufacturing technologies. OJSC "Novosibirsk Plant of Chemical Concentrates" (a part of the corporation "TVEL") is the only Russian manufacturer of pure Lithium products. OJSC "NZKH" supplies Lithium products to both the domestic market and abroad cooperating on the long-term basis with companies in the North America, Canada, Europe and the South-East Asia. Therefore, Russia has a large supplier of Lithium chemicals, which is an advantage, for transportation and customs costs are decreased.

In the territory of Russia, potential buyers of cathode materials are manufacturers and developers of Lithium-ion batteries: SMC Rigel (Saint-Petersburg); CJSC "NIIHIT-2", (Samara); CJSC IF "Orion-HIT", (Novocherkassk); OJSC "NIIAI "Istochnik", (Saint-Petersburg); OJSC "Lithium-Element", (Saratov); OJSC "LioTech", (Novosibirsk) and others. Considering their high cost, Lithium-ion batteries made in Russia are mainly used in specialized machines. It is especially important for military production to manufacture all the components inside the country.

In highly developed industrial countries, the manufacturing technologies for Lithium-ion batteries are being continuously improved with new developments regularly implemented into manufacturing, in particular, for cathode materials. It is expected that using nano-technologies will bring maximum effect both in characteristics improvement and cost decrease. In this respect, foreign manufacturers support many projects in the sphere of manufacturing new materials and, in particular, cathode materials and cathodes based on them and a new generation of Lithium-ion batteries using innovative technologies (program DOE – USA, EC programs).

Currently, the most used cathode material is lithiated Cobalt oxide. However, in the medium-term perspective, the share of lithiated oxides of Nickel-Cobalt-Manganese (with higher Nickel content) and new materials – Lithium- and Manganese-enriched nano-composite lithiated oxides with laminated structure, materials with two or more atoms of Lithium in the structural formula (Fluorine-phosphates etc.)

It is noteworthy that, since first cathode material (Lithium cobaltate) was invented in the 1980-ies by John B. Goodenough [5] and used in manufacturing in early 1990-ies by Sony, less than ten years have passed. In 2008, industrial use started of the cathode material based on Lithium-Ferrum-phosphate (LFP) obtained in 1997. Therefore, development of new and improved cathode materials for Lithium power sources and their implementation for manufacturing has only been done very recently, about 10-15 years ago.

Currently, more sophisticated cathode materials are being introduced, such as $LiNi_{0,33}Co_{0,33}Mn_{0,33}O_2$ (NCM), $LiNi_{0,8}Co_{0,15}Al_{0,05}O_2$ (NCA) etc. (Table 1), where the content of transitory metals can vary depending of the conditions of use [2].

Table 1. Characteristics and use of the main cathode materials.

Cathode materials			Characteristics (10 is the maximum)				
Name	Metals content	Main use	Energy capacity	Power	Safety	Life cycle	Price
NCA	**Li/Ni/Co/Al**	Electric vehicles/ hybrid vehicles	10	10	3	6	6
NCM	**Li/Ni/Mn/Co**	Electric vehicles/ hybrid vehicles	6	6	6	10	10
LFP	**Li/Fe/P**	Uninterrupted power sources	2	10	10	6	6
LCO	**Li/Co**	Hybrid vehicles/ portable electronics	8	10	2	10	10

Among the methods of synthesizing cathode materials are the following: depositing from solutions with subsequent thermal processing and crystallization, solutions (or aerosols) drying with air-spraying, hard-phase caking (including the mechanically activated chemicals) with certain temperature-time intervals, the sol-gel method and others. When comparing generis methods for synthesizing cathode materials, a conclusion can be drawn that using the sol-gel method is a more technologically complicated solution as it includes many auxiliary processes such as: flushing ions out of the cathode material and multi-stage drying. Besides, in order to cut the manufacturing cost, it is necessary to filtrate and recycle by-products of the cathode materials synthesis.

At the moment, due to high price of Cobalt, one of the most expensive cathode materials is Lithium cobaltate (LCO), but, as it has a number of undeniable advantages, (Table 1) it is the most widely used. The only drawback of $LiCoO_2$ is its low safety that can be significantly improved through passivation (protective coating) with aluminum oxide [6-9]. As a perspective material for passivation, tin dioxide can also be considered that is also a feasible anode material for thin-film LIB [10-12]. Besides improving the safety, protective coating can increase the life cycle and capacity maintaining LIB [13, 14].

Among the methods for applying the coating on the surface of cathode materials, a method of atomic layer deposition (ALD) can be considered [15]. This technology is widely used for micro-processors manufacturing and passivation (encapsulation) of modern electronic displays; however, its use for manufacturing and modifying cathode materials has only been introduced recently. The main advantage of this method is the possibility to apply ultra-thin coatings (to several nano-meters) with high uniformity and integrity, directly on the material of the electrode that usually consists of micro- and nano-particles. For example, in the research of Dutch scientists [16] two main methods are described for manufacturing cathode materials with passivation coatings: applying coatings directly on the powder of the cathode material and on the cathode material in the structure of the LIB electrode. The authors said that, as the passivation coating is applied directly on the cathode material in the composition of the electrode, the electric contact between the particles is preserved (Fig. 3), which improves the electric-chemical characteristics.

https://doi.org/10.1051/shsconf/20184400048

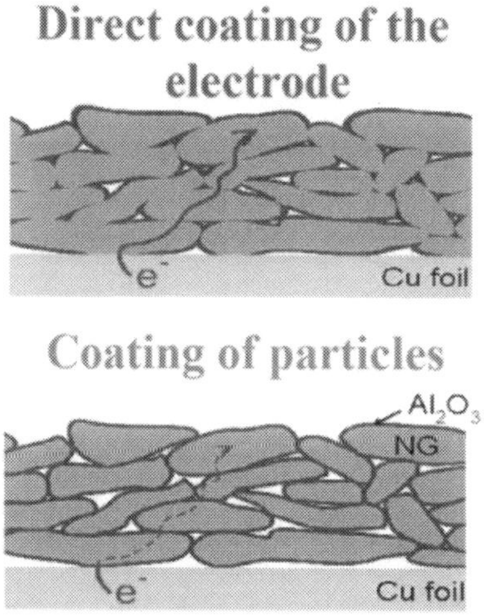

Fig. 3. A scheme of electrons transport with the coating applied on the electrode and the powder KM [16].

It is noteworthy that the technological method for applying functional coatings on electrodes can be introduced into the manufacturing cycle of LIB. This technological process has been already implemented in practice, and equipment manufacturers have presented industrial samples that can be adapted for particular uses. A schematic illustration of the principle of operation of actual manufacturing installations using the ALD method for flexible base plates that is called "Roll-to-Roll Spatial ALD" in the English-language literature is shown in Fig. 4. The process of application can be carried out under atmospheric or lower pressure, but does not require vacuum, which reduces the costs and simplifies manufacturing. This technology can be used not only for applying passivation coatings but also for other types of functional coatings, for example, the conductive coatings of various chemical compositions. Therefore the ALD technology has high adaptability and is also potentially usable for various electrode materials.

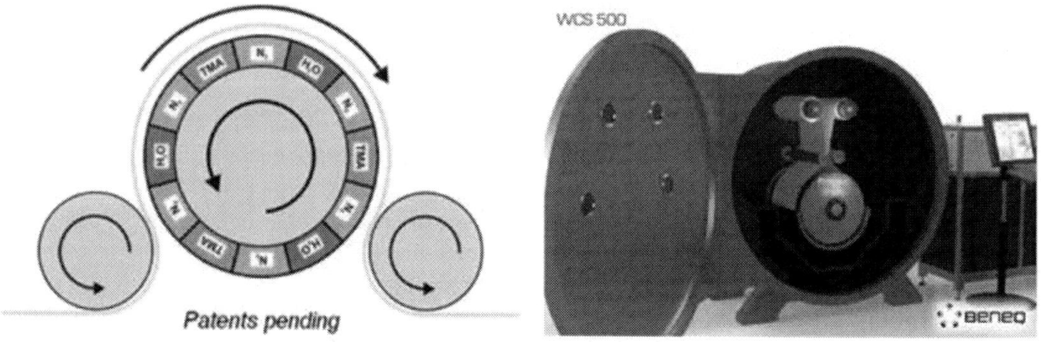

Fig. 4. A scheme of applying aluminum oxide coating on a film using the "Roll-to-Roll Spatial ALD" method and the equipment from Beneq Oy, Finland [17].

Using the atomic-layer depositing method for developing and manufacturing cathode materials can help achieve the leading position in the market of Lithium-ion batteries. The company "Pneumaticoat Technologies" (USA) already uses this technological approach for mass-production of cathode materials [18]. Fig. 5 shows a scheme and a photograph of the equipment.

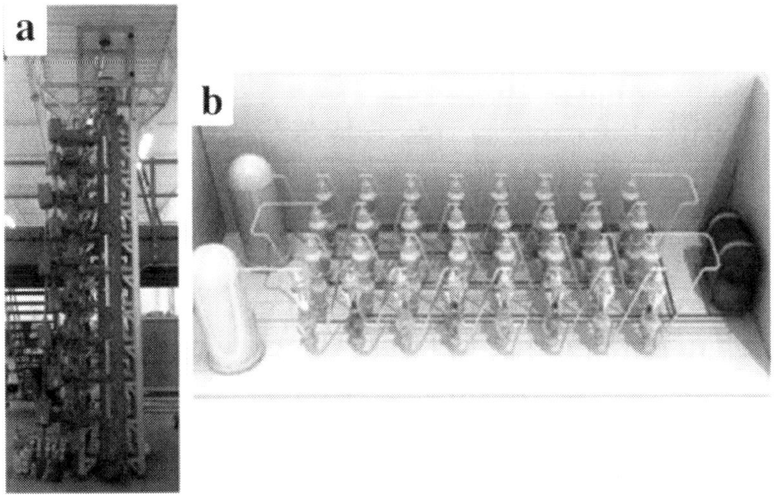

Fig. 5. Industrial implementation of the technology for applying thin film of various chemical compositions on powders using the ALD method. a) Equipment of the company "Pneumaticoat Technologies" based in Broomfield, Colorado (USA); б) A scheme of the applying process [18].

The red cylinder contains the metal-organic chemical that makes it possible to apply one nano-coating of Al_2O_3, TiO_2, ZrO_2, BN, AlN, Pt, W, Co, Fe or others; the blue cylinder contains the additional chemical (water); Nitrogen is continuously fed from gray cylinders to maintain the suspended state of the powder in each of the small cameras, forming the "boiling layer". The consumption of all the three gases is monitored with electronic sensors so that the flow of the chemical or inert gas can be increased or decreased depending on the process stage of atomic-layer depositing.

In Russia, such projects were implemented in the R&D group led by A.A.Popovich; in particular, a research was carried out to investigate the influence of the coating of aluminum oxide formed with the ALD method on flat electrodes (cathodes) for LIB manufacturing. As a result of the research for applying the coating and examining its electric-chemical properties according to newly developed programs and methods, it was estimated that, after 10 cycled of atomic-layer depositing of aluminum oxide with the layer thickness about 1 nm, the cyclic life cycle of LIB grew by more than 30 % [9]. The possibility was shown to apply ultra-thin aluminum oxide films with the ALD method on powder materials using a pseudo-suspended layer [19]. Therefore, a technology was developed to increase the life cycle of the battery by more than 30 %, which, at the present time, is a significant achievement under implementation.

As a conclusion, it is noteworthy that the leading LIB manufacturers widely use nano-technologies and high-tech equipment to reinforce their leading position in manufacturing cathode materials and Lithium-ion batteries. In Russia, nano-technologies are primarily used for R&D purposes. In particular, there are a number of R&D laboratories and research centers in the leading universities and branches of the Academy of Sciences in Moscow, Saint-Petersburg, Novosibirsk, and Saransk developing the ALD technology; they have made scientific progress that enables achieving a significant breakthrough in using up-to-date technologies for developing new materials for LIB manufacturing.

The research was carried out with financial support from the grant of the President of the Russian Federation for the state support of young Russian scientists – candidates of sciences; grant No. MK-2961.2018.3.

References

1. G. E. Blomgren, Journal of the Electrochemical Society, **164 (1)** (2017)
2. G. Berckmans, M. Messagie, J. Smekens, N. Omar, L. Vanhaverbeke, J. Van Mierlo, Energies, **10** (2017)
3. According to materials published by vedomosti [online], Available at: https://www.vedomosti.ru/business/articles/2017/12/07/744439-proizvoditeli-akkumulyatorov-gotovyatsya (2017)
4. K. Palmer, J. E. Tate, Z. Wadud, J. Nellthorp, Applied Energy **209** (2018)
5. K. Mitzushima, P. C. Jones, P. J. Wiseman, J. Goodenough, Materials Res. Bull., **15** (1980)
6. D. H. K. Jackson, M. R. Laskar, S. Y. Fang, S. Z. Xu, R. G. Ellis, X. Q. Li, M. Dreibelbis, S. E. Babcock, M. K. Mahanthappa, D. Morgan, R. J. Hamers, T. F. Kuech, J. Vac. Sci. Technol., A., **34 (3)** (2016)
7. M. Xie, T. Hu, L. Yang, Y. Zhou, RSC Adv., **6 (68)** (2016)
8. J. S. Park, X. B. Meng, J. W. Elam, S. Q. Hao, C. Wolverton, C. Kim, J. Cabana, Chem. Mater., **26 (10)** (2014)
9. A. A. Popovich, M. Yu. Maximov, A. M. Rumyantsev, P. A. Novikov, J. Appl. Chem, **88** (5) (2015)
10. D. V. Nazarov, M. Yu. Maximov, P. A. Novikov, A. A. Popovich, A. O. Silin, V. M. Smirnov, N. P. Bobrysheva, O. M. Osmolovskaya, M. G. Osmolovsky, A. M. Rumyantsev, J. Vac. Sci. Technol., A., **35 (1)** (2017)
11. M. Yu. Maximov, P. A. Novikov, D. V. Nazarov, A. M. Rymyantsev, A.O. Silin, Y. Zhang, A. A. Popovich, J. Electr. Mater., **46 (11)** (2017)
12. A. A. Popovich, M. Y. Maximov, D. V. Nazarov, P. A. Novikov, A. O. Silin, A. I. Shamshurin, Rus. J. Appl. Chem., **89 (5)** (2016)
13. J. Liu, X. Sun, Nanotechnology, **26** (2015)
14. A. A. Popovich, M. Yu. Maksimov, P. A. Novikov, A. O. Silin, D. V. Nazarov, A. M. Rumyantsev, Rus. J. Appl. Chem., **89 (4)** (2016)
15. S. M. George, Chem. Rev., **110** (2010)
16. M. E. Donders, H. C. M. Knoops, W. M. M. Kessels, P. H. L. Notten, J. Electrochem. Society, **160 (5)** (2013)
17. According to materials published by https://beneq.com/ [online], Available at: https://beneq.com/en/thin-films/products/roll-roll-ald/beneq-wcs-600 (2018)
18. Pneumaticoating [online], Available at: http://www.pneumaticoat.com/rd-systems.html (2018)
19. M. Yu. Maximov, A. S. Verevkin, A. A. Orlova, P. A. Novikov, A. O. Silin, O.V. Panchenko, A. A. Popovich, Journal of Ceramic Processing Research, **18 (2)** (2017)

Digital platforms based marketing innovations: new development trends

Alex Krasnov[1], *Valentin* Nikonorov[1*], and *Marina* Yanenko[1]

[1] Peter the Great St. Petersburg Polytechnic University, Institute of Industrial Management, Economics and Trade, 195251 Polytechnicheskaya st. 29, Russian Federation

Abstract. Marketing innovations in the digital economy are considered as the most important factor for the further digital economy growth. The main trends for development of the information and communication technologies market are studied. The basic types of innovations are analyzed. An algorithm for generation of competitive innovative marketing strategies is proposed. A business strategy that takes into account the digital technologies development is supplemented by a number of innovative components. The main lines for generation of a digital platform for marketing activities transformation with subsequent disclosure of the content of each line are indicated. The digital platform design for the marketing activities transformation is developed. There are three cornerstones of this platform are arrangement of interaction with consumers in the digital environment; improvement of digital methods for processing marketing information; automation of planning and implementation of marketing activities. The marketing complex specifics in the digital economy are specified and supplemented.

1 Introduction

Relevance. The ICT development results in revolutionary changes in the society and the economy, forces to talk about the generation of the information society that differs significantly from the industrial and post-industrial societies. Even now there is a significant contribution of information and communication technologies to the gross domestic product of the Russian Federation.

Foreign specialists also note the ICT importance specifying the need to use new innovative tools for development of economy and marketing such as Internet of things, BigData, Cloud computing, etc. [1,2,3].

Under modern globalization conditions the marketing system turns into an integrated unified system for coordinating supply and demand at all levels of economic ties in the use of tangible and intangible assets. At the same time, the virtualization of market processes, their communication and communicatory integration contribute to generation of an objective hierarchical marketing structure, which, in turn, affects the business processes efficiency.

*Corresponding author: Nikanorv@mail.ru

The marketing is developed through multimedia communications: the Internet, call centers, mobile phones, interactive television, etc., which allow to establish individual contacts with customers at a faster rate and at lower cost and to provide long-term after-sales service. Here is the place to especially highlight a number of trends for development of the information and communication technologies (ICT) market, and especially Foresight marketing technologies [4, 5]:

1. Growing of the Internet role and influence on economic processes.
2. Companies' focus on the purchase of ready IT tools and solutions.
3. Convergent solutions become more popular when the Internet is connected with mobile devices and IP-telephony.
4. Cloud technologies development and application.
5. DATA-centers organization by domestic companies.
6. Appearance of high-speed communication technologies and Internet access.
7. Individualization of needs satisfaction and customer service personalizing.
8. Internet of things market growth.
9. "Nuclear" growth in a number of social networks including ones of professionals and professionals.

The marketing management that is developed on the basis of media technologies under constant changes in the economy, science, practice requires rethinking, formulating of the conceptual foundations of innovation development. Marketing innovations will play a key role in the development of markets in the global economic space.

2 Development of marketing innovations

Under the global competition, innovations make it possible to provide leading positions in world commodity markets and to receive solid financial dividends through the introduction of new technologies. Therefore, the developed countries purposefully support the innovation processes. A share of new or improved technologies containing advanced knowledge or solutions is up to 80% of GDP growth in the developed countries. At the same time, scientific-and-technical and innovation activities in the Russian Federation are featured by a sharp decline against the innovations development in the world community. The contribution of Russian innovative products to the world bank of innovations is only 0.3% and tends to further decrease [6]

Therefore, under the sanctions, the transition to an innovation development model is a necessary strategic choice that in mid-term perspective can assist to overcome the production crisis, industry restructuring and market saturating with competitive products. In the long term, such a strategy shall help Russia to restore its position in the developed countries community.

J. Schumpeter interprets the innovations as "a change for the purpose of implementing and using new types of consumer goods, new production and transportation means, markets and forms of industry organization" [7].

The majority of theorists and practitioners in the management adheres to the innovation concept presented by J. Schumpeter. It is also taken as a basis for the development of the regulatory and legal framework for innovations in our country, in the development of innovation concepts, programs, and other strategic documents. There are two main approaches to innovation: 1) as a result of the creative process; 2) the process of innovations implementation.

U. King and D. Cleland mean by innovation a process including generation of a new idea of products, technology, material, management, form of production organization –

analysis and selection of received proposals; approbation of development in production conditions; mass production and assessment by consumers [8].

According to V. E. Gordin and M. D. Suschinskaya et al. [9] it is possible to identify the main innovation criteria: scientific-technical or social-cultural novelty; practical incarnation; commercial feasibility.

From the above definitions, the following conclusion may be drawn that the specific innovation content composes the changes. These innovations cover a very wide range of activities – from research and development to marketing activities, include both the innovation process itself and its result.

In practice, there are four types of innovation: product, process, marketing and organization.

Product innovation is the introduction to the use (implementation) of a product or service that is new or significantly improved in terms of their properties or methods of use.

Process innovation is the introduction of a new or significantly improved way for product production or delivery.

Organizational innovation is the introduction of a new organizational method in the enterprise business standard, in the organization of workplaces or external relations.

Marketing innovation is the introduction of a new marketing method including significant changes in the product design or packaging, its placement, promotion to the market, or in setting prices [10].

The marketing innovations are aimed at the best satisfaction of the needs of the consumer, opening of new markets or winning of new positions for the enterprise's products on the market for sales increasing.

A distinctive feature of the marketing innovation compared to other changes in marketing tools is the implementation of the marketing method. The digital technologies implementation to solve marketing challenges (consumers' analysis, product selection at the request of individual customers, etc.) can also be considered a marketing innovation.

The digital technologies development stimulates appearances of spatial relationships between enterprises, creates unprecedented abilities in establishing mutually beneficial relations with customers. Due to the rapid spread of wireless networks, smartphones and tablets, mobile applications and cloud computing technologies, there are significant changes in the consumers lifestyle, activation of e-commerce [11].

ICTs create new conditions for market interaction, allow to significantly increase the level of consumers' confidence. The overwhelming majority of authors agree that ICT fundamentally change the company's external and internal marketing environment, approaches to marketing research, analysis of markets and competitors, development of marketing strategies and marketing programs [12].

It seems that the implementation of digital technologies in marketing activities will mainly facilitate the transition in communication with a client from the impressions to the creation of its constant involvement in the firm's activities. The effect is created by channels and means of digital technologies due to new ways to attract consumers and to increase a rate of communication with them.

The results of our research [12, 13, 14] allow to conclude that most of the surveyed companies (more than 70%) in one form or another actively use marketing innovations in their daily marketing activities

The innovative marketing activity of the enterprise is based on constant work with various sources of information, knowledge about technologies, practical experience, available and accessible human and financial resources.

Marketing innovations research includes the analysis of possible response of potential consumers to the innovations, the analysis of innovation from the point of view of the consumer, as well as comprehensive analysis of the innovative market environment. It shall be ensured that the scientific, technical and economic information relevant to the marketing strategy development is monitored continuously and on its basis corrections are made both to the strategic decisions of the firm and to the tactical means for achieving the priority objectives.

To generate competitive innovative marketing strategies, we propose the following algorithm.

Stage I. Identification of the main trends affecting the business environment.

1. Analysis of trends in the development of the world and Russian economy.
2. Analysis of trends in the industry development.
3. Analysis of trends in the business environment development.
4. Analysis of marketing innovations.

Stage II. Definition of prospective directions of innovation development of the enterprise.

Stage III. Assessment of the prospects for integration in the innovation environment.

1. Assessment of participation in government programs
2. Assessment of participation in federal targeted programs.
3. Assessment of participation in design and survey work.
4. Assessment of participation in the generation of the knowledge economy.

IV. Generation of the strategy for participation in the innovation process.

V. Choice of innovation tools for marketing strategy implementation

1. Mobile technologies.
2. BigData technologies.
3. Geoinformational technologies.
4. Video analytics technologies.

VI. Generation of competitive innovation marketing strategy.

The algorithm can work both at the enterprise level and at the industry level.

Its main features are that to reduce the costs and time of marketing research, the economic phenomena concept is used that allows moving from time-consuming and long-term studies of environmental factors to the formation of a generalized description of the processes taking place in the economy and the enterprise business environment. Identification of the main trends affecting the business environment allows to determine the prospective lines of innovation enterprise development and to assess the prospects of its integration in the innovation environment.

Generation of the innovation marketing strategy is impossible without the use of innovation tools, with the help of which the program will be implemented. Along with the marketing innovations listed, for example, in [12,13,14], we consider the innovative marketing tools based on the use of mobile, BigData, Internet of Things technologies, etc., and being not yet sufficiently described in the marketing literature are prospective .

3 Further learning of the concepts of organization digital platform development and management of the organization marketing activities

According to M. B. Yanenko and M. E Yanenko.who studied mobile technologies in marketing services in [14], the business strategy considering the development of mobile technologies shall include such innovation components as:

– adaptation of the corporate site, promo-sites for mobile devices;

– adaptation of the existing company services for mobile devices and creation of special applications;

– development of the company's IT infrastructure to ensure high-quality, stable communications;

– the maximum coverage of potential buyers and constant information impact on them;

– increase the volume and quality of on-line advertising;

– provision of the client's access to the account from any device;

– new pricing policy and loyalty programs for customers viewing on-line advertising and buying it from mobile devices;

– individualization of work with a client and strengthening of feedback, etc.

The authors proposed the digital platform design for the marketing activities transformation (Fig. 1).

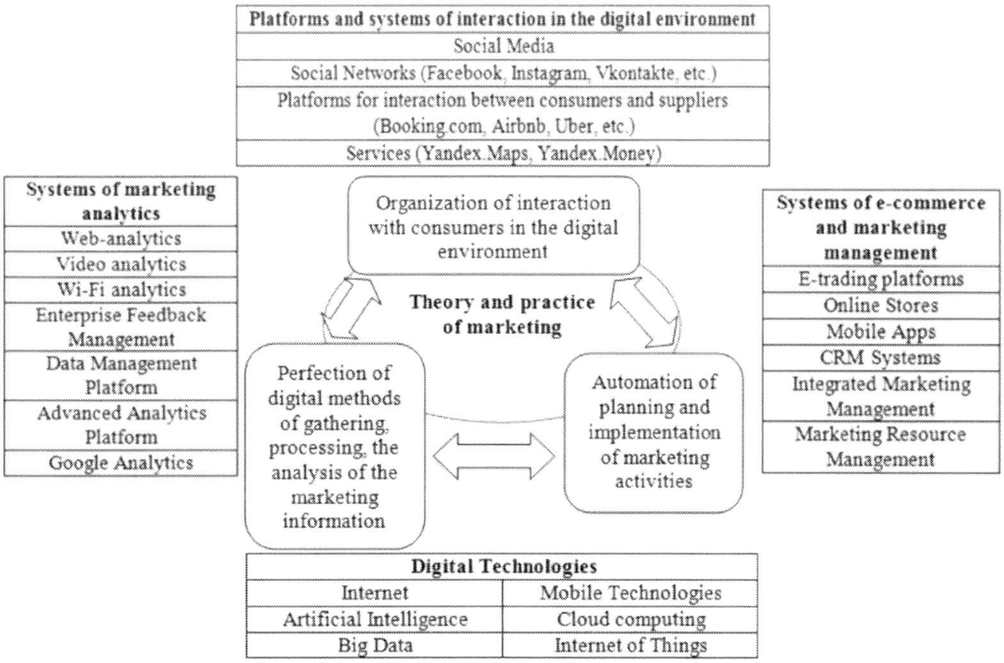

Fig. 1. The main elements of marketing innovations based on the digital platforms.

Based on the marketing theory and practice, it is possible to identify the following basic lines for generation of the digital platform for marketing activity transformation

– improvement of digital methods for collection, processing, analyzing of marketing information;

– arrangement of interaction with consumers in the digital environment;

– automation of planning and implementation of marketing activities.

The first line is improving the methods for collection, processing, analyzing of marketing information; it is aimed primarily at creating systems of marketing analytics, specialized tools for marketing data analysis. Web analytics, video analytics, Wi-Fi analytics, etc. can be used as an example.

The second line of digital platform generation is the improvement of arrangement of interaction with consumers in the digital environment.

Development of marketing activities under marketing functions digitizing implies, along with such conventional channels as Internet advertising, direct mailings, mobile communication, etc., the use of social media, social networks (Facebook, Instagram, Classmates, etc.), digital platforms of interaction of consumers and suppliers (Booking, Momondo), various services [15].

Identification of the automation of planning and implementation of marketing activities, and the development of e-commerce and marketing management systems as a third line is due to that, along with the electronic trading platforms, on-line stores, mobile applications, CRM systems widely used in practice and already described in the marketing literature, there are new marketing activities automation systems such as Integrated Marketing Management, Marketing Resource Management.

Under real conditions there is a continuous process of integration of various computer and software products aimed at creating platforms and systems of continuous interaction between the consumers and the suppliers. In this case, the conventional cycle of marketing activities including marketing research, planning and implementation of marketing activities is implemented as software products that provide instant system response to changing customer requests.

In terms of the generation of the digital platform for marketing activities management, it is necessary to clarify certain provisions of the marketing theory.

In particular, the marketing complex elements (Fig. 2) will have a number of features that characterize the abilities of interaction in the digital environment (for more details see our paper 12,13).

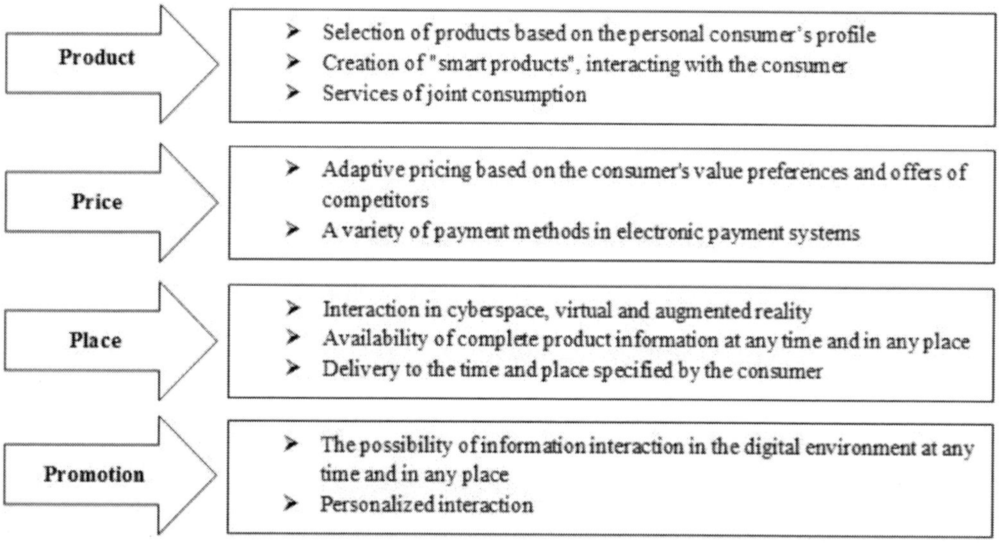

Fig. 2. The marketing complex specifics in the digital economy.

The above considerations show that the transformation of the marketing activities management in the digital economy is complex and requires an in-depth analysis of the practice of using the digital technologies, rethinking a number of key theoretical marketing provisions.

The main challenges for generation of the organization digital platform and marketing activities management shall include the following:

– onrush of digital technologies; computer technologies grow and change faster than the business can adapt to them;

– explosive growth of data volumes; they are extremely difficult to process to find data that can help make the right decisions.

– increased competition.

Thus, the creation of the organization digital platform and marketing activities management is not a one-off event, but one of the key innovation lines of the business development strategy, a continuous process that allows monitoring environmental changes and using the digital technologies to strengthen competitive positions in the digital economic space.

The main point of the marketing activities management transformation is the accelerated application of rapidly developing digital technologies to solve key marketing problems such as: competitive situation analysis; prices monitoring; activities to promote goods and services in a virtual environment; presentation of goods and services to customers; the desire to involve the consumer in the interaction process, that is, during identifying and satisfying the needs.

The lag in the transfer of functional and technological subdivisions to the use of digital technologies can lead to additional costs associated with loss of consumers, decrease in the sales of goods or services provided.

The digital technologies development, innovation economy building will require significant changes in the marketing activities arrangement. Among the most significant changes there are the following.

1. Participation in the development (as a customer) of new analysis tools and subsequent application of these tools allowing to process large amount of marketing information.
2. Search for optimal combinations of digital and classical marketing methods.
3. Ideas generation, super-fast (thanks to the digital technologies) spread of the generated ideas among a large number of potential consumers.

4 Conclusions

The analysis of extensive literature, publications on information resources and technologies in marketing, statistical data makes it possible to obtain the following important results:

1. Knowledge and skillful use of information technologies, resources, systems provide the unlimited possibilities for the successful work of the marketer allowing him/her to navigate the information space, to find and effectively use valuable information to achieve the firm's goals.
2. The skills of handling information can become an important competitive advantage of a marketer in the modern labor market.
3. Expanding use of the digital technologies in marketing processes is explained by the desire of enterprises to increase competitiveness and profits through effective processing of marketing information and creation of new business lines. A systematic approach to the use of ICT becomes an important competitive advantage of the company, allowing it to occupy a leading position in the market. The changes in the elements of the marketing complex allow to identify and include innovation measures in the marketing strategy aimed at increasing economic efficiency and securing the company's long-term competitive advantages.

References

1. New Skills for the Digital Economy [online], Available at: http://dx.doi.org/10.1787/5jlwnkm2fc9x-en (2017)
2. The Internet of Things [online], Available at: http://dx.doi.org/10.1787/5jlwvzz8td0n-en (2017)
3. Cloud Computing: The Concept, Impacts and the Role of Government Policy [online], Available at: //dx.doi.org/10.1787/5jxzf4lcc7f5-en (2017)
4. G. L. Bagiev, A. A. Dligach. Yu. N. Soloviyova, *Marketing foresight technologies Relationship marketing: system reflexive marketing. Benchmarking.Competence management. Value measurement and assessment* (Asterion, Saint Petersburg, 2016)
5. V. N. Naumov, *Information and communication technology markets and sales arrangement* (INFRA-M, Moscow, 2017)
6. Yu. Samsonov, Maket of Russian innovations [online], Available at: http://www.center-inno.ru/materials/library/06-2 (2015)
7. J. Schumpeter, *TheTheory of Economic Development* (Progress, Moscow, 1983)
8. U. King, *Cleland Strategic planning and policy* (Progress, Moscow, 1982)
9. V. E. Gordin, M. D. Sushinskaya, *Service management* (Pub. House "Business-Pressa", Saint Petersburg, 2007)
10. Oslo management, *Recommendations for collection and analysis of innovation data* ZISN, Moscow, 2010)
11. E. V. Popov, *Minieconomic institution evolution* (Nauka, Moscow, 2007)
12. M. B. Yanenko, M. E. Yanenko, Izvestiya of Ural State University of Economics, **2 (24)** (2009)
13. M. B. Yanenko, M. E. Yanenko, *Methodology for formation of innovative marketing strategies under digital technologies introduction* (Saint Petersburg State University of Economics, Saint Petersburg, 2015)
14. M. B. Yanenko, M. E. Yanenko, Modern economic problems, **2 (50)** (2014)
15. E-mail marketing mobilization [online], Available at: https://subscribe.ru/archive/media.vox/201410/30171621.html (2015)

An empirical study of information technology clusters and regional economic growth in Russia

Tatiana Kudryavtseva[1], *Dmitry* Rodionov[1], and *Angi* Skhvediani[1*]

[1] Peter the Great St. Petersburg Polytechnic University, Engineering and Economical Higher School, 195251, Politekhnicheskaya st., 29 Russian Federation

Abstract. The paper is devoted to the identification of the "Information Technologies" cluster in the regions of the Russian Federation and verification of the assumption that there is an interaction between the degree of cluster representation in the region and the GRP size. The authors considered the main theoretical and methodological provisions concerning the identification of clusters with the Top-down approach. Based on the develops of M. Porter and G. Lindqvist, the "Information Technologies" cluster characteristics such as local content, size and focus were calculated for 80 regions of the Russian Federation. The conclusions about the specifics of the cluster development in the country were made. Using the methods of regression analysis, the authors tested a number of hypotheses and revealed the presence of a positive interaction between the GRP volume and the "Information Technologies" cluster presence in the regions of the Russian Federation, as well as the local content, size and focus of this cluster in the regions of the Russian Federation.

1 Introduction

Regional economic growth is a relevant studies trend [1]. Issues related to the relationship between the economic growth and development of information technologies in separate countries and regions are also the subject of many scientific studies [2, 3, 4, 5, 6]. In particular, in terms of the development and institutionalization of the concepts "digital economy" [7, 8] and "sixth technological mode" [9] which is based on the convergence of nanotechnologies, biotechnologies, information technologies and cognitive science, the authors deem that it is advisable to perform an empirical study on the analysis of information technologies cluster development in the regions of the Russian Federation and the identification of the relationship between its characteristics and regional economic growth.

The information technologies are one of the drivers of economical growth in the modern world. Mainly, the studies related to the assessment of ICT effect on the economical growth at the national level are divided into two large categories. The first category includes the studies which reflect ICT interest bearing deposit to GDP growth. For example, the studies of M. Timmer, G. Ypma & B. Van Ark [10], D. Jorgenson & K. Vu [12] et al. The second group includes the studies using the cross-country methods of regression analysis to assess the ICT effect on the economical growth. This category include studies of Z. Latif, S. Latif,

* Corresponding author: aeskhvediani@mail.ru

L. Ximei, Z. H. Pathan, S. Salam, & Z. Jianqiu [13], T. Niebel [14], et al. In this case, the studies of the second group are usually devoted to two problems:

- assessment of the impact of investments in ICT on the economic growth of the regions;
- assessment of the impact of technologies penetration and distribution, their level of use on economic growth.

In this case, the problem of the influence of the cluster structure considered from the perspective of the macro level and, in particular, the ICT cluster on the economic growth of the regions remains open and little presented in the literature.

Thus, the study purpose is to find the relationship between the regional economic growth and the development of the "Information Technologies" cluster in the Russian Federation. To achieve this goal, the authors revealed the main theoretical and methodological provisions related to the identification of clusters using the top-down approach, estimated the local content, size and focus of the cluster group "Information Technologies" in 80 regions of the Russian Federation in the period from 2008 to 2016, marked the significant clusters and built four groups of regression models reflecting the positive relationship between the development of the "Information Technology" cluster and the real GRP growth in the region.

2 Cluster and its identification

One of the key aspects of the cluster theory is the problem of clusters identification within separate territories – regions. As foreign experience shows, the existing methodological approaches with a low variety of tools differ considerably in practice. There are many pairs of categories for characterizing the process and techniques for clusters identification, however, most of them are based on two main approaches [15]. In the first approach that can be called "down", the clusters are identified in a specific area based on the presence of enterprises and industries-leaders known in advance. The second approach uses a technique conventionally called "top" where spatially localized industries oriented to the specific types of economic activity are detected. Further, to detect and perform initial analysis of specific regional clusters, a nationwide reference sample is used.

The meaning of "reference" clusters is to determine the types of economic activity which are most often located near each other, and, therefore, have the effect of complementarity. Since "the degree to which the industries actually colocalized in the space indicates the importance of local inter-industry contacts" [16], if spatial affinity is between two or more industries, it will serve to synergy the cluster specialization industries.

The approaches to identification of clusters "top", taking into account two invariable characteristics of clusters – functional connectivity and geographical proximity – are conventionally divided into 2 types: 1) functional, focused on detection of certain types of the clusters;2) spatial, focused on detection of the geographic clusters.

It is now generally recognized that the best results of identification of the clusters "top" are achieved through a combination of functional and spatial approaches. Such synthetic approaches include the approach of M. Porter. The M. Porter's method became classic and one of the most widespread in other countries. Many European and a few domestic attempts to identify and map the clusters do not just use the Harvard approach as the technique, but are based on its results.

As a result of numerous studies, M. Porter was able to fully determine the structure of "reference" clusters based on the variety of activities represented in the American Classifier SIC (Standard Industrial Classification) [17].

Subsequently, the "reference" cores of the cluster groups were widely used by the US Department of Commerce, which supports the project of US clusters mapping [18]. The composition of the "reference" cluster core was adapted for the European Union taking into account the application of the European NACE classifier in the project of the European cluster observatory for identification and mapping of economic agglomerations of the EU countries [19].

Full adaptation of foreign Standard Industrial Classification to the Russian analogue – OKVED has not been carried out to date.

The solution of this problem by adapting the structure of the "reference" cluster cores for the Russian economy in accordance with the Standard Industrial Classification OKVED will allow determining the composition of the most probable cores of cluster groups of RF entities and can be widely used as an adequate basis for approbation of foreign methods of cluster analysis.

3 Top – down approach for cluster identification

In the framework of the "top" approach, the filling of cluster groups within the territory of the federation entities in accordance with the identified "standards" allows to form conditional clusters, but the clusters identification suggests confirmation of the hypothesis of their existence within the specified territory that can be achieved with the use of statistical tools in accordance with the methodology proposed by the European cluster observatory [19].

The presence and development of positive economic externalities affecting the activities of enterprises included in the cluster is determined by the presence of a certain "critical mass" of the cluster group core. As a consequence, the formed "reference" cores of the cluster groups shall be investigated for the presence of specified "critical mass" that determines the relative strength and competitiveness of the local cluster.

This method is based on the assumption that the volume and qualitative level of knowledge circulating between enterprises and organizations included in the cluster under investigation depends on the cluster size, its specialization level, and the extent to which the studied region is aimed at products production in related areas included in the cluster. These 3 factors are determined by the European cluster observatory as the "Localization Coefficient" (1), "Size" (2), "Focus" (3). The factor values within the threshold values reflect whether the studied cluster has achieved a sufficient "critical mass" to generate the positive external effects and relations. These indicators are calculated according to the employment statistics and are specified in the following formula:

$$LQ = \frac{Emp_{ig}}{Emp_g} / \frac{Emp_i}{Emp} \quad (1)$$

where LQ is the "localization coefficient"; Emp_{ig} is a number of employees in the cluster group i in region g; Emp_g is the total number of employees in the region g; Emp_i is a number of employees in the cluster group i; Emp is the total number of employees.

$$Size = \frac{Emp_{ig}}{Emp_i} \tag{2}$$

where Size is the "Cluster group size"; Emp_{ig} is a number of employees in the cluster group i in region g; Emp_i is a number of employees in the cluster group i.

$$Focus = \frac{Emp_{ig}}{Emp_g} \tag{3}$$

where Focus is the cluster group "focus"; Emp_{ig} – is a number of employees in the cluster group i in region g; Emp_g is a number of employees in the region g.

G. Lindqvist, a Swedish economist from the European Cluster Observatory [20] sets the following criteria as the threshold values that feature the meaningful cluster groups in the region:

1) "Localization coefficient" (3.1) ≥ 2;

2) the region shall be among the 10% of the regions leading by "Size" (3.2);

3) the region shall be among the 10% of the regions leading by "Focus" (3.2);

Fulfillment of the constraint conditions for each indicator means assignment of a "star" to the cluster group 1. Thus, as much as possible, one or another cluster group can receive 3 "stars". A number of "stars" determines cluster group strength.

In addition, none of the "stars" can be assigned if the total number of workers in the cluster core does not exceed 1000 persons.

As a result, the implementation of the described methodology makes it possible to obtain data on a number and strength of the studied cluster groups in all regions of the studied country (group of countries).

It should be noted that the restriction by the "Localization coefficient" is a variable value. Thus, M. Porter, when studying the "core" of clusters (i.e., the clusters in the strict sense), determined the threshold value of the localization coefficient at 1.0 [17], and the US Department of Commerce uses the threshold value 1.3 [18]. In our study, when selecting the strong clusters, it is proposed to use a threshold value of 1.3.

Thus, in the course of the cluster analysis, adaptation of the results of the synthetic approach to the Russian economy makes it possible to identify the cluster "standards" typical for the studied area, and the use of the European Cluster Observatory criteria makes it possible, firstly, according to employment statistics, to check the hypothesis of a specific cluster groups strength in one region or another by a number of assigned "stars", and secondly, to identify the regions where the studied clusters are significant. The identification of such regions allows speaking both of the existence of interterritorial clusters, which accounting allows for a more effective regional policy, and the existence of competing "centers" of concentration of relevant industries capable of "draining" the employment of other cluster groups through the action of more significant positive agglomeration externalities within their territory.

The application of criteria for the level of cluster groups' development makes it possible to identify strong clusters within the country and its regions, but does not provide sufficient information about the factors of the cluster geographical concentration – agglomeration external effects which determine a level and potential of cluster group development within the studied territory.

4 The results of assessment of the "Information Technologies" cluster development in the regions of the Russian Federation in the period from 2008 to 2016

To assess the development of the "Information Technologies" cluster in the regions of the Russian Federation, the authors compared the activities according to the NACE classifier, which M. Porter assigns to the "Information Technologies" cluster with the corresponding activities according to the OKVED-2001 classifier (see Table 1).

Table 1. Correlation of activity types included in the "Information Technology" cluster according to the NACE and OKVED-2001 classifiers.

Cluster	Activities according to NACE (Europe)		Activities according to OKVED (Russia)	
Information Technology	26.20	Manufacture of computers and peripheral equipment	30.0	Production of office equipment and computer technologies
	58.21 58.29 62.01	Publishing of computer games; Other software publishing; Computer programming activities	72.20	Software development and consulting in this field

Further, the authors calculated a level of localization, size and focus of this cluster for 80 regions of the Russian Federation for the period from 2008 to 2016 and identified 13 regions, where at least once per this period a cluster was identified in accordance with the criteria presented above. The calculation results for Moscow and St. Petersburg are presented in Fig. 1.

As of 2016, the "Information Technologies" cluster is represented in the following regions (see Table 2): St. Petersburg, Moscow, Yaroslavl Region, Novosibirsk Region, Tatarstan and Penza Region. The cluster is the largest in Moscow and St. Petersburg – 30.52% and 16.14% of all persons employed in the cluster in the Russian Federation, in this case, the cluster focus – a share of persons employed in the cluster in relation to all ones in the region – in Moscow it is increased from 0.96% to 1.2%, and in St. Petersburg – from 0.58% to 1.47%. High cluster localization in these cities with relatively small values of focus and size is explained by the higher population in them and by the fact that they are the main administrative, managerial and economic centers of the country.

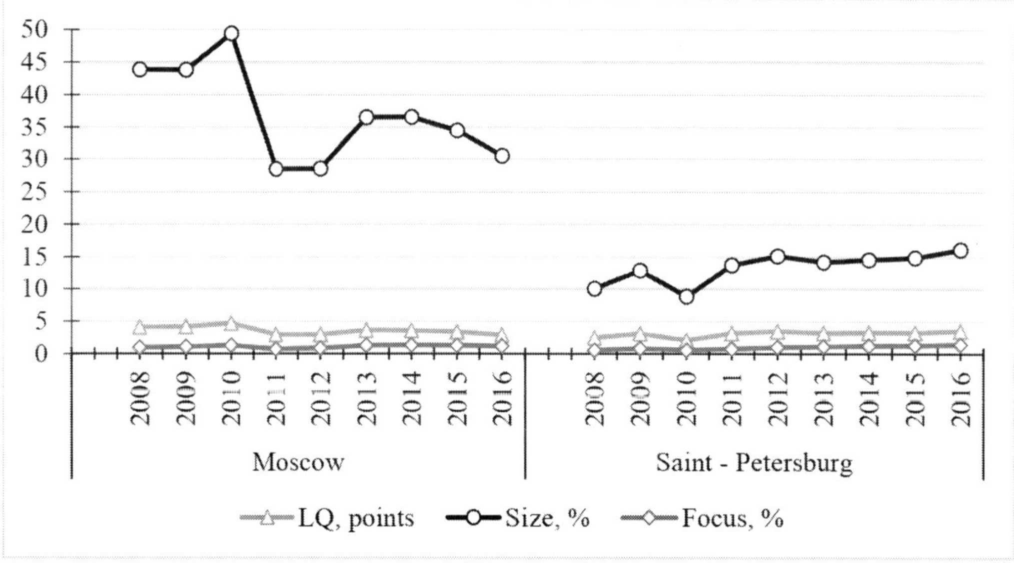

Fig. 1. Dynamics of changes in the level of localization, size and focus of the"Information Technologies" cluster in Moscow and St. Petersburg.

Table 2. A number of stars assigned to the "Information Technology" cluster in some regions of Russian Federation.

	2008	2009	2010	2011	2012	2013	2014	2015	2016
Republic of Bashkortostan	2	1	2	3	1	1	1	0	0
Republic of Tatarstan	1	1	1	1	1	1	2	2	3
Khabarovsk Territory	0	0	0	2	2	1	0	0	0
Vladimir Region	0	0	3	0	0	0	0	0	0
Kaluga Region	2	1	0	0	0	0	0	0	0
Novosibirsk Region	3	1	0	3	3	3	3	3	3
Penza Region	2	2	2	2	2	2	2	2	2
Perm Territory	0	0	0	0	1	0	1	2	0
Yaroslavl Region	0	1	1	2	2	2	2	2	2
Kursk Region	3	2	0	0	0	0	0	0	0
Nizhny Novgorod Region	2	2	2	3	3	2	2	1	1
Moscow	3	3	3	3	3	3	3	3	3
Saint Petersburg	3	3	3	3	3	3	3	3	3

In the period from 2008 to 2016, a stable growth of indicators characterizing the cluster development occurred only in two regions: St. Petersburg and the Republic of Tatarstan. So, in St. Petersburg, the growth of the level of the localization (ELQ) for nine years was 1.05 units, the size (ESize) by 6.09 percentage points and the focus (EFocus) by 0.89 percentage points. In Tatarstan, the level of localization increased by 0.71 units, the focus – by 0.43 percentage points, and the size by 2.24 percentage points. The simultaneous increase in all three indicators reflects the increase in specialization of these regions on the "Information Technologies".

As well as the stable presence of the "Information Technologies" cluster is observed in the Penza and Novosibirsk regions although the dynamics of its development in these regions is not unambiguous. Thus, in the Penza region there is cluster weakening over the past nine years for all three indicators. While in Novosibirsk region, despite the general trend to its increasing, the cluster development dynamics is characterized by constant downturns and upturns.

5 The relationship between the regional economic growth and the development of the "Information Technologies" cluster in the Russian Federation.

5.1 Model, hypothesis and study method

The relationship between the regional economic growth and the development of the "Information Technology" cluster in the Russian Federation was measured using the regression analysis tools available in the STATA MP14 program.The basic study tool was the Linear regression with panel-corrected standard errors proposed by Beck and Katz as an alternative to the feasible generalized least squares (FGLS) based algorithm proposed by Parks and Kmenta in 1986 [21, 22].

In the framework of this study, 12 models were built and tested, in the framework of which the presence or absence of relationship between the characteristics of the "Information Technologies" cluster and the GRP size was assessed. These models are divided into 4 groups depending on the hypotheses to be tested.

The first group of models can be represented as an equation as follows:

$$\mathrm{lnGRP}_{it} = \beta_0 + \beta_1 \mathrm{lnRIiFA}_{it} + \beta_2 \mathrm{lnTRE}_{it} + \Upsilon_i \mathrm{ClusterIT}_{it} + \phi_t \mathrm{Year}_t + \mathcal{E}_{it} + \mathrm{U}_t \quad (4)$$

where:

lnGRP_{it} –base logarithm of GRP (rub., in constant prices of 2008) generated in region i at time t;

$\mathrm{lnRIiFA}_{it}$ –base logarithm of investments (rub., in constant prices of 2000) in the fixed capital carried out in region i at time t;

lnTRE_{it}- base logarithm of a number of workers employed in the region (million persons) in region i at time t;

$\mathrm{ClusterIT}_{it}$- a binary variable that takes the value 1 if there is an "Information technology" cluster in the region, and otherwise, it is 0.

$Year_t$ – binary variables that take the value 1 if the observation refers to a certain year t, and otherwise, it is 0.

For dependent and independent control variables to graduate heteroscedasticity resulting from the uneven social and economic position of the regions, the functional form of the basic logarithm was taken. In addition, the logarithmic specification of the regression equation made it possible to linearize the presented function by analogy with the Cobb-Douglas production function, which allows interpreting their coefficients as elasticity.

The H1 hypothesis is tested in the framework of the first group of models, according to which there is a statistically significant relationship between the GRP volume and the presence of the "Information Technologies" cluster in the region.

The second, third and fourth groups of models were constructed by analogy with the first one:

$$\mathrm{lnGRP}_{it} = \beta_0 + \beta_1 \mathrm{lnRIiFA}_{it} + \beta_2 \mathrm{lnTRE}_{it} + \Upsilon_i \mathrm{LQ}_{it} + \phi_t \mathrm{Year}_t + \mathcal{E}_{it} + \mathrm{U}_t \quad (5)$$

$$\mathrm{lnGRP}_{it} = \beta_0 + \beta_1 \mathrm{lnRIiFA}_{it} + \beta_2 \mathrm{lnTRE}_{it} + \Upsilon_i \mathrm{Size}_{it} + \phi_t \mathrm{Year}_t + \mathcal{E}_{it} + \mathrm{U}_t \quad (6)$$

$$\mathrm{lnGRP}_{it} = \beta_0 + \beta_1 \mathrm{lnRIiFA}_{it} + \beta_2 \mathrm{lnTRE}_{it} + \Upsilon_i \mathrm{Focus}_{it} + \phi_t \mathrm{Year}_t + \mathcal{E}_{it} + \mathrm{U}_t \quad (7)$$

where:

LQ_{it}- the value of the localization coefficient of the "Information technology" cluster in region i at time t;
$Size_{it}$ – the size of the cluster group i at time t, %;
$Focus_{it}$ – the focus of the cluster group i at time t, %.

In the second model the H2 hypothesis of statistically significant relationship between the localization level of the "Information Technology" cluster in the region and with the GRP volume, the third – the H3 hypothesis of the presence of positive relationship between the size of the"Information Technology" cluster in the region and with the GRP volume, the fourth – the H4 hypothesis on the presence of positive relationship between the focus of the"Information Technology" cluster in the region and with the GRP volume.

In groups of models 2, 3 and 4, the indexes: 1 corresponds to the models built based on 80 regions of the Russian Federation, 2 – based on 13 regions, where the minimum required value for two parameters of three was achieved at least once per 2008 – 2016 according to the "Information Technology" cluster, 3 – based on 13 regions with an adjustment for annual fixed effects.

5.2 Empirical results of the study

The main empirical results of the study are presented in the Appendix. Based on these calculations, we can conclude that there is an interaction between GRP volumes and the main characteristics of the "Information Technology" cluster (see Tables 3 and 4).

So, according to the results of models 1.1 – 1.3, there is a statistically significant interaction between the GRP volume and the cluster presence in the region. That is, in regions, where the presence of this cluster is recorded, the GRP level is higher on average (hypothesis H1 is confirmed).

Models 2.1 – 2.3 show the presence of positive interaction between the level of local content of the "Information Technologies" cluster in the region and the GRP volume. That is, in regions, where the employment level in the "Information Technologies" cluster is higher, the GRP level is higher on average (hypothesis H2 is confirmed).

Models 3.1 – 3.3 show the presence of positive interaction between the size of the "Information Technology" cluster in the region and the GRP volume. That is, in regions, where the employment share in the "Information Technologies" cluster is more relative to everybody employed in the region, the GRP level is higher on average (hypothesis H3 is confirmed).

Models 4.1 – 4.3 show the presence of positive interaction between the focus of the "Information Technology" cluster in the region and the GRP volume. That is, in regions, where the employment share in the "Information Technologies"cluster is more relative to everybody employed in the region, the GRP level is higher on average (hypothesis H4 is confirmed).

In this case, these interactions are maintained even when we control in the models the volumes of investment in fixed assets by organizations, manpower in the region and annual fixed effects.

Table 3. Empirical results of the estimation relationship between "Information technology" cluster characteristics and Gross regional product (models 1 and 2).

MODELS / VARIABLES	Model 1			Model 2		
	1.1	1.2	1.3	2.1	2.2	2.3
Whether cluster "Information technologies" presented in the region or not	**1.290***** (0.144)	**0.153***** (0.0265)	**0.152***** (0.0265)			
LQ				**0.930***** (0.0417)	**0.0999***** (0.0207)	**0.104***** (0.0189)
Natural logarithm of real investments in fixed assets		0.720*** (0.0293)	0.725*** (0.0284)		0.476*** (0.0536)	0.474*** (0.0489)
Natural logarithm of total regional employment		0.345*** (0.0343)	0.340*** (0.0337)		0.821*** (0.0784)	0.820*** (0.0724)
Constant	12.13*** (0.0297)	4.500*** (0.332)	4.356*** (0.328)	11.73*** (0.0277)	7.179*** (0.624)	7.104*** (0.571)
Observations	640	640	640	640	104	104
R-squared	0.104	0.944	0.948	0.266	0.971	0.976
NumberofRegionID	80	80	80	80	13	13
Year FE	No	No	Yes	No	No	Yes
chi2	79.94	34153	35068	496.1	3765	3791
rmse	1.052	0.262	0.256	0.952	0.184	0.174

Standard errors in parentheses
*** $p<0.01$, ** $p<0.05$, * $p<0.1$

Table 4. Empirical results of the estimation relationship between «Information technology» cluster characteristics and Gross regional product (models 3 and 4).

MODELS / VARIABLES	Model 3			Model 4		
	3.1	3.2	3.3	4.1	4.2	4.3
Size	**0.0271*****	**0.0217*****	**0.0222*****			
	(0.00176)	(0.00141)	(0.00137)			
Focus				**0.584*****	**0.351*****	**0.303*****
				(0.0504)	(0.0556)	(0.0668)
Natural logarithm of real investments in fixed assets		0.449***	0.435***		0.483***	0.469***
		(0.0484)	(0.0411)		(0.0489)	(0.0492)
Natural logarithm of total regional employment		0.699***	0.710***		0.804***	0.834***
		(0.0647)	(0.0576)		(0.0734)	(0.0762)
Constant	4.592***	7.564***	7.630***	4.334***	7.094***	7.205***
	(0.321)	(0.550)	(0.471)	(0.339)	(0.567)	(0.574)
Observations	640	104	104	640	104	104
R-squared	0.953	0.983	0.988	0.951	0.972	0.975
Number of Region ID	80	13	13	80	13	13
Year FE	No	No	Yes	No	No	Yes
chi2	47263	6055	6511	43222	2778	3128
rmse	0.242	0.142	0.123	0.247	0.180	0.178

Standard errors in parentheses
*** $p<0.01$, ** $p<0.05$, * $p<0.1$

6 Conclusion

The relevance of measuring the impact of the information technology development on the GRP level is difficult to overestimate in the modern world. This work shows that the assessment of this contribution can be made from different sides including using macroeconomic data based on the cluster structure of the regions. Based on the theoretical and methodological developments of M. Porter and G. Lindqvist, the authors analyzed the main characteristics of the "Information Technology" cluster identified on the basis of employment data in the regions of the Russian Federation. Using the methods of econometric analysis, the authors have revealed the existence of positive interaction between the GRP volumes and the characteristics of the "Information Technologies" cluster based on the example of the regions in the Russian Federation. In this case, the positive significant interaction remained both in models built across all the regions and in models built around the regions where at least once in 2008 – 2016 the cluster existence was recorded.

It should be noted that the conclusions drawn under this study reflect the situation in the Russian Federation and the authors of future studies shall interpret these results with care when their extrapolation to other regions.

As guidelines for future studies, the authors consider it important to perform a more detailed examination of the «Information Technologies" cluster and its impact on GRP of the regions. In particular, in addition to the characteristics of the cluster based on the employment level, the assessment aspects Jacobian proximity effects and "Marshallian" proximity effects and their interaction to GRP volumes in the regions are relevant.

Acknowledgment: The study was performed under support of the Russian Federation President Council on Grants (project НШ – 3792.2018.6).

References

1. N. Rogge, Empirical Economics, 1-22 (2018)
2. D. G. Rodionov, I. A. Rudskaya, International Journal of Ecology & Development, **32** **(4)** (2017)
3. D. G. Rodionov, I. A. Rudskaia, V. A. Degtereva Proceedings of the 29th International Business Information Management Association Conference – Education Excellence and Innovation Management through Vision 2020: From Regional Development Sustainability to Global Economic Growth (2017)
4. K. M. Vu, Information Economics and policy, **25 (4)** (2013)
5. T. Niebel, World Development, **104** (2018)
6. J. Kowal, and G. Paliwoda-Pękosz, Information Systems Management, **34 (4)** (2017)
7. D. Tapscott, The digital economy: Promise and peril in the age of networked intelligence, (McGraw-Hill, New York 1996)
8. M. Peitz, and J. Waldfogel, (Eds.). *The Oxford handbook of the digital economy (*Oxford University Press, New York, 2012)
9. J. A. Mathews, The sixth technoeconomic paradigm. In 35th DRUID Celebration Conference 2013, Barcelona, Spain, June 17*,* **19** (2013)
10. K. M. Vu, Telecommunications Policy, **35 (4)** (2011)
11. M. Timmer, G. Ypma, and B. Van Ark, *Groningen Growth and Development Centre*. [online] Available at: http://www.ggdc.net/publications/memorandum/gd67.pdf. (2003)
12. D. Jorgenson, and K. Vu, *German Economic Review*, **8 (2)** (2007)
13. Z. Latif, S. Latif, L. Ximei, Z. H. Pathan, S. Salam, and Z. Jianqiu, Telematics and Informatics (2017)
14. T. Niebel, World Development, **104** (2018)
15. L. S. Markov, V. M. Markova "Identification of reference clusters: methodological issues and practical application to the domestic industry". Vestnik NGU. Series: social and economic sciences, **12** (1) (2012)
16. E. J. Feser, S. H. Sweeney, Journal of Geographical Systems. **2**, 349–373 (2000)
17. M. E. Porter, Carfax Publishing, **37 (6/7)** (2003)
18. U.S. Cluster Mapping | Mapping a nation of regional clusters. (n.d.). [online] Available at: http://www.clustermapping.us/ (2018)
19. European Cluster Observatory [online] Available at: http://www.clusterobservatory.eu (2018)
20. G. Lindqvist, (Stockholm 2009)
21. N. Beck, J. N. Katz, American political science review, **89 (3)** (1995)
22. D. Hoechle, Stata Journal, **7(3)** (2007)

Detection of cyber threats to network infrastructure of digital production based on the methods of Big Data and multifractal analysis of traffic[a]

Daria Lavrova[1*], *Maria* Poltavtseva[1], *Anna* Shtyrkina[1], and *Pyotr* Zegzhda[1]

[1] Peter the Great St. Petersburg Polytechnic University, Institute of Computer Sciences and Technologies, 195251 Polytechnicheskaya st. 29, Russian Federation

Abstract. The article offers an approach to analyzing data security of network infrastructure of digital production providing for contraction of network traffic size and detecting anomalies in the network traffic on the basis of multifractal analysis. The contraction of data size will be provided due to extraction of significant parameters from the network packets and dropping the rest data, as well as due to application of such Big Data method as aggregation. The experimental investigations on contracting data size on analyzing security have proven the operability and efficiency thereof. The method of contracting data size has demonstrated a possibility of traffic volume contraction from hundreds of Gbit to several Mbyte. The suggested approach to security analysis using the assessment of width of multifractional spectrum as a criterion of anomaly presence has detected both simulated attacks of denial of servicing SYN-flood and smurf. Thus, the suggested approach can be efficiently used for analyzing big volumes of dissimilar traffic of network infrastructure of digital production.

1 Problem of providing security of digital infrastructure

The digitization of key and vital field of human activity has resulted in that the ability of data exchange and the works with the use of Internet became the most important demand of the modern community. The use of M2M technology and incorporating an Internet of things concept into production branches have triggered the emergence of cyber-physical systems (CPS) consisting of interrelated sensors, networks, cloud systems of data storage, applications and devices. CPS differ from information and computer systems by the principles of work organization: a collective functioning of the elements of cybernetic and

[a] With financial support from the Ministry of Education and Science of the Russian Federation in the framework of the Federal targeted program "Investigations and developments in the priority field of development of Russian science and technology complex for 2014-2020", Agreement No. 14.578.21.0231, agreement unique identifier RFMEFI57817X0231).
* Corresponding author: lavrova@ibks.spbstu.ru

physical environments integrated with computational resources, with minimal participation of an individual or without him is provided.

CPS implements a technological concept of digital environment bringing all the field of country's activity to the new level of competitive ability [1]. At that, according to source [2], more than half of the modern CPS have been integrated with critical field of life-sustaining activity, such as power engineering, defense industry, communication, public health services and transport. It makes the problem of cyber security of such systems highly relevant.

The structural intricacy of CPS, high heterogeneity and low computational capability of the components thereof significantly obstruct a development of a unified methodology of ensuring cyber security of digital infrastructure. The most promising approach to detecting cyber threats in complex intellectual systems according to sources [3, 4] is the analysis of security of infrastructure network data, since the implementation of production processes in CPS takes place in the way of network data exchange by the components thereof, including commands and informing/status messages.

The network infrastructure of digital production systems is highly diversified, it includes both traditional network devices and components of systems of Internet of things (sensors and actuators, "smart" devices). The availability of a great number of "smart" devices brings about heterogeneity of the used network protocols and an essential growth of the network traffic volume.

The cyber security of digital production implies the analysis of security of super-high data volumes, since the development of cloud, mobile, sensor technologies and technology of Internet of things integrated with the digital production has resulted in a vigorous growth of volume of the global IP-traffic. According to data of Cisco corporation the volume of global IP-traffic will increase 3 times by 2021, attaining 3.3 ZettaByte. At that, the share of traffic of devices of Internet of things and devices interacting with respect to M2M technologies (which is characteristic for digital production) will amount to about 5% of the global IP-traffic, while a share of connections of M2M supporting Internet of things will constitute more than half of the total number of devices and connections constituting 27.1 billion devices. A super-high volume of heterogeneous network traffic influences negatively the quality of detecting security threats, since the "surges" caused by abnormal traffic are much less distinguishable in big data volumes. In view of this fact a risk of omitting cyber attacks and compromising digital infrastructure increases.

In order to timely detect cyber threats and counteract them, the analysis of network traffic security shall be performed in the real-time mode, which is complicated by the enormous traffic volumes. Taking into account the above peculiarities of the network infrastructure of digital production, the following is required for solving the task of effective analysis of its data security:

1) provide contraction of size of super-high volume of network traffic for increasing the rate of security analysis [5];

2) develop methods of network traffic security analysis able to detect anomalies under conditions of big data scales with high accuracy.

This article offers an approach to detecting anomalies in the super-high volumes of network traffic based on the assessment of multifractal spectrum of traffic parameter time series. It also describes an approach to preliminary network traffic processing with the use of Big Data technology providing for traffic size contraction on the basis of extracting essential traffic parameters "on-the-fly" and aggregation of the extracted values with the use of hierarchically-dependable windows.

2 Methods of contracting size of super-high network traffic volumes with the use of hierarchically-dependable windows of aggregation

Big Data corresponds to a combination of methods and tools of processing big volumes of heterogeneous data with the aim of extracting information important from the point of view of the task to be solved. The Big Data methods include the methods of data aggregation, normalization, filtration, classification and clusterization.

This article offers to use such Big Data method as aggregation combining values of parameters extracted from the network traffic into a unified indicator [5]. It is proposed to perform total contraction of traffic size in two stages: an extraction of traffic parameters important from the point of view of further security analysis takes place at the first stage, the aggregation of values of parameters with the use of hierarchically-dependable windows is performed at the second stage. The following traffic network parameters have been distinguished for security analysis:

1) IP-addresses of sender and receiver;
2) ports of sender and receiver;
3) timestamp;
4) network packet size;
5) number of network packets in a flow;
6) type of network protocol of transportation level;
7) number of network packets of protocols of every type;
8) number of outgoing and incoming connections for a host.

This list can be expanded, besides, these values shall be a subject to certain statistical processing in future in order to make it possible to handle such statistics as an average, maximum and minimum number of packets, packet size, flow length, etc.

The rate of analysis increases significantly and the data size decreases due to extraction of these parameters, it is related to the fact that there is no need to analyze the payload network packets – all the required data get obtained as quick as possible in the way of analyzing predominantly the packets of the network and transportation levels.

However, such size contraction will be insufficient under conditions of intensively arriving network traffic and a necessity of providing quick data processing. Therefore, a second stage is introduced – an aggregation of extracted values of parameters being implemented with the use of hierarchically-dependable windows [6]. Every window corresponds to a structure describing aggregated data over a certain period of time with the aim of calculating statistical indicators. An upper-level window is the aggregation interval for the inferior windows taking into account the aggregation coefficient α expressed as a positive integer. The window is described by a finite sequence: $Window\langle Id,\ Dt,\ N,\ Parent,\ Fr,\ \alpha,\ \alpha_{cur},\ Par\rangle$, where Id is a window identifier, Dt is an aggregation time period, N is a length of numerical rows of parameters the same for all window parameters *(100 < N < 1000),* N_{cur} is a number of values in the window time rows, $Parent$ is a parent window located higher in the hierarchy of windows (for all window except a minimal one), Fr are related methods of calculation of statistical parameters applied to data of window under consideration, $Par = \{Qp_1,\dots,Qp_m\}$ are the time rows or waiting lines of parameters. The window structure is shown in accordance with Fig. 1.

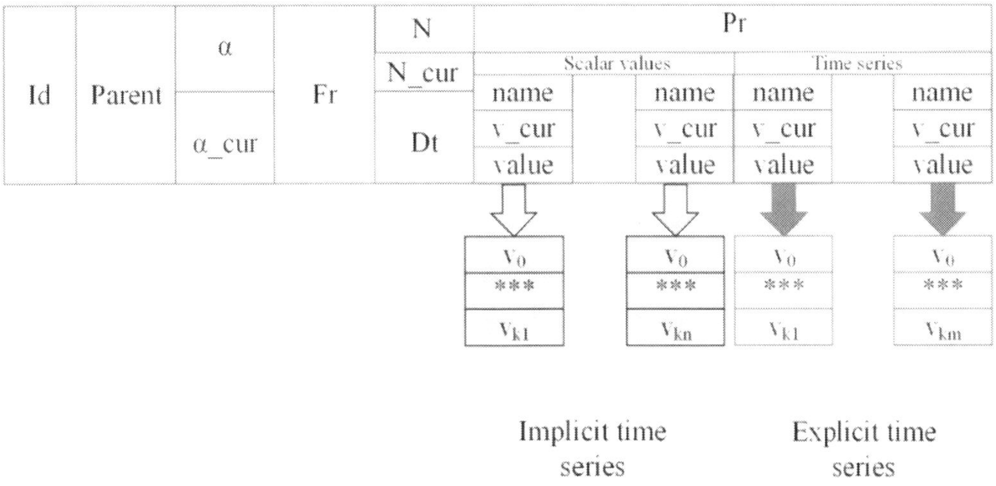

Fig. 1. Structure of hierarchically-dependable aggregation window.

Parameters α and α_{cur} are used in the course of shifting time rows of windows and organizing hierarchic dependence thereof. α is a coefficient of dependence between windows, α_{cur} is a number of accumulated shifts of the superior window. Upon attaining $\alpha_{cur} = \alpha$ a counter of current shifts is reset, while the current window shifts by one value in the aggregation row.

The shaping of hierarchy of dependable time windows is implemented in the way of selecting windows of analysis in accordance with specified values, selecting the preceding host window for every time window, shaping a tree of windows and shaping a "virtual" window of tree root not taking part in the analysis. General diagram of functioning method of size contraction is shown in Fig. 2.

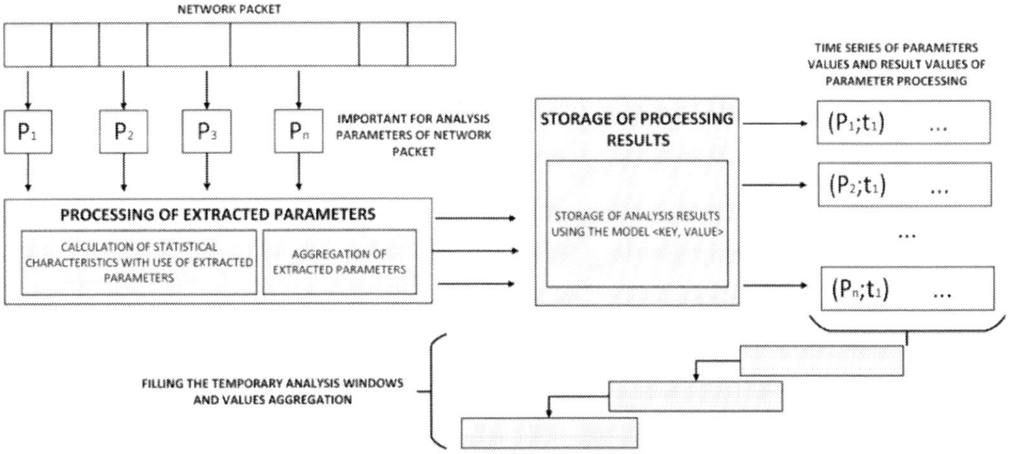

Fig. 2. Diagram of functioning method of size contraction of super-high volumes of network traffic.

A general assessment of contracting data size with the use and support of dependable aggregation windows will be determined in the following way (1):

$$V = N*P*B*m\ , \tag{1}$$

where:
1) N – number of aggregation windows;
2) P – number of parameters in every window;
3) B – size of one value of one parameter;
4) m – length of time row for window parameters.

Thus, the developed method provides for contraction of direct size of the stored information for getting an opportunity of its prompt processing and analyzing without losing significance.

3 Analysis of network traffic security with the use of multifractal characteristics

In order to detect anomalies under conditions of big volumes of the network traffic, it is necessary to use metrics and characteristics providing for high accuracy of detecting even insignificant deviations of traffic behaviour from a normal one. A big volume of traffic according to the data of many investigations features a self-similarity property, i.e., it looks qualitatively in the same way with any rather irresistible proportions of time axis [7]. The self-similarity property is used for simulation of the network traffic and for solving tasks of information security after revealing anomalies [8].

The fractal methods, which are gaining the ever-growing popularity in the recent times, are built just on this peculiarity. The main focus in the fractal analysis of traffic is made on calculating Hurst exponent, which a measure of stability of statistical phenomenon or measure of duration of a long-time process dependence [9]. However, the investigations show that under conditions of real networks the traffic not always possesses fractal properties, more frequently the network data exhibit the multifractal properties [10]. At that, the self-similarity property can be seen on the big scales of traffics, while the multifractal properties are characteristic within smaller time sections of the network. Thus, the property of scale invariance, or fractality reflects the long-term signal behaviour, while multifractal metrics reflect its momentary behaviour.

The authors suggest in this article to calculate the multifractal heuristics providing for detection of anomalies invisible in the big traffic volumes and making it possible to describe the network traffic in the form of a multifractal. The multifractal is assigned by several algorithms changing in sequence, each of them generates a pattern with its fractal size.

It is offered in this article to use a value of multifractal spectrum width as a criterion of whether the network traffic is normal or abnormal [11].

In order to build the spectrum, one can suppose that there is a certain fractal object. Let us assume that its surface is covered with cubes measuring ε, then a probability of hitting a cell i with an arbitrary point will be designated as ρ_i. In this case the spectrum of fractal sizes will be expressed by formula (2):

$$D_q = \frac{\tau(q)}{q-1} = \lim_{\varepsilon \to 0} \frac{1}{q-1} \left(\frac{\ln\left(\sum_{i=1}^{N(\varepsilon)} \rho_i(\varepsilon)^q\right)}{\ln \varepsilon} \right), \tag{2}$$

where, $\tau(q)$ is referred to as a scaling function.

In practice it is convenient to use variables $f(\alpha)$ and α, which are acquired from $\tau(q)$ and q by means of Legendre transformation [11]. The value $f(\alpha)$ is referred to as multifractal Legendre spectrum, while the variable α – is referred to as a local Lipschitz-Helder indicator. In order to build the Legendre spectrum, a row of process of incrementations $Z_1, Z_2, \ldots, Z_n$ is assigned and an aggregated sequence corresponding to it $\{Z^{(m)}\}$ is determined at the level of aggregation m (3):

$$Z_k^{(m)} = Z_{(k-1)m+1} + Z_{(k-1)m+2} + \ldots + Z_{km}, \tag{3}$$

where, $k, m = 1, 2, \ldots$. Further, a sum of separation is determined (4):

$$S_m^Z(q) = \sum_{k=1}^{N/m} \left(\overline{Z_k}^{(m)}\right)^q, \tag{4}$$

where, Z – vector of data, for which a multifractal spectrum is built, while $\overline{Z_k}^{(m)} = \sum_{l=1}^{m} Z_{(k-1)n+1}$ – discretization of measure μ on scale $\delta_m = \frac{m}{N}$, $m = 1, 2, 2^2, \ldots, 2^n$ – size of summation unit [11].

It is widely thought that Z_i is a multifractal, if $\log S_m^Z(q)$ with approximation linearly depends on $\log(m)$. The inclination of approximation is designated $\tau(q)$ and calculated with the use of linear approximation (5):

$$\log S_m^Z(q) \approx \tau(q) \log m + c(q), \tag{5}$$

The multifractal spectrum is the Legendre transformation from separation function $\tau(q)$ (6):

$$f_L(\alpha) = \inf_{q \in R} (\alpha q - \tau(q)), \tag{6}$$

Thus, the multifractal Legendre spectrum will be built in the course of performing experimental investigations [11]. From the point of view of security analysis one can assume that the width of multifractal spectrum will either decrease or increase during network attacks implementation. The increase of width of multifractal spectrum testifies to the fact that the process under investigation became more heterogeneous. Regarding the network traffic and its parameters it can denote the emergence of the new traffic and new dependencies in the traffic testifying to an attempt of attack implementation. The decrease of width of multifractal spectrum testifies to the fact that the process became more homogeneous. Regarding the network traffic, it can denote the increased percentage of the identical traffic (e.g., attacked with the repeating packets).

4 Conducting experimental investigations

The conducted experimental investigations concerned the assessment of contracting size of the network traffic and detection of network attacks on the basis of multifractal analysis. The intensively arriving network traffic of super-high volumes has been simulated in the work framework. The speed of traffic under investigation equals 100 Gbit/s, i.e., during 1 hour of observations the volume of accumulated data equals 100 Gbit×3 600=360 000 Gbit=360 Tbit. Hence, that during one day only more than 8 Pbit of information are to be subject to information, where, 1 Pbit = 10^6 Gbit = 10^{15} bit.

The first stage of method of data size contraction consists in the extraction of key parameters from the network traffic. The average size of network packet equals 1,500 byte. Let us assume that around 50 parameters get extracted from every packet taking into account derived parameters from the flows and packets of higher level. If 10 bytes are allotted to every parameter, the total volume required for one packet storage is 500 byte. Thus, this method helps keep 500 byte out of 1,500 byte of data only in the course of the first stage, i. e., the saving of space in data storage will amount to 66%.

Figure 3 presents results of experimental investigations on data size contraction following the first stage of method functioning.

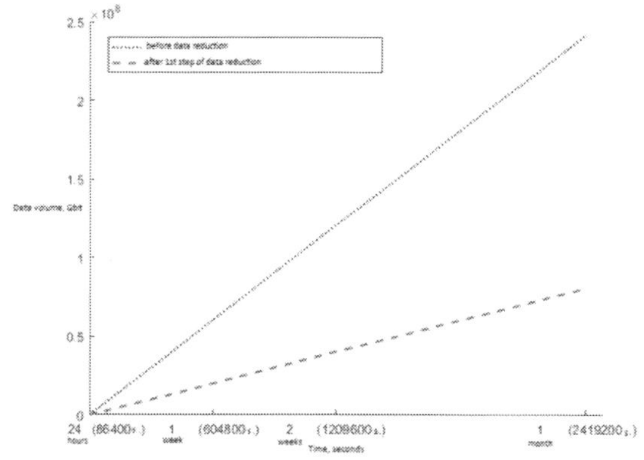

Fig. 3. Result of Functioning method of size contraction at the first stage for different time intervals.

In order to provide for greater contraction of data size at the second stage, the aggregation of acquired values of parameters will be carried out with the use of hierarchically-dependable windows. The efficiency of decreasing data volume at this stage depends on the parameters selected by investigator. 10 aggregation windows corresponding to time intervals from seconds to a month have been used in the conducted experiment.

The volume of "clean" data for traffic under investigation without taking into account auxiliary structures has amounted to about 5 Mb of memory for an average length of time row of $m = 1000$ elements, number of aggregation windows $N = 10$, number of parameters $P = 50$, and $B = 10$ byte required for storage of one parameter. Taking $N = 5$ aggregation windows, about 2.5 Mb of memory will be required for data storage.

Consideration has been given to dump network traffic without attacks, dump with attack SYN-flood and dump with attack smurf in the course of conducting experimental investigations related to detection of anomalies in the network traffic [12, 13].

A parameter characterizing the number of TCP-packets of definite type over a period of time of Δt=5 seconds has been used when conducting attack SYN-flood or shaping time row. A change of spectrum in the course of conducting attack SYN-flood is demonstrated in Fig. 4 a) and b).

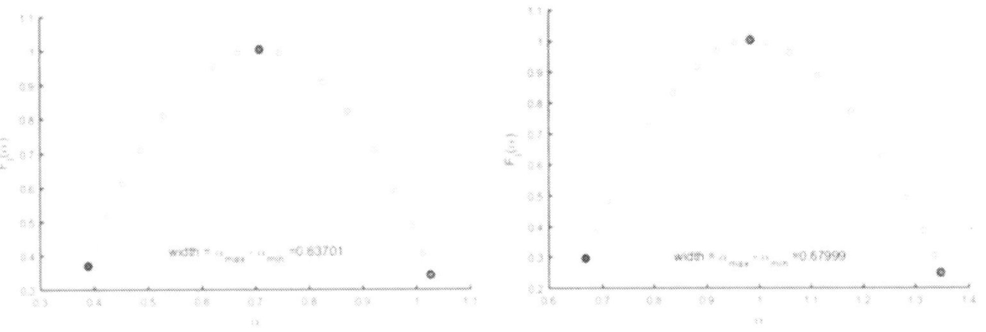

a) b)

Fig. 4. Multifractal legendre spectrum for time rows of network packets of traffic without attack (a), with attack SYN-flood (b).

The increase of width of multifractal Legendre spectrum by more than 0.4 is observed in this experiment. Such a phenomenon is explained by the fact that the number of TCP-packets in the normal traffic did not vary and remained approximately at the same level. In the course of attack the number of TCP-packets began to increase gradually, as a result of which the network traffic became more heterogeneous over the investigated period of time, which resulted in manifestation of more multifractal properties.

In the course of conducting attack smurf the other network traffic parameter has been investigated – an average size of network packets. Figure 5 presents multifractal spectra for the cases of attack smurf and without it.

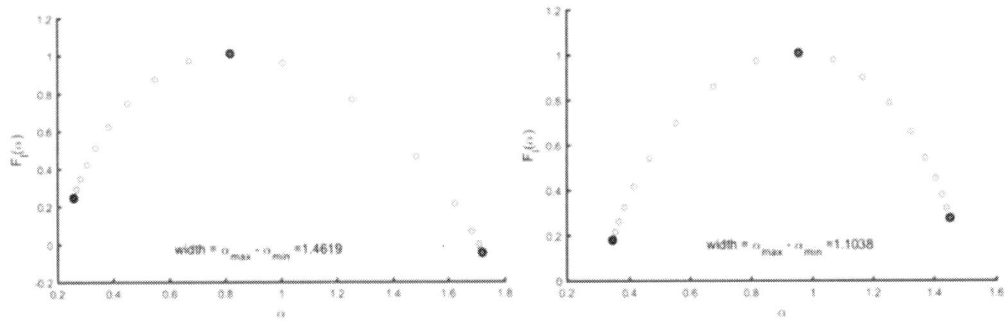

a) b)

Fig. 5. Multifractal legendre spectrum for time rows of average size of traffic network packets without attack (a), with attack smurf (b).

Apparently, in case of availability of attack of smurf type a great number of identical ICMP-packets appear in the traffic. As a result, the network traffic gets saturated with identical packets and becomes less heterogeneous, therefore, a degree of time row multifractality (of width of multifractal spectrum) decreases.

5 Conclusions

This article offers an approach to detecting cyber threats in the network infrastructure of digital production taking into account specific features of application environment. The network infrastructure of digital production features high volume and heterogeneity of its composition, which entails a necessity of super-high volumes of network traffic. At that, the traffic shall be processed as quick as possible for efficient detection of security threats and immediate counteracting them, which is an unconventional problem under conditions of big volumes of intensively arriving data.

The approach offered in the article includes a method of contracting size of super-high volumes of network traffic on the basis of Big Data technology and method of detecting anomalies in the network traffic based on multifractal analysis.

The contraction of traffic size takes place in two stages, an extraction of parameters important from the point of view of security analysis takes place at the first stage, the aggregation of the extracted values of parameters on the basis of hierarchically-dependable windows is performed at the second stage. The performance of this method has been proven by the contraction of data size approximately by 2/3 after the first stage of contraction. The efficiency of data volume contraction at this stage depends on parameters selected by the investigator. The experimental investigations have demonstrated the contraction of traffic volumes down to several Mbyte, which testifies to high efficiency of using hierarchically-dependable windows of aggregation.

In order to analyze security of network traffic, an assessment of such traffic characteristic as multifractal spectrum has been performed. The assessment of multifractal properties of network traffic required a significantly lower data volume, since the multifractality is distinguishable particularly at relatively small volumes. From the point of view of security analysis it is reasonable to monitor the multifractal traffic properties, the multifractal describes the network traffic with more accuracy demonstrating dependencies, which are not distinguishable at big data volumes. It is especially relevant under conditions of big traffic volumes from the objects of network infrastructure of digital production.

The conducted experimental investigations have proven the functionality of the proposed approach to security analysis: the value of width of multifractal spectrum appeared to be sensitive to the network traffic changes. At that, the use of different characteristics of network traffic is possible when building the multifractal spectrum. In particular, the medium size of network packets and a number of TCP-packets in the traffic have been used, both characteristics have reflected the emergence of anomalies.

A further direction of investigations will be devoted to establishing boundaries of values of spectrum width for shaping a certain confidential interval. The system of security analysis will not need to generate a signal on the possible cyber attack, if it enters this interval. Besides, further investigations will be dedicated to searching other network traffic characteristics capable of reflecting presence of anomalies in the network traffic with high accuracy.

References

1. R. Seiger, S. Huber, P. Heisig, U. Assmann, LNBIP, **248** (2016)
2. Y. S. Vasiliev, P. D. Zegzhda, D. P. Zegzhda, Aut. Cont. and Comp. Scien., **63** (2016)
3. D. S. Lavrova, A. I. Pechenkin, IJCNIS, **7** (2015)
4. D. S. Lavrova, Aut. Cont. and Comp. Scien., **50** (2016)
5. M. A. Poltavtseva, A. I. Pechenkin, D. S. Lavrova, Soft. & Sys., **2** (2016)
6. N. Karthick , X. Agnes Kalarani, IJCTT, **17** (2014)

7. D. E. Sokolov, N. G. Trenogin, SibSUTIS, **34** (2001)
8. D. E. Sokolov, N. G. Trenogin, Mod. probl. of inf. in tech. and technologies., **10** (2004)
9. R. Yan, Y. Wang, IT Journ, **11**, (2012)
10. F. H. T. Vieira, G. R. Bianchi, L.L. Lee, J. High Speed Netw, **17** (2010)
11. A. N. Pavlov, V. S. Anishchenko, Physics-Uspekhi, **50** (2007)
12. N. Wattanapongsakorn, INC, **98** (2011)
13. C. Fachkha, E. Bou-Harb, M. Debbabi, Wireless Com. and Mob. Comp., **15** (2015)

Wavelet-analysis of network traffic time-series for detection of attacks on digital production infrastructure[a]

Darya Lavrova[1*], *Pavel* Semyanov[1], *Anna* Shtyrkina[1], and *Peter* Zegzhda[1]

[1] Peter the Great Saint Petersburg Polytechnic University, Institute of Applied Mathematics and Mechanics, 195251 Polytechnicheskaya st. 29, Russian Federation

Abstract. Digital production integrates with all the areas of human activity including critical industries, therefore the task of detecting network attacks has a key priority in protecting digital manufacture systems. This article offers an approach for analysis of digital production security based on evaluation of a posteriori probability for change point in time-series, which are based on the change point coefficient values of digital wavelet-transform in the network traffic time-series. These time-series make it possible to consider the network traffic from several points of view at the same time, which plays an important role in the task of detecting network attacks. The attack methods vary significantly; therefore, in order to detect them it is necessary to monitor different values of various traffic parameters. The proposed method has demonstrated its efficiency in detecting network service denial attacks (SlowLoris and HTTP DoS) being realized at the application level.

1 Complexity of security assurance in digital manufacture systems

The modern level of science and equipment development is characterized by active transition from automated manufacture to digital manufacture practices. This transition goes along with transformation of existing process infrastructure, with combination of technologies and up-to-date developments bringing it into a global multi-level, multi-component system that is capable of changing the existing process practices and bringing all the industrial sectors to a new level of competitive ability.

Digital manufacture systems allow processing and systematization of data from all production process areas, organizational structures and business process data, a deep and comprehensive analysis of all these data makes it possible to take managerial decisions.

---

[a] With financial support from the Ministry of education and science of the Russian Federation as part of the Federal target program "Research and development of priority areas for Russia's research and process complex for 2014-2020" (Agreement No.14.578.21.0231, unique identifier of this agreement RFMEFI57817X0231)

[*] Corresponding author: lavrova@ibks.spbstu.ru

The key role in digital production is given to such technologies as artificial intelligence, sensor and cloud technologies aimed at supporting effective operation of complex industrial systems. The complexity of these systems, a great number of various components incorporated in them makes the data analysis and knowledge extraction tasks rather difficult but still very important. Bearing in mind the large scale of these systems the task of mitigating the human factor effects on the operation of digital manufacture systems becomes relevant, because only machine intelligence is capable of processing large amounts of different data with high accuracy and extracting dependencies and properties that may go unnoticed for people.

Intellectualization and transition to artificial intelligence will significantly speed up both technological and business processes. However, functional transition from automated systems to automatic ones comes with a great number of complex tasks that need to be implemented before commissioning digital manufacture systems. The key problem is to provide security of digital manufacture systems.

Integrating these digital manufacture systems with such critical industries as power engineering, defense industry, health care, transport highlights the relevancy of this problem. Incorrect operation of the systems in these industries may cause harm to people's lives and health as well as bring the state significant financial losses [1].

Resolving this problem is complicated by the following causes:

– big difference in types of digital manufacture system components caused by both technical difference of components by intended use and a great number of component manufacturers;

– low output capacity of most components;

– Intensive generation of large and diverse data volumes by digital manufacture systems;

This high diversity of system components brings about a great number of generated data formats and different interfacing protocols to be applied and integrated. This imposes a requirement on these protection systems proposed to be developed to ensure that different data types can be processed.

Low output capacity of most components does not allow classic security systems such as attack and intrusion detection systems, information leakage detection systems etc, to be integrated with digital manufacture systems in an efficient manner. Therefore, the solutions proposed to provide security should consider this feature of application environment for digital production.

Intensive generation of huge data volumes requires from these security assurance systems to be capable of analyzing data on a real time basis. In combination with resource intensiveness requirements for these security solutions the task of developing digital production security systems becomes much more complicated.

Systems operating on standalone servers instead of running on the end nodes of digital manufacture systems could be a solution to this problem in accordance with sources [2-4]. These systems should be handling data from all the system components and be capable of processing them quickly and detecting data abnormalities with high accuracy signaling that the system may be running incorrectly due to a technical fault or a cyber attack on the system.

In this article the authors offer an approach to analyze digital manufacture system data for abnormalities based on assessment of digital wavelet-transform parameters of time-series. The use of these time-series especially for a traffic analysis is justified by the fact that the same network traffic volume can generate several time-series containing various traffic parameters. The following can be referred to these parameters: quantity of network packets for certain protocols, average quantity of network protocols per time unit representing a time series step, average packet size etc. Thus these time-series make it possible to consider the network traffic from different sides at the same time, which plays an important role in detecting network attacks. Attacks of different type, even if they refer to the same class (for example, to service denial attack class) are carried out by intruders in a different way and to be detected it is necessary to monitor different characteristics.

2 Abnormality detection method based on wavelet-transform

One of the advantages of wavelet-transform is that it makes it possible to analyze a signal within the frequency-and-time region and allows researching the abnormal process on the background of other components. This article offers to implement digital wavelet-transform.

Its idea consists in the fact that any digital sequence is represented as a combination of decomposition coefficients as per basic scaling and wavelet-functions [5]. Thus, wavelet-transform decomposes the analyzed sequence into two sequences of coefficients: approximation coefficients $coeffA$, which are linked with a scaling function and detailing coefficients $coeffD$, which are linked with wavelet-function. If the level of decomposition is higher than one, then at further steps, the approximation coefficients obtained at each level are subject to wavelet-transform. Thus the algorithm outcome at decomposition level j is a set of coefficients, $[coeffA_j, coeffD_j, coeffD_{j-1}, coeffD_{j-2}, \dots, coeffD_2, coeffD_1]$.

The set of approximation and detailing coefficients has its statistical properties. The detailing coefficients characterize the local changes of analyzed sequence. Their distribution is described by Gaussian law with zero mean (Fig. 1a)). The distribution density of approximation coefficients, which provide information about global trend, are best of all described by distribution of exponential type [6], as it is shown in Fig. 1 b).

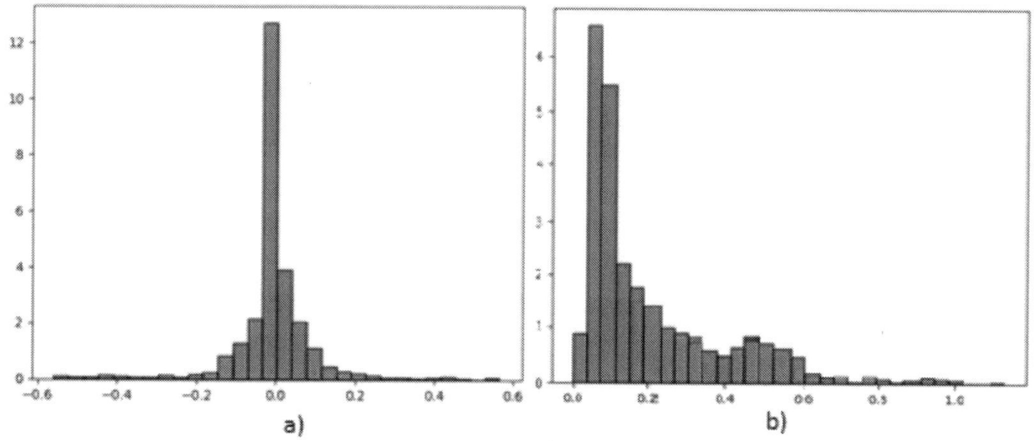

Fig. 1. Analysis of normal traffic time-series elaborated by average size of the HTTP-packets.

While elaborating an autocorrelation function (Fig. 2) of detailing coefficients obtained as a result of wavelet-decomposition of time-series containing a number of network packets of certain type an insignificant relationship between considered values has been identified. This fact tells us that the detailing coefficients (or as they are also called wavelet-coefficients) are independently distributed random values.

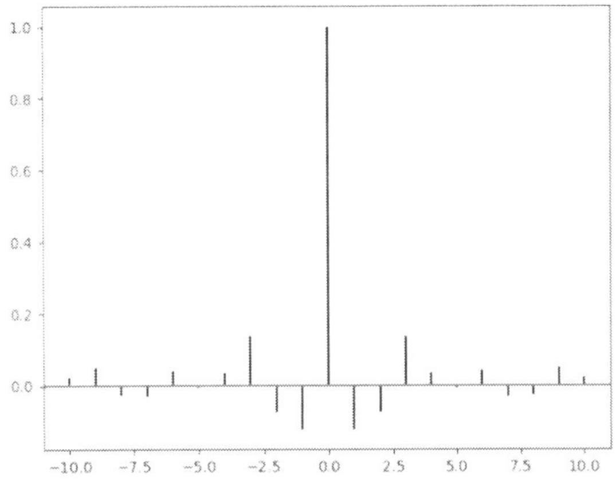

Fig. 2. Autocorrelation function of detailing coefficients.

The abnormality detection methods using digital wavelet-transform are mainly aimed at analyzing detailing and approximation coefficients. In particular, within a number of methods researchers apply approaches related to the change detection task, which is one of widely distributed tasks of data sequence analysis [7-10].

It is obvious that the statistical properties of time-series may vary in time. However, if there is an abrupt change in the properties of analyzed sequence than the assessment of time point of this jump can significantly help during time-series analysis. In this paper the change point accompanied by a rapid jump in distribution parameters can indicate that there is a network abnormality.

As discussed, the detailing coefficients are described by normal distribution with zero mean value. It means that it is necessary to detect change points caused by a rapid change in dispersion of detailing coefficients in order to detect abnormalities in local traffic trend. In a number of works it is offered to use ICSS criteria (iterative algorithm of cumulative sum of squares) [7, 8], SIC (Shwartz information criterion) [9], Fisher criterion making it possible to trace dispersion equality [5] and etc. This paper offers to use a Bayesian on-line change detection algorithm [10]. In original research this method is applied to analyze various data time-series. In this case, this article offers to apply the Bayesian algorithm to detailing coefficients obtained as a result of wavelet-transform of time-series. The analyzed data processing time is reduced due to a lesser sequence generated by detailing coefficients. Moreover, wavelet-coefficients make it possible to analyze data within various frequency regions which allows detecting abnormalities at several decomposition levels.

The algorithm is based on the idea that the analyzed time-series $(x_1 \cdot t_1), (x_2 \cdot t_2), \ldots, (x_n \cdot t_n)$ is broken down into disjoint intervals. The delimiters between the intervals represent the points of appearance of the fault. With the algorithm running a posteriori probability is evaluated throughout the length of sequence, which starts with the last appearance of the change point. Let us symbolize the length of each of these sequences at time points t as r_t Let an average value be symbolized as μ and dispersion as ν. According to the Bayesian theorem the following equation is true:

$$P(r_t|x) = \frac{P(r_t,x)}{P(x)}, \tag{1}$$

The new monitored data collection process occurs after initialization step [10]. The following is calculated:

- Forecasting probability (using Student's distribution) $P(r_t \mid \mu, \nu)$;
- Quality of evidence $P(x)$;

– Growth probability $P(r_t = r_{t-t} + 1, x)$;

– Fault probability $P(r_t = 0, x)$.

The last two probabilities are calculated using Hazard functions. The following is calculated according to Bayes' formula $P(r_t \mid x)$. Once the change point is identified the main distribution parameters are initiated once again.

The proposed method's operability has been checked during detection of attacks from the traffic dump collected and posted by New Brunswick University.

3 Experimental tests to detect abnormalities in network traffic by proposed method based on digital wavelet-transform

CIC IDS 2017 dataset contains backbone network dumps over five work days including both normal network traffic and traffic with attacks such as service denial. Traffic with SlowLoris and HTTP Flood application level attacks was used for these experimental tests.

A SlowLoris attack occurs when an intruder sends a huge amount of data to a victim with slow speed, which makes it possible to use the server resources much longer than required. It is done by opening links with a target web-server and sending a partial request. At regular intervals this intruder sends further HTTP headers but never completing the request. The servers under attack will be opening these connections and filling the connection pool will not allow the clients to connect to it.

While identifying time-series from the network traffic it is necessary to consider both the number of HTTP protocol packets over a particular period of time and an average size of HTTP-packets. The time-series received were decomposed using digital wavelet-transform. Detailing coefficients were analyzed using the Bayesian change point detection method. The following results were received during these experimental tests (Fig. 3-6).

Three charts are shown in each figure:

– Upper chart – time-series based on average HTTP-packet size parameter

– Middle chart – detailing coefficient values received and based on digital wavelet-transform of time-series;

– Lower chart – change point probability chart calculated in accordance with the Bayesian algorithm.

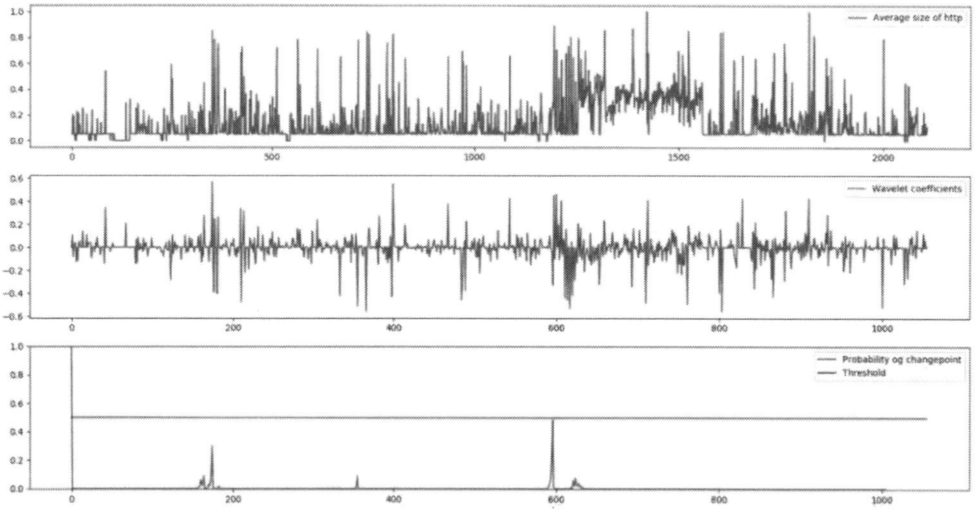

Fig. 3. Analysis of normal traffic time-series plotted as per an average size of HTTP-packets.

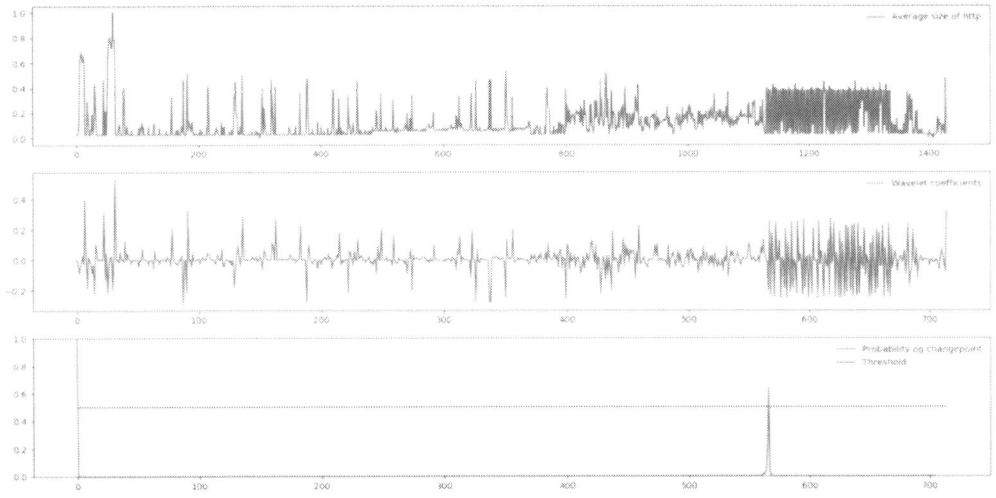

Fig. 4. Analysis of abnormal traffic time-series with SlowLoris attack being carried out.

It is possible to see in Fig. 5 that the developed method detected a change point between the intervals 500 and 600: the posteriori probability assumed the value that is greater than the threshold one (threshold value is 0.5). The rapidest jumps within the distribution parameters most likely will be a change point and consequently will define a possible attack.

The second attack to be considered is HTTP Flood, which is initiated by sending HTTP-requests GET to the 80th port. It loads the server so much that it cannot process the other requests. This flood attack can be aimed both at the server root and its script that is busy carrying out resource-intensive tasks. This attack can be identified by detecting a rapid increase in the number of requests to the same or several scripts on the servers and a rapid increase in the server logs.

The time-series plotted and based on the "number of HTTP packets" parameter were used to detect this attack. Fig. 5 shows the normal traffic time-series plotted by the number of packets and Fig. 6 shows the time-series chart for traffic under attack.

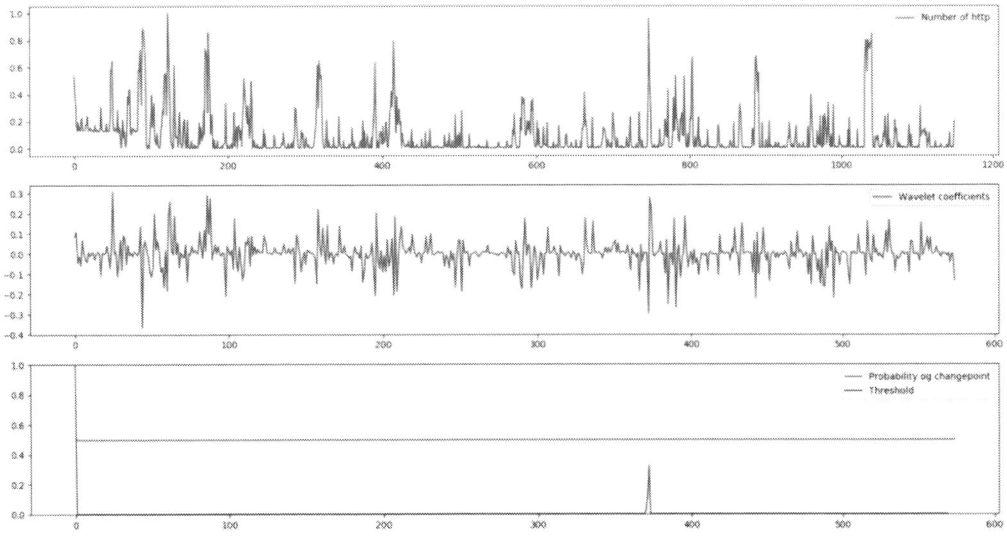

Fig. 5. Analysis of time series of normal traffic plotted as per the number of packets.

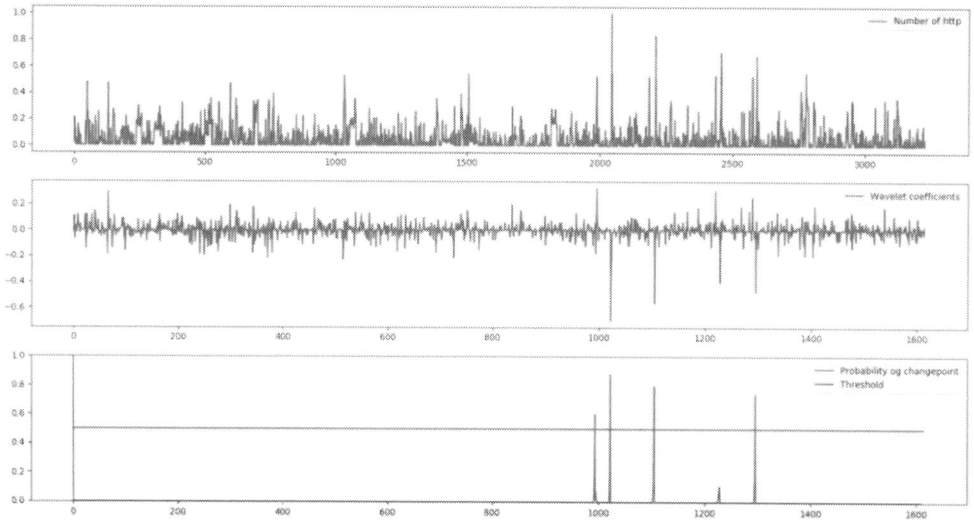

Fig. 6. Analysis of abnormal traffic time-series with SlowLoris attack being carried out.

In Fig. 5 there is a slight jump in data, however in accordance with the developed method implementation it is not a characteristic of abnormality. In Fig. 6 it is possible to see 4 intense jumps in data and all of them coincide with the attack time. In this case, it should be noted that the developed method does not initiate false responses. The noticeable jump after value 1200 on the middle chart looks like an abnormality, however, the lower chart showing the change point posteriori probability value demonstrates that the change point probability is very low: less than 0.2.

Thus, it has been experimentally proved that the developed method demonstrating the application of Bayesian algorithm to the network traffic time-series parameters transformed using wavelet-transform was efficient.

4 Conclusion

This article has offered a method of wavelet-analysis for network traffic time-series to detect attacks on the digital manufacture infrastructure. This method is based on evaluation of change point probability by the Bayesian method, however this method applies not to the data series containing the network traffic parameters but to the time-series of detailing coefficients received using the digital wavelet-transform of traffic series.

This approach is quite new, its comparison with the methods based on the analysis of time-series without wavelet-transform applied shows efficiency in terms of operation speed and possibility for a more deep traffic analysis. The analyzed data processing time is reduced due to a lesser sequence generated by detailing coefficients. Moreover, wavelet-coefficients make it possible to analyze data within various frequency regions which allows detecting abnormalities at several decomposition levels. High operating speed and consideration of various frequency regions have an important value during security analysis of digital manufacture network infrastructure, because a wide spectrum of managerial and industrial processes to be implemented should be considered at various time intervals. In addition, the high operating speed of this method increases the speed of detecting network attacked on the digital manufacture infrastructure.

The network traffic data provided by researchers of New Brunswick University were used to assess the proposed method's efficiency. The traffic dump contained both normal traffic and traffic circulating within the network during simulation of service denial attacks at the application level, in particular, SlowLoris and HTTPDoS that were used to carry out experimental test of the developed method. Both attacks were successfully detected: The a posteriori probability value exceed the preset threshold equal to 0.5 when the abnormal traffic was observed.

References

1. Y. S. Vasiliev, P. D. Zegzhda, D. P. Zegzhda, Aut. Cont. and Comp. Scien., **63** (2016)
2. D. S. Lavrova, A. I. Pechenkin, IJCNIS, **7** (2015)
3. D. S. Lavrova, Aut. Cont. and Comp. Scien., **50** (2016)
4. D. P. Zegzhda, E. Yu. Pavlenko, Aut. Cont. and Comp. Scien., **51** (2017)
5. O. I. Sheluhin, A. A. Atayero, IJCSIS, **10(1)** (2012)
6. O. I. Sheluhin, A. V. Pankrushin, SAI Conf. (2013)
7. C. Inclan, G. C. Tiao, Journ. of the Americ. Stat. Ass. (1994)
8. O. I. Shelukhin, Y. A. Ivanov, V. Y. Rogov, TComm-Telekom. i Transp. (2011)
9. O. Y. Rodionova, A. L. Pomerantsev, Progr. in Chem. Research (2005)
10. R. P. Adams, D. J. C. MacKay, *Bayesian Online Changepoint Detection* (University of Cambridge, Cambridge, 2007)

Esse homo or esse kiborg: Anthropologic perspective in the information technology world

Sergey Lebedev[1], *Vera* Lobastova[1*], *Oleg* Samylov[2], and *Tatyana* Simonenko[1]

[1] Saint Petersburg State University, the Institute of Philosophy, 199034 Universitetskaya Naberezhnaya 7/9, Russian Federation
[2] Emperor Alexander the 1st Saint Petersubrg State Transport University, Economics and Management Department, 190031 Moskovsky pr. 9, Russian Federation

Abstract. The article traces a transition from non-classical understanding of the digital world as reality created by people to develop tools for resolution of theoretical and practical tasks to postnonclassical awareness of information space as distant from people. It has been shown that the digital reality arising out of the subjective world of people and increasingly acquires independent and self-sustaining existence. The information revolution expands the artificial world as interactive and makes actual a new type of interaction of a human being with the world, with himself or herself and other people. Interpersonal communication acquires a digital nature and loses direct connection with certain people dealing with a great number of technical gate-keepers. A man begins to form a template, fragmentary mind-set, which blunts the criticality and reflectivity in perceiving the world. All this makes the education a priority in the development of society, clearly defines its targets related to the formation and development of human potential for each subject of education.

Within the bounds of classical philosophic paradigm the virtual reality cannot be set aside as the one with its own existence, in non-classical (for example, phenomenological) one the digital world is a reality, that is created by a subject based on his or her theoretical and practical goals and tasks bearing both personal and common to humanity nature. The postnonclassical type of rationality offers the virtual world to be reviewed as an objective, independent and self-sustaining reality. This analytic logic of virtual (or digital, information) space is by no means chosen randomly.It reflects the real process of forming a new type of reality, its place and meaning in human life.

At first thought, a significant and inherent property of the digital world is its stable relatedness to a subject, who makes the digital reality possible because only a subject can determine the existential authenticity of the digital world. In this situation, no matter how global and all-encompassing it seems to be the digital world as part of immanent experience of a subject cannot overshadow and thus substitute the physical world and quite a different situation develops when this immanent experience actively starts to multiply and unfold in an endless perspective of various options for intesubjective interactions.

[*] Corresponding author: hist@pgups.ru

To understand true reality of the digital world in a more precise and clear manner we should turn to a phenomenological model of consciousness in order to describe the structure of conscious activity in more detail and thoughtfully as Edmund Husserl did in his transcendental-phenomenological philosophy. The fundamental property of consciousness, which makes conscious activity itself possible, is its intentionality. According to this property every act of consciousness is directed at something and tries to capture this something and hold as an object experiencing and perceiving it in various ways available to consciousness here and now.

All conscious activity of a subject is encompassed by an intentional approach of this consciousness to a variety of intentional objects, which make up a vast field of his or her immanent experience. According to Frantz Bretano's standpoint, who in his descriptive psychology applied the principle of intentionality to analyze the structure of consciousness, there is no and there cannot be objectless consciousness and unconscious experiences [1]. In the act of reflectivity a subject directly finds himself or herself existing only when he or she notices that something happens to him or her. For example, when a subject perceives assumingly, sees something, some object, he or she simultaneously realizes that it is him or her who experiences this something, some object in his or her perception but not any other individual.

Each object experienced in consciousness is located in the intentional act as its integral part. The intentional act arising out of consciousness and identifying active conscious activity of a subject puts its object into the immanent field of experiences thus making it part of consciousness. An intentional object in the act of experience becomes dependent, because it is correlatively linked with consciousness and cannot exist beyond consciousness. A subject obviously experiences the existence of this intentional object in the sphere of immanent experience and also experiences the actual existence of his or her consciousness on the whole, in its unity.

Consciousness is a single stream of intentional acts continuously running one after another in synthetic relations with different level of complexity and flowing within the all-encompassing internal time of a subject. E. Husserl emphasized:-"On two sides, psychology is an unlimited flow of phenomena with a single intentional line passing through it, which would seem to be a list of all-encompassing unity, namely the line of immanent time without beginning and end- the time that cannot be measured by any chronometers" [2].

Intentional acts differ by types in accordance with the methods intentional objects are given to one's consciousness. So experiences can include sensory perceptions, memories, imaginations, speculations, desires, assessments, interest and emotions. An intentional object is always given to consciousness as an important one to it; it is experienced not only in isolation as all by itself but also in the open space of previous and further intentional acts. The single immanent experience of consciousness is passed through in a flow of interchanging ways of a given in particular as defined and undefined, contemplating and non-contemplating and only assumed methods. Intentional objects can also be experienced by a subject in different existential modalities such as actual, doubtful and others. This demonstration of various changeable methods of a given for intentional objects results in synthetic interrelation, which constitutes immanent experience of a subject as unified, and single and permanently existing one for consciousness. The virtual reality is an expression and exemplification of this stable interaction.

The action of consciousness manifests itself in its constituting activity, the backbone if which consists in assigning such a meaning to an intentional object that is used by a subject to experience this object in consciousness. This meaning assumed by a subject still requires a procedure for multiple repetition and adequate confirmation. This procedure is implemented in a continuous flow of harmonized intentional acts. The unity of a subject's immanent experience extends much further of separate and single intentional objects because any intentional act can be surrounded by others still being hidden and able for actualization by experiences.

After conducting clarifying phenomenological reductions in the sphere of a subject's immanent experience it is possible to clearly distinguish the two levels of experiences – empirical and transcendental. Empirical experiences fill up the psychophysical structure and exist in an individual, random and doubtful way. Transcendental experiences make up the eidetic structure and demonstrate the universal, necessary and apodictic status of existence. A transcendental subject takes the central position of his or her immanent experience and surrounded by a great deal of intentional objects. Close and remote location of intentional objects depends on the degree of actuality and significance to a subject.

Alongside with own primordial experience a subject notices other psychophysical structures with independent existence. In the act of appresentation or comparing apperception a subject conceives other subjects having the same structure of consciousness, which is although not accessible to him or her. Subjects form the intersubjective world based on communicative experience. "The ego is no longer an isolated thing alongside other such things in a pre-given world. The serious problem of personal egos external to or alongside of each other comes to an end in favor of an intimate relation of beings in each other and for each other" as quoted by E. Husserl [2]. In a process of various verbal and non-verbal interactions subjects through joint efforts constitute intentional objects being common to them, harmonizing and enriching the immanent experience of each subject participating in the intersubjective world. The digital world's resources used to accumulate information and expand contacts are applied here.

Digital technologies are first of all a tool. A man always depends on something – on external physical reality, on communication with other people and on their internal world. The well-being is acquired by him after successful influence on these areas. This well-being is stated by consciousness in the form of experiencing the states of happiness, pleasure, enjoyment etc. Internal states are the initial point of human activity and its ultimate goal. Therefore, the internal sphere of human brain has the signs of self-sustainability, although, needless to say that a finite creature can have it slightly deferent. People would certainly not have been people if they had neither developed tools nor accumulated technologies to interact with reality. The more primitive a tool is the more it is connected with the body and the more obvious it plays a utility role and does not lay claim for something more. Tools used to influence the physical world are perceived by the human consciousness as just tools that cannot substitute the content of internal experiences.

Technical capabilities at the end of the 20th century allowed people to realize and automate one of their intellectual functions – a calculating function by developing appropriate machines. A tool being primarily internal one in the past is being detached now and takes on the form of an external device being accessible to any individual. Those who are busy making IT-equipment more complex should enhance their intellectual abilities and skills and those who do not have to deal with computations may get relaxed and enjoy machine capabilities. There are preconditions being developed for intellectual stratification of society and degradation of its majority and as it usually happens this does not set off alarm bells straight away.

The simulation and objectivization of rational calculating ability is still a tool, which is not self-sufficient performing a utility function. But transiting to the simulation of visual and sound images has actually become a move not only to the simulation of intelligence but the entire human mental life. The tool function ceases to be noticeable. A picture on the screen allows people to minimize contact with reality and build up their own virtual external world in conformity with offered rules and inherent tastes. The choice of virtual reality provides people with a distorted image of physical reality; the simulation that pictures the physical world more beautiful in many cases than it is in reality and has a better position compared to the original. The physical world's illusion created by digital technologies inside consciousness is no less real for this consciousness than the physical world itself (which by the way is not the physical world in itself but only its psychic and intellectual image). Why do people need to come out of the world's image where they can do almost everything into the world where they can do almost nothing? Easy solutions to the problems take on the form of speedy search of ready answers in the internet. Another individual comes out as a network chat name and communication with him or her is limited to an exchange of short information between chat names. Digital technologies in contrast to others to a greater extent detach an individual from physical reality from the necessity to communicate with other individuals. The tool becomes an individual's "other self". If people still remain to people physically then their consciousness exists under the laws of digital reality.

As a result the digital reality takes on a number of properties overriding the inherent subjective world of its separate users. Self-sufficiency, self-sustainability and self-determinacy are among the digital world's acquired characteristics. Gradually the virtual world containing a sphere of information technologies introducing algorithms and thus making the intellectual process easier due to its tool attractiveness and visible variety practically captures and absorbs the human world completely, brings it under control of its logic and its laws.

This situation is reflected in a philosophical discussion over the recent years. So in modern ontology the understanding of existence as a subject-to-object interaction gives way to the concepts in which this subject-to-object interaction gives place to object-oriented ontology. As an example, we can give Graham Harman's immaterialism concept, which debates traditional European ontology. For Harman objects are– "sleeping giants holding their forces in reserve and do not unleash their energies at once" [3]. The world according to Harman is similar to Parmenides' cosmic space – "one homogeneous existence on one side and an unreliable game of opinions and visions on the other side" [3]. The world of subjects and objects is undermined following the information revolution and establishing a new type of people's interaction with the worlds and each other. The philosophical topics of virtual object ontology have been developed since recently by the Centre of Virtualistics attached to the Institute of Human Studies (Russian Academy of Science). If the first studies of virtual reality were about an analysis of mental state and mental training in conditions of extreme situations [4] then further on this analysis picked up philosophical aspect as well [5, 6]. It is emphasized in a philosophical analysis of virtual reality that virtual objects characterize "creation, actuality, self-sustainability" [5], that the world in aspect of virtual paradigmatics is polyontolodical, each created virtuality does not exist forever but in a situation of its action or interaction – interactivity and there is "another reality" existing objectively [5]. This new reality is characterized by a huge informative component with exclusive self-sustainability makes it possible to form special types of culture and education. Modern education involving the maximum amount of certain knowledge as one of its actual tasks cannot but use new computer-based telecommunication technologies that are used to create a well-ordered and transparent world image. Therefore, developing new methods for transfer of knowledge and its permanent transformation is an objective and inevitable process.

First of all let us indicate the characteristics of knowledge itself as an educational phenomenon. According to a representation widely spread in philosophy knowledge bears a true educational meaning only in that case when its object is included in human activity in a human co-being system representing an event for him or her because the objectness is not only the characteristic of objective reality, it is the characteristic of consciousness itself preconditioned by expanding the boundaries of its activity. As noted, for example, S.L.

Frank to a large extent following the logic of phenomenological trend in philosophy, the object is not a transcendental object beyond consciousness but the moment of objectness in consciousness itself, in which some contents of our consciousness take on an objective nature for us"[7]. However, the continuously growing flow of information perceived by people is far away for its educational meaning to be recognized: As a result knowledge is obtained without objective values. The thing is that as a rule it reflects simulated phenomena having no place in reality, what is more important is that human consciousness loses its objectness because the global, unified reality absorbing it does not consider understanding and acceptance of cultural diversity, emotional-active attitude towards the sociocultural contest of knowledge being. Knowledge becomes plain and ethically neutral.

Being captured by virtual reality, which becomes increasingly understandable, actual and interactive, close and more preferable than actual reality, people have less abilities for creative work, who cannot and do not want to evaluate or create something really new. The goals of education correspond to this position of things: They shift towards the training of not only specialists being able to resolve creative tasks and reproduce knowledge but successful users of information cyberspace, in other words, the tasks of educations only unless they are comprehended on the ground of spiritual positions mostly have a tool orientation.

Due to the total effects of a new reality on human consciousness, people lose critical and reflexive properties in perceiving the world and form template, fragmentary thinking, which makes it impossible to consider knowledge as the most important side of human life connected through diverse meanings and demonstrations with the physical, natural world on one side and with the world of human feelings and relations on the other side. This tendency in the development of modern education becomes more relevant, this what O.D Shipunova and L.I Evseeva write about in their article: "A hyperactive communicative network is capable of transforming the informative field and message meanings thus creating potential conditions for destructing the commonality and mental structures of collective, unconscious, practical and discursive consciousness" [8].

As a result of total influence the information environment have on people the nature and style of communication are changed within the educational space. The quantitative indicators – speed and volume of messages transferred from a network to a user and back are a criterion of success in the sphere of information technologies. As for interpersonal communication, its conceptual certainty and completeness then it clearly undergoes transformation becoming multiple-valued, digital and dependent on an endless succession of various virtual intermediate carriers and as a result – not quite directed at an individual subject. That is why a user loses his or her meaning as a human subject –feeling, worrying, reasonable and spiritual, which completely changes the educational situation. In this new information reality everything is done to make a man passive, personally primitive, not being able for truly reflexive activity, which is born exclusively out of communication and live exchange of knowledge, opinions, impressions with the world as well as in the process of active attention towards self ego.

Reflections on a new reality created by people, which becomes more and more detached from them and begins to stand against them, inevitably bring worries over the prospects of humanity. A well-known statement "Esse homo" becomes irrelevant. In conditions, when the real human world is being replaced by the artificial world absorbing and substituting everything in people that is attributed to humanity – mind, feelings, worries, will, freedom, creative works, love and when a man becomes part of the digital reality, its appendage a future man's new image "Esse kiborg" is being developed, because the anthropological perspective moves in this direction. Despite the objective nature of this process, it can and must be counteracted. For this purpose, society has an excellent tool – a system of education, which is developed in accordance with the objectives and tasks of social developmet. These objectives are important to perceive and articulate clearly and take as a basis of modern educational paradigm.

References

1. F. Bretano, *Selected works* (House of the intellectual book, Moscow, 1996)
2. E. Husserl. *Logic investigations. Cartesian meditations. The crises of European sciences and transcendental phenomenology. The crisis of European man and philosophy. Philosophy as rigorous science* (AST, Moscow, 2000)
3. G. Harman, *Immaterialism. Objects and Social Theory* (Gaidar Institute, Moscow, 2018)
4. N. A. Nosov, *Virtual psychology* (Agraf, Moscow, 2000)
5. M. A. Pronin, *Virtualistics in the Institute of Human Studies* (Russian Academy of Science, Moscow, 2015)
6. M. A. Pronin, *Existence: Forgotten Chernobyl: Liquidator's notes: A philosophical-anthropological essay* (Kanon+, Moscow, 2016)
7. S. L. Frank, *A subject of knowledge. Human sole* (AST, Moscow, 2000)
8. O. D. Shipunova, L. I. Evseeva, *Philosophy of communication: University education in sociocultural dynamics of information society* (Saint Petersburg Polytechnic University, Saint Petersburg, 2015)

Mathematic model of production technology transformation

Valery Levensov[1], *Anton* Radaev[1*], and *Sergey* Salkutsan[1]

[1] Peter the Great Saint Petersburg Polytechnic University, Institute of Industrial Management, Economy and Trade, 195251, Politechnicheskaya st., 29, Russian Federation

Abstract. Modeling the processes of creating and improving production technologies is one of the most important tasks in the sphere of providing competitiveness for enterprises, branches and complexes in the strategic aspect. For the moment, the model Gartner's Hype Cycle is used for the specified tasks, which describes changes in expectations from technologies in the course of a determined period of time from the moment when this technology appears to the moment of its complete development. At that, the results of analysis of literary sources on the explored theme speak about the lack of effective instruments for mathematical description of the process of developing and implementing production technologies in the practice of industrial enterprises. The given circumstance has validated the necessity of working out a mathematic model for the specified process; its elements should have a determined functional designation and it enables comparing the processes of development of different technologies.

1 Introduction

In modern conditions of development of the world economy and organization of functioning of innovative production systems on the basis of progressive digital technologies is the key factor for providing the state competitiveness in the respective branches of industry and economy. At that, the significance of every separate technology is determined by the spheres of applying this technology, the scales of respective markets and the volumes of resources which the supposed clients possess, rather than by the cost and labor inputs for implementing this technology. Currently, to describe the process of development and implementation of progressive technologies Gartner's hype cycle model [1] and Arthur D. Little's technology lifecycle model [2], also known as McKinsey's S-curve model, are used. Despite extensive application of the specified instruments in the wide sphere of fields (metal-rolling industry, manufacturing of microelectronic integrated circuits, etc.) including the sphere of planning scientific-research works, currently, instruments for mathematical description of the process of development and implementation of progressive technologies are practically absent. This problem is responsible for relatively low adequacy (objectivity) of the indicated models and, consequently, low effectiveness of their use for solving a wide range of applied tasks. The specified circumstance has determined the necessity of creating (based on the Gartner's hype cycle model) a mathematic model of the process of development and implementation of a

* Corresponding author TW-inc@yandex.ru

progressive production technology which will be a frame for creating methods of solving application tasks for justifying the characteristics of the indicated process with different variants of structuring primary data.

2 Review of literature

At the initial stages of research a review of scientific works on the considered subject was made.

The generalized mathematical description of the Gartner's hype cycle model represented in the works of the scientists M. Steinert, L. Leifer [2], J. Fenn, M. Raskino [3] and others presupposes distinguishing in its composition a respective curve (which describes functional dependence of expectations (the technology development characteristics) from the time factor) of two components:

- Hype curve (in the form of a bell) which describes primarily positive and, as a rule, irrational perception of the considered technology in regard to perspectives and opportunities expected from it in the absence of concrete results of complete or partial implementation of the ideas which constitute the basis of the technology;
- S-curve which describes the maturity of the considered technology which, in its turn, is defined by the effectiveness of the performed experiments and, as a consequence, by the volumes of the respective investments.

It is important to note that the resulting curve which corresponds to the Gartner's hype cycle models and includes the above mentioned components in the general case is not the sum of the latest and is described by each component separately in different sections of the time factor scale: in the primary section the resulting curve repeats the form of the Hype curve, in the next section – the form of the S-curve. At that, the local minimum of the curve within the framework of the Gartner's hype cycle model (see Fig. 1) corresponds to the point of transition between sections.

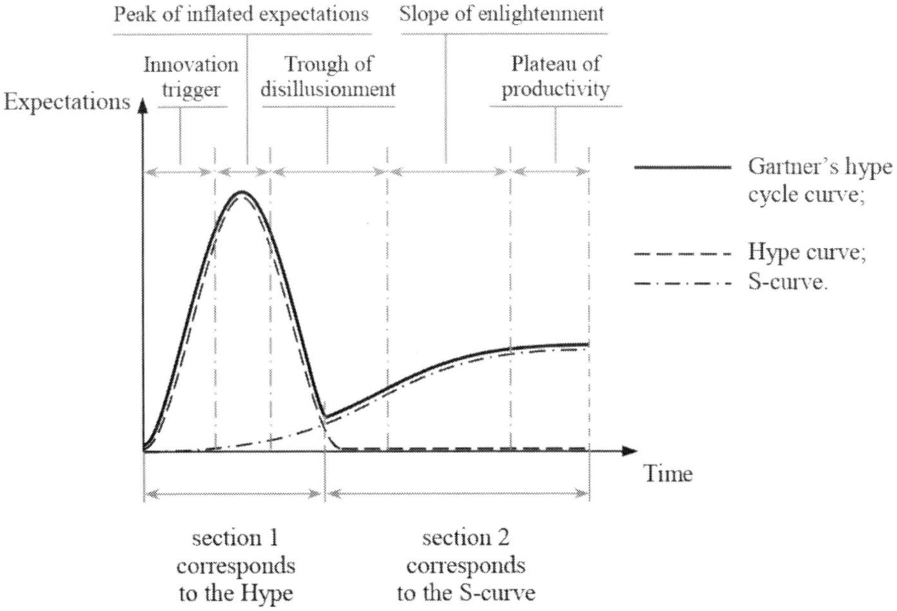

Fig. 1. The generalized mathematical description of the Gartner's hype cycle model.

A significant number of works is devoted to applying the Gartner's hype cycle model for estimating the current condition and forecasting the future development of informational technologies [4] including those in the sphere of education [5, 6], business [7–9] and entertainment [9], technologies for manufacturing innovative production – graphene [10], metamaterials [11], superconducting materials [12], transport vehicles with hydride engine and on fuel elements [13], fuel cells for stationary units [14, 15], etc. At that, for qualitative measuring of expectations from the technology and in every separate case one indicator is used, as a rule, which is objectively estimated on the basis of information obtained from reliable sources. As the specified indicator within the framework of the corresponding studies the specific (in the period of, as a rule, one year) quantity is considered in current events newspapers [7, 12, 13, 15, 16], the quantity of popular-scientific publications [4, 14], the quantity of the registered patents [13, 14], the distribution of the number of studies on separate kinds of production and technologies [8], the quantity of queries in the search systems of the Internet (Google, Yahoo, etc.) [13].

We should particularly distinguish the works of M. Steinert and L. Leifer [2] and also J. Kim et. al. [17] that contain the results of analysis of the large quantity (more than 40 in use [2], about 500 in use [17]) of applied and developed technologies in the field of power industry, public services, etc., in the part of correlating the stages of technologies development (in accordance with the Gartner's hype cycle model) with the concrete time periods.

However, it is important to mention that in a number of works [5, 6, 9–11] application of the Gartner's hype cycle model for estimating the current condition and the development prospects of technologies under research is carried out expertly (without analyzing any quantitative factors), on the basis of the published data of the former publications.

A relatively small quantity of works is devoted to the questions of mathematical description of separate components of the Gartner's hype cycle model. Thus, H. Sasaki in his research work [18], by analogy with the work of M. Steinert and L. Leifer [2], suggests to describe the Gartner's hype cycle model in the form of two components based, relatively, on non-cumulative (a bell-type curve) and cumulative (S-curve) values of the indicator of expectations from the technology, and in the research work by M. Fries and M. Lienkamp [19] analysis of dependencies of the effectiveness indicator for realization of the technology on the time factor (S-curve model) with the aim of determining the type and characteristics of the corresponding mathematic model – approximating function – is carried out. The main disadvantages of the above-mentioned research works [18, 19] are the primary inconsistency (compliance with different scales) of the values of the model components, the difficulty of qualitative interpretation of coefficients of approximating functions, and also the lack of distinct functional correlation (based, for instance, on the principle of summing up or multiplication) of the common indicator of expectations from the technology with its components.

Thus, according to the results of analysis of the literary sources regarding modeling the processes of developing and implementing technologies with the use of the Gartner's hype cycle model the following conclusions were made:

– a significant number of works concerning applying the Gartner's hype cycle model to exploring the processes of development of separate technologies does not address the questions of justification of the characteristics of mathematical interpretation of the model, and it contains only qualitative justification of the current or future stages of technology development on the basis of either expert estimation or the results of statistic analysis of quantitative data of the publishing or patent activity;

- a relatively small number of the developed mathematic models which describe the process of working out and implementing the technologies in accordance with the Gartner`s hype cycle model have a relatively low practical significance and a limited sphere of application on account of the difficulty of interpretation of separate model characteristics.

3 The description of the mathematic model

The results of analysis of scientific publications on the topic under consideration represented in the previous section have defined the necessity of creating (within the framework of the next research stage) a mathematic model of the process of developing and implementing the production technology into the activity of industrial enterprises, based on the Gartner`s hype cycle model. The main provisions of the worked out model are as follows:

- the mathematic model describes the process of working out and developing the technology of producing innovative materials and products which begins at the moment the idea of creating the material (product) appears and ends at the moment of realizing the technology in the full-scale production (single-piece production, batch production, mass production);
- the model represents the correlation of the characteristics of expectations from the technology with the time factor; the correlation has analytical and graphical description; both the quantitative categories are measured in percents, correspond to the range of values from 0 to 100;
- the time factor measured in the limits from 0% (the idea appears) to 100% (full-scale production is organized), is identified with the indicator of completeness of the technology development (Technology Development's Completion Indicator – TDCI);
- the main characteristics of the technology expectations – the generalized expectation indicator (Aggregate Expectation Indicator – AEI) – represents a sum of two components (secondary characteristics) – the indicators of subjective expectation (Subjective Expectation Indicator – SEI) and the indicators of objective expectation (Objective Expectation Indicator); the units of measure and the ranges of changing of the SEI и OEI values are analogous to AEI;
- SEI characterizes hypothetic expectations (from the studied technology), not confirmed by objective results of the undertaken studies – practical experiments, procedures of prototype or physical modeling, implemented pilot projects, etc.;
- OEI characterizes objective expectations confirmed with the cumulatively gathered results of the undertaken studies.

Analytical dependencies of the values AEI, SEI and OEI on the values of the time factor or TDCI are described by the determined mathematical expression of the form

$$E_{\Sigma}(t)=E_{\text{sub}}(t)+E_{\text{obj}}(t)\,, \tag{1}$$

$$E_{\text{sub}}(t)=a_1\cdot t\cdot b_1^{\,c_1\cdot t}\,, \tag{2}$$

$$E_{\text{obj}}(t)=a_2\cdot t\cdot b_2^{\,c_2\cdot t}\,, \tag{3}$$

where E_{Σ}, E_{sub}, E_{obj} – relatively AEI, SEI, OEI, %;

t – time factor or TDCI, %;

$a_1, b_1, c_1, a_2, b_2, c_2$ – the parameters of functional dependencies of SEI and OEI on the time factor (TDCI), their designation is described in Table 1.

Graphic interpretation of the specified dependencies is demonstrated in Fig. 2.

Thus, the diagram of dependency of AEI on TDCI which characterizes the process of developing and implementing production technology into the activity of industrial enterprises can be represented in the form of a sequence of sections identified with the separate stages of the considered process.

1. Development of ideas in regard to research methods and spheres of application of the technology – the number of the formed hypotheses grows faster than the number of the tested hypotheses on account of the small number of the studies undertaken.
2. The objective estimation of the opportunities ensured by the technology – the number of the formed hypotheses virtually does not change (the limits are reached), at this the greater part of the growing number of tested hypotheses is constituted by negative (from the perspective of technologies development) results.
3. Implementation of the technologies in full-scale production – the number of tested hypotheses approaches the total number of formed hypotheses (and finally reaches it), at this, the part of the tested hypotheses with a positive result grows faster than the part of the hypotheses with a negative result.

Table 1. Description of parameters of functional dependencies of SEI and OEI on the time factor (TDCI).

No. of item	Parameter name	Indication	Designation	Note
1	The coefficient of the standard growth of SEI	a_1	Displays by what value in fractional expression the expectations from the technologies would increase in case the TDCI is increased by 1% if all the proposed hypothetic judgments turned out to be true	$a_1 > 0$
2	The coefficient of cumulative decrease of the SEI growth	b_1	Displays how many folds the standardly increasing SEI value decreases taking into account the accumulated data on the results of the undertaken studies in the part of objectively estimated opportunities ensured by the technology	$b_1 > 0$; $b_1 < 1$
3	The coefficient of influence of the TDCI on cumulative decrease of the SEI growth.	c_1	Displays how many folds the break between the standardly growing and the actually reached the SEI values increases in case the TDCI increases by 1%	$c_1 > 0$; $c_1 < 1$
4	The coefficient of the standard growth of the OEI	a_2	Displays by what value in fractional expression the expectations from the technologies would increase in case the TDCI increased by 1% if all the succeeding studies were undertaken independently of the preceding ones.	$a_2 > 0$
5	The coefficient of cumulative increase of the OEI growth	b_2	Displays how many folds the standardly increasing the OEI value increases taking into account the studies already undertaken in the studies which are being undertaken	$b_2 > 0$; $b_2 < 1$
6	The coefficient of influence of the TDCI on cumulative increase of the SEI growth.	c_2	Displays how many folds the break between the standardly growing and the actually reached the OEI values increases in case the TDCI increases by 1%	$c_2 < 0$; $c_2 > -1$

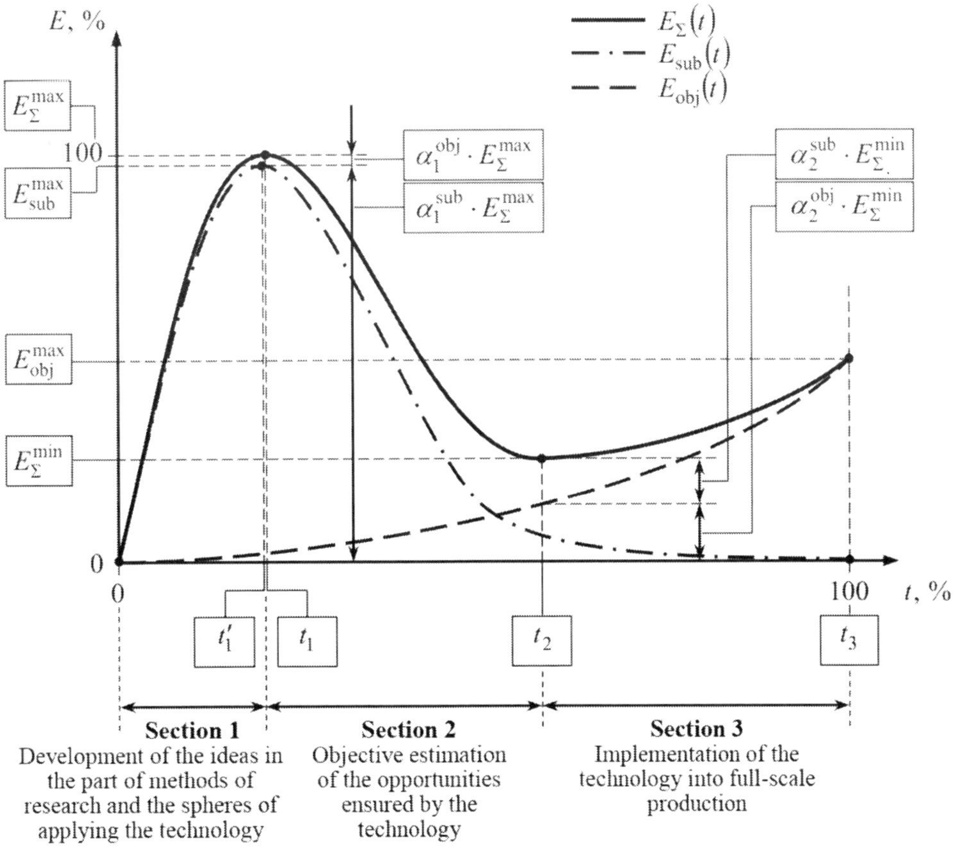

Note:

t_1', t_1, t_2, t_3 – TDCI values corresponding to the characteristic points of the dependencies diagrams $E_{sub}(t)$, $E_{\Sigma}(t)$;

$E_{sub}^{max}, E_{obj}^{max}, E_{\Sigma}^{min}, E_{\Sigma}^{max}$ – SEI, OEI, AEI values in the characteristic points of the dependencies diagrams $E_{sub}(t), E_{\Sigma}(t)$;

$\alpha_1^{sub}, \alpha_1^{obj}, \alpha_2^{sub}, \alpha_2^{obj}$ – parts of SEI and OEI in the maximum and minimum AEI values.

Fig. 2. Graphical interpretation of the developed mathematic model

4 Conclusions and directions of the further studies

Thus, the developed mathematic model describes the key peculiarities of the process of development and implementation of the production technology and its components have a concrete functional designation (qualitative description) that helps to use the developed instrument for solving a wide range of tasks which, in their turn, can be divided into two groups:

– the tasks of justifying the characteristics of the processes of developing and implementing the production technologies into the activity of industrial enterprises with the aim of their further comparative analysis in the historical aspect within the framework of retrospective studies;

– the tasks of justifying the characteristics of the processes of developing promising production technologies with the aim of forming possible schemes of developing the technologies in future.

At the further stages of research it is planned to work out methods of justifying the characteristics of the suggested mathematic model within the framework of the two categories of tasks mentioned above.

It is suggested to implement these methods as exemplified by the technologies of manufacturing innovative materials (metamaterials, thermoelectric materials, bioceramics, etc.) and also by the new ways of constructing (including additive technologies, 3D-printing, etc.) necessary for the most effective functioning of innovative production systems with the use of advanced digital technologies [20].

The results of study are published within the context of implementing the project "Working out the estimation of realizing the priority of scientific-technological development specified in item 20a of the Strategy of scientific-technological development of the Russian Federation (transition to advanced digital intellectual production technologies, robotic systems, new materials and methods of constructing, creating the systems of processing large volumes of data, computer-aided learning and artificial intellect)", financed by the Ministry of Education and Science of the Russian Federation out of the subsidy within the framework of the Federal Program "Studies and workings according to the priority directions for developing the scientific-technological complex of Russia for 2014-2020", Action item 1.1, the Agreement on the Grant Policy No. 14.572.21.0008, October 23, 2017, unique identifier: RFMEFI57217X0006.

References

1. Gartner.Inc. Gartner Hype Cycle [online], Available at: https://www.gartner.com/technology/ research/methodologies/hype-cycle.jsp (2018)
2. M. Steinert, L. Leifer, IEEE Proccedings of Technology Management for Global Economic Growth (2010)
3. J. Fenn, M. Raskino, *Mastering the Hype Cycle: How to Choose the Right Innovation at the Right Time* (2008)
4. G. Vahid, Software & Systems Modeling, **11 (2)** (2012)
5. R. Nikolov, E. Shoikova, M. Krumova, E. Kovatcheva, V. Dimitrov, A.Shikalanov, Journal of Communication and Computer, **13** (2016)
6. J. Laru, S. Järvelä, CSCL, **1** (2013)
7. K. Konrad, Technology Analysis & Strategic Management, **18 (3/4)** (2006)
8. G. Gray. V. Chiu, Q. Liu, P. Li, International Journal of Accounting Information Systems. **15** (2014)
9. N. Ukwuani, E. Bashir, International Journal of Information Systems in the Service Sector (2017)
10. K.S. Siow, Sains Malaysiana. **46 (7)** DOI: 10.17576/jsm-2017-4607-06 (2017)
11. G. Palikaras, E. Kallos 8th International Congress on Advanced Electromagnetic Materials in Microwaves and Optics – Metamaterials (2014)
12. H. Lente, C. Spitters, A. Peine, Technological Forecasting and Social Change, **80(8)** (2013)
13. S.-P. Jun, Technological Forecasting and Social Change, **79 (8)** (2012)

14. B. Budde, F. Alkemade, M. Hekkert, Environmental Innovation and Societal Transitions, **14** (2015)
15. K. Konrad, J. Markard, A. Ruef, B. Truffer, Technological Forecasting and Social Change, **79(6)** (2012)
16. A. Ruef, J. Markard, Technology Analysis & Strategic Management. **22 (3)** (2010)
17. J. Kim, M. Hwang, D.H. Jeong, H. Jung, Expert Systems with Applications, **39 (16)** (2012)
18. H. Sasaki, IJMIT. **7 (2)** DOI : 10.5121/ijmit.2015.7201 (2015)
19. M. Fries, M. Lienkamp, Advances in Science, Technology and Engineering Systems Journal. **2 (3)** (2017)
20. V. Leventsov, A. Radaev, N. Nikolaevskiy, Lecture Notes in Computer Science. **10531** (2017)

Ontology as mapping of material world

Irina Leshcheva[1*], and *Dmitry* Leshchev[2]

[1] Saint Petersburg State University, the Institute "Graduate School of Management", 199004 Volkhovsky per. 3, Russian Federation
[2] Peter the Great Saint Petersburg Polytechnic University, Centre for Advanced Studies, 195251 Polytechnicheskaya st. 29, Russian Federation

Abstract. This paper reviews currently available approaches and methods of automated population and enrichment of ontologies or ontology-based knowledge bases by structured data stored in various heterogeneous sources. Advantages and disadvantages of each approach are pointed out. The results of the analysis allow concluding that the existing methods are not effective enough to solve practical problems. A new method suggested does not have any of the specified disadvantages. The suggested method allows integrating data from different types of sources and considering the distributed nature of data and the necessity of authentication during accessing network resources. The method also suggests a solution to the problem of integrated data conflict resolution so that it will reduce the complexity of populating and enriching ontologies using the collected data arrays, irrespective of the format in which data are stored or represented.

1 Introduction

The term "ontology" came from Philosophy where it means the theory of existence; the subdiscipline of Philosophy that studies the fundamental principles of existence, the most general entities and their categories [1]. In the end of the 20th century, the term "ontology" started to be used in the artificial intelligence, in particular, knowledge engineering [2].

There are many approaches to defining the term "ontology". Tom Gruber formulated one of the most well-known definitions of ontology: "Ontology is a specification of conceptualization" [3]. "Conceptualization" is understood as a rigorous description of the system of concepts, objects and other entities and relationships between them [4]. In other words, conceptualization is a simplified model of the world created for certain purposes using the systems approach. Accordingly, ontology may be considered as mapping of the material world to a certain structured verbal or symbolic space and, finally, in the age of digital technology, as a mapping of our knowledge about the material world in the digital world.

In the context of convergence of digital and physical worlds, ontology is a suitable mechanism to store and convert knowledge. As a universal tool to record knowledge, ontology may do even without formal verbalization of knowledge which makes knowledge digitalization and revisualization simpler. Logical inference based on ontologies allows

* Corresponding author: leshcheva@gsom.pu.ru

digital devices to use recorded knowledge and even generate new knowledge providing a turn of the convergence spiral in the reverse direction.

A detailed practically oriented definition of the term may also be given: "Ontology means a specification or a formal representation of a subject domain which includes an index of terms within the subject domain and logical expressions which describe what the terms mean, how the terms correlate with each other and how the terms may or may not be interrelated" [5].

This study broadens the standard formal definition of ontology by introducing a new component related to data types. The formal model of ontology shall imply an ordered quintuple $O=\langle C,T,\Re,A,I\rangle$ where C is the plurality of notions (classes, concepts) which form ontology; T is the plurality of data types; $\Re=\langle\Re o,\Re d\rangle$ is the plurality of relations, wherein $\Re o \subseteq C\times C$ is the plurality of relations between concepts; $\Re d \subseteq C\times T$is the plurality of properties of concepts; A is the plurality of axioms, i.e. statements on concepts which further allow to make logical inference of other statements; and I is the plurality of individuals (class instances).

Ontology which plurality of axioms is not empty ($A\neq\varnothing$) is called heavyweight, and such ontologies are of the most practical interest since they allow to make inference of new knowledge.

If the plurality of individuals is not empty ($I\neq\varnothing$), such ontology is called an ontology-based knowledge base. Thus, ontology may be divided into two parts. The first part includes ontological knowledge itself that is descriptions of concepts, and relationships between concepts, that is rules describing the subject domain. These rules remain unchanged or change very rarely. The examples of such rules are as follows: "Employee (of an enterprise) is a human", "Head of department X is an employee who manages the operations of the department X". The second part describes particular individuals. For example, "Mikhail Smirnov is Head of department X." This part is subject to constant expansions/changes and may include large amounts of data (data may be evaluations, prices, exchange rates etc. depending on the subject domain).

2 Problem of definition

Information infrastructure of a modern enterprise or company is a complex system. Various technology solutions may be used to support management. Such solutions include both large information systems, covering a full range of business processes and small programs used to solve one routine problem. Some examples of industrial systems are given below:

- ERP (Enterprise Resource Planning)
- MES (Manufacturing Execution System)
- LMS (Learning Management Systems)
- HIS (Hospital Information System)
- LIMS (Laboratory Information Management System)
- CAD (Computer-Aided Design)
- EDMS (Electronic Document Management System).

Examples of a program to solve more specific problems are "working time-keeping system" or "electronic schedule". Moreover, an organisation keeps large amounts of disembodied information which is contained in separate documents (for example, in design documentation, reports, tables etc.) or which is not documented at all.

Tasks requiring retrieval and integration of information from various sources regularly arise in operations management to sample data during the process of making various managerial decisions. For example, combining the data from ERP and MES, consistent roll-out from HIS and LIMS etc. These tasks are often implemented manually or with minimum automation, although a lot of methods and tools have been developed to solve them. In fact, this is rather difficult to combine all knowledge, information and data of a company into a common knowledge base, e.g. due to segregation of documentation access rights, high rates of new information generation etc. However, it is possible and urgent to define a common development method which would allow creating and maintaining an ontology-based knowledge base to solve highly-specific knowledge integration tasks.

This study is devoted to the description of such methodology: creation and population of an ontology with individuals and relationships between individuals based on structured data stored in various heterogeneous sources. The focus is made on developing an open method which would enable to integrated data of various nature.

3 Approaches to creating ontology-based knowledge bases

There are three basic approaches to creating ontologies and ontology-based knowledge bases [6]:

1. Integration of existing ontologies. During the process of integration, an attempt is made to identify common data in ontologies describing the same or similar subject domains to create a new ontology. Several methods were suggested, namely:
   - merging of ontologies for the purpose of creating a common consistent ontology
   - alignment of ontologies by identifying relationships between them which will allow them to repeatedly use information from each other
   - mapping of ontologies by determining correspondence between elements of the ontologies.
2. Development of ontology from scratch or expansion (population and enrichment) of the existing ontology generally based on the information retrieved from the subject-oriented content.
3. Specialisation of a common ontology to adapt it to a specific subject domain.

Ontology population is understood as adding individuals, with their properties, to the ontology, and ontology enrichment implies addition of new relationships and axioms which use such relationships.

3.1 Currently available approaches to populating ontologies

It is necessary to specify the peculiarities of data integration into knowledge bases. Two approaches are used depending on the problem to be solved. The first approach, mapping on-demand, in similar to ontology mapping, but the relationship is established between the ontology and data stored in distributed data sources, rather than the two or more ontologies.

The approach has proven itself to be useful in the context of very large arrays of decentralised data. It ensures that return values are always relevant as no data copying is done into the ontology. Moreover, it provides the observance of access control policies implemented in the database management system. However, when a large number of data sources is integrated or logical inference machines are used to process complex requests, the performance may become extremely low [7]. A supposition was made [8] that expressiveness of requests to a knowledge base should be limited, as some request types may cause exponential growth in the number of generated requests to data sources.

The second approach is data inclusion (consolidation) in the knowledge base as values of properties of the objects (data materialization). It is used to build data warehouses. After consolidation is completed, all necessary data are put into the ontology and this allows to take all the advantages of knowledge bases as compared with databases, namely logical inference tools and means of visualisation of the relationships between objects. However, this approach conflicts with the principle of separation of ontology code from data and this makes it difficult to develop and, mainly, maintain the ontology. When a new individual appears or properties of the previously described individual are changed, it its necessary to create/find the respective object in the knowledge base and set/modify values of its properties. To solve the problem of data deterioration, the process of consolidation must be regularly started. That is why, it is necessary to find a compromise between expenses on data updating and sensitivity of the application to deteriorated data. The second limitation may be an amount of data because the obtained knowledge base virtually doubles the data volume. There are Direct Mapping and Domain Semantics-Driven Mapping depending on what structure, the structure of ontology or the structure of data sources is primary or more critical [9].

Direct Mapping is implemented automatically, and the resulting ontology completely inherits the structure of the data source. But the structure of the data source may rarely serve a good description of the subject domain [10]. That is why the result of Direct Mapping is used as a starting point for developing the ontology. Otherwise, Domain Semantics-Driven Mapping is applied.

When the second approach is used, the ontology of the subject domain serves as a basis and the rules for ontology population are established using a certain mapping description language processed by a specialised (pre)processor.

3.2 Sources of data to be integrated

Main types of sources of structured data are relational databases, XML documents, electronic tables and text files with a proprietary structure. Methods of integration of data from various source types are currently being developed in parallel. Let us consider main of them.

Translation of relational databases into ontology. Relational databases are mainly used to store structured data sources. For Direct Mapping, the database schema is directly translated into ontology using a special translating program. The rules of mappings are established by developers, so if different programs are used, a wide range of similar but not identical ontologies may be obtained from one database.

When the database schema is transformed into ontology with account of the subject domain semantics, the mapping rules are explicitly set using mapping description languages. Such languages may be divided into two groups. Languages of the first group are mainly rely on SQL queries to describe data mapping and this is a potential disadvantage because such languages cannot be used to describe complicated cases of mapping. However, SQL popularity facilitates the acceptance of this approach because there is no need to learn a new language. Second group languages use specialised mapping description languages, hence, they may be developed/expanded so that any specific needs are met, for example, keyword search or regular expression search. In practice, expressiveness of the second group languages is very limited [9].

Main features to be provided by mapping languages and tools to implement them:

1. Generation of unique identifiers determined by the user (ability to generate Uniform Resource Identifiers (URI) along with a simple use of primary key values, for example, by combining values in columns etc.)
2. Logical tables (ability to read tuples not only from tables but also from the SQL view or SQL query result).
3. Field selection (ability to select only a subset of table columns for translation).
4. Field renaming (ability to map a column in the RDF property with another name).
5. Selection condition (ability to translate a subset of table tuples only by setting the WHERE conditions in the SELECT operator).
6. Use of the existing ontology (ability to map relational objects into instances of

existing ontologies).

7. Mapping of one table to n classes (ability to use values of a column as a categorization template: tuples of the table will be translated into instances of various ontological classes based on the value of this field).

8. Conversion of the many-to-many relationship into simple triples (ability to translate a combined table representing a many-to-many relationship into a simple triple, unlike direct mapping where the combined table will be translated into a separate class).

9. Creation of blank nodes (ability to create blank nodes and refer to them within a graph obtained in the translation process).

10. Translation of data types (ability to process relational data types into RDF data types).

11. Data processing (ability to apply the conversion function to the values prior to formation of RDF triples, for example, complex conversion of a type like computation of a value using several columns, line processing etc.)

The urgency of the issue of populating ontologies with data from relational databases with account of the subject domain semantics has resulted in development of a wide range of mapping description languages, such as DR2 MAP [11], R2O [12], DR2Q [13]. We should also mention languages which were created and developed within one and the same project, for example, METAmorphoses [14], RDBToOnto [15], Relational.OWL [16], but they are no longer supported.

In 2012, the W3C RDB2RDF Working Group issued two Recommendations: A Direct Mapping of Relational Data to RDF [17] and R2RML: RDB to RDF Mapping Language [18]. As it follows from its title, the first Recommendation regulates direct mapping of relational databases to RDF. The other document defines a language for describing mapping from a relational database to RDF but includes no guidance on implementation of the R2RML processor, that is why there is a number of R2RML compatible tools with unique approaches to implementation, for example, Ultrawrap [19], DB2Triples [20]. The R2RML uses the best features of its predecessors: it is developed as a result of learning of its predecessors, is based on their experience and includes most of their expressiveness. That is why; it seems that using of the R2RML is inevitable when it comes to conversion of relational databases into RDF. Moreover, tools appeared earlier than R2RML also support it now. For example, Virtuoso [21] includes a simple adapter which translates R2RML in syntax of its own language. However, the authors [9] believe that the R2RML cannot be considered as a comprehensive solution, so new suggestions will appear. This is due to the fact that some approaches rely on complex templates which cannot be expressed using the R2RML language. For example, RDBToOnto [15] analyses data redundancy to define categorisation templates. The publication [22] describes an intelligent data analysis method used to automatically define mappings between the database and the existing ontology. And, finally, the R2RML does not provide data manipulation functions. It relies on the functionality of a relational DBMS, but not on its internal interface.

Integration of data from XML documents. XML (Extensible Markup Language) [23] is an extensible markup language, a simple flexible Internet-oriented textual format developed to structure, store and transmit information between applications. XML documents may be divided into two categories, such as data-oriented and content-oriented categories, but only the first one is considered in the context of XML schema conversion to ontology.

First methods of converting XML documents to an ontology [24, 25] implemented Directed Mapping, then the methods allowing to convert XML schemas to an ontology, for example [26, 27], were developed. One of the well-developed methods as regards to the functionality provided by them is described in [28]. This method enables, in particular, to map several XML schemas to one existing ontology, including creation of individuals. For this purpose, the authors have developed their own mapping language which is used to describe how XML nodes are converted to ontology elements.

It should be noted that none of the suggested methods could become a standard and each project where XML document conversion to ontology is required uses its own tools especially developed to meet the needs of the project and to consider its peculiarities.

Conversion of electronic tables into ontology. Despite of the fact that electronic tables are a prevailing tool to represent and process structured data, the issue of converting tables into ontology is relatively rare discussed. We may suggest that it is so due to the fact that tables may be represented in the form of relational databases for which a number of methods have already been developed. However, for projects where many separate tables of different structures are used, an extra conversion may become a significant limitation. That is why; it is practical to develop a method for converting tables into ontology.

The publication [29] suggests TANGO (Table ANalysis for Generating Ontologies) which is explained as follows: firstly, tables are "canonized", i.e. tables are converted into a standard form suitable for further analysis; secondly, a set of "mini-ontologies" is created where each "mini-ontology" describes the structure of one canonized table; and thirdly, the "mini-ontologies" are merged into one resulting ontology. Thus, TANGO implements Directed Mapping, and the ontology created as a result of TANGO application describes the structure of tables and, in general, cannot be considered as ontology of a subject domain.

3.3 Limitations and disadvantages of existing solutions

A vast number of approaches to integrating data into ontologies have been suggested. However, all of them have some limitations. The disadvantages of the existing solutions include:

1. The need to use and, accordingly, to learn the syntax of several specific mapping description languages. In addition, a convenient tool must be created for each of the languages being used to ensure effective performance.
2. A vast number of various methods for integrating data to RDF have bee suggested, but each method is suitable for one data source type only.
3. It is unclear how simultaneously integrate data from multiple sources. If it is necessary to integrate data, for example, from a database or a XML document into one ontology, the operations should be carried out consequently, using existing methods. For example, at first, populate the initial ontology with data from the DB and then populate the ontology obtained at the previous step with the data from the XML document. Due to constant modifications of data in sources, the above mentioned procedure must be regularly repeated and that will cause unreasonable expenses.
4. Conflicts may arise during integration of data from various sources. The authors of the above mentioned method focus on integration of data from one source, so the ways to resolve such conflicts are not discussed.
5. It is unclear how the connection with the data source is established, how authentication is carried out etc.
6. Companies may use proprietary data storage formats and new formats may be created in the future. No recommendations concerning data integration in this case are given.

The problem analysis allows concluding that it is necessary to develop a new method which will enable to integrate data from various source types. Development of such method will reduce the complexity of populating and enriching ontologies using the collected data arrays, irrespective of the format in which data are stored or represented.

4 Suggested method

A method of automated population and enrichment of ontologies or ontology-based knowledge bases by consolidation based on structured data stored in various heterogeneous sources is suggested. Main types of structured data sources are relational databases, XML documents, electronic tables and text files with a proprietary structure. The algorithm of data consolidation process is shown in Fig. 1.

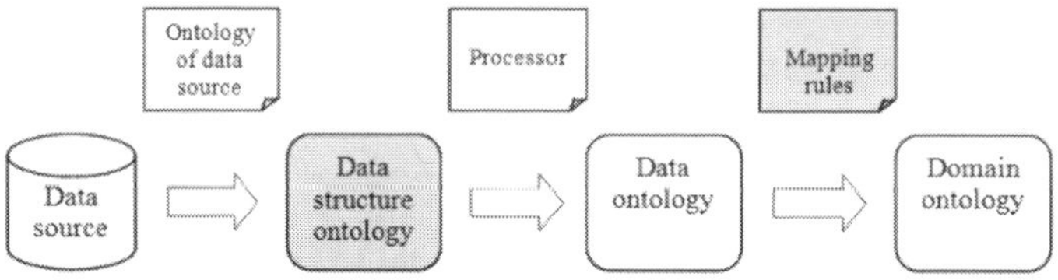

Fig. 1. Algorithm of data consolidation process.

In order to ensure processing of data from various source types, ontologies generally describing the structure of such sources have been created. For example, ontology of a relational database is shown in Fig. 2 in a simplified form. It should be noted that ontologies are a considerably expressive tool to describe structures of data of any type and format.

Using the ontology of data source type, a developer describes the structure of the source which data have to be put in the knowledge base. A special processor program generates an intermediate ontology based on the ontology of data structure; such intermediate ontology including required data from the described source.

The developer applies the mapping rules to describe in detail how the data will be integrated in the ontology. The rules may also govern integration process behaviour if any conflicts arise in data from different sources. Due to application of the rules, ontology of the subject domain is enriched by the data from intermediate ontologies.

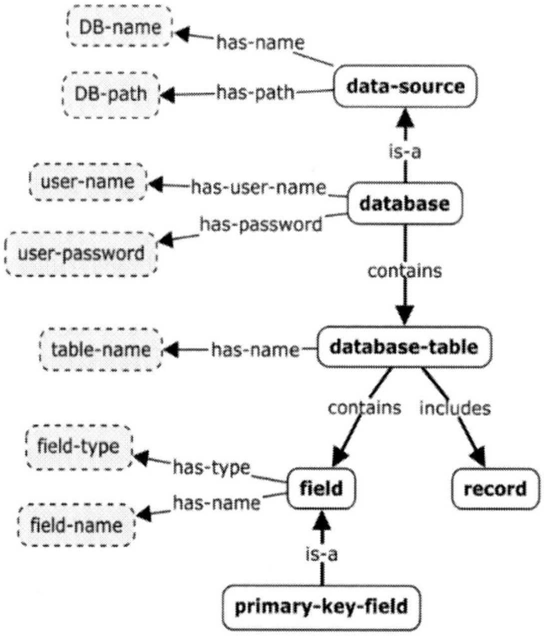

Fig. 2. Ontology of a relational database.

The suggested method has a modular architecture and enables to integrate data from different source types and to consider the distributed nature of data and the necessity of authentication during accessing network resources. The method also suggests a solution to the problem of integrated data conflict resolution so that the complexity of populating and enriching ontologies is reduced using the collected data arrays, irrespective of the format in which data are stored or represented. The method is devoid of the majority of the above mentioned disadvantages. In particular, a developer may describe ontology of the data structure and mapping rules using ontology tools known to him/her. The suggested solution is also extendible to provide a capability to be used with new data formats.

5 Conclusion

The problem of creation of integrated and automated knowledge management systems becomes more and more relevant for companies to ensure that a company's intelligent assets are stored and critical business processes are supported.

Effectiveness of managerial decisions depends, in particular, on completeness and consistency of the information available as well as the possibility to process it flexibly, including at the semantic level. Business processes are often automated using software solutions of in-house and outsourced developers without taking into account of their interrelationships; data are stored in different formats and different sources. Due to constant changes in business processes, knowledge management system developers have to correct data models that results in structural and semantic heterogeneity of information elements. The use of such solutions leads to an increase in complexity and, therefore, reduces effectiveness and convenience of knowledge management systems.

Ontologies and knowledge bases may be used to describe not only business processes but also products, documents, competences, technologies, functions, strategies, financial flows etc. This tool is oriented on interoperability which means the possibility to be used at different hierarchical levels, in different departments, on different hardware and software platforms by differently qualified staff. The aggregate of corporate ontologies serve as a universal framework of the company and, simultaneously, a bridge to understand and transfer knowledges and technologies. But generating such ontologies is a first step only. All advantages of ontology-based knowledge bases are revealed only when they are populated and enriched with data arrays collected by the company.

This study is supported by grant no. 17-07-00228 issued by the Russian Foundation for Basic Research.

References

1. A. L. Dobrokhotov, *New Encyclopaedia of Philosophy* (Mysl, Moscow, 2010)
2. R. Studer, et al., *Knowledge Engineering and Agent* Technology (IOS Press, Amsterdam 2000)
3. T. R. Gruber, Knowledge acquisition, **5(2)** (1993)
4. M. R. Genesereth, N. J. Nilsson, *Logical Foundations of Artificial Intelligence* (Morgan Kaufmann, Los Altos, 1987)
5. T. A. Gavrilova, D. I. Muromtsev, *Intelligent Technologies in Management – Tools and Systems* (Hidher School of Management, St. Petersburg, 2007)
6. G. Petasis et al., *Knowledge-driven multimedia information extraction and ontology evolution* (Springer-Verlag, Berlin, 2011)

7. S. S. Sahoo et al., W3C RDB2RDF Incubator Group Report [online], Available at: http://www.w3.org/2005/Incubator/rdb2rdf/RDB2RDF_SurveyReport_01082009.pdf (2009)
8. O. Erling, Requirements for relational to RDF mapping [online], Available at: http://www.w3.org/wiki/Rdb2RdfXG/ReqForMappingByOErling (2008)
9. F. Michel, J. Montagnat, C. Faron-Zucker A survey of RDB to RDF translation approaches and tools, Research report [online], Available at: http://hal.archives-ouvertes.fr/hal-00903568 (2014)
10. C. Dolbear, J. Goodwin, *W3C Workshop on RDF Access to Relational Databases*, (2007)
11. C. Bizer, *Proceedings of the 12th International World Wide Web Conference* (2003)
12. J. Barrasa, Ó. Corcho, A. Gómez-pérez, *Proceedings of the 2nd Workshop on Semantic Web and Databases* (2004)
13. R. Cyganiak, C. Bizer, O. Maresch, C. Becker, The D2RQ mapping language v0.*8* [online], Available at: http://d2rq.org/d2rq-language (2012)
14. M. Svihla, I. Jelinek, *Proceedings of Electronic Computers and Informatics (ECI)* (2004)
15. F. Cerbah, *Learning highly structured semantic repositories from relational databases* (Springer Berlin, Heidelberg, 2008)
16. C. P. De Laborda, S. Conrad, *Conceptual Modelling-ER 2006* (Springer Berlin, Heidelberg 2006)
17. A Direct Mapping of Relational Data to RDF [online], Available at: https://www.w3.org/TR/rdb-direct-mapping/ (2012)
18. R2RML: RDB to RDF Mapping Language [online], Available at: https://www.w3.org/TR/r2rml/ (2012)
19. Ultrawrap [online], Available at: http://capsenta.com/ultrawrap (2014)
20. DB2Triple*s* [online], Available at: https://github.com/antidot/db2triples (2018)
21. Virtuoso [online], Available at: http://virtuoso.openlinksw.com/dataspace/doc/dav/wiki/Main/ (2016)
22. W. Hu, Y. Qu, Discovering simple mappings between relational database schemas and ontologies, Springer Berlin Heidelberg, 225-238 (2007)
23. M. Ferdinand, C. Zirpins, D. Trastour, *Lifting XML Schema to OWL, Web Engineering* (ICWE 2004, Munich, 2004)
24. R. García, O. Celma, *Semantic Integration and Retrieval of Multimedia Metadata* (ISWC, Galway 2005)
25. N. Anicic, N. Ivezic, Z. Marjanovic, *Mapping XML Schema to OWL, Enterprise Interoperability* (Springer, London, 2007)
26. C. Cruz, C. Nicolle, ODBIS, **2008** (2008)
27. T. Rodrigues, P. Rosa, J. Cardoso, Mapping XML to Exiting OWL ontologies, International Conference WWW (2006)
28. Y. A. Tijerino et al., World Wide Web, **8(3)** (2005)

Digitalization – quo vadis?

Juho Mäkiö[1], *Andrey* Miroliubov[2], and *Valeria* Zhgun[2*]

[1] Emden/Leer University of Applied Sciences, 26723 Constantia pl. 4, Germany
[2] Peter the Great Saint Petersburg Polytechnic University, 195251 Polytechnicheskaya st. 29, Russian Federation

Abstract. Digitalization is changing the global business ecosystem at an unimaginable speed. Although previous industrial revolutions took dozens of years to transform the existing markets, internet-based companies like Google, Amazon and Uber have done it in less than ten years. Business models in the nearest future – how will they look like? Where will the extensive process of the fourth industrial revolution take us? How will our role as entrepreneurs, managers or consumers change in the new business ecosystem? In this paper we consider the changes concerning the process of digitalization as the main prerequisites for transformation of business models. We combine them into three main aspects that influence modern business modeling approaches: technological, social and economic. This prospective gives insight into the way the future business models will look like and leads us to practical recommendations for companies to follow when digitizing their business.

1 Introduction

In context of digitalization, which has been penetrating the market with digital products, digital services and digital solutions, businesses of all industries are in front of a challenge: to adapt to the changes or to initiate the changes. In the new business ecosystem, the relations between companies (competition/cooperation) increasingly depend on this decision. According to McKinsey [1], in 2017 Europe was a net importer of US digital services, running a digital trade deficit amounting equal to nearly 5.6% of total services trade between the EU and the US. However, if its laggards double their digital intensity, EU can add €2.5 trillion to GDP in 2025, boosting GDP growth by 1% a year over a decade.

Can the process of digitalization be stopped? Probably, it cannot. The economic benefits are obvious. Despite this, 42.6% of businesses in the world do not recognize digitalization as a priority strategy [2]. Other companies realize the need to transform their business models in terms of integration and other processes that dictate the direction of digitalization, but they do not know what to start with.

* Corresponding author: International_office@igms.info

The question of digitalization and its consequences was studied by various researchers. The economic role of software platforms was investigated by D. Evans, A. Hagiu and R. Schmalensee with a case-based analysis [3]. B. Jullien performs a theoretical analysis of double-sided markets, highlighting the role of business in online intermediation. The researcher looks at efficiency and price issues of monopoly intermediation and competition between the intermediary businesses [4]. E. Dinlersoz and P. Pereira discuss the viability of adoption of e-commerce by retailers and construct a theoretical model to explain these facts focusing on market characteristics (technology, consumer loyalty, and preferences) [5].

From practical point of view, different companies apply various approaches to digitize business:

- digitizing products;
- digitizing processes when implementing diverse business management systems/online platforms/applications;
- combining both approaches (using the products of data science, cognitive technology and processing power to create 'intelligent enterprises').

Amazon transformed its online paper bookseller's model by launching the Kindle e-book reader at the expense of its physical books sales ("how to cannibalize yourself" strategy [6]). This way they digitized the content.

WhatsApp used a lean operating model approach in digitization of its business processes and achieved astonishing growth with just 35 employees (in 2014) [6].

Philips Healthcare is working with Salesforce on building a platform that will transform and optimize the way healthcare is delivered. They plan to create an ecosystem of developers with healthcare applications that will support collaboration between doctors and patients [6].

IP Soft elaborated a virtual agent Amelia (AI platform) that is capable to understand customer's questions and even emotions when they call or email [6].

Do these examples of new business models use a universal approach to innovation of the models? Probably, it is a more individual question. Can we come up with initial steps and key directions for the companies – this is another question. Even those that started the process and adapted their business to some extent need to change fundamentally the way they identify, develop and launch new business models. A company producing digital software embedded in cars that inform the user about the nearest services to pump a tire or change the color is to cooperate with those services not only in terms of communication, but also in terms of correspondence to the same technical standards. This is an example of a prerequisite to the model transformation.

2 Hypothesis

In this paper we discuss the future prospects of business modeling in context of digitization of business and, in this regard, we ask the question: is it possible to define a dominate business model, and to reveal the key directions for business model transformation in context of the fourth industrial revolution? To reach the goals, we will complete the following tasks:

- to clarify the process of digitalization;
- to observe the digitalization process as a milestone on the timeline of technological evolution (historical aspect);
- to consider the impact of digitalization on business modeling from three aspects: technological, social and economic.

The results of the discussion give a chance to set certain process metrics and indicators for companies to follow when digitalizing their businesses in the future. How well is it possible to measure the success of digitalization in practice? Which leverages will we be able to use later to benefit more?

3 Digitalization or digitization?

When we say that businesses of all industries are increasingly involved in the process of digitalization, we mean different things. Some assume that it is connected with companies digitizing their products or implementing an online retail. Economists evaluate the share of the digital economy: in Russia it is equal to 2.1% of GDP [7]. "Business dictionary" defines digitalization as an "integration of digital technologies into everyday life by the digitization of everything that can be digitized" [8]. Three synonyms (an adjective, a verb, and a noun) are used in this definition of the initial term on purpose. All of these realities ("digital technologies", "digitization" and "digitized everything") are to be integrated together to show that digitalization is a process that involves the economy on the whole, instead of just one business or a product or even a business process.

Digitalization is connected with the use of technologies, products and data in order to maximize revenue, improve business models, replace/change business processes. Digitalization creates an environment for digital business.

Digitization is connected with the digitized units, IOT (Internet of Things). It is the process of converting information into a digital form. As a result, we have the representation of an object, image, sound, document or signal by generating a series of digits that describe a discrete set of its points or samples.

Digitalization neither means preservation of business into a digital copy. The essence of digitalization is not concluded in maintaining business over a long period of time.

When we digitize an object, we convert it into a numerical format. When we digitize business ecosystem in general – we mean the same act. The result of digital camera creation – is digital photos. What is a product of business digitalization?

4 From industry 1.0 to industry 4.0

The difference indicated between the terms "digitization" and "digitalization" leads to understanding of the process of evolution of the industry 4.0. From the historical point of view, digitalization term appeared as a necessity to involve the whole economy in this process.

Industry 3.0, for instance, grew through the use of electronic and IT systems that automate production and other processes. It started as a result of appearance of the first programmable logic controller, development of computer technologies, and Internet. Automated solutions to the business problems allowed speeding up the operations management. Internet connected businesses of different industries and contributed significantly to international business development. We have technologies. We have communication. We have access to BIG data. Next step was adaptation (digitization) and creation of the products that would be able to process and function based on these processes.

Each industrial shift was accompanied by diverse social and economic processes that also influenced business modeling approaches. One of such processes became globalization. The integration of political, economic and social spaces in the world by the means of communication technologies resulted in appearance of new business models based on sharing economy principle and internet trade throughout the world. In its turn, it led to creation of a new business ecosystem with its digital products and processes. We have processes. We have a new business ecosystem. We need these processes connected that will allow the elements to function in a more effective way.

Industry 4.0 is initiated by the active use of cyber-physical systems. "Systems thinking" approach is a key element essential for the success of such ecosystem. It is a holistic understanding of how it works, including the micro-perspective of any individual part of the system, as well as the macro-perspective of how all the individual parts work together as part of the whole. This became a prerequisite to creation of new business models.

5 Industry 4.0 business model transformation

What do we mean by a "business model"? Business model provides a simplified, conceptual view on business development and the mechanism of its operation (business logic), with its separate design elements (business system, business function) that can be modeled in various ways along with an operating enterprise. Business model covers the concept of building a company specific value proposition, key processes and mechanisms for the management, competitive strategy and ways to generate income. It defines the way to grow competitiveness and achieve higher effectiveness of business and characterizes flexibility and stability of business under different scenarios of economic and political trends. Finally yet importantly, the concept of business model includes the company's employees with the skills of system and strategic thinking.

Typical parameters, defining the business model characteristics include the following:

a) business concept (value proposition of a product/service for the consumer);
b) the focus on the client segment;
c) intra-procedure and qualification characteristics (competences) of staff;
d) processes that provide the profit;
e) strategy for achieving competitiveness;
f) company's goals in the market [9].

Typically, business model is based in the present period of existence of an enterprise and covers the near future. In a number of requirements for a business model, the following should be highlighted: 1) adequately respond to changes in the external environment, 2) align the reaction of the business model on the environment with the approved strategic objectives of the company, and 3) match skills of personnel with strategic goals and ways of growth (or change) of these competences. Thus, the quality criteria of a business model should correspond to the factors of a company success in achieving its strategic objectives, and reflect changes in the external environment in the short term.

The key approach used in development of business models is a holistic thinking method. A business-processes analyst evaluates the relations between different internal elements of business and the relations that connect these elements with stakeholders. The analyst is to plan how to improve the way business elements function and interact based on this evaluation [10].

In context of industry 4.0, the relevance of an approach analyzing the ecosystem of business is increasing. New business models will be built on stronger interdependence between the internal and external agents of business environment. The role of the analyst in the new conditions is to consider a more integrated approach. It may be fulfilled by the CDO (Chief digitalization officer) or CEO (Chief executive officer) that has to possess the certain skills to draw the new roadmap to convert the traditional business to digital one and sustain the new system. Digitalization process embraces the whole business system, it is not just a value-added service implemented in one of the business processes. Moreover, it provides valuable opportunities in terms of sustainable growth of business. With easier connection and access to the data of different departments, the roles of the key business model executives are changing. Where is the place of top-management, customer, supplier and product in the new firm infrastructure? Where is the place of digitalization between them? In fact, it is not between, it is in the basis of their relations (Fig. 1).

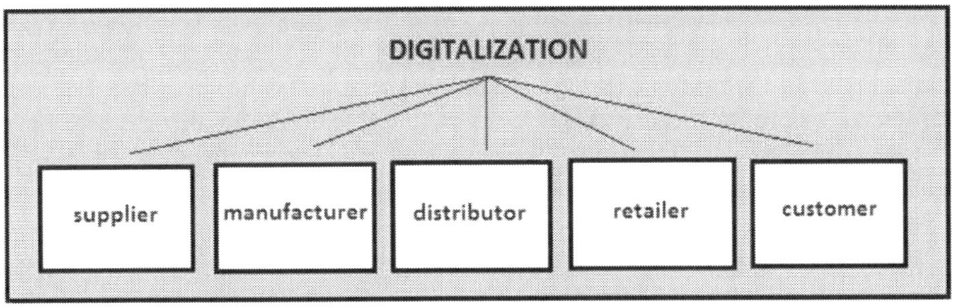

Fig. 1. The place of digitalization process in a value-creation system.

In terms of the listed transformations, it is essential to look at the changes in the future approaches to business modeling from the perspective of three angles (Fig. 2).

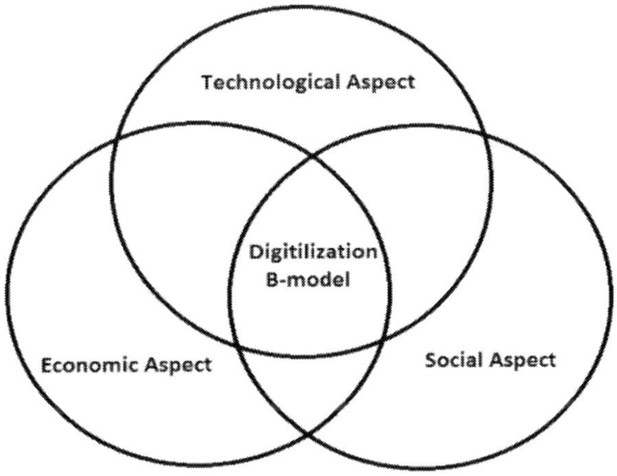

Fig. 2. Business model in context of digitalization process.

6 Technological aspect

From the technological point, we can find several novelties that course the transformation of business models.

First feature is the *comprehensive nature of digitalization process*. New technologies, used in businesses have to correspond technically to the environment's capabilities. Mobile applications require access of the final user to the smartphone and Internet. They require smartphone companies to provide certain technical functions. Online CRM, CIS systems cannot function by themselves. Marketing of digital goods is fulfilled by internet social media channels because that is where the target customer is present most of the time. Someone has to adapt or lose.

Second aspect is the *change of the focus* of the customer towards the company and its product/service. What characteristics did we expect to see in our cellphones five years ago? Today, one of the most important things is for the cellphone to be able to connect to the internet, perform services/applications of other companies. The relations between the businesses of different industries are transforming. There is a strong need in closer cooperation. The "Iphone – Itunes" business model is functioning on the level of macro-environment, not only in terms of one business. If the manufacturer uses QR-coding, the retailers need the system that will be able to recognize the codes.

Previous business models revolved around the core of the product (responding the core need of the customer, answering the question why the customer wants to make a purchase) and plus IT -based service that was adding value to the product. If we think of traditional air conditioner and voice-/mobile phone controlled air conditioner – what would be the reason to purchase the first one and the second one? Service is turning to be the new core of the product. According to Chavez [11], smart functionalities for devices can be grouped into five categories: information storage, information collection, communication, information processing and performance of actions.

Finally, codification of knowledge makes *communications carriers the cores in this new business model*. The way business processes, production and distribution of the products is organized, depends on communication capabilities of the participating actors. In modern business ecosystem business-processes analyst does not have to be a person. The relations that new business models have to consider include people+people, people+machines, machines+machines types.

7 Economic aspect

From the economic perspective, digital processes embedded in business have a strong *impact on the way cashflows are organized*. Digitalization process has led to creation of digital money that speed up cashflow circulation in the business model. The cost of transaction is less, and the time is shorter. Venture capital, crowdsourcing and crowdfunding platforms are some of examples of the globalization influenced business modeling. It also concerns relation between customer and retailer. The latter must provide the opportunity for the first to pay right away.

One of the key benefits that digitalization provides to businesses is *economy of resources*. Various studies [12] have shown that conventional markets are less efficient than internet-based markets with respect to price levels and price elasticity. As the access to the information about the products is getting easier, the competitive environment is also changing. [13]

In fact, *the value of the fourth production factor [information] is increasing*. Economic growth does not come from people working harder now but rather from working smarter. That means using new technologies and new techniques of production to create more value without increasing the labor, capital, and other resources used [1].

As a result, *the way the cost of the product (revenue) is formed is also to be reconsidered*: indicators of rent/warehouses are replaced by the cost of installation of the service, CDO salary, etc. Digital services as new objects of intellectual capital and are to be also considered in the cost of the product.

8 Social aspect

Social impact consequences are analyzed from the point of structural changes in the labor market.

First of all, the digitalization strategy realization results in appearance of new professions (digitalization officer, information officer). There is a correlation between unemployment and structural changes in a new economy. One of consequences is the high unemployment rate in the countries that are the engines of this progress (China, USA). From the employer's prospective, there is a strong demand for the new professions. Current educational approaches do not provide the necessary skills required by the labor market.

The demand for IT skills and knowledge is constantly growing. These skills allow for larger contribution to income of the company and, consequently, to the income of the employee.

Undoubtedly, one of the strongest impacts of such business model transformation is connected with *labor market changes*. We can define two types of structural changes in terms of labor market demand: appearance of jobs that require collaboration with machines and disappearing of jobs that can be replaced by machines that match or exceed human capabilities. Thirty percent of new jobs created in the US in the past 25 years were types that did not exist, in areas including IT development, hardware manufacturing, application creation, and IT systems management.

According to ILO estimates, in 2019 the global unemployment rate is expected to remain essentially unchanged, but the number of unemployed is projected to grow by 1.3 million. Technological progress, capital accumulation, globalization, demographics and government policies will promote the tendency of reallocation of employment across sectors of production: increasing number of workers is projected to be employed in the service sector. The share of manufacturing employment is expected to continue its decline in upper middle-income and developed countries ("deindustrialization" trend).

Business managers need to consider the change in labor relations from three aspects: skills, time and place. According to McKinsey [1] research, 20% to 30% of the working age population in the US and the EU is engaged in independent work. 70% choose this type of work, 30% use it out of necessity because they cannot find a traditional job, or one that meets their income and flexibility needs.

From the social aspect we can derive a number of *issues that businesses and the society face*: digital divide, disability of conventional economy co-live with digital economy, security problems and others challenges.

Digitalization is also dramatically changing the social behaviors and interaction between business agents. As *the point where customers and companies meet changes,* it becomes a *continuous interaction* during the time a customer uses a product or service.

At the beginning of 2000s, neuro-marketing allowed to predict and analyze customer's behavior in order to plan product output. With the total digitalization of business environment, there will be no need to analyze when the signal will come directly from machine to machine (*M2M relations*). Uber systems capture and provide information on people behavior when choosing routes and schedule (route patterns) to logistics companies. This *information is also a new product that has a value*. M2M relations change the way such products are bought and sold.

The roles of business agents on a micro-environment level are also modified or even lose their relevance. The integration of digital processes in the business model may result in *self-controlled organization* – this is the level of management that just a couple of years ago did not seem real on the macro-level.

Another challenge for society is the necessity to adjust legislation to the changes. As in case of a sharing economy business model, many countries faced the problem of the existing tax policy that cannot be applied to the services. As an intermediary online business, online platform cannot be subject to taxation in certain countries.

9 Conclusion and future research

As a result of the research on three main aspects influencing modern business modeling approaches and clarification of the key terms concerning the process of digitalization, we came up with the following directions for business model transformation in context of the fourth industrial revolution and recommendations for companies to digitize their business. It is essential:

1. To consider the transformation of a business model by a holistic approach. Digitalization is not is not a process that connects supplier, manufacturer, distributor, retailer and customer. It lies at the basis of these relations.

2. To understand that digitalization concerns digitization of business in general (products and processes). The core of the product is digital service that allows it to function or supports the key value of the product.

3. To focus on processes: information storage, information collection, communication, information processing or performance of actions.

4. To remember that communication carriers (people/machines) are the cores in the new business model.

5. To apply digitization in organization of the cashflows in the business model: the transaction time will be shorter. Reconsider the cost of the final product. Analyze the new sources of revenue in the business model.

6. To perceive information derived in the process of value creation as another source of value.

7. To consider the new type of the relations in the new business model – P2M (people to machines), M2M (machines to machines).

8. To be ready for the social challenges: digital security, digital divide on the local and external business level.

The future research will concern the answer to the question based on the outcomes above, how to make a roadmap for the companies that need to digitize their business, what indices should be run to evaluate the results of a business model transformation when digitizing the business.

References

1. Report McKinsey Global Institute [online], Available at: https://www.mckinsey.com/~/media/McKinsey/Business%20Functions/McKinsey%20Digital/Our%20Insights/Digital%20Europe%20Pushing%20the%20frontier%20capturing%20the%20benefits/Digital-Europe-Full-report-June-2016.ashx (2016)
2. Digital Vortex. How Digital Disruption Is Redefining Industries. Global Center for Digital Business Transformation [online], Available at: https://www.cisco.com/c/dam/en/us/solutions/collateral/industry-solutions/digital-vortex-report.pdf (2015)
3. D. S. Evans, A. Hagiu, R. Schmalensee, *Invisible Engines: How Software Platforms* (MIT Press, Cambridge, 2006)
4. C. Crampes, C. Haritchabalet, B. Jullien, Journal of Industrial Economics, **57 (1)** (2009)
5. E. M. Dinlersoz, P.Pereira, International Journal of Industrial Organization, **25** (2007)
6. World Economic Forum White Paper. Digital Transformation of Industries: In collaboration with Accenture [online], Available at: http://reports.weforum.org/digital-transformation/wp-content/blogs.dir/94/mp/files/pages/files/digital-enterprise-narrative-final-january-2016.pdf (2016)
7. Regnum Information Agency: Digitalization of Russian economy: apply or postpone [online], Available at: https://regnum.ru/news/2305956.html (2017)
8. Business dictionary online, [online], Available at: http://www.businessdictionary.com/definition/digitalization.html (2017)
9. M. Morris, M. Shindehutte, J. Richardson, Journal of Business research, **58 (6)**, (2005)
10. Science-engineering, University of Houston [online], Available at: http://sce.uhcl.edu/helm/rationalunifiedprocess/process/workers/wk_bpan.htm (2017)

11. E. Chávez, S. Dobrev, E. Kranakis, J. Opatrny, L. Stacho, J. Urrutia, Latin American Symposium on Theoretical Informatics (2006)
12. M.D. Smith, J. Bailey, E. Brynjolfsson, Understanding Digital Markets: Review and Assessment (1999)
13. Bosch White Paper Series Part I: Internet of Things Strategy: Capitalizing on the Internet of Things – how to succeed in a connected world (2014)

Information technologies and transformation of models for implementation of investment-construction projects in modern Russia[a]

Xeniya Malinina[1], *Juriy* Shamara[2*], and *Zhanna* Petukhova[3]

[1] Saint Petersburg State University of Architecture and Civil Engineering, 190005 2-ya Krasnoarmeiskaya st. 4, Russian Federation
[2] Investment-Engineering holding "KNGK-Group", 350000 Budionnogo st. 117/1, Russian Federation
[3] Norilsk State Industrial Institute, 663300 50 years of October st. 7, Russian Federation

Abstract. In this article we carry out the analysis of the possible directions and consequences of transformations of the existing models for implementation of investment-construction projects in relation with integration of information technologies and the construction industry in modern Russia. Such integration is considered as the most useful tool to solve such chronicle problems of the construction industry as low quality of works, missed deadlines and sustaining the best ratio "price-quality" for the customer. The basis for such integration is the technologies of informational modeling of construction objects. We investigated two basic models: disintegrated purchases and integrated purchases whose transformation will be directed towards development of mechanisms of partnership between participants of investment-construction projects, expanded use of "integrated" contracts in the system of state purchases of construction works and further centralization of control in the system of construction for state purposes.

1 Introduction

We will assume the digital economy as a business activity where the key factor for production is the data in the digital form, processing of large volumes of information and using the results of the analysis to significantly increase the efficiency of production and economic processes [1]. In the report of the Organization of the Economic Co-operation and Development (OECD) published in 2016 the conclusion is made that the digital economy is an unconditional imperative for the effective development of any sphere of human activity and will require, along with the introduction and mastering of information technologies, also a revision of the whole complex of production and, in a broader sense, social relations [2, 3]. This topic is important in view of the "Strategy for Developing

[a]The article was prepared as part of the work on the grant of the President of the Russian Federation NSh-4028.2018.6
*Corresponding author: info@kngk-group.ru

Information Society in the Russian Federation for the Period 2017 – 2030" adopted in 2017 and the State program "Digital Economy of the Russian Federation" [4].

The investigation of the consulting company McKinsey "Digital Russia – a New Reality" published in July 2017 showed that the economic effect of digitalization of the economy in Russia can increase the GDP by 4.1–8.9 trillion rubles by the year 2025, which will constitute 19% to 34% of the total expected GDP growth [5]. In construction, the digital environment is formed on the basis of the technological platform based on the technology of informational modeling of construction objects (BIM technologies). A group of Russian researchers in the work "Digital Economy – Various Ways for Efficient Use of Technologies" showed that a very important characteristic of the digital environment in construction is the integrated character and openness of the information on the object for all the interested parties. This information is contained in the information model of a building (or facility) created during the projecting stage and utilized during construction and operation of the object [6]. The information model is integrated with the existing and prospective information systems supporting the construction, and, in the future, we should anticipate integration of technologies of information modeling of buildings with technologies of the distributed register, including the context of using "smart" contracts [7]. In general, according to the evaluation of Russian and foreign researchers, it is obvious that there is institutional and technological readiness of the construction industry in the developed countries for integration into the digital economy.

After analyzing the publications we can draw the conclusion that creating an all-encompassing digital environment in the construction industry will significantly influence the investment-construction processes and the character of contract relationships between their participants. In this article we made an attempt to identify the basic directions of such influence and the possible consequences.

In the world practice, a few organizational-methodical approaches are used to implement the investment-construction process and regulate the contract relationships between their participants. In accordance with the classification by J. Masterman [8], there are two models to implement investment-construction projects (ICP). Each of them includes several schemes of interaction between their participants.

1) The model of disintegrated purchases implying distribution of responsibility for different types of project works between different workers, with each of whom a separate contract is signed (the designer makes the project, the subcontractor carries out construction, the engineer carries out designer's supervision etc.). The scheme of interaction within the framework of this model is called different names in different sources: "traditional" [9], "distributed" [10], the "projecting-tender-construction" scheme [11] and are primarily characterized by disintegration between the design and construction functions.

Within the framework of the described model, a "managerial contract" scheme is also used, when the general contractor only under the project management and outsources 100% of construction works to subcontractors.

2) The model of integrated purchases basing on the so-called "complex contract" implying integration of works carried out during various stages of the project, in the hands of one contractor, includes the following contract schemes:

- Project-construction contract (integration between designing and construction);
- "Turnkey" contract (the contractor takes on responsibility for the entire complex of works for designing and construction of the object and commissioning it to full capacity);
- "Engineering-Procurement-Construction-Management" contract (EPCM) (used for construction of high-tech industrial objects and means not only commissioning of a new plant but also transferring a new innovative technology);

– A concession scheme based on complex contracts for designing, construction and operation of objects within the framework of the state-private partnership.

A brief comparative characteristic of models and schemes to implement investment-construction projects is shown in Table 1.

Table 1. A comparative characteristic of models and schemes to implement investment-construction projects.

Scheme	Advantages	Drawbacks	Sphere of use	Development trend
Disintegrated model				
Distributed scheme	Maximum economy of invested money. Highly controllable parameters of the project. Even distribution of risks between the customer and contractor.	Loose coordination between designing and construction. Significant growth of the actual costs and length of construction works as compared to the accepted ones. High requirements for the customer's expertise level.	Construction for state contracts. Large infrastructural projects.	Partial integration of designing and construction. Tighter co-operation between the parties of the contract.
Managerial contract	High quality of project management. Not too high requirements for the customer's expertise level.	Insufficient "transparency" and controllability of works.	Customers with low managerial expertise level.	
Integrated model				
Design-construction contract	Decreased risks for the customer. Not too high requirements for the customer's expertise level.	Insufficient "transparency" and controllability of works. Relatively high costs.	Commercial construction.	Better controllability of the project. Tighter co-operation between the parties of the contract.
EPCM and "turnkey" schemes	Low risks for the customer. Not too high requirements for the customer's expertise level. Implementation of innovative technologies.	Insufficient "transparency" and controllability of works and high costs of the project. Focusing on imported technologies as opposite to own development.	Industrial construction where the cost of technologies is much more than the cost of construction and assembly works.	Better controllability of the project. Tighter co-operation between the parties of the contract. Focusing on acquiring experience and localizing the technologies.
Concession, SPP-MPP	Economy of budget investment. Increased quality of state-controlled works.	Long-term risks. Low "transparency" and controllability of the project.	A wide range of projects implemented in the public sphere.	

As we can see in the table, the main trend of development of the investment-construction process, disregarding the selected model and scheme, is tendency for a deeper co-operation between the participants of investment-construction projects and a better transparency, controllability and, therefore, stability of the ICP. Implementation of information technologies into construction industry and using them as a basis for digital environment has the purpose to create pre-requisites for such co-operation, which, in its turn, will require transformation of the entire system of interaction between the participants of the ICP, that has already started and whose analysis for the two described models for implementation of investment-construction projects has made it possible to highlight the basic trends of this process, as presented below.

2 The model of disintegrated purchases

2.1 Forming a mechanism of partnership between participants of investment-construction projects

The term "partnership" means a documented co-operation between the customer and the contractor, and other participants of ICP, implying combination of their resources and effort to achieve the target of the project in the conditions of complete availability of information with the use of established rules and procedures that are mandatory for all the parties.

The technological basis for forming partnerships within the framework of an investment-construction project will be an informational model of the object of construction, which is an informational resource used by everyone and ensuring the capability for co-operative work of all the involved parties during the entire life cycle of the object. Partnership in the conditions of the digital environment can be supported by the following:

– Saving the investor's money due to co-operative use of the method of function-cost analysis;

– Decreasing the number of critical conflicts during implementation of ICP due to co-operative risk management;

– Decreasing the gap between designing and construction due to contractor's involvement in creating the information model of the object during the designing stage and organizing tight co-operation between the contractor and the designer during the construction stage;

During the last years, in the economy of Russia, including the construction industry, important changes have happened, which makes it possible to speak of a transition into a new quality from the viewpoint of forming conditions for wide use of digital technologies:

– Adopting a strategy of development of an informational society in the Russian Federation and the corresponding state program;

– Creating national and regional information systems (including the technical, software, organizational and professional support of their operation) in the sphere of state purchases (IIS SP), in the system of price-forming, including stock exchange of commodities for construction, in the system of overhaul and servicing of buildings and facilities, in the sphere of self-regulation etc.;

– Creating an institution of state technical customers providing professional support of investment-construction projects;

– Increasing the role of the Ministry of Construction and Housing as an institutional basis and the basic center of expertise in construction encompassing not only urban planning and construction for state purposes but also large-scale corporative construction projects in the sphere of industry and infrastructure development, as well as construction in the commercial production;

– Wide implementation of mechanisms of state-private partnership in the form of concession and gaining the corresponding experience in this sphere;

– Employing the professional community for regulating relationships in the industry (self-regulating through SRO, normative-technical regulating through updating the existing normative-technical documentation and creating new one etc.).

All these changes create material institutional and economic basis for transformation of the model of disintegrated purchases in the direction of forming partnerships between the participants of investment-construction projects.

2.2 Management centralization in the system of construction for state purposes

In accordance with the changes in the Urban-planning code of the RF, the key participant of the modern investment-construction process is the technical customer acting in the name of the developer and bearing full responsibility for efficient spending of investors' money, observing deadlines and ensuring the quality of construction. On the part of the state, efforts are made to centralize the activity of technical customers in the system of construction for sate purposes by forming a state structure of a new type – the universal technical customer (UTC) whose task is to ensure efficient spending of budget investment and increased quality of works. Using BIM technologies and integration of federal and regional information systems enforces this process due to creating an information-technological basis for efficient management of many projects at once.

2.3 Intensifying the use of the managerial contract scheme

Increasing the role of technical customers in the investment-construction process on the basis of digital technologies creates conditions for inclusion of technical customers into the system of general contract as general contractors, which will demand that they acquire the technical and technological expertise they currently do not have. This, in its turn, will create conditions for wide use of the managerial contract scheme that is very rarely used in modern Russia. An indirect indication of this trend is the explanation of the Ministry of Construction and Housing dated 28 April, 2017, saying that the function of the technical customer can only be fulfilled by a member of the corresponding self-regulating organization in the sphere of engineering research, architectural-construction designing, construction, reconstruction and overhaul of capital construction objects [12].

3 The Model of Integrated Purchases

3.1 Increasing the transparency and controllability of integrated purchases that will result in their wider use in construction

The model of integrated purchases implying transfer of responsibility for designing, construction and commissioning of the object to the contractor is primarily used in commercial and industrial construction. In the USA and Great Britain, more than 70% of ICP in these spheres are carried out within the framework of the integrated purchases model, whereas in Russia the share of such projects is as low as 40%. Implementing the technology of informational modeling of construction objects on the basis of integrated databases on construction resources and universal methods of cost estimation in the Russian

Federation will enable increased accuracy of cost calculation and better transparency and controllability of the investment-construction process for the customer. This will eliminate the existing obstacles for wider use of the integrated purchases mechanism: excessive cost of construction and non-transparency of spending the investors' money, and will create conditions for wider use of the corresponding schemes in construction in the RF.

3.2 Expanding the use of the design-construction contract scheme onto the system of state purchases

Due to the reasons described above, the design-construction contract scheme is very rarely used in the system of state purchases in the RF. However, considering the perspectives of a wider use of informational modeling and assuming quick development of the institution of the integrated technical customer in construction, who has managerial, engineering and often also construction expertise, as well as professional and technical resources in the sphere of digital technologies, we should anticipate expanded use of the design-construction contract scheme in construction for state purposes. This will require changes in the effective legislature on state purchases (in particular, in federal laws No. 44 and No. 223, as well as in similar legal acts at the regional and municipal levels) in the parts regarding elimination or decreasing limitations imposed on combining lots in order to improve competitive advantage of the sales.

3.3 Expanded use of the state-private partnership mechanism

In the Russian Federation, the state-private partnership in construction is implemented in the form of concession for the objects in the state ownership, and in the form of the state-private and municipal-private partnership (SPP-MPP) for other objects. Currently, the state-private partnership has limited use, primarily in the sphere of transport infrastructure and residential areas development.

Implementing informational modeling technologies for construction objects to ensure efficient interaction between partners will make it possible to find the optimal balance between the parties' interests, decrease or eliminate long-term technical and financial risks for projects of this type while keeping their main advantages: increased efficiency of state investment and the quality of state-controlled works. This will create conditions for wider use of the state-private partnership mechanism in other spheres: construction and operation of schools, hospitals and social services objects.

4 Conclusions

Integration of the construction industry into digital economy will significantly influence the organization of the investment-construction process and will require transformation of the two existing models of implementation of investment-construction projects. Transformation of the disintegrated purchases model will be directed towards development of the mechanisms of partnership between participants of investment-construction projects; using "complex" integrated contracts in the system of state purchases of construction works; further centralization of management in the system of construction for state purposes through development of the institution of the integrated state customer. The model of integrated purchases will transform towards increased transparency of the investment-construction process, which will ensure its wider use in the system of construction for state and municipal purposes.

References

1. Order of the President of the Russian Federation dated 09.05.2017 No. 203 "On the Strategy of Development of Informational Society in the Russian Federation for the Period 2017 – 2030"[online], Available at: http://kremlin.ru/ acts/bank/41919 (2017)
2. OECD "New Forms of Work in the Digital Economy", OECD Digital Economy Papers, No. 260, OECD Publishing, Paris [online], Available at: http://dx.doi.org/10.1787/5jlwnklt820x-en (2016)
3. OECD "Stimulating digital innovation for growth and inclusiveness: The role of policies for the successful diffusion of ICT", OECD Digital Economy Papers, No. 256, OECD Publishing, Paris [online], Available at: http://dx.doi.org/10.1787/5jlwqvhg3l31-en (2016)
4. Order of the RF Government dated 28 July 2017 No. 1632-p on approving the program "Digital Economy of the Russian Federation" [online], Available at: http://static.government.ru/media/files/9gFM4FHj4PsB79I5v7yL_VuPgu4bvR7M0.pdf (2017)
5. Digital Russia – a New Reality [online], Available at: https://www.mckinsey.com/~/media/McKinsey/Locations/Europe%20and%20Middle%20East/Russia/Our%20Insights/Digital%20Russia/Digital-Russia-report.ashx (2017)
6. A. P. Dobrynin, K. Yu.Chernykh, V. P. Kupriyanovsky, P. V. Kupriyanovsky, S. A. Sinyagov, International Journal of Open Information Technologies, **4 (1)**(2016)
7. N. Alekseyenko Block-Chain without Intermediaries: Development in the Digital Economy [online], Available at: https://realty.rbc.ru/news/59788fab9a7947d94ee1ddcb acts/bank/41919 (2017)
8. J. W. E. Masterman, *An Introduction To Building Procurement Systems* (E & FN Spon, London, 1992)
9. A. E. Churbanov, *Forming a Mechanism of Contract Relationships in Modern Construction* (Saint Petersburg, 2006)
10. M. V.Demidenko, A. S. Philippov, Proceedings of Civil Engineering, **4 (57)**(2016)
11. C. Hendrickson, *Project Management for Construction* (Carnegie Mellon University, Pittsburgh, 1999)
12. Ministry of Construction and Housing of the Russian Federation. Letter dated 28 April 2017 No. 15175-TB/02 [online], Available at: http://rulaws.ru/acts/Pismo-Minstroya-Rossii-ot-28.04.2017-N-15175-TB_02/ (2017)

Twisted particles as a new tool to study micro world phenomena and processes[a]

Anna Mayorova[1*]

[1] Peter the Great Saint Petersburg Polytechnic University, Centre for Advanced Studies, 195251 Polytechnicheskaya st. 29, Russian Federation

Abstract. Twisted or vortex particles are a new powerful tool to study atomic and molecular processes as well as phenomena that occur at the level of nano-objects. The main feature of such particles is that they carry a non-zero projection of orbital angular momentum along the beam propagation direction. The process of twisted electron scattering from diatomic molecule targets has been studied in this paper for the first time. The Yukawa potential is selected as a model potential. Numerical calculations are carried out for the case of scattering from a hydrogen molecule H_2.

1 Introduction

Over the last two decades, conceptually new tools became available to be used in studying such micro world phenomena as twisted, or vortex, particles. Twisted photons were theoretically predicted [1] and experimentally implemented [2] in the end of the 20th century. In 2007, the properties of twisted electrons were described in detail, the behaviour of twisted electrons in external fields was studied, and a number of experiments to obtain twisted electrons was proposed in the publication [3]. The publication gave rise to a series of experimental work on obtaining twisted electron beams. Today, it is possible to produce twisted electron beams with an energy of about a few hundreds keV and projections of the angular momentum $m\hbar{\sim}100\hbar$. Moreover, first steps to obtain twisted neutron beams [4] and even twisted matter waves [5] have recently been taken. Twisted particles serve as a powerful research tool in various fields of modern physics. For example, in quantum information theory, twisted photons may be used to transmit data since the information capacity of twisted states is significantly higher than that one of preset helicity states, as well as to multiplex data flows. Furthermore, twisted photons may be used to manipulate individual atoms, to carry out fundamental verifications of the STR and the GTR, and to analyse fundamental processes of the interaction of light with matter. Twisted light in optical traps enables not only to trap a nano-object (e.g. a biological structure or the Bose-Einstein condensate), but also to rotate it. Twisted electrons may be used to study structural and electronic properties of a matter or magnetic properties of surfaces and solid bodies.

---

[a] This study was supported by the Foundation for the Advancement of Theoretical Physics "BASIS" and the Ministry of Education and Science of the Russian Federation (grant no. 3.1463.2017/4.6)
[*] Corresponding author: majorova_av@spbstu.ru

2 Theory and results

The state of a twisted particle is described by a wave; the wave front represents a helical curve. Therewith, there is a relationship between the wave phase and the azimuth angle φ (Fig. 1 a). The intensity profile of such wave in the plane perpendicular to its direction of propagation is a set of concentric rings with a central null-intensity spot (vortex) (Fig.1 b). Moreover, the state of a twisted particle in momentum space may be described by a superposition of plane waves with the wave vector $\mathbf{k} = (\mathbf{k}_\perp, k_z)$ which lays on the surface of a cone with the opening angle θ_k (Fig. 1 c). When the opening angle θ_k becomes zero, the twisted wave turns into a common plane wave.

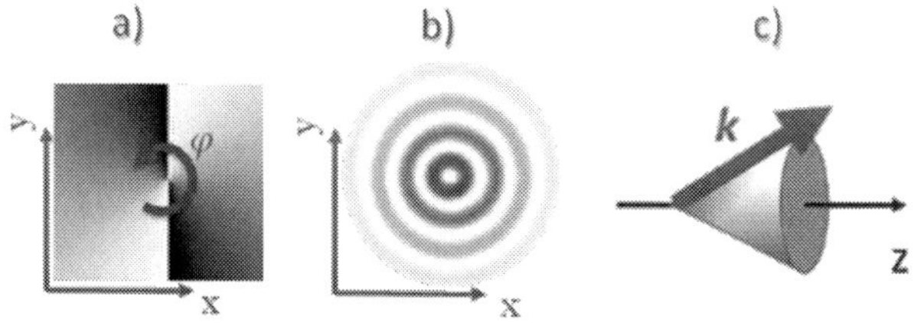

Fig. 1. a) twisted wave phase, b) twisted wave intensity, c) wave vector **k** of the twisted wave in momentum space.

Twisted waves may be described by what is known as the Bessel wave. The Bessel wave is a stationary state having a definite energy ω, a longitudinal momentum k_z, helicity λ, and an orbital angular momentum projection m:

$$\Psi_{tw}(\mathbf{r}) = \int \frac{d^2\mathbf{k}_\perp}{(2\pi)^2} a_{æm}(\mathbf{k}_\perp) e^{i\mathbf{kr}} \quad (1)$$

where

$$a_{æm}(\mathbf{k}_\perp) = (-i)^m e^{im\varphi} \delta(|\mathbf{k}_\perp| - æ) \frac{1}{æ} \quad (2)$$

A series of studies of various processes of collisions with twisted electrons was carried out over the last decade. However, in all these studies, twisted electron beam interacted with either a single counter-propagating beam (Compton scattering [6], electron-electron scattering [7]) or a target consisting of atoms (radiative recombination [8-9], Mott scattering [10]). The process of twisted electron scattering on target molecules has been studied herein for the first time. It is well known that when colliding with a molecule, high-speed electrons generally interact with nuclei and electrons of the inner shell of atoms which form the given molecule. Therewith, molecular centres play the role similar to that one of optical slit in light scattering, since they are localized in space and distinctly separated from each other. As a result of the interaction of electrons with the molecule, a strong interference occurs in the differential cross-section. The use in this experiment of such twisted electrons instead of the usual electrons described by a plane wave leads to a number of peculiarities. Three possible scenarios are studied in this paper: (I) scattering from one molecule which centre of gravity lays on the beam axis (Fig. 2), (II) scattering from a molecule with one of its atoms laying on the beam axis (Fig. 3), and (III) scattering from a macroscopic target consisting of a plurality of molecules (Fig. 4).

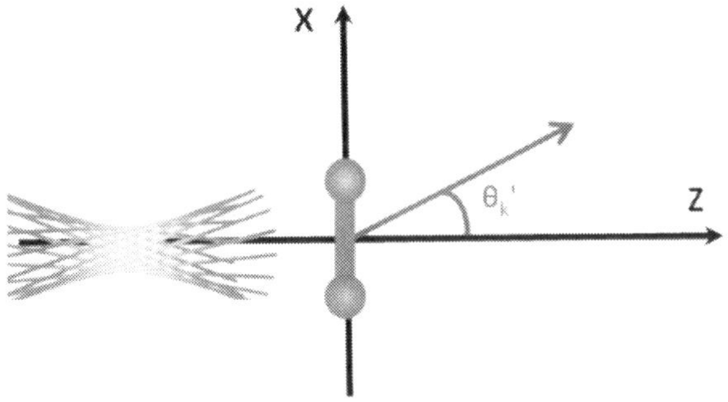

Fig. 2. Scenario (I) geometry: the centre of gravity of the molecule lays on the beam axis.

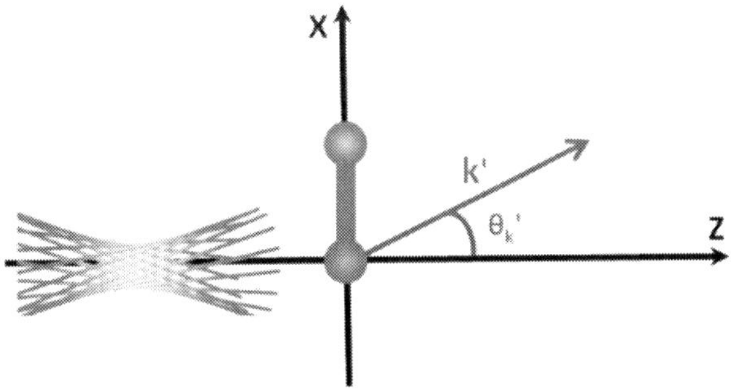

Fig. 3. Scenario (II) geometry: one of the atoms in the molecule lays on the beam axis.

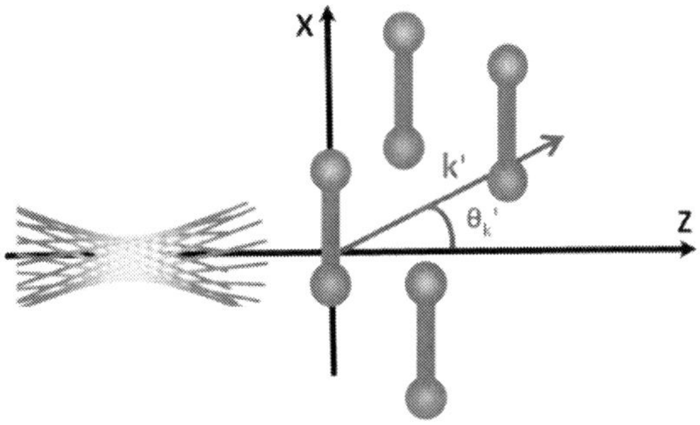

Fig. 4. Scenario (III) geometry: macroscopic target.

Numerical calculations of angular distributions and cross-sections for different scenarios have been carried out for the hydrogen molecule H_2. This study uses the relativistic system of units $\hbar = c = m_e = 1$. The Yukawa potential is selected as a model potential:

$$V(r) = A\frac{e^{-r/a}}{r} \tag{3}$$

All calculations have been carried out in the first Born approximation. The amplitude of twisted wave scattering from two centres takes the following form:

$$f_2^{tw}(\mathbf{k},\mathbf{k}') = (-i)^m e^{i\mathbf{k}_\perp\mathbf{b}} \int \frac{d^2\mathbf{k}_\perp}{(2\pi)^2} e^{im\varphi - i\mathbf{k}_\perp\mathbf{b_0}}\, \delta(|\mathbf{k}_\perp| - æ)\frac{1}{æ}(1+e^{i\mathbf{qb}}) f_1(\mathbf{k},\mathbf{k}') \tag{4}$$

where

$$f_1(\mathbf{k},\mathbf{k}') \;=\; -2\int_0^\infty rV(r)\sin qr\, dr \tag{5}$$

is the amplitude of plane wave scattering from one centre, $\mathbf{b}$ is the atomic spacing in the molecule, $\mathbf{b_0}$ is the distance between the beam axis and the nearest atom, $\mathbf{q} = \mathbf{k}' - \mathbf{k}$ is the momentum transferred. The calculation results are shown in Fig. 5 to 7. As is clear from Fig. 5, when the molecule centre is on the beam axis (Scenario (I)), there is a strong dependence from the projection of angular momentum m, and the maximums and minimums of the angular distribution are interchanged. As the energy increases, the number of minimums (and maximums) grows. This scenario is a quantum analogue of the classical Young's double-slit experiment. Scenario (II) corresponds to a classical experiment when one of the slits is closed. The strong dependence from the projection of angular momentum m is still observed (Fig. 6). However, the interference disappears, depending on the projection and the opening angle. Scenario (III) corresponds to scattering from a macroscopic target. In this case, the scattering cross-section no longer depends on the angular momentum projection. As one should expect, the contributions of multiple slits are non-coherently summed, which results in disappearance of the interference pattern (Fig. 7).

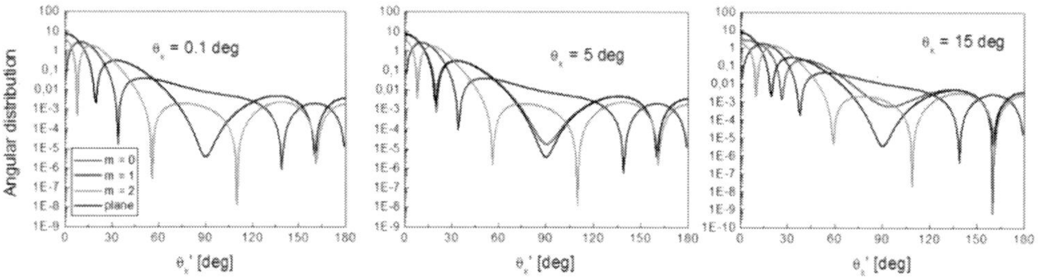

Fig. 5. Results of numerical calculations for Scenario (I). Angular distribution in case of scattering of twisted electrons with E= 300 eV from the hydrogen molecule H_2.

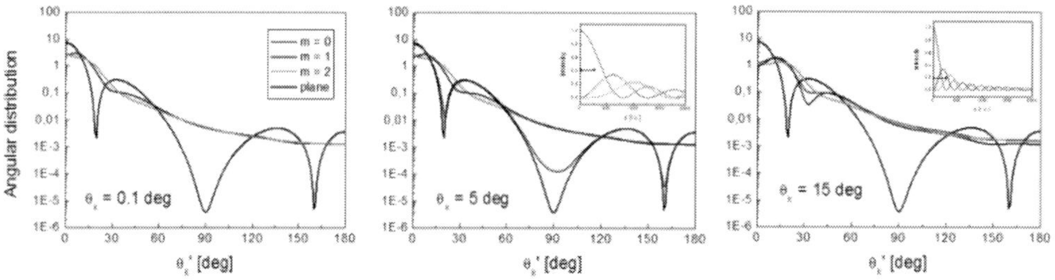

Fig. 6. Results of numerical calculations for Scenario (II). Angular distribution in case of scattering of twisted electrons with E= 300 eV from the hydrogen molecule H_2.

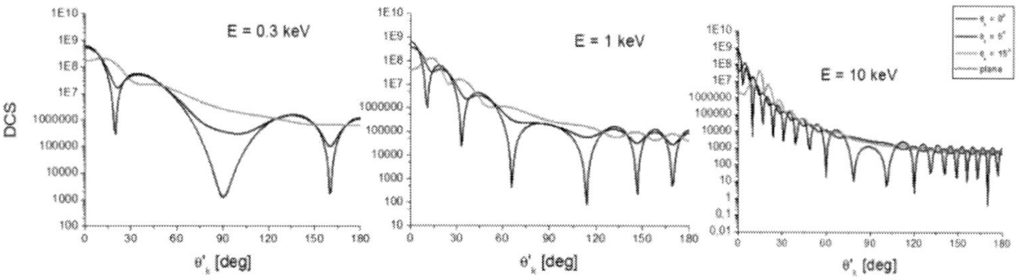

Fig. 7. Results of numerical calculations for Scenario (III). Scattering of twisted electrons from a macroscopic target.

3 Conclusion

The theoretical study of the process of twisted electron beam scattering from a diatomic molecule have been carried out for different geometries of the process for the first time. The numerical calculations are given for the hydrogen molecule. Studying the interaction of twisted electrons with target molecules is an important step to studying such fundamental phenomenon of living systems as chirality.

References

1. L. Allen, M.W. Beijersbergen, R.J.C. Spreeuw, J.P. Woerdman, Phys. Rev. A, **45** (1992)
2. H. He, M.E.J. Friese, N.R. Heckenberg, H. Rubinsztein-Dunlop, Phys. Rev. Lett. **75** (1995)
3. K.Y. Bliokh, Y.P. Bliokh, S. Savel'ev, F. Nori, Phys. Rev. Lett., **99** (2007)
4. C.W. Clark, R. Barankov, M.G. Huber, M. Arif, D.G. Cory, D.A. Pushin, Nature, **525** (2015)
5. C. Ryu, K.C. Henderson, M.G. Boshier, New Jour. of Phys, **16** (2014)
6. D. Seipt, A. Surzhykov, S. Fritzsche, Phys. Rev. A, **90** (2014)
7. I.P. Ivanov, D. Seipt, A. Surzhykov, S. Fritzsche, Phys. Rev. D, **94** (2016)
8. O. Matula, A.G. Hayrapetyan, V.G. Serbo, A. Surzhykov, S. Fritzsche, New J. Phys., **16** (2014)
9. V.A. Zaytsev, V.G. Serbo, V.M. Shabaev, Phys. Rev. A, **95** (2017)
10. V. Serbo, I.P. Ivanov, S. Fritzsche, D. Seipt, A. Surzhykov, Phys. Rev. A, **92** (2015)

A processing center for using digital hybrid technologies

Dmitry Masailo[1*], *Alexey* Orlov[1], *Vadim* Sufiyarov[1], and *Andrey* Volkov[1]

[1] National Technological Initiatives Center "New Industrial Technologies" of Peter the Great St. Petersburg Polytechnic University", 195251, Polytechnicheskaya st., 29, Russian Federation

Abstract. The role of additive technologies in industrial development was highlighted, in particular, for implementation of the concept "Industry 4.0". We discussed their significance for digital manufacturing of parts having complex configuration with internal cavities and functionally gradient properties. We analyzed the main drawbacks of additive technologies and suggested the ways to overcome them. We described the problem in creating the equipment for hybrid technologies on the basis of a processing center and an industrial robot. We developed a concept for creating a Russian-made machine-tool for using hybrid technologies. Solutions are proposed for improving the structure of the material of parts.

At the present moment, digital technologies for the parts manufacturing cycle are being quickly developed in the leading industrial countries. First of all, this regards manufacturing billets or articles made of metallic materials. Traditionally, mechanical processing is used that are named "deducing technologies". Among new world trends, there is "additive manufacturing" [1] that makes it possible to manufacture articles having complex geometry that cannot always be made using the traditional processing technologies of cutting, die molding, casting etc. [2, 3] In the concept of transition to "Industry 4.0", this new method of manufacturing is undoubtedly promising. Besides that, additive technologies have the following important advantages: firstly, manufacturing complex-geometry articles with internal cavities, including completely closed cavities; secondly, the possibility to obtain functionally gradient properties of the material the article is made of. However, additive technologies also have some significant drawbacks: firstly, at the moment and, possibly, in the foreseeable future, using the technology of laser melting of powder, wire or tape with focused laser radiation does not allow obtaining the geometry accuracy better than 100 micron and roughness of the surface better than Rz 20; secondly, as using additive technologies implies a metallurgic process, the structure of the material is still not sufficiently predictable, with large internal stresses and defects.

Currently, hybrid technologies for manufacturing metallic parts are widely used, with a combination of additive technologies and traditional mechanical processing.

The pioneer of this development is the German company DMG MORY that manufactured a processing center with an integrated module for powder weld deposition in 2015 (Fig. 1) [4].

* Corresponding author: dmasaylo@gmail.com

Fig. 1. A hybrid installation DMG MORI LASERTEC 65 3D.

Such approach, with alternating use of different methods of processing in the same working place (weld deposition and mechanical processing) makes it possible to manufacture complex-configuration parts with accurate size and geometry, as well as with good quality of surfaces. However, this solution has rather significant drawbacks of its own. Firstly, the process of direct build-up is carried out in the main working position of the processing center with the use of precision drives of the machine-tool (the feeding mechanism with the tolerance up to several microns is used for build-up of elements with the tolerance of hundreds of microns), and high hardness, which is not very feasible, from the technical point of view. Secondly, in the operating zone of precision drives of the machine-tool, up to ten or more kW of thermal power is emitted, which definitely causes a significant decrease in the total life cycle of the machine-tool modules due to overheating. Thirdly, the process of the part build-up by direct depositing is accompanied by diffusion of thin powder in the operating zone, with its highly abrasive properties, which also shortens the life cycle of the machine-tool. Fourthly, with small-series manufacturing, it is not possible to use experiments to thoroughly adjust the technological process for each part, so significant internal stresses can form, which may cause defects and cracks (usually, stresses are detected in laboratory conditions and relieved by the corresponding thermal processing).

Analysis of the above-listed problems makes it possible to suggest the following scientific-technical measures to improve the efficiency of hybrid technologies. For example, to improve the efficiency of using precision drives of the processing center for hybrid technologies, we suggest introducing an additional working position with a turntable of the normal accuracy, a system for repositioning a part installed on a satellite from one position to the other and back, as well as a technological robot-manipulator of the normal accuracy equipped with a laser head for powder, wire or tape weld deposition. A dedicated zone for 3D depositing makes it possible to separate the zone of mechanic processing so as to eliminate the negative influence of the powder and high temperatures on the mechanisms and units of mechanic processing modules. In order to prevent defects, cracks and unacceptable stresses, it is necessary to install the means to monitor stresses, such as an X-ray diffractometer or an ultra-sound device in the additive module. Additionally, this module can be equipped with inductive heaters with changeable inductors for thermal processing of the most responsible elements of the manufactured article.

In order to enable selective influence on the structure of the material of the manufactured part, the technological complex can be equipped with a vibrational module for transmitting oscillations to the zone of metal melting, which will have the required effect on the process of crystallization [5-7].

Fig. 2 shows the structure of samples obtained by weld deposition with and without vibrations in the zone of crystallization, where Fig. 2 a shows the case without using vibration, and 2b shows the case with using 400 Hz vibration in the zone of melting and crystallization.

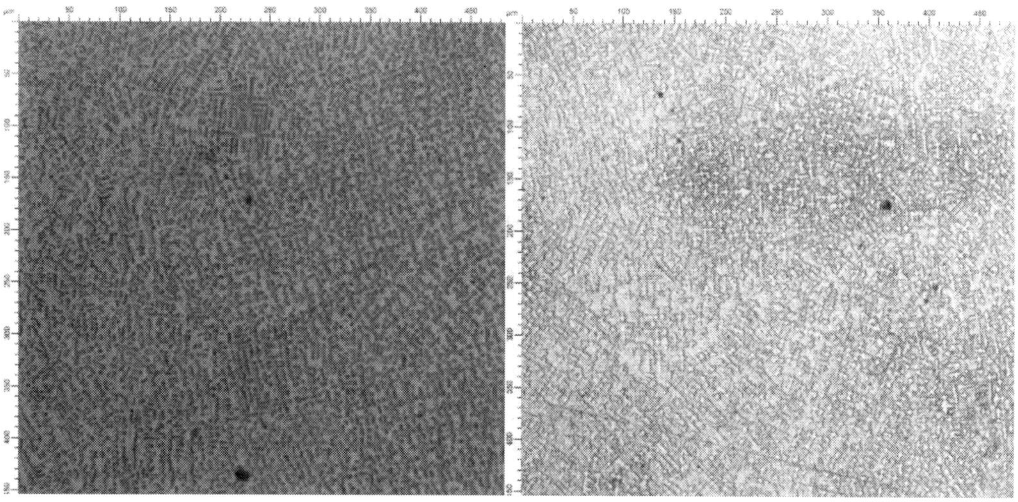

a) b)

Fig. 2. The structure of samples obtained by weld deposition with and without vibrations in the zone of crystallization.

In Fig. 2a, we can clearly see dendrites of the first, second and third kind, whereas, with using vibrational processing (400 Hz), in Fig. 2b, only dendrites of the first and the second kind can be seen. Their number is also significantly smaller than in the case of weld deposition without using vibration. Also, it can be added that, when using vibration, the average hardness of the material was 10 % higher (Brinnell scale).

The above-listed measures can improve the efficiency of processing complexes for hybrid technologies.

The work for developing a hybrid complex was divided into 2 stages. During the first stage, only the module for additive build-up of articles was created. It consists of a source of laser radiation, a weld deposition head, a powder feeder and a robot-manipulator.

The weld deposition head is the main working organ of the DED installation combining several systems: a system for laser beam focusing, a cooling system, a material feeding system and control systems (sensors, cameras etc.).

The main purpose of the head is feeding powder to the melting zone. The most widely used variants of the system are as follows:

– lateral single-jet – the powder is fed from the side. As a result, the deposited bead is elongated. The process must be strictly vertical.

– multi-jet (usually, three or for jets) – feeding from several nozzles. It is a modification of the lateral feeding method that ensures symmetrical feeding of the powder relative to the direction of movement. This method of feeding is not sensitive to the movement direction relative to powder feeding and allows inclination of the head in a wide range, up to 45 degrees from the vertical.

– coaxial – the powder is fed with a coaxial laser beam. It ensures the thinnest gas-powder stream, and, therefore, the deposited bead. It ensures the best material use factor. The process must be strictly vertical.

Therefore, the preferred tool is the multi-jet weld deposition head manufactured by the company Fraunhofer. It allows the processing angle up to 90 deg., the laser beam power up to 5 kW, and the best factor of material use (up to 95%).

In comparison with CO_2-lasers, optic-fiber lasers have 2-3 times higher performance index (about 25-30%) and require smaller operating costs. From this viewpoint, optic-fiber lasers are more cost-efficient, despite their higher price.

In Russia, industrial optic-fiber lasers are only manufactured by STA "IRE-Polus" (Friasino, Moscow district) that is a part of "IPG Photonics Corp." — an international scientific-manufacturing group of the Russian origin. The share of IPG is above 75% of the world amount of optic-fiber lasers production, with most types of optic-fiber lasers that are of the most relevance for industrial use, in particular, in the kilowatt power range, are only manufactured by IPG Photonics.

Due to the selection of the particular weld deposition head, an optic-fiber laser ЛС-3 was used – maximum power is 3 kW, wavelength is 1070 nm.

At the present moment, there are a lot of companies in the market that manufacture modules for feeding gas-powder mixture. They all are based on the same principle: the powder is transported by gas (Argon or Nitrogen depending on the weld deposition material). Powder feeding is controlled by a rotating dosing disc. With increasing rotation speed, the system receives a larger volume of powder. As a result, the powder feeder with two flasks was selected (manufactured by the company "Plaqart").

For the manipulator, the industrial robot Fanuc M20i was selected. Due to its loading capacity, the large number of degrees of freedom and accurate positioning. Fig. 3 shows an installation assembly with a protective cover.

Fig. 3. A laser installation for powder weld deposition.

For creating a digital model and adjusting the technology, the CAM system "SprutCam" was used. Basing on the parameters of the process (track thickness and width, speed of movement, article geometry) this software develops strategies for the robot to move the weld deposition head (Fig. 4).

The software makes it possible to:
– develop the strategy of additive manufacturing of the article;
– develop the strategy of repairs of the article;
– develop the strategy of coating application.

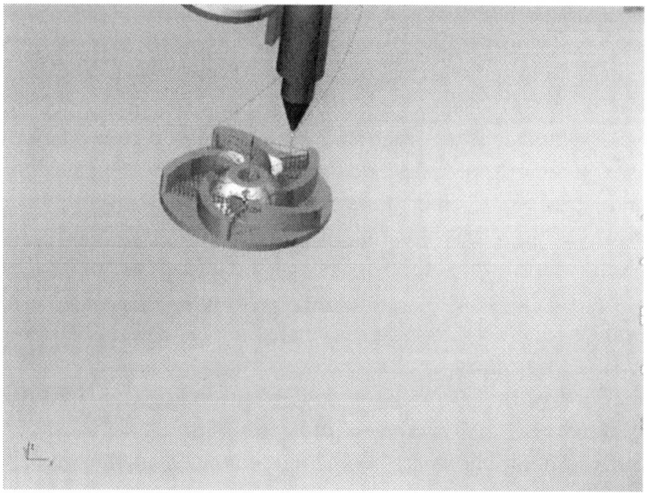

Fig. 4. Interface of the software complex “Sprut” for creating a digital model for manufacturing.

In the future, the software complex “Sprut” can also be used for a hybrid system. Fig. 5 shows a variant of the structural scheme of the hybrid complex.

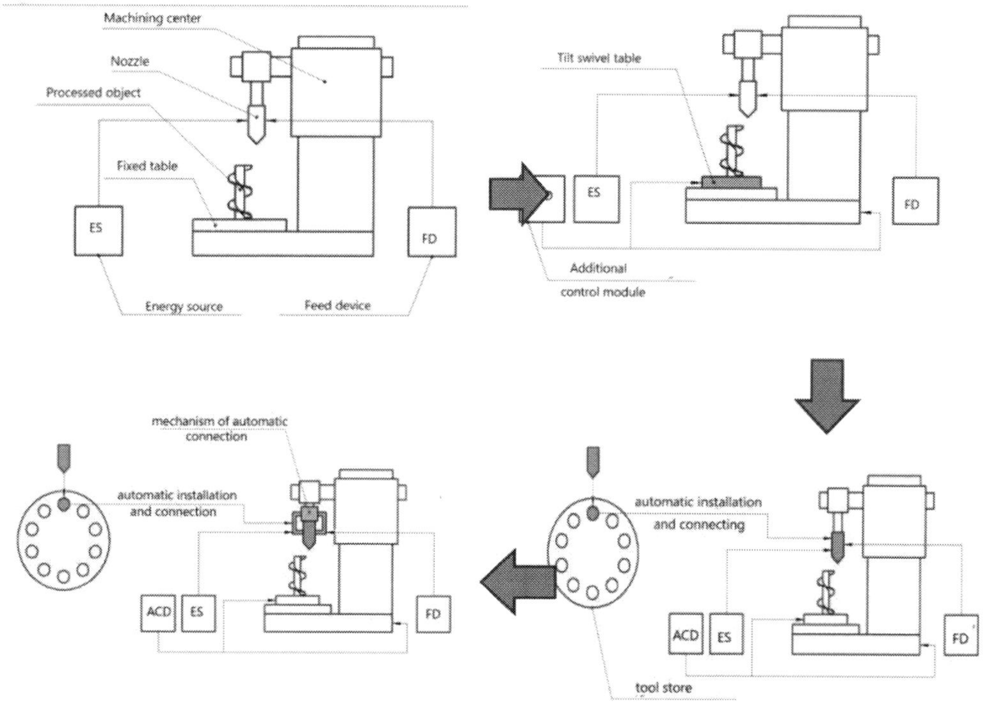

Fig. 5. The algorithm for creating a processing complex for using hybrid technologies

This algorithm is not final. Similarly to the module for gas-powder weld deposition, modifications are possible, in particular, modernization of the hybrid system.

Conclusion

In this work, we analyzed the equipment for a laser installation for powder weld deposition. We presented the software to create control programs for this installation. We indicated the possible drawbacks regarding the hybrid technologies available in the world market. We presented a variant of the conceptual scheme for developing Russian equipment for using digitally-controlled hybrid technologies.

References

1. M. Zlenko, A. A. Popovich, I. N. Mutylina, *Additive technologies in mechanical engineering*. (Publishing house Polytechnic University, Saint Petersburg, 2013)
2. B. Mueller, Assembly Automation. **32(2)** (2012)
3. Frazier W. E, Journal of Materials Engineering and Performance. **23(6)** (2014)
4. Electronic resource DMG MORI [online], Available at: https://en.dmgmori.com/ (2018)
5. L. Qin, W. Wang, G. Yang. Applied Mechanics and Materials, **271-272** (2012)
6. F. Ning, W. Cong. Materials Letter, **179** (2016)
7. X. Chen, T. Sparks, J. Ruan, F. Liou, Advance Materials Research. **189-193** (2011)

Up-to-date mathematical models lines of development of information technologies in the field of numerical methods of structures strength calculations

Vladimir Meleshko[1]*

[1] Saint Petersburg State University of Architecture and Civil Engineering, Faculty of civil engineering, 190005 2-ya Krasnoarmeiskaya st. 4, Russian Federation

Abstract. In order to carry out reliable calculations of structures adequate to reality, in particular, for taking into account plastic resource, it is necessary to use complex program systems and build finite element models of high dimensionality. This work provides a comparison of different mathematical models, which can be used for numerical analysis. Consideration was given to basic variation principles and methods of calculating structural mechanics. Distinctive features of forming systems of equations of classical methods of structural mechanics and known numerical methods were demonstrated. Possible advantages of methods with respect to accuracy and rate of calculations were revealed. Consideration was given to possible improvements of existing mathematical models in elastoplastic domain. Possible directions of development in the field of engineering methods for calculating strength were proposed.

1 Introduction

The information technologies, which rapid development makes it possible to essentially expand the instrument base of investigations in different fields, play an important role in modern construction. The structures of greater complexity are used more and more frequently, in the wake of developing trends characterizing a process of architectural creative work. The work under extreme conditions, efficient use of new materials, all this determines a necessity of development of more efficient approaches to calculation of structures proper, being based on up-to-date tools, in which development the key role belongs to innovative mathematical models and derivatives to product programs.

A permanent improvement of structures and equipment brings the development of existing calculation methods of mechanics to the first place. A considerable amount of time has passed since the emergence of finite-elements method, during which it has succeeded to prove itself as a universal method for solving tasks of mechanics, gas-dynamics and electrical engineering. Nevertheless, there exist narrow opportunities of improving the

* Corresponding author: vl-meleshko@yandex.ru

method of finite elements in separate domains. The improvements resolve basically into application of modern algorithms of calculating systems of equations, improving a process of repeatability. The improvement can manifest itself in accuracy and rate of calculation and can be performed in elastoplastic domain, if it can not be performed in the elastic domain.

The improvement of the existing methods of numerical analysis resolve itself into different hybrid wordings, which associate analytical expressions with numerical methods and solving integral equations, which brings about a reduction of unknown degrees of freedom.

The purpose of this work consists in revealing peculiarities of different methods of construction mechanical equipment for optimization of calculations of elastoplastic deformations.

2 Methods of Solving Problems of Construction Mechanical Equipment

2.1 Classical methods

Let us give consideration to classical methods of structural mechanics: force method, displacement method and mixed method. The classical methods of structural mechanics are described quite in details in equation [1]. The first two have been obtained on the basis of variation Lagrange and Castigliano principle [2, 3]. The mixed method presents a combination of method of forces and displacements. A variation Reissner principle corresponds to this method. The meaning of mixed method consists in the fact that different parts of trussed system can have different degrees of static and kinematic non-definability. Discriminating the least degree in every part of trussed system, it is possible to optimize the system of canonical equations making it mixed, i.e. consisting of unknown displacements and forces and, thus, reduce the number of equations in the system.

The canonical equations of classical methods get received through selection of the main system, which characterizes continuous function in corresponding composed functions of potential energy. This continuous function is expressed through unknown displacements of kinematically non-definable system or efforts in the discarded links of statically non-definable system. For instance, a system of canonical equations for the method of displacements looks as follows:

$$\begin{cases} r_{11}u_1 + \ldots + r_{1n}u_n + R_{1P} = 0 \\ \ldots\ldots\ldots\ldots \\ r_{n1}u_1 + \ldots + r_{nn}u_n + R_{nP} = 0 \end{cases}, \tag{1}$$

where, r_{ij} – rigidity factors; u_i – unknown displacements.
Let us present equations (1) in a matrix form

$$[R]\{u\} = \{P\} \tag{2}$$

$$[R] = \begin{bmatrix} r_{11} & \cdots & r_{1n} \\ \vdots & \ddots & \vdots \\ r_{n1} & \cdots & r_{nn} \end{bmatrix} \tag{3}$$

$$\{P\} = [R_{1P} \quad \ldots \quad R_{nP}]^T \tag{4}$$

$$\{u\} = [u_1 \quad \dots \quad u_n]^T \tag{5}$$

The main drawback when compiling equations in these methods is a selection of the main system, which complicates the process of automation and, accordingly, integration into program complexes.

2.2 Numerical Methods of Calculation

Let us further give consideration to the known approximation methods, such as Ritz method, method of weighted residuals (minimization of residual errors, errors, in particular, Bubnov-Galerkin method and variation-difference method.

The idea of Ritz method consists in that a finite number of basic functions f_1, f_2, ... , f_i is selected and a combination providing minimum of composed function is looked for among all linear combinations of $\sum u_i \cdot f_i$ type. It is Ritz approximation [4, 5, 6]. The unknown coefficients u_i are determined already not from differential equations, but from system n of discrete algebraic equations, for solution of which it is possible to use computer. In other words, we change from continual problem with an endless number of degrees of freedom with respect to the form of body deformation we turn to the problem for a system with a finite number of degrees of freedom. The theoretical substantiation of this method is very simple: minimization process automatically gives a combination nearest to function $y(x)$. Thus, the purpose consists in selecting the basis functions f_i, taking into account boundary constraints quite convenient for calculation and minimization of potential energy and at the same time provide for good approximation of unknown solution $y(x)$.

Let us review a composed function of full potential energy for the trussed system [7].

$$\Pi = U - W \tag{6}$$

The approximation Ritz method consists in direct minimization of full potential energy of system Π. Let us set the change of displacements as the following function

$$y(x) = \sum_{i=1}^{n} u_i \cdot f_i(x), \tag{7}$$

Then

$$W = \frac{EI}{2} \cdot \int_0^l y''^2(x)dx = \frac{EI}{2} \cdot \int_0^l \left(\sum_{i=1}^{n} u_i \cdot f_i(x)'' \right)^2 dx \tag{8}$$

$$U = \int_0^l p(x) \cdot y(x)dx = \int_0^l p(x) \cdot \sum_{i=1}^{n} u_i \cdot f_i(x)dx \tag{9}$$

Let us substitute (8) and (9) in (6) and differentiate according to u_i.

$$\frac{\partial \Pi}{\partial u_i} = \int_0^l p(x) \cdot \sum_{i=1}^{n} f_i(x)dx - \frac{EI}{2} \cdot \int_0^l \sum_{i=1}^{n} u_i \cdot f_i(x)'' \cdot f_k(x)''dx \tag{10}$$

The first variation of full potential energy equals zero (condition of potential energy stationary state) on the basis of variation Lagrange principle. As a result, we obtain n of equations

$$\frac{\partial \Pi}{\partial u_i} = \frac{\partial U}{\partial u_i} + \frac{\partial W}{\partial u_i} = 0 . \tag{11}$$

These equations form a system of algebraic linear equations (1) with respect to generalized displacements u_i in case of linearly deformable system with due account of equation (10).

Let us apply Ritz method in the variational formulation of Castigliano. Let us review statically undeterminable beam on two supports. There exists an infinite aggregate of equilibrium bending-moment curves set by the equality

$$M = M_P + X_1 \overline{M}_1 , \tag{12}$$

where, M_P and M_1 are the bending-moment curves (Fig. 1), while X_1 is an arbitrary variate of bearing reaction.

The Castigliano principle in an integral form expresses conditions of compatibility of body deformations and zero equality of the first variation of potential energy. Let us find X_1 using a principle of least work (physical entity of Castigliano principle). The deformation energy taking into account bending moments only will equal:

$$U = \frac{1}{2}\int_0^l \frac{M^2}{EI} ds = \frac{1}{2}\int_0^l \frac{\left(M_P + X_1 \overline{M}_1\right)^2}{EI} ds . \tag{13}$$

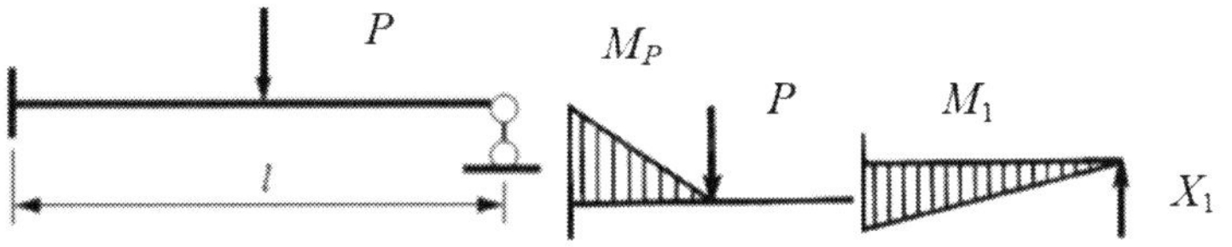

Fig. 1. Beam on two supports and moment curves.

A condition of minimum of deformation energy U according to Castigliano gives:

$$\frac{\partial U}{\partial X_1} = \left(\int_0^l \frac{\overline{M}_1^{\,2}}{EI} ds \right) \cdot X_1 + \int_0^l \frac{M_P \overline{M}_1}{EI} ds = 0 . \tag{14}$$

Let us present integral equations in the form of

$$\delta_{11} = \int_0^l \frac{\overline{M}_1^{\,2}}{EI} ds , \tag{15}$$

$$\Delta_{1P} = \int_0^l \frac{M_P \overline{M}_1}{EI} ds . \tag{16}$$

As a result we will get a known equation for solution of statically undeterminable systems by the method of forces expressing a zero equality of deflection at pivot bearing

$$\delta_{11} \cdot X_1 + \Delta_{1P} = 0 . \tag{17}$$

Let us consider statically undeterminable trussed system n times and select the undefined efforts such that the system remains geometrically invariable. Let us present the moment in the form of a function:

$$M = M_P + \sum_{i=1}^{n} X_i M_i \ . \tag{18}$$

Having calculated the potential energy $U(X_i,\ P)$ (i = 1,2,….n), on the basis of Castigliano variation principle:

$$\delta U = \sum_{i=1}^{n} \frac{\partial U}{\partial X_i} \cdot \delta X_i = 0 \ . \tag{19}$$

In view of arbitrariness of variations δX_i, we will get n of equations of forces method

$$\frac{\partial U}{\partial X_i} = 0 \ , \tag{20}$$

or in detail:

$$\begin{cases} \delta_{11} X_1 + \ldots + \delta_{1n} X_n + \Delta_{1P} = 0 \\ \qquad \cdots\cdots\cdots\cdots \\ \delta_{n1} X_1 + \ldots + \delta_{nn} X_n + \Delta_{nP} = 0 \end{cases} . \tag{21}$$

Let us give brief consideration to the following two methods. The variation-difference method makes it possible to confine solution of differential equations for continuous functions to numerical solution of a system of algebraic equations in the way of difference approximation of derivatives in a composed function. As a result of solving such task, it becomes possible to determine the values of the sought-for function in the finite number of points. The idea of method of weighted residuals is based on selecting a solution. The method is based on the requirement of orthogonal origin of functions to a residual error. If a residual error equals zero, it is orthogonal to a fundamental system of functions. Let us set forth an approximated solution in the following form:

$$\tilde{y}(x) = \psi(x) + \sum_{i=1}^{n} u_i \cdot f_i(x) \ , \tag{22}$$

at that, function $\psi(x)$ positively meets boundary conditions, while basis functions f_i (x) assume zero value at the boundary. Let us introduce a residual error or an error

$$R = y(x) - \tilde{y}(x) \ . \tag{23}$$

In order to minimize a residual error

$$\int_{\Omega} R_{\Omega} d\Omega = 0 \ , \tag{24}$$

where, Ω is a field of determining functions.

But in this case (with $n > 1$) after expansion of integral equation we arrive at incomplete system of equations with respect to u_i. Since we want that the residual error equals zero ($R_\Omega = 0$), multiplying of the residual error by some function shall not change a value of integral equation, i.e.

$$\int_\Omega W_k \cdot R_\Omega d\Omega = 0 , \qquad (25)$$

where, W_k are the weight functions.
When $i = 1, 2, \ldots, n$ we will arrive at incomplete system of equations with respect to coefficients u_i. The peculiarity of Bubnov-Galerkin method consists in the fact that basis functions are accepted as the weight functions.

All these methods are based on the fact that the approximating function is continuous. Based thereupon we obtain a definite system of equations with respect to indefinite approximation coefficients. The following two methods make it possible to present a solution in the form of piecewise continuous function.

2.3 Finite Elements Method

The finite elements method (FEM) is a powerful tool of approximated direct finding of unknown functions on the basis of any variation principle in elasticity and structural theory problems. It can be interpreted as a specific form of Ritz method, which provides a key for theoretical substantiation.

There are several FEM versions: direct method, variation method, residual method and energy balance method; and there are several FEM forms: displacement method, force method and mixed method [8, 9, 10, 11]. In order to reveal the key peculiarities and differences from Ritz method, let us give more detailed consideration to variation FEM in the form of displacements method.

FEM can be described in a couple of words. Let the task to be solved is set in a variation form: it is necessary to find function $u(x, y, z)$ minimizing the set composed function of potential energy. The composed function of energy is presented here for the entire region under consideration in the form of a sum of composed functions of its separate parts – finite elements. A dedicated law of distributing the sought-for functions is specified for the region of every element independently from the other ones. Such a piecewise continuous approximation will be made by means of specifically selected approximating functions, also referred to as coordinate functions or interpolating functions. They are used to express the sought-for continuous values (displacements, strains, etc.) within the limits of every FE through the figures of these values in nodal points, while an arbitrary preset load gets replaced with a system of equivalent nodal forces.

A difficulty of applying Ritz method consists in that it is practically impossible to select such a system of basis functions $fi(x, y, z)$ for the intricate-shaped solid, which being set within entire field of the region, would take into account different local peculiarities of its stress and strain state. The finite elements method eliminates this basic difficulty by introducing piecewise continuous functions, which equal zero everywhere, except for limited sub-regions, which are the finite elements. As a result, the matrix of coefficients of resolving system of equations it assumes a banded unloaded structure.

A physical problem definition corresponds, as a rule, to a certain structure with the loads applied thereto. The idealization of physical problem definition and further acquisition of mathematic model there from contemplates availability of assumptions, which all together bring about a system of differential equations corresponding to mathematical formulation of the problem.

If the task is being solved in displacements, i.e., their values are set at the boundaries, the potential system energy shall be minimized. If the task is being solved in stresses, while the external loads are set at the boundaries, an additional system operation will be minimized.

An assumption is made in the finite elements method, according to which the displacements of all element points get expressly determined by its nodal displacements (Fig. 2)

$$\{u^e\} = [N] \cdot \{\Delta^e\}, \quad (26)$$

$$\{u^e\} = [u_x \quad u_y \quad u_z]^T, \quad (27)$$

$$\{\Delta^e\} = [\{\Delta_i\} \quad \{\Delta_j\} \quad \ldots]^T, \quad (28)$$

$$\{\Delta_i\} = [\Delta_{ix} \quad \Delta_{iy} \quad \Delta_{iz}]^T, \quad (29)$$

where, $[N]$ is a rectangular matrix, where the quantity of lines equals the number of components u, while the number of columns corresponds to a number of vector Δ components. The approximating coordinate functions are the matrix elements.

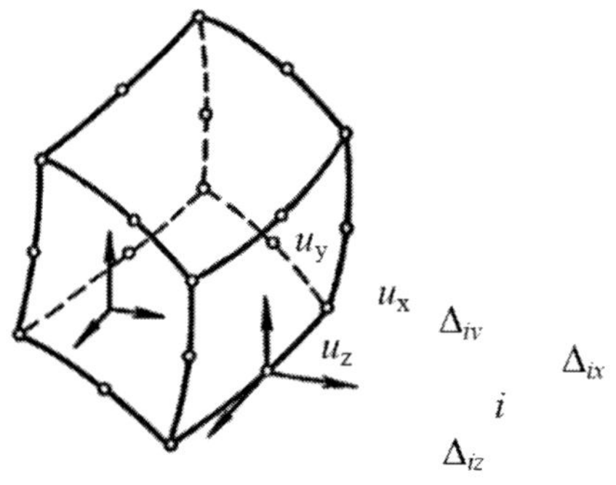

Fig. 2. Element displacements.

Let us express deformations in every point of finite element using Cauchy geometrical relationships [6] through its nodal displacements

$$\{\varepsilon^e\} = [D] \cdot \{u^e\}, \quad (30)$$

$$\{\varepsilon^e\} = [D] \cdot [N] \cdot \{\Delta^e\}. \quad (31)$$

Let us present $[N]$ in such a form

$$[N] = [N_x \quad N_y \quad N_z]^T, \quad (32)$$

where, N_x, N_y, N_z are the matrices of a line, where the known approximating functions are its elements.

$$[A]=[D][N]=\begin{bmatrix}\frac{\partial}{\partial x} & 0 & 0\\ 0 & \frac{\partial}{\partial y} & 0\\ 0 & 0 & \frac{\partial}{\partial z}\\ \frac{\partial}{\partial y} & \frac{\partial}{\partial x} & 0\\ 0 & \frac{\partial}{\partial z} & \frac{\partial}{\partial y}\\ \frac{\partial}{\partial z} & 0 & \frac{\partial}{\partial x}\end{bmatrix}\cdot\begin{bmatrix}N_x\\ N_y\\ N_z\end{bmatrix}=\begin{bmatrix}\frac{\partial N_x}{\partial x}\\ \frac{\partial N_y}{\partial y}\\ \frac{\partial N_z}{\partial z}\\ \frac{\partial N_y}{\partial x}+\frac{\partial N_x}{\partial y}\\ \frac{\partial N_z}{\partial y}+\frac{\partial N_y}{\partial z}\\ \frac{\partial N_z}{\partial x}+\frac{\partial N_x}{\partial z}\end{bmatrix}. \quad (33)$$

Let us put down Hooke's law in such a form

$$\{\sigma^e\}=[c]\cdot\{\varepsilon^e\}, \quad (34)$$

where, $\{\sigma^e\}$ is a vector of stresses; $[c]$ is an elastic-constant matrix. Let us substitute (30) and (32) in (33), then

$$\{\sigma^e\}=[c]\cdot[A]\cdot\{\Delta^e\}. \quad (35)$$

It is seen from the obtained relations that the stress and strain state of finite element will be expressly determined by nodal displacements Δ with the known function of approximating functions $[N]$.

If the received interrelations are substituted into composed function for full potential energy and summarized for every finite element, after minimization of cumulative composed function taking into account boundary conditions we will get a system of FEM resolving equations

$$\{P\}=[k]\cdot\{\Delta\}, \quad (36)$$

$$\left[k^e\right]=\int_V [A]^T[c]\cdot[A]dV, \quad (37)$$

where, k is a matrix of system rigidity; k^e is a matrix of finite-element rigidity.

In order to solve simultaneous linear algebraic equations (SLAE), both the exact and (with high system order) iteration methods are used. The effective numerical procedures built thereupon take into account symmetry and banded structure of system rigidity matrix.

2.4 Boundary-Element Method

FEM helps to solve the tasks of calculating different trussed and continual systems. An extensive experience of using FEM has revealed not only the advantages of this method, but the expressed drawbacks too, which can be eliminated on the basis of fundamentally new approaches, e.g., the theories of integral equations in the boundary-element method (BEM). The methods of solving boundary value problems on the basis of integral equations are considered more exact and economical than the methods based on approximation of differential operators (FEM).

As compared with FEM, BEM can exceed the existing methods with respect to accuracy and authenticity of the results by duration of processor operation and memory footprint.

The substance of BEM consists in solution of potential Laplace and Poisson equations with different boundary conditions (Dirichlet, Neumann, Robin) using integral Gauss-Greene and Gauss-Ostrogradsky transformations, under condition of boundary discretization by the finite number of segments, which are referred to as the boundary elements (Fig. 3).

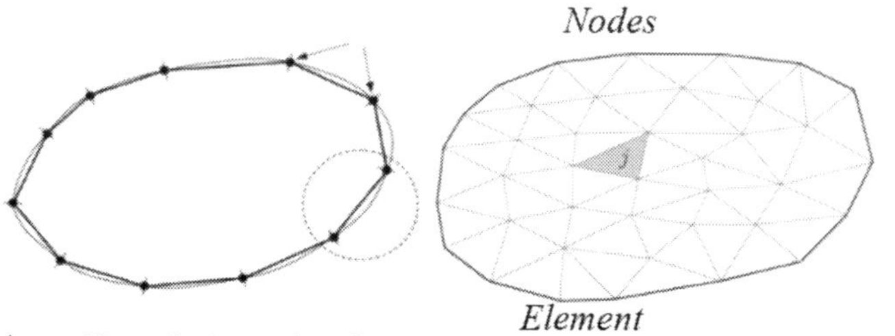

Fig. 3. Discretization of boundaries and region Ω.

Let us put down the potential theory main equation, in particular, in case of bidimensional problem [12]

$$\nabla^2 u = f(x,y) \quad (x, y \in \Omega) \,, \tag{38}$$

where, ∇^2 is a Laplace operator or harmonic operator. It will be determined in the following way:

$$\nabla^2 \equiv \nabla \cdot \nabla = \left(i\frac{\partial}{\partial x} + j\frac{\partial}{\partial x} \right) \cdot \left(i\frac{\partial}{\partial x} + j\frac{\partial}{\partial x} \right) = \frac{\partial^2}{\partial x^2} + \frac{\partial^2}{\partial y^2} \,. \tag{39}$$

Equation (1) in case of $f = 0$ is referred to as Laplace equation, and in case of $f \neq 0$ – as Poisson equation. Its solution u = $u(x, y)$ presents a potential determined in point (x, y) of region Ω of source function $f(x, y)$ distributed to Ω. The solution shall meet the task boundary conditions at boundary Γ. The boundary problems (Dirichlet, Neumann, Robin and mixed problem) for potential equation can be joined by consolidated wording

$$\begin{cases} \nabla^2 u = f, & \Omega \\ \alpha u + \beta \dfrac{\partial u}{\partial n} = \gamma, & \Gamma \end{cases} , \tag{40}$$

where,

$$\frac{\partial}{\partial n} \equiv n \cdot \nabla = (n_x i + n_y j) \cdot \left(i\frac{\partial}{\partial x} + j\frac{\partial}{\partial x} \right) = n_x \frac{\partial}{\partial x} + n_y \frac{\partial}{\partial y} \,. \tag{41}$$

is an operator, which differentiates the scalar function in direction n; $\alpha = \alpha(s)$, $\beta = \beta(s)$ and $\gamma = \gamma(s)$ are known functions defined at boundary Γ.

Every of four boundary problems can be obtained from equation (3) by means of corresponding identification of functions α, β, γ [12]. Equation (4) is referred to as the second Green identity for harmonic operator. The fundamental and numerical solution of these equations is presented in [12].

The issues of theory and practical application of BEM numerical and analytical variant with respect to unidimensional structural models of linear truss and plate systems are considered in [13, 14].

The basic advantage of BEM is an exact compliance with the initial differential equation inside of computational domain. In the problems with infinite boundary BEM features an advantage due to the ease of its accountability. A completely filled matrix of the resulting simultaneous linear algebraic equations (SLAE) can be attributed to method drawbacks unlike the loose (unloaded) one in BEM, where it comprises a great number of zeroes. Since the mesh is applied to the region boundary only, the matrix dimensionality will be the next lower order, than with BEM. In case of solving integral equations analytically a presence of flat boundary is necessary, since the singular integrals do not exist in angular points of piecewise-smooth boundary.

3 Conclusion

It proceeds from the above that presently the finite-elements method in classical form is not exclusion for solving mechanics problems and in many cases it can be irrational. For instance, an alternative method of boundary elements makes it possible to reduce the number of equations by an order of magnitude using numerical integration across the region and discretization across the boundary. In case the trussed systems are given consideration in elastoplastic domain, the finite-elements method in the form of forces method can increase the accuracy of determining internal efforts. In case of using generalized formula of Mohr [15] it is possible not to divide rods into finite elements. In such case the order of system of equations for long rods can be reduced significantly.

There is an extensive scope of functions, in which structural models are used with a great number of degrees of freedom. It increases time of numerical calculation as a result of exponential dependence on the number of resulting BEM equations unknown in the system. In order to optimize expenditures, a plastic resource is considered most frequently in many problems, which brings about a more reasonable material utilization. The operation of construction structures takes place not infrequently under extreme conditions, where the existing linear approaches are not always justified and it is necessary to take into account the non-linear behavior of structures. All this results in definite complications in the course of designing.

In spite of the fact that BEM has proven itself well in the elastic zone, the problems with a great number of degrees of freedom and the problems related to determining elastoplastic deformations feature possibilities for the development of existing methods. Hence, one can make a conclusion on a possibility of development of additional wordings for particular problems, and elastoplastic, in particular.

References

1. A.V. Darkov, N.N. Shaposhnikov, *Structural Mechanics* (Publishing house Vysshaya shkola, Moscow, 1986)
2. V.I. Slivker, *Structural Mechanics. Variation Basics* (Publishing house ASV, Moscow, 2005)
3. K. Vasidzu, *Variation Methods in the Theory of Elasticity and Plasticity* (Publishing house Mir, Moscow, 1987)
4. N.S. Bakhvalov, N.P. Zhidkov, G.M. Kobelkov, *Numerical Methods* (Nauka, Moscow, 1987)
5. V.P. Ilyin, V.V. Karpov, A.M. Maslennikov, *Numerical Methods of Solving Problems of Structural Mechanics* (Vysheishaya shkola, Minsk, 1990)
6. V.I. Samul', *Fundamentals of Theory of Elasticity and Plasticity* (Vysshaya shkola, Moscow, 1982)
7. A.V. Ignatiev, Vestnik MGSU, **1(3)** (2015)

8. M. Sekulovich, *Finite Elements Method* (Stroyizdat, Moscow, 1993)
9. I. N. Serpik, *Finite Elements Method in Solving Problems of Mechanics of Carrier Systems* (Publishing house ASV, Moscow, 2015)
10. R. Gallaher, *Finite Elements Method. Fundamentals* (Publishing house Mir, Moscow, 1984)
11. S.I. Trushi, *Finite Elements Method. Theory and Problems* (Publishing house of Association of construction HEI, Moscow, 2008)
12. J. Katsikadelis, *Boundary Elements. Theory and Applications* (Publishing house ASV, Moscow, 2015)
13. V.A. Bazhenov, V.F. Orobei, A.F. Dashchenko, L.V. Kolomiets, *Structural Mechanics. Special Course. Application of Boundary Elements Method* (Astroprint, Odessa, 2001)
14. P. Benardji, R. Batterfield, *Boundary Elements Method in Applied Sciences* (Mir, Moscow, 1984)
15. V.A. Meleshko, U.L. Rutman, Materials physics and mechanics, **31** (2017)

Software complexes and new approaches to non-linear analysis of framed structures

Vladimir Meleshko[1*]

[1] Saint Petersburg State University of Architecture and Civil Engineering, Faculty of Civil Engineering, 190005 2nd Krasnoarmeiskaya st. 4, Russian Federation

Abstract. There is a great number of non-linear tasks which can be solved with the use of computer-based simulation and finite elements method (FEM). But in order to ensure high speed and accuracy of calculations it is necessary to use new mathematical models and algorithms. The analysis of the known FEM forms and approaches to numerical solution of tasks based on force method is performed in this work. Represented in the document is formulation of the finite-element stress method and algorithmization of the classical force method for calculation of framed structures based on the equation of strain compatibility – contour forces method. Statement of problems which can be more effective from the point of view of elastic-plastic deformations at numerical solution is considered. In particular, the hybrid finite-element method based on the generalized Mohr formula for determination of long bar stiffness coefficient with account of non-linear behavior. The main relationships for creation of finite-element method equation system in the form of force method are represented.

1 Introduction

The modern tendencies in modeling of building structures are characterized by continuous increase in dimensionality of the solvable problems which requires advanced development in the sphere of software products. The necessity of solving the problems within the acceptable terms becomes common practice in the engineering activity. Engineers must pay more and more attention to the model physics and mathematical computational algorithms.Solution of complex problems, non-linear in particular, would be challenging without implementation of the necessary mathematical models. Besides, the important factor is productivity of computer programs which is directly connected with the applied mathematical tool. All this stipulates a necessity in elaboration of new approaches to calculation of building structures the main role in development of which belongs to software complexes.

The finite-element method (FEM) is taken as a basis for strength analysis of structures in the modern software complexes. In order to determine the elastic-plastic deformation the use is made of FEM in the classical form of a deflection method [1]. The main unknown quantities here are displacements of junction points; stresses are of secondary importance and

* Corresponding author: vl-meleshko@yandex.ru

shall be determined by numeric differentiation of displacements. But for non-linear problems the more convenient can be the hybrid FEM scheme in the form of displacement method [2, 3] and force method, especially in regard to obtaining stress values. The main advantage of FEM in the form of force method is that the main unknown values here are stresses. Besides, application of the Castigliano principle [4] gives the upper limit of the approximate solution (i.e. stresses are overstated), which is better at strength calculation than the understated value.

The finite-element method belongs to the discrete analysis method. Unlike the rest numerical methods it is based on the physical discretization of the investigated area. The area, the continuous medium with an infinite number of the degrees of freedom, is replaced with a discrete model of interconnected finite elements with a finite number of the degrees of freedom which in aggregate determine the piecewise continuous interpolation function. Unlike classic variation methods [5] where selection of interpolation functions depends on configuration of the considered problem, this does not takes place in FEM since the interpolation functions are determined exclusively within individual finite elements. These functions represent a family of functions independent of one another which are taken as an element, so that their values along with all other elements, except for elements they belong to, equal to zero. This is the main distinction between FEM and classical numerical methods where the interpolation functions are taken for the whole area.

In order to carry out the elastic-plastic calculation it is necessary to know the fields of stress (force) occurring in the deformable body points. From the point of view of stress determination at numeric calculations, setting of problems in displacements has significant deficiency. Since the result of the approximate solution for such scenarios is displacement values in individual points (grid nodes) of the body, stress calculation is brought to numeric differentiation of functions set by points. This leads to loss of accuracy in stress (force) determination as compared to the accuracy of displacement determination.

One method to improve accuracy of stress determination at numeric solution is elaboration and application of problem scenarios in stresses (forces), i.e. such problem scenarios of the deformable solid body mechanics where the unknown functions are stresses immediately. This work is devoted to this very range of issues.

The variational formulation of elasticity problems in stresses – the principle of minimum complementary energy (Castigliano variational principle) is well known [6]. However, the conventionally extreme character of the Castigliano functionality makes creation of the finite elements and the analysis of FEM convergence significantly more complicated than that in the scenario of displacements. Studied in works [11, 12] is a possibility of obtaining the definitely extreme variational problem on the basis of Castigliano functionality with the use of penalty method. There are certain difficulties occurring here and connected with a necessity to select the optimum value of penalty parameter and application of discontinuous approximation of stresses. The known method to avoid a necessity in creation of statically admissible stress fields is application of stress functions. However, occurred in the functionality are the second derivatives from the required functions and it is necessary to use finite elements complicated enough for creation, which provide continuity of both the function itself and its first derivatives. Such element is considered in [11].

The FEM diagrams have gained practical application, where the Castigliano functionality is used, actually, as an auxiliary means for creation of the so called equilibrium finite elements of the displacement method. The hybrid FEM is studied in works [2, 3] with the use of generalized Mohr formula within the finite element for non-linear analysis of framed structures. Nevertheless, the variational problem based on the Castigliano functionality can be more effective for calculation of framed structures in the elastic-plastic domain than the classical FEM.Execution of two-value calculation on the basis of two opposite FEM forms makes it possible to obtain the two-way evaluation of the accurate solution of the corresponding problem.

A purpose of this work was to perform the analysis of the known approaches on the basis of force method, to show peculiarities of equation system generation. Consider the statement of problems which can be more effective from the point of view of elastic-plastic deformations at numerical calculation.

2 Numerical methods based on structural engineering force method

2.1 Method of contour forces

Let's consider the contour force method proposed in [7] for algorithmization of classical force method. The main problem of the force method implementation on computer is conditioned by nonuniqueness of the main system selection.

The algorithm of the contour force method consists in direct generation of strain compatibility equations on the basis of the previously generated strain compatibility matrix of individual framed structure contours [8]. The matrix of the general solution of homogeneous equilibrium equations is created by transposition of compatibility equation matrix. As a result, no analysis of the nodal equilibrium equations matrix is required [L]. The yield matrix structure is unambiguously determined by numeration of the statically undeterminable contours of the system [8].

Let's write the node equilibrium equation for the framed structure

$$[L]^T \cdot \{\sigma\} = \{P\}, \tag{1}$$

where $\{P\}$ – a vector of external forces; $\{\sigma\}$ – a vector of internal forces in bars; $[L]^T$ – a matrix of internal forces transformation according to the main coordinate axis.

The framed structure connected in nodes must remain connected in these very nodes after deformation as well. Equations showing this condition are called compatibility equations. Let's write geometrical constrained equations of nodes displacement with deformations of bars

$$[L] \cdot \{U\} = \{e^y\} + \{e^0\}, \tag{2}$$

and physical equations

$$\{e^y\} = [\delta^e] \cdot \{\sigma\}, \tag{3}$$

where $\{U\}$ – a column of nodes displacement; $\{e^y\}$ – a column of generalized displacements (deformation of bars); $\{e^0\}$ – a column of the specified initial deformations; $[\delta^e]$ – a matrix of the specified bar yield coefficients.

Further, these formulas will be used at obtaining the equations of strain compatibility and the corresponding matrix.

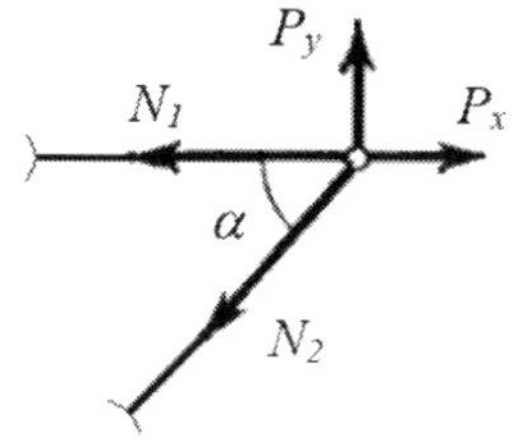

Fig. 1. External and internal forces in the node.

The main problem of the force method algorithmization consists in generation of the common solution of the homogeneous equilibrium equations

$$[L]^T \cdot \{\sigma\} = 0 \,, \tag{4}$$

For statically indeterminate systems a number of lines and the matrix rank $[L]^T$ is less than a number of columns and, consequently, the homogeneous equilibrium equations (4) have non-zero solutions. Let's assume that solutions of equations are obtained (4). Let's present these solutions as matrix lines $[B]$, then, as defined by the system (4), the identity is true

$$[L]^T \cdot [B]^T = 0 \,, \tag{5}$$

or by transposition rules

$$[B] \cdot [L] = 0 \,. \tag{6}$$

Let's multiply equations (2) by $[B]$ and taking into account (6) we obtain the formula

$$[B](\{e^y\} + \{e^0\}) = 0 \,, \tag{7}$$

in which the equations of strain compatibility are presented.

In the absence of external load, let's write the general solution of the homogeneous equilibrium equations

$$\{\sigma\} = [B]^T \cdot \{\phi\} \,, \tag{8}$$

where $\{\phi\}$ – a column of strain functions (or "excessive" unknown values through traditional terminology of structural mechanics).

By substituting (3) in (7) and taking into account (8) we get the final system of force method equations

$$[B] \cdot [\delta^e] \cdot [B]^T \cdot \{\phi\} + [B] \cdot \{e^0\} = 0 \,, \tag{9}$$

where

$$[\delta] = [B] \cdot [\delta^e] \cdot [B]^T \tag{10}$$

–a matrix of system yield.

Upon solution of the system (9) we find the unknown values $\{\phi\}$ and forces in bars by the formula (8). If the load is given in the form of forces and moments, it must be reduced to initial strains [8, 10].

Determination of forces, strains and matrix of their connection for an individual bar with equal nodal connections is given in [10]. Depending on conditions at bar ends: with two rigid joints, with two hinged joints and with one rigid and one hinged joint the matrix of bar yield

coefficients can be obtained by differentiation of the potential strain energy for each internal force [7]:
–for the bar with two rigid joints

$$\left[\delta^e\right]=\begin{bmatrix} \frac{l}{EF} & 0 & 0 \\ 0 & \frac{l}{kGF}+\frac{l^3}{12EI} & 0 \\ 0 & 0 & \frac{l}{EI} \end{bmatrix}, \tag{11}$$

–for the bar with two hinged joints

$$\left[\delta^e\right]=\left[\frac{l}{EF}\right], \tag{12}$$

–for the bar with one rigid and one hinged joint

$$\left[\delta^e\right]=\begin{bmatrix} \frac{l}{EF} & 0 \\ 0 & \frac{l}{kGF}+\frac{l^3}{3EI} \end{bmatrix}, \tag{13}$$

where F – a cross-section area; E – elasticity modulus; G – shear modulus; k – coefficient taking into account the shearing stress distribution; l – bar length.

The flexibility matrix for the curved bar is given in [10].

Let's consider generation of the strain compatibility matrix $[B]$. This matrix for the whole framed structure is obtained by integration of strain compatibility equations of individual statically indeterminable contours. At that, the strain compatibility matrix of the individual contour is obtained from the condition that the algebraic sum of strains in the closed contour is equal to zero (Fig. 2). These strains for an individual bar must be expressed through displacement of nodes [10]. Meant by strains will be such combinations of nodal displacements which, firstly, energetically correspond to generalized forces, i.e. multiplication of strains by forces must be equal to operation of nodal forces in nodal displacements; secondly, they are identically zero at any rigid shift of the bar. Each contour of the structure gives a number of equations of strain compatibility corresponding to the degree of the contour static indetermination.

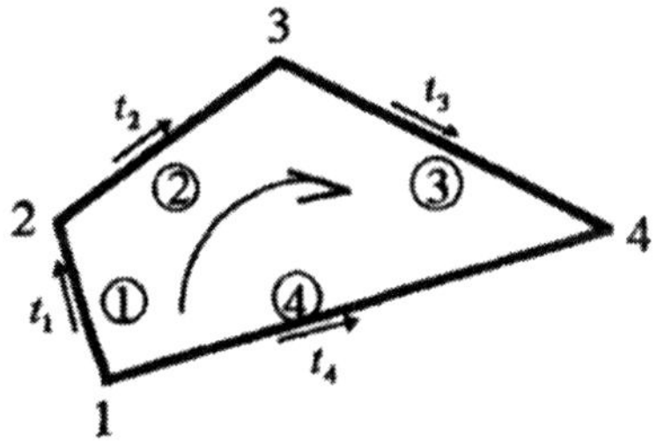

Fig. 2. Statically indeterminable contour

Let's write the equation of strain compatibility in the closed contour (Fig. 2) with sequential connection of bars with the guide unit vectors t_i. The degree of contour static indetermination is equal to 3.

$$\{e_1\}+\{e_2\}+\{e_3\}-\{e_4\}=0, \tag{14}$$

let's represent (14) as

$$[B]\cdot\{e\}=0, \tag{15}$$

$$\{e\}^T=[\{e_1\}\ \ \{e_2\}\ \ \{e_3\}\ \ \{e_4\}]=0, \tag{16}$$

where $[B]$ – a matrix of contour strain compatibility with a , dimension of (3x12).

For the example shown in Fig. 2 the matrix of strain compatibility is given by

$$[B]=[I\ \ I\ \ I\ \ -I], \tag{17}$$

where $[I]$ – a unit matrix with a dimension of (3x3).

Knowing the yield matrix of individual bars and taking into account (14) we can get the matrix of strain compatibility for different statically indeterminable contours. In the actual framed structure containing a lot of contours the matrix of the system strain compatibility consists of the unit lines, each containing a compatibility matrix of the corresponding contour. Peculiarities of the system calculation with a statically determinable contour are given in [9].

Such approach allows formulation of the force method algorithm comparable by complexity and by properties with the finite-element method algorithm. In the contour force method the selection and numeration of independent contours of the framed structure uniquely determine the block structure of the yield matrix [δ]: as soon as the contours are numbered the location of zero and non-zero blocks in the matrix can be specified unambiguously [δ]. But nonuniqueness of this matrix structure remains which is connected with a possibility to select different systems of independent contours in the initial structure. In spatial structures it is more complicated than numeration of nodes and bars for calculation by finite-element method.

2.2 FEM in the form of force method

Let's consider one variant of FEM in the form of force method for calculation of continual systems. It is based on approximation of discontinuous stress fields and application of penalty method [11] for satisfying equilibrium equations. The corresponding variational adjustment with a penalty has a form of complementary energy functional stationarity condition

$$\Pi(\sigma)=-\frac{1}{2}\int_{\Omega}\{\sigma\}^T[E]^{-1}\{\sigma\}d\Omega+\int_{S}\{u\}^T[L]^T\{\sigma\}dS+\vartheta\int_{\Omega}\left([A]^T\{\sigma\}+\{P\}\right)^T\cdot\left([A]^T\{\sigma\}+\{P\}\right)d\Omega, \tag{18}$$

where

$$[L]^T\{\sigma\}=g_s \tag{19}$$

–static boundary conditions in the form of distributed load,

$$[A]^T\{\sigma\}+\{P\}=0 \tag{20}$$

–equilibrium equations in the differential form; $\{\boldsymbol{\sigma}\}$ – a stress vector; $\{\mathbf{u}\}$ – a displacement vector; Ω – field; S – contour; $\{\mathbf{P}\}$ – a volumetric force vector; $[E]$ – a flexibility matrix of the generalized Hook's law; $[A]$ – a differential operator; υ – a penalty characteristics.

Whenusingthevariational formulation in stresses the solution is sought in a multitude of statically admissible stress fields satisfying the static boundary conditions and equilibrium equations.It is necessary to provide existence of piecewise continuous derivatives from stress components. For example, for plane stress problem of the elasticity theory the differentiability of stresses σ_x only by x, σ_y – only by y, a τ– and by x, and by y is obligatory. So, normal stresses can have discontinuities in areas perpendicular to the boundaries of elements. Application of such discontinuous approximations results in a necessity to use special class of finite elements [11, 12].

Shown in Fig. 3 is one of simple elements of such type representing a rectangle the four nodes in the tops of which respond to tangent stresses, the two nodes in lateral sides of which respond to normal stresses σ_x, the two nodes in the upper and lower sides respond to σ_y. Location of nodal points here must satisfy discontinuity conditions for normal stresses.

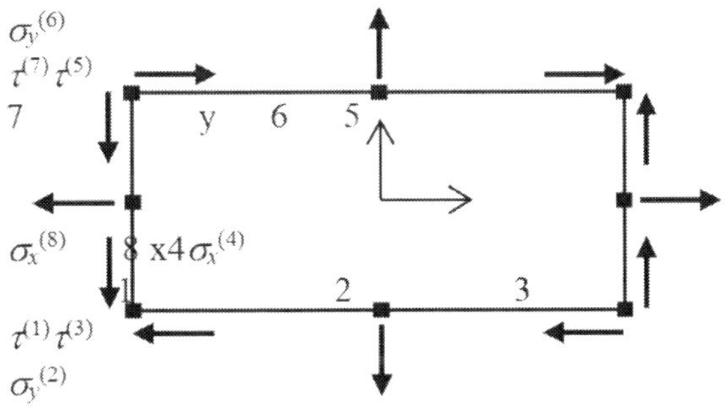

Fig. 3. Finite element

Distribution of stresses here is represented by the following polynoms:

$$\sigma_x = \alpha_1 + \alpha_2 x; \quad \sigma_y = \alpha_3 + \alpha_4 y; \quad \tau = \alpha_5 + \alpha_6 x + \alpha_7 y + \alpha_8 xy. \tag{21}$$

By applying the approximation data in the equilibrium equations (20) we get

$$\alpha_2 + \alpha_7 + \alpha_8 x + p_x = 0; \quad \alpha_4 + \alpha_6 + \alpha_8 y + p_y = 0. \tag{22}$$

With the volumetric forces p_x, p_y constant by element the conditions (22) can be satisfied only in case the following condition is identically met:

$$\alpha_8 x = \alpha_8 y = 0. \tag{23}$$

Since this does not ensure exact integration of the penalty summand of a functional (18), it is defined to synthetically decrease the integral calculation accuracy for the given element, which helps vanishing the expression in the integral part of the penalty term.

Whereas the given finite element gives the acceptable accuracy and reproducibility, the deficiencies connected with integration of the penalty summand take place. Determination of nodal functions of forms and flexibility matrix is given in [11].

2.3 FEM in the form of force method for calculation of framed structures. Creation of generalized force method equation system

The idea of the generalized force method consists in application of finite-element method in one of two forms: displacement method and force method. At that, determination of unknown values along the bar is carried out analytically with the use of integral expression – generalized Mohr formula [13] with a matrix of tangent rigidity [2, 3, 13], which is an integral characteristic of the stress-strain state of all points in the bar cross-section. From this the rigidity change is considered. As a result, two hybrid methods for elastic-plastic calculation are obtained. At that, the finite-element method in the form of force method has advantages: there is no necessity in determination of the intermediate rigidity matrix of the bar element, it is possible to immediately proceed with creation of the resolvent equation system.

In order to distinguish two methods let's consider that:

– finite-element method in the form of displacement method with the generalized Mohr method – this is a non-linear hybrid finite-element method;

– finite-element method in the form of force method with the generalized Mohr method – this is a non-linear generalized force method. Considered in works [2, 3] is a non-linear hybrid finite-element method for elastic-plastic calculation of plane grids. Here the integral function of cross-section state law is used as a tangent rigidity matrix [16, 17].

When using the classical force method [14] the availability of geometrically unchangeable main system is required. Since the finite-element method is a discrete method, there is no necessity in selecting the main system, but equilibrium equations under external force action must be taken into account if stresses are approximated. At that, if the action is in the form of displacements, the equilibrium equations shall be considered through the additional work (24).

Let's consider creation of FEM equations in the form of force method for framed structures. On the basis of the Castigliano variational principle let's write the functional for complete potential energy of the system in stresses [1, 15]

$$\Pi(\sigma)=\sum_{e}\left(-\frac{1}{2}\int_{\Omega}\{\sigma\}^{T}[E]^{-1}\{\sigma\}d\Omega+\int_{S}\{u\}^{T}\{X\}dS\right), \tag{24}$$

where the first member represents the complementary deformation energy from the stress change functions, and the second member represents the force potential in contour S with the given displacements u.

At that, if the external displacements are not specified ($u = 0$), then expression for complementary energy in the finite-element method will be equal to

$$\Pi(\sigma)=-\sum_{e}\frac{1}{2}\int_{\Omega}\{\sigma\}^{T}[E]^{-1}\{\sigma\}d\Omega, \tag{25}$$

But in this case, it is necessary to satisfy the equilibrium equation in order to determine the complete energy [15]. This is taken into account for continual systems with the help of penalty summand [11].

Since the potential energy in the framed structure can be expressed directly through internal forces and moments X, then the external forces P can be theoretically added to a functional for potential strain energy and differentiated, particularly, by approximation coefficients. As a result, a system of resolvent equations of the finite-element method in the form of the force method must be created for calculation of framed structures

$$[\delta]\cdot\{X\}+\{\Delta_P\}=0, \tag{26}$$

which is similar in appearance to the classical force method, but internally represents the piecewise continuous approximation. With the specified external displacements the system will take the following form

$$[\delta]\cdot\{X\}=\{u\}. \tag{27}$$

Matrix equations (26) and (27) represent the systems of FEM resolvent equations in the form of force method. It is supposed that no penalty summand in the functional for complete energy must be taken into account for elastic-plastic calculation of the framed structures. The coefficients δ will be calculated using the generalized Mohr formula [13].

3 Conclusion

Simplicity and substantiation of FEM classical scheme based on the minimum potential energy principle retard, in some measure, development of the finite-element formulations supported by the alternative variational principles. Nevertheless, the finite-element method in displacements suffers significant difficulties at resolution of problems with absolutely rigid bars and has an error at determination of stresses, which is important at elastic-plastic calculation.

In particular, FEM in the form of force method based on the Castigliano variational principle makes it possible to avoid such difficulties. Also, at solution of big systems of linear algebraic equations (SLAE) (more than thousand of equations) the important factor is a significant accumulation of rounding errors occurred in the process of a great number of arithmetic operations. In this case it is recommended to use double accuracy of calculations. Application of hybrid methods may lead to decrease in a number of equations, i.e. decrease in computational operations and, correspondingly, to increase in calculation accuracy.

Unlike the classical force method and contour force method a number of unknown values in the system of FEM resolvent equations in the form of force methods will be a little more, but the advantage will consist in simplicity of calculation scheme and equation system creation. Difficulties can be connected with the approximating functions. But since the bar is a one-dimensional continuum, the processes of impact on it (mechanical, thermal) in the most cases are described by relatively simple differential equations.

Thus, application of the proposed hybrid formulations may significantly increase calculation accuracy and speed at determination of elastic-plastic deformations.

References

1. M. Sekulovich, *Finite element method* (Stroyizdat, Moscow, 1993)
2. V. A. Meleshko, Procedia Structural Integrity, **6** (2017)
3. V. A. Meleshko, U. L. Rutman, Procedia Structural Integrity, **6** (2017)
4. S. P. Timoshenko, J. Gudier, *The theory of elasticity* (Science Publ., Moscow, 1979)
5. V. P. Ilyin, V. V. Karpov, A. M. Maslennikov, *Numerical methods for solution of structural engineering problems* (Higher School Publ., Minsk, 1990)
6. K. Vasidzu, *Variation methods in the theory of elasticity and plasticity* (Mir, Moscow, 1987)
7. V. V. Lalin, *Equations of strain compatibility as a basis for force method algorithmization. Structural mechanics and calculation of structures.* Collection of studies (Saint Petersburg, 1992)
8. V. V. Lalin, T. N. Bugaeva, News of higher educational establishments, **10** (1998)

9. V. V. Lalin, *Equations of strain compatibility for calculation of statically indeterminate trusses by force method. Structural mechanics and calculation of structures. Collection of studies* (Saint Petersburg, 1992)
10. T. N. Bugaeva, *Algorithmization of structure calculation by force method* PhD thesis (Saint Petersburg, 2000)
11. A. A. Lukashevich, *Modern numerical methods of structural engineering* (KhSTU, Khabarovsk, 2003)
12. Yu. S. Sukhodulova, N. A. Truphanov, *PNIPU Bulletin*, **1** (2012)
13. V. A. Meleshko, U. L. Rutman, *Materials physics and mechanics*, **31**, 67-70 (2017)
14. A. S. Volmir, Yu. P. Grigoryev, A. I. Stankevich, *Structural performance of materials* (Drofa publishing house, Moscow, 2007)
15. A. S. Sakharov, I. Altenbach, *Finite element method in mechanics of rigid bodies*. (Higher School, Kiev, 1982)
16. N. V. Ostrovskaya, V. A. Meleshko, *Marine intellectual technologies*, **4 (38)** (2017)
17. N. V. Ostrovskaya, *Bulletin of Civil Engineers*, **51** (2015)

Features of information modeling in the design of pre-school buildings in Russia

Yury Minkinen[1], and *Liya* Movsesova[1*]

[1] Saint Petersburg State University of Architecture and Civil Engineering, Faculty of civil engineering, 190005 2-ya Krasnoarmeiskaya st. 4, Russian Federation

Abstract. In the context of modern industrial base establishment on the new technology platform, the tendencies of IT-technologies penetration into building and structure design, construction and operation and transition to Building Information Model are getting more and more emphasized. This article focuses on BIM-modeling employment in the design of pre-school educational institution. Advantages of IT-modeling for buildings complying with modern ecological and safety demands are illustrated. Integration of data on building architecture, structure, interior decoration and utilities into integrated data model effectively saves time and allows making right decisions at all stages of object life cycle. The model allows making optimal decision accounting for such factors as weather conditions analysis, building shape, amount of people to be hold, periodicity of their stay, materials to be used, natural light level, utilities design etc.

1 Introduction

IT-technologies make up the basis of new social digital infrastructure. The new industrial base on new technology platform is mostly established by means of technology diffusion. It is by means of diffusion that digital technologies penetrate into the area of building and structure design, construction and their operation and the fact destined the birth of the new trend – Building Information Modeling.

The new technology, BIM (Building Information Modeling), allows creating construction object multivariate model containing full information on the object [1]. Object information model consists of virtual items that exist or will exist in reality and also contains data on their specific geometric and physical properties.

The new technology has very powerful capabilities [2]. With information modeling, even before actual construction beginning (with sufficient model detailed elaboration) all processes at all life cycle stages can be determined and fully estimated in advance. Thus, a brand new approach to building construction and managing is expected. Full-fledged building information model allows business process improvement at all stages: facility design, planning of required resources volumes and delivery schedule, planning of construction operations, facility operation process, its demolition after its service life depletion or in case of other necessity [3–5]. As advantages of using BIM-technology, they

* Corresponding author: yury-m@mail.ru

are – the decrease of project cost and design development period, improvement of coordination and communication between design engineers of different departments, project quality improvement and decrease of collisions/errors at the ready made model output [4].

BIM-technologies are in sufficient detail described in special literature [6–7]. At present modern methods of information modeling are actively introduced into Russian construction practices [8]. BIM-technologies are used for the design of office and industrial buildings as well as medical, educational ones and in the sphere of transportation [9–12], surrounding amenities [13], apartment buildings [14]; they are widely used not only in construction but also for reconstruction of existing buildings [15, 16]: historical [17] and industrial [18] ones, schools [19] and etc. One of the information modeling new trends is Green BIM [20]. It is used to design environmentally friendly buildings when such factors as temperature conditions, power supply, materials, utilities etc are to be accounted for, and the fact makes BIM employment for pre-school buildings design particularly topical.

Since 2011 in Russia the work has been carried out to select economically efficient projects for their reusing, among them one can mention pre-school buildings which are built with the involvement of budgetary funds. At the end of 2016 Ministry of Housing and Building of Russia resolved to create a register of economically efficient design documentation to be reused. Project selection criteria were approved: project cost estimate shall not exceed construction expected (limit) value and the facility energy efficiency class shall be at least class "C". As of December 2017 the register included 17 kindergarten projects. BIM-technology employment in the design is just the factor that allows approximating construction ultimate cost to initial budget value due to exact calculation of materials assortment and quantity.

2 BIM-Modeling in Pre-School Building Design

Information model of "Pre-School Educational Institution for 180 Inhabitants" facility was made with the use of Autodesk Revit software. The appearance of a 3-storey building with a basement is shown in Fig.1.

Fig. 1. Information Model of Pre-School Educational Institution.

From the model all the necessary information on the architecture, design, interior decoration and engineering systems of the kindergarten can be obtained.

The color solution of the facades of the kindergarten matches surrounding accommodation buildings has the same outside finish and makes up unified composition. Bright accents on the facades give the building an individual look.

The information model shows that the facade is decorated with white lining ceramic bricks; bright accents are accomplished by façade plastering on top of mineral wool board. The color solution emphasizes the volumetric composition of the building and is based on combination of green, green-yellow, yellow, turquoise and light-blue colors. The facade is visually divided into spaces and every space has its own color accent. The base is decorated with grey facing block with relief surface. There are visors and canopies over the porches of the building entrances, which are a continuation of the floor slabs. For all materials and elements there are volume indicators.

The facility is to accommodate 12 groups (each comprising 15 kids) of children of different age. The kindergarten model consists of five functional groups of compartments: entrance group; group compartments; additional compartments for lessons (halls for musical and physical training lessons, club rooms, logopedist room, study room); related compartments (medical, kitchen and laundry); service rooms. Compartment specification with area and space indicated as well as finishing material list is available.

The model comprises data on the specific type of materials to be used for finishing of any particular compartment. For wall internal finishing, plastering, vitreous tile, water paint and polyvinyl acetate paint are used. Flooring material is linoleum (its warm-keeping type is used on the ground floor) and ceramic tile with nonskid surface. Floors in the game rooms, located on the ground floor, are equipped with a "warm floor" device. Ceilings are decorated with liming, water-proof emulsion paint or hung ceiling is used.

Data on structural system is also integrated into building information model. The model of the load carrying structure system (Fig. 2) if necessary can be extracted from unified information model.

Load carrying structure system of a monolithic reinforced concrete building of a kindergarten consists of a foundation supported by vertical bearing elements (columns and walls) and integrating them into a single spatial system of horizontal elements (slabs and cover plates). Building structural system is of a column type, structural diagram of the building is of a cross-over design. Building transverse and longitudinal strength as well as its buckling resistance are ensured by a system of transverse and longitudinal reinforced concrete walls of stairways enclosures 200 mm thick joined with horizontal monolithic intermediate floor discs 220 mm thick. The building is designed monolithic: walls are 200 mm and columns are 400x400 mm. Monolithic reinforced concrete flooring 220 mm thick serves as horizontal stiffening diaphragm.

Foundation is in the form of monolithic reinforced concrete slab 600 mm thick made of grade B25W10F150 concrete. Basement wall material is grade B25W10F150 concrete; wall material for 1 to 3 floors is grade B25W4F75 concrete; ceiling material is grade B25W6F150 concrete above basement, grade B25W6F75 concrete above 1 to 3 floors. All flights of steps and window wells are made of class B25W10F150 monolithic reinforced concrete; link beams are monolithic of B25 concrete. Partition walls are of tongue-and-groove gypsum-cardboard sheet 160 mm thick. Information model comprises data on concrete quantities and reinforcement consumption specified item-wise, by diameter and length for all monolithic structures.

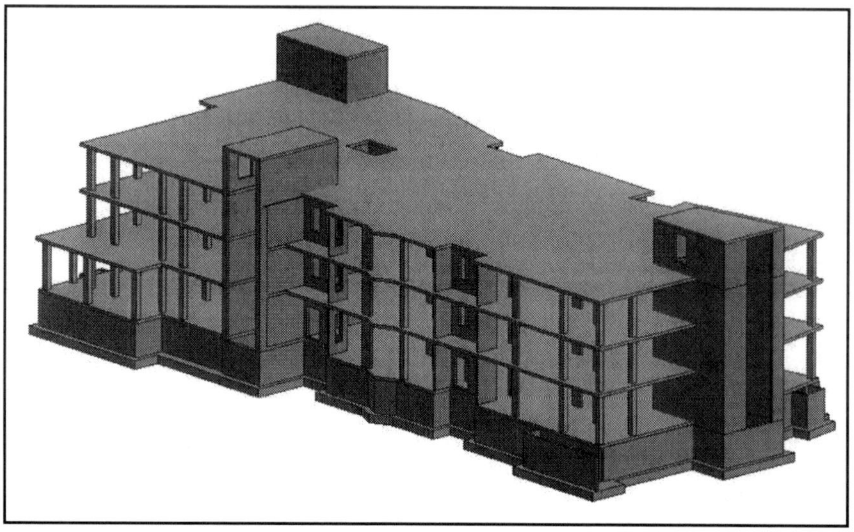

Fig. 2. Load Carrying Structure Model of Pre-School Educational Institution.

Undeniable advantage of correct building information model is the possibility of extracting models of load-carrying structures with their prompt export to design computer complex.

Autodesk Revit software is provided with an export file (with R2S extension) and load-carrying structure model was exported to SCAD Office computer complex, then loads and constraints were set and all required design calculations were made. Kindergarten computer model is given in Fig.3.

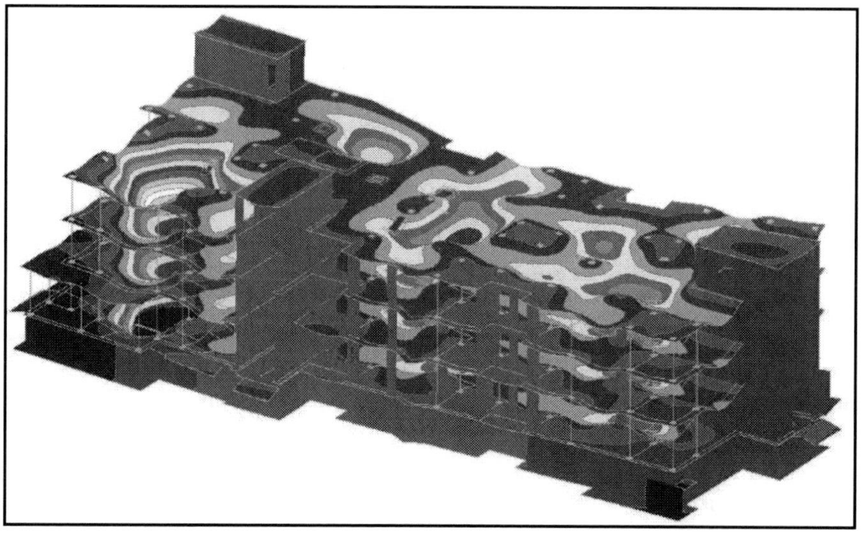

Fig. 3. Computer model of Pre-School Educational Institution.

Data on building technical equipment and the design compliance with sanitary norms are also included into integrated information model and can be easily extracted with all technical specifications.

For vertical connection of the building floors and for the purpose of evacuation, the design provides for three stair enclosures for people including those with limited mobility and also a passenger lift. Kindergarten main compartments have natural light. Natural light level complies with demands which is achieved by means of group and study compartments optimal orientation, location and dimensions of window areas filled with reinforced-plastic double-pane insulated window for protection against outdoor noise.

For protection against internal noise sources, the design provides for lift and winder without machine rooms; spaces enclosing lift hall and lift shaft are separated from adjacent compartments by monolithic reinforced concrete walls 200 mm thick. Lift and winder compartments do not border on permanent human presence compartments. Heat supply station, boiler and pump rooms in the basement are also arranged under compartments with temporary stay.

For noise protection, design measures have been taken: all technical compartments with noise generation are provided with acoustic joints between the floor and adjacent wall structures; engineering equipment with the lowest noise and vibration levels is installed; floating floors with acoustic joint are provided for noise-producing equipment; sound-insulated walls, floorings and partition walls are adopted by acoustic computation.

3 Conclusion

Employment of BIM-technologies opens a wide range of opportunities. Information model rapid development and design options allow online presenting the Investor/Client with technical-economic values and selecting optimal solution of a variety of options. Full conversion of the project into digital form with interactively changing indicators and application of interactive visualization of the project speeds up the consideration of options and allows substantiating the technical literacy of the adopted project solutions. Operation and technical department automatically receives all data online with respect of quantities of materials and resources required for facility construction, resource models curves for all construction stages. Construction subdivisions receive soft copy of complete set of design documentation supported in updated mode without collisions.

Brand new approach to building design and management in the form of an integrated and full-fledged information model helps to effectively save time and allows making right design and managerial decisions improving business processes at all stages of object life cycle.

References

1. C. Eastman, P. Teicholz, R. Sacks, K. Liston, *BIM handbook: A guide to building information modeling for owners, managers, designers, engineers, and contractors* (Wiley, New York, 2011)
2. R.G. Kreider, J.I. Messner, *The Uses of BIM: Classifying and Selecting BIM Uses* (The Pennsylvania State University, University Park, 2013)
3. S. Azhar, Leadersh. Manag. Eng., **11(3)** (2011)
4. D. Bryde, M. Broquetas, J. M. Volm, International Journal of Project Management, **31 (7)** (2013)
5. K. Barlish, K. Sullivan, Automation in Construction, **24** (2012)
6. R. Santos, A. A. Costa, A. Grilo, Automation in Construction, **80** (2017)
7. X. Li, P. Wu, G.Q. Shen, X, Wang, Y. Teng, Automation in Construction, **84** (2017)
8. A. Vysotskiy, S. Makarov, J. Zolotova, E. Tuchkevich, Procedia Engineering, **117** (2015)
9. Building Information Modeling (BIM). Transforming Design and Construction to Achieve Greater Industry Productivity [online], Available at: http://images.autodesk.co

m/latin_am_main/files/mcgraw-hill_construction_bim_smartmarket_report_december_2008.pdf (2008)

10. The Business Value of BIM. Getting Building Information Modeling to the Bottom Line. [online], Available at: http://fiatech.org/images/stories/research/2009_BIM_SmartMarket_Report.pdf (2009)
11. The Business Value of BIM in Europe. Getting Building Information Modeling to the Bottom Line in the United Kingdom, France and Germany [online], Available at: http://images.autodesk.com/adsk/files/business_value_of_bim_in_europe_smr_final.pdf (2010)
12. Green BIM. How Building Information Modeling is Contributing to Green Design and Construction [online], Available at: https://www.construction.com/market_research/freereport/greenbim/MHC_GreenBIM_SmartMarket_Report_2010.pdf (2010)
13. A. Bradley, H. Li, R. Lark, S. Dunn, Automation in Construction, **71** (2016)
14. J. Jia, J. Sun, Z. Wang, T. Xu, Procedia Engineering, **180** (2017)
15. R. Volk, J. Stengel, F. Schultmann, Automation in Construction, **38** (2014)
16. L. Joblot, T. Paviot, D. Deneux, S. Lamouri, IFAC PapersOnLine, **50(1)** (2017)
17. E. Gigliarelli, F. Calcerano, L. Cessari, Energy Procedia, **133** (2017)
18. M. Pavlovskis, J. Antucheviciene, D. Migilinskas, Procedia Engineering, **172** (2017)
19. G.M. Di Giuda, V. Villa, P. Piantanida, Energy Procedia, **78** (2015)
20. S. Azhar, W. A. Carlton, D. Olsen, I. Ahmad, Automation in Construction, **20** (2011)

Evolutionary processes in nature, technology and society –a few common trends[a]

Yekaterina Myasnikova[1*], and *Aleksandr* Spirov[2]

[1] Peter the Great Saint Petersburg Polytechnic University, Centre for Advanced Studies, 195251, Politechnicheskaya st., 29, Russian Federation
[2] Sechenov Institute of Evolutionary Physiology and Biochemistry of the Russian Academy of Sciences (IEPhB RAS), 194223, Toreza av., 44, Russian Federation

Abstract. The diversity of branches of knowledge, within which evolutionary approaches are applied to significantly different objects and processes, includes those branches which are especially interesting due to the implementation of the Darwin's concepts of variation, heredity and selection. This is what is interpreted by some authors as universal selectionism. In this case, objects of evolution may be represented as sequences of symbols, code lines or graphs. This is a method to record heredity of an individual. The recording format allows for mutation (substitution, addition or deletion of certain elements of an individual) and crossing-over during production of offspring from a pair of parent individuals. The approach also allows for a quantitative assessment of the "value" of an individual for evolutionary selection. Such evolution includes, first of all, evolutionary computation, computer-aided modelling of evolution, directed evolution of biomolecules, biological evolution, evolution of technology etc. If we consider the above mentioned examples successively, from computer-based examples to humanitarian one, we can observe definite trends. Firstly, we can see a trend of using "languages" of higher levels to implement an evolutionary problem. Secondly, we can observe a trend of forming "building blocks" in heredity structures as well as a crossing-over mechanism which retains the said blocks. Thirdly, "variation" of an individual is carried out by increasingly high-intelligent methods. Studying of main trends and mutually enriching interchange of experience between such different branches of knowledge may enable to make more reasonable and exact predictions of the results of evolutionary processes and to achieve higher effectiveness of evolutionary search in application areas.

1 Introduction

In modern scientific literature, the term "evolution" is applied to a very wide range of processes and phenomena. Studying of the basic principles of evolution allows explaining

[a] This study is supported by Grant no. 16.8549.2017/8.9 issued by the Ministry of Education and Science of the Russian Federation.
* Corresponding author: myasnikova_em@spbstu.ru

development of various processes and making well-grounded predictions in such different branches of knowledge as Natural and Life Sciences, Technology, and Human Sciences. Some examples are software evolution [1], social (sociocultural) evolution [2], evolutionary linguistics [3], evolutionary economics [4] etc. From a biological point of view, evolution is a natural process of development of life on Earth. Inspired by evolutionary biology, an attempt to develop a new constructive trend of research often allows obtaining such results and making such conclusions which cannot be achieved by other approaches.

Table 1. Evolutions which the concept of selectionism may be applied to.

Evolutionary Computations (genetic algorithms and genetic programming)
Computer-based Evolution Modelling (evolution of "digital" and virtual organisms and gene network models)
Directed evolution of biomolecules (SELEX)
Biological micro- and macroevolution
Evolution of equipment/technologies

We focus on those cases of evolution which the main concepts of Darwin's theory may be applied to. Table 1 lists such branches where similar features may be found between such different evolutionary processes and biological evolution.

The types of evolution in question are characterized by Darwin's variation, heredity and selection. Heredity is determined so that it is possible to represent an individual in the population as a sequence of symbols, code fragments, sentences of (formalized) language or, e.g., as a graph. Such records are often called "chromosomes". These objects are understood as a method to record heredity of an individual. Consistently, variation is understood as changing such representation. The format of the record allows mutating it (by substituting, adding or deleting its certain elements). Moreover, the possibility of crossing-over of parental chromosomes is implemented during production of offspring from a pair of parent individuals.

For selection, it is important to have a possibility of quantitative assessment (fitness) of desired properties of the individual for the evolutionary process (selection), i.e. "value" of the individual. Then, high-value individuals and/or their offspring substitute low-value individual in the population and this corresponds to selectionism.

Key features of evolutions listed in Table 1 are considered in the comparative aspect in the main section of this paper below.

2 Unity and diversity of "Darwinian" evolutions

In this paper, we attempt to track general trends in the evolutions listed in Table 1. The above mentioned trends are differently expressed in various evolutionary branches and the depth of their study also varies.

2.1 Evolutionary computations and computer-based evolution

Our analysis starts with the first two evolutions from the list which are probably the simplest cases. This is a set of evolutions implemented using a computer. These are branches where the problems and approaches significant for developing and understanding other more complex cases of non-biological evolutions are formulated.

Computer evolution is a very large branch which includes both strictly academic (biological evolution modelling) and strictly application fields (techniques of evolutionary computation in real applied problems) [5-6].

Computer evolution has been considerably strictly and mathematically formalized [7]. As a large branch called evolutionary computation or evolutionary algorithms, it includes such well-known subdisciplines as genetic algorithms, genetic programming, evolutionary programming, evolution strategies, learning classifier systems and many others.

Evolutionary computations are a kind of schematized and simplified representation of selectionism. Evolutionary algorithms solve problems working with a population of a plurality of randomly taken solutions. Individuals/solutions in the population undergo mutations and then are assessed based on pre-defined criteria (fitness of individuals). One part of them is selected to produce an offspring population; the other part is eliminated so that the number of individuals in the population remains unchanged after reproduction. During reproduction, a crossing-over, i.e. recombination of parent chromosomes in offspring, is carried out to qualitatively increase diversity of offspring of the given pair. Then, the renewed population undergoes mutagenesis, and the cycle repeats until a satisfactory solution is found (i.e. an individual with the required fitness level).

2.1.1 Genetic algorithms and genetic programming

Genetic algorithms (GA) [8] are the most well-developed branch of evolutionary computations. As a rule, individuals/solutions represent a line of symbols or figures which is called a "chromosome", and this is just one of the common features of GA and biological molecular evolution. Changes in symbols/figures in the line are mutations. Since chromosomes are sequences of "elements" here, just as in DNA, the crossing-over is implemented similar to the biological one in the form of a "crossing" of parent chromosomes in one or two points (sometimes in many points) to allow offspring to receive recombined copies of the parent chromosomes. The significance of crossing-over for effective evolutionary search has been specifically assessed in GA [5].

In GA, almost any optimization problem (i.e. seeking and arriving to a best solution) may be solved by formalizing it in such a way that it is reduced to manipulations with sequences of figures, numbers or symbols [8]. In this case, computer-based evolutionary search is (often easily) feasible.

Schema theorem and building blocks. As a rather simple and intensively researched branch, GA has its theoretical justifications. The schema theorem [5] suggested by John Holland (one of the GA founders) in 1975 influenced much not only GA itself but also other evolutions. The definitions of schemata and building blocks follow from the above mentioned Holland's considerations (which are omitted here).

Building blocks as fragments of the desired solutions. The building-block (BB) hypothesis states that evolutionary search is carried out in GA though finding individual blocks, i.e. parts of solutions [9]. (Despite that not all problems may be properly decomposed into individual blocks for the given problem implementation, it will work for many cases).

Crossing-over combines BBs, crossing-over destroys BBs. Holland's theorem implies that crossing-over plays a critical role in the evolutionary search in GA [10-11]. Crossing-over is first necessary to combine various parent BBs in offspring, thereby increasing the fitness level of the offspring. However, (common) crossing-over tends to destroy (break) BBs, thereby slowing the evolutionary search down [8]. The gist of it is that the crossing over points in a routine crossing-over algorithm are either fixed or arbitrary. Hence, if parent chromosomes are separated and shuffled in offspring during crossing-over so that parental BBs remain unbroken and are received integral by offspring, the fitness level of the offspring will increase. But if crossing over is carried out through a parent BB and such block is not received by any offspring in its integral state, the fitness level of the offspring will not increase (as compared with that one of the parents), and the said BB will be lost in the evolutionary search. A problem arises that the evolutionary process must be such that BB appearance, multiplication and recombination are maintained.

2.1.2 Crossing-over operators retaining building blocks

The demand for crossing-over operators retaining BBs (as well as the hopes put on them) has been recognized in evolutionary computations in the course of development of the theory and practice of GA and GP application. In parallel with and independently from them, molecular engineering approaches has been developed to manipulate domains (BB) in directed evolution of biological macromolecules ([12], see Section 2.2). Moreover, modern biological engineering has adopted the idea of modular design (presence of BBs) in many respects from common engineering ([13], see Section 2.3).

Crossing-over retaining BBs is required in GA and GP, evolutionary design of gene network models, directed evolution of macromolecules and some other fields. Many special crossing-over operators retaining BBs are being developed in evolutionary computations [14-18]. There is a chance that such operators will be applied in other evolutions.

Thus, the cross-cutting issue of our analysis is the demand for such crossing-over operator which would retain BBs in the evolution.

2.1.3 Evolution of virtual organisms

Now, let us consider the evolution of virtual and "digital" organisms (Table 1) as they are a good illustration of the statements set forth in the previous paragraphs.

Evolution of virtual creatures and virtual robots: Let us consider the evolution of virtual creatures by the example of Karl Sims's work [19-20]. The approach suggested by Sims is similar to GA and GP, and the issue of modularity (BB) found its expression in this field as well.

These creatures are a kind of virtual robots which move on the plane or swim in a virtual water environment. They have a modular body and modular (block) limbs. They also have sets of sensors, simple signal-processing systems and decision-making systems to decide where to move. They are able to walk, hop, or swim; they can even follow their "targets" and compete with each other for loot (in a virtual environment). Evolving virtual robots is an intensively developing branch of evolutions where approaches to designing real evolving robots are being tried out [21].

From building blocks to modular design. Sims's creatures are implemented as modular ones. Genetically, a creature is an oriented graph, i.e. the design of a creature is represented by a graph. In particular, the segmented body and limbs are represented by points and the links between the segments are determined by arrows (oriented verges). Similarly to GP, crossing-over of genotypes is implemented here in the form of an exchange of graph parts. The assembly of a virtual creature is carried out according to the graph as a block design, and this is what can be defined as single-value mapping from a genotype into a phenotype.

Genotype modularity and corresponding phenotype modularity allow to promptly find series of designs of (virtual) robots becoming more complicated. Thus, if the evolutionary problem is implemented in such a way that BBs appear in the genotype and are retained during crossing-over (and mapping from a genotype into a phenotype determines and maintains modularity), this may provide essential advantages e.g. in evolutionary robotics.

2.2 Directed evolution of biomolecules and biological evolution

The following branch of evolution important for us is popularly called evolution in vitro. Evolution in vitro is also known as SELEX (Systematic Evolution of Ligands by Exponential

Enrichment), or directed evolution [22]. Evolution in vitro is also a very large branch which includes both strictly academic fields (as it is directly connected to the range of problems of biological molecular evolution) and strictly applied problems (obtaining chimeric proteins and enzymes with new properties).

Modular structure of RNA and proteins. Modularity of biological macromolecules of proteins and nucleic acids is studied extensively by biologists. Evolutionary significance of modularity of macromolecules is also the subject of wide speculation. In particular, special crossing-over mechanisms are required to maintain modularity. Such mechanisms have been developed, for example, in directed evolution of macromolecules.

Real crossing-over to retain modules. Experimental molecular biological procedures have been developed for sexual methods in protein engineering [23]. These biotechnological approaches imply exon shuffling similar to that is supposed to have occurred in biological evolution.

As is known, an eukaryotic gene consists of exons and introns. Exons code protein parts, and introns are "service" inserts (sequences) between them. Exon often but not always corresponds to a domain (module, as the BB is called in this branch). These blocks may be cut out of different genes and shuffled as desired. As a result, chimeric proteins that do not exist in nature are obtained. Some of them have new properties. The said approaches use ferments and the peculiarities of gene structure. May be it is the way of evolution of proteins and RNA in living nature.

Thus, the idea of BBs is a mainstream of modern biology, and the mechanisms of genetic material recombination to retain and propagate BBs in evolutions have been the subject of active discussions over recent decades.

2.3 Evolution of technology

Modular design in engineering. The module principle is being actively developed in modern engineering (a modular air plane may be even represented). Modular design of a smartphone is a good example for the man or woman in the street, and the expectations are that smartphones will become modular soon. An important thing for us within the said branch of evolution is the modularity principle which is systematically tracked in our evolutions [24].

Building blocks and design modularity. The idea of BB may be illustrated by the example of the results of computer evolution. So, design modularity allows to easily upgrading a computer by adding new blocks.

It should be noted that the modularity principle in engineering is discussed much in modern literature in the context of a number of branches where the modularity of engineering developments is of importance, and has been repeatedly compared to the ideas of modularity in modern biology [13].

From BASIC to English. The trend of developing high-level programming languages is also being observed in computer sciences. High and very high level programming languages are becoming more like human languages. For example, program codes written in the Inform programming language are read almost just as a text written in the English language which significantly simplifies the work of users not being experts in programming [25]. We arrive to a conclusion that the higher the level of evolutionary process in the direction of "humanitarity" is, the higher the level of languages generally used for implementation of individuals in the evolving population is.

3 Findings and conclusions

The brief analysis of evolutionary processes and phenomena allows arriving to the following conclusions. The following trends are observed in branches of knowledge where "Darwinian" evolutionary processes may be formulated, formalized and applied; the branches being ranked from their lowest to highest levels of "humanitarity".

In the simplest case, heredity of "individuals" is implemented as a sequence of symbols. In more complex forms, it is represented as programs (e.g., trees) and structures (e.g. graphs). The exception is biology where, in spite of the complexity of evolutionary processes, the hereditary apparatus is based on sequences of symbols.

Mutations of "genes"/ "chromosomes" of individuals are implemented by increasingly high-intelligent approaches: in standard GA, mutation means substituting the binary number in a random position; a lot of examples of non-random mutations may be given in biology; in computer-based evolutions, both mutations and crossing-over become increasingly intelligent and make functional substitutions, extensions and complications rather than random (often senseless) changes. Finally, a human plays the role of an intelligent mutator in "humanitarian" branches. As a result, "languages" of an increasingly high level are used to implement the evolutionary problem: from binary codes in GA to human languages.

Heredity of "building blocks" observed in the evolving material requires using crossing-over mechanisms which retain the blocks during the production of offspring from parent pairs. The more complex evolutionary problems become, the more complex crossing-over operators are; they are, for example, complex algorithms, evolving algorithms.

During selection, the individual fitness assessment in evolving populations demonstrates the trend for implementation by increasingly high-intelligent approaches (artificial intellect or human experts).

It should be noted in conclusion that the exchange of experience between various evolutions may be mutually enriching. In particular, "simple" computer-based evolutions are well-formalized and provide mathematical and software tools for complex, more humanitarian branches. And vice versa, more complex evolutionary processes may be the source of ideas of particular mechanisms in evolution which may be formalized into new computational algorithms and approaches.

References

1. N. Chapin, J. E. Hale, K. M. Khan, J. F. Ramil, Tan W-G. *J. Software Maint. Evol.: Res. and Practice*, **13** (2001)
2. A. V. Korotayev, *SocialEvolution* (2003)
3. W. Croft Ann, Rev. Anthropology. *Annual Reviews*, **37** (2008)
4. D. J. Friedman *Evol. Econ.,* **8** (1998)
5. J. H. Holland, *Adaptation in Natural and Artificial System* (1975)
6. G. C. Onwubolu, B. V. Babu, *New Optimization Techniques in Engineering* (2004)
7. L. N. deCastro, *Fundamentals of Natural Computing: Basic Concepts, Algorithms, and Applications* (2006)
8. M. Mitchell, *An Introduction to Genetic Algorithms. Cambridge, MA: MIT Press* (1996)
9. D. Goldberg, *Genetic Algorithms in Search, Optimization and Machine Learning* (1989)
10. Z. Li, E. D. Goodman In ISICA 2008. *Lec. Notes Comp. Sci.* **5370** (2008)
11. Sudholt D. *EvolComput.,* **25** (2017)
12. C. A. Voigt, C. Martinez, Z. G. Wang, S. L. Mayo, and F. H. Arnold *Nat Struct Biol.*, **9**, 553-558 (2001)
13. L. H. Hartwell, J. J Hopfield., S. Leibler, A. W. Murray *Nature*, **402**, 47-52 (1999).
14. C. Skinner, P. Riddle, *Parallel Problem Solving from Nature* (2004)

15. A. Zaritsky, M. Sipper *IEEE Trans. Evol. Comp.,* **8** (2004).
16. F. Li, Q. H. Liu, F. Min, G. W Yang. Int. Conf. Mach. Learn. Cyber (2006)
17. Y. Kameya, C. Prayoonsri IEEE Cong. Evol. Comp (2011)
18. A. J. Umbarkar, P. D. Sheth *ICTACT J. Soft Comp.,***06**, 1083-1092 (2015)
19. K. Sims *In: Art. Life IV Proc*. Available at: http://www.karlsims.com/evolved-virtual-creatures.html (1994)
20. K. Sims *In: 21st Int. ACM Conf. Comp. Graph. and Interactive Techniques*. Available at: http://www.karlsims.com/evolved-virtual-creatures.html (1994)
21. P. A. Vargas, E. A. DiPaolo, I. Harvey, P. Husbands, *The horizons of evolutionary robotics* (2014)
22. S. Lutz, S. J. Benkovk, *Protein Engineering by Evolutionary Methods* (2008)
23. S. Lutz, *Curr Opin Biotechnol*, **21** (2010)
24. M. A. Schilling, *Managing in the Modular Age: Architectures, Networks and Organizations* (2002)
25. G. Nelson, Available at: http://inform7.com/learn/documents/WhitePaper.pdf (2005)

Conceptual model of information support for taking decisions

Yury Nurulin[1*], and *Inga* Skvortsova[1]

1 Peter the Great St. Petersburg Polytechnic University, Institute of Industrial Management, Economy and Trade, 195251 Polytechnicheskaya st. 29, Russian Federation

Abstract. The modern society is characterized by qualitative changes in the volumes, composition and significance of collected and processed data. This data reflects the condition of the real and virtual world surrounding people and it is used for respective impact on the real and virtual world. All this requires theoretical generalizations that form a single conceptual platform as for managers working with the real world and for knowledge management professionals who work with the virtual world. The traditional model of taking decisions in management indirectly reflects the significance of knowledge and other elements of the virtual world for taking effective decisions which have impact on the real world. However the process of forming knowledge is not reflected in these models. Traditional models of knowledge management mainly concentrate on the internal transformation processes "data-information-knowledge-wisdom" which further are used for taking decisions.

1 Introduction

1.1 Classical model of taking decisions

Back in 1954 Peter Drucker called the process of taking effective decisions the essential function of a manager. He suggested a model of the process of taking decisions which consists of a logically connected sequence of actions aimed at finding the best decision [1].

Later this model was developed by G. Simon who suggested the conception of limited rationality [2]. He noted that though the problem has the best solution it is not always possible to find it because of limited cognitive ability of the person who takes decisions – decision maker (DM). In reality DMs often don't have enough information for determining the problem, they don't see all the available alternatives and the knowledge used by them for taking decisions is not full. As a result, the decision usually leads to satisfactory but not optimal consequences. Relying on this observation Simon replaced the task of finding the best decision by the task of finding effective decisions.

Later this model was elaborated and making more detailed and it is still in the focus of the analysis of the Russian and foreign scientists [3-5].

[*] Corresponding author: yury.nurulin@gmail.com

1.2 Informational model

Since the 80-ies of the last century in the scientific literature there is a lively discussion about the nature of information and the process of cognition. A significant role in this discussion belongs to R. Ackoff who suggested a model of data transformation in 1989 [6]. This model has been called a DIKW-model in the English-language literature as an abbreviation of the English words Data, Information, Knowledge and Wisdom. The model is based on the assumption that data can be used for obtaining information, information – for obtaining knowledge and knowledge – for developing wisdom. The studies where the DIKW-model is used note its main features.

1. The model has hierarchical structure which describes the processes of transformation of the essence of the lowest level of hierarchy into the essence of the top level, at this, each level adds some new properties to the previous one [7, p. 164]. Quite often this hierarchy is displayed in the form of a pyramid (Fig. 1).

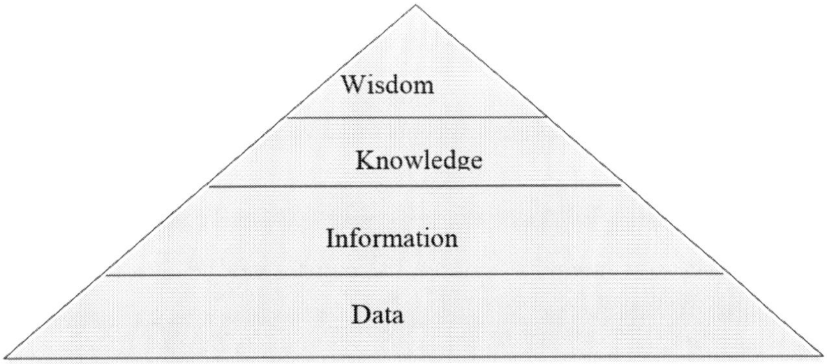

Fig. 1. Pyramid of the DIKW [7].

2. The hierarchy possesses the property of continuity both in relation to the process and in relation to the object of transformation [8].

3. There are no unified definitions for the main terms which are used in the DIKW-model. [9].

2 The principles of model convergence in taking decisions

Currently both the models mentioned above are developing independently. Specialists of the information field improve methods and means for knowledge management, at this, questions of using the obtained knowledge are not the subject of analysis. Specialists working in the sphere of management develop models of taking decisions taking into account business-processes and their environment, at this, the questions of informational support for taking decisions are analyzed insufficiently. Two significant elements are indirectly present in the classic model of taking decisions: information on the condition of the observed object and its environment and also cognitive abilities of the DM which reflect his knowledge and ethical and moral standards and values. In this regard, a significant part of discussions on the nature of the process of making decisions is devoted to exploring the principles of rational behavior of a DM [10]. This reflects the general tendency: the impact of psychology on the models and methods used in economy and management increases [11]. The DM is considered as a socially active agent (an individual or a group) whose system of preferences is one of the key factors determining his behavior in the process of making decisions. However, it is necessary to note an insufficient number of works connected with exploring the influence of the informational component on the process of taking decisions,

2.1 Information support for taking decisions

The indispensable link between information and making decisions was first noted in 1958 by March and Simon: processing of information and taking decisions of different levels should be considered as the key types of activity [12] for any organization.

The pyramid, as a visual reflection of the DIKW-model, shows that the number of elements at each level decreases while we move upwards through the hierarchy. Informational overload takes place when the DM receives for analysis too many elements of the lower level of the DIKW-hierarchy and that, in its turn, happens when data replaces information for describing a problem, information replaces knowledge, etc. From here it follows that there are two quite evident conclusions about the principles of information support of the decision-making process.

1. Information support of business processes should be organized according to the principles of the DIKW hierarchy. Transition to a new hierarchy level of making decisions should be accompanied by changing the information essence. It correlates well enough with the known principles of effective management which are based on the statement that the problem should be possibly solved on the level of hierarchy where it appeared.

2. Basic competencies of a manager should include the ability for effective knowledge management, the ability to acquire information from data and knowledge from information, and also the skills of using modern instruments of knowledge management.

2.2 The models of the manager and the business-environment cooperation

The conscious process of interplay between the human and the surrounding world can be represented as a sequence of the following stages:

observation→description→explanation →impact (use).

At the first and the last stages of the process the subject cooperates with the real world, and the central stages belong to the virtual world which doesn't exist without the subject. The classic DIKW-model reflects the virtual world and has only indirect connections with the real world. For using in management it should be adjusted to the stages of cooperation of the subject with the real world.

In general terms, in the context of direct engineering of business "from top downward" these tasks can be represented as an iterative answer to the following sequence of questions:

what for → how → why → what → who → when → how many

In the context of the business-analysis "from top downward" in accordance with the classic model of taking decisions these tasks are transformed in the following way:

how many, where, when, who, what (*happened*) → ***why*** (*it happened*) → ***how (is it possible*** *to correct it*) → ***what for*** (*it should be done*)

Taking decisions complies with the rules of business-analysis that is why it is necessary to solve two tasks for developing an integrated model:

– put the elements of the DIKW-hierarchy and the key questions of the business-analysis according to the classic model of taking decisions in direct correlation;

– suggest subject-oriented statements of the main elements of the DIKW-hierarchy from the perspectives of management.

3 The integrated model of taking decisions

The basis for developing an integrated model is the model of the W2T-cycle which reflects cyclical pattern of cooperation of the real and virtual world through the subject: "from objects to data, information, knowledge, wisdom, services, subjects and back to objects" [14]. In this model the DIKW-hierarchy is based on the signals which come from the real world. The signals reflect the condition of the objects from the real world and transform into data through results of observation. The virtual world is connected with the real world through services (business-processes) and subjects (DM). The DM place in business-processes and also cooperation of the DM with the elements of the DIKW-hierarchy are not reflected in the model.

As the DM is the key element of the decision-making process the integrated model should reflect both the procedures of information support for the DM and also the basic procedures of his cooperation with the business-environment. Taking into account the fact that observations can be carried out for objects both of the real and also of the virtual world we suggest the following definition of the main categories of the DIKW-hierarchy from the perspectives of management.

Data - results of observations and measuring objects of the real and virtual world collected without context processing and available for analysis and further processing. In other words, data is a category of the virtual world which describes the real world independently from cognitive components of the observed subject. The key words in this definition are "independently from cognitive components of the observed subject". While moving upwards through the DIKW-hierarchy the results of processing become more and more dependent on cognitive capacities of the subject. That is why the hierarchy level following the data can be represented as the result of describing the world formed by the subject on the basis of context analysis of data.

Information - combination of data unified by the context for adequate description of the world. In other words, information is the description of the real of virtual world obtained by the subject on the basis of context processing of results of observation and measuring. The role of cognitive abilities of the subject in extracting information from data is relatively small.

Active discussion of the nature of knowledge is carried out in scientific literature. A number of authors underlined the indispensable link between the levels of hierarchy and defined information as simplified knowledge and, on this basis, they stated that the notions "information" and "knowledge" are synonims [15, 16]. However, the majority of research workers note the presence of qualitative differences of essences which belong to different levels of hierarchy. Considering the nature of knowledge, Polany [17] and also Nonaka and Takeuchi and then Bennet and other research workers distinguished direct and indirect types of knowledge [17, 18]. The bsis of this classification is a degree of formalizing knowledge. In this work [19] a break between the given classification and practical problems which are being solved by management are noted.

The analysis from literature mentioned above shows that the connections between knowledge and taking decisions are not studied in the direct form. At the same time such connections are present in implicit form because the distinguished types are associated with the key questions analyzed when taking decisions.

For building a combined model of the decision process in the work the following subject-oriented definition of knowledge is suggested.

Knowledge is a category characterized by cognitive abilities of a subject according to contextual selection, analysis and use of information for describing problems of both the virtual and the real world (*why* it happened).

The interpretations of the term "knowledge" mentioned above do not ensure smooth transition to the top level of the DIKW-hierarchy from the perspectives of taking effective decisions. For eliminating this disadvantage in the work it is suggested to introduce an additional level into the DIKW-model - *Understanding,* as an intermediate stage of transition from knowledge to wisdom. The necessity of constructing this level is explained by the following reasons. Knowledge is the last category of the hierarchy which is focused on the past and the present whereas a number of elements of the classic model of taking decisions is focused on the future. Wisdom reflects strategic view of the consequences of a decision including those in the distant future whereas it is important to form and analyze the scenarios of the nearest future for taking decisions. Besides, a combination of moral and ethical values forms the basis of wisdom whereas the classic model of taking decisions is based on the planned condition of the object. The essence of *understanding* as the level of the DIKW-hierarchy consists in transforming knowledge from the past to the future through the combination of cause-effect relationship of the analyzed events. Thus, ***understanding*** is a category which characterizes the abilities of the subject to extrapolate modern tendencies on the future which are defined as a result of analyzing the events which has taken place in the virtual and real world.

The finishing stage of decision-making in the DIKW-model is *wisdom*. Zeleny (M. Zeleny) explains wisdom as a category which is associated with the term know-why [20]. Rowley and [20] underline that wisdom has moral, social and practical measuring (wisdom is the result of integration of knowledge with moral principles) [21].

As the highest level of abstraction wisdom characterizes the ability to "look ahead". In the Russian-language literature on the theory of decision-making it corresponds with the term "the system of preferences of a DM" to a significant extent [22]. Wisdom associates with the DM's opportunities for choosing effective alternatives in the classic model. Thus, in the combined model of taking decisions, ***Wisdom*** is a category characterizing ethical principles of a DM and his cognitive abilities to foresee technical, economic and social-ethical consequences of the decisions taken Fig. 2.

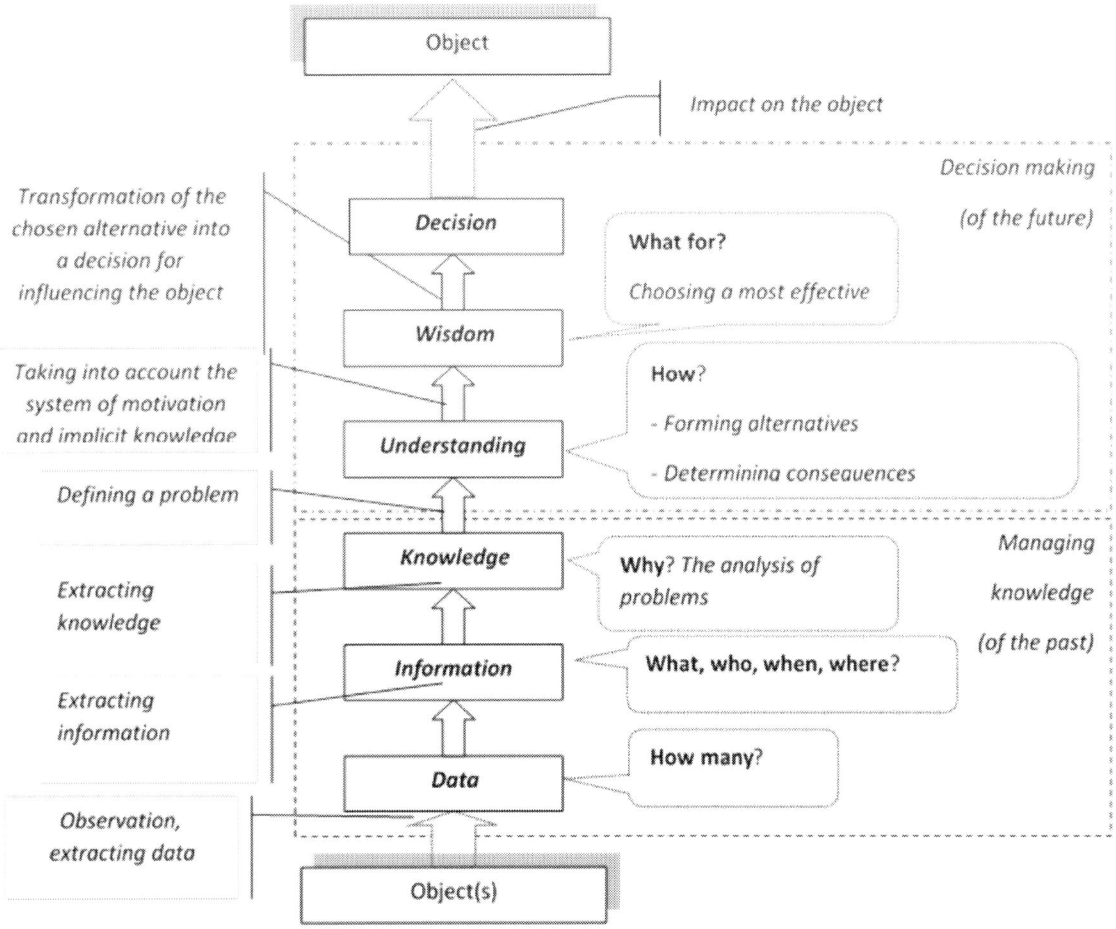

Fig. 2. The integrated model of taking managerial decisions.

We can distinguish the following basic components of the real world: material technical components (products, services, technologies); economic components (finances, organizations, business-models, market) and social components (code of behavior, jurisprudence, culture). The virtual world created by the man is also multi-component. Except data, information, knowledge it reflects the system of opinions, mentality, language, arts, entertainment, etc. Acting on the basis of wisdom DMs should directly or indirectly take into account all these components while making decisions.

4 Conclusion

The suggested model has conceptual character and reflects the main approaches to organizing the processes of taking decisions from the perspectives of management and knowledge management. At the stage of strategic control it enables forming general principles of constructing business-processes oriented at taking effective managerial decisions on the basis of the DM knowledge system. At the level of tactical management it emphasizes the effective information support of the decision-making process for excluding informational overloads of the DM and providing him with necessary information. At the contextual (technical) level it underlines the necessity of using contemporary instruments for collecting and analyzing information in the process of taking decisions, extracting information from them and generating knowledge. Integration of the considered approaches forms the necessary methodological base for forming the future economy structure.

References

1. P. Drucker, *The Practice of Management* (Harper & Brothers, New York, 1954)
2. H. Simon, *Administrative Behavior* (The Free Press, New York, 1976)
3. V. G. Smirnova et al., *Organization and its business environment: 17-module environment for managers "Organization development control" Module 2* (INFRA-M, Moscow, 2000)
4. F. Adam, Journal of Decision Systems, **21 (2)** (2012)
5. A Chaabounia, I. Yahiab, Journal of Decision Systems, **23(3)** (2014)
6. R. Ackoff, Journal of Applies Systems Analysis, **16** (1989)
7. J. Rowley, Journal of Information Science, **33** (2007)
8. D. Pan, Computing in Science and Engineering, **5** (2010)
9. S. Baškarada, A. Koronios, Australasian Journal of Information Systems', **18 (1)** (2013)
10. J. Basel, R. Jörn, European Management Journal, **31** (2013)
11. S. Della Vigna, Journal of Economic Literature, **47 (2)** (2009)
12. J. March, H. Simon, *Organizations* (Wiley and Sons, New York, 1993)
13. P. Hemp, Harvard Business Review, **87 (9)** (2009)
14. N Zhong, J Ma, R. Huang, J. Liu, Y. Yao, Y. Zhang, & J. Chen, Journal of Supercomputing, **64 (3)** (2013)
15. M Swigon, Journal of Information Science, **39 (6)** (2013)
16. M. Fricke, J. Inf. Sci, **35(2)** (2009)
17. M. Polanyi, *Personal knowledge: Towards a post-critical* philosophy (Routledge, London, 1958)
18. D. Bennet, A. Bennet, J. Inf. Know. Man. Syst, **38** (2008)
19. P. Hulme, J. Appl. Ecol., **51** (2014)
20. J. Rowley, F. Slack, J. Inf. Sci., **35 (1)** (2009)
21. M. Zeleny, Human Syst. Man., **7 (1)** (1987)
22. Z. P. Rumyantseva et al., *General organization control: principles and processes: 17-module program for managers "Organization development control". Module 3* (INFRA-M, Moscow, 2000)

Application of numerical integration methods to continuously variable transmission dynamics models[a]

Orlov Stepan[1*]

[1] Peter the Great St. Petersburg Polytechnic University Russian Federation, 195251, St.Petersburg, Polytechnicheskaya, 29

Abstract. The expansion of digital engineering technologies in the framework of the fourth industrial revolution relies on core technologies for mathematical modeling and computer simulation of physical processes. Time required for a computer simulation and the quality of numerical solutions are key factors that ultimately have impact on product quality and the amount of waste at product design stage. This paper is aimed on the reduction computer simulation time for continuously variable transmission (CVT) models. The modeling of the device as a set of deformable rigid bodies with numerous contact interactions is an extraordinary problem addressed in [1]. Model dynamics is described in terms of ordinary differential equations (ODE) of motion. The system of ODEs has about 3600 variables (generalized coordinates and speeds). Despite relatively low dimension of the model, computer simulation using traditional numerical integration methods takes long time to run. The reason for this is the stiffness of the ODE system. In this paper, we present the results of an investigation aimed on finding a numerical integration method appropriate for problems of this kind.

1 Introduction

The world scientific and industrial society is now entering a new phase of its development, called Industrie 4.0 in Europe. One of the main features of this phase is the expansion of digital engineering technologies, which dominated until recently, in the direction of the development of virtual engineering concepts based on the latest achievements of virtual and augmented reality technologies. Motivating factors for that are a high level of competition of industrial enterprises, the search for new technologies for design, modeling, verification of modeling results, the creation of industrial products, marketing and sales of enterprise products.

The newest technologies of virtual engineering are of key importance in the modern industrial world in the design and modeling of complex industrial facilities, since they allow to significantly reduce the amount of waste at the design stage of the product. The core of the newest virtual engineering technologies are the newest methods of mathematical modeling

[a] This work was supported by Russian Science Foundation grant No. 18-11-245.

* Corresponding author: majorsteve@mail.ru

for solving extraordinary problems in the industry. Solving those problems requires the development of a complete simulation cycle from creating a physical model, deducing up constitutive equations, selecting or creating numerical schemes for solving the equations and creating an industrial software system for the predictive modeling of product behavior.
In this paper we consider numerical simulations of CVT dynamics. The system of ODEs of motion contains about 1800 generalized coordinates, plus the same number of generalized speeds, totaling in about 3600 variables. Initial value problems for those equations need to be solved to simulate CVT dynamics.

The dimension of our ODE system is relatively low, compared to that of ODE systems in other fields like structural mechanics, computational fluid dynamics, and others. However, computer simulation times are high: one second of real time needs several hours of CPU time to perform a simulation. It is highly desirable to reduce simulation times since that would allow users to modify CVT parameters in a desired manner much faster, resulting in better quality product. One obvious approach to this goal is to parallelize the simulation code. We already have some success with the parallelization [2]. But in this paper we consider the other approach, focused on a search for a numerical method that would run simulations faster than the classical Runge – Kutta 4-th order method (RK4) [3] that we have been using in production versions of CVT software. A combination of both approaches promises to have much faster simulations.

Next sections are as follows. In sec. 2 we provide an overview of CVT model, which helps reader understand the sources of its numerical stiffness. Section 3 presents the result of the investigation of numerical integration methods applied to CVT dynamics. Section 4 summarizes the results obtained and outlines future work.

2 CVT Model overview

The model of CVT includes two elastic shafts, the input and the output one, on nonlinearly elastic supports. There are two pulleys on each shaft, one motionless and one moving (Figure 1). The pulleys have toroidal (almost conical) contact surfaces. There is a chain consisting of rocker pins and plates (Figure 2). Each pin has two halves that roll over each other during chain motion. End surfaces of pin halves are in contact with the pulleys. The application of clamping forces to pulleys leads to certain chain configuration such that pins are at certain contact radius at each pulley set; the gear ratio can be changed by shifting the moving pulleys along the shafts. The torque is transmitted due to the friction forces at pin-pulley contact points.

A number of mathematical models of CVT parts for dynamics simulation have been developed [1]. Most advanced models consider rocker pins bending elasticity and the rolling of pin halves. Chain models have up to 21 generalized coordinates per link, totaling in 1600+ degrees of freedom per typical chain.

There are many contact interactions in the CVT model: between pin and pulley; between pins and plates; between pin halves (Figure 3).

Elastic normal forces acting at contact pairs are modeled according the Hertz' theory [4]. Importantly, there are also tangential friction forces. Those are proportional to normal forces and the friction coefficient f depending on relative speed v_r. The friction law $f(v_r)$ used is close to the Coulomb's one, but is regularized: is constant at relative speeds greater than the saturation speed v_0, and depends on speed linearly at speeds less than v_0. Therefore, the friction law is piecewise linear. The non-smoothness of the friction law may affect the behavior of numerical methods investigated in this paper, that's why we also consider an alternative system in which the friction law is smoothed using a parabola connecting straight parts (Figure 4).

Two factors make the developed CVT mathematical models computationally stiff: elasticity (of model bodies and of normal contact force) and friction in contact pairs. Taking elasticity and inertia into account results in natural frequencies of linearized system up to 10^6 rad/s. On the other hand, friction results in even more serious "numerical stiffness", as we will see in sec. 3.1.

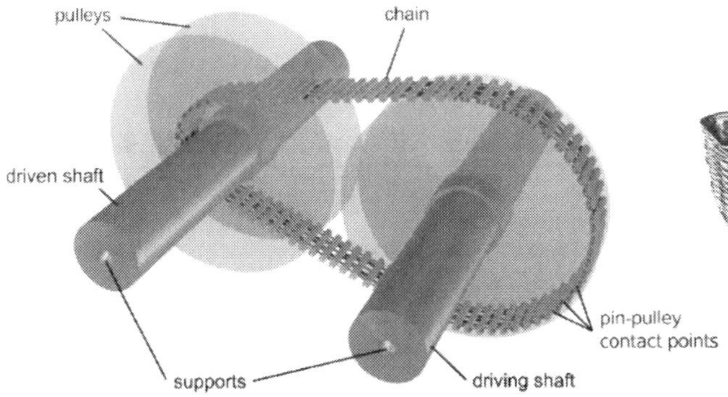

Figure 1. CVT model general view.

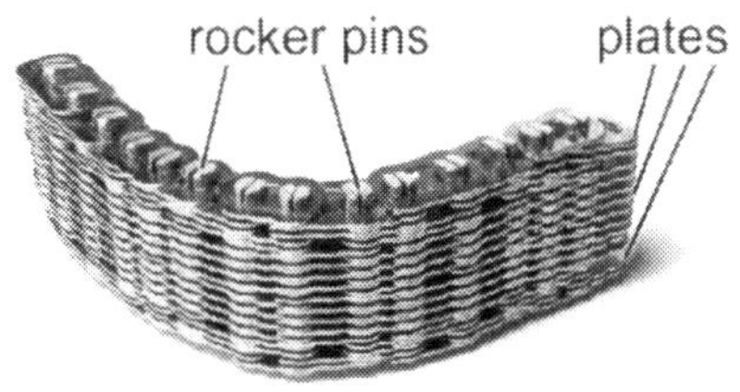

Figure 2. CVT chain.

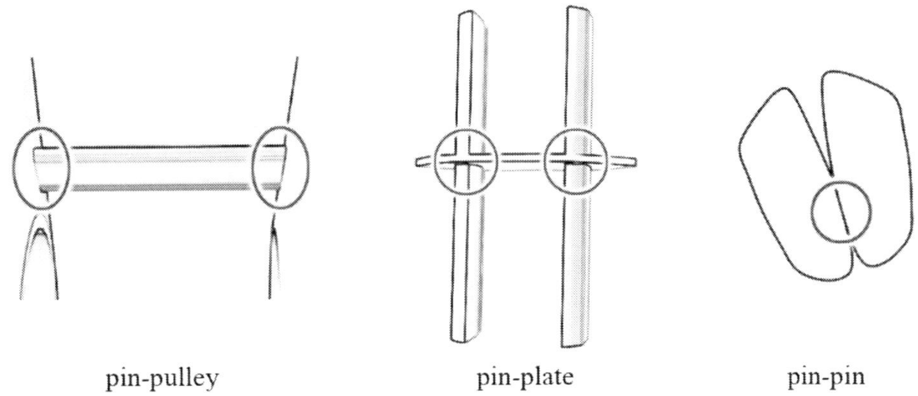

Figure 3. Types of contact interaction in CVT.

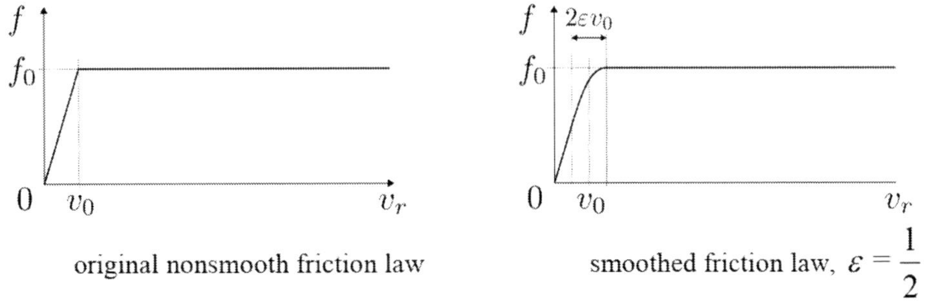

Figure 4. Friction laws used in numerical experiments.

Differential equations of motion for the CVT model are obtained in the framework of Lagrangian mechanics, so they have the following form:

$$\frac{d}{dt}\frac{\partial L}{\partial \dot{q}_k} - \frac{\partial L}{\partial q_k} = \tilde{Q}_k, \quad k = 1,\ldots,n, \qquad (1)$$

where t is the time, q_k are generalized coordinates, L is the Lagrange's function, $\tilde{Q}_k$ are non-potential applied generalized forces, and n is the number of degrees of freedom.
Equations of motion can be rewritten in the normal form:

$$\dot{x} = F(t,x),\ x = \begin{bmatrix} q \\ v \end{bmatrix},\ F = \begin{bmatrix} v \\ A^{-1}P \end{bmatrix},\ P(q,v,t) \equiv \left(\frac{\partial L}{\partial q} + \tilde{Q} - \dot{A}v \right)$$

(2)

(we took into account that the system is scleronomous), where $q = [q_1,\ldots,q_n]^T$ is the vector of generalized coordinates, $A(q)$ — symmetric positive-definite matrix of inertia with elements $A_{ij} = \dfrac{\partial^2 L}{\partial \dot{q}_i \partial \dot{q}_j}$, v — vector of generalized speeds, $P(q,v,t)$ — essentially nonlinear function, in particular due to $\tilde{Q}$ containing friction forces.

3 Investigation of numerical methods

Production versions of the CVT simulation software have been using the classical Runge – Kutta numerical integration scheme of fourth order (RK4) [3] to solve the initial value problem of CVT dynamics. It is known that the RK4 scheme, as well as other explicit numerical integration schemes, have a step size limitation due to the stability requirement: in general, the value $h\lambda$, where h is the step size and λ is an eigenvalue of ODE right-hand side Jacobian matrix, must belong to the stability region of the method.

Due to that limitation, step sizes that can be used with RK4 vary in the range [10^{-8} s, 10^{-7} s], which leads to long CPU time required for a simulation. In next subsection we analyze ODE system Jacobian matrix and explain the origin of its high eigenvalues. Then we proceed with the investigation of a number of numerical integration methods in application to CVT dynamics equations (2). The goal of the investigation is to find a method allowing much longer step sizes than RK4 and having the potential to run significantly faster than RK4.

3.1 Eigenvalues of ODE right hand side Jacobian matrix

To make the search for an appropriate numerical method more purposeful, we have numerically solved the full eigenvalue problem at some typical state in a stationary regime of CVT operation. The eigenvalues found split into two groups: firstly, there are complex eigenvalues corresponding to damped oscillations; secondly, there are real negative eigenvalues corresponding to non-oscillatory dissipation processes. Absolute values of eigenvalue imaginary parts have maximum at approx. 10^6 s^{-1}, while absolute values of real parts — at approx. 10^8 s^{-1}. Figure 5 (left) shows the computed eigenvalues of the Jacobian matrix.

Further we proved that the largest negative eigenvalues are caused by friction forces acting between pin halves, and the operating points in the friction law are at the linear part ($v < v_0$). The idea of the proof is to change (e.g., increase 10 times) the saturation speed v_0

in the friction law, then recompute the Jacobian matrix and find its eigenvalues. The results of evaluation are shown in Figure 5 (right) for the case of v_0 increased 10 times for the friction law between pin halves; changing v_0 for other contact types (pin-plate, pin-pulley) results in changes of other eigenvalues, while those with maximum absolute values remain the same. Notice that "the worst" eigenvalues are proportional to the tension force in the most loaded straight part of the chain, and, consequently, vary from one CVT operation regime to another.

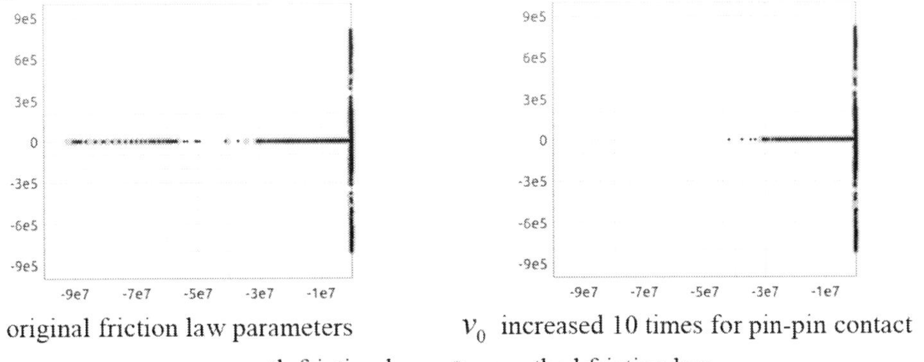

Figure 5. Eigenvalues of ODE right hand side Jacobian matrix.

3.2 Numerical experiment setup

For each numerical integration scheme, two tests have been done. In the first test, the dependency of step local error norm e on the step size h is investigated. The error is computed simply by comparison with the "exact" reference solution obtained with a very small step size of $2\cdot10^{-9}$ s using the RK4 scheme. In the second test, a dynamics simulation is performed during 0.005 second of real time; a sample history curve is obtained (namely, the axial force in a pin half entering a pulley set, $P_{\bar{z}}(t)$ at certain pin — Figure 6) as an evident indicator of the acceptability of numerical results. Relative global error E of a numerical solution is estimated as

$$E \equiv \max_{t\in[t_*,0.005\mathrm{s}]} |P_{\bar{z}}(t)-P_{\bar{z}}^*(t)| / \max_{t\in[t_*,0.005s]} |P_{\bar{z}}^*(t)|, \quad (3)$$

where $P_{\bar{z}}^*(t)$ is the reference curve; $t_* = 0.001$ s has been chosen to avoid culling out some numerical solutions due to a small time shift resulting in a large error at $t \in [0,t_*]$, which is not representative because the reference curve has a large slope at some pints in the range $[0,t_*]$.

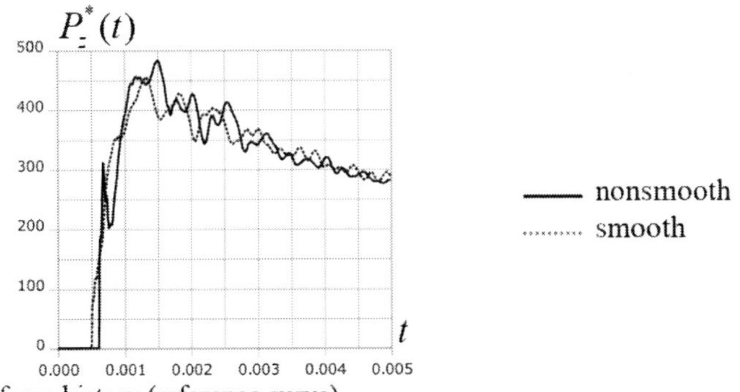

Figure 6. Pin axial force history (reference curve).

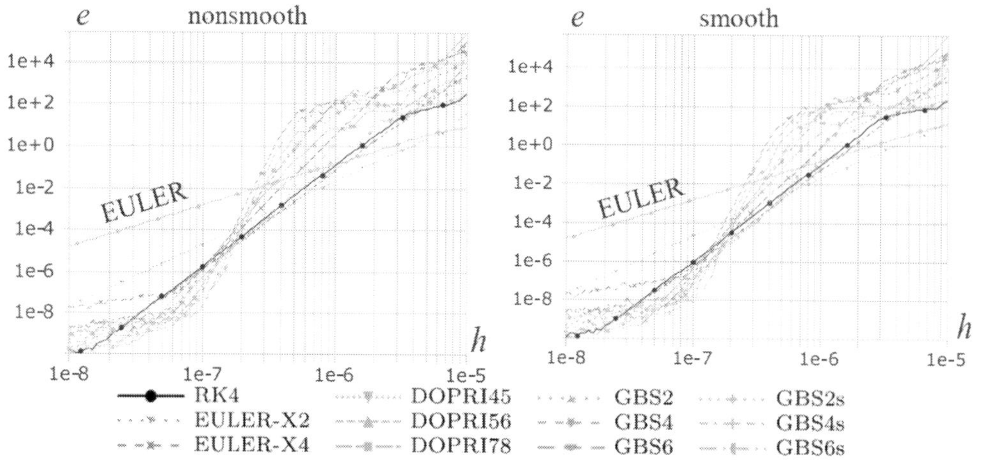

Figure 7. Step local error for explicit methods.

To illustrate the impact of the nonsmoothness of friction law on the accuracy of numerical results, we included numerical results for two modifications of the model, differing only by the friction law (nonsmooth and smoothed, see Fig. 4, left and right respectively).

3.3 Explicit methods

Explicit methods covered in this subsection are the following classical ones.

- Three embedded Dormand – Prince schemes with step size control [3]. The step size control was disabled in test simulations. An embedded scheme provides two solutions of different orders of accuracy at each step, which can be used to control the step size; those orders are encoded in the name of the scheme. The three schemes are DOPRI45 (orders 4, 5), DOPRI56 (orders 5, 6), and DOPRI78 (orders 7,8).
- Gragg – Bulirsch – Stoer method with (GBS p s) or without (GBS p) smoothing step [3]. It is an extrapolation method with the symmetric Gragg's scheme used as the reference scheme. We tried this method with a fixed extrapolation order p (2, 4, 6) and the harmonic step size sequence.
- Extrapolated explicit Euler scheme, with p extrapolation stages and the harmonic step size sequence (referred to as EULER-X p below).

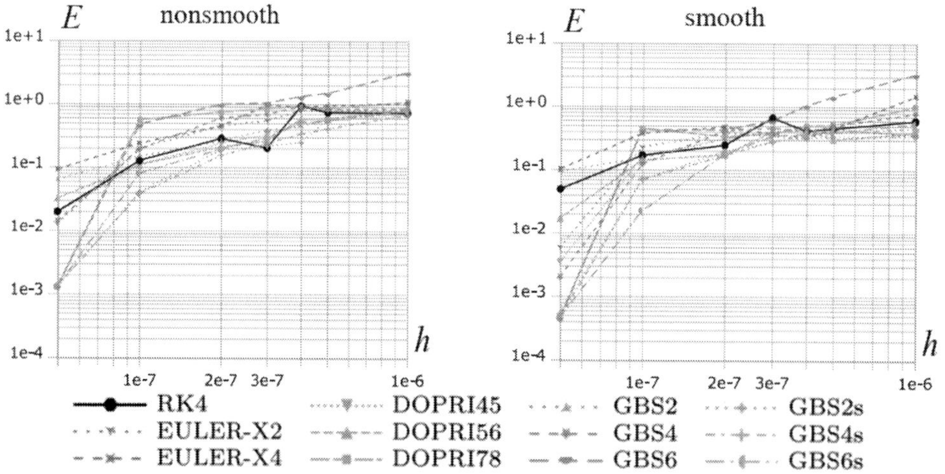

Figure 8. Global error for sample curve, explicit methods.

The step local error test (Figure 7) shows that the local error is generally less for smooth friction law; further data processing also indicates that the local error behaves according to scheme order only in a limited step size ranges, different for different schemes; some schemes (DOPRI45, DOPRI78, GBS4, GBS6) do not show the expected behavior at all, although they do so in tests with simple ODEs.

Global error in the dynamics test (Figure 8) confirms that all explicit schemes considered have severe step size limitation that is about 10^{-7} for nonsmooth friction law and schemes GBS2, DOPRI56, and is less for other schemes; for smooth friction law, the limit is higher yet it is less than $5\cdot 10^{-7}$. We can also conclude that low order schemes (2–4) are preferable in model with both smooth and nonsmooth friction low; although some higher order schemes (e.g. GBS6s) give less error in model with smooth friction law, they are not an appropriate choice due to their complexity.

3.4 Linearly implicit methods

There was a hope that a W-method [5] is capable of producing acceptable numerical solution at steps much greater than 10^{-7}, because those methods generally have better stability properties than explicit ones. However, in our case all W-methods tested failed for some reason, though they worked good in tests with simple ODEs.

The schemes considered in this subsection are SW24-d [5] (where d is a parameter) and the W1 method extrapolated according to the Richardson's procedure [3]. The W1 scheme is as follows:

$$x_{k+1} = x_k + hF(t_k, x_k) + hdA(x_{k+1} - x_k), \qquad (4)$$

where x is the numerical solution vector, the subscript k denotes the step number, h is the step size, t is the time, F is the ODE right-hand side vector, d is a parameter (usually between 0 and 1), and A is a matrix approximating the ODE system Jacobian DF/Dx. W-methods are attractive compared to Rosenbrock methods [6] due to the ability to keep A constant during many time steps, thus eliminating the necessity to compute it and factorize the matrix $I - hdA$ at each time step. Schemes resulting from p extrapolation stages of W1 are further referred to as W1-Xp-d.

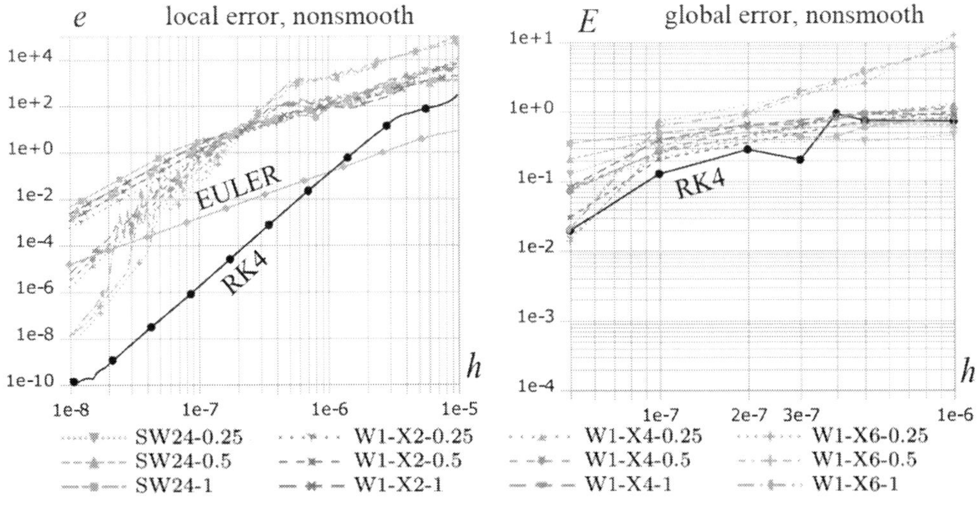

Figure 9. Local step error and global error for sample curve, linearly implicit methods compared to RK4 and explicit Euler methods.

Figure 9 (left) shows that all schemes tested have much greater local step error than explicit schemes. The expected order of schemes is observed at step sizes less than 10^{-7} ; the higher the order, the narrower the range in which scheme order is obeyed. Figure 9 (right) shows that all W-method schemes produce inacceptable solution ($E > 0.05$) even at step 10^{-7} . We have to conclude that they didn't work in our case.

3.5 Trapezoidal Rule Method

Among many implicit methods, we chose the trapezoidal rule (a 2-nd order scheme), further abbreviated as TRPZ:

$$x_{k+1} = x_k + \frac{h}{2}[F(t_k, x_k) + F(t_k + h, x_{k+1})], \qquad (5)$$

Figure 10 shows the step local error for the trapezoidal rule. Notice that it is less than for any other scheme tested at steps greater than $4 \cdot 10^{-7}$.

Sample curves obtained at step size $2 \cdot 10^{-6}$ practically coincide with reference curves; global error E is $1.4 \cdot 10^{-3}$ for nonsmooth friction law and $5.6 \cdot 10^{-4}$ for smooth friction law. It is possible to use larger step sizes, but only with step size control because the Newton's method used at a time step may fail to converge.

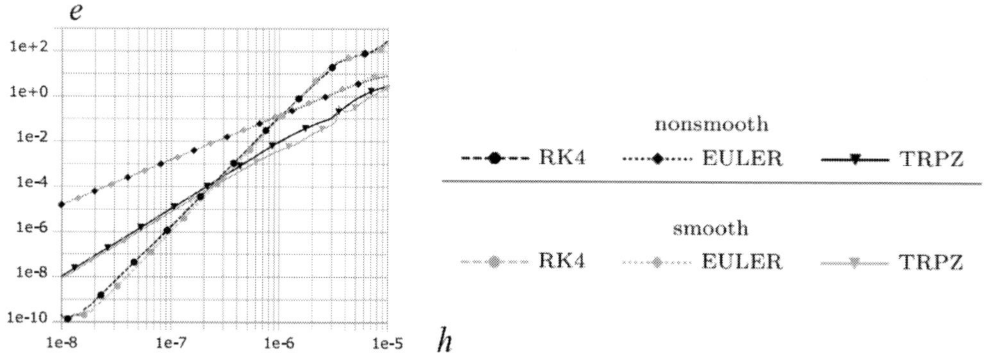

Figure 10. Step local error for trapezoidal rule, compared to RK4 and explicit Euler methods.

Notice that, despite the large step size in the trapezoidal rule method, it does not currently run faster than RK4. The reasons are the necessity to solve a system of nonlinear algebraic equations at each step using an iterative Newton-like method, and the need to compute the Jacobian matrix. We omit details here, but in short, the number of Newton's iterations is low (2–3) when the Jacobian matrix is recomputed at each iteration, and is significantly higher (10–20) in cases with approximated Jacobian matrix (e.g., using an update formula similar to the Broyden's one [7]).

3.6 Stabilized explicit method

Having investigated the stiffness properties of the ODE system, we decided to consider so called stabilized explicit, or Chebyshev – Runge – Kutta [8, ch. IV.2], numerical integration methods. Among those we picked the one called DUMKA3 [9]. The choice of that particular method was based on public availability of solver implementation code in C programming language.

A stabilized explicit scheme has stability region, defined by the condition $|R_s(h\lambda)| \le 1$, extended into real negative direction of complex plane $h\lambda$. The function R_s is a polynomial of degree s, called the *stability polynomial*.

The DUMKA3 solver actually implements a family of s-stage Runge–Kutta schemes, each of which realizes stability polynomial of degree s varying from 3 up to 324. The solver implements automatic step size control, based on step local error estimation, and polynomial degree control, based on the estimation of ODE right hand side Jacobian matrix spectral radius. Preliminary tests have shown that solver performance with both control options enabled is far from optimal in our system. Besides, numerical estimation of Jacobian spectral radius don't work well due to discontinuities of the ODE right hand side in the case of nonsmooth friction law, resulting sometimes in too large values. We disabled both control options. The motivation was to obtain best performance at fixed step for each fixed polynomial degree. Giving each polynomial an index k from 0 to 13 (DUMKA3 implements 14 polynomials), we denote corresponding schemes by suffixes -Pk. In particular, we tested degrees $s=21$ ($k=4$), $s=27$ ($k=5$), $s=36$ ($k=6$), $s=48$ ($k=7$), $s=63$ ($k=8$), $s=81$ ($k=9$). Polynomials $k \le 4$ and $k \ge 9$ have shown poor performance: in the first case the stability region is too small in the real negative direction, and in the second case it is too small in the imaginary direction.

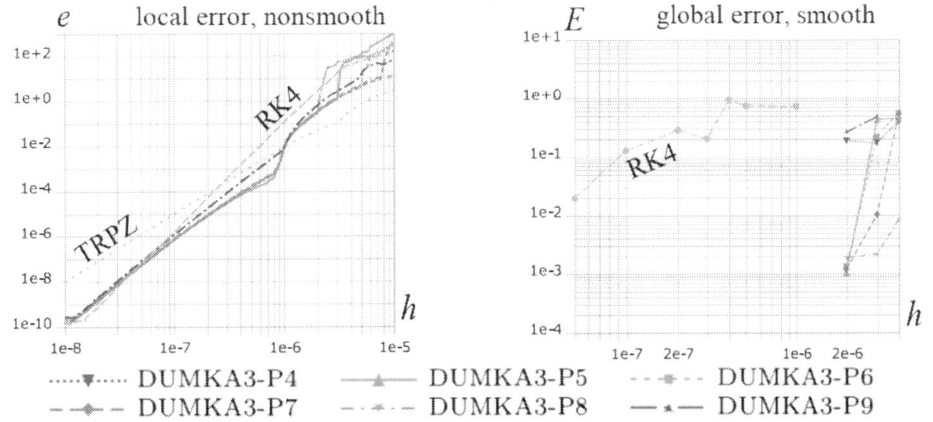

Figure 11. Local step error and global error for sample curve for DUMKA3, compared to RK4 and explicit Euler methods.

Figure 11 (left) shows the dependency of step local error norm on the step size. DUMKA3 results are compared against RK4 and the trapezoidal rule; the latter one is known (see sec. 3.5) to give sufficiently accurate solution at $h = 2\cdot 10^{-6}$ s. It can be shown that the slope for each curve at steps below 10^{-6} corresponds to the order of the scheme (3 for DUMKA3, 4 for RK4, and 2 for TRPZ). Notice also that at steps above 10^{-6} local error for all DUMKA schemes rises sharply at some point; additional error jumps can be seen at step 10^{-6} for nonsmooth friction law. At large step sizes, local error for DUMKA schemes is approximately the same as for the trapezoidal rule, in the case of smoothed friction law; for nonsmooth fricion law, the trapezoidal rule gives smaller error.

Figure 11 (right) shows the global error for sample curve. It follows from the figure that schemes DUMKA3-P5 – DUMKA3-P8 give sufficiently accurate solution at step $h = 2\cdot 10^{-6}$, and at step $h = 4\cdot 10^{-6}$ only the scheme DUMKA3-P8 does so.

Table 1. Performance of DUMKA3 schemes compared against RK4.

scheme	h, s	n_{RHS}	speedup against RK4
RK4	$5 \cdot 10^{-8}$	400824	1
DUMKA-P5	$2 \cdot 10^{-6}$	75817	5.9
DUMKA-P7	$3 \cdot 10^{-6}$	95425	4.7
DUMKA-P8	$4 \cdot 10^{-6}$	104821	4.4

Comparing simulation times, we can conclude that the DUMKA3 solver can perform simulations several times faster than RK4, which is summarized in Table 1. Notice that the value n_{RHS} in the table is the total number of ODE right hand side evaluations in the test simulation (the one used to obtain the sample curve).

4 Conclusions and Future Work

This paper represents the results of an investigation of application of different numerical integration methods to the ODEs of CVT dynamics model, in a hope to find a potentially faster method. The investigation has shown that traditional explicit numerical integration schemes and W-methods don't work in our case. Implicit methods give good results; however, to make those methods run faster than RK4, additional efforts are required: for example, ODE right-hand side Jacobian could be computed much faster but it requires tedious programming (the idea is to combine the approach presented in [10] with the decomposition of the ODE right-hand side into a sum and providing faster code for the Jacobian of contact forces). The attempt to use stabilized explicit Runge – Kutta solver, RK4, has proven to be successful in terms of performance. However, the original polynomial order control implemented in the solver doesn't work: it tends to increase polynomial order, but in that case Jacobian eigenvalues with maximum imaginary parts fall outside the stability region. This motivates us to consider other stabilized explicit solvers, first of all RKC and SERK2 [11], and probably others, constructed according to the approach presented in [12], because there is a way to construct a method with stability region that best fits the spectrum of ODE right hand side Jacobian.

References

1. N. Shabrov, Yu. Ispolov, S. Orlov, ZAMM **94(11)** (2014)
2. S. Orlov, A. Kuzin, N. Shabrov, CCIS **793** (2017)
3. E. Hairer, S. Nørsett, G. Wanner, *Solving Ordinary Differential Equations I: Nonstiff Problems* (Springer-Verlag, New York, 1993)
4. K. Johnson, *Contact mechanics* (Cambridge University Press, Cambridge, 1987)
5. T. Steihaug, A. Wolfbrandt, Math. Comp. **33(146)** (1979)
6. H. Rosenbrock, Comput. J. **5** (1963)
7. C. Broyden, Math Comp. **19** (1965)
8. E. Hairer, G. Wanner, *Solving Ordinary Differential Equations II: Stiff and Differential-Algebraic Problems* (Springer-Verlag, Berlin Heidelberg, 1996)
9. Medovikov, BIT Numerical Mathematics **38(2)** (1998)
10. T. Ypma, J. Comput. Appl. Math., **18(1)** (1987)
11. J. Martín-Vaquero, B. Janssen, Comput. Phys. Commun. **180(10)** (2009)
12. M. Torrilhon, R. Jeltsch, Numerische Mathematik **106(2)** (2007)

Homeostatic approach to assessing digital manufacturing security[a]

Evgeny Pavlenko[1*] and *Dmitry* Zegzhda[1]

[1] Peter the Great Saint Petersburg Polytechnic University, Institute of Computer Science and Technology, 195251, Politechnicheskaya st., 29, Russian Federation

Abstract. This study suggests a new digital manufacturing security paradigm based on the bio-inspired homeostasis concept to provide structural and functional cyber resilience of digital manufacturing to external destructive actions. Digital manufacturing management state indices, in particular, cyber resilience indices, have been determined. Possible approaches to calculating indices of consistency of the information layer with the physical layer, self-adaptation capability, self-similarity of performance parameters and homeostatic capability have been formulated. The analysis of the suggested approach to ensuring cyber resilience of digital manufacturing has been carried out using the software-configurable network technology. The experimental results have demonstrated the effectiveness of the suggested approach. The developed homeostatic approach lays the groundwork for building a proactive security strategy due to development of predictive methods of processing the system status monitoring results.

1 Introduction

The analysis of modern science and technology development tendencies demonstrates that world industry is currently on the threshold of the forth technological revolution which means the adoption of completely automated digital manufacturing controlled by intelligent systems on a real-time basis, constantly interacting with the external environment, implying the prospect of uniting into a global industrial network of things and services.

Digitalization of life-building branches of activity has triggered appearance of a new type of entities and systems – cyber-physical entities and systems associated with manufacturing processes and having an informational control circuit constructed using sophisticated computer technologies.

Cyber-physical systems (CPS) are multi-component distributed systems which function independently of human being and monitor areas which are vital for the population. Such systems combine information modules with physical process implementation modules [1]. The CPS includes a set of interrelated physical components implementing a manufacturing process; information components controlling the process at different layers of automation;

[a] The work was funded by the Russian Federation Presidential grants for support of leading scientific schools (NSh-2992.2018.9), Contract No. 14.Y31.18.2992-NSh. January 17, 2018

* Corresponding author: pavlenko@ibks.spbstu.ru

and a communication environment providing information exchange within the system and with the external environment and transmitting control commands to actuating mechanisms.

Tight integration of the CPS with manufacturing processes associated with industrial manufacturing and management of a large number of complex objects capable of changing their behavior resulted in the necessity of modifying the existing security paradigm for digital manufacturing. This is due to the fact that direct transfer of information security concepts, such as confidentiality, availability and integrity, is impossible in digital manufacturing because in contrast to informational processes, physical processes are irreversible and cannot be monitored and control at the same layer as informational processes [2]. Therewith, the concept of availability as sustainability of manufacturing processes comes into the forefront.

With regard to a CPS for digital manufacturing, control over the system is the main target of an intruder rather than obtaining data on the operations being carried out. A digital manufacturing security paradigm should be based on new security principles which have to be invariant to attack mechanisms because the components of digital manufacturing are heterogeneous, digital manufacturing standardization is impossible in the foreseeable future and technologies are being actively developed and modified.

After being introduced into manufacturing, computer technologies have added one more requirement to digital manufacturing system security that is system control resilience to targeted external actions. Probability of such adverse actions is an inherent peculiarity of the modern architectural and algorithmic platform of computer systems which is proved by current practice. In general, adverse actions may occur on both the information layer and the physical layer. A system's ability to function within the pre-determined input and output characteristics despite of targeted external information actions is defined as cyber resilience [2].

2 Researches on CPS sustainability and reliability control

A large number of researches on sustainability and reliability control of digital manufacturing and CPS is known.

The publication [3] addresses the problem of assessing electric network intelligent system efficiency and reliability in case of cascade failure. To solve the problem, the authors calculate stability (sustainability) of the network at different load levels based on the estimated length of the transient state graph.

This approach is oriented on high-voltage networks; equipment reliability and uncertainty of external disturbances affecting system performance are not taken into account. The said approach cannot be applied to assessing resilience and stability of cyber-physical systems because a large number of uncertain external disturbances are characteristic of cyber-physical systems. Moreover, the structure of an electric network is static, and that cannot be applied to most cyber-physical systems a priori.

The research paper [4] is focused on maintaining stability of cyber-physical systems, in particular, maintaining stability of both the information component (computer network) and the physical component at the same time. The mathematical apparatus used in the research is represented by planning invariants and system physical state invariants which together allow maintaining system stability. The authors developed an adaptive algorithm to plan capacity migration between smart grid nodes.

Applying the approach requires complex mathematical models of a cyber-physical system to take into account, particularly, possible component dynamics and migration, that involves immense time expenditures and depends heavily on the type of a cyber-physical system and its operation conditions. The mathematical apparatus of invariants implies a long-term manual derivation of invariants and a vast object-oriented knowledge of the system. Moreover, invariants are obtained for particular expected physical relationships and they do not include implicit internal relations between system components. Thus, the said approach is not effective enough for controlling sustainability of cyber-physical systems.

The publication [5] introduces the concept of stability for determining reliability of cyber-physical systems. This approach is oriented on providing reliability of cyber-physical system and aimed at ensuring control stability. However, it is focused on controlling the physical component of cyber-physical systems only and does not consider the possibility of system security violation by information actions. Thus, the said approach cannot be applied to resist security threats to cyber-physical systems.

It may be concluded that researches on providing cyber resilience of digital manufacturing are focused on ensuring proper CPS performance only, but the problem of information component security assurance and integration is not addressed.

3 Researches on developing approaches to digital manufacturing self-regulation and self-adaptation

The homeostatic approach to assuring CPS security consists in self-adaptation of the system when destructive actions occur.

The study [6] suggests an approach to adaptation of complex systems at the architectural level based on formal determination of limitations of the system architecture, architecture elements and supported adaptation operations.

Firstly, the said approach requires preliminary time-consuming work on preparing formal description of the system which is not always possible for large-scale cyber-physical systems. Secondly, it is aimed at determining such adaptation strategies which would transfer the system from an invalid state to a state meeting the architectural requirements.

Hence, the said approach cannot be applied to cyber-physical systems, because it considers structural and functional system properties, but does not take into account the system's target function which is a crucial factor for cyber-physical systems.

The research [7] is focused on performance check of self-adaptive systems and aimed at solving the problem of system efficiency and reliability assurance in case of self-adaptation. The said approach includes a model check of system behavior at the design stage, model-based testing at the design stage and post-adaptation diagnostics during operation.

However, it cannot solve the problem of self-adaptation assurance in cyber-physical systems. The said approach requires development of a formal model which is a time-consuming task in case of large-scale cyber-physical systems. In addition, a formal model may be used only to describe the target function of the system and limitations on operations implemented in the system.

Moreover, adaptation correctness diagnostics during operation of a cyber-physical system involves a considerable hazard if errors occur during adaptation. Incorrect functioning of cyber-physical systems may cause a significant financial loss and even harm to human health and environment.

Therefore, the said approach is not focused on security, but it is aimed at controlling the system performance and it does not solve the problem of self-adaptation of cyber-physical systems.

The research [8] suggests a model of an adaptive system as a multi-agent structure where the main role belongs to agents, i.e. autonomous entities located in the environment.

The said research is aimed at formulation of an approach to developing self-adaptive systems with well-defined and undefined requirements to self-adaptation.

The approach cannot be applied to cyber-physical systems because it does not consider that adaptation is necessary for not only the structure, but the content as well. Moreover, development of agents, effective sharing of tasks and functions between them and their integration into the system are very time-consuming and system-specific tasks.

However, self-adaptation must ensure correctness of both performance and the control data flow. The majority of researches associated with assurance of self-regulation and self-adaptation of digital manufacturing are aimed at maintaining system performance ability, and the information component is ignored.

4 Researches on homeostasis in digital manufacturing

The existing studies suggesting application of the concept of homeostasis to technical systems are connected to the theory of control of complex systems.

The research paper [9] considers homeostasis as an ability of cyber-physical systems to self-adapt, i.e. maintain their operational condition in case of any disruptions. The suggested approach is aimed at assuring CPS sustainability by modifying the system's architecture based on pre-defined self-adaptation strategies. The approach is initially oriented on assurance of correct system operation rather than assurance of cyber security. However, it may be partially applied to building a new cyber security paradigm.

The research [10] further develops the study [9] and suggests a formal model to ensure reliable operation of the system by simultaneous control of system requirements, possible system configurations and the state of the environment. The suggested model and a self-adaptation method to implement it allow for modifications in the system architecture during manufacturing processes.

It should be noted that all researches on CPS self-adaptation are oriented on maintaining correct CPS performance and ignore the information component that is why the homeostatic approach has never been applied to cyber security issues.

However, there are studies which include attempts to formulate key features of CPS control systems to response to attacks. In the research paper [11], redundancy is identified as a CPS characteristic to response to denial-of-service attacks. The above mentioned approach may be used for the purpose of implementation of the homeostatic approach to assure CPS security.

The prospects of applying the homeostatic approach suggested herein are substantiated by the fact that it will simultaneously assure both information security and functional/process security consisting in maintaining correct CPS performance in case of destructive actions.

5 Self-similarity as a criterion of digital manufacturing sustainability

Sustainability of a cyber-physical system may be identified by assessing the capability of the system to stay in a stable state [2], and such assessment must be carried out for the entire system, not just for its separate elements. In this case, cyber-physical system sustainability indices are applied as set forth in [12]. Self-similarity of a system is determined using the fractal method based on the Hurst coefficient (1) and the Fano factor (2).

$$H = 1 - \frac{\beta}{2} \tag{1}$$

$$\Phi(n) = \frac{\delta^2(n)}{m(n)} \tag{2}$$

Self-similarity is applicable to assessing sustainability of cyber-physical systems which enable functioning of digital manufacturing due to the fact that the key feature of such cyber-physical systems is periodicity of manufacturing processes to be carried out. Periodicity is explained by a target function of each cyber-physical manufacturing system which is implemented when digital manufacturing components implement a finite set of functions transferring the digital manufacturing into different states, the aggregate of which is finite and, possibly, countable.

Periodicity of manufacturing processes implemented by transferring the control flow of commands and messages between digital manufacturing components suggests stationarity of manufacturing processes. According to [13], this means that statistical properties of a process do not change in time, so its characteristics are invariant with respect to time shifts. Invariance of characteristics allows suggesting that the manufacturing process under study have a property of fractality or self-similarity.

Assessment of self-similarity of digital manufacturing is so important because it is self-similarity which is able to comprehensively characterize manufacturing performance both on the layer of information flows and at the physical layer where its components function. Any cyber security violation aimed at illegitimate modification of control data flow, disruption of communication channels between digital manufacturing components, or its particular components will be reflected in the data flow because digital manufacturing is managed by the information component. Therefore, cyber threats may be effectively monitored due to assessment of self-similarity of time series characterizing the control data flow during the manufacturing process.

6 Concept of homeostatic control and self-similarity assessment of digital manufacturing

Due to the need to simultaneously assure both information and process security, a common mechanism has to be developed to control and maintain cyber resilience of the entire digital manufacturing; such cyber resilience meaning resilience to circulating information and its functioning. Hence, it is necessary to consider the capability of digital manufacturing to self-adaptation.

The ability of a system to self-adaptation is defined by cross-correlational relationships within the system which are defined as (3),

$$r(t,\tau) = E[c_n^T(t+\tau)X(t)] \tag{3}$$

the system's controllability (4),

$$CT_p(t) = \begin{cases} \dfrac{\sum\limits_{i=1}^{N} path\_num\_t_i}{\sum\limits_{i=1}^{N} path\_num_i}, \text{если} \sum\limits_{i=1}^{N} path\_num_i > 0 \\ 0, \text{если} \sum\limits_{i=1}^{N} path\_num_i = 0 \end{cases} \tag{4}$$

constancy of performance (5)

$$Op = \frac{\partial \operatorname{Re} s_{sp}}{\partial t} \tag{5}$$

and the degree of scalability of the system (6).

$$S_c[k,n] = (\Delta CT(t), \Delta R_{\max}, \Delta O_p, \Delta T) \quad (6)$$

The use of sustainability and self-adaptation assessment in the context of CPS specifics results in a modification of the concept of digital manufacturing system security management. In view of the above mentioned features, we believe that arrangements for digital manufacturing security should be classified as dynamic systems, the security policy must provide for:

– maintenance of the manufacturing process according to the pre-defined dynamics in case of destructive actions;

– maintenance of correct addressing of the control data flow;

– ability to adapt digital manufacturing parameters and structure to response external and internal destructive actions and maintain sustainability of the manufacturing process;

– in prospect, in view of intellectualization of certain digital manufacturing components, maintenance of the ability to analyze the state of the environment and the digital manufacturing in order to decide on proactive adaptation of the digital manufacturing to external attacks by way of anticipation and reasoning ability when choosing an adaptation strategy.

The concept of homeostatic control better corresponds to the above listed requirements to ensure cyber resilience. Homeostatic control is a bio-inspired concept of managing intelligent technical systems and consists of provision of a relational balance of the system maintained by self-regulation mechanisms. Homeostasis implies a combination of mechanisms which ensure constancy of the system's internal environment and its structural and functional resilience to external destructive actions [12].

By analogy with biological systems, three homeostasis layers are defined in digital manufacturing:

1. Homeostasis at the layer of parametric control of manufacturing processes.
2. Homeostasis at the layer of control of the relationships between digital manufacturing components.
3. Architectural homeostasis to completely readjust digital manufacturing: control parameters and relationships between components.

A distinctive feature of the homeostatic approach to security management is that digital manufacturing is controlled by two independent systems having opposite purposes, thus, a homeostat is a mechanism of contradiction management. As any conflict, such contradiction is twofold: on the one hand, it is a threat of loss of stability, on the other hand, in case of self-regulation; it is a tool to develop behavior strategies for self-improvement of the system by modifying its structure. The range of permissible structural variations within which the system remains tolerant to external actions includes space for permissible strategies of managerial decisions to maintain dynamic sustainability of the entire system. To implement homeostatic control, a system must be redundant to some extent and have a well-developed structure defining the limits within which structural variations in the system are permissible without the permissible loss of functionality. The specific feature of the homeostatic approach is impossibility to control the external circuit (an intruder) while the intruder may control digital manufacturing due to errors in the digital manufacturing security subsystem. Thus, the homeostatic paradigm in assuring security differs from the adaptive strategy by the ability to solve the problems of Pareto optimization i.e. find areas of best possible solutions to maintain the criteria of security and functionality within pre-defined limits.

7 Approaches to assessing digital manufacturing sustainability

When developing approaches to assessing self-similarity and sustainability, the type of digital manufacturing must be take into consideration since types of digital manufacturing vary much and, consequently, have key differences with regard to functioning organization.

The source [12] includes the CPS systematization which allows distinguishing five main types of digital manufacturing:

1. The Internet of Things is a network of physical entities united by embedded technologies to communicate, response and interact within themselves and with the external environment, independently of humans
2. Multi-agent systems (MAS) are systems built by several interacting intelligent agents and the industrial Internet of Things
3. Computer-aided manufacturing (CAM)
4. Moving object systems (VANET – Vehicular Ad Hoc Networks, FANET – Flying Ad Hoc Networks)
5. Robot intelligent systems.

For the above listed types of digital manufacturing, the source [14] also suggests cyber resilience assessment indices which characterize consistency of the information layer with the physical one, self-adaptation capability, self-similarity of performance parameters, and homeostatic capability.

The information-and-physical-layer consistency index is suitable for all types of digital manufacturing and can be calculated using the coefficient of concordance in dynamics (7).

$$k_S = \frac{\sum_i \bar{\Delta}^i y \bar{\Delta}^i x}{\sqrt{\sum_i (\bar{\Delta}^i y)^2 \sum_i (\bar{\Delta}^i x)^2}} \quad (7)$$

The self-similarity index of digital manufacturing CPS functional parameters may also be applied to all types of digital manufacturing. It is calculated based on the Hurst coefficient (1) and the Fano factor (2).

The homeostatic capability index of the system for the simplest digital manufacturing types based on the Internet of Things concept can be calculated using the method of principal components and estimation of eigen values, the matrix of functional indices of the system (8).

$$a_k = \arg\min_{\|a_k\|=1} \left(\sum_{i=1}^{m} \|x_i - a_k(a_k, x_i)\|^2 \right) \quad (8)$$

For more complex digital manufacturing systems, such as MAC and SCADA, the homeostatic capability index may be calculated using the assessment of adjacency matrix and reachability matrix of a graph representation of the given digital manufacturing system (9).

$$E^* = E \vee E^2 \vee ... \vee E^n = (e_{ij}^*)_{n \times n} = (e_{ij} \vee e_{ij}^2 \vee ... \vee e_{ij}^n) \quad (9)$$

For the most complex digital manufacturing systems, such as systems of unmanned vehicles and intelligent robots, the homeostatic capability index may be calculated using the method of calculation of an autocorrelation function (10).

$$K(\tau) = \mathrm{E}\{X(t) X^*(t - \tau)\} \quad (9)$$

8 Experimental studies

A series of experiments consisting of emulation of a destructive action have been carried out for the purpose of analyzing applicability of the suggested homeostatic approach to assuring cyber resilience by controlling a digital manufacturing systems based on the software-configurable network technology.

The SCN technology was chosen as a technology for organizing network interactions because it allows structural reconfiguration of a network in accordance with homeostasis mechanisms. The SCN technology provides for [15]:

1) separation of the network infrastructure control layer from the data communication layer using a dedicated software which provides communication between a network device and a control system (PCS controller) operating on a dedicated computer;

2) transition from controlling separate units of network equipment to configuring the entire network as a whole, which enables to distribute the load in the network and ensure network traffic with required parameters.

A SCN uses a common, unified, supplier-independent interface between the control layer and the data communication layer; logically centralized network control by a controller with an installed network operating system and network applications and by virtualization of physical resources of the network. The architecture [15] includes an infrastructure layer (in fact, a set of network devices), a control layer (system software) and a network application layers which actually control network operation.

The following control parameters are used:

- network capacity
- the number of network ports
- packet capacity
- the number of lost packets
- round-trip delay
- device recovery time after restart

For the purpose of security management, a mechanism of homeostasis was initiated (availability of more than one SCN controllers in the system meant that the distributed system is capable of homeostasis).

Three different attacks on the software-configurable network have been emulated during the experimental study of the possibility to use the suggested homeostatic control technology:

- a DoS attack aimed at disabling one of the network nodes;
- a substitution attack aimed at substitution of operating parameters of one of the network infrastructure components;
- an attack aimed at disruption of the communication channel between the server and the OpenFlow switch.

The mathematical apparatus of the method of principal components was used to assess cyber resilience, since, due to a strong correlation relationship of parameters; the state of a CPS may be described by one variable, i.e. the first principal component in the following form (10),

$$PC_1(X) = \alpha_i X \tag{10}$$

where α_i are weighing coefficients which are components of the respective eigen vector of the covariance matrix of the CPS control parameters. In addition, the following condition must be met (11),

$$\lambda_1 \geq 0{,}9 \sum_{i=2}^{n} \lambda_i \tag{11}$$

which represents the condition of considering the first principal component of 90% parameter spread of the entire system. Thus, cyber resilience is assessed by meeting the following condition (12).

$$PC_1(X) \in W \,\&\, \lambda_1 \geq 0,9 \sum_{i=2}^{P} \lambda_i \tag{12}$$

The results of the experiments shown in Fig. 1 demonstrate that the condition of sustainability is not met during attacks on digital manufacturing systems aimed at substitution of control parameters. The area of sustainability during attacks on the digital manufacturing systems is shown by a dashed line.

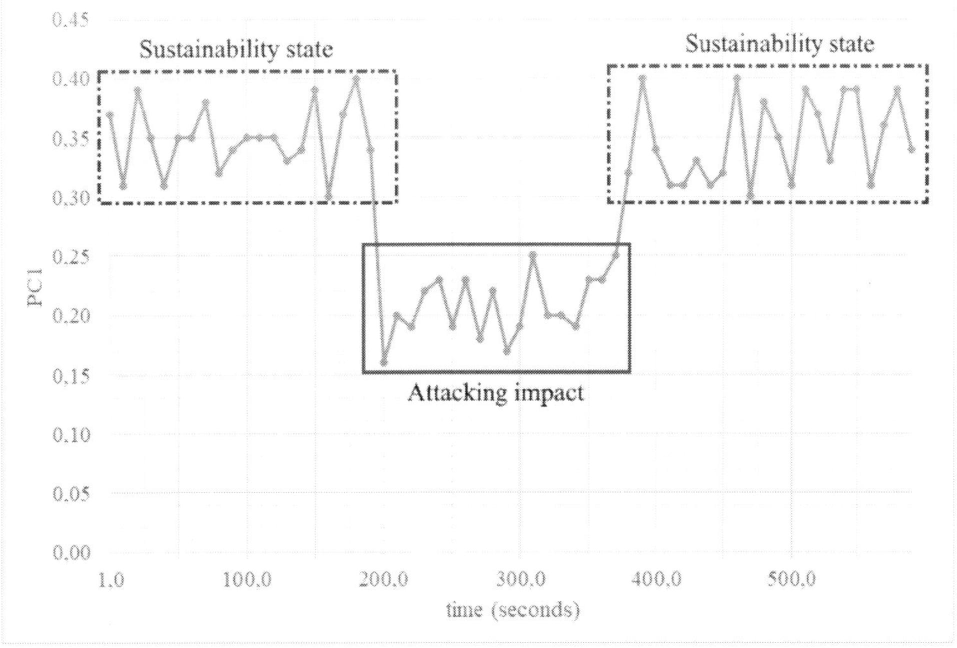

Fig. 1. Principal component value.

We can conclude that digital manufacturing security may be expressed in terms of cyber resilience. Cyber resilience of digital manufacturing should be understood as a capability to maintain self-similarity of the system in case of external actions. The simplest method to develop a control, that is selecting one of the pre-defined homeostatic scenarios, has been implemented as a part of the experiments:

– for the DOS attack, the volume of traffic to the network node under attack was limited by reconfiguration of the OpenFlow switch;

– for the substitution of operating parameters of one of the network infrastructure components, the OpenFlow switch which made the substitution was disconnected and the data communication routes in the network were changed;

– for disruption of the communication channel between the server and the OpenFlow switch, the data communication routes were also changed and a new route was implemented for the given server.

9 Conclusion

The study suggests a new digital manufacturing security paradigm based on the bio-inspired homeostasis concept to provide structural and functional cyber resilience of digital manufacturing to external destructive actions.

The possibility to apply the concept of homeostasis to digital manufacturing systems has been demonstrated; digital manufacturing control state indices, in particular cyber resilience indices, have been identified. Possible approaches to calculating indices of consistency of the information layer with the physical layer, self-adaptation capability, self-similarity of performance parameters and homeostatic capability have been formulated.

The suggested approach is invariant to attacks on digital manufacturing and suitable for different digital manufacturing systems; moreover, the suggested approach solves all security issues for the new-type systems: attack detection, control, interaction optimization, incident management etc. The developed approach combines information security and physical sustainability and gives an opportunity to automate the synthesis of homeostatically stable structures for digital manufacturing systems of any complexity.

The analysis of homeostatic approach applicability to assurance cyber resilience of digital manufacturing have been carried out using the software-configurable network technology which allows to effectively simulate the digital manufacturing control process due to flexible modifications to its structure.

Thus, the suggested homeostatic security control technology enables the implementation of multi-layer control of digital manufacturing by combining distributed and centralized hierarchical control which increases the number of control loops and expands the range of control factors (parameters and structural characteristics).

To assess the system security state, the approach suggests using universal indices which consider both information and functional components aimed at system self-similarity which is represented by the hierarchical set of criteria. System self-similarity allows maintaining the balance of external factor compensation which is the essence of homeostatic control.

The homeostatic approach lays the groundwork for building a predictive and proactive security strategy due to development of predictive methods of processing of the system status monitoring results.

References

1. R. Seiger, S. Huber, P. Heisig, U. Assmann, LNBIP, **248** (2016)
2. D. P.Zegzhda, Aut. Cont. and Comp. Scien., **50** (2016)
3. C. Liang, Z. Wu., Int. J. Electr. Pow. Ener. Syst., **33** (2011)
4. A. Choudhari, H. Ramaprasad, T. Paul, J. W. Kimball, M. Zawodniok, B. McMillin, S. Chellappan, COMPSAC (2013)
5. M. Rungger, P. Tabuada, IEEE Trans. on Aut. Con., **59** (2014)
6. K. M. Hansen, M. Ingstrup, SAC (2010)
7. D. Weyns, WODA, **24-29** (2012)
8. X. Mao, M. Dong, L. Liu, H. Wang, J. of Inform. Scien. and Eng., **30** (2014)
9. I. Gerostathopoulos, D. Skoda, F.Plasil, T.Bures, A.Knauss, ECSA (2016)
10. I. Gerostathopoulos, T. Bures, P. Hnetynka, J. Keznikl, M. Kit, F. Plasil and N. Plouzeau, The J. of Syst. and Soft., **122** (2016)
11. A. Cardenas, S. Amin, B. Sinopoli, A. Giani, A. Perrig, S. Sastry, Work. on fut. direct. in CPS sec. (2009)
12. D. P. Zegzhda, M. A. Poltavtseva, D. S. Lavrova, Aut. Cont. and Comp. Scien., **51** (2017)
13. D. S. Lavrova, Aut. Cont. and Comp. Scien., **50** (2016)

14. D. P. Zegzhda, E. Yu. Pavlenko, Aut. Cont. and Comp. Scien., **51** (2017)
15. M. O. Kalinin, E. Yu. Pavlenko, Aut. Cont. and Comp. Scien., **49** (2015)

Architecture of homeostatic security control for digital manufacture systems based on software-defined networks[a]

Evgeny Pavlenko[1*], and *Dmitry* Zegzhda[1]

[1] Peter the Great St. Petersburg Polytechnic University, Institute of Applied Mathematics and Mechanics, 195251, 29, Politechnicheskaya st., Russian Federation

Abstract. The authors have offered the homeostatic control system architecture for digital manufacture security based on the software-defined network technology.We have highlighted the development features of digital manufacture systems and defined the technology advantages of software- defined networks, which allow these networks to be successfully applied with flexible and adaptive topology for a highly efficient new generation of cyber-physical systems. We have also described the main operating principles of software-defined networks in digital manufacture systems. A description of homeostatic security control technology, which includes a combination of engines to provide stability of the system's internal environment and structural and functional resistance to external disturbances, is provided. We have proposed and described in detail the homeostatic security control system architecture including three generalized components: monitoring unit, decision-making unit, protection and control unit.

1 Introduction

Active development of information technologies made it possible to develop a new type of industrial systems. Unlike industrial systems that are available now and include separate components interacting with each other through special interfaces, digital interfaces provide throughout integration and uniform data formats at all process stages. For this purpose, data from all the digital manufacture system components is collected in one center, where they are systemized and processed using up-to-date methods Data Mining and transmitted in the form that is convenient for decision making process with artificial intelligence method. This approach makes it possible to significantly enhance the performance of industrial systems, the decision- making speed with automatic systems exceeds that of automated ones. Digital manufacture systems are based on cyber-physical systems, which are multi-component, distributed systems operating independently from people and monitoring areas that are critical and important to population. These systems combine information modules physical process implementation modules [1].

[a] The work was funded by the Russian Federation Presidential grants for support of leading scientific schools (NSh-2992.2018.9), Contract No. 14.Y31.18.2992-NSh. January 17, 2018
* Corresponding author: pavlenko@ibks.spbstu.ru

Digital manufacture systems are based on network interfacing technologies. Classic methods and network infrastructure and data stream control technologies, which are available in the computer networks now, cannot allow network interaction to develop in distributed digital manufacture systems. The development of such distributed systems has pushed for the need for flexible, reliable, scalable, well-controlled network backbones. A network interfacing system in large-scale digital manufacture systems cannot be set up by configuring each element separately and manually. A technology is needed to be developed that will allow controlling the network infrastructure as a single system. All the requirements for network interfacing systems are met by the software-defined network technology (SDN) in which the network infrastructure control level is separated from the data transmission level by automating the control functions and by transferring them into specialized software, which runs on a standalone computer [2].

In order to implement this idea open protocol OpenFlow is developed to control network equipment that is not designed for products of certain manufacturers of multi-protocol products. By using this protocol system administrators can set and monitor: who with whom, in what conditions, with what quality can interact within the network.

All the network equipment is combined under control of a SDN controller, which the network operating system is installed on: The network control system installed in OS provides the following functions:

– Network control access;
– Generation of data on status of network resources.
– Network infrastructure monitoring.

This technology makes it possible to implement strict data transmission rules within the network regardless of its topology as well as to provide intelligent response of the system to changes occurring within the network infrastructure.

Close integration of cyber-physical systems with manufacturing processes related to industrial manufacture and control of a great number of complex objects has brought up the requirement to change the existing security paradigm for digital manufacture. It is associated with the fact that direct transition of information security features such confidentiality, accessibility, integrity is impossible in digital manufacture because unlike information processes, physical processes are irreversible and it is impossible to implement the same monitoring and control level as for the information processes [3].

2 Software-defined network security control research

The topic of integrating the SDN technology with cyber-physical systems (in particular the Internet of Things systems) is widely covered in foreign publications. However, it should be noted that there are very few research papers dedicated to cyber-physical system security control based on SDN. The latest publications mainly focus on the integration process but not on the development of flexible and adaptive security control process by means of SDN engine.

In this paper [4] the authors offer a system architecture that is based on SDN controllers executing control over the infrastructure of various systems in the Internet of Things. We have also considered the issue of overriding a semantic break between the abstractions of high-level tasks and certain network devices and resources. A heuristic algorithm for planning streams for centralized coordination of resources, whose simulation has shown the best performance results in comparison with existing solutions. However, the offered infrastructure does not make the Internet of Things stable in relation to targeted destructive disturbances and requires more complex and reliable tools to be developed to ensure security.

In research [5] the authors offer architecture based on the software-defined network technologies taking into account the horizontal model of Internet of Things, whose aim is to provide the total infrastructure for a wide range of application and to support functional compatibility at various levels. The system architecture includes four levels: device level collecting data, interaction level containing SDN-gates and routers, control level containing SDN-controllers and mechanisms for service billing and metering and application level. The proposed solution makes it possible to support new services quickly as well as to use devices and data jointly by several different applications. A significant disadvantage of this architecture is no security mechanisms to protect the central SDN-controller, provide stable operation of the overall system and security of separate connected resources and information.

In paper [6] the UbiFlow system is presented, which controls flows and coordinates resources in the Internet of Things employing the SDN technology. The key feature of this UbiFlow system is that it divides the entire network into small clusters, which are controlled by SDN controllers. Devices of the Internet of Things located inside a cluster can be connected to another access point to make different requests providing fault-free operation and scaling. However, the proposed system does not make it possible to forecast further behavior of the system and does not provide for compensation and control engines for functional stability of the entire system.

Publication [7] presents the architecture of protected Internet of things including transmitted data confidentiality, identification and authentication control, key control and protected routing blocks based on SDN. This architecture makes authentication of heterogeneous devices possible, at the same time the SDN controllers as a third, confidential party and control routing between the Internet of Things devices. However, this paper does not cover the issue of fall-over protection, stable operation of the system and its adaptation to external disturbances.

Publication [8] offers the security control architecture for the Internet of Things network based on SDN. The main focus area is to provide authentication of the Internet of Things devices using a SDN-controller. Thus, the controller itself acts as an interlink providing data source authenticity. In case of malfunction, the border controller will perform the security controller's functions, however these complex cyber physical systems such as the Internet of Things need intelligent stability engines to be implemented, which would not only allow optimizing the operating scenarios and timely response in case of malfunction of critical system components but also support the internal environment state in case of targeted sustained attacks by implementing additional compensating actions.

3 Operating principle of software-defined networks in digital manufacture systems

The main idea of this SDN technology is to create a single general-purpose control engine for stream table regardless of a network device manufacturer. The OpenFlow protocol is an open protocol, which successfully implements software control of network stream table regardless of a switch or router, where it is implemented. With this OpenFlow protocol help the network administrator can classify traffic depending on the operating environment of network equipment and monitor network streams, packet forwarding routes Data plane in the SDN network equipment is defined by the stream table and appropriate action associated with every rule given in this table [2].

The network equipment supporting the OpenFlow protocol-based operation includes three main components:

– Network stream table with action rules associated with every record;

– Control channel, which provides safe connection of network device and SDN controller to transmit control commands and network packets via the OpenFlow protocols;

– OpenFlow protocol support components, which implements standard controller and network device interfacing mechanisms.

Network switches supporting the OpenFlow protocol-based operation forward packets between ports depending on those set by the network stream and rules table controller; in this situation, it is possible to isolate network traffic streams according to different information. Each record in the network stream table associates with action that should be applied to packets belonging to this stream [9]. The main actions are as follows:

– Forwarding of packets of this stream, further to a set port or to several ports, in other words, traffic switching;

– Encapsulation and transmission of packets belonging to this stream to SDN controller via safe channel This rule always applies to the first packet from a new stream, in order to allow the controller to make a decision on adding a new network stream on the device.

– Discarding of all packets belonging to this stream. This rule can be utilized to provide security, deter "service denial" attacks or filter network traffic.

Each record within the stream table has the following structure:

– Rule for selecting packets belonging to this stream.

– Actions determining how this stream elements should be processed;

– Statistics, which monitors the quantity of this stream packet bytes as well the time that has passed since the last pocket from this stream popped up in order to delete inactive streams.

The SDN controller's main functions are to add and delete records from the network stream tables on the device. The controller dynamically analyzes the entire network status, which allows the system administrator to assess the network infrastructure state at the present moment. Thus, the software-defined network technology meets all the necessary requirements for efficient control of network resources and data streams within digital infrastructure system, which enables to:

– Separate the network equipment control plane and data transmission place, which is traditionally done by the switches. Features related to data plane are still implemented on the switch but the controller is now responsible for making decisions on high-level routing in SDN, as a rule, it is based on a standard server, which makes it possible to increase the network infrastructure traffic capability as well as enhance the digital manufacture system flexibility;

– Create a convenient and flexible control system for the entire network but not for standalone devices. It is possible to monitor the entire network on the SDN central controller, which greatly enhances control, security assurance and other tasks. Because the SDN technology allows the administrator to clearly see all the traffic streams, it will be easier for him to notice intrusions and identify other problems;

– Afford an opportunity to implement a customized model for network traffic classification. The SDN technology makes it possible to assign priorities to different traffic types. For example, the controller can order the switches to implement rules for certain network traffic streams. In particular, these rules can ensure that data are forwarded via the fastest routes or via the routes with minimum quantity of transit points, in other words, enhance the data transmission system performance as well as make it possible to control data streams [10];

– Enhance network performance and provide quick recovery after errors. With switches no longer responsible for processing traffic associated with control plane, the SDN allows these devices to allocate all their resources to speed up traffic as well as develop network action plans to be followed during clogging or equipment problems [11];

– Provide efficient data transmission with due consideration of infrastructure and network purpose. The SDN technology makes it possible to create virtual network topologies, build up, when necessary, virtual or global networks without physical changing the main network. For this purpose, it is possible to develop centralized virtual control plane, providing network administration functions.

With the SDN technology applied the controller directly sets rules and settings for processing network traffic streams on equipment. Using a special language defines what action needs to be taken on an incoming packet: send a packet further, discard a packet or change some field in the header. Selecting any action depends on many parameters, such as: Presence of some specific bits in a network packet; priority to process network packets of this configuration; status of network equipment processing this packet. Thus, the SDN technology makes it possible to break down the entire network infrastructure into logical parts, in other words, it is possible to define potential routes for some network stream.

4 Homeostatic security control

The task of implementing digital manufacture in all the branches of activity is slowed down at the moment in connection with the fact that it is necessary to develop a strategy that will provide security and stable running of digital manufacture in conditions of targeted destructive disturbances. The relation of digital manufacture systems with critical branches of activities makes them an attractive target for intruders' attacks.

The specific features of digital manufacture systems shaping the developed protection strategy requirements are laid down in source [12]. These features presume that the digital manufacture security methodology should be based on the methods that support and ensure that the manufacturing process continues in preset dynamics in conditions of destructive disturbances, safeguard correct addressing of control commands and allow parameters and structure to adapt in order to counteract external and internal destructive disturbances and keep the manufacturing process stable. In this case, what significantly complicates this task is the fact that these digital manufacture systems are dynamic.

The authors of this article earlier offered a homeostatic control idea, which imply a combination of mechanisms providing stability of the system's internal environment and system's structural and functional resistance to external destructive disturbances. This control technology is implemented on the basis of homeostat – a self-organizing specialized subsystem aimed at supporting the system's key parameter values within a great variety of allowable values [13, 14].

In this situation, this subsystem shall always come up with a resolution to controversy of two control loops, one of which characterizes intruder's destructive actions during attacks on the system and the second one tries to make changes to the system in such a manner so that to eliminate destructive influence and maintain the system's target functions. On one side this contradiction provokes a threat of stability loss and on the other side self-regulation, which involves a mechanism for developing behavior strategies for system's self-improvement by changing its block diagram. The specific features of homeostatic security paradigm consist in resolving the Pareto-optimization task, in other words, finding the area of unimprovable solutions [15] ensuring that security and functionality are maintained within preset limits. This is connected with the fact that an intruder can control the cyber physical system components exploiting errors and weaknesses in the security subsystem and homeostat cannot control this intruder.

The range of allowable structural changes that allows the system to counteract external disturbances is a domain of permissible strategic managerial solutions in order to support the entire system's dynamic stability. The system that allows homeostatic control to occur should have a capability for structural changes; consequently it should have some "reserve" of key units that can be activated when the system gets closer to unstable state. In this cases, it is also required that the system would have a well-developed structure defining the limits, which allow the system's structure to vary without permissible loss of functional features.

5 Architecture of homeostatic security control system for SDN-based digital manufacture

With approaches and evaluations proposed [12] the authors offer a general architecture of security control unit for cyber-physical systems and digital manufacture as a whole, which is shown in Fig. 1. This security control unit includes three generalized components. Monitoring unit, decision-making unit and protection and control unit.

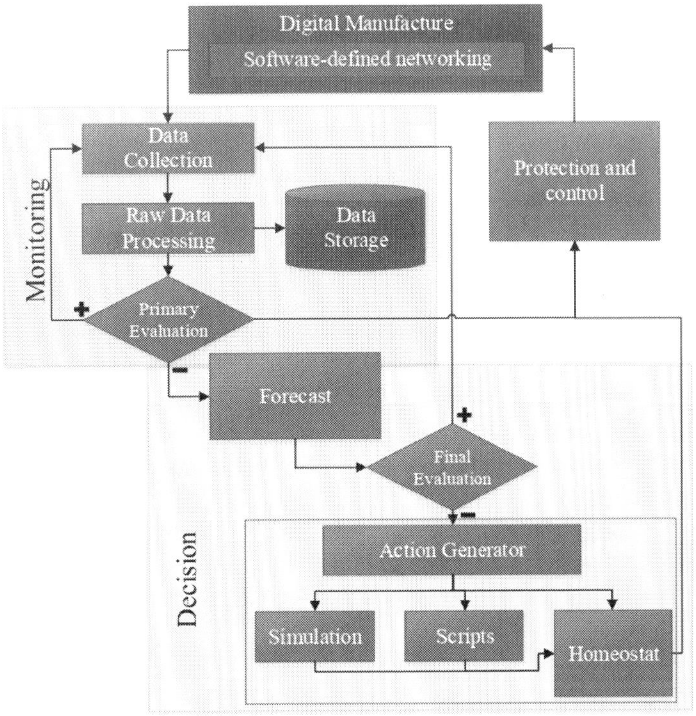

Fig. 1. General architecture of digital manufacture system control unit.

Monitoring of the digital manufacture system status and diagnostics of malfunctions and possible security problems are an integral part of general control process. The purpose of monitoring is to determine primary evaluation of the system's status to make a decision on required interference. This unit implements the following functions:

- Data collection from digital manufacture system components;
- Data processing to bring them to the same format and reduce their size;
- Data storage management;
- Data analysis to obtain primary evaluation.

In conditions of digital manufacture for the purpose of data collection it is necessary to implement MDC-systems (MachineDataCollection) making it possible to control operation of all the digital infrastructure objects: equipment, workstations, services etc.

To process digital manufacture system data it is expedient to use such BigData methods as aggregation, normalization and filtration. Aggregation in accordance with time parameter makes it possible to combine a great number of messages from one device into a single message, thus to reduce data size. The data aggregation diagram of digital manufacture systems in accordance with a time parameter is shown in Fig. 2.

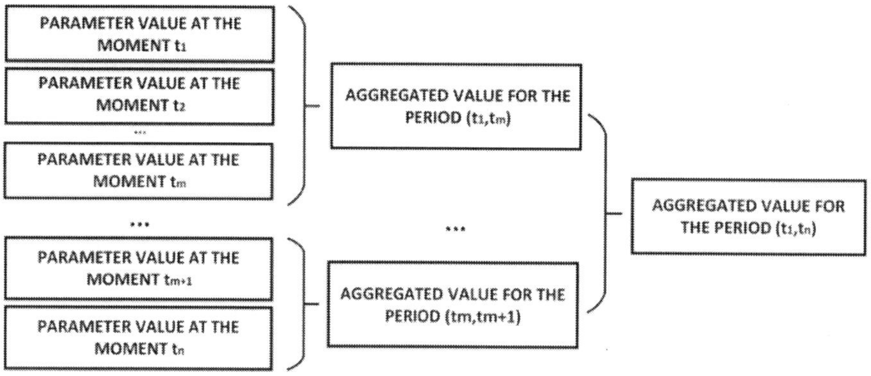

Fig. 2. Data aggregation diagram of digital manufacture system in accordance with time parameter.

In addition, it is possible to aggregate data coming from similar type devices implemented within the same digital manufacture subsystem. Data normalization will bring data to the same format, which may be relevant in conditions of no interaction standards for digital manufacture systems as well as in conditions of a great number of vendors supplying industrial automation devices (transmitters, actuators and controllers). Data filtration will make it possible to discard information, which is not needed by the analysis module for primary evaluation.

Data storage management is closely interrelated with the type of digital manufacture systems and prevailing data type circulating in them. In this case, it is necessary to determine what time periods should cover stored data in order to arrange the data storage and update process in an efficient manner.

The primary system status evaluation consists in calculating metrics and indicators characterizing the range that covers the monitored system parameter values. In accordance with obtained values the system makes a conclusion whether it is necessary to interfere in the system's operations in order to correct it.

On the border of the monitoring and decision-making unit there is a forecast component determining the system's behavior trends. A forecast model should also be selected taking into account the digital manufacture system features. For complex systems it is expedient to apply simulation modeling methods during forecasting and use the formal apparatus of mathematic logic, the theory of probabilities and statistic method, the image discrimination theory, the fuzzy-set theory, artificial neural and immune networks, research and information model methods. Following the forecast results the decision-making unit makes the final conclusion whether it is necessary to interfere in the production complex operation.

In case of unsatisfactory forecast the compensation action generation unit activates, which enables an action generator and action development components based on simulation and known response scenario database and homeostatis unit, which implements an integrated approach to control interference synthesis based on the abovementioned principles.

A certain number of response scenarios allowing the system to self-adapt in order to bring the system back to stable state and maintain its correct operation should be introduced in accordance with key features of each digital manufacture system.

Response scenarios can be divided into 3 groups:

– Scenariosresponsible for creation of new system objects or activation of already existing one, in this situation in order to implement this strategy it is expedient to provide for some redundancy within the system, this will enhance its stability;

– Scenarios being responsible for interaction of system object and their joint operation;

– Scenarios defining the entire system's behavior and setting connection between the digital manufacture system object and control action stream circulating between them.

In this case for some digital manufacture systems it is expedient to provide possible setting to return to previous stable state.

Introducing changes to the system's operating process should not be rapid, for this purpose the compensation action generation unit is provided with a simulation function that prepares a plan of operation changes on the already operating system.

5 Conclusion

In this article the authors have offered the general architecture of security control unit for cyber-physical systems and digital manufacture systems. This unit is a key module within digital manufacture systems, it is the unit that detects security problems (monitoring), predicts further system's behavior trends and makes a decision on whether it is necessary to introduce changes to current operation of the system, exercises compensating effects on the system using built-in response scenarios.

In order to implement control functions in accordance with the proposed architecture we have applied a technology of software-defined networks being a single general-purpose control engine for stream table regardless of a network device manufacturer. The SDN technology makes it possible to divide the network equipment control plane and data transmission plane, which significantly enhances the SDN-based digital manufacture system security level. Applying the SDN technology in complex, large-scale systems makes it possible to efficiently control all the network nodes and monitor traffic streams, which is achieved by transferring the main network control logic onto the SDN controllers. In this case, an important feature of the SDN technology is possible implementation of your own network traffic control model, therefore, for each digital manufacture system, it is possible to arrange network interaction in accordance with system's specific features.

Digital manufacture systems are mainly large-scale systems, therefore, an importation task in their operation is to provide high performance in conditions of intensive network interaction. Applying the SDN technology will make it possible to enhance the network communications performance; because the switch load will be reduced and consequently these network switches will be able to allocate all the resources to speed up the data exchange process.

References

1. R. Seiger, S. Huber, P. Heisig, U. Assmann, LNBIP, **248**, (2016)
2. M. O. Kalinin, E. Y. Pavlenko, Aut. Cont. and Comp. Scien., **49** (2015)
3. D. P. Zegzhda, Aut. Cont. and Comp.Scien., **50** (2016).
4. Z. Qin, G. Denker, C. Gianelli, P. Bellavista, N. Venkatasubramanian. NOMS (2014)
5. Y. Li, X. Su, J. Riekki, T. Kanter, R. Rahmani. IEEE Int. conf. on ICC (2016)
6. D. Wu, D. Arkhipov, E. Asmare, Z. Qin, J. McCann. INFOCOM (2015)
7. S. Chakrabarty, D. Engels. CCNC (2016)
8. K. Sahoo, B. Sahoo, A. Panda. MAMI (2015)
9. I. Z. Bholebawa, R. K. Jha, U. D. Dalal, Wir. Pers. Comm., **86** (2016)
10. B. Ng, M. Hayes, W. K. Seah, IFIP Net. Conf., IFIP, 1-9 (2015)
11. S. Kaur,J. Singh, AISC, **434** (2016)
12. D. P. Zegzhda, E. Yu. Pavlenko, Aut. Cont. and Comp. Scien., **51** (2017)
13. I. Gerostathopoulos, D. Skoda, F. Plasil, T. Bures, A. Knauss, ECSA (2016)
14. I. Gerostathopoulos, T. Bures, P. Hnetynka, J. Keznikl, M. Kit, F. Plasil and N. Plouzeau, The J. of Syst. and Soft., **122** (2016)
15. I. Kuwajima,Y. Nojima,H. Ishibuchi, Artif. LifeandRobot., **1**(2008)

Application of deep neural networks for security analysis of digital infrastructure components[a]

Alexander Pechenkin[1*], and *Roman* Demidov[1]

[1] Peter the Great St. Petersburg Polytechnic University, Institute of Computer Sciences and Technologies, Department of Computer Systems Information Security, 195251 Polytechnicheskaya st. 29, Russian Federation

Abstract. In this article the authors give a consideration to a problem of detecting errors and vulnerabilities in software components of different digital devices. The article shows an ever-increasing criticality of this problem in the course of time related to development of modern concepts the Industrial Internet and the Industry 4.0. It gives an overview of modern approaches to application of methods of computer-assisted learning and artificial intellect in the sphere of cyber security, problems and prospects of application thereof. A new approach is offered to searching software vulnerabilities on the basis of application of deep learning. The approach is based on building semantically significant vector representations of software code and multistage instructing the deep neural network on revealing hierarchical abstractions in computer code testifying to presence of vulnerabilities. The authors describe specific features of the goal of analyzing software code for presence of vulnerabilities and proceeding thereof it is offered to use a neural network with long short-term memory (LSTM). In order to solve a problem of the learning set, the authors offer to use learning with transfer in case of building vector representations of instructions. The article also provides results of experimental investigations on application of offered solutions.

1 Security of digital infrastructure components

1.1 Trends of developing information and computer sphere

The world industry is now on the verge of the fourth technical revolution [1] denoting a transition to automated digital production controlled by smart systems in real-time mode with permanent interaction with the environment extending beyond the boundaries of one

[a] This work is supported by the Russian Science Foundation under grant No.17-71-10065
* Corresponding author: pechenkin@ibks.spbstu.ru

enterprise with a perspective of being associated into a global industrial network of goods and services. The integration of a great number of fields of activity with information and network technologies has brought about a result that a possibility of data exchange and operations with the use of Internet became the most important need of the modern society. The ever-growing number of produced devices in all spheres of vital activities (medical services, power engineering, housing services and utilities, industry, etc.) are digital and get integrated into a unified digital information and computer environment. In this case, the solution of task of providing cyber security is essential for overcoming restrictions in the development and incorporation of up-to-date technologies. For instance, according to Peter Tren, Director General of RSA Security, the provision of cyber security is a top priority for building "smart cities" [2]. Moreover it is relevant in such spheres as unmanned means of transportation, where incorrect electronics operation can bring about catastrophic consequences [3].

The mobile technology and all-round automation have brought about an interesting result – a number of devices connected to Internet a way back has exceeded the number of people inhabiting the Earth. As of the present moment, more than 10 billion devices in the world already use the network protocols for connecting to the Internet, and it means, that the security thereof depends directly on timely detection of network vulnerabilities (vulnerabilities in implementations of network protocols), therefore, they help an intruder remotely perform an arbitrary code at the device connected to the network (including Internet). Everything surrounding us in the digital world of future will become a potential source of cyber threats and a potential target for cyber attacks. The cyber threats appear to be one of the biggest sources of danger for community, economics and states. Therefore, the provision of cyber security of final products is an important and even critical element of digital designing of new devices. It underlines a necessity and relevancy of new methods of searching vulnerabilities in the software of devices.

1.2 Software components analysis for availability of vulnerabilities

The availability of vulnerabilities in the software components of various devices is one of the most critical problems in the sphere of cyber safety. The "Kaspersky laboratory" points out a trend in its forecast for 2017 [4] to conducting goal-oriented attacks of high complexity, which are based most frequently on implementation of vulnerabilities. The methods of detecting vulnerabilities are divided into two classes: static conducting code analysis without its execution, and dynamic based on checking different parameters in the course of SW operation. The modern methods have a number of drawbacks (exponential complexity, availability of limitations for a code to be analyzed, requirement of code availability in high-level programming languages, etc.), which do not allow to efficiently use them in practice. At present there is no universal method, which helps reveal software vulnerabilities in the software encountered actually over acceptable period of time. In the general case the task of searching vulnerabilities is confined to NP-complete task of SAT-feasibility of Boolean formulae. All heuristic approaches to searching vulnerabilities are aimed at revealing not the vulnerabilities proper, but the assigned features (criteria) thereof in advance, and therefore, they have a strictly limited field of application.

Widespread is the proprietary software, which source code corresponds to an intellectual property of this or the other company, which are, as a rule, not interested in publication or transfer of its developments to the third parties. Such a situation contributes to occurrence of both occasional errors and vulnerabilities, and software bugs intentionally introduced into a code. Besides, the analysis of source software text does not allow revealing some types of errors, which can be related to peculiarities of compilators. In some systems (e.g., firmware of transmitters and sensors, field programmable gate array, etc.) the software components are initially presented in the form of binary codes. It emphasizes the necessity and relevance of developing new methods of searching vulnerabilities based on the analysis of software code being executed.

All the described factors demonstrate a necessity and relevance of developing new technologies for analyzing components of digital infrastructure for availability of vulnerabilities meeting the following requirements: (1) possibility of analyzing programs represented by binary code; (2) intricacy of developed algorithms shall provide for a possibility of analyzing programs by means of modern computation devices over acceptable period of time. The solution of this problem offered in this article is based on modeling cognitive perception of images for presentation of highly-abstract software characteristics. Such a decision is not based on exponential attack of input data and search of expected features of vulnerabilities, at that, the application of neural networks with deep learning will provide revealing deep trends uniting a vulnerable code. The implementation of the offered approach will help get an algorithm, which will identify the root reasons and characteristics hidden in the code, which bring about vulnerabilities over time polynomial from code size.

1.3 Application of machine learning methods in the sphere of cyber security

The recent years were marked with rampant development of methods of machine learning and cognitive analysis and cognitive analysis. In fact, a breakthrough has taken place in different spheres, e.g., such as identification of images (disclosure of faces in photos, identification automobile license plates) and analysis of texts (revealing focus and subjects, machine translation). Fig. 1 shows statistics of registration of rights for intellectual property in the field of cyber security [5].

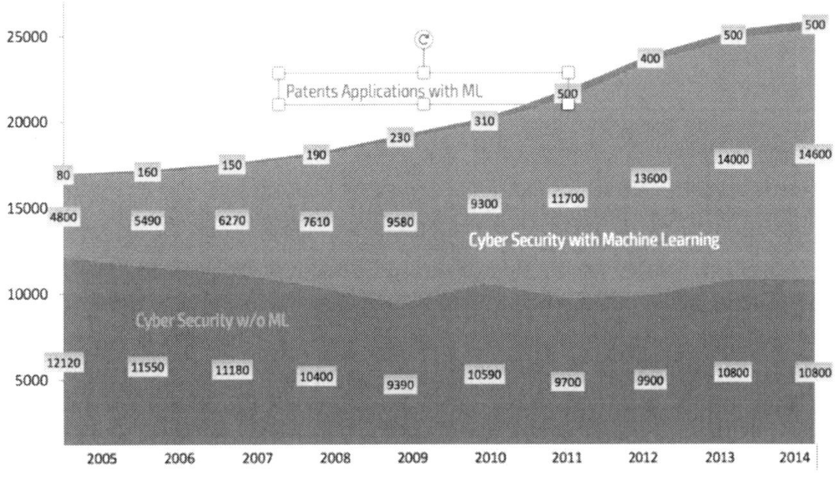

Fig. 1. Statistics of registrations of intellectual property in the sphere of cyber security.

It can be seen that the number of requests for solutions of machine learning remains approximately at the same level, while with the use thereof – it increases sharply in the recent years. In this case a growth of requests for registration of program solutions in the sphere of cyber security based on using methods of machine learning takes place. The methods of machine learning are used in different directions of cyber security: spam filtration, searching bots in social media, revealing botnets, data leak prevention (DLP), analysis of network traffic, analysis of signals from systems of detecting intrusions, etc. [6, 7, 8]. In this case the authors offer an approach to revealing vulnerabilities based on using neural networks and machine learning. Particularly, the development of methods of machine learning and artificial intellect will help to solve a problem of revealing vulnerabilities in future in great numbers of various digital devices.

2 Neuro-semantic approach to searching vulnerabilities

2.1 Analysis of high-abstract program characteristics

It is proposed to consider vulnerabilities in the code as the abstract code properties as a whole, which get expressed only in terms of presence/absence any machine instructions therein. These properties are based, in turn, on less abstract properties of the same code (Fig. 2). All this shapes a hierarchic structure of the code properties. The purpose consists in developing approach that provides revealing these properties in the incoming code samples with the aim of revealing vulnerabilities.

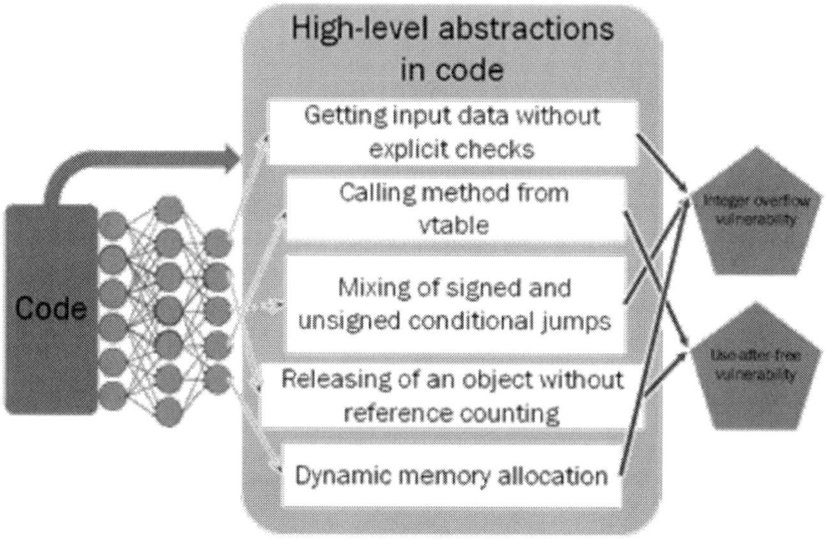

Fig. 2. Analysis of high-abstract program characteristics.

In order to attain this goal, it is recommended to use methods of deep learning of neural networks for building algorithm classifier capable of identifying deep reasons of emergence of vulnerabilities in the machine code and classify the code by classes of vulnerabilities on this basis.

2.2 Building vector representations of program instructions

The application of methods of machine learning for revealing vulnerabilities faces a number of problems; one of such problems is a compilation of learning sample. The availability of a great number of samples is the main requirement for application of machine learning methods. For instance, the methods of machine learning in the sphere of analyzing photos gained momentum particularly after appearance of bases comprising a great number of marked images (indicating what is depicted thereat). Since the majority of companies do not strive after dissemination of information about vulnerabilities, the acquisition of a great number of examples of a vulnerable code is difficult task from organizational point of view. In order to solve this problem, the authors offer to use learning with transferal. It will also help oppose a problem of disappearing gradients in neuronets [8]. Instead of solving a task of searching vulnerabilities with "expensive" learning data (for which it is difficult to get a big learning sample) initially the auxiliary neural network is being learned on solving simple auxiliary task with "cheap" learning data (for which it is easy to build a great learning set). It is proposed to use emulation of the simplest programs as such a task. A preliminary setting of weights of neural network in the initial layers (Fig. 3, network A+B) takes place as a result of solving an auxiliary task. As a result a representation of individual instructions with coding semantics thereof in the form of dense vectors of real numbers is shaped in the initial layers (Fig. 3, part A) of neural network. Later on the weight coefficients of a part of network with vector representations of instructions (Fig. 3, part A) do not change and get connected to the inlet of neural network for solving the main task of searching vulnerabilities (Fig. 3, network C+D). The stage of building vector representations is described in the article of authors with more details [9].

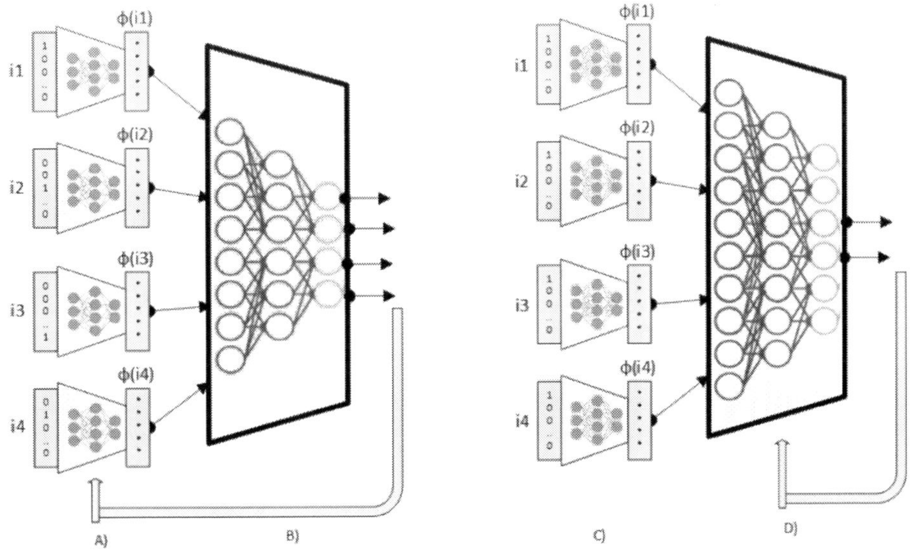

Fig. 3. Left side: stage of building vector representations (A) with the use of network (A+B) for solving auxiliary task. Right side: learning network (C+D) for solving the main task with the use of fixed vector representations (C).

2.3 Architecture of deep neural network

The program code as data form features the key peculiarities:

- discreteness – data on code corresponds to a sequence of locally non-correlated objects;
- availability of semantics of instructions in terms of impact on memory;
- high variability of code – small changes sometime entail radically different program behavior;
- duality of data – presence of instructions, and numerical parameters thereof in the code.

Proceeding from these peculiarities it is offered to use cascade of several layers of recurrent networks LSTM (Long Short-Term Memory) as architecture of neural network for revealing vulnerable code areas [10]. The recurrent neural networks make it possible to process serial data (time rows, series, sequence of non-commutative operations). LSTM networks as a subtype of recurrent networks are tailored for operation with long-term dependencies between the members of incoming sequence the same as it happens in long texts and in code of programs. A fundamental layout of the network is shown in Fig. 4.

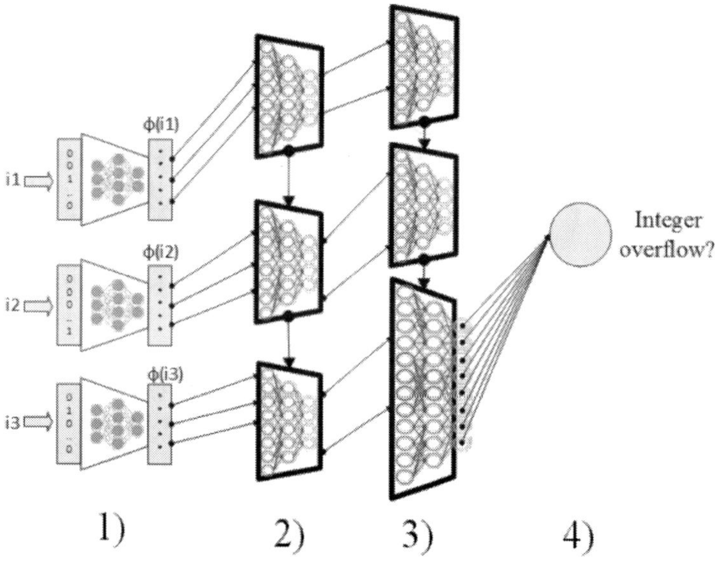

Fig. 4. Architecture of neural network for task of searching vulnerabilities of integer overflow.

A code specimen in the form of sequence of program instructions is fed to the network input. The network consists of the following parts (Fig. 4):

1. Embedding layer. Layers pre-learned earlier, which reflect the indices of instructions and vector representations thereof. The weights of this part of network have been acquired by method of learning with transferal on auxiliary sub-task [11, 12].

2.-3. Layers *consisting of sequence of LSTM cells*. It is a recurrent type of neural networks intended for work with time rows or sequential data in the form of tests. Every LSTM cell in the layer is connected with the next module and receives information of vector representation of current instruction to the input.

4. *Output fully connected layer*. It receives information to the input from the last LSTM module in the last layer and outputs a number from 0 to 1 – probability of presence of vulnerability in the input code sample.

It is possible to classify a new code with respect to availability to vulnerabilities in future by learning such a network in the plurality of marked code samples. The corrective adjustment of weight coefficients is carried out by algorithm of reverse error propagation for the recurrent LSTM networks [13, 14]. A difference between mark for every code example and network response to this example shapes the error signal. In order to minimize the network error, the weights of neural network change in the order reverse to the order of signal passage through the network in the test example. First of all a change takes place in the weights running to the resulting neural of the last layer (in Fig. 4 – 4), then the weights in the last LSTM cell (in Fig. 4 – 3) and ending by the weights in the first such module of the initial layer (in Fig. 4 – 4). Depending on learning parameters, the weights can regenerate only after some test examples, but not after every example. It speeds up learning, however, makes its result less accurate, especially under conditions of deficiency of training examples. The acceleration of learning without losing quality will be attained due to parallelizing process at GPU.

2.4 The data for network machine learning

The performance of approach in general is provided in many respects by data size and integrity for learning at every stage. Different representative sets of training data get shaped for learning different model parts: vector representations of individual instructions and code classifier as a whole with respect to presence of vulnerabilities therein. The semantics of every instruction is to be derived to the fullest in the process of building vector representations of instructions. In order to do so, the training data shall comprise the exhaustive information about using every instruction under different conditions. The fullest set of marked data is required for correct building of all levels of abstraction of goal-oriented algorithm-classifier of the code. The training code samples comprise a mark on availability/absence of vulnerabilities of definite classes.

The data for learning vector representations correspond to a set of short code sectors together with marks. The learning with transferal is used at this stage, while the marks describe several code properties; the implicit learning of semantics of individual instructions takes place during analysis thereof. The marks depend on the particular auxiliary task and proceed from emulation of code of the corresponding architecture. In general, an indicator of any side effect emerging in the course of its fulfillment is the mark of the code sector. The marks get generated automatically; the learning of semantics of individual instructions takes place at this stage; no presence of code of real programs is required. In order to generate marks to training examples, Open Source projects – Keystone assembler [15], Unicorn emulator are used [16]. The code sectors get shaped randomly with maximization of coverage of possible variants of using machine instructions (Fig. 5).

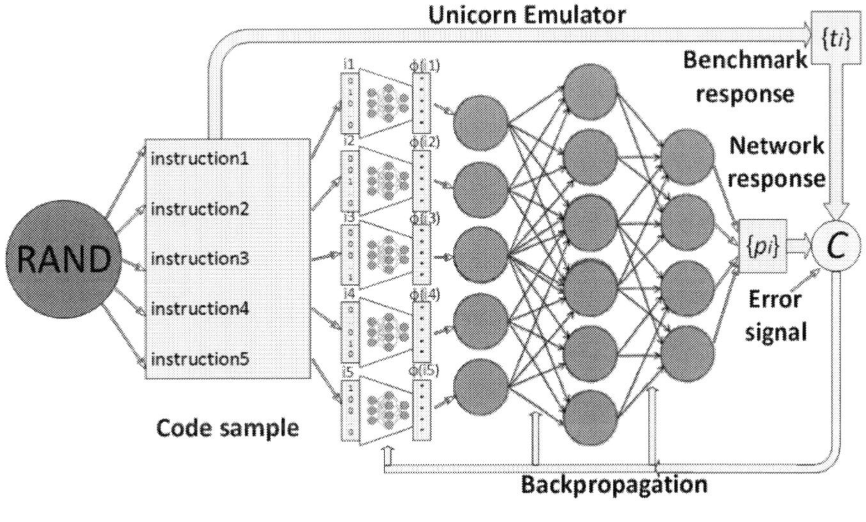

Fig. 5. Learning vector representations using emulation of side effects of code short sectors.

The marked data for learning the main network get shaped from two sources. First of all, the synthetic code examples get shaped automatically with vulnerability and without it. Some classes of vulnerabilities can be entered into a code artificially, equally as vise versa – a vulnerable code can be intentionally corrected with vulnerability removal. Secondly, the data about a vulnerable code will be extracted from data bases on vulnerabilities (CVE, Microsoft Security Bulletin), as well as generated on the basis of renovations (they comprise information about code binary patches). The vulnerable code examples denote a code before patch application, a code without presence of vulnerability is the code after patch application. It helps learn the network to differentiate between "bad" or "good" code and, by the same, identify vulnerabilities in the real code.

3 Experimental results

The authors have carried out experiments demonstrating correct work of the offered approach for searching vulnerabilities of the integer overflow in machine code. The vulnerability of the integer overflow is one of the most frequently encountered and consists in uncontrolled overflow of the integer register as a result of fulfilling arithmetic operations and future use of this register when fulfilling critical operations (e.g., memory allotment). A task being solved by neural network consisted in searching the integer overflow in machine code of different length. A sub-plurality of instructions of processor of x86-archtecture has been used – a limited number of instructions and registers, reduced number of possible numerical values.

Analyzed instructions:

Every instruction is represented by one of five commands:

- nop
- mov REG, REG/NUM
- add REG, REG/NUM
- sub REG, REG/NUM
- call malloc

Three eight-byte registers of general purpose REG = {ax, bx, cx}, all eight-byte numerical values NUM = [0, 1, .., 255] are supported. Collectively there are 2,332 different variants of program instructions.

Input data of neural network:

In this experiment the programs represented by the sequence of instructions are supplied to the input of neural network LSTM (Ref. item 2.3). The last command – a call of function of dynamic memory allotment with the size located in register ax. The initialization of registers prior to code fulfilling has taken place by random values in the range of values [25,.., 32].

Configuration of neural network:

The network architecture in general is described in item 2.3 of this article. The enabling layer compares a real vector of physical dimension 11 with every input instruction. Three LSTM layers, physical dimension of output for LSTM modules: 8, 5, 3, accordingly. The network output in the range [0.1] describes a probability of yes/no decision for the assigned task.

Vector representations of instructions:

The fixed weights in the enabling layer have been acquired in the course of implementing other experiments [9] during learning on the auxiliary task of forecasting the code emulation results. These values are used in this experiment as a carrier of knowledge about instructions as they are.

Learning sample:

The network has been learned for operation with three different program sizes. In order to solve such tasks, three synthetic data sets have been generated (Table 1). Every example has been marked using a back tracing method, the markers have been placed on the presence/absence of vulnerability in the code (taking into account permissible boundaries of external data).

Table 1. Parameters of test sets.

Experiment No.	Length of programs (number of instructions in a program)	Size of learning sample	Size ofchecking sample
1	20	18000	2000
2	30	15000	5000
3	50	6500	500

Learning results:

15 sequential epochs have been used; the network weights have been renovated after every training example in the course of learning. The network has been correctly learned to find vulnerabilities in programs for every used length (Table 2).

Table 2. Parameters of test sets.

Experiment No.	Accuracy at all samples (%)	Accuracy at vulnerable samples only (%)	Accuracy at non-vulnerable samples only (%)
1	79	80	78
2	81	82	80
3	83	84	82

Finding:

The acquired results presented in the table demonstrate the network's capability to classify the incoming code for availability of the integer overflow with a sufficient accuracy. The result has been significantly enhanced by the presence of prebuilt vector representations for instructions under conditions of a small number of examples for learning.

4 Conclusion

The development and implementation of this approach will help develop solutions providing automatic detection of vulnerabilities in the program components of different digital devices over acceptable time without using exponential memory consumption. This is especially relevant under conditions of dashing increase of the number of digital devices accessible through Internet. The incorporation of this approach in practice will help, if necessary, to additionally learn the network with new examples of the vulnerable code (with new types of vulnerabilities). Besides, a modular architecture of computation architecture provides for a possibility of supporting different hardware architectures of processors in the way of learning vector representations for different sets of instructions. These results can be used for advanced detection of and removal of program vulnerabilities in the code of different digital devices being protected.

References

1. K. Schwab, *The Fourth Industrial Revolution* (Crown Business, New York, 2016)
2. P. Tran, Navigating Smart Cities: A Q&A with RSA's Peter Tran [online], Available at: http://www.itproportal.com/features/navigating-smart-cities-a-qa-with-rsas-peter-tran/ (2017)

3. M. Kalinin, P. Zegzhda, D. Zegzhda, Y. Vasiliev, V. Belenko, Proceedings of 7th International Conference on Information and Communication Technology Convergence (ICTC2016) (2016)
4. Kaspersky Security Bulletin 2016, Forecast for 2017: the end "of virus indicators" [online], Available at: https://securelist.ru/files/2016/11/KSB_Predictions_2017_RUS.pdf (2016)
5. L. Rokach, When Cyber Security Meets Machine Learning [online], Available at: http://ucys.ugr.es/jnic2016/docs/MachineLearning_LiorRokachJNIC2016.pdf (2016)
6. CS259D: Data Mining foe Cyber Security [online], Available at: https://web.stanford.edu/class/cs259d/lectures/Session2.pdf (2017)
7. D. Barbara, S. Jajodia, Applications of data mining in computer security [online], Available at: http://www.cs.odu.edu/~mukka/cs795sum10dm/Lecturenotes/Day7/Barbara%20Jajodia%20Data%20Mining%20Book.pdf (2002)
8. R. Pascanu, T. Mikolov, Y. Bengio, Proceedings of the 30th International Conference on International Conference on Machine Learning, on the difficulty of learning recurrent neural networks, **28** (2013)
9. R. Demidov, A. Pechenkin, Approach to software security analysis based on vector representation of a machine code, **4** (2017)
10. H. Sak, A. Senior, F. Beaufays, Proceedings of the Annual Conference of the International Speech Communication Association, Long short-term memory recurrent neural network architectures for large scale acoustic modelling (2014)
11. L. Bottou, Machine Learning, From machine learning to machine reasoning, **94 (2)** (2014)
12. T. Mikolov, W.-T. Yih, G. Zweig, Proceedings of NAACL-HLT "Linguistic regularities in continuous space word representations" (2013)
13. Y. Lecun, L. Bottou, Y. Bengio, P. Haffner, Proceedings of the IEEE "Gradient-based learning applied to document recognition", **86 (11)** (1998)
14. B. Bakker, IEEE International Symposium on Approximate Dynamic Programming and Reinforcement Learning, "Reinforcement learning by back propagation through an LSTM model/critic (2007)
15. Keystone, The Ultimate Assembler [online], Available at: http://www.keystone-engine.org/ (2018)
16. Unicorn, The Ultimate CPU emulator [online], Available at: http://www.unicorn-engine.org/ (2018)

Mathematical model for the evaluation of risk of emergency situations at a dangerous technical object based on artificial neural networks

Nikolay Peganov[1], *Aleksandr* Tumanov[1*], and *Vladimir* Tumanov[2]

[1]Peter the Great Saint Petersburg Polytechnic University, 195251 Polytechnicheskaya st.29, Russian Federation
[2]St. Petersburg State Forest Technical University, 194021 Institutskij pereulok 5, Russian Federation

Abstract. In the work performed adaptation of artificial neural networks in modern security systems potentially dangerous technical objects — high-rise buildings as tools for assessing and forecasting in management decision. The study obtained the main scientific results: the mathematical model of risk assessment of man-made emergencies based on artificial neural networks; the mathematical model, adapted to the cumulative model of development technogene emergency-fire; provided risk assessment technique manmade emergencies based on artificial neural networks; represented private man-made fire risk assessment methodology using artificial neural networks.

1. Introduction

Modern methods of risk assessment are nothing more than a set of all possible methods of assessment, analysis and security of a particular object. At the moment the number of known methods of tens, but not all of them found practical application, and left only a hypothetical model in relation to security. In addition, it is worth noting that the problem is that not all existing modern knowledge applied in the field. So, for example, a great impetus to the development of the security management system has been the emergence of risk assessment [1, 2], based on the theory of probability. Therefore, we can conclude that any of the promising direction or even a parallel region will be able to give impetus to the further development of the theory of security. Proof of this is the extensive integration in the safety of the most advanced ideas: modern integrated security systems [3], based on the software-hardware complex; the application of mathematical analysis in reliability. Despite the large number of methods, the quality of the risk assessments have not yet at a sufficient level therefore requires consideration of innovative methods in this area. This can be attributed, and the adaptation of artificial neural networks, further ANN.

The aim of this work is to improve the quality of risk assessment of emergency situations at hazardous activities through adaptation of artificial neural networks (ANN) in

*Corresponding author: toumanov@mail.ru

modern security systems. The targets set for the implementation of the above objectives the following: an analysis of concepts of artificial neural networks, their architecture; adaptation of neural network by applying an integral development model for evaluating the development emergency hazards of man-made fire.

2. Mathematical model

Artificial neural networks in general understanding constitute a mathematical model and its software or hardware incarnation, built on the principle of organization and functioning of the biological neural networks-networks of nerve cells alive the body [4]. Generalized model of biological neuron was introduced back in 1943 year Makkalak and Pits [4], presented in Fig. 1 and the analytical version (1).

$$a(x,w) = \sigma(\langle w,x\rangle) = \sigma\left(\sum_{j=1}^{n} w_j f_j x\right)$$

Where is, $f_j; X \to R, j = 1, \ldots, n$ – numeric signs

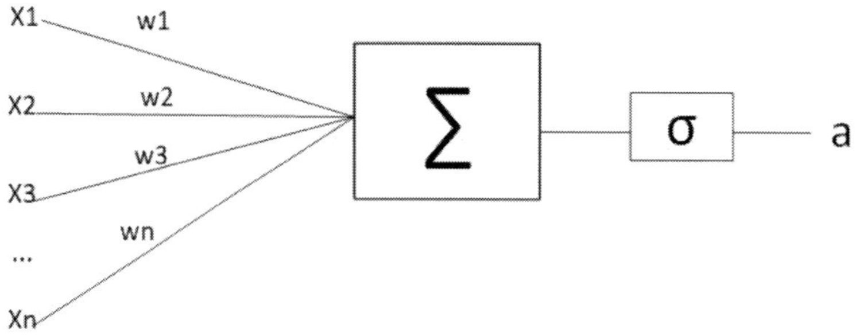

Fig. 1. Biological neuron Model [4] where x 1, ...Xn-input parameters; W_{11}, w_{1h} ... w_{nH}-weight of the relevant parameters; σ-neuron activation function.

The figure shows that the neuron is a "black box", which enters a few parameters, and leaves only one option, provided that the neuron active according to a specific function activation. Because neural network consists of more than one neuron, then it follows that the network itself is superposition of individual neurons. This hypothesis is reflected in the ideas, and then the Perceptron in layered neural networks, Fig. 2.

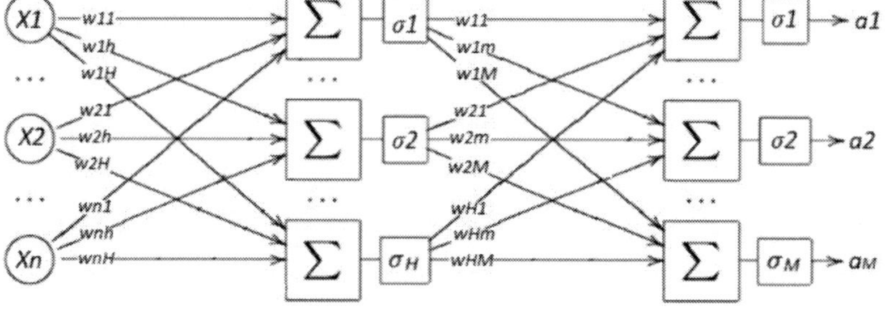

Fig. 2. Multilayer neural network where σ1, σ2, ...,σM-activating neurons; A1, a2, am-output parameters relevant neurons.

To solve the problems by using ANN, consider the following situation: indoor complex dangerous technical object, such as a high-rise building or a floating nuclear power plants going explosion and fire, which resulted in the fire and hazardous factors of fire (hereinafter

FHF). The problem is adequately predict fire development and its FHF and then deciding to manage the system. In General, this question has a solution in the form of modern security systems installations (hereinafter SS), automatic fire extinguishing systems, preliminary modeling of fire development, with a view to analysing the proliferation FHF, etc. [5]. However, this work will be considered a special case of this adverse event. Namely, the design, configuration and run ANN in the hardware-software complex of modern SS.
In this scenario, the neural networks based on a mathematical model for calculating cumulative laid gas exchange during a fire in the building [5]. Basis of this model make up expression of gas flow between rooms (1), the equation of mass balance and optical density (2), (3) energy conservation equation (4), the equation for determining gas temperature and concentration of combustion products in the premises buildings (5), main gas law equation:

$$G_{ji} = sign\left(\Delta P_{ji}\right)\cdot\xi\cdot F\cdot\sqrt{2\cdot\rho\cdot\left|\Delta P_{ji}\right|}$$

where:

G_{ji} – Gas consumption through a doorway between the two (j and i) adjacent premises, kg/s;

ξ – discharge coefficient of aperture (ξ = 0.8 for closed openings и ξ = 0.64 for open);

F – cross-sectional area of the doorway, m^2;

ρ – the density of the gases passing through the doorway, kg/m^3;

ΔP_{ji} – the average difference between complete j and i location, PA.

$$d\left(\rho_j\cdot V_j\right)/dt = \psi + \sum_k G_k - \sum_i G_i$$

where:

V_j – room volume, m^3;

t – time, c;

$\sum_k G_k$ – expenditure included in the room rate, kg/s;

$\sum_i G_i$ – the cost of premises, kg/s;

ψ – burnout speed of fire load, kg/s.

$$d\left(C_v\cdot\rho_j\cdot V_j\cdot T_j\right)/dt = C_p\cdot\sum_k\left(T_k\cdot G_k\right) - C_p\cdot T_j\cdot\sum_i\left(G_i + Q_r - Q_w\right)$$

where:

C_v, C_p – specificizohornaja and isobaric heat capacity, KJ/(kg * k);

T_i, T_j – the temperature of the gases in the i and j indoors, K;

Q_r – the amount of heat generated indoors by combustion, kW;

Q_w – heat flow absorbed by structures and emitted through openings, kW.

$$V_j \cdot d\mu_j / dt = \psi \cdot D_m + \sum_k (\mu_k \cdot G_k) / \rho_k - \mu_j \cdot \sum_i G_i / \rho_j$$

where:

μ_i, μ_j – optical smoke density in the i-m and j-m premises;

D_m – forming ability of fire load,

$$T_{nj} = \frac{\sum_{k=1}^{n} (C_{PB} \cdot G_k \cdot T_k) + Q_j}{C_{vz} \cdot \left(\sum_{k=1}^{n} G_k - \sum_{i=1}^{m} G_i \right) + C_{pr} \cdot \sum_{i=1}^{m} G_i + \alpha^*_{jn} \cdot F_{jn} + \alpha^*_{jcT} \cdot F_{jcT}} +$$

$$+ \left[T_{(n-1)j} - \frac{\sum_{k=1}^{n} (C_{PB} \cdot G_k \cdot T_k) + Q_j}{C_{vz} \cdot \left(\sum_{k=1}^{n} G_k - \sum_{i=1}^{m} G_i \right) + C_{pr} \cdot \sum_{i=1}^{m} G_i + \alpha^*_{jn} \cdot F_{jn} + \alpha^*_{jcT} \cdot F_{jcT}} \right] \cdot$$

$$\cdot \exp \left[- \frac{C_{vz} \left(\sum_{k=1}^{n} G_k - \sum_{i=1}^{m} G_i \right) + C_{pr} \cdot \sum_{i=1}^{m} G_i + \alpha^*_{jn} \cdot F_{jn} + \alpha^*_{jcT} \cdot F_{jcT}}{C_{vz} \cdot \rho_j \cdot V_j} \cdot \Delta\tau \right]$$

where:

Q_j – the amount of sources (sewage) heat in a volume of j-facilities and equipment to heat, retiring in enclosures;

$\alpha^* = \alpha \cdot \left[\frac{T(\tau) - T_w(\tau)}{T(\tau) - T_0} \right]$ – given the coefficient of heat transfer;

T_0 – initial temperature indoors;

F_{jcT} – the surface area of the frame structures in j indoors.

When adapting an integrated mathematical model [5] in artificial neural networks, in the above expressions one can distinguish two kinds of parameters: the constant (the volumes of space, initial temperature, the initial pressure, specific heat capacity, etc.), as well as calculated parameters (number of heat in a room different coefficients, etc.). Regarding both types of neural network parameters will be initial parameters to find the summary results that need user for management decision. If you apply these settings regarding a multi-layer neural network (fig. 2.), you can propose a mathematical model of primary and result parameters in ANN, proposed in table 1.

Table 1. Mathematical model adapted for integrated development model of fire at a dangerous technical object.

Serial number	Intervals of variable values of input parameters, $X_1 - X_n$	Weights, w	Intervals of output parameters, *a*
1	Values with an electronic thermometer, 20…Nt°C		Design temperature of gas indoors, 0…T_{nj}, K
2	Volumes of premises, 0…Nv, $м^3$		Concentrations of hazardous factors of fire, 0…Ad, %
3	Dynamic pressure, 100…N, КПа	Calculated on the basis of the learning process ANN	Change optical density, No…Ao
4	Unit heat, C_v , C_p , KJ/(kg * k);		
5	Optical smoke density in the i and j (measured by instruments) 0…No		The concentration of the individual components of a gas mixture, $X_{Lj(n)}$, kg/kg

On the basis of intervals of values, you can perform the initial configuration of ANN, and further her education, with a view to forecasting the FHF as well, further, and the adoption on the basis of this management decision. Training a neural network consists of the following aspects:-the destination array data (Fig. 2) is a collection of numbers, based on which, in the future maybe the adoption of managerial decisions (intervals of variable values of the input parameters, X, 1-Xn); -Once became known the output (output parameters and intervals) it is possible to perform learning ANN. The process of machine learningwill occur at this stage. The user specifies the input parameters, as well as settings that wait. Training will automatically pick weights w, and configures the dependence between input and finite intervals.

3 Results

It is worth noting that learning occurs in several iterations, until the rejection of the results:

– as a result of the above transactions the neural network as a tool for forecasting was formed. To solve the problem of management decision to build additional ANN, who is trained in the same way as neural network for prediction, only without the prior calculations. As a result of the work of the neural network to the output we get managerial decision. If you think of an example, the following view is emerging:

– output array data from previous neural network and become inputs for new neural networks;

– you know that under certain parameters some result occur (favourable or adverse event), so the output will be determined ANN. In other words, this operation will produce an automatic decision, and provide it to the user in the system security;

– as a result of neural network learning system will turn the decision in accordance with [6] (in the context of the considered emergency decision based on providing user information with a reasonable degree of accuracy, for example, about case of fire and its dangerous affect factors). Thus, in the course of this work carried out adaptation of artificial neural networks in modern security systems as tools for assessing and forecasting in management decision.

4 Conclusions

The study obtained the main scientific results:

the mathematical model of risk assessment of man-made emergencies based on artificial neural networks;

the mathematical model, adapted to the cumulative model of development technogene emergency-fire;

provided risk assessment technique manmade emergencies based on artificial neural networks provided private man-made fire risk assessment methodology using artificial neural networks.

References

1. D. Tarkhov, A. Vasilyev, Optical Memoryand Neural Networks (Information Optics), **14 (1)** (2005)
2. A. Vasilyev, D. Tarkhov, G. Guschin, Proceedings of the 10th IMEKO TC7 International Symposium onAdvances of Measurement Science, **2** (2004)
3. V. Gumenyuk, A. Tumanov, Technology of civil safety, **1 (51)** (2017)
4. A. Tumanov, Nauchno-tekhnicheskie vedomosti SPbGPU, **2 (171)** (2013)
5. V. Gumenyuk, A. Tumanov, Problemy bezopasnostii chrezvychainykh situatsii, **1** (2017)
6. V. Gumenyuk., E. Ryabinina, A. Tumanov, N. Khlobystin, *Security management in emergency situations* (Ed. Polytech, Saint Petersburg, 2017)

International experience of state support and encouragement of digital economy processes[a]

Elena Pesotskaya[2], and *Ivan* Petrov[1*]

[1] Saint Petersburg State University of Architecture and Civil Engineering, 190005 2-ya Krasnoarmeiskaya st. 4, Russian Federation
[2] Saint Petersburg State University of Economics, 191023 Sadovaya st. 21, Russian Federation

Abstract. The World Economic Forum estimates that digital transformations have a huge potential for developing business and society within the next decade and the global economy can earn over 30 trln $ additionally for a period up to 2025 [1]. A significant portion of the advantages will be given to the countries, which will deeply and comprehensively implement information and communication technologies to allow the state, society and business to interact. A high speed of data transmission and exchange of information allows innovations to diffuse both at the intra-industry and cross-industry levels, which promotes competitive strength of companies, countries and world's regions by increasing labor efficiency. In this article we have considered the programs being implemented in developed and developing countries to promote conditions for digital transformation of society and industry, boost industrial cooperation in the research and development, innovative and production areas, develop industrial and innovative infrastructure facilities, upgrade existing production facilities and create new innovative sectors of economy.

1 Introduction

"Digital economy" is a certain economic order, which naturally involves active use of advanced information technologies to collect, store, process, transform and transfer data in all areas of human activity. It is also a system of technical, organizational, program, normative and legislative elements with distributed interaction and mutual use by economic agents to exchange knowledge in permanent development conditions.

A wide application of digital technologies in the economy today is a reality and necessity to support competitive strength and meet consumer demands. Many states elaborate special programs at the national level due to their high efficiency. The tasks of these programs are as follows:

- Building and stable development of society, state and business;
- Improvements to support innovations being implemented at a system level;

[a] The article was prepared as part of the work on the grant of the President of the Russian Federation NSh-4028.2018.6
[*] Corresponding author: petrovrf@mail.ru

- Further development and binding of legislative environment to support the set-up of a "digital government";
- Arrangement of cross-border, legally relevant digital document management;
- Rendering of services in electronic format;
- Intellectual property protection;
- Information security;
- Electronic trade development;
- Development of electronic and distance learning technologies and other areas.

At the present time state programs and strategies for digital economy development have been elaborated and being implemented in different countries of the world as well as at the interstate level. So, only EU countries according to official data of the European Commission as of March 2017 there are over 30 national and regional initiatives for industrial digitization [2].

Let us consider the main provisions and peculiarities of digitization programs in developed and developing countries.

2 Programs of EU countries

One of the leading players in digitization and a key architect of "Industry 4.0" concept is Germany that already in 2011 officially introduced a state strategy under the same name. This program is based on the internet of things and industrial Internet of things inclusive (industrial Internet) [3]. "Industrie 4.0" was initiated by Germany's scientific and business society in 2011 and being implemented with the assistance of German chancellor Angela Merkel. By 2030 Germany's plan is to move forward to a completely different level of production, where the Internet is used to achieve maximum productivity and efficiency in industry. Apart from general concept Industry 4.0 several other strategies and initiatives of similar type have been developed and being implemented in Germany at the state level including Smart Networking Strategy [4], which formed a basis for introducing Digital Agenda program.

In July 2015, Alliance pourl' Industrie du Futur [5] was established in France to combine different organizations from private business, research society and a number of state institutes and establishments.

A new digital strategy (UK Digital Strategy 2017) was published officially relatively recently, March 1, 2017 [6].

Ambitious program Smart Industry [7] was adopted by the Government of the Netherlands. The Netherlands is one of the world's most "digitized" countries being highly rated by different global ratings for in the sphere of digital technologies. So it is number 4 in DESI rating (Digital Economy and Society Index) 2017 and is among the global leaders in terms of Internet penetration among population (number 2 worldwide in MGI rating Connectedness Index) and digitization of state services [8].

The Government of the Netherland in its general industrial policy lays emphasis on four areas:

- Strengthening of national economy's competitive power at a global level;
- Further growth of productivity in industrial sectors;
- Sustaining and increase in employment rates in industry and service sector;
- Overall improvement of business climate in the country and involvement of foreign high technology companies.

An important element of the Netherlands's industrial policy today is Smart Industry Action Agenda. A preliminary plan to launch this new strategy was first announced by the country's government in April 2014. In January 2015 this strategy was officially approved at the highest level. The general task tabled in this strategy is "to allow the national economy to achieve leading positions in the world by means of quick and efficient use of Information technologies in combination with advanced industrial technologies" [7].

In this case the most important objective of Smart Industry Action Agenda is to set up effective ecosystems (smart ecosystem) – interlinked networks of private companies and research and education institutions. The key practical objective of this Smart Industry program (at least at its initial stage) was a strategy to set up a wide network so called FieldLabs (field laboratories) in the country. According to the architects of this concept, FieldLabs are different physical objects within the industrial and process infrastructure, where private companies and state research organizations jointly carry out experimental developments, testing and commercially implement efficient solutions and products of "smart industry". In this case, an emphasis is laid on an interdisciplinary approach, – FieldLabs should promote more efficient interaction of high-tech companies and research organization from very different industrial branches, service sector and agriculture (it should be noted that the agricultural sector is considered to be one of the most technology intensive in the Netherlands's economy). One more essential element of this strategy is to apply a bottom-up approach, when the main initiative comes from the bottom level while setting up new experimental FieldLabs (representative of private business and regional authorities of the Netherlands) [10].

As reflected in TNO's latest report (a research company being one of organizations-coordinators of the overall big project Smart Industry), the program of setting up a network of new "field laboratories" has caught the most interest of regional authorities, which view it as an effective mechanism of strengthening "smart specialization" and clustering of their territories [11]. According to the latest information posted on the official web site of Smart Industry program at the present time in the Netherlands there are already 32 these "field laboratories" being at different stages of establishment and practical operation [12].

Over the last decade European countries have been also taking certain efforts to develop "common digital agenda" in other words, joint effective solutions and control mechanisms for digitization process at the interstate level. EU leaders have defined a general long-term task to create a digital single market in Europe. For the first time the need to work out such a common strategy was officially called for by Chairman of the European Commission Jean-Claude Junker in October 2015 [13].

In 2010, EU countries launched special initiative Digital Europe as part of the implementation of more common strategy Europe 2020, the main objective of which was to stimulate the growth of common European internet economy. In the same year of 2010 so called Digital Agenda of Europe was published, it called for the development of common approaches and priorities for EU member states concerning further development of digital sectors of European economy and stimulation measures for digital innovations. In April 2016 the European commission made public a new integrated initiative under a temporary name "Digital single market- digitizing European industry, which contained a wide range of new tools and mechanism to support further digitalization of European industry and service sector [14].

3 Programs of Asia-Pacific countries

Countries in this region have been rationally supporting a wide use of new technologies in all economic sectors; therefore digital technologies are of no exception. In Japan the main governmental document defining the country's long-term objectives and tasks in the sphere of digital technologies is SmartJapan ICT Strategy [15], officially published in June 2014. The concept consists of two parts: National and international. Its purpose is to ensure Japan's economic growth and significant contribution to the international society and economy through innovations and information and communication technologies.

Special attention should be drawn to China's development of its digital society and economy. Prerequisites to this program were developed at the start of the century and in 2007 China's State Council put forward a first draft system, whose tasks were to collect data on bank clients and determine their creditworthiness in accordance with available information, payment and credit history [14, 17]. It is worth noting that as of today these systems are already in place in many developed European countries and USA [18].

The full-scale SCS system has been designed since 2014. The program should start in 2020 according to the plan. It should be noted that up to now the government keeps the SCS system design details in secret. It is only known that the population rating will be individual for every citizen and will be identified in accordance with ID card, it is also known that certain measures will be taken in case of refusal to use this system.

In 2018, it is planned to start an experimental version of this "credit-social system" for several cities in China. It is planned to assign an initial base rating equal to 1000 points to citizens and monitor its dynamics: a model citizen will be that person whose rating will be growing. In accordance with its growth he or she will be getting certain preferences in the form of preferential credit interest, travel privilege, medical service etc. At the same time, certain sanction measures will be introduced for citizens, whose rating will be decreasing [18].

Moreover, the rating will be assigned not only to individuals but to legal entities as well. Thus, companies will be motivated to timely submit financial statements, without notice pass all audits and inspections in exchange for favorable business conditions [19].

After this reform was presented to society, the state has made a decision to set the SCS system with 10 companies including such giants as Alibaba and Tencent. Two world's largest internet companies have launched similar applications for gadgets, which after receipt of registered user's permission can receive all available information about him or her. Tencent mainly uses messenger programs to send short messages. They have managed to collect over billion users [20]! Internet-giant Alibaba through its corporate application Alipay gets information about users' transactions, paid purchases etc. It involves over half a million users [17]. In addition, the both applications receive information about people's activities from municipalities, police stations, research centers and private companies. A user's rating is built according to this database: The higher it is the more bonuses a person gets.

State authorities in the sphere of law enforcement also benefit from these programs. For example, Sesame Credit helps the PRC's High court in its search of suspects and criminals by providing all available data on some people in the public interest. According to 2015 statistics it helped detain around 6000 people later made accountable for criminal, civil and administrative actions [18].

South Korea does not lag behind in digitizing its economy either. The main current state documents in the sphere of South Korea's research and manufacturing policy is the Third Basis Plan for the development of science and technologies that was implemented in a period from 2013 to 2017. It separately states an accelerated development strategy so called 13 future growth engines, in this case all these new industries and sectors are referred to a number of "breakthrough digital technologies" (smart cars, 5G networks, smart robotic engineering, smart portable devices etc.) Special Manufacturing Innovation 3.0 Strategy is being implemented in parallel; it lays emphasis on the internet of things, 3D-printing technologies and BigData technologies [19].

As for integration and international organizations, today the Organization for Economic Cooperation and Development (OECD) has adopted its Strategy for common digital market development. Special interstate treaties in the sphere of telecommunications and electronic commerce have been developed within the framework of Trans-Pacific Partnership (TPP).

In 2015, ASEAN countries agreed a common Master-plan for the development of information and communication technologies [20].

4 USA

There is no common state program for the development of digital technologies in the United States of America; however, special technological initiatives were launched jointly with private business and scientific society in different years. As an example we can mention such programs as a federal initiative in the sphere of "cloud" computations (2009) or Barak Obama's initiative to create a new network of institutes-centers for advanced manufacturing ((AMP – Advanced Manufacturing Partnership, in 2011) involving the key federal departments and largest US high-tech companies. In addition, following an initiative of leading representatives of American private business (first of all – GE, AT&T, IBM, Intel and Cisco) special Industrial Internet Consortium (IIC) was established in March 2014. Its main mission was declared to be "accelerated development, industrial implementation and wide distribution of interconnected machines, devices as well as intelligent analytics, in other words, industrial internet of things" [21].

5 Eurasian Economic Union (EAEU)

Russia also tries to keep pace with its competitors. Speaking about the creation of Russia's digital economy, one event should not go unnoticed, a meeting of the Counsel for strategic development and priority projects under the President of the Russian Federation, which discussed the planning and implementation of "RF digital economy" project. The aim of this project is to transform Russia's current economy, digitize it and improve its efficiency. This project involves large-scale changes in many key spheres of society's life, namely state and municipal administration, officialdom, education, management etc. The project frames precise objectives and tasks as wells as timelines.

The project makes provision for wide state support in five areas: regulatory control, human resources and education, development of research competence and technical capabilities, information infrastructure and information security -basis areas. The applicable areas include – state control, "smart city" and health care.

The program should result in countrywide connection of high-speed internet, implementation of 5G networks, enhancing the role of national servers and increasing their share up to 95%, setting-up of new high-tech corporation, increasing the number of population with basic digital knowledge up to 50% and higher [22].

In 1997, in order to improve information support of research and technical sphere the Council of Ministers of the Republic of Belarus found it expedient to create a single research and information computer network in the republic [23]. From that moment the country started developing a Single research and information computer network of the Republic of Belarus (RICN), which includes networks of the Ministry of Educations, Belarus State University and scientific computer network of National Academy of Science of Belarus – BASNET. RICN incorporates a library network, a ground segment of Belarus's space remote probing system, a national grid-network, RINC provides off-line access to global computer networks through pan-European research and education network GEANT combining users from more than 8000 research and education organizations in 40 European countries. In 2016, the Government approved the State digital economy and information society development program for 2106-2020 [24]. The program includes nationwide subprograms, which contain backbone measures in the sphere of ICT development: information-communication infrastructure; information system development infrastructure; digital transformation. Herein the research results within the framework of the Program are subject to mandatory integration with the national automated information system (NAIS) in order to provide electronic services to citizens and legal entities. The Belarus high technology park (HTP) is the largest IT-cluster in Central and Eastern Europe. The most popular mobile application developed by this NTP is Viber, which is used by over 82 mln people [27].

In Kazakhstan, by the President's decree in 2003 [26] a special economic zone was created (SEZ) "Innovative technologies park". Techno park "Alatau" was selected to be a service company within the territory of this SEZ, it also carries out activities as part of the implementation of state programs (technological business incubation of innovative projects, assistance in developing innovations and development of favorable conditions). The center of research laboratories including 4 laboratories was set up to stimulate the development of information and communication and digital technologies: laboratories of cloud technologies, laboratories of mobile technologies, laboratories of "Electronic government" architecture, Big Data laboratories. The state program "Digital Kazakhstan" was developed and approved for a period of 2017-2020, which includes four areas: digital Silk Road, creative society, digital transformation in economic sectors and proactive state. The key areas of the effective state program "Informational Kazakhstan-2020" are to make information and communication infrastructure accessible to population, develop telecommunication industry, create optical access networks in all large cities of the country, and provide the high-speed Internet to population.

The integration unions, in which the EAEU countries participate, also implement projects in the sphere of digital economy, which were initiated by state authorities, research societies and business. The Strategy for cooperation of CIS member states in building and developing information society for a period until 2025 and Implementation action plan were approved by a Resolution of the Council of the Heads of Governments the Commonwealth of Independent States dated October 28, 2016 [27]. This is already the second strategic document within the SIC framework in this area, the first one was approved in 2012. In 2016, in Saint Petersburg heads of the EAEU countries made a Statement on digital agenda of the Eurasian Economic Union, in which they declared to provide required conditions for forming "EAUE's digital agenda" [28].

6 Conclusions

Having analyzed the existing digital economy development concepts we can make a conclusion that there is no uniform plan of measures and actions, which can be used in all countries. State digital transformation support and stimulation programs are developed taking into account national features, capabilities of modern and future innovations being available here and there. At the same time they are aimed to leveling the fragmentation of markets, the standardization of data sources, which are obstacles on the way to digital transformation of global economy. The technological compatibility of architectures, standards, data, processes, platforms, infrastructures and networks at the interstate level making global integration possible has a crucial significance to the development and implementation of electronic ecosystem based on digital economy.

References

1. The World Economic Forum, Digital Transformation of Industries Demystifying Digital and Securing $100 Trillion for Society and Industry by 2025 [online], Available at: http://reports.weforum.org/digital-transformation/wp-

content/blogs.dir/94/mp/files/pages/files/wef-digital-transformation-2016-exec-summary.pdf (2016)

European Commission, Coordination of European, national & regional initiatives [online], Available at: https://ec.europa.eu/digital-single-market/en/cordination-european-national-regional-initiatives (2018)

Plattform-i40 [online], Available at: https://www.plattform-i40.de/I40/Navigation/DE/Home/home.html (2018)

Smart networking [online], Available at: https://www.bmwi.de/Redaktion/EN/Dossier/smart-networking.html (2018)

The Industry Technology Guide of the Future [online], Available at: http://www.industrie-dufutur.org/ (2018)

Department for Digital, Culture, Media & Sport, UK Digital Strategy 2017 [online], Available at: https://www.gov.uk/government/publications/uk-digital-strategy/uk-digital-strategy (2017)

Smart Industry has the ambition that in 2021 the Netherlands will have the most flexible and the best digitally connected production network in Europe [online], Available at: https://www.smartindustry.nl/ (2018)

McKinsey Global Institute. Digital globalization: The new era of global flows [online], Available at: https://www.mckinsey.com/~/media/McKinsey/Business%20Functions/McKinsey%20Digital/Our%20Insights/Digital%20globalization%20The%20new%20era%20of%20global%20flows/MGI-Digital-globalization-Full-report.ashx (2016)

G. Landheer, Digital revolution in industry. The Dutch approach [online], Available at: http://www.eesc.europa.eu/resources/docs/guido_landheer.pdf (2015)

Eurasian Economic Commission. Information and analytical report "An analysis of global experience in developing industrial sectors and approaches to digital transformation of industry in Eurasian Economic Union state members (2017)

C. Stolwijk, M. Punter, 101 ICT Developments in Smart Industry Field labs (TNO, Hague, 2017)

Smart Industry Field labs [online], Available at: https://www.smartindustry.nl/wp-content/uploads/2018/02/SI-Fieldlabposter-A2-2018-NL-LR.pdf (2018)

Building the digital industrial Europe (2015) [online], Available at: http://europa.eu/rapid/press-release_SPEECH-15-5938_fr.htm (2015)

Digital Single Market – Digitizing European Industry [online], Available at: [http://europa.eu/rapid/press-release_MEMO-16-1409_en.htm (2016)

Ministry of Internal Affairs and Communications of Japan, Smart Japan ICT Strategy [online], Available at: http://www.soumu.go.jp/main_content/000301884.pdf (2014)

FICO At a Glance [online], Available at: http://www.fico.com/en/about-us#at_glance (2018)

Tencent Announces 2017 Third Quarter Results [online], Available at: https://www.tencent.com/en-us/articles/15000651510741924.pdf (2017)

Alipay [online], Available at: https://intl.alipay.com/ (2018)

J. Kallio, Disruption Brief, **6** (2016)

Asean ICT masterplan 2015 completion report [online], Available at: http://www.asean.org/storage/images/2015/December/telmin/ASEAN%20ICT%20Completion%20Report.pdf (2015)

21. The Industrial Internet Consortium [online], Available at: http://www.iiconsortium.org/ (2018)
22. Program "Digital economy of the Russian Federation" [online], Available at: [http://static.government.ru/media/files/9gFM4FHj4PsB79I5v7yLVuPgu4bvR7M0.pdf (2017)
23. Resolution of the Council of Ministers of the Republic of Belarus No.1677 (1997)
24. State Program for the development of digital economy and information society for 2016 – 2020" approved by Resolution of the Council of Ministers of the Republic of Belarus 23.03.2016 No 235) [online], Available at: http://www.government.by/upload/docs/file4c1542d87d1083b5.PDF (2016)
25. The number of Viber users in Russia has exceeded 82 million people [online], Available at: https://www.rbc.ru/rbcfreenews/58d0f1ab9a794704cbebce1d (2017)
26. Decree of the President of the Republic of Kazakhstan dated August 18, 2003 No.1166 "On creation of special economic zone "Park of innovative technologies" (2003)
27. Digital agenda of the Eurasian Economic Union until 2025. Outlooks and recommendations [online], Available at: http://www.eurasiancommission.org/ru/act/dmi/SiteAssets/%D0%9E%D0%B1%D0%B7%D0%BE%D1%80%20%D0%92%D0%91.pdf (2017)
28. Statement on digital agenda of the Eurasian Economic Union [online], Available at: [http://www.eurasiancommission.org/ru/act/dmi/workgroup/materials/Pages/docs.aspx (2018)

The model of system predicting with the use of dynamic arrangement schemes[a]

Oksana Pirogova[1], *Vladimir* Plotnikov[2*], and *Andrey* Prolubnikov[3]

[1] Peter the Great St. Petersburg Polytechnic University, Institute of Industrial Management, Economics and Trade, Higher School of Service and Trade, 195251 Politekhnicheskaya st. 29, Russian Federation
[2] The Saint Petersburg State University of Economics, Faculty of General Economics and History of Economic Thinking, 19102321 Sadovaya st. 21, Russian Federation
[3] Dushanbe Subdivision of National University of Science and Technology "MISIS", Nazarshoyeva st. 7, Tajikistan

Abstract. The basic problems are considered in the paper connected with solving the problems of forecasting development of enterprises in the conditions of growth of volumes and intensity of information flows in consequence of digitalization of economic processes. The aspects of using a cost approach and also life cycle models of enterprises in the tasks of building the system of planning and predicting activity are considered. An approach to forecasting development of an enterprise on the basis of a dynamic model of the cost growth is proposed by the authors. As the main general indicator fundamental cost of an enterprise is considered, which includes four basic elements. A principle which takes into account dynamic cosubordination of basic indicators of growth of the fundamental enterprise cost is accepted as a basis for the predicting model. A variant of a structure of an adaptive model of dynamic cosubordination of basic indicators is suggested; the structure changes depending on the stage of the life cycle. The represented approach enables taking into account contradictory requirements to the choice of key indicators of development, changing at different stages of the life cycle, and also estimating and predicting the activity of an enterprise from unified positions.

1 Introduction

The millennium of transformation to digital economy reveals new opportunities in the sphere of managing business [1]. By means of increasing flexibility in processing significant volumes of information arrays and expanding opportunities for accessing the information enterprise management gets new resources for generating new knowledge in

[a] This paper is an output of the science project of the government task of Ministry of education and science of the Russian Federation # 26.3546.2017/PCH "Development fundamentals of analysis and prediction of structural and dynamic parameters of the regional economy are based on the integration of the Russian and world experience of management of territorial development and modern scientific doctrines"
*Corresponding author: plotnikov_2000@mail.ru

real time scale [2]. This knowledge, in its turn, facilitates growth of management efficiency and, consequently, competitive ability of enterprises. New knowledge and new models of its extracting and using enable shortening the time for analysis and taking decisions enable considering a greater number of factors and modeling future problems and challenges which deal with effective development of enterprises.

Thanks to digital economy even a very small enterprise becomes the owner of a huge volume of information about its activity, on condition that its system of business and management accounting is correctly organized. The growth of information volumes about the enterprise activity in different aspects increases awareness of managers and owners of the enterprise activity state. On the other hand, development of digital economy gives new opportunities for accessing and using external information which is also important for making management decisions. This information becomes more extensive, cheaper and the promptness of its obtaining constantly grows. At that, as the technology of distributed data storage develops, possibilities for using actual information in enterprise management become more and more accessible [3].

Consequently, the value of the models increases: the models make building the process of enterprise development possible with the use of the entire array of aposteriori information on the activity of the enterprise, also using external information which preconditions the activity of the enterprise and data on macroeconomic and regional forecasts [4]. In addition to that, formulation of such models is connected with certain hardships which are preconditioned, first of all, by a great number of correlation relationships between indicators which reflect the activity of the enterprise. A very important factor is the possibility for accounting changes of goal sets in such models and also taking into account behavior of enterprises at different stages of their life cycle.

2 The problems of predicting the development of an enterprise at the current stage

Planning and, especially, predicting the activity and development of an enterprise are the most complex elements in the activity control circuit of the enterprise and they are connected with strategic planning which is aimed at providing the enterprise managers and owners with information on possible alternative directions for its development depending on the condition of the internal and external environment. Predicting is one of the main procedures of strategic planning; it's about composing alternative long-term and medium-term forecasts of the activity of the enterprise and estimating the degree of executability of the given forecasts [5, 6].

Currently, the methods of simulation and economic-statistical modeling are most widely spread [7, 8]. They are based on the use of statistical regularities as one of the forms of expressing the variety of economically stable connections between separate elements of an enterprise as a system and also between enterprises in the external environment which is constantly changing. That is to say, digital economy enables using the advantages of external and internal information awareness of the enterprise management to the full extent.

Currently, methods of predicting the activity of an enterprise based on the complex of economic and financial indicators are worked out in detail. At the same time, the approach to predicting the development of an enterprise may be built on the basis of the cost approach [9, 10]. Without going into all the peculiarities of this approach, we will mark its most important aspects, namely:

– fixation of the activity on the growth (gain) of cost and not on its concrete value;

– commitment to providing stable long-term active existence of the enterprise (that is, the life time of the enterprise is not limited and not considered as a project limited in time);

– commitment to the future of the enterprise and that implicates finding answers to the question: "What is it necessary to do today in order to provide the required rates of growth of the cost in future?"

– fixation not only on the managers' and owners' interests but also on the interests of other groups of people interested in the activity of the enterprise (stakeholders);

– an objectively proved possibility of influencing the cost of an enterprise through managing its operational, financial and investment activities.

The suggested theoretical projects, as a rule, don't take into account the stage of the life cycle of an enterprise. At the same time, competent accounting of this factor at each stage enables concentrating on the most important, from the point of view of cost ideology, indicators and, in doing so, ensure stable and sequential development of the enterprise [11].

While predicting the development of the enterprise it is important to define basic models which are in the basis of its activity at each stage of its life cycle, to determine the horizon and the goals of predictive modeling. This approach allows the enterprise to select the most effective development pathway at each stage of its life cycle, ensuring in doing so progressive stable development.

3 Integration of life cycle models with the conception of the cost approach for managing the enterprise

The main task of life cycle models is distinguishing periods in the development of an enterprise; each one of them is characterized by certain stable features. At this, control models should directly consider these features and they should be built on the basis of a detailed report.

Historically, the appearing and development of life cycle models was connected with the analysis of organizational problems in the enterprise activity which is associated with distributing rights, privileges and responsibility [12]. However, further it became clear that expansion of life cycle models to aspects of financial, operational and investment activity of an enterprise may also bring significant positive effects. This idea was mostly widely used for managing enterprise finances [13]. Thus, it is suggested to consider cost models (of the *EVA*, *MVA* types) only at the stage of maturity in the work [14], and in our opinion that is not enough. It is also suggested to use cost models at different stages of the life cycle in the work [15], however, there are no specific recommendations in this work.

A deep economic analysis of cost and its dynamics through the prism of the life cycle stages of an enterprise is carried out in the works [8, 16] and it is shown that the cost growth indicator of an enterprise defined through money flows is dependent on the complex internal structure of the cost generation system and is formed thanks to money flows from operational, investment and financial activity of an enterprise. Dynamics of these components of the money flow and integral value of the net cash flow of an enterprise at life cycle stages is represented in Table 1.

Table 1. Dynamics of rates of growth, components of net cash flow of an enterprise.

Life cycle stage	**Main task**	**Basic profile of a dynamically harmonized system**
Founding stage	To prove viability and consistency of a business-project	$T(CF_O)>T(CF_F)>1>T(CF_I)$ $T(CF_\Sigma)<0$
Growth stage (youth)	Transformation of the money flow into the formed market share	$T(CF_O)>T(CF_F)>T(CF_I)>1$ $T(CF_\Sigma)>>1$
The stage of stability (maturity)	Building up an effective competitive business-model	$T(CF_O)>T(CF_I)>T(CF_F)>1$ $T(CF_\Sigma)>1$
		$T(CF_I)>T(CF_F)>T(CF_O)>1$ $T(CF_\Sigma)<>1$
The stage of decline	Preparing to effective transformation of an enterprise in accordance with the requirements of competitive conditions	$T(CF_O)>1>T(CF_F)>T(CF_I)$ $T(CF_\Sigma)<0$

The following designations are used in this table: $T(CF_O)$ – the rate of growth of the money flow from operational activity, $T(CF_F)$ – the rate of growth of the money flow from financial activity, $T(CF_I)$ – the rate of growth of the money flow from investment activity, $T(CF_\Sigma)$ – the rate of growth of integral value of the net cash flow of the enterprise.

The authors introduced a transition line in Table 1 between the stages of stability and decline (marked by color filling in the table). This addition has not technical but conceptual character. This transition situation corresponds to the point of bifurcation – the situation in which an enterprise may be. Development after its passing may follow two scenarios: optimistic (maintaining competitive ability and stable functioning, preserving and increasing value of an enterprise) or pessimistic (losing competitive advantages, reduction in value of an enterprise).

At this, the first scenario, in case of taking decisions of an innovative type by the management of the enterprise, may lead to transition to the next cycle of its life. In this case the enterprise, owing to the implemented technological, organizational, market and other innovations, passes to a new stage of growth and stability, that is, a new phase of development is implemented which presupposes repeating the stages of youth and maturity. Such a transition to a new stage of development is possible only in the event when benefit from investments into expanded production on the innovative basis starts to bring income which is comparable to the main activity of the enterprise.

The main idea of the considered approach reflected in the form of Table 1 is that at different life cycle stages of an enterprise dynamics of components of its value differs and, definitely, it is necessary to take it into account when building up a system of enterprise management on the basis of its value. Nonhomogeneity of the value indicator as an economical category is considered and justified in detail in the works [17, 18].

To estimate each component of the cost value a chain of private indicators may be used which characterizes the value and quality of this or that component of the cost. Moreover, in a general case these indicators may be combined in a system on the basis of principles of dynamic concurrence. This approach was earlier developed by the authors and represented in the article [16]. The chain of dynamic concurrence of separate elements of the fundamental cost [8] is the basic one according to the approach suggested by us:

$$I(V_{DF})> I(V_I)> I(V_O)> I(V_B)>0, \tag{1}$$

where $I(V_B)$, $I(V_O)$, $I(V_I)$, $I(V_{DF})$ are rates of gain of balance, operational, investment components and the component of dynamic flexibility (potential) of the fundamental cost of a trade enterprise, respectively. The cost component of dynamic flexibility is the cost of direct and indirect abilities of an enterprise to adapt to changes of external environment and also to transform it for its own benefit.

The represented model is true only at the stage of maturity, at the same time; the task of achieving the cost growth at other stages of the life cycle requires applying other kinds (schemes) of dynamic arrangement. The schemes of dynamic arrangement of private factors suggested by us are represented in Table 2. It should be noted that the moment of transition from the stability (maturity) stage to decline stage is specially emphasized in this table like in the previous one.

But, unlike Table 1, where the growth rates of the components of the company's cash flow are considered, the rate of increase in the value of the enterprise is considered here. A very important contribution into the cost growth at the maturity stage and passing over to a new development cycle is made by the component of dynamic flexibility value (VDF) which is an estimation of competitive advantages, intellectual capital and also other direct and indirect abilities of the enterprise to change its internal environment in the context of external environment changes. If this cost component is developed insufficiently it won't allow the enterprise to implement the required internal transformations and it will lead it to the stage of decline.

Table 2. Schemes of dynamic arrangement of gain rates of the basic factors of the enterprise value growth system.

Life cycle stage	**Basic profile of a dynamically harmonized system**
Founding stage	$I(V_O)>0$
The stage of growth (youth)	$I(V_O)> I(V_I)>I(V_B)>0$
The stage of stability (maturity)	$I(V_O)> I(V_I)>I(V_D)>I(V_{DF})>0$
	$I(V_{DF})>I(V_I)>I(V_O)>I(V_B)>0$
The stage of decline	$I(V_B)>0$

4 Predicting development of an enterprise with the use of schemes of dynamic arrangement

The variant of the adaptive variant of dynamic arrangement of growth rates for basic factors of an enterprise value growth suggested above can be used for building up a scheme of predicting development of the enterprise.

In order to account for correlation between the main factors of value growth through basic factors – growth rates, the method of system predicting can be used, suggested in the work [11]. The theory of potentials is at the core of analytical methods of system analysis. According to this theory any object or system represents a multidimensional dynamic object or a system because it is described with multiple factors. A notion of "shalanovskiy process" is suggested for predicting; it is a non steady accidental process the state of which at a moment of time depends on the state at the previous stage. The basic element of the approach is the Shalanov's chain which is built on the basis of recurrent relation:

$$X(t+1) = B(t-1, t, \sigma_j)\, X(t)\,, \tag{2}$$

where $X(t)$ is the state of the system at the moment of time t.
$X(t+1)$ – the state of the system at the moment of time $t+1$.
$B(t-1, t, \sigma_j)$ – transfer matrix based on accounting for retrospective data;
σ_j –mean-square deviation of attributes which characterize the system development level.

Predicting the system state is implemented on the basis of Shalanov's chains on the basis of the following algorithm:

$$X(t+1) = B(t-1, t, \sigma_j(1,t))\, X(t);$$

$$X(t+2) = B(t, t+1, \sigma_j(1,t+1))\, X(t+1);$$
$$X(t+n) = B(t+n-2, t+n-1, \sigma_j(1,t+n-1))\, X(t+n-1). \qquad (3)$$

Calculating the transfer matrix at each stage is implemented on the basis of using the potential theory. While using the given method it is suggested to work not with the factor values influencing the cost but with the rates of their changing. In this case the model of prediction includes growth rates of separate factors of activity.

A system of factors for forming a dynamic model of development of a trade enterprise on the basis of the cost growth by using the system of factors for estimating different components of the cost value is suggested in the work [8, 9]; the system reveals all the main components of each type of the fundamental cost of the enterprise. The scheme of the noted dynamic model at the maturity stage can be expressed in the following way:

$$I(V_B)=I(NA)>I(IC)>0;$$
$$I(V_O)= I(NP)>I(OI)>I(GI)>I(R)>0; \qquad (4)$$
$$I(V_I)=I(RI)>I(NPV)> I(I)>0;$$
$$I(V_{DF})= I(InC)>0.$$

In the system of equations and inequations (4): $I(NA)$ – net assets gain rate; $I(IC)$ – gain rate of the invested capital, $I(NP)$ – gain rate of the net profit; $I(OI)$ – gain rate of the sales profit; $I(GI)$ – gain rate of the gross income; $I(R)$ – gain rate of sale proceeds; $I(RI)$ – gain rates of investment profitability; $I(NPV)$ – gain rate of the net present value, $I(I)$ – investments gain rate; $I(InC)$ – gain rate of the innovation capital. On the basis of dynamic models represented in Table 2 and the equations (4) an algorithm of predicting the enterprise cost value can be made which includes the following sequence of actions.

The calculation of the current cost value of an enterprise V on the basis of *MVA* or *CVA* methods.

Calculation of historical values of basic factors determining the cost of the enterprise: *NA, IC, R, GI, OI, NP, I, NPV, RI, InC*, and also their gain rates.

Estimating the stage of the enterprise development and selecting the model of the cost growth in accordance with Table 1.

Calculating the transfer matrix at the predicting stage:

$B(t+n-2, t+n-1, \sigma_j(1,t+n-1))$ based on accounting for the retrospective data (here n is an iteration step)

Calculating the predicted values of gain rates of basic factors determining the cost of the enterprise at the stage of predicting $(t+n)$:

$X(t+n) = B(t+n-2, t+n-1, \sigma_j(1,t+n-1))\, X(t+n-1)$.

Calculating the predicted values of gain rates of the fundamental cost of the enterprise at the stage of predicting $(t+n)$, using the components – balance, operational, investment and the component of dynamic flexibility respectively:

$\Delta V_{f(t+n)}= \Delta V_{B(t+n)}+ \Delta V_{O(t+n)}+ \Delta V_{I(t+n)}+ \Delta V_{DF(t+n)}$.

Calculating the predicted value of the fundamental cost of the enterprise:

$V_{f(t+n)}= V_{f(t+n-1)}+ \Delta V_{f(t+n)}$.

Stages connected with calculating the matrix of transition may be repeated the required number of times depending on the size of the predicting period.

Unlike algorithms of predicting considered within the framework of development of Shalanov school methods where dimensional values of enterprise activity factors are used, this approach deals with predicting gain rates of the main factors of the enterprise financial economic activity, as relative factors which first of all characterize the quality of the system.

It allows to avoid the influence of trend changes in the original data and from the other side it enables preserving the main advantage of the given method of predicting –

systematic approach as complex accounting for all basic factors influencing the results of functioning of the system being modeled.

5 Conclusions

A modification of the method of predicting the cost of an enterprise on the basis of Shalanov's chains is suggested; this modification enables implementing the concept of system predicting. The represented method differs from the known methods in using principles of system dynamics when growth of private cost parameters is considered together with other factors of financial and economic activity of an enterprise. The structure of fundamental cost of an enterprise is taken into account in the suggested approach, and also principles of dynamic compatibility of the parameters used for evaluating the quality of the enterprise development on the basis of its cost are observed.

The second important distinguishing feature of the suggested approach is flexibility in selecting the basic model of cost growth which enables adequate accounting of changes in the enterprise goals at each stage and adjusting differences between the change in basic factors of productivity and efficiency of its activity at each stage of development on the one hand and fixation on cost growth as integral factor of development efficiency of an enterprise on the other hand.

References

1. E. J. Malecki, B. Moriset, *The digital economy: Business organization, production processes and regional developments* (Routledge, London, 2007)
2. D. Helbing, *Thinking ahead-essays on big data, digital revolution, and participatory market society* (Springer International Publishing, Cham, 2015)
3. S. Graham, D. Wood, Critical Social Policy, **23 (2)** (2003)
4. Y. Vertakova, O. Grechenyuk, A. Grechenyuk, S. Emelianov, Proceedings of the 29th International Business Information Management Association Conference - Education Excellence and Innovation Management through Vision 2020: From Regional Development Sustainability to Global Economic Growth (2017)
5. N. V. Shalanov, *Economic Diagnostics of Efficiency of a Trade Enterprise Activity* (Publishing House "Omsk Economics Institute", Omsk, 2008)
6. E. V. Sokolov, A. Y. Kiselev, Controlling, **3 (27)** (2008)
7. Z. K. Likhanova, Economic Analysis: Theory and Practice, **2** (2009)
8. O. E. Pirogova, V. A. Plotnikov, News of the Saint Petersburg University of Economics, **2 (104)** (2017)
9. O. E. Pirogova, V. A. Plotnikov, News of the Saint Petersburg University of Economics, **4 (106)** (2017)
10. V. V. Belov, V. I. Chistyakova, Business-informatics, **4 (06)** (2008)
11. N. V. Shalanov, *Economic Aspects* (NGTU, Novosibirsk, 2008)
12. I. Adizes, *Corporate Lifecycles: how and why corporations grow and die and what to do about it* (Prentice Hall, New Jersey, 1988)
13. Y. Vertakova, V. Plotnikov, Economic Annals-XXI, **156 (1-2)** (2016)
14. J. Stern, G. Stewart, D. Chew, Journal of Applied Corporate Finance, **8 (2)** (1995)
15. L.E. Greiner, Harvard Business Review, **50 (4)** (1972)
16. O. Pirogova, V. Plotnikov, Proceedings of 17th International Scientific Conference Proceedings (Part IV) (2017)

17. J. D. Martin, J. W. Petty, *Value Based Management – The corporate response to the shareholder revolution* (Harvard Business School Press, Harvard, 2000)
18. G.B. Stewart, *The Quest for Value: A Guide for Senior Managers Harper Business* (HarperCollins Publishers, New York, 1991)

Effect of heat treatment on the structure and magnetic properties of Sm-Fe alloys obtained by mechanical alloying

Nikolay Razumov[1*], and *Aleksandr* Verevkin[1]

[1] National Technology Initiative Center of Excellence in Advanced Manufacturing Technologies at Peter the Great Saint-Petersburg Polytechnic University, 195251, 29, Polytechnicheskaya st., Saint-Petersburg, Russian Federation

Abstract. The effect of heat treatment on the structure and magnetic properties of Sm-Fe alloys obtained by mechanical alloying was investigated. The crystallization temperature of Sm_2Fe_{17}, an amorphous alloy obtained by mechanical alloying, was determined using differential scanning calorimetry. Based on these results, various samples were annealed at different isothermal holding temperatures, and those with the best magnetic properties were found. Experimental studies show that decreasing the isothermal holding temperature from 750 °C to 630 °C increases magnetic characteristics nearly four times. The saturation magnetization, romance and coercivity of the Sm_2Fe_{17} powder were 121 emu/g, 28.5 emu/g and 800 Oe, respectively.

1 Introduction

The development of civilization and technological progress necessitate the production of devices of a higher level and a new purpose. Along with new design and design solutions in many cases, such devices require the use of special or new materials. New materials may be subject to special requirements for functional, technological or economic reasons. Magnetic materials are of particular interest.

Magnetic materials are used by mankind for several millennia. However, the great significance of magnetic materials for technological progress humanity felt only in the middle of the XIX century after Faraday discovered the law of electromagnetic induction. Then it became possible to design and manufacture power generators, motors, transformers and other apparatuses and devices for electrical engineering and communications equipment. The development of electronics means of generation and transmission of data is not possible without the development of magnetic materials.

Many researchers have become interested in the nitrides and carbides of the intermetallic compound Sm_2Fe_{17} by reasone of their excellent magnetic properties, discovered by Coey and Sun in 1990 [1]. This intermetallic material is a promising replacement for permanent magnets that is different from widely-used Nd-based magnets. It has uniaxial anisotropy with a high anisotropic field and a Curie temperature exceeding 450 °C.

* Corresponding author: n.razumov@onti.spbstu.ru

Several techniques have been developed for syntheszing Sm_2Fe_{17}-type magnetic materials, including casting [2], melt spinning, hydrogen disproportionation desorption recombination [3], reduction–diffusion [4], and mechanical alloying (MA) [5]. In all cases, MA proved to be an efficient technique for the low cost, large scale production of powders [2, 6]. Mechanical alloying has been recognized as a technique for synthesizing ultrafine powder materials through solid-state diffusion under intense mechanical deformations [7, 8], and MA elevates coercivity [9].

Numerous published reports have established that the master alloy, Sm_2Fe_{17}, produced via MA, consists of two main parts: nanosized crystalline α-Fe and an amorphous Sm-Fe phase [10, 11]. Heat treatment of the as-milled powder in a vacuum is required to obtain fully crystalline Sm_2Fe_{17}. The grain size can be modified by heat treating. Generally, the Sm-Fe alloy is isothermallly held between 700 °C and 850 °C; greater temperatures have been used [5, 8, 12, 13]. A single-phase Sm_2Fe_{17} intermetallic compound with a rhombohedral Th_2Zn_{17} crystal structure forms during heat treatment. A strong relationship between particle and grain size and magnetic properties exists.

In this paper, we describe studies of the effect of heat treatment on the structure and magnetic properties of non-nitrogenated Sm-Fe alloys obtained by MA. The crystallization temperature of partially amorphous Sm-Fe alloys was determined using differential scanning calorimetry (DSC). The results led us to anneal various samples at different isothermal holding temperatures and compare their magnetic properties. Grain size, lattice parameters, and magnetic properties were functions of the isothermal holding temperature.

2 Experimental

Materials

High purity Fe (d90 < 300 μm, 99.96% purity; NevaReaktiv, LLC, Russia) and Sm (d90 < 700 μm, 99.9% purity; Huizhou Gl Technology Co., LTD, PRC) were used as initial components.

Preparation of Sm-Fe powders

Sm-Fe-based alloys were prepared by MA of initial powders using a Pulverisette-4 vario-planetary mill (Fritsch GmbH, Germany). This technique applies a short isothermal holding time. The obtained nanocrystalline powders are very reactive and are easily subjected to nitriding. Moreover, nanocrystalline materials have an adapted microstructure for extrinsic magnetic properties [14].

To prevent oxidation of the initially-formed powder, all operations were handled inside a glove box under a high-purity nitrogen atmosphere. Powders initially nominally composed of Fe and 15 at.% Sm (5 at.% excess Sm) were milled for 10 h using a planetary ball mill with hard metal vials and balls under an argon atmosphere and a ball-to-powder mass ratio of 10:1 using a disc rotation velocity of 200 rpm. The main-to-planetary disc rotation velocity ratio was 1:-1.5. The as-milled powders were annealed in a vacuum furnace (VBF-1200X; MTI Corporation, USA) under a medium vacuum of about 150 mtorr at 630 °C to 750 °C for 30 minutes. The excess 5 at. % Sm was used to compensate for possible Sm evaporation during the isothermal hold.

Characterizations

The powder morphology and distribution of elements per volume of powder particle were examined using a scanning electron microscope (Mira 3 Tescan; Tescan Orsay Holding a.s, Czech Republic) at 20 kV equipped with an Oxford INCA Wave 500 add-on device.

Thermal analysis was performed using a DSC device for thermal testing of materials (Setaram SETSYS Evolution 16; Setaram Instrumentation SAS, France) under an argon flow of 30 ml min-1, a heating rate of 5 °C min-1, and a temperature range of 20 °C to 1000 °C.

The crystal structures of the obtained powders were characterized by X-ray diffraction (XRD) on a Brucker D2 Phaser (Bruker Corporation, USA) in Co-Kα-radiation (λ = 1.79026 Å) at a scanning step of 0.05° (2θ scale) for 0.5 s in the range of 2θ = 30° to 100°. TOPAS software was used to carry out the Rietveld refinement of the XRD patterns and to analyze the crystal structures and calculate the lattice parameters and grain size. The quality of the Rietveld refinement was evaluated in terms of goodness of fit (GOF) and the R factor (R_{wp}). Generally, when GOF is close to 1 and R_{wp} is less than 10%, the result can be considered reliable.

Magnetic properties were measured at ambient temperature (300 K) using a vibrating sample magnetometer (Lakeshore 7410 model VSM; Lake Shore Cryotronics, Inc, USA) at the maximum magnetic field of 22 kOe, a measurement sensitivity of 4 emu, and a measurement step of 200 Oe.

3 Results and discussion

Powder Morphology

The SEM micrographs in Fig. 1a and 1b show the morphologies of as-milled Sm_2Fe_{17} powders. The as-milled powder appeared in the form of irregular highly agglomerated particles with an average size of 8 µm. The elemental analysis obtained by energy-dispersive X-ray spectroscopy indicated uniform and homogeneous distribution of each initial element in the particle. The XRD results showed that a two-phase mixture of amorphous Sm-Fe and α-Fe was formed in the powder. The broadening peaks corresponded to α-Fe (110) and (200) planes and showed grain refinement and an accumulation of defects and strains induced by MA.

Fig.. 1. SEM micrographs of as-milled powder.

DSC Measurements

The crystallization temperature of the amorphous Sm_2Fe_{17} alloy was determined using DSC, yielding three characteristic peaks as shown in Fig. 2. The first peak corresponded to the formation $SmFe_3$ phases. Tan [13] showed that the free energy barrier for the nucleation of $SmFe_3$ is smaller than that of Sm_2Fe_{17}, thus the reaction $Sm + 3Fe \rightarrow SmFe_3$ proceeds at lower temperatures. Small thermal fluctuations at 510 °C to 570 °C cannot agitate nucleations in Sm_2Fe_{17} at appreciable rates. The second peak corresponded to the formation Sm_2Fe_{17} phases. This stable chemical compound was found to form at 626 °C to 719 °C, and this was confirmed by XRD. The third peak was not determined, but the XRD phase compositions did not change with increasing heat treatment temperature. Therefore, this peak likely corresponds to the formation $SmFe_2$ phases, though this was not indicated by XRD analysis. As shown in [13], the free energy barrier for nucleation of $SmFe_3$, $\Delta G(SmFe_3)$, is lower than those for $SmFe_2$ or Sm_2Fe_{17}. $\Delta G(SmFe_3)$ being less than $\Delta G(Sm_2Fe_{17})$ can be associated with the elimination of a larger number of Sm/Fe interfaces during nucleation of $SmFe_3$, and $\Delta G(SmFe_3)$ being less than $\Delta G(SmFe_2)$ can be associated with lower driving forces for the reaction leading to the formation of $SmFe_2$. Based on these results, a series of experiments was designed to determine the effect of heat treatment on the magnetic properties of Sm_2Fe_{17} alloy.

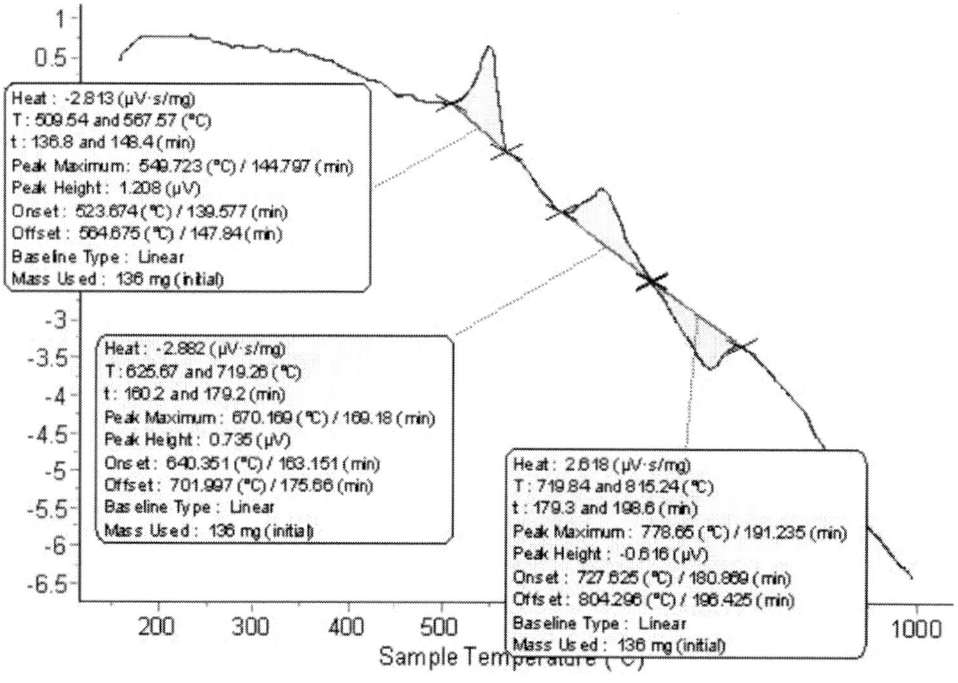

Fig. 2. Differential scanning calorimetry curve of the Sm_2Fe_{17} alloy obtained by mechanical alloying.

XRD Measurements

Fig. 3 shows the XRD patterns after isothermal holds at 630 °C, 660 °C, 690 °C, and 750 °C. All XRD patterns for these annealed powders were successfully indexed based on Sm_2Fe_{17}, $SmFe_3$, and Sm_2O_3. The Sm_2Fe_{17} rhombohedral Th_2Zn_{17}-type phase was shown by the main diffraction peaks (00-051-0910 pattern) at 34.92°, 42.44°, 49.42°, 49.85°, 51.09°, and 56.13°, corresponding to the (113), (300), (220), (303), (006), and (223) crystal planes. The peaks on all three XRD patterns at 40.35°, 41.85°, 47.22°, 48.03°, and 64.17° corresponded to the (110), (113), (021), (202), and (211) crystal planes of $SmFe_3$ (00-050-1450 pattern). The diffraction peaks at 33.45°, 35.95°, 38.85°, and 55.15° corresponded to the (222), (321), (400), and (440) crystal planes of Sm_2O_3 (00-015-0813 pattern). The $SmFe_3$ was formed because the Sm content in the initial powder mixture was higher than that required for formation of a nominal Sm_2Fe_{17} phase. This excess was included to account for possible losses of Sm during heat treatment or additions of α-Fe from wear debris from the vials and balls during MA. Peaks for the free α-Fe phase were not detected. Decreasing the isothermal holding temperature from 750 °C to 630 °C led to a simultaneous broadening and shifting of the Sm_2Fe_{17} diffraction peaks.

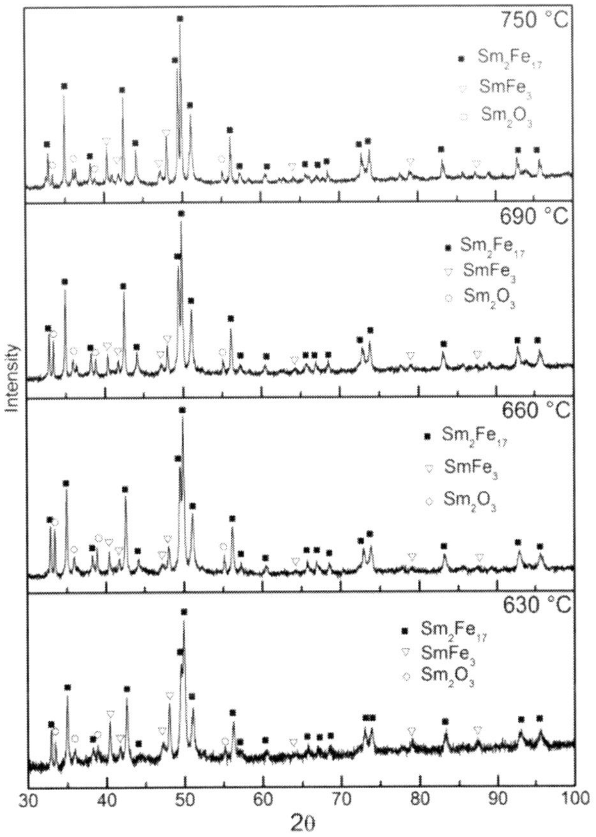

Fig.. 3. X-ray diffraction patterns of Sm_2Fe_{17} alloy after isothermal hold at various temperatures.

The best Rietveld refinement (GOF = 1.23; R_{wp} = 3.34%) was for powder annealed at 630 °C, resulting in three crystalline phases. One was Sm_2Fe_{17} with lattice parameters a = 8.5425(7) Å, c = 12.4692(15) Å, and V = 788.03(15) Å^3. Another was $SmFe_3$ with lattice parameters a = 5.1837(5) Å, c = 24.856(7) Å, and V = 578.4(2) Å^3. The third was Sm_2O_3 with lattice parameters a = 10.9350(15) Å and V = 1307.6(5) Å^3. Increasing the isothermal holding temperature to 750 °C changed the lattice parameters from a = 8.5425(2) to a = 8.55253(14) Å and from c = 12.4692(2) to c = 12.4374(3)Å. The largest lattice volume was achieved at 660 °C and was 788.46(8) Å^3. The relative changes in the lattice parameters a, c, and V can be seen in Fig. 4. The corresponding Rietveld refinement GOF and R_{wp} values were 1.47 and 2.55% when the hold temperature was 660 °C, 1.44 and 2.61% when it was 690 °C, and 1.41 and 2.57% when it was 750 °C. The Rietveld refinement results of the Sm_2Fe_{17} alloy XRD patterns are shown in Table 1.

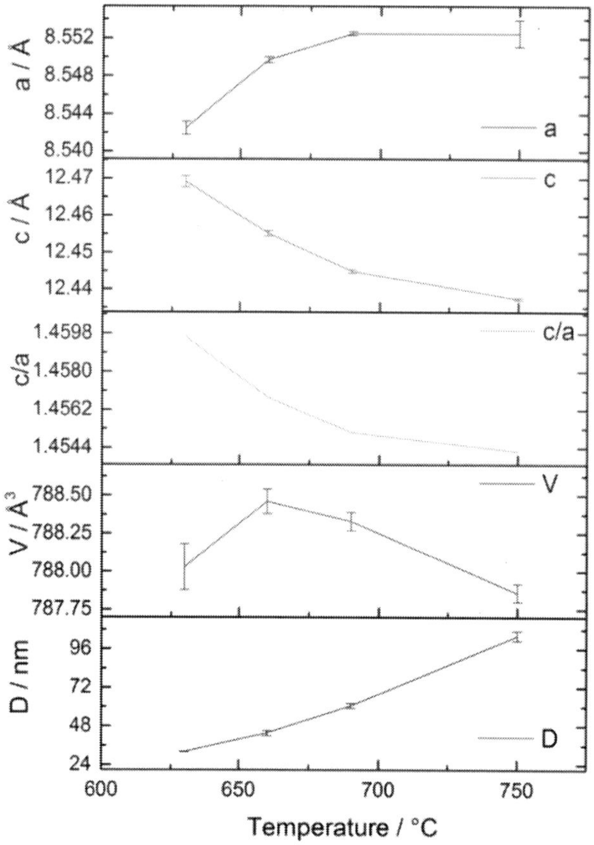

Fig. 4. Lattice parameters a and c, c/a ratio, unit-cell volume (V), and grain size (D) of Sm_2Fe_{17} alloy as a function of heat treatment temperature.

Table 1. Crystallographic parameters from the Rietveld refinement of Sm_2Fe_{17} alloys annealed at various temperatures.

Heat treatment temperature, °C	Lattice parameters			D (nm)
	a (Å)	c (Å)	V (Å^3)	
630 °C	8.5425(7)	12.4692(15)	788.03(15)	32.2(2)
660 °C	8.5497(3)	12.4552(7)	788.46(8)	43.7(16)
690 °C	8.5525(2)	12.4449(5)	788.33(6)	60.7(15)
750 °C	8.5525(14)	12.4374(3)	787.86(1)	104(3)

Notes: V = unit cell volume; D = grain size.

The c parameter of the Th_2Zn_{17}-unit cell decreased, and the a parameter increased, with greater isothermal holding temperatures (Fig. 4). The c/a ratio showed that the c parameter grew at a higher rate than the *a* parameter decreased. This preferential distortion of the Th_2Zn_{17}-unit cell along the a- and c-axes may be indicative of remaining defects and strains after low-temperature isothermal holding. The diffraction peaks of the Sm_2Fe_{17}, $SmFe_3$, and Sm_2O_3 phases narrowed with rising isothermal holding temperature, indicating better crystallinity at higher temperatures. The volume of the Th_2Zn_{17} phase was extracted by Rietveld refinement of the XRD data. The overall volume of the unit cell increased with increasing temperature, up to 660 °C. Thereafter, it decreased with temperature (Fig. 4).

The XRD data also showed that, as a result of isothermal holding at 630 °C, a nanocrystalline structure was formed with a grain size of 32(2) nm. Crystal size increased with isothermal holding temperature to 100 to 110 nm.

Magnetic Measurements

Hysteresis loops for non-magnetized samples are presented in Fig. 5. It can be seen that the coercive force of the samples increased from 200 to 800 Oe through increases in isothermal holding temperature (Fig. 5a). Coercivity increased with grains size reduction (Table 1). Yosida [15] and Khazzan et al. [16] showed that the coercive field value and the magnetization reversal process depend not only on chemical composition, temperature, and magnetic anisotropy, but also strongly on microstructure. Higher coercivities can be achieved when grains are finer [15, 18]. When isothermal holding temperature is low, the sample often has many defects resulting from high-energy milling; in this case, crystallite sizes are very small. It is well known that crystalline size increases with isothermal holding temperature. Therefore, grain size is optimal after an isothermal hold at 630 °C. The c parameter and grain size were found to be strongly correlated to magnetic properties.

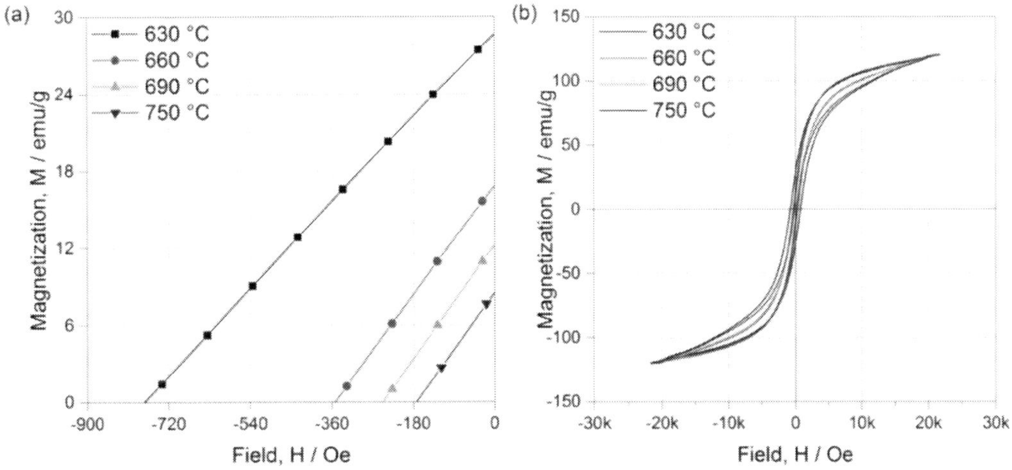

Fig. 5. Hysteresis loops of Sm_2Fe_{17} alloys formed using isothermal holds at various temperatures.

As depicted in Table 2, most Sm_2Fe_{17} powders, produced using different processes that resulted in much larger grain or particle sizes, (0.3 to 20 μm), showed much lower coercivities, ranging between 240 and 480 Oe. This is the result of the size effect of the Sm_2Fe_{17} powder. Only Yun et al. [19] used a modified reduction-diffusion process to synthesize Sm_2Fe_{17} nanopowders, achieving coercivities greater than 1000 Oe.

Table 2. Magnetic properties of Sm_2Fe_{17} alloy synthesized by various processes.

Process	Particle size, D (μm)	Coercivity, H_c (Oe)	Saturation Magnetization, M_s (emu/g)	Ref.
MA	8	800	121	This study
MRD process	0.1-0.3	1000	128	**[19]**
Arc melting	<50	300	110	**[23]**
Induction melting	<25	550	117	**[24]**
R-D process	5-10	300	110-130	**[4]**
HDDR	<3	600	130	**[3]**

4 Conclusion

Formation temperature range of the stable chemical compound Sm_2Fe_{17} was determined using DSC. Best magnetic properties archived 630 °C. This temperature corresponds to the beginning of the Sm_2Fe_{17} formation. In Sm_2Fe_{17}, the single domain is approximately 350 nm [20]. Below this grain size, coercivity should rapidly reduce with grain size; we observed abnormal coercivity in ultrafine crystallite powders. The field of 22 kOe which may be generated by VSM magnetometer are below magnetization field required for saturation of approx. 40 kOe [21] of Sm_2Fe_{17} intermetallic compound. Proper magnetization might result in better magnetic values [22].

5 References

1. J. M. D. Coey, H. J. Sun Magn. Magn. Mater., **87(3)** (1990)
2. N. Imaoka, T. Iriyama, S. J. Itoh Alloy Comp., **222(1)** (1995)
3. J. Sun, C. Cui, Y. Zhang, L. Li, J. Gao, et al. Mater. Chem. Phys., **97** (2006)
4. J.-G. Lee, S.-K. Kang, P.-Z. Si, C.-J. J. Choi Magn., **16(2)** (2011)
5. A. A. Popovich, A. S. Verevkin, N. G. Razumov, T. A. Popovich, ARPN J. Eng. Ap. Sc., **11(3)** (2016)
6. Q. Fang, X. An, F. Wang, Y. Li, et al. J. Magn. Magn. Mater., **410** (2016)
7. C. H. Lee, T. Fukunaga, Y. Yamada, U. Mizutani, H. J. Okamoto, Phase Equilibria., **14** (1993)
8. C.-H.Lee, Y.-S. Kwon Met.Mater. Int., **8(2)** (2002)
9. X. Lv, W. Liu, W. Cui, X. Zhao, W. Ren, Z. Zhang, J.Appl.Phys., **103** (2008)
10. L. Schultz, K. Schnitzke, J. Wecker, M. Katter, C. Kuhrt, J. Appl. Phys., **70(10)** (1991)
11. K. Majima, N. Niimi, S. Katsuyama, H. Nagai, H. Tomizawa, J. Alloy Comp., **193(1)** (1993)
12. C. Kuhrt, K. Schnitzke, L. Schultz J.Appl.Phys., **73(10)** (1993)
13. M. J. Tan, Mater. Sci., **29(5)** (1994)
14. I. Nehdi, L. Bessais, C. Djega-Mariadassou, M. Abdellaoui, H. Zarrouk, J. Alloy Comp., **351** (2003)
15. Y.Yoshida, The International Forum on Magnetic Applications, Technologies and Materials (Magnetics 2016), Jacksonville, Fl, USA, 21-22 January (2016)
16. S. Khazzan, L. Bessais, G. Van Tendeloo, N. J. Mliki, Magn. Magn. Mater., **363** (2014)
17. K. Uestuener, M.Katter, Rodewald W, IEEE Trans. Magn., **42(10)** (2006)
18. C. H. Chen, S. Kodat, M. H. Walmer, S. F. Cheng, M. A. Willard, V. G. Harris J. Appl. Phys., **93(10)** (2003)
19. J.-C. Yun, S.-M. Yoon, J.-Y. Lee, J.-P. Choi, J.-S. Lee, Mater. Trans., **55 (10)** (2014)
20. K. Kobayashi, X.-L. Rao, J. M. D. Coey, D. Givord, J. Appl. Phys., **80** (1996)
21. O. Isnard, S. Miraglia, M. Guillot, D.J. Fruchart, Appl. Phys. **75(10)** (1994)
22. M. Przybylski, D. Kapelski, B. Ślusarek, S. Wiak. Sensors **16(4)** (2016)
23. L. Zhao, L. Zheng, Funct. Mat. Let. **6(4)** (2013)
24. T. Saito, H. Miyoshi, D.J. Nishio-Hamane, Alloy Comp. **519** (2012)

A digital method for correcting planned electric energy consumption as a step to the Energynet market

Oleg Russkov[1*], and *Sergei* Saradszhivili[1]

[1] Peter the Great Saint Petersburg Polytechnic University, 195251 Polytechnicheskaya st. 29, Russian Federation

Abstract. Creating the modern high-tech industry should be viewed as a fusion of material and digital production and control methods. Industrial enterprises with uneven electric energy consumption, which have failed to adapt to the requirements of modern digital wholesale electricity market, have to spend significant money to pay for hourly deviations of electric energy, whose price constantly grows. A digital method for correcting planned electric energy consumption based on the theory of games is offered to reduce the costs of these enterprises, which have no possibility for regulating own load on a real time basis. The updating is carried out depending on hourly relations of prices on the wholesale electric energy market in order to exclude the risks of making unprofitable hourly transactions. An algorithm of the proposed method is provided and a predictive model developed on its basis is described and positive results of its testing on the basis of a metallurgical enterprise.

1 Introduction

Nowadays, digital technologies have found their way into all the areas of human activity. In particular, the digital economy is impossible without high-tech industry based on digital "future factories, within which a product passes through design stage to production at the shortest time and with minimum expenses. Several plans for developing perspective future markets, in particular, cross-industrial "Technet", "Autonet", "Energynet" markets have been approved in Russia to support this strategy at the Government level. Active participation of an electric energy consumer during on-line dispatching control of local energy system using digital algorithms and new generation devices is assumed within the framework of the latter. This will make it possible to develop transparent and accurate planning of loads for electric power generators within all the energy system segments. Within the framework of "Energynet" it is proposed to create digital algorithms and devices allowing optimal self-dispatching of the energy system. Thus, a future consumer will switch over from passive electric energy consumption to on-line participation in minimization of own hourly deviations of planned electric energy consumption from actual one. It should be noted that the task of adequate planning of consumption of any type of

* Corresponding author: zenit-che@mail.ru

resources has been relevant at all times. The main characteristic determining the accuracy of this planning is an uneven load curve. In particular, a metallurgical enterprise has an uneven nature of electric energy consumption due to the steel melting process peculiarities. Applying the quick-acting computing means and up-to-date predictive algorithms will allow combining the effects of digital methods on the functional process of an industrial enterprise and its economics improving the most important production and economic indicators of the country's entire industrial sectors, thus taking care of environmental problems, because active participation of industrial enterprises in the process of electric energy consumption will make it possible to refuse from loading inefficient electric energy generator by saving non-renewable resources to be used for electric energy generation.

2 Brief review of existing prediction methods

There is a great number of methods, which are actively applied to predict electric energy consumption. At present time, mathematical time series models prove to be the best, they include autoregressive models, exponential smoothing models, neural network models, Markov's chain models and those based on classification and regression trees CART [1]. These models are used by industrial enterprises as well in conditions of wholesale electric energy market [2]. However, a significant decrease in predictive accuracy with irregularity of time series are referred to well-known disadvantages of these models [3]. The human factor and non-stationary nature of steel melting process are the main causes of irregular electric energy consumption during metallurgical production [4]. Some metallurgical enterprises, in particular, Oskolsky electrometallurgical plant, try to use neural network models to plan their hourly electric energy consumption [5]. Works on an analysis of hourly electric energy consumed by Magnitogorsk metallurgical plant show the inefficiency of time series models and correlative-regression analysis [6]. For example, Volzhsky pipe plant carries out involuntarily planning activities according to average previous day's consumption based on an expert judgment made by personnel of the chief power engineer department [7]. Foreign researchers ironically call this approach a "straw man's prediction" [8]. Due to no generally accepted solution available for planning irregular consumption there are prediction methods for market price indicators actively developed, which are used to predict intermediate electric energy consumption [9]. Therefore, at present time there is a big field for experiments and improvement of digital methods and models including those within the "Energynet" area.

3 Cost elements of electric energy consumed by a large enterprise

Electric energy cost S on the wholesale energy market (EM) at every hour of day is calculated in accordance with market regulations [10, 11] as per the formula below:

$$S = C_{DAM} \cdot V_p + \begin{cases} \left(V_f - V_p\right) \cdot C_{BM+}, if \left(V_f - V_p\right) \\ \left(V_f - V_p\right) \cdot C_{BM-}, if \left(V_f - V_p\right) \end{cases}, \tag{1}$$

Where C_{DAM} is a price on the day ahead market (DAM), V_p is planned, V_f is actual consumption, C_{BM+} is a buying price, C_{BM-} is a selling price on the balancing market (BM).

In this case the EM with the purpose of stimulating the market participants for accurate planning of hourly electric energy consumptions sets the DAM and BM prices in accordance with the following formula:

$$C_{BM-} \leq C_{DAM} \leq C_{BM+}. \tag{2}$$

Every hour the price of one of the BM prices matches the DAM price (Fig. 1), determining the profitable type of transaction: type 0 – C_{DAM} coincides with C_{BM+} (a white rectangular), type 1 – C_{DAM} coincides with C_{BM-} (a black rectangular):

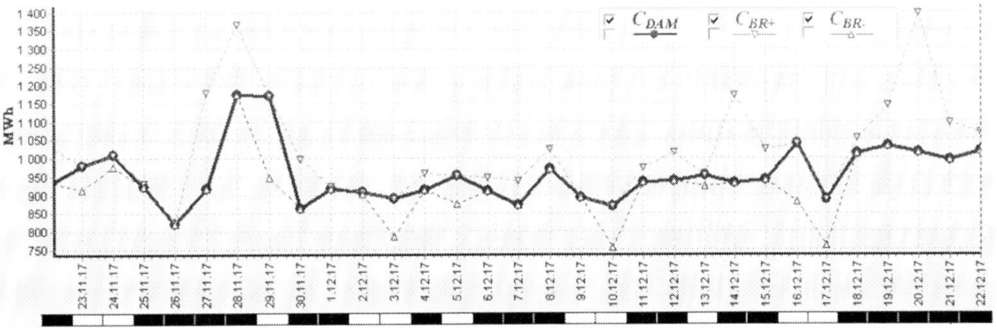

Fig. 1. DAM and BM price ratio for a metallurgical enterprise in Volgograd region at time of day 5:00-6:00.

For an EM consumer there are 2 types of costs related to payment for hourly electric energy deviations.

-total cost of hourly deviation to be paid at high BM prices relative to the DAM ones. This type of costs can be reduced without changing the total volume of deviations.

-cost of EM out-of-balance adjustment interest invoiced by the commercial market operator upon completion of settling period according to a ratio of certain consumer's total hourly deviation volume to all the EM participants' total deviation volume [11]. This type of costs can be reduced by only changing the total volume of consumer electric energy deviations.

The characteristics of enterprise's load curve determine an option to be selected to reduce costs. If the consumer has a relatively even load curve then he can use well recommended existing time series models and reduce the total volume of his deviations. If the consumer can control the load on a real time basis then he will be able to minimize his deviations without any predictive models. If the consumer has an uneven load curve that does not allow planning in-house electric energy consumption by means of existing predictive models [7] as well as if he cannot regulate the load on a real time basis due to reasons that are not related to the production technology then he has to deal with a great amount of electric energy deviations. A metallurgical enterprise has this type of electric energy consumption in particular as it has been mentioned above. Consequently for these EM participants there is only one way to reduce the costs of both types – avoiding unprofitable hourly transactions on the BM by switching over from quantitative prediction of electric energy consumption to qualitative prediction of BM and DAM price ratios. Thus, planned consumption V_p is predicted in a vicarious manner.

4 Digital method for updating of planned electric energy consumption

At the first stage the enterprise calculates its load curve for the next days based on the production plans of its main process facilities. The main task of this first stage is to form such a planned hourly load curve that will be close to an average value of actual electric energy consumption on the next day as much as possible. Calculation is carried out according to the following formula:

$$V_p = \frac{\sum_{j=1}^{k} Pl_j * U_j}{24}, \tag{3}$$

Where j is the serial number of facility, k is the number of facilities, Pl_j is the production plan, (tn), U_j is the specific consumption of facility j, (kW·h/tn).

The preliminarily calculated planned curve for each hour separately is updated at the second stage. In this case it is taken into account that all the EM participants have no full information about DAM requests from each other neither about existing limitations of the unified energy system cross-flows nor about actual changes in demand for electric energy by consumers of their region [10]. Consequently, the enterprise with uneven uncontrolled consumption needs to solve the task of making decisions and selecting the optimal option from a variety of alternate values for updating the planned electric energy consumption in uncertain conditions related to the future ratios of both hourly DAM and BM prices and the volumes of planned and actual electric energy consumption [7]. The mathematical mechanism that is mostly suitable for resolving this type of task is a mechanism of game theory. The EM participant competes to get the maximum profit by sending their requests in attempts to predict the requests sent by other participants (Fig. 2).

Fig. 2. “A game" of wholesale electric energy market participants.

For example, the buyer indicating 24 3-stage pairs of "volume-prices in the DAM bid establishes the price value that he agrees to pay for the given volume of electric energy at a certain hour of day, trying to predict the prices values set by the generators in similar bids. If we consider the influence of participants’ moves on each other in a day following the predicted one then these participants use the statistic values of DAM and BM prices of the previous day that in their turn have been determined by earlier moves made by all the EM participants (Fig. 3).

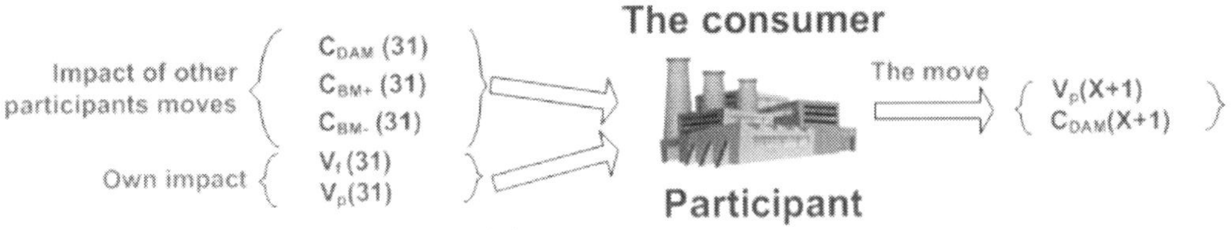

Fig. 3. Influence of other EM game participants.

Thus, the EM game is consistent, because the hourly price values received from the market Operators in accordance with Regulations [10, 11] indirectly depend on the previous moves made by all the participants. Taking into account the presence of uncertainty relative to other participants' bids placed on this current day it is possible to say the consistent game of the EM participants is a game with incomplete information in accordance with generally accepted classification. Presuming that the determination of each main analyzed parameters – type of price and electric energy volume ratios- is a nondeterministic experiment in which only one of the two mutually exclusive outcomes can be implemented (Fig. 4) for formal description of the outcome implementation process during the analyzed interval being equal to the EM settling period, it is possible to apply the tools of the theory of probability [12].

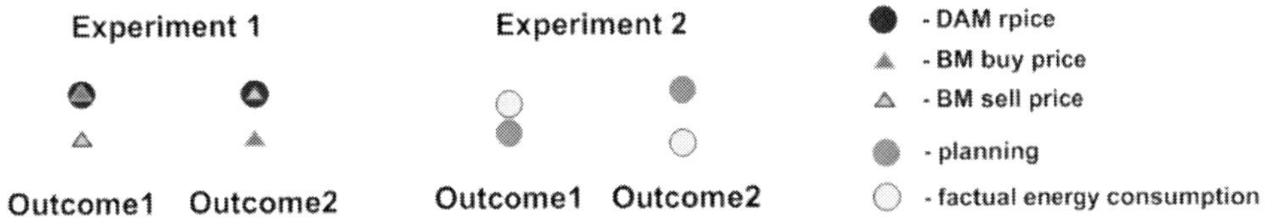

Fig. 4. Non deterministic experiments during determination of price and volume ratios.

Because the principle of optimality that is used to select a suitable alternative from a number of possible update values V_p is unknown, it should be found by solving the selection task in accordance with the decision – making theory. The final decision will be a function of utility or profit. The target function of a model for solving the set task in opinion of a person making the decision can be described as follows [7]:

$$\begin{cases} \sum_{i=1}^{N} S^{i}_{DAM+BM} < \sum_{i=1}^{N} S^{*i}_{DAM+BM}, \\ \sum_{i=1}^{N} V_i \leq \sum_{i=1}^{N} V^{*}_{i}, \end{cases} \tag{4}$$

Where S^{i}_{DAM+BM} is electric energy cost and V_i is the amount of deviations after updating the planed electric energy consumption, S^{*i}_{DAM+BM} is electric energy cost and V^{*}_{i} is the amount of deviations before updating, i is the number of hour, N is the number of hours within a reporting month.

Thus, in this case the decision-making task is a multi-criterion task: one criterion is to reduce electric energy cost and another one is to reduce the amount of deviations. However, considering the fact that the amounts of deviations can be expressed in their costs and presuming the EM-out-of-balance update fraction as the second type costs [11], the task becomes a single-criterion one: its criterion is electric energy cost.

Summarizing the abovementioned information makes it possible to say that in order to ensure that only the profitable BM transactions are made, the enterprise needs to solve the task of selecting such an update value for preliminarily calculated planned electric energy consumption task that will make the expected hourly profit prevail over the loss within this settling period by calculating the utility function based on one criterion. In order to calculate the utility function, it is necessary to consider all possible options in the electric energy price-to-volume ratios during updates of V_p. Let us repeat briefly the outcome of utility functions earlier calculated by the authors [4, 7] by an example of negative update function F_0, which makes planned volume V_p go down to updated value V_c based on 6 main price-to-volume ratios (Fig. 5). In this situation, the actual, uneven and uncontrolled consumption V_f can assume any values. Let us remind that there are 12 possible options of price-to-volume ratios (6 for each update type).

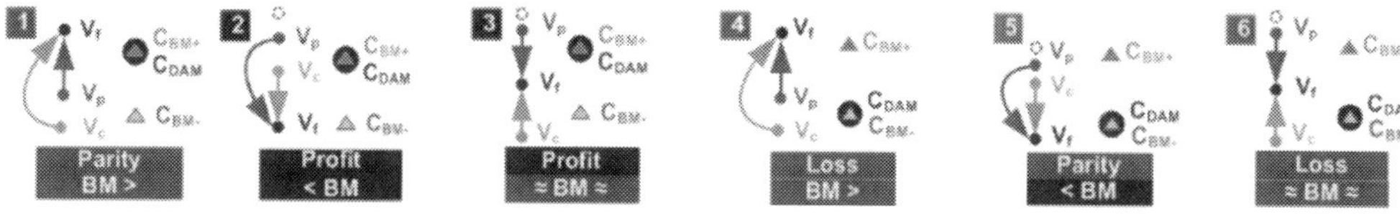

Fig. 5. Outcomes of experiments during determination of main price-to-volume ratios for negative update.

Let us record the possible profit for each option under consideration in accordance with probabilities of price-to-volume ratios obtained as a result of their analysis over 31 previous days – an interval being equal to the EM reporting period:

$$\begin{cases} P_1 | P_2 : -V \cdot C_{dif}; \\ P_1 | P_3 : V \cdot \Delta_0 + V \cdot C_{dif}; \\ P_1 | P_4 : (V_p - V_f) \cdot \Delta_0 + (V_p - 2 \cdot V_f + V_c) \cdot C_{dif}; \\ 1 - P_1 | P_2 : -V \cdot \Delta_1 - V \cdot C_{dif}; \\ 1 - P_1 | P_3 : V \cdot C_{dif}; \\ 1 - P_1 | P_4 : -(V_f - V_c) \cdot \Delta_1 + (V_p - 2 \cdot V_f + V_c) \cdot C_{dif}, \end{cases} \tag{5}$$

Where P_1 is probability of price ratio determination, when DAM and BM+ coincide; P_2, P_3 are probabilities that V_f will be higher or lower than V_p respectively; P_4 is probability that V_f will be between V_p and V_c; V is the update value equal to $|V_p$-$V_c|$; Δ_0, Δ_1 is an average difference in prices during the analyzed interval for BM price ratios of type 0 and 1 respectively; C_{dif} is an average price of deviations according to the enterprise unbalance share on the EM within the analyzed month [11].

The presence of BM price difference values Δ_0 and Δ_1 in these formulas is very important, because this BM price difference determines the profit or loss cost, which the economic effect for each day hour depends on:

$$Effect^{+}_{-} = (C_{BM+} - C_{BM-}) * \mathrm{V} \ , \tag{6}$$

The second possible parameter, as seen from the formula, is update size V.

Function F_0 is calculated using the full probability formula provided that less common options 3 and 6 are neglected (their total probability at average hourly consumption of enterprise equal to about 150 MWt·h and update size equal to 5 MWt·h amounts to ≈0.03), transformation of P_3 into $(1- P_2)$ and reduction of P_4:

$$F_0 = V \cdot (P_1 \cdot d_0 - P_2 \cdot d_1 + P_1 \cdot P_2 \cdot (d_1 - d_0) - 2 \cdot P_2 \cdot C_{dif} + C_{dif}) \tag{7}$$

The utility function of positive update F_1 is opposite by sign to function F_0. The update sign and volume of hourly electric energy consumption initially expressed by “even curve” is determined according to the values of utility functions F_0 and F_1 [7]:

$$\begin{cases} F_0 > 0 : V_c = V_p - V; \\ F_1 > 0 : V_c = V_p + V; \\ F_0 = F_1 = 0 : V_c = V_p; \end{cases} \tag{8}$$

An update carried out in accordance with the calculated values of these functions makes the profit prevail over loss within a reporting month in accordance with statistical stability property. In this situation it is worth noting the positive moment for the planned consumption update method. The BM prices BM C_{BM+} and C_{BM-} are determined by the EM System Operator (SO) based on the calculation of price indicator C_{ind} [11]:

$$C_{BM+} = max(C_{DAM}; C_{ind}) \tag{9}$$

$$C_{BM-} = min(C_{DAM}; C_{ind}) \tag{10}$$

In case of negative update V_p, when it is expected that the price ratio of type 0 is established (with profitable buy on the BM), and the SO predictive model is stimulated towards a decrease in BM price-indicator and consequently towards an increase in probability of price ratios of expected type (Fig. 6).

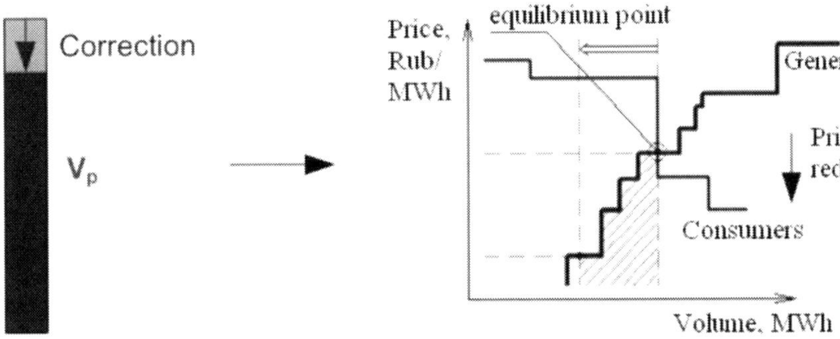

Fig. 6. Influence of negative update on profitable price ratios of type 0.

And on the contrary, when V_p is updated towards an increase in expectation of price ratios of type 1 (with profitable sale on BM), the SO predictive model is stimulated towards an increase in BM price indicators and formation of price ratio of type 1 (Fig. 7). The influence of this factor depends on the enterprise's electric energy consumption share in its region and update size of its planned hourly electric energy consumption.

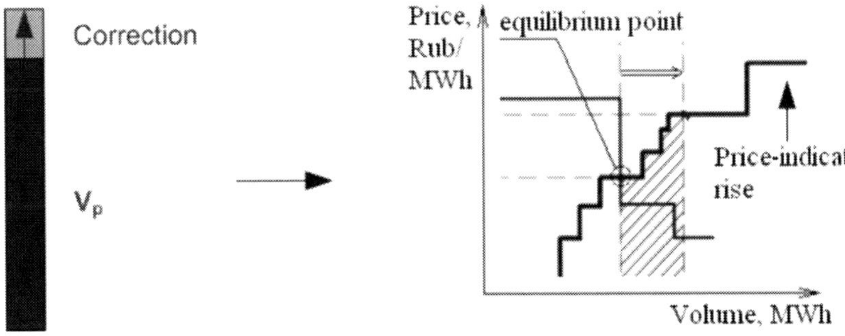

Fig. 7. Influence of positive update on profitable price ratio of type 1.

The DAM and BM price ratios are virtually the signals given by the SO to the consumer about how the generators are loaded at a certain hour and how electric energy should be consumed. That is why following these signals makes it possible to avoid unprofitable transactions made on the BM with no excessive load of inefficient generators and as a consequence, save non-renewable resources such as coal, gas, black oil, which helps solve environmental problems within an energy consumption region and the country as a whole.

5 Algorithm of proposed method

The scaled-up algorithm of this method, which is used to implement the proposed method is shown in Fig. 8. The actions described are carried out for each hour of day, and calculations can be made in parallel in this situation. It is presumed that the enterprise has runs a database on electric energy consumption V_p ,V_f and prices C_{DAM} ,C_{BM+} ,C_{BM-} for each hour of day as deep as 31 days for the future period.

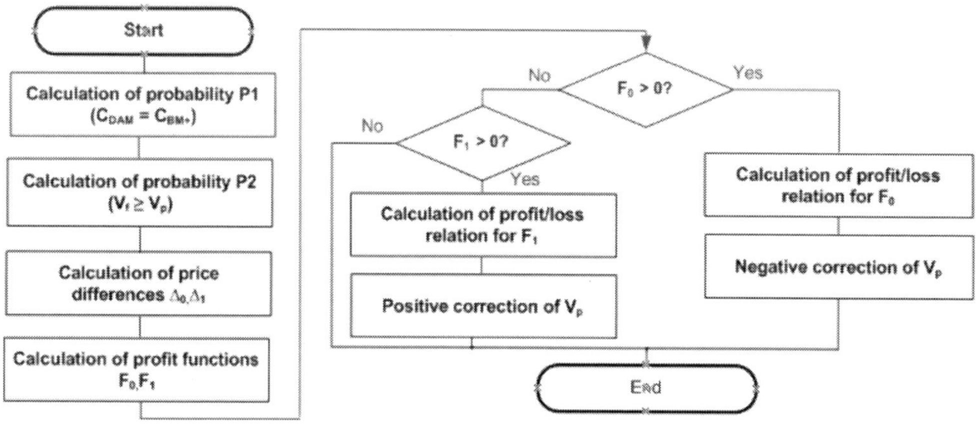

Fig. 8. Algorithm of digital method for updating of planned electric energy consumption.

The computer software operating in accordance with the described algorithm received state registration certificate in 2017 as per the established procedure.

6 Method validation

The software module in C++ language implementing the above-mentioned algorithm operates within the electric energy data measuring complex of metallurgical enterprise operating in the Volgograd region. Every day the module analyzes the values of electric energy prices and volumes over the previous 31 days for every 24 hours, issuing recommendations for updating its planned electric energy consumption. Profit is determined by comparing the financial results of original and updated DAM bids (fig. 9).

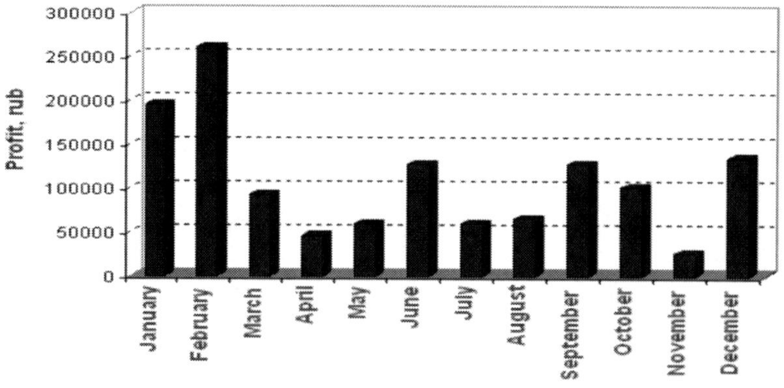

Fig. 9. Profit from recommendations of digital method broken down into months of 2017.

Total profit gained from recommendations for updating the enterprise's planned electric energy consumption amounts to about 1.3 mln rubles for 2017.

Actual distribution of price-to-volume ratio experiment outcomes (Fig. 5) is shown in Fig. 10. As seen in the figure for the current software version the maximum quantity of outcomes corresponds to the option when the algorithm finds it difficult to choose an alternative for update, as a result the planned electric energy consumption remains unchanged.

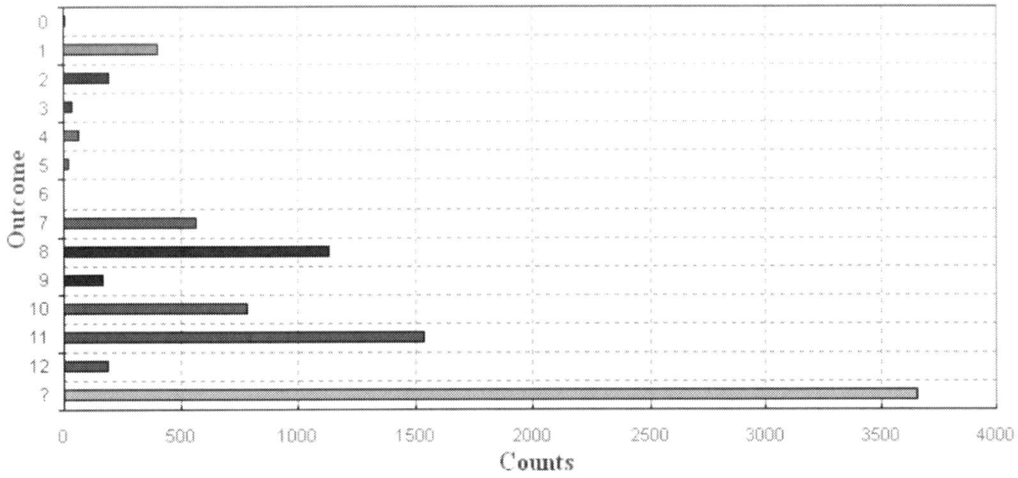

Fig. 10. Distribution of DAM and BM price options from 1.01.17 to 31.12.17.

Thus, with recorded economic effect there is a significant margin for further improving the algorithm by adjusting its main parameters.

7 Conclusion

The proposed digital method for updating the planned electric energy consumption allows solving the main task to be faced during planning of uneven, unregulated electric energy consumption by an industrial enterprise – reducing the electric energy consumption cost with no possible direct influence on the deviations of actual electric energy consumption from planned one. In this case the method is a step in creating a new high-tech industry using digital algorithms and means for optimizing the production process with minimum costs of all resources. In particular, the proposed digital algorithms allows enterprises that use it to be ahead on the developing prospective "Energynet" market, because these enterprises stop being passive energy consumers and become smart participants in the energy market, which makes it possible, among other issues, to minimize the cost of in-house hourly deviations of planned electric energy consumption from actual one. In modern conditions of financial crisis it allows large industrial enterprises, many of which are city-forming ones and have to fill city and regional budgets, to have an additional high-tech tool to reduce their running costs and enhance their competitiveness. It is also important that updating the planned electric energy consumption in accordance with electric energy market signals results in no excessive load of inefficient generator and as a consequence saves non-renewable natural resources.

References

1. H.K. Alfares, M. Nazeeruddin, Int. J. of Sys. Sc., **33.1** (2002)

2. P.V. Val, *Short-term forecasting of power consumption of a mining enterprise in the conditions of the wholesale electricity and capacity market* (SibFY, Krasnoyarsk, 2012)
3. B.I. Makoklyuev, V.F.Ech, Electric Power Plants, **5** (2005)
4. O.V. Russkov, S.E. Saradzhishvili, ICIEAM, **1-4** (2017)
5. S.S. Novikov, *Technique of operational planning and management of power consumption of large-capacity electric steelmaking furnaces when operating in the wholesale electricity market* (MEI, 2008)
6. V.Sh. Trofimova, A.V. Lipatnikov, Newspaper of G. I. Nosov MSTU, **3** (2014)
7. O.V. Russkov, S.E. Saradgishvili, IOP Conf. Ser.: Earth and Env. Sc., **90** (2017)
8. M. Harris, *Inside the crystal ball: how to make and use* forecasts (Wiley, New York, 2015)
9. A.P. Dzuba, *Energy management of industrial enterprises* (SUSU, Chelyabinsk, 2014)
10. DAM Regulati [online], Available at: https://www.np-sr.ru/ru/regulation/joining/reglaments/1971 (2018)
11. BM Regulations [online], Available at: https://www.np-sr.ru/ru/regulation/joining/reglaments/1975 (2018)
12. I. G. Chernorytsky, *Methods of decision making* (BXV-Petersburg, Saint Petersburg, 2005)
13. M. Shahidehpour, H. Yamin, Z. Li, *Market operations in electric power systems: forecasting, scheduling and risk management* (Wiley, New York, 2002)

Building partnering in construction under conditions of a new information space

Yury Shamara[1,2], and *Evgeny* Smirnov[1*]

[1] Saint Petersburg State University of Architecture and Civil Engineering, 190005 2-ya Krasnoarmeiskaya st., 4, Russian Federation
[2] "KNGK-Group" Investment and Engineering Holding, 350000 Budennogo st. 117/1, Russian Federation

Abstract. The analysis of institutional and technological prerequisites is given in this article to implement the partnering mechanism in the Russian building with respect to the declaration of the state policy for formation of the digital economy and adoption of the relevant strategy and state program. Three elements of information environment which are under formation at present and that can form a technological basis for the wide application of the mechanism of partnering in the investment and building process are identified as the reference ones: technologies for building information modeling, information analysis systems which unite various construction aspects in a single complex, and banks of regulatory documents and standard forms of contracts for use by building participants. It was concluded that the conditions for transition from the conventional models for implementation of the investment and building process to the models based on the building participants' partnership have been created in Russia.
Key words: partnering, investment and building project, digital environment, BIM technologies, partnering agreement

1 Introduction

A modern investment and construction project unites and contractually binds many participants of the investment and building process. In this case, the central, system-forming element of contract relations in framework of the project is a general contract as A. E. Churbanov aptly notes [1]. Formation of the unified information space and implementation of new digital technologies in the building will require to review production relations both in this branch, and in the economy as a whole that is discussed in the reports of the Organization for Economic Cooperation and Development published in 2016 [2, 3].

With historical hindsight, the building contract was primarily considered as a document establishing the "game rules" and sanctions for their violation: In this case, the contact parties are mainly represented as rivals, and their contract is the enforcement means to fulfill their obligations under the building project. However, since the 1990s of the past

* Corresponding author: pnr@spbgasu.ru

century, the conceptual approach is increasingly being used in the foreign building practice according to which the participants of the investment and building project (IBP) are not considered as rivals, but, first of all, as partners progressing the same goal – project implementation. In this case, the building contract is represented less as the document where the game conditions and rules mandatory for observance by the Customer and Contractor, than as the document describing the conditions of the partnership between these two entities [4].

A significant number of studies abroad and a number of publications in Russia are devoted to the building partnership. The content of the partnership formed to implement the investment and building project is quite fully described in the paper of S. Børve, A. Rolstadås, I. Andersen and W. Aarseth [5], in the study of J. Bennett and A. Baird [6], as well as in the guidance papers of the Institution of Civil Engineers of the UK. This partnership means the following:

- open relationships that ensure transparency of pricing and project costs;
- joint management of project risks;
- mutual efforts for provision or improvement of preset project parameters;
- mutual efforts towards investor's cost cutout.

Chris Skeggs, summarizing the experience of partnering in the Australian building sector, points to the advantages of building partnering contracts in comparison with conventional ones: less disagreements and arbitrations, better characteristics of project results in terms of cost, time and quality, greater opportunities for saving the investor funds [7]. In support of the above mentioned, I. K. Pinkevich and E. B. Smirnov present a number of indicators obtained in Great Britain and that characterize the partnerships advantage over the conventional building contracts: increasing the ICP profitability by a mean of 25%, reducing the building cost by 10%, reducing the building time by 20% [8].

J. Bennett and S. L. Jayes point to extra costs as the partnership disadvantages; the partners bear these costs due to arrangement of cooperation at a higher (in comparison with normal construction contracts) level, a great number of meetings as well operation of a permanent coordinating body [9].

The papers of A. Howlett [11] and E. B. Smirnov [4] are devoted to the questions of building partnerships classification according to the conclusions of which the partnerships shall be classified as per three main characteristics: urgent or indefinite as per the nature of the partnership; a number of partners; the way of partnership documenting for.

Unfortunately, in the presence of a significant number of publications concerning the partnering between participants of the investment and building projects, insufficient attention is paid to assessment of a location and importance of information technology for the development and efficiency of these processes, while, according to the British Association of Building Products Manufacturers, the formation of national and regional information platforms in the field of building support will allow reducing investment costs by more than 30% [11]. As well as the study, the results of which are presented in the paper of W. Bouck [12], indicate the readiness of modern building for the transition to digital technology platforms. The analysis performed in 2013 by I. K. Pinkevich and E. B. Smirnov showed the conditions for implementation of partnering mechanisms in building practice starts to form in the Russian Federation, but this process is not quick due to insufficient support from the state and the professional community, and the absence of proper infrastructure [8]. The topic under consideration is actual in terms of the "Strategy of Information Society Development in the Russian Federation for 2017-2030" [13] and the state program "Digital Economy of the Russian Federation" [14] adopted in 2017, which provide the creation and development of the digital environment based on new business models, one of which can be a model of partnering between the participants of the investment and building process for the building sector.

The purpose of this article is to assess the existing institutional and process prerequisites for implementation of the partnering mechanism in the Russian building sector including for the state needs.

In the state program "Digital Economy of the Russian Federation", the digital environment is understood as a set of interconnected information systems based on the relative process platforms. The digital environment for the building industry shall be considered as the one consisting of three elements:

1. The process platform based on the building information modeling technologies (BIM technologies).
2. Information and analytical systems that unite various building aspects in a single complex and are updated based on the incoming information on resources and external environment changes.
3. The regulatory documentation banks, standard projects, standard forms of contracts, etc. for application by the building participants.

Let's consider in detail the specified elements of the digital environment and their importance for the formation of the partnering mechanism.

2 Information Modeling Technologies of Construction Objects

The information model of a building or structure is defined as a shared resource of information about an object which basic function is to provide team operations of all concerned parties with the project throughout its full life cycle [15]. Let's compare this definition with the one of the building partnerships which:

- are open for all the participants of the investment and building project;
- cover all stages of the investment and building project: from the concept development to finishing building operations and handover the object to the Customer, and in some instances it includes the object operation stage including running and capital repairs, registration and renovation;
- provide complete procedural project performance.

Taking into account the above definitions, it is obvious that information modeling technologies, when applied in full, are an ideal process base to implement building partnering mechanisms. The problem is that now the use of information modeling technology in the Russian Federation is limited, mainly, to pre-design studies and building design, that is, it is not beyond CAD (computer-aided design systems) that were developed and used in the days of the Soviet Union. To create full information environment based on the object information model that can form the basis for partnership relations, the object information model shall be combined with information systems that ensure continuous receipt and processing of data from the external sources.

3 National and Regional Information and Analytical Systems Used during Building

According to the experts, at present in the country there are about four hundred federal state information systems and about a thousand regional ones representing data on suppliers, goods, services, prices, etc. [16]. Let's consider the most important of them in terms of providing the partnering conditions.

3.1 Unified Information System (UIS) in the Field of State and Municipal Procurements

According to the experience of Commonwealth Nations, the partnerships have the greatest advantages over the conventional construction contracts when implementing projects in conditions of unstable financing, and those which are innovative, city-forming or emergency in nature. These include a significant number of construction projects for the state and municipal needs, which are often implemented in Russia in conditions of underfunding that reduces the effectiveness of relationships based on the commercial contracts, and where unformalized quasi-partnership relations are often formed spontaneously between the state customer and the contractor. It should be noted that the partnership does not contradict with the principle of competitiveness of public procurements, as partners are selected on a competitive basis like any other supplier of building activities and services. The analysis showed that in the Russian Federation as a whole there is the created institutional, process and information base that can provide competitive selection of partners in building projects for state needs including the following:

– unified information system in the field of public procurements;
– system of electronic platforms for electronic tenders;
– system of authorized organizations that provide the digital infrastructure functioning and are the centers of competence in this sphere.

The created digital environment can serve as a good basis for the wide implementation of partnering mechanisms in the building for public needs, but it will require a certain innovation to ensure the following:

– implementation of the "open book" principle;
– mechanism for joint management of project risks;
– the possibility of total package procurement contracts that integrate different types of operations at several stages of the investment and construction project.

3.2 Unified Pricing Information Systems and Building Products Telemarketing Systems

In December 2017, the Russian Federation introduced the federal government information system for building pricing (FGIS BP) that is intended to increase the reliability and transparency of building cost determination at all stages of the investment and building project. The FGIS BP focused on fixing the resource method of cost determination as the main method for building cost estimation and being one of the main peripheral interfaces of the building information models can provide ample opportunities for dynamic functional-cost analysis in the frameworks of partnerships to save investors' funds and increase the investment and building projects efficiency. The federal and regional pricing information systems are added by trade-information exchange-type systems, one of which is established in the Republic of Tatarstan. The analysis of the regional pilot project showed that the exchange mechanism allows removing the extra links in the procurement process, making the process of building costs forming as transparent as possible, and improving the calculations accuracy.

3.3 Other Information Systems and Data Bases

The following can be presented as the examples of other information-analytical resources relevant to the study topic:

– urban development support information system (UDSIS) including a classified set of documented information on territories development, their construction, availability of land and other information required for the public authorities, local government authorities;

– the Unified State Register of Design Documentation Appraisal Reports of Capital Construction Objects (FAI Glavgosexpertiza of Russia);

– database of objects white tag created in accordance with Federal Law No. 261 "On energy saving and increase of energy efficiency";

– databases of technical and economic of buildings and structure certificates created in various cities of Russia.

The integration of information and analytical systems and databases into a unified information network and their integration in the building information modeling system is the most important prerequisite for the development of the building partnering mechanism of the Russian Federation.

4 Regulatory Documents Banks, Development of Standard Contract Forms for Partnering Application

The partnership represents a new model of relationship for Russia between the participants of the investment and building process, and therefore it requires the proper provision of regulatory, methodological and contractual documentation. The partnership can be documented by inclusion a unified additional section describing the partnering terms obligatory for all participants in all contracts awarded under the building project. This method is implemented as a series of model building contracts NEC (New Engineering Contract) developed by the Institute of Civil Engineers of Great Britain (ICE) for application in national and international building projects [17]. The second way of partnering registration provides for the conclusion of the investment and building project of a separate multilateral partnership agreement by the participants that is complementary relative to the awarded bilateral contracts, or completely replacing them. Such an agreement should be open so that, while progressing the project, all of its key participants: the customer, the designer, the general contractor, the technical consultants, and the most important suppliers can be involved. A partnership agreement of this type provides for establishing a coordinating body, which includes the representatives of all partners. The model partnering agreement can be given as the example for application in building projects PPC 2000 (Project Partnering Contract 2000) issued in 2000 by the British National Association of Consulting Engineers [18].

The performed analysis showed that the absence of regulatory, methodological and contractual support of partnerships is currently the main obstacle to implement the partnering model in the building of Russia.

5 Conclusions

The creation of the institutional and technological base is under completion in the Russian Federation, and it generates the unified information space in the building sector creating the prerequisites for a transition from the conventional models of the investment and building process implementation to models based on the partnership of building participants.

The partnership will be developed based on the information environment generated with the support of concerned public authorities, and that is based on the process platform of the building information modeling integrated with the federal, regional and corporate information and analytical systems, databases and information banks, which will ensure continuity, continuity and high efficiency of management under a dynamically changing environment during a full life cycle of objects.

For the successful implementation of partnering mechanisms in building practice, the state and the professional community shall pay the attention to development of legislation, methodological support and preparation of the standard documentation including standard forms of partnering agreements, and generation of the interaction and experience exchange system in this field.

References

1. A. E. Churbanov, Generation of contracting relations in modern building (SaintPetersburg State University of Engineering and Economics, St. Petersburg, 2006)
2. OECD, OECD Digital Economy Papers, **260** (2016)
3. OECD, OECD Digital Economy Papers, **256** (2016)
4. E. B. Smirnov, Civil Engineers Bulletin, **2** (2012)
5. S. Børve, A. Rolstadås, B. Andersen, W. Aarseth, International Journal of Managing Projects in Business, **10(4)** (2017)
6. A. Baird, J. Bennett, *NEC and Partnering: A Guide to Building Winning Teams* (Thomas Telford, London, 2001)
7. C. Skeggs, *Project Partnering in the International Construction Industry* (Abigroup Contractors, Sydney, 2000)
8. I. K. Pinkevich, E. B. Smirnov, Modern economic problems, **4 (48)** (2013)
9. J. Bennett, S. L. Jayes, *Seven Pillars of Partnering: A Guide to Second Generation Partnering* (Thomas Telford, London, 1998)
10. A. Howlett, International Construction Developments-What Comes After Partnering [online], Available at: http:// wwwljonesday.com/practices/puLdetail (2002)
11. The Future for Construction Product Manufacturing Digitalization, Industry 4.0 and the Circular Economy. Report (October 2016) by Construction Products Association, London [online], Available at: https://www.thefis.org/wp-content/uploads/2016/10/cpa-future-of-construction-product-manufacturing-report-2016.pdf (2016)
12. W. Bouck, Mapping the Information Economy: A Tale of Five Industries [online], Available at: https://blog.box.com/blog/mapping-the-information-economy-a-tale-of-five-industries (2014)
13. Decree of the President of the Russian Federation, 203 dated 09.05.2017 "On the Strategy of Information Society Development in the Russian Federation for 2017-2030" [online], Available at: http://kremlin.ru/acts/bank/41919 (2017)

14. Regulation of the Russian Federation Government No. 1632-p dated July 28, 2017 "On approval of the program "Digital Economy of the Russian Federation" [online], Available at: http://base.garant.ru/71734878/ (2017)
15. National BIM Standard – United States. National Institute of Building Sciences [online], Available at: https://www.nationalbimstandard.org/files/NBIMS-US_FactSheet_2015.pdf (2015)
16. A. P. Dobrynin, K. Yu. Chenykh, V. P. Kupriyanovsky, P. V. Kupriyanovsky, S. A. Sinyagov, International Journal of Open Information Technologies, **(4)** 1 (2016)
17. The NEC Partnering Option: First Edition, June 2001 (Thomas Telford Limited, Heron Quay, London, 2003)
18. Standard Forms of Contract for Project Partnering (Trowers & Hamlins, London, 2005)
19. W. Bouck, Mapping the Information Economy: A Tale of Five Industries [online], Available at: https://blog.box.com/blog/mapping-the-information-economy-a-tale-of-five-industries (2014)

Interrelation model capital/output in the conditions of a new technological platform[a]

Valentin Sokolov[1*], *Galina* Karpova[2], and *Alena* Kuryleva[3]

[1] Saint Petersburg State Economy University, Center for fundamental Studies of Development Processes in the Russian Economy, 191002 Marat st. 27, Russian Federation
[2] Saint Petersburg State University of Architecture and Civil Engineering, Faculty of economics and management, 190005 2nd Krasnoarmeiskaya st. 4, Russian Federation
[3] Saint Petersburg State Economy University, dept. of Applied Mathematics and Economical-Mathematical Methods, 191023 Sadovaya st. 21, Russian Federation

Abstract. Many experts relate rehabilitation of the world economy to forming a new technological platform. In this work we made an attempt to show the trends in the interrelation between capital and output in the conditions of forming new technological platform. In order to do that, we used a modified productive function with technical progress saving labor consumption. Even though this model bears a simulative character, it has all the required capabilities to calculate interrelations “capital/output” for long periods of time and can be a tool to investigate the economical dynamics with consideration of the new character of the economic progress.

1 Introduction

The scholars who analyzed stagnation in the Japanese economy that had lasted more than 10 years, pointed out such a reason as low efficiency in using the capital [1, 2]. In their co-operative research, the Japanese and Korean economists see the reason for stagnation of the Japanese economy in very low tempo of capital investment into its development [3]. One of the ways to solve the problem of the economic stagnation is a search of new technological solutions to dramatically change the entire economic landscape and give a new incentive to development. Here we would like to highlight the strategic recommendations for development of "the Industry 4.0" for German manufacturers [4], two American concepts: "Industrial internet" [5] and "Internet of Things" [6]. The research on the artificial intelligence [7] issued in 2003 laid a basement for industrial development of artificial intelligence systems. At the World Economic Forum a wide-scale discussion was started on the "Fourth industrial revolution" [8]. It is easy to notice that accumulation is taking place of the “critical mass” of new knowledge and technologies that can work as an explosion to create new conditions for development. It is obvious that this development will require sufficient amount of capital and expenditures to support human resources. In this respect

[a] This article was prepared with financial support of the RUSSIAN Scientific fund (Grant No. 18-18-00099)
[*] Corresponding author: svn@engec.ru

we consider it important to investigate capital accumulation and the interrelation "capital/output" in the conditions of forming a new technological platform.

2 Some initial provisions

Nickolas Kaldor [9] in 1961 formulated 5 empirical regularities (sometimes referred to as "formalized facts") that are relevant in the long-term perspective, when consequences of various economical and financial crises have leveled out. For our research, two empirical regularities of Kaldor [9] have relevance:

1. The ratio between the physical capital and the output – which is almost a constant value.

2. The share of labor and physical capital in the growth of the national income – these are, too, almost constant values.

The first of these regularities can be formalized as follows:

$$Y = \kappa \cdot K, \kappa = const, \tag{1}$$

where κ is the coefficient of capital return. We assume that the equality (1) will be observed in the first half of the XXI century. This is directly derived from the results obtained by Thomas Piketti and presented in his work "Capital in the XXI Century" [10][a].

As for the second Kaldor's regularity mentioned above, our opinion is that it will not be observed anymore in XXI c., because the share of the capital in the national income growth will steadily increase, which conforms to the results obtained by T. Piketti.

3 Model

Our model is based on the productive function (PF) with labor-saving (labor-intensive) technical progress:

$$\tilde{Y} = K^{\alpha} \cdot (A \cdot L)^{1+\sigma-\alpha}, \tag{2}$$

where $\tilde{Y}$ is the theoretical volume of the Gross Domestic Product (GDP); K is the physical capital; L is the number of the workforce in the economy; A is the technical progress; α is the share of the capital in the GDP growth; σ is the parameter characterizing a growing yield from the production scope ($\sigma \geq 0$).

In the long-term perspective, the capital-output ratio is directly related to the amount of savings (s) in the economy and averaged growth rates (g) of its Gross Domestic Product (Y):

$$\beta = \kappa^{-1} = \frac{s}{g}. \tag{3}$$

T. Piketti considers interrelation (3) as the second basic regularity of capitalism. This regularity is asymptotic: in the long-term perspective, the capital-output ratio β will tend to approach an equilibrium determined by the interrelation$\beta = {}^{s}/_{g}$. It is easy to see that this

[a] During XVIII-XIX cc. this ratio, which is a capital-output ratio $\beta = \kappa^{-1} = {}^{K}/_{Y}$, in the leading European economies was pretty stable and was equal to $\beta \cong 7$ in France and Great Britain, whereas in Germany it was $\beta \cong 6.5$ [10]. In the USA this ratio reached quasi-stability in the early XX c., at the level $\beta \cong 4.5$, and then, beginning from mid-XX c., it was stabilized at the level $\beta \cong 4$ [10]. We can see that the capital-output ratio in the USA was much more limited than in the Western-European countries, i.e., the corresponding Kaldor's regularity for the USA also worked in the XX century. In the XXI c., the capital-output ratio raised high again, close to values of the XVIII-XIX cc. T. Piketti explains the transition to the regime of the slow economic growth [10]. In this respect, T. Piketti predicted that, on the global scale, the capital-output ratio (β), which has once approached the value of 5 and reached the level of the year 1910, will later be about 6 in mid-XXI and will reach 7 by late XXI c. In our opinion, a significant growth of capital will actually take place, but the ratio (β) will remain essentially the same, which we are going to illustrate later on the basis of model calculations.

interrelation results from the theory of the economic growth by Harrod-Domar and is unstable in the dynamic aspect. Therefore, the equality (1) will determine the PF (2). So, the accumulation of the capital and new revolutionary technologies and innovations will become a dominating moving force influencing the economic growth in the first half of the XXI century.

Let us consider the regularities of capital accumulation in the conditions of forming new technological platforms. It is well known that the dynamics of the capital growth is estimated by the capital accumulation equation:

$$\dot{K}(t) = I(t) - \mu \cdot K(t), \tag{4}$$

where $I(t)$ is industrial investment, μ is the norm of capital retirement. Due to the fact that $I(t) = s \cdot Y(t)$, the equation (4) will transform into:

$$\dot{K}(t) = s \cdot Y(t) - \mu \cdot K(t). \tag{5}$$

Considering the basic equality (1), basing on (5), we obtain the final equality capital accumulation:

$$\dot{K}(t) = (s \cdot \kappa - \mu) \cdot K(t). \tag{6}$$

This differential equation is solved as follows:

$$K(t) = K_0 \cdot \exp[(s \cdot \kappa - \mu) \cdot (t - T_0)]. \tag{7}$$

Therefore, on the basis of the assumption (1) there will be an exponential growth of the accumulated volume of the industrial capital.

However, considering that, in accordance with the theory of Big Cycles by Kondratiyev (BCK) during its descending stage, the effect of capital saturation is to take place, in reality it is to be expected that capital accumulation will take place according to the logistic regularity:

$$K(t) = \frac{K_m}{1+\left(\frac{K_m}{K_0}-1\right)\cdot\exp[-v_k\cdot(t-T_0)]}, \tag{8}$$

where K_0 and K_m are the initial and the maximum values of the accumulated capital within the limits of the 6-th BCK (2018-2050); v_k is the parameter describing the rate of capital accumulation. The parameters K_m and v_k in the formula (8) shall be determined from the condition of coincidence of trajectories of he accumulated capital growth (7) and (8) at the section of the increasing stage of the 6-th BCK (2018-2034). That is why it is very important to predict, with sufficient accuracy, the parameters s, κ and μ in the formula (7).

In the new conditions of an accelerated capital accumulation (8), it is most natural to adopt the type of the technical progress related to the amount of knowledge, skills and experience obtained during practical work with the new equipment, which, in its turn, depends on the volume of the employed capital, i.e. there will be a model of training in the process of production necessity, proposed by Kenneth Arrow in 1962 [11]:

$$\text{a) } A = K^{\theta}; \text{b) } A = \left(\frac{K}{L}\right)^{\theta}, 0 < \theta < 1, \tag{9}$$

where θ is the parameter describing the efficiency of the education. For traditional economy branches, typical are the values $\theta = 0.3$. For most modern economies, it is obviously true that the following inequality applies: $0.1 < \theta < 0.7$.

Earlier in the work [12], it was shown that, in the conditions of Great Cycles by Kondratiyev, the graph of the capital growth share in the GDP increase α will be close to the logistic one:

$$\alpha = \frac{\alpha_m}{1+\left(\frac{\alpha_m}{\alpha_0}-1\right)\cdot\exp[-v_\alpha\cdot(t-T_0)]}, \quad (10)$$

where α_0 and α_m are shares of capital in GDP increase at the beginning and the end of the 6-th BCK (2018 and 2050); v_α is the rate of growth of the capital share. T. Piketti predicts the value α_m to be 10 per cent higher than α_0.

Therefore, the formulas (1), (8), (9b) and (10) describe the trends of development of highly profitable economies while new technological platforms are formed. Using these formulas, the basic PF (2) can be converted into an equation to calculate the predicted dynamics of the basic economic variables Y, L and A. In order to do that, let us substitute the formulas (1) and (9b) into the production function (2). The result will be:

$$\begin{aligned} &\text{a) } Y(t) = \kappa \cdot K(t); \\ &\text{b) } q_y = \frac{\dot{Y}}{Y} = q_k = \frac{\dot{K}}{K}; \\ &\text{c) } L(t) = \kappa^{\frac{1}{(1-\theta)\cdot(1+\sigma-\alpha)}} \cdot K(t)^{\frac{1-\alpha-\theta\cdot(1+\sigma-\alpha)}{(1-\theta)\cdot(1+\sigma-\alpha)}}; \\ &\text{d) } A(t) = \left(\frac{K}{L}\right)^\theta = \kappa^{-\frac{\theta}{(1-\theta)\cdot(1+\sigma-\alpha)}} \cdot K(t)^{\frac{\theta\cdot\sigma}{(1-\theta)\cdot(1+\sigma-\alpha)}}. \end{aligned} \quad (11)$$

Whereas the dynamics of the capital accumulation $K(t)$; will be described by the logistic function (8):

$$K(t) = \frac{K_m}{1+\left(\frac{K_m}{K_0}-1\right)\cdot\exp[-v_k\cdot(t-T_0)]}. \quad (12)$$

In the formulas (11) the value α is changed according to the graph (10):

$$\alpha(t) = \frac{\alpha_m}{1+\left(\frac{\alpha_m}{\alpha_0}-1\right)\cdot\exp[-v_\alpha\cdot(t-T_0)]}. \quad (13)$$

As we can see from the formula (11b), the rates of the economic growth will only be determined by the rates of the capital accumulation and will not depend on the increase in redundancy. Considering (12), we obtain the result:

$$q_y = \frac{\dot{K}}{K} = v_k \cdot \frac{K(t)}{K_{(m)}} \cdot \left(\frac{K_m}{K_0} - 1\right) \cdot \exp[-v_k \cdot (t - T_0)]. \quad (14)$$

For the countries where there is a constant or decreasing yield from the scale ($\sigma = 0$), the equations (11) will take the following form:

$$\begin{aligned} &\text{a) } Y(t) = \kappa \cdot K(t); \\ &\text{b) } q_y = q_k; \\ &\text{c) } L(t) = \kappa^{\frac{1}{(1-\theta)\cdot(1-\alpha)}} \cdot K(t); \\ &\text{d) } A(t) = \kappa^{-\frac{\theta}{(1-\theta)\cdot(1-\alpha)}}. \end{aligned} \quad (15)$$

Despite that the proposed model bears a simulative character, it has sufficient potential that can be demonstrated during verification of the actual statistical data for the economies of some well-developed countries.

4 Preliminary results

Within the framework of this research, despite the simulative character of the proposed model, we have tried to verify it for the economy of the Great Britain, when we used the data from the World Bank [13] and University of Groningen [14] as the data base. The calculation results are presented below in figures 1-4.

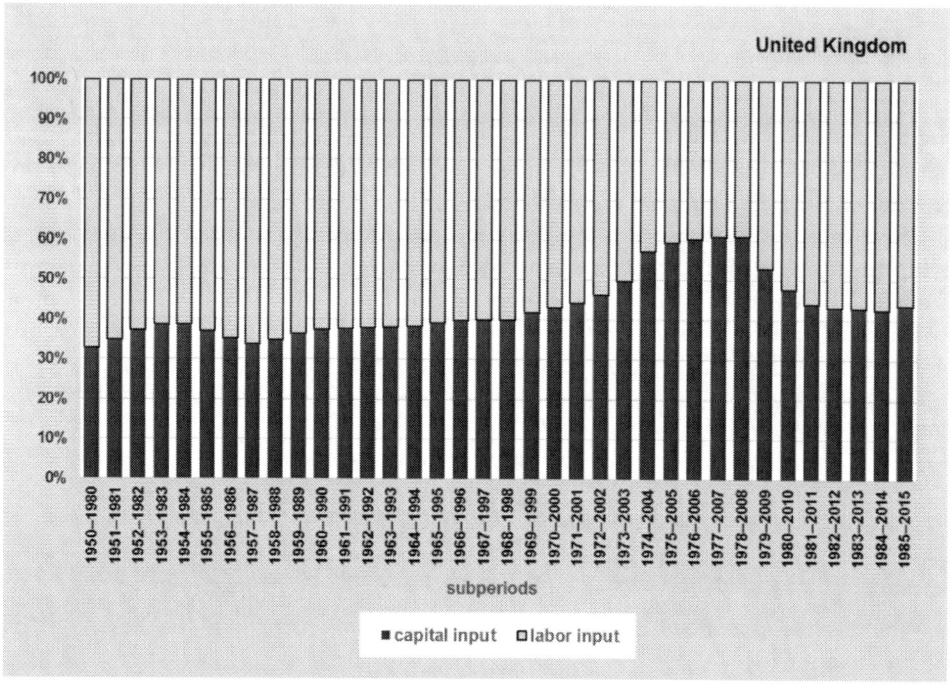

Fig. 1a. Preliminary processing of source data.

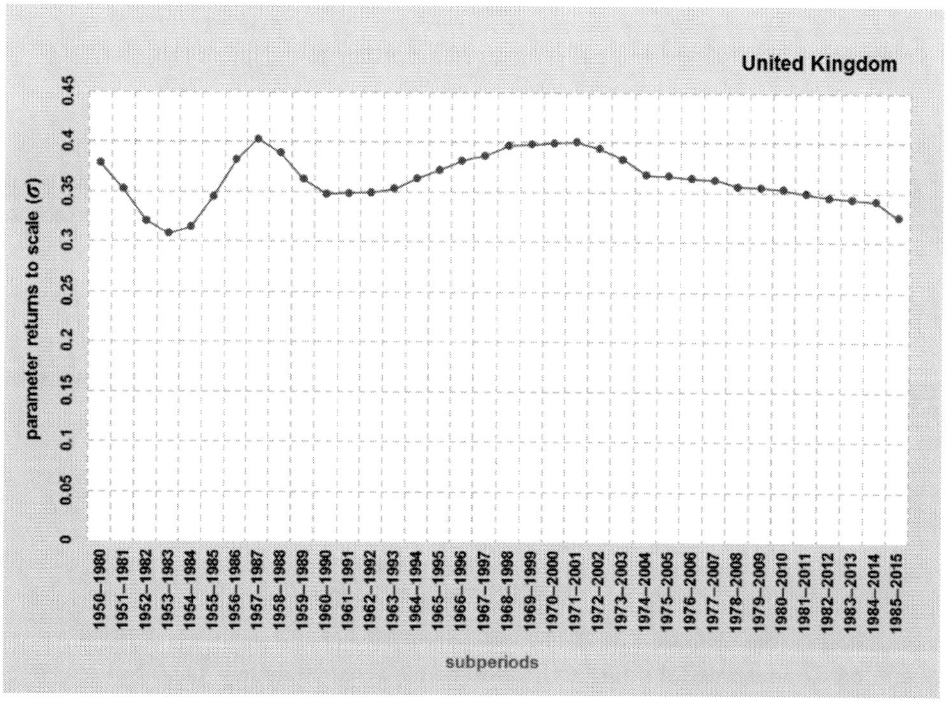

Fig. 1b. Preliminary processing of source data.

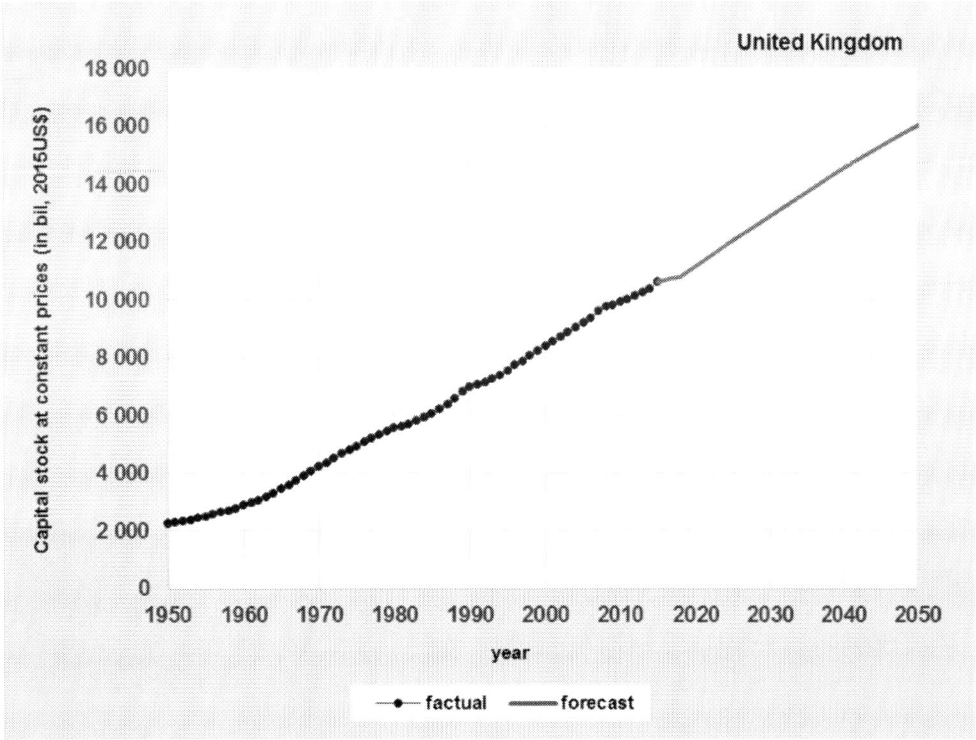

Fig. 2. Dynamics of the volume of physical capital at constant prices 2015.

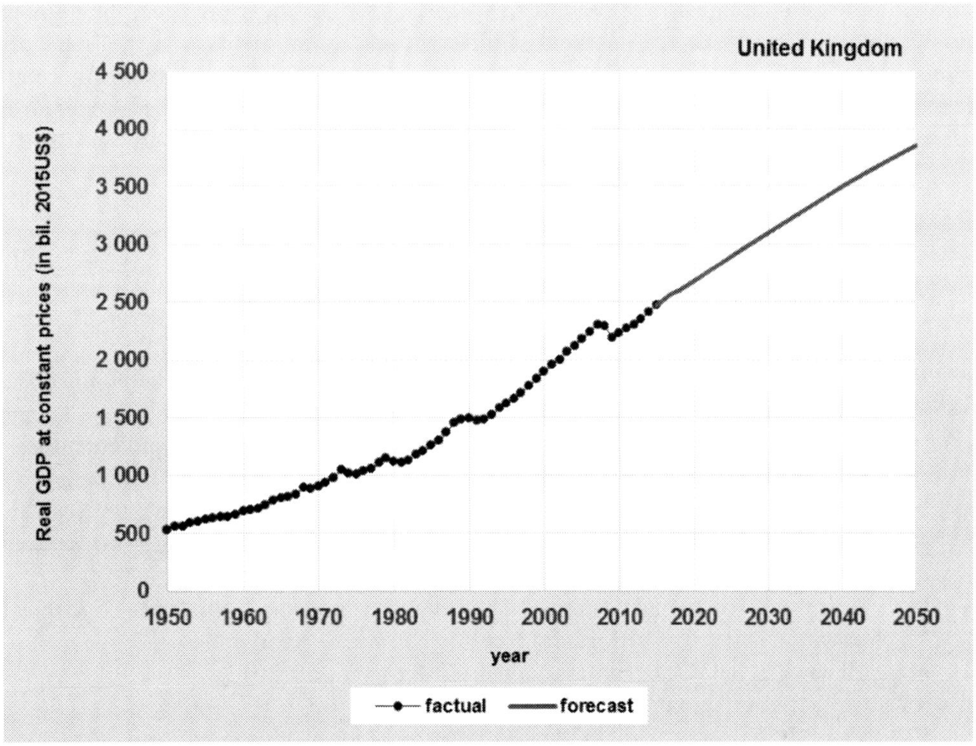

Fig. 3. Dynamics of the volume of GDP at constant prices 2015.

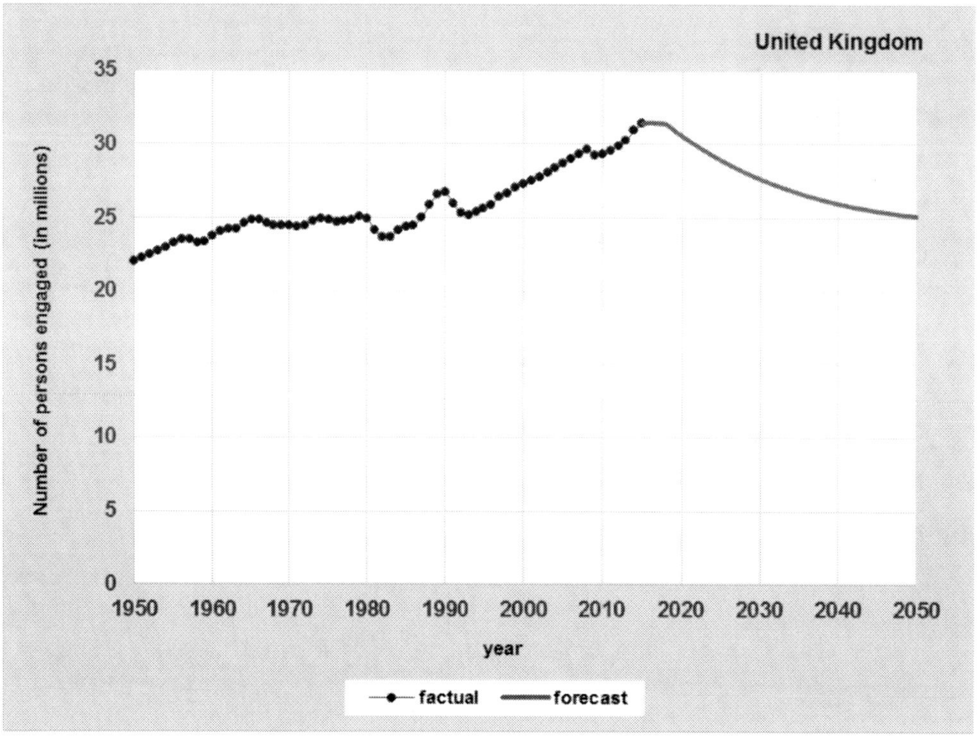

Fig. 4. Dynamics of employment.

It should be expected that in the long term for the UK, the capital / output ratio will be constant and the relationship between them will be linear. At the same time, the number of employees will tend to decrease, which is likely to lead to an increase in the share of the capital factor in the formation of gross output. This will reflect already emerging trends in economic development, when new technological platforms will be able to generate new value with much less involvement of a person directly into the production process itself.

References

1. A. Ando, D. Christelis, T. Miyagawa, NBER Working Paper, **9444** (2003)
2. F. Hayashi, *Long-Run Growth and Short-Run Stabilization: Essays in Memory of Albert Ando* (Edward Elgar Publishing, Cheltenham, 2006)
3. H. Chun, T. Miyagawa, H. K. Pyo, M. Takizawa, K. Tonogi, The Fourth World KLEMS Conference Asia KLEMS session (2016)
4. H. Kagermann, W. Wahlster, J. Helbig, Recommendations for implementing the strategic initiative INDUSTRIE 4.0. [online], Available at: http://www.acatech.de/fileadmin/user_upload/Baumstruktur_nach_Website/Acatech/root/de/Material_fuer_Sonderseiten/Industrie_4.0/Final_report__Industrie_4.0_accessible.pdf (2013)
5. P. C. Evans, M. Annunziata, Industrial Internet: Pushing the Boundaries of Minds and Machines [online], Available at: https://www.ge.com/docs/chapters/Industrial_Internet.pdf (2012)
6. M. Swan, J. Sens. Actuator Netw., **1** (2012)
7. S.J. Russel, P. Norvig, *Artificial Intelligence: A Modern Approach* (2nd ed.) (Prentice Hall, New Jersey, 2003)
8. K. Schwab, *The Fourth Industrial Revolution* (World Economic Forum,

Cologne, 2016)
9. N. Kaldor, *Capital Accumulation and Economic Growth* (St. Martin Press, New York, 1961)
10. T. Piketty, *Capital in the Twenty-First Century* (Harvard University Press, Harvard, 2014)
11. K. Arrow, Review of Economic Studies, **29 (80)** (1962)
12. A. Akaev, A. Rudskoi, *Economic Potential of Social Consequents, Industry 4.0 – Entrepreneurship and Structural Change in the New Digital Landscape* (Springer Verlag, Berlin, 2016)
13. World Bank Open Data [online], Available at: http://data.worldbank.org/ (2017)
14. Penn World Table - international comparisons of production, income and prices 9.0 [online], Available at: http://febpwt.webhosting.rug.nl/ (2018)

Numerical simulation of environmentally-safe technologies in power engineering

Alexei Trinchenko[1*]

1 Peter the Great St. Petersburg Polytechnic University, Institute of power Engineering and Transportation Systems, 195251 Polytechnicheskaya st. 29, Russian Federation

Abstract. One of the effective tools of solving engineering problems is the mathematical simulation of newly built and reconstructed industrial equipment. A necessity of solving identical problems fully belongs to generating equipment of thermal power plants too, which makes the use of methods of mathematic simulation quite a promising one in the course of designing power-generating units. The work presents the results of simulation and subsequent incorporation of the method of low-temperature vortex fossil solid-fuel combustion. Based on the developed algorithms and calculation program the assessment of environmental indicators of reconstructed boiler equipment has been carried out and compliance with environmental standards with respect to the level of emissions of gaseous pollutants into environment confirmed. The incorporation of the method being considered into power-generating production has made it possible to reduce emissions of gaseous nitrogen oxides during combustion of coals of different types by 30%.

1 Introduction

The incorporation of big heat-and-power units into power industry, sophistication of process diagrams and operating conditions, increasing requirements to economical efficiency, reliability and environmental indicators thereof will be accompanied by the necessity of building numerical models and conducting simulation studies. It is impossible to carry out such investigations within a short period of time without using modern computers and methods of mathematic simulation [1, 2]. The numerical models make it possible to view an object on a real scale, change geometry of the plant, fuel characteristics, orientation of action of burner jets and parameters thereof, promptly make assessment of effect of performed changes on the efficiency of operation of power-generating equipment and its environmental indicators in a relatively short time [3].

There appeared a possibility to include into viewing the ever-growing determining factors and assess the influence thereof on the intensity of pollutants generation and on the burning process as a whole as much as the computer equipment gets developed. The methods of mathematic simulation, models and programs for expert calculations of processes in the furnace are more and more widely used in the process of building the new boiler equipment in world practice in the most recent decades, which help assess the

* Corresponding author: trinchenko@spbstu.ru

efficiency of influence of different technical and mode-related factors, which reduces the labor content and increases reliability of substantiating technical solutions significantly. Such an approach is especially required in the process of development of new technologies of combustion and optimization of burning processes.

The low-temperature vortex (LTV) method of burning developed under the guidance of Professor V. V. Pomerantsev [4] has proven itself presently to be one of the up-to-date and advanced methods for incorporation into power industry. The use of LTV method helps significantly reduce the emissions of pollutants into atmosphere, increase efficiency of using energy resources, increase reliability and economic efficiency of electric power installations [5, 6]. The LTV burning opens great opportunities for decreasing overall dimensions of boilers and reducing metal expenditures as a result of increasing intensity of combustion and heat-exchange processes. The application of LTV technology makes it possible to install new boilers into existing building boxes, and in some cases – increase the capacity of an installation [7]. It is especially important when replacing the worn-out Central Heating and Power Plant equipment (in the course of upgrading thereof).

The purpose of this work consists in the development of model of low-temperature vortex burning process for increasing environmental indices of boilers and incorporation of LTV method in power industry.

2 Principles of organization and simulation of low-temperature vortex method

The mathematic description of investigation object (Fig. 1) has been obtained in the way of building a three-dimensional model on the basis of coordinates of characteristic points restricting a furnace of the low-temperature vortex boiler and reflecting the incorporated design solutions (Fig. 2). The model gives a chance of changing geometry of the burners, furnace and its individual assemblies for optimizing design characteristics of mode-related parameters of boiler operation.

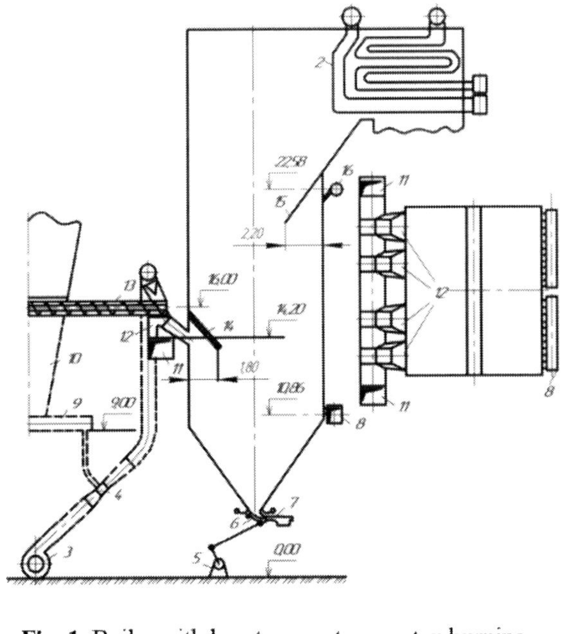

Fig. 1. Boiler with low-temperature vortex burning technology

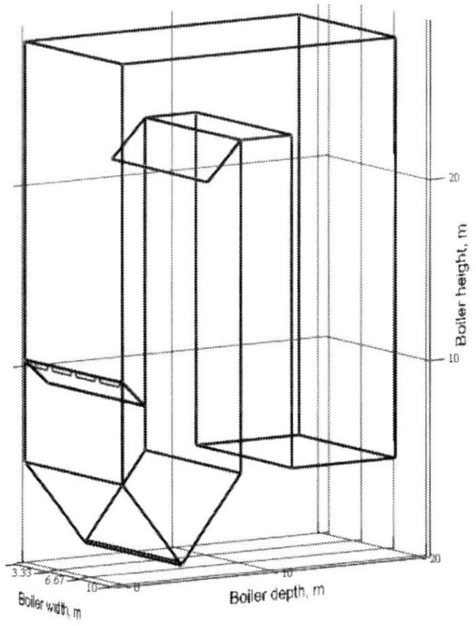

Fig. 2. Model of boiler with low-temperature vortex burning technology

The implementation of LTV method is based on building special aerodynamics of moving flows provided by the furnace chamber design, which includes individual areas (Fig. 3): I – hot air flow arriving at the furnace from beneath (downdraft (DD) jet), II – flow arriving at the furnace via burners; III – vortex area of furnace formed during interaction of flows I and II; IV, V – vortex zones in the volume of furnace chamber. The velocities of gas and air flows can be described by the corresponding dependences for every characteristic flow zones.

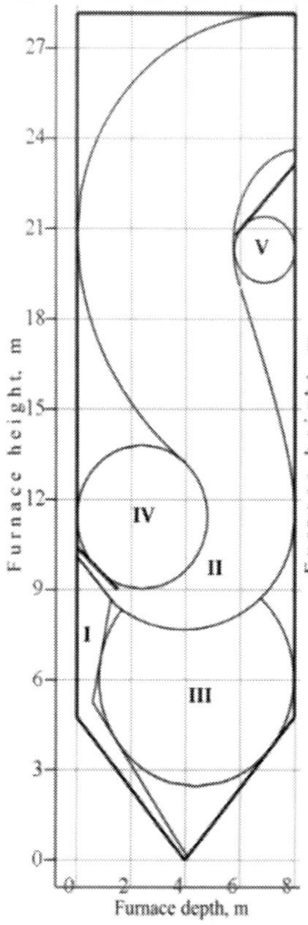

Fig. 3. Pattern of low-temperature vortex burning organization

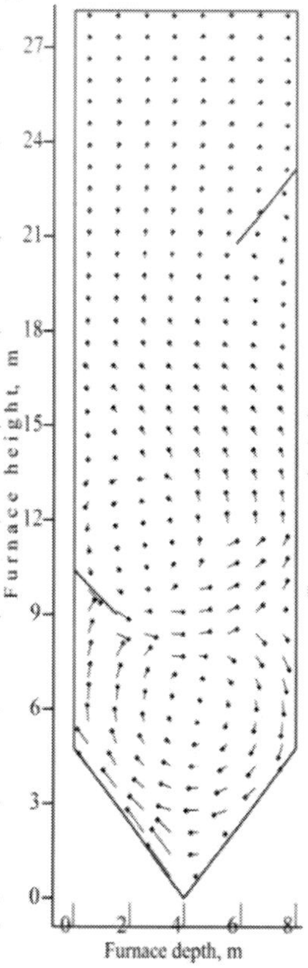

Fig. 4. Design vector field of velocities in ltv furnace chamber

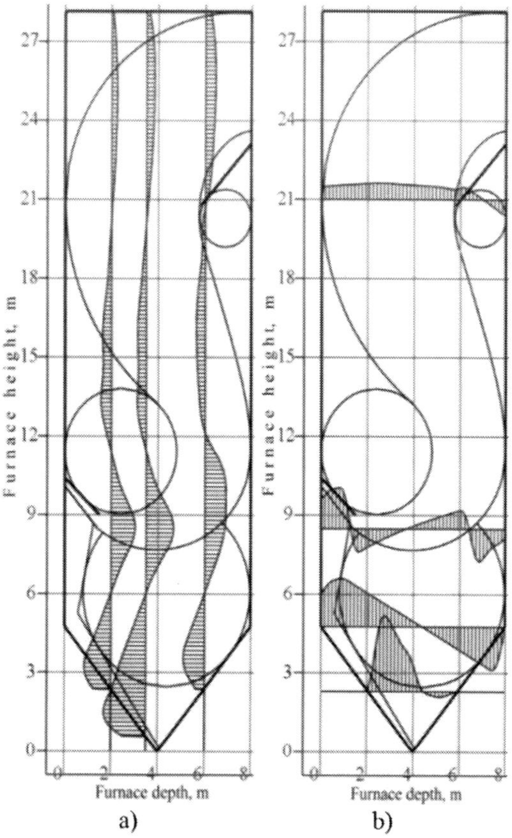

Fig. 5. Profiles of velocities of gas and air flows: a) – by furnace height; b) – by furnace depth

The profile of external portion of semi-restricted downdraft jet (zone I) will be described by the dependence according to the theory of Prandtl-Schlichting, as follows:

$$\overline{w}_{ext} = \overline{W}/W_m = \left\{1 - \left[(Y - Y_{\overline{W}m})/(Y^{ext} - Y_{\overline{W}m})\right]^{3/2}\right\}^2, \tag{1}$$

while the internal portion of downdraft jet will be described by the dependence, as follows:

$$\overline{w}_{int} = \overline{W}/W_m = 1 - 0.5 \cdot \left[(Y - Y_{\overline{W}m})/(Y_{0,5\overline{W}m} - Y_{\overline{W}m})\right]^{2.3} \tag{2}$$

The path of jet axis (zone II) is described according to [8] by the equation for the system of jets in the cross-flow:

$$\frac{a \cdot y}{b_0} = 1.9 \cdot \left(\frac{\rho_c \cdot (273/T_c) \cdot W_c^2}{\rho_0 \cdot (273/T_0) \cdot W_0^2}\right) \cdot \left(\frac{a \cdot x}{b_0}\right)^{2.5} + \frac{a \cdot x}{b_0} \cdot ctg\alpha, \tag{3}$$

where, a – coefficient characterizing the jet structure, its initial turbulence and non-uniformity of field of velocities at the nozzle outlet (with a uniform field at nozzle outlet a = 0.10...0.12); ρ_0 and ρ_c – densities of jet and cross-flow, accordingly; W_0 and W_c – initial velocities of jet and cross-flow; b_0 – nozzle width; x – distance from nozzle exit section along jet axis; α – angle of attack.

Zones III, IV and V are described by the model of quasi-solid body:

$$(\omega R) = \text{const}, \tag{4}$$

where, ω – angular velocity, R – distance to vortex zone center.

Describing velocities of gas and air flows by the dependencies (1)...(4) for characteristic regions grants a chance to get the vector field of velocities (Fig. 4) and use it for calculating the paths of motion of burning fuel particles of variable mass. The model makes it possible to get the vector of velocity in any point of furnace chamber (Fig. 5), and close the balance of flow rates in the cross sections along coordinate axes.

3 Model of low-temperature vortex burning process and generation of gaseous nitrogen oxides

An investigation of generation of toxic nitrogen oxides (NO) in case of operation on Cheremkhovo black coal, Azeiskoye and Irsha-Borodinskoye brown coals has been performed by means of numerical simulation with the use of developed fuel burning model taking into account the renowned NO generation mechanisms [9], and decomposition of nitrogen oxides to carbon particles in the process of multiple circulation. Combustion theory takes into consideration occurrence of process in stages for the particles of natural solid fuel and makes it possible to study its separate stages: drying, ignition and burning of volatile matter, burning of coke carbon as well as includes blocks of calculation of screening characteristics, field of temperatures, furnace aerodynamics, motion and destruction of reacting particles of polifraction fuel, generation of nitrogen oxides and decomposition thereof on coke surface.

The model of burning in LTV furnace involves a theory of "reduced film" offered by V.V. Pomerantsev and S.M. Shestakov [8]. Burning of big coke particles of high-moisture fuel is described by the set (5) of chemical reactions (thermal effect in kJ/mole) taking into account reaction No.5 – decomposition of nitrogen oxides on the surface of burning fuel particles:

$$\left\{\begin{array}{ll} \multicolumn{2}{c}{\text{heterogeneous}} \\ \text{at "dry" gasification} & \text{at "wet" gasification} \\ 1.\ C + O_2 = CO_2 + 394.6 & 3'.\ C + H_2O = CO + H_2 - 130.4 \\ 2.\ 2C + O_2 = 2CO + 219.6 & 3''.\ C + 2H_2O = CO_2 + 2H_2 - 132 \\ 3.\ C + CO_2 = 2CO - 175.6 & 3'''.\ C + 2H_2 = CH_4 - 74.8 \\ \multicolumn{2}{c}{\text{homogeneous}} \\ 4.\ CO + O_2 = 2CO_2 + 570.2 & 4'.\ 2H_2 + O_2 = 2H_2O + 231.5 \\ & 4''.\ CH_4 + 2O_2 = CO_2 + 2H_2O + 891 \\ & 4'''.\ CO + H_2O = CO_2 + H_2 + 40.4 \end{array}\right. , \tag{5}$$

$$5.\ 2NO + C = N_2 + CO - 180.2. \tag{6}$$

The consideration of burning process from the diffusion-kinetic positions has made it possible to compile a system of non-linear differential equations of diffusion and kinetics of the following type:

$$dG_j = -\frac{D}{RT}\cdot\frac{d^2 p_j}{dx^2}dx;\quad G_j = \frac{\alpha_D}{RT}\cdot(p_j - p_{j0});\quad \frac{dG_i}{d\tau} = C_i \cdot k_i, \tag{7}$$

taking into account oxidation and reduction reactions taking pace on the surface of particles, and homogeneous reactions taking place within the limits of boundary layer. The calculations have shown that the process of burning takes place in the intermediate area following a pattern of double burning boundary layer, a case of "wet" gasification (Fig. 6).

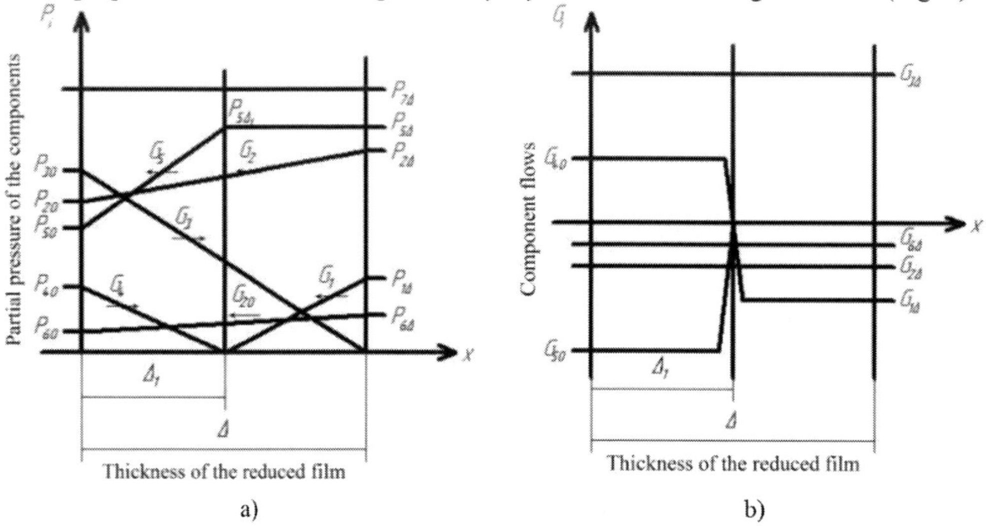

Fig. 6. Distributions of Partial Pressures (a), and Flows of Components (b) in Shown Film for Case of "Double Burning" Boundary Layer, "Wet Gasification":
1 – O_2; 2 – CO_2; 3 – CO; 4 – H_2; 5 – H_2O; 6 – NO; 7 – N_2. Indices "0" – Particle Surface; "Δ" – Flow

As a result of solving a system of equations (7) an expression has been obtained for carbon flow burning out from the surface of particle, (kmole/(m^2·s)):

$$G_c = \frac{\alpha_D}{RT}\left[\frac{N_3}{1+N_3}p_{CO_2\Delta} + \frac{N_{3'}}{1+N_{3'}}\left(p_{O_2\Delta} + 0.5p_{H_2O\Delta}\right) + \frac{N_5}{1+N_5}p_{NO\Delta}\right], \tag{8}$$

and dependences for calculating loss of mass and particle dimensions:

$$\frac{dm}{d\tau} = \frac{dm_{W'}}{d\tau} + \frac{dm_{vol}}{d\tau} + \frac{dm_c}{d\tau},\ \text{kg/s};\quad \frac{dm_C}{d\tau} = -G_C \cdot M_C \cdot \pi \cdot \delta^2,\ \text{kg/(m}^2\cdot\text{s)};\quad \frac{d\delta}{d\tau} = -\frac{2M_C}{\rho_C}\cdot G_C,\ \text{m/s}, \tag{9}$$

where, $M_c = 12$ kg/kmole – molar mass of carbon; $m = \pi/6\cdot\delta^3_{eq}\cdot\rho$ – mass of spherical particle, kg; $f_{surf} = \pi\cdot\delta^2_{eq}$ – area of external surface, m^2.

The distribution of NO concentrations across furnace cross section (after concentrations) in the known field of gas flow velocities has been determined in the way of numerical solution (diagram "against flow" [10]) of differential equation of mass exchange, in case of presence of source term (zones of NO generation):

$$\frac{\partial}{\partial\tau}(\rho\cdot C_{NO}) + \nabla\cdot(\rho\bar{w}C_{NO}) = \rho D_{NO}\nabla^2 C_{NO} + J_{NO}, \tag{10}$$

where, C_{NO} – mass concentration of nitrogen oxides; w – gas flow velocity; D_{NO} – average effective coefficient of NO diffusion in the mixture of furnace gas; J_{NO} – intensity of generation of nitrogen oxides (power of NO source [11]):

$$J_{NO} = \begin{cases} dN_{2i}/d\tau_i = k_{01\_N_2} \cdot exp(-E_{1\_N_2}/(RT_i)) \cdot (1/T_i) \cdot [N_i]^2 \\ dNO_i/d\tau_i = k_{02\_NO} \cdot exp(-E_{2\_NO}/(RT_i)) \cdot (1/T_i) \cdot [O_2]_i^{1.8} [N]_i \end{cases} \quad (11)$$

The amount of nitrogen oxides decomposed on the surface of burning carbon particles is calculated proceeding from the balance of reaction No.5.

The motion of reacting particles has been described by Meshchersky equation:

$$m\frac{d\bar{V}}{d\tau} = \sum_{i=1}^{k} \bar{P}_i + (\overline{W_{fl}} - \bar{V})\frac{dm}{d\tau}. \quad (12)$$

The calculations of paths of particles motion in the known field of velocities have been conducted in the way of numerical solution of equation (12) taking into account influence of two major forces: force of aerodynamic resistance and gravity force recorded in projection at the axis of rectangular coordinate system:

$$\begin{cases} m\frac{dV_x}{d\tau} = \frac{cf\rho_g}{2}(W_x - V_x)\sqrt{(W_x - V_x)^2 + (W_y - V_y)^2 + (W_z - V_z)^2} \\ m\frac{dV_y}{d\tau} = \frac{cf\rho_g}{2}(W_y - V_y)\sqrt{(W_x - V_x)^2 + (W_y - V_y)^2 + (W_z - V_z)^2} \\ m\frac{dV_z}{d\tau} = \frac{cf\rho_g}{2}(W_z - V_z)\sqrt{(W_x - V_x)^2 + (W_y - V_y)^2 + (W_z - V_z)^2} - mg \end{cases} \quad (13)$$

As Re ≤ 1: $c = 24/Re$; as Re > 1: $c = 24/Re + 4/Re^{1/3}$; as Re > 1000: $c = 0.48$. In this case the particles of fuel of irregular shape have been replaced with the spherical ones equivalent by volume:

$$\delta_{eq} = \sqrt[3]{6abc/\pi}. \quad (14)$$

The consumption of natural solid fuel of polifraction composition has been recalculated to equivalent consumption of spherical particles. The size of fuel particles, the quantity thereof per 1 kg of designed fuel, mass within the limits of every fraction and area of the initial surface of response have been determined in the way of processing the screening curve. The distribution of particles by fractions has been described by Rosin-Rammler-Bennet formula:

$$R_{0i} = exp(-b \cdot \delta^{n}_{0i}), \quad (15)$$

where, b and n – are experimental coefficients [8].

Thus, the burning out of polifraction composition fuel is calculated with the use of equivalent consumption as the sequence of calculations of burning out single particles, where every particle corresponds to one of fuel fractions. At that it is assumed that particles in the process of moving interact with screen heating surfaces only restricting the furnace chamber.

The comparison of calculation and experimental paths of particles movement in LTV furnace has demonstrated close agreement thereof (Fig. 7).

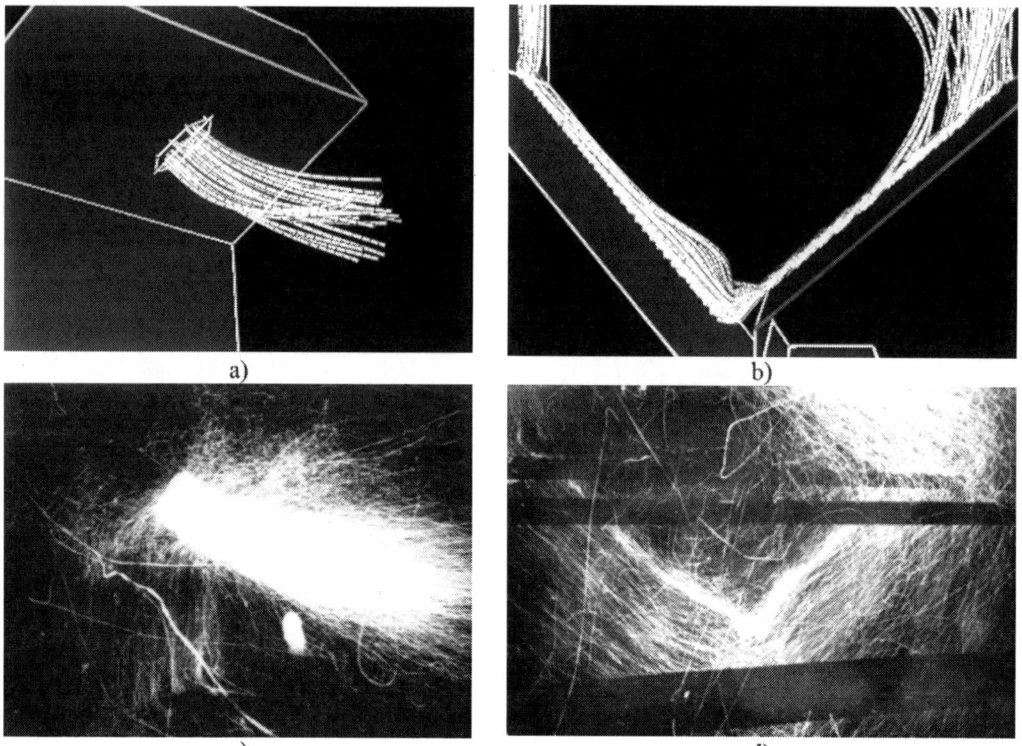

Fig. 7. Comparison of calculation and experimental paths of particles movement in LTV furnace of boiler БКЗ-210-140ф: a), b) – Calculation paths of particles; c), d) – Experimental paths of particles (visualization of flows by means of burning sawdust moistened in kerosene; a), c) – Development of burner jet in initial area; b), d) – Movement in bottom vortex zone of LTV furnace

The distribution of temperatures in LTV furnace has been determined by the zonal heat calculation in he way of numerical solution of balance equations recorded for every of eight zones (two by depth and four by height) of the furnace.

More accurate two-component scheme recommended for utilization during analysis of process of thermolysis of fuel rich in volatile matter has been used in the developed model for calculating volatile matter yield. The constant values of the rate of decomposition reactions shown in [8] have been used during calculation.

4 Results of numerical investigation of burning process, analysis of generation and transformation of nitrogen oxides

The results of calculation according to the presented model have been shown by the example of Azeiskoye brown coal.

The comparison of calculation curves of volatile matter yield from a particle measuring δ=5 mm acquired according to one-component and two-component schemes has been carried out with due account of particle temperature change in the process of heating. This comparison has demonstrated that the time of volatile matter yield calculated according to a two-component scheme is bigger than that of one-component scheme. Two time sectors, within which limits the intensive yield of the first and the second groups of volatile matter takes place, appear at the curve acquired according to two-component scheme. A decrease of particles density in the process of drying and volatile matter yield (Fig. 8), takes place to a value of density of fuel dry coke (Fig. 9).

The calculation of process of pneumatic and thermal destruction of particles has shown that in case of shock (basically, against the rear slope of furnace funnel) the particles bigger than $\delta > 6 \cdot 10^{-3}$ m get destructed (Fig. 10); at that, the surface of response increases by 2…5 %.

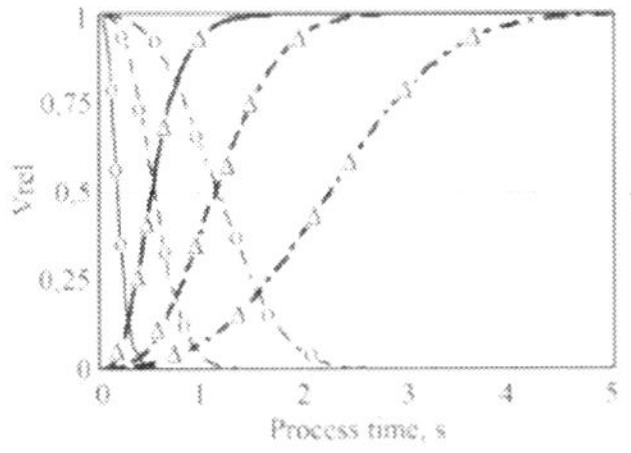

Fig. 8. Drying (o – W/W_0^r) and yield of volatile matter (Δ – V_{rel}) from particles of Azeiskoye coal in environment with temperature T_{av}=1500 K: ——— – $\delta = 2 \cdot 10^{-3}$ m; – – – – $\delta = 4 \cdot 10^{-3}$ m; · – · – – $\delta = 8 \cdot 10^{-3}$ m

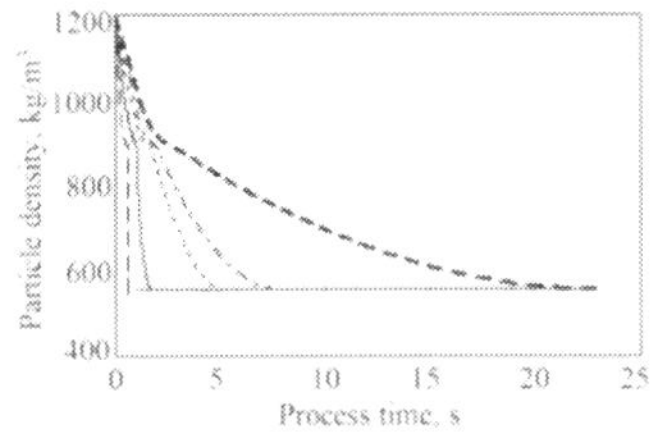

Fig. 9. Changing density of particle material in the process of drying and yield of volatile matter($\delta = 2.5 \cdot 10^{-4} \ldots 0.016$ m)

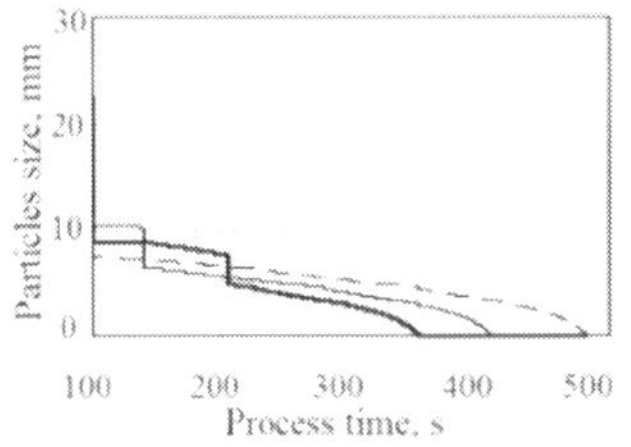

Fig. 10. Time of burning out of particles of different fractions ($\delta > 8 \cdot 10^{-3}$) of Azeiskoye coal

The design field of temperatures in LTV furnace for determining constant values of speeds of chemical reactions is shown in Fig. 11.

The analysis of paths of particles movement has shown (Fig. 12) that coarse particles ($\delta > 600 \cdot 10^{-6}$ m) get accumulated at the front slope of the bottom vortex zone forming a zone of high near-wall concentrations of fuel and coke particles. The main emission of NO takes place in this zone (Fig. 13) – an area of maximum NO concentrations. A vertical area over burners can be also attributed thereto. The burning of coarse particles continues up to a moment, when effected by the downdraft jet they can be carried to a straight-flow portion of the flame.

The maximum amount of NO gets decomposed at the front slope of the bottom vortex zone, since maximum concentrations of nitrogen oxides are available in this area, while the big fuel particles dwell for the maximum period of time of the entire combustion process.

Due to decomposition of nitrogen oxides on coke particles in calculating the process of burning of crushed Azeiskoye deposit coal, the reduction of NO concentration in the smoke gas equals 28 % (NO''_T = 500 mg/nm^3); burning time – 383 s, value of mechanical underburning q_4=1.4 %.

In case of burning of coarse dust of Azeiskoye deposit brown coal (R_{90}=80 %, R_{200}=50 %) small fuel particles ($\delta \leq 600 \cdot 10^{-6}$ m) coming into fuel chamber immediately go to straight-flow flame portion, while the big ones ($\delta > 600 \cdot 10^{-6}$ m) turning at the rear furnace wall come to the bottom vortex zone. The zone of maximum NO decomposition on the coke particles is arranged in the bottom vortex zone, NO decomposition equals 15% of the initial emission; time of particles burning– 10 s. The maximum amount of nitrogen oxides decomposition is accounted for by the particles $\delta_{10} = 959 \cdot 10^{-6}$ m, which is explained by rather significant time of oxides presence in the bottom vortex zone. Therefore, the coarsening of particle-size distribution of the burnt fuel (within the limits down to the particles of crushed fuel), will contribute to the increased NO decomposition.

In case of combustion of fine-grained pulverized brown coal (R_{90}=50 %, R_{200}=0.2 %) of Azeiskoye deposit, the burning of all particles takes place in the straight-flow flame portion (analog of straight-flow pulverized coal flame), Fig. 12. The maximum concentrations of generated nitrogen oxides are located at the level of burners, while the zones of NO maximum decomposition are located further in the direction of flame travel. During 1.5 s of burning NO decomposition has amounted to 0.58% of the initial emission.

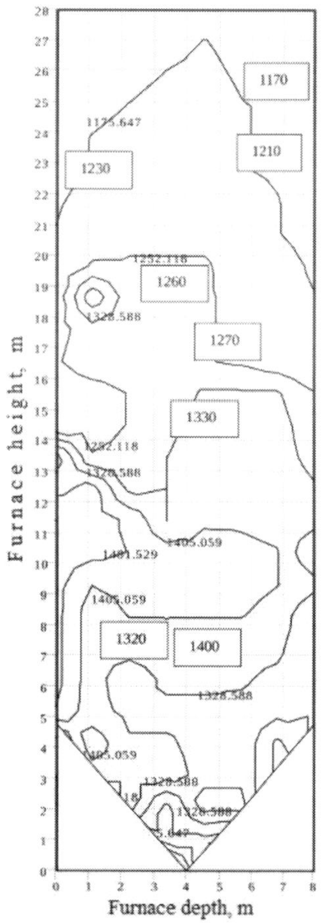

Fig. 11. Design field of temperatures (K) in LTV furnace (experimental values are shown in boxes)

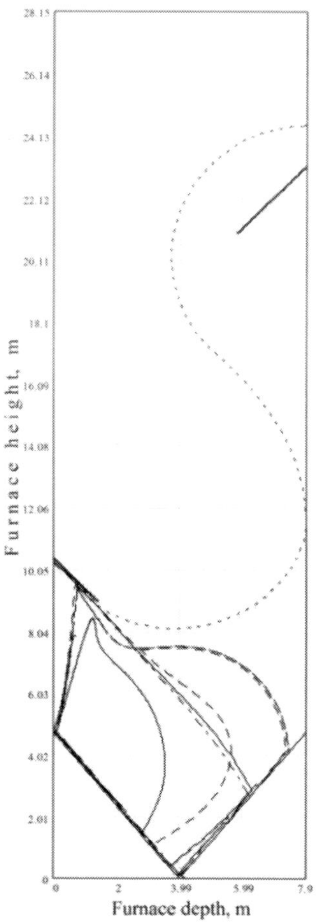

Fig. 12. Design paths of motion of burning particles in boiler LTV furnace:
– – – – $\delta=2\cdot10^{-6}$ m;
——— – $\delta=0.016$ m

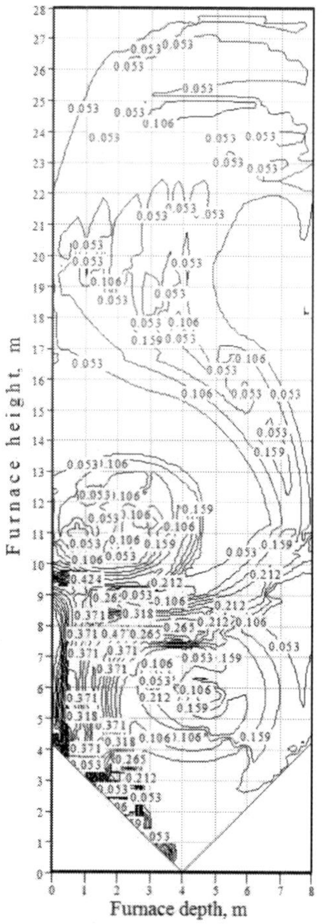

Fig. 13. Design field of concentrations of nitrogen oxides (by volume, %) in case of burning fuel in LTV furnace

The calculations of burning and decomposition of nitrogen oxides for Irsha-Borodinskoye brown coal and Cheremkhovo black coal are made in a similar way. The calculation results are shown in Table 1.

Table 1. Results of calculated analysis of influence of particle-size distribution on decomposition of nitrogen oxides in the course of burning of Irsha-Borodinskoye brown coal and Cheremkhovo black coal

Fuel	Irsha-Borodinskoye brown coal $A^r=6$ %, $W^r=33$ %, $C^r=43.7$ %, $N^r=0.6$%; $Q^r_i=15.67$ MJ/kg			Cheremkhovo black coal $A^r=27$ %, $W^r=13$ %, $C^r=45.6$%, $N^r=0.7$%, $Q^r_i=17.89$ MJ/kg		
Particle-size distribution	crushed fuel	coarse dust	fine dust	crushed fuel	coarse dust	fine dust
NO decomposition in furnace, kg/s	0.015	0.0056	$2.95\cdot10^{-4}$	0.011	0.0031	$2.52\cdot10^{-4}$

Reduction of NO emissions, %	31	12	0.6	25	6.6	0.54

According to acquired calculation results the value of nitrogen oxides decomposition (as compared with initial emission) is within the limits: in case of crushed fuel burning of 20...31 %; in case of coarse dust burning of 5...15 %; in case of fine dust burning of 0.5...0.7 %, and depends on fuel composition (first of all, composition of nitrogen and carbon in as-received basis) and kinetic constant values of system reactions (5). Thus, the coarsening of fuel grind burnt in the low-temperature vortex furnace contributes to the reduction of emissions of gaseous nitrogen oxides, reduction of plant explosion hazard as well as reduces electric power expenditures for fuel grinding.

5 Conclusive provisions and findings

The algorithm and program of calculation of process of burning of organic fuel in the low-temperature vortex furnace have been developed on the basis of presented model. The use of model has made it possible to authentically predict emissions of gaseous nitrogen oxides in case of reconstruction to the low-temperature vortex method of boilers of low (БКЗ-75 Southern thermal plant of Rubtsovsk town) [12], medium (БКЗ-210 of Kirovskaya CHPP-4 and БКЗ-220 of Novomoskovskaya regional hydro-electric power plant (RHEPP) [13–20] and high (П-49 Nazarovskaya RHEPP) [21, 22] capacity. The acquired calculation data have been used as the basis for environmental substantiation of reconstruction projects and proven a possibility of fulfilling applicable standards for the level of emissions of nitrogen oxides to environment in case of burning of a wide range of fuels: peat, brown and black coals of different grades.

As a result of incorporation of low-temperature vortex burning in the foregoing boilers a significant reduction (up to 30 %) of emissions of nitrogen oxides to atmosphere has been attained proving by the same high efficiency of this method, while LTV technology can be referred to as a promising method of reducing ecological burden on the environment.

References

1. A. Rodionov, *ECM in aerodynamics* (1985)
2. V. Antonov, *Mathematics. Mathematic models of thermal power-engineering processes* (2008)
3. E. Volkov, L. Zaichik, V. Pershukov, *Simulation of solid fuel burning* (Nauka, Moscow, 1994)
4. Y. Rundygin, K. Grigoriev, V. Skuditsky, *Low-temperature swirl technology of burning: experience of implementation, perspective of use* (Publishing house Politekh, St. Petersburg, 2006)
5. K. Grigoriev, V. Skuditsky, Y. Rundygin, A. Trinchenko, Swirling-type furnace. Eurasian patent of 008691 (2007)
6. K. Grigoriev, V. Skuditsky, Y. Rundygin, A. Trinchenko, Swirling-type furnace. Patent of 2253801 Russia. Publ. 10.06.2005. Bulletin No 16 (2005)
7. K. Grigoryev, Y. Roundyguine, V. Skuditskii, R. Anoshin, A. Paramonov, A. Trinchenko, Proceedings of the 7th International Symposium on Coal Combustion (2012)
8. V. Pomerantsev, K. Arefyev, D. Akhmedov, S. Shestakov, *Bases of the practical theory of burning* (Energoatomizdat, Leningrad, 1986)

9. V. Kotler, *Nitrogen oxides in combustion gases of boilers* (Energoatomizdat, Moscow, 1987)
10. M. Patankar, *Numerical methods of problem solving of heat exchange and fluid dynamics* (1984)
11. V. Babiy, *Burning of coal dust and calculation of coal-dust torch* (1986)
12. A. Trinchenko, A. Paramonov, IOP Conf. Ser.: Earth Environ. Sci., **90** (2017)
13. V. Osmanov, SPbPU J. of Eng. Sci. and Tec., **4 (183)** (2013)
14. A. Trinchenko, A. Paramonov, SPbPU J. of Eng. Sci. and Tec., **23_(02)** (2017)
15. A. Trinchenko, A. Paramonov, Advances in Intelligent Systems and Computing, **692** (2017)
16. K. Grigoriev, V. Skuditsky, Y. Zykin, Power Tech. and Eng., **4** (2010)
17. K. Grigoriev, V. Skuditsky, R. Anoshin, Energetik, **1** (2009)
18. A. Paramonov, M. Kadyrov, A. Trinchenko, Procedia Engineering, **206** (2017)
19. A. Paramonov, M. Kadyrov, A. Trinchenko, Procedia Engineering, **206** (2017)
20. V. Osmanov, *Improving heat measurements on the basis of heat flow gradient transmitters* (Saint Petersburg Polytechnic University, Saint Petersburg, 2015)
21. A. Trinchenko, A. Paramonov, V. Skouditskiy, R. Anoshin, J. Phys.: Conf. Ser., **891** (2017)
22. V. Skuditsky, R. Anoshin, Y. Rundygin, V.Mikhailov, N. Ryzhikov, K. Grigoriev, Power Tech. and Eng., **2** (2017)

Key performance indicators of high-tech enterprises

Tatyana Verevka[1*]

[1] Peter the Great St. Petersburg Polytechnic University, Institute of Industrial Management, Economics and Trade, Higher Engineering-Economical School, 195251 Polytechnicheskaya st. 29, Russian Federation

Abstract. In the conditions of the transition to innovative development and digital economy, the unconditional priority is shifted to restoration and transformation of high-tech enterprises. The stability of their strategic developing greatly depends on the efficiency of their business activity and the system of the enterprise strategic management. This article defines the basic performance indicators of high-tech enterprises, the particular features of the system to evaluate the efficiency of strategic management of a high-tech enterprise: innovative, scientific-technological and intellectual potential. On the basis of the analysis of the methods widely used all over the world, we developed a system key performance indicators to evaluate the efficiency of high-tech enterprises, with consideration of particular features of operation and development of high-tech enterprises, to enable evaluating the efficiency of their business activities and management through analyzing the inter-related financial and non-financial performance indicators. The practical implementation of this system will make it possible for high-tech enterprises to form a data base for making strategic solutions to ensure competitive advantage of these enterprises and, as a consequence, facilitate their steady development.

1 Introduction

In the conditions of the transition to innovative development and digital economy, the unconditional priority is shifted to creating and developing new technologies, restoration and transforming high-tech industrial enterprises, as well as ensuring their steady strategic development aimed at manufacturing innovative product. Such enterprises cannot find solutions to these tasks without creating a system of informational-spatial strategic milestones and implementing up-to-date evaluation tools.

The purpose of the research is theoretical-methodological substantiation and development of practical recommendations for forming a system of key performance indicators to evaluate the efficiency of management of high-tech enterprises in four most important strategic perspectives (customers, finance, internal processes and workforce) on the basis of the approaches used worldwide.

*Corresponding author: verevkatv@mail.ru

Due to direct state support – federal target programs, the state program for the development of the defense industry complex.

With the general theoretical comprehension of the usefulness of a modern system of performance indicators to evaluate the efficiency of the enterprise management, the content and the selection criteria of performance indicators, as well as the calculation methods proposed by authors of research works are quite various, which emphasizes the importance of this topic and highlights the perspectives and the direction of further scientific research.

One of the most widely used methods to evaluate the efficiency of strategic management of financial and business activity are as follows:

– performance indicators*EVA*to evaluate the increase in the price of the capital;
– a system of balanced performance indicators *(BSC)* [1];
– key performance indicators of efficiency developed by David Parmenter*(KPI)* [2];
– multi-factormodels*DuPont* [3] and some others.

The basis of all these methodsis the system of strategic performance indicators forming an informational-spatial base in accordance withthe specified purpose of the enterprise.

An outstanding place among thesemethods is occupied by a balanced system of performance indicators developed by American scholars R.Kaplan and D.Norton *(BSC, Balanced Scorecard)* [1]. This concept is made of four components: "Finance", "Customers", "Business processes" and "Workforce"that are inter-related through the cause-and-effect relations. While solving the problems of evaluating the efficiency of their activity, enterprises focus on the*BSC*approach more and more actively.However, the main deficiency of the *BSC* approach is lack of concise performance indicators (with their calculation methods) to evaluate the strategic objectives, which greatly hampers their applicability to enterprises of various industries and, especially, in the high-tech sphere.

In most information sources high technologies are defined differently, as science-intensive, progressive, new, innovative, break-through, new-wave technologies etc.

In thedocuments adopted by the European community, high technologies are defined as a "system of knowledge, industrial and otheroperations, methods and processescorresponding or surpassing world analogues in their quality performance indicators..." [4].

According tothe rules of international and Russian statistics, grouping the products, enterprises and industries by their technological level (high-, medium- and low-technology) is carried out on the basis of the performance indicator ofscience intensity.

High-technologyindustries (products) are those whose level of science intensitycalculated as a ratio between the total cost of R&D and the revenueis above the average level for the investigated combination. For example, RosStat (Russian Statistics administration)considers pharmaceutics, electronics, telecommunication, aviation and space industries as high-tech level, whereas chemical industry, engineering, motor car industry, shipbuilding and other transport industry are considered as high-level medium-technology level.

It should be noted that science intensity of Russian enterprises is much lower than that of their foreign competitors in the corresponding industries. Obviously, the low level of interest from enterprises towards technological innovations during many years, insufficient investments into the innovative sphere from the business and the state, has led to sufficient technological weakness of the Russian industry. In order to correct that, the state took extraordinary measures to stimulate perspective directions of development of modern technologies (transport, space systems, nano-technologies, nuclear industry etc.). As a result, the enterprises carrying out research and development in these spheres have significant taxation advantages causingthe decrease in the taxation base for revenue one-and-a-half as to the actual costs of R&D.

The objective of the state strategy of innovativedeveloping in the RF is reaching the performance indicator for science intensityfor the largest Russian enterprises to the level of similar foreign enterprises in the respective industries.

However, large investment into the R&D does not guarantee the result. For example, in motor car manufacturing, the industry-average level of science intensity is 4-5% (*Volkswagen*– 5.3%, *Toyota Motor Corporation*– 3.8%, *General MotorsCompany*– 4.9%, *Ford MotorsCompany*– 4.8%, *Daimler AG*– 4.2%, *Honda Motor Co., Ltd*– 4.9%). The performance indicator for science intensity of *Porsche* is twice as high as the industry-average, whereas this value for*Hyundai Motor*is five times as low [5]. Nevertheless, during the last decade, the price of the brand*Hyundai* has grown three times (from 4.1 to 12.5 billion dollars), and, as a result, *Hyundai*has become the sixth largest motor car brand, overtaking *Volkswagen* (11.4 billion dollars) and *Porsche* (9.5 billion dollars), and the 35-thworld-largest brand in all the industries [6].

Another very spectacular illustration is not only the most expensive brand but also the most efficient innovator in the world – *Apple Inc.*that, even though spending less than 5% of revenue for R&D (3.5% in 2016and 4.7% in 2017), i.e.almost three times less than their competitor *Cisco Systems, Inc.* (12.6% in 2016and 12.8% in 2017), shows one of the highest growth in the revenue and market capitalization, and,during seven years, is number one on the list "*The 10 Most Innovative Enterprises*", as selected by the world experts in the sphere of innovations.Moreover, as noted by the experts of the consulting-auditing company *PwC*, during the entire period of this list rating, starting from 2010,the ten most innovative enterprises are ahead of the ten enterprises leading in the level of expenditures for R&D from the viewpoint of key performance indicators of efficiency of their business and financial activity [7].

Therefore, the stability of the strategic innovativedevelopment of high-tech enterprises is greatly affected by the efficiency of their business and financial activity and the efficiency of their managementsystem.

Definitely, as we develop the strategic map and the efficiency evaluation performance indicators, we should consider the particular features of the operating system of high-tech enterprises, whose common attributes are the following:

- science intensity and high significance of R&D results during the entire manufacturing cycle, which makes it possible to attribute R&D to the basic internal operating processes of high-tech enterprises;
- highly qualified (intellectual)workforce potential;
- a significant share of non-material assets (intellectual property) in the stock;
- a powerful industrial and technological platform that makes it possible to develop and implement innovations (scientific-technological or other potential of commercialization);
- a large added valuein the final product;
- high risks and input of the innovative process.

These particular features will cause certain difficulties while developing a systemof key performance indicators for efficiency evaluation for high-tech enterprises.

As a universal set of performance indicators for efficiency evaluation of a high-tech enterprise, the following can be included.

2 Financial activity evaluation of the enterprise

The financial evaluation of the efficiency of a high-techenterprise, with consideration of a high added value in the final product, can be carried out on the basis of dynamics of the economic added value (*EVA,Economic Value Added*) calculatedby the formula (1):

$$EVA = NOPAT - CE \times WACC, \quad (1)$$

where*NOPAT* is the net operating profit after taxes, without the interest; *WACC* is the weighted average cost of capital;*CE*is the capital employed.

The positive dynamics of this performance indicator means that the enterpriseoperates efficiently and its market value is increasing.

An advantage of this method in comparison to*DuPont* models is focusing not as much on the profitability of capital but on the increase in the price of the enterprise, which is especially important for diagnosing efficiency in the innovative sector. A drawback of this method, similarly to *DuPont* models, is focusing on the financial targets of the enterprise, which does not allow accurate evaluation of all the components of the system [8].

3 Evaluation of customer satisfaction

An integrated indicator reflecting the quality of the services provided is the index of actual and potential customers' satisfaction*(CSI, Customer Satisfaction Index)* calculated by the formula from the points received with a questionnaire for customers (2):

$$CSI = \sum_{n=1}^{N} F_n \cdot W_n , \quad (2)$$

where *CSI*is the customer satisfaction index; $F_n$is the evaluation of the index number n; N is the total number of indexes; $W_n$is the relevance (weight) of the index number$n$ ($\sum_{n=1}^{N} W_n = 1$).

Evaluation of the competitive advantage of the enterprise is usually done by calculating the index of competitive advantage. However, when calculating this index for high-tech enterprises, their product should be compared with world analogues. This process includes the following: analysis of similar industries and similar products; finding additional features and performance indicators for the products that ensure their competitive advantage; finding the basic performance indicators to be used forevaluation; evaluation of perspective products from competitors.

At the same time, besides using the general strategic performance indicators, the system of performance indicators for evaluation of high-tech enterpriseshas its own particular featuresconditioned by the specific character of this sphere, whose attributes have been investigated above. The primary particular performance indicators of the system is the innovativepotential, which the author considers as a complex of all the resources required to solve the innovative tasks and defining the readiness of the enterprisefor solving them. In the author's opinion, two main components of the innovativepotential are the intellectualpotential and the scientific-technological potential (potential of commercialization).

Let us comprehend how these aspects can be taken into consideration when developing a system of strategic performance indicators of the activity of high-tech enterprises.

4 Evaluation of the innovative potential

Innovation is the main factor influencing the increase of the value of a high-tech enterprise. Therefore, the efficiency of innovations greatly contributes to the success of such enterprises.

Within the framework ofthe strategic managementsystem of the enterpriseit is important that innovative projects be carried out in the specified volume and in due time. Therefore, to control the innovative activity, both the preliminary evaluation and continuous monitoring are necessary for the process of innovative projects of the enterprise [9].

Efficiency of using the innovative potential of the enterprisecan be evaluated as the ratio between the cost and the result. The index of using the innovative potential can be expressed as the following formula (3):

$$R_{IC} = \frac{1}{A} \cdot \sum_{t=1}^{T} \frac{EVA_t}{(1+r)^t}, \quad (3)$$

where R_{IC} is the index of using the innovative potential; $A$is thebook value of the enterprise assets; $EVA_t$is the economic added valueof innovative projects during the year number t; r isthe rate of discounting.

5 Evaluation of the scientific-technological potential (potential of commercialization)

New inventions should not only be developed at the enterprise but be implemented in the practical use. As a rule, not all the inventions at high-tech enterprises have practical implementation (commercialization). Therefore, the efficiency of thescientific-technologicalpotential (potential of commercialization) of the enterprisecan be evaluated asthe ratio between the implemented inventions and the inventions that have been developed or purchased. An index of using the scientific-technological potential (R_{com}) is calculated by the following formula (4):

$$R_{com} = \frac{q_i}{q_d}, \quad (4)$$

where R_{com} is the index of using the scientific-technologicalpotential (potential of commercialization); q_i is the number of implemented inventions (technical solutionsetc.); q_d is the number of developed inventions.

6 Evaluationof the intellectual potential

The index of using the intellectual potential (I_{IP}) can be calculatedby the following formula (5):

$$I_{IP} = IP(hr) \cdot R_{com}, \quad (5)$$

where I_{IP} is the index of using the intellectualpotential; $IP(hr)$is the intellectual potential of the workforce; R_{com} is the index of using the scientific-technological potential (potential of commercialization).

The intellectual potential of the workforce can be calculatedby the following formula (6):

$$IP(hr) = \sum_{j=1}^{J} \frac{IP(hr)_j}{J}, \quad (6)$$

where $IP(hr)$ is the intellectual potential of the workforce; $IP(hr)_j$ is the intellectual potential of the worker number$j$; J is the total number of workers.

The intellectual potential of each worker can be calculatedby the following formula (7):

$$IP(hr)_j = \sum_{n=1}^{N} Pj_n \times W_n , \qquad (7)$$

where $IP(hr)_j$ is the intellectualpotential of the worker number$j$; Pj_n isevaluation of the parameter number$n$of the worker number j; $N$is the total number ofparameters; $W_n$is the importance (weight) of the parameter number n $\left(\sum_{n=1}^{N} W_n = 1 \right)$.

The author of this research did not set the task of developing a complete list of performance indicators for the efficiency of high-tech enterprises described in the modern literature on economybut only limited oneself to only some most important key performance indicators for evaluation of strategic managementefficiency ofa high-tech enterprise as shown in Fig. 1.

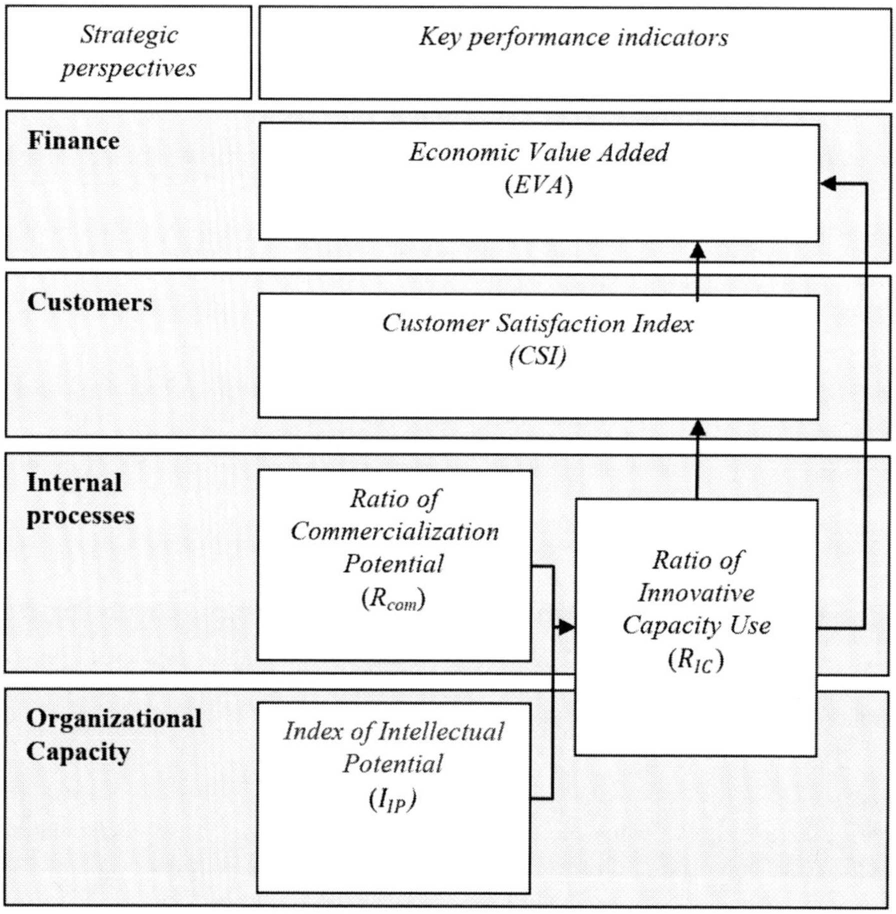

Fig. 1. Strategic perspectives and key performance indicators of a high-tech enterprise.

The scientific novelty of this research consists in the following provisions:

– we defined the basic attributes of a high-tech enterprise and particular features of a system for strategic evaluation of high-tech enterprises conditioned by the specific features of their operating system and the main factors ensuring their competitive advantages: innovative, scientific-technological and intellectual potential of the enterprise;

- we offered relevant performance indicators for evaluation of the innovative, scientific-technological and intellectual potential of a high-tech enterprise, with formulas to calculate them;
- we developed a general system of key performance indicators to evaluate the efficiency of a high-tech enterprise in four most important strategic perspectives:
  1) customers – evaluation of customer satisfaction (*CSI*);
  2) finance – evaluation of the financial efficiency of the enterprise *(EVA);*
  3) internal processes – evaluation of the efficiency of using the innovative (R_{IC}) and scientific-technological (R_{com}) potential;
  4) workforce – evaluation of using the intellectual potential (I_{IP}).
  2.

7 Conclusions

The proposed system of strategic performance indicators takes into consideration the particular features of operating and developing high-tech enterprises and makes it possible to evaluate the efficiency of their financial and business activity and the efficiency of thesystem of strategic management on the basis of inter-related financial and non- financial performance indicators.

The results of the research are presented in the form of concise recommendations and proposals for forming a system of key performance indicators to evaluate the efficiency of high-tech enterprises and can be used when developing a strategic map of a high-tech enterprise. Using this system of performance indicators in combination with definitions of their normative and target values will enable an objective analysis of the state and long-term development of the enterprisewith consideration of its strategic purpose.

References

1. R. Kaplan, D. Norton, *Balanced indicators system. From strategy to action* (Olymp-business, Moscow, 2006)
2. D. Parmenter, *Key Performance Indicators. Development, implementation and application of decisive indicators*(Olymp-business, Moscow, 2009)
3. M. Phillips, The DuPont invention that changed how things work in the corporate world [online], Available at:https://qz.com/569738/the-dupont-invention-that-forever-changed-how-things-work-in-the-corporate-world/ (2015)
4. Decision of the Interstate Council of the Eurasian Economic Community on December 11, 2009, No. 475 "On the Concept of the Establishment of the Eurasian Innovation System". The document was not published. Access from the legal system "ConsultantPlus" [online], Available at: http://www.consultant.ru/law/ref/ju_dict/word/vysokie_tehnologii/ (2018)
5. Strategy & 2017 Global Innovation 1000. Annual Strategy &pwc [online], Available at: https://www.pwc.fr/fr/assets/files/pdf/2017/10/2017-global-innovation-1000.pdf (2018)
6. Best Global Brands – 2017 (Interbrand) / Ranking The Brands [online], Available at:http://interbrand.com/best-brands/best-global-brands/2016/ranking/ (2018)
7. The 10 Most Innovative Companies. [online], Available at: https://www.pwc.ru/en/press-releases/2016/global-innovation-1000.html (2018)

8. T. V. Verevka, Russia in the global world, **9 (32)** (2016)
9. S.V. Koledinov, T.V. Verevka, Science Week SPbPU: materials of a scientific conference with international participation, **38** (2017)

Digital technologies and development of clusters in the light industry of the PRC

Yuan Zheng[1*]

[1] Saint Petersburg State University of Industrial Technologies and Design, 191186 Bolshaya Morskaya st. 18, Russian Federation

Abstract. China has demonstrated during the last thirty years the highest and the most stable GDP growth rate. It has helped the country become the biggest world exporter and significantly increase the social standard of living. However, the growth potential within the boundaries of engineering capability existing before has its limits and during the next 10-15 years the country will not be able to demonstrate the two-digit growth rate again. The same as the other industrially developed countries China has outlined the national prospects in the sphere of wide use of digital technologies. In this respect the development of textile sector of economics with more than 11 mln. people engaged is of a considerable interest. The article gives analysis to the new trends in industry development and offers new organizational models. It has been shown that in case of implementation of innovative development scenario and wide use of digital technologies the average annual growth rates in the period of 2018-2025 will be by 0.8 – 1.0 percentage points higher than in 2015-2016.

1 Introduction

China has gone through three stages of development in the light industry sector by this time [1]. The first stage is a prereform one (1949-1978), the second stage is a transitional one (1978-2000) and the third stage is the stage of renovation (2000-2013). The high average annual growth rate of the industry of 14% has been characteristic for the second stage, which ensured the domination of China in the world market of textile by 2000. At the same time it should be noted that the world market environment and internal conditions too have changed greatly by this time. First of all, a trend has emerged to the drop of sector's share in the volume of added tax and industry's export. If the value of the first indicator in 1990 equaled 14.8%, in 2007 it equaled 9.9%, as for the second indicator, its share decreased from 16.3% in 1997 to 9% in 2010 [1]. It took place against the background of root changes in the structure of ownership. By 2011 the share of state enterprises in the sector dropped down to 1.2% (124 enterprises), when the share of private enterprises grew up to 59.9% (6,060 enterprises) and enterprises based on the foreign capital and with their participation grew up to 36.9% (3,938 enterprises). Thus, the number of medium and big enterprises in the sector (with the number exceeding 270 pers.) amounted to 10, 122 with 3.24 mln. people employed thereat. Totally there were already 18,547 enterprises by that time in the

* Corresponding author: yuanzheng.chaos@gmail.com

sector including small and private households [1]. Two trends of macroeconomical nature have been characteristic for the third stage; they have taken the attractiveness and competitiveness of the sector down: the average annual growth rate of the salary amounted to 8.21% against the background of decreasing volumes of foreign investments into Chinese industry from 1.9 bln. dollars to 1.6 bln. dollars [1]. It has taken place against the background of a considerable deceleration of economic growth: in 2013 and 2014 the results were the lowest during the last six years. At the same time the number of newly established working places in the period since January till March 2013 appeared to be lower by 200 thousand, than over the same period of 2012: 3.24 million against 3.44 million. The level of unemployment in China in 2013 was about 4.1%. The maximum value of indicator was registered in 2012 and 2011 over the last ten years [2].

Since 2000 China had launched a wide expansion of financial investments to foreign countries and by 2011 the total volume of such investments had amounted to 430 bln. dollars. In particular, already by 2005 more than 780 mln. dollars have been invested into textile production of such countries as Cambodia, Bangladesh and Myanmar [3]. Thus, one can acknowledge that a necessity overdue by 2013 in the sector of light industry of China to identify new lines of development [4] as a result of:

– involvement of Chinese textile industry into a global chain of supplies and location of new production capacities outside of China;
– sharp reduction of the share of sector in the added value and export of industry;
– cycle between production and end user extended in time (it makes ten weeks instead of two weeks);
– beginning of wide structural reforms in Chinese industry with the launched transition from textile production to the production of goods of industrial application and durable goods, hi-tech produce and development of real estate sector.

In this respect the incorporation of innovations, for instance, based on digital technologies becomes especially relevant: automated systems of developing new models of clothes (CAD), automated systems of manufacture (CAM), systems of planning results at enterprise (ERP).

2 Innovations and digital technologies

A great number of small and family enterprises work in textile industry of China, which main focus is the survival, but not the technological innovation. The other problem is a low educational level of managers at the textile enterprises, which brings about the insufficient competencies, information about market and, as a result, weakening positions in the struggle for leadership. In parallel to that, most frequently no strategic plans are available, while the information systems are imperfect and poorly integrated with the other part of companies' activity.

An important direction in mastering new segments of the market is the concept of personalization of satisfying the mass-consumer's request being actively developed in the world, which contemplates a number of new innovative capabilities for the manufacturers of clothes. In order to use this capability, the customers should understand better what is possible from the point of view of product and clothes personalization under particular production facility capabilities.

A Program of development of digital community and economy of China initiated by the State Council of the PRC in 2007 in the form of system of data acquisition about clients of banks with the aim of determining paying capacity thereof in accordance with the available information, payment and credit record shall become one of the possible tools for implementing this concept [5]. Similar programs exist already in some countries, for instance, in the USA [6].

The designing of full-scale system Social Credit Score (SCS) began in China since 2014, the beginning of experimental version of "credit social system" is planned for 2018 for several cities in China. This system envisages that the ratings will be awarded not only to physical persons but to legal entities too. Thus, the companies will be motivated to provide reports in time, pass all the checks and inspections in good faith in exchange for the privileged business conditions.

The government has adopted a decision to build SCS system with 10 companies, including giants Alibaba and Tencent. Two biggest Internet companies have launched identical applications for gadgets, which after receiving authorization from the registered user; have received all the available information about him. Tencent Company mainly uses the messenger programs for transmitting brief messages. They managed to collect more than a billion of users [7]; the Internet giant Alibaba acquires information via proprietary application Alipay about effected payments of the users, paid purchases, etc. More than half-million of the users [8] are involved in it. Additionally, both applications get information about actions of an individual from municipal authorities, police departments, research centers and private companies. The user's rating is built on its basis: the higher is the rating, more bonuses receives an individual.

High, stable and long-standing high rate of Chinese economics growth have contributed to the emergence of nodal points; the following are to be specifically singled out among them:

– deficit of qualified workers, technicians and engineers in line with high unemployment of wide public lacking required competences and skills;

– necessity of advanced development of machine-building, which produce shall provide for furnishing new and upgrading existing light industry enterprises;

– vertical integration of light industry enterprises and bunching thereof with the aim of increasing the scale of production, increasing level of yield and proceeds, build-up and increase of efficiency of economic activity, reduction of tax burden.

In order to solve these nodal problems in the sector of light industry of China, it is absolutely essential to shape a national innovative system, including such components as R&D purpose-oriented programs for the development of inherent patents and process renovation and wide use of the up-to-date digital technologies: automated systems of developing new models of clothes (CAD), automated systems of manufacture (CAM), systems of planning results at enterprise (ERP), data transfer technologies (EDI, RFID and bar-codes), information platforms on markets, products, consumers and contents (MAP, PIM, CRM, CMC).

3 New configuration of clusters

The further development of light industry of China is associated with the establishment of clusters maximizing its presence in the global chain of produce added value. The basic principles of building clusters have been suggested in due time by M. Porter [9, 10].

The investigators point out: "…the cluster policy has acquired an ever more significance in the sewing and textile production during the last decade" [11]. The clusters contribute to:

– steady and efficient networking between enterprises of different industries;

– information exchange aimed at improving technical and economical characteristics and consumer properties of manufactured produce, used technology and equipment;

– coordination of investment and innovative activity;

– reduction of expenses, increasing volume of output and competitiveness.

The "supplier-consumer"-type relations are used as a basis of one of the developed forms of building clusters. For instance, the textile industry of Shaoxing consists of the production chain formed by such sectors as the production of chemical fibers, weaving industry, printing and fabrics dyeing [12].

Apart from the factories focusing activity on the main business processes from the chain of added value of product line, the industrial cluster shall include enterprises and organizations providing its activity. The following is to be attributed to such enterprises and organizations with respect to light industry:

– universities, professional educational institutions and other educational establishments training personnel;

– machine-building enterprises specializing in manufacturing products for the cluster enterprises;

– centers conducting scientific, experimental-and-design and engineering activity in the cluster's interests as well as coordinating the marketing, innovative, investment and product policy determining specialization capabilities thereof;

– bank organizations, which provide financing;

– wholesale and retail organizations engaged in produce selling.

The detailed information about composition of the light industry clusters in Jiangsu and Zhejiang provinces is comprised in [13].

The conducted analysis makes it possible to offer a number of additions to the light industry clusters of China, which can be considered by the example of clothes production. The suggested cluster as compared with the existing ones shall feature an extended composition.

It is offered to include not only educational institutions into composition of the extended cluster as it is implemented, for instance, in the Russian legislation [14], but the banking institutions as well as machine-building enterprises specializing in manufacturing equipment for the cluster. The suggested cluster composition makes it possible to implement in principle the entire chain of clothes production added value, since:

– cluster core is formed by the enterprises of several light industry branches, which are to be integrated. The integration implies synchronization of produce output volumes and coordination of price policy with the aim of minimizing expenses and taxation burden with restricting prices for final produce.

– interests of owners of enterprises producing raw materials and intermediate produce can be satisfied by means of receiving a share of ownership in the sewing industry and trading enterprises featuring high profitability.

Thus, it is proposed to attribute the following to the necessary participants of the light-industry cluster providing its functioning and development:

– bank providing budgeting of current activity of all enterprises and organizations as well as implementation of innovative and investment policy;

– universities and secondary technical educational institutions, which basic function is to train personnel. The universities play a central role, since they train personnel for all enterprises, including inherent needs. Besides, a part of, and maybe all scientific investigations and experimental-and-design developments shall be concentrated also there;

– fashion houses fulfill a function of renovation and forming product line, develop and catch up fashionable trends, perform promotion of cluster's produce due to use of its brands;

– engineering center is engaged in the development of new products, technologies, equipment, fulfillment of scientific investigations in technical and economic field, forms and effects implementation of innovative and investment policy;

– machine-building participates directly in implementation of investment policy. The equipment is to be manufactured within time limits recorded in the cluster's investment program for every enterprise participating in implementation of this program.

4 Model and results of its verification

The innovations, digital technologies and new models of business organization for the light industry of China set more complete saturation of the market with goods, provision of personal requests of the customers and, as a result, growth of volumes of the manufactured produce as the final goal.

In order to assess the industry's potential; we have offered one of modifications of Cobb-Douglas production model widely used in economical literature in the following form:

$$\tilde{Y} = \gamma \cdot K^{\alpha} \cdot [A \cdot L]^{1-\alpha+\varepsilon}$$

where:

Ỹ – design volume of added value of the light industry of the PRC in comparable prices of 2010.

K – capital assets in the light industry of the PRC in comparable prices of 2010.

A – change of multifactor productivity in the PRC.

L – number of employees in the light industry of the PRC.

γ, α, ε – model parameters.

In order to provide for higher accuracy of calculating according to the model, we have processed the dynamic rows of actual values for such indicators as the cost of fixed assets (capital), quantity of employed people and multifactor productivity on the basis of four data sources – National Statistical Office of PRC [15], University of Groningen (the Netherlands) [16], Organization for Economic Cooperation and Development (OECD) [17], and World Bank [18]. In view of specific features of running a system of national accounts in the PRC, it is not always possible to provide for correct data comparability, therefore, it is necessary to address the other sources providing more accurate data, especially in terms of industrial product prices, multifactor productivity (to be calculated for the whole economics) and inflation rate. Therefore, in order to carry out calculations, the cost of fixed assets was recalculated in prices of 2010, while the multifactor productivity was corrected to 1998, the baseline one for making calculations. The volume of added value of the light industry has been determined as the sum of volumes of three sub-industries: production of fabrics, threads and fibers (textile); sewing industry; leather and footwear industry, fur industry and headgear production.

The calculation results according to the suggested model are shown in Table 2, at that, the values of basic parameters were as follows: $\gamma = 0.101$; $\alpha = 1.174$; $\varepsilon = 0.796$.

Table 2. Results of forecast calculations for light industry of PRC.

Year	Capital in prices of 2010	Q-ty of employed	Multifactor productivity	Added value in prices of 2010	
	bln. yuan	mln. people	1998=1	bln. yuan	growth rate, %
	$\tilde{K}$	$\tilde{L}$	$\tilde{A}$	$\tilde{Y}$	$\tilde{T}_Y$
2017	152.8	11.7	1.609	230.8	9.0
2018	161.0	11.6	1.625	245.4	6.3
2019	169.2	11.5	1.639	260.0	6.0
2020	177.2	11.4	1.651	274.5	5.6
2021	185.1	11.3	1.661	288.8	5.2

Year	Capital in prices of 2010	Q-ty of employed	Multifactor productivity	Added value in prices of 2010	
	bln. yuan	mln. people	1998=1	bln. yuan	growth rate, %
	$\tilde{K}$	$\tilde{L}$	$\tilde{A}$	$\tilde{Y}$	$\tilde{T}_Y$
2022	192.7	11.3	1.669	302.8	4.8
2023	200.2	11.2	1.675	316.3	4.5
2024	207.3	11.2	1.679	329.3	4.1
2025	214.1	11.2	1.681	341.6	3.8

According to our calculations the average-annual growth rate of light industry of PRC in the forecast zone will amount to 5.5%, which exceeds the industry's indicators in 2015-2016 (4.7 and 4.2 percent, accordingly), but is significantly lower than the average-annual growth rate for the entire retrospective period (12.4%). According to our opinion the provision of such high growth rate is impossible under the present-day economical conditions, since the measurement reference proper has changed, and the consumer itself has become more demanding to quality and range of produce of the sector. At the same time it should be noted that the industry growth rates obtained on the basis of the model exceed significantly the growth rate of gross domestic product (GDP) of China for the same period, which have been calculated by a number of reputable research centers: two reputable research centers – RAND Corporation [19] and the Conference Board [20] have published the forecasts of annual-average growth rate of China's GDP for a period of 2016-2025 within an interval of four years (2011 and 2015). It is notable that in the first forecast such growth rates are evaluated in the interval from 3.8 to 9.0 percent (average of 5.7), in the second forecast these rates are considerably lower: 4.5 percent for a period of 2016-2020 and 3.6 percent for a period of 2021-2025.

Since the annual-average growth rate of the volume of industry's added value in the forecasting period amounted to 5.5 percent, we will interpret the difference in rate characteristics between the forecast and actual indicators for 2015-2016 (4.7 and 4.2 percent) as an effect, which can be obtained by the industry as a result of cluster-type organization model and new tools of implementing the innovative policy in the industry. The graphical trajectory of industry development itself for a period until 2025 is shown in Fig. 1.

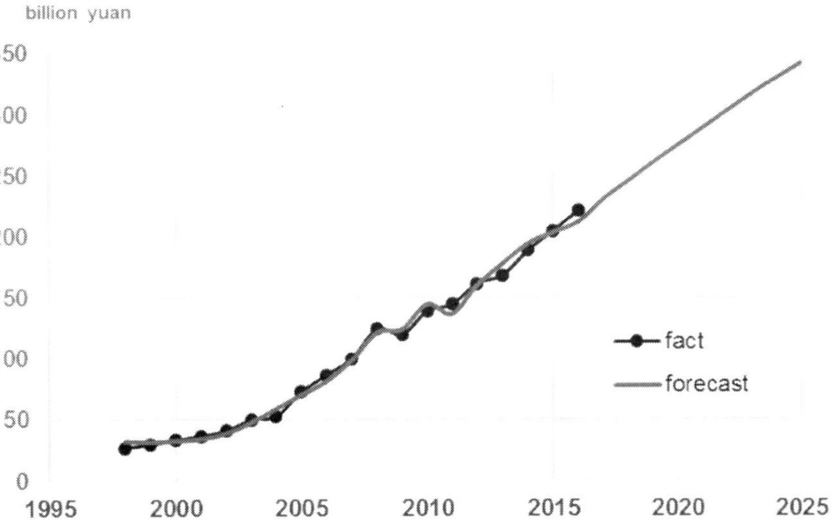

Fig. 1. Forecast of added value of china's textile industry.

The graph shows that the model suggested by ourselves gives quite an accurate description of dynamics of the industry's dynamic growth, while the model's error does not exceed 0.6%. Such a high accuracy of calculation has been provided due to correct selection of models describing dynamics of the model's basic factors – capital, quantity and multifactor productivity.

5 Conclusion

The development of textile sector of China on a new technological basis can play a role of stabilization factor for the national economy for two reasons. The first one consists in that the internal market will be provided with the proper-quality goods by the affordable prices. The second reason consists in that the sector can become a reliable source of export proceeds due to a wide use of new digital technologies. In combination these two factors can make a basis for the new qualitative growth of the country's textile industry in the nearest 10-15 years.

References

1. M. Zhang, ERIA Discussion Paper Series, **12** (2015)
2. E. Bazhenova, A. Ostrovsky, Otechestvennyye Zapiski, **3** (2008)
3. S. Wang, H. Liu, F. Qian, J. Chen, X. Zhang (eds.), *Report on Development of China's Outward Investment and Economic Cooperation* (Ministry of Commerce of the People's Republic of China, Beijing, 2011)
4. Ch. Yuan, Problems of Modern Economics, **2 (62)** (2017)
5. Digital Single Market – Digitizing European Industry [online], Available at: http://europa.eu/rapid/press-release_MEMO-16-1409_en.htm (2016)
6. FICO At a Glance [online], Available at: http://www.fico.com/en/about-us#at_glance (2018)
7. Tencent Announces 2017 Third Quarter Results [online], Available at: https://www.tencent.com/en-us/articles/15000651510741924.pdf (2017)

8. Official website of Alipay [online], Available at: https://intl.alipay.com/ (2018)
9. M. Porter, *On Competition* (Harvard Business Press Books, Boston, 2008)
10. Yu. I. Efimychev, I. V. Zakharov, Bulletin of Nizhni-Novgorod Lobachevsky University, **1** (2005)
11. O. Korkmaz, T. D. Medeni, International Journal of Business and Government Studies. **4 (1)** (2012)
12. Distinctive Features of Industrial Clusters of China [online], Available at: http://sapsan-logistics.ru/otlichitelnye-osobennosti-proizvods (2018)
13. List of Clusters by Specialization [online], Available at: http://sapsan-logistics.ru/spisok-klasterov-po-specializacii (2018)
14. On Industrial Clusters and Specialized Organizations of Industrial Clusters. Resolution of Government of RF No. 779 [online], Available at: http://gov.garant.ru/document?id=71050302&byPara=1 (2015)
15. National Bureau of statistics of China [online], Available at: http://data.stats.gov.cn/english/easyquery.htm?cn=C01 (2018)
16. Groningen Growth and Development Centre [online], Available at: http://www.rug.nl/research/ggdc/data/pwt/pwt-9.0 (2018)
17. Key Short-Term Economic Indicators [online], Available at: http://stats.oecd.org/index.aspx?DatasetCode=KEI# (2018)
18. United Nations Industrial Development Organization [online], Available at: http://data.un.org/Data.aspx?q=value+added&d=UNIDO&f=tableCode%3a20 (2018)
19. Jr. Wolf Ch., J Dalal S., J. Da Vanzo, V. Eric, E. V. Larson, A. Akhmedjonov, H. Dogo, M. Huang, S. Montoya, China and India, 2025 A Comparative Assessment [online], Available at: https://www.rand.org/content/dam/rand/pubs/monographs/2011/RAND_MG1009.pdf (2011)
20. A. A. Erumban, K. de Vries, Global Growth Projections for The Conference Board Global Economic Outlook 2016 [online], Available at: https://www.conference-board.org/attach/GEO_Methodology_Oct20151.pdf (The Conference Board. NY. 2015)

AUTHOR INDEX

AUTHOR INDEX